FOOD ON THE MOVE

PROCEEDINGS OF THE OXFORD SYMPOSIUM ON FOOD AND COOKERY 1996

FOOD
ON
THE MOVE

PROCEEDINGS OF THE OXFORD SYMPOSIUM ON FOOD AND COOKERY 1996

EDITED
BY
HARLAN WALKER

PROSPECT BOOKS
1997

ISBN 0907325793

© 1997 as a collection Prospect Books (but © 1996 in individual articles rests with the authors)

Published in 1997 by Prospect Books, Allaleigh House, Blackawton, Totnes, Devon TQ9 7DL, England

Printed by Antony Rowe, Bumper's Farm, Chippenham, Wilts

Designed and typeset by Wendy Baker and Tom Jaine.

The cover illustration is taken from the cover of Czibulya Ferenc, 'Bulgarian Horticulture on Hungarian Soil' referred to and illustrated in Maria Kaneva-Johnson's paper, below.

Contents

Introduction

This volume of papers presented at the Oxford Symposium on Food and Cookery follows the pattern of previous collections. The Symposium was held in September 1996 at Saint Antony's College, Oxford under the joint chairmanship of Alan Davidson and Dr Theodore Zeldin.

I must again record our thanks to the staff of Saint Antony's, who helped us in all our unreasonable requests as they have always done. We are particularly grateful for the way that they coped with our increased numbers; we were able to accept about twenty-five more people than ever before.

On Saturday evening the college chef, Mark Walker, again prepared our splendid dinner, which was planned by Claudia Roden to illustrate her paper, printed below (where the menu for the dinner may also be found).

For our lunch on Sunday, symposiast and baker Dan Schickentanz, also illustrating his paper, presented us with a delicious selection of his sourdough breads. With these we ate a salad dressed with lovely olive oils given by Spanish producers and arranged by Maria José Sevilla, of 'Foods from Spain' of the Spanish Embassy Commercial Department. We are very grateful to both of them for their help.

Finally, I must record our thanks to all those people who have helped to make the symposium possible – symposiasts, friends and relations. Without this endless detailed assistance before, during and after the event, we couldn't do it.

Harlan Walker,
May 1997

Assyrian Flat Bread: from Mesopotamia to Sweden

Michael Abdalla

Bread is the most important and the most frequently consumed product in human nutrition. Its unique organoleptic value make it a universal food, always up-to-date and irreplaceable, which for centuries has accompanied man almost all over the globe. It has become a synonym of life, and that is not only with respect to the spiritual rebirth through the Eucharist. In search of bread people wander from one country to another, from one continent to another. Some people believe that ones homeland is where bread is. There are also those who express their patriotism through the cult of bread. A Polish poet, C.K. Norwid, suffering from nostalgia, wrote that he missed the country where out of respect a crumb of bread is picked from the ground.

Bread in ancient Mesopotamia

Information about bread in ancient Mesopotamia dates back to the beginning of the fourth millennium BC. In that period of the development of cuneiform writing the activity of eating was represented by a pictogram of a head with a piece of bread.[1] In archaeological records one may find information about 'grinding houses', number of employed millers and types of flour, also about bakers and bakeries and kinds of bread. We know a few kinds of Sumerian bread such as beer, royal, permanent, common, ritual, wheat, wheat-and-barley and others. This range of bread types was continuously enriched by the Babylonians and the Assyrians. It is worth noticing that in those records bread is frequently mentioned next to beer. In the letters of Eridu disciples to their parents, they complain about small bread and beer allowances. During a banquet arranged for about 70,000 people on the occasion of the completion of the rebuilding of the Assyrian capital Nemrud (9th century BC), King Assurnasirpal II ordered the preparation of 10,000 loaves of bread and the same number of amphoras of beer and skinfuls of wine. These products were served during celebrations devoted to the gods. Kings were also treated with them.

It is worthwhile mentioning the position of bakers in Sumerian society. In these remote times bakers enjoyed exceptional privileges and the good graces of the authorities. The evidence of that may be their exemption from military service and the fact that they were usually invited to participate in the biggest annual celebration of welcoming spring.[2] After introducing 'gods of goodness' from the central temples in Nineveh, there were competitions organised along the procession route for the largest loaf (or flat cake) of bread. The ceremony was accompanied by presentations by the master bakers. The inhabitants of the Assyrian capital could admire the skills of their bakers, who were said to bake on this day loaves of bread weighing 30 kilograms. Since that time the first of April has become a special date for many Middle Eastern nations. It has been continuously celebrated by the Assyrians as a national feast, a peculiar New Year celebration.

The reflection of the primary character of bread in the culture of Mesopotamia can be found in the poem on Gilgamesh, which is the world's oldest, most perfect and valuable literary work. The inscription preserved in plaque 11 helps us to realise that bread was probably the first food product remembered by both those suffering from hunger and those wanting to give them food. When after the exhausting quest for the 'herb of life', Gilgamesh reached the place where rivers flow, his immortal host Utnapishti said to his wife, 'Start baking bread; you shall place one loaf next to his head every day and make a sign on the wall according to how many times you have baked bread'. Descriptions of specific loaves are particularly fascinating, since Gilgamesh's dream lasted for seven days.[3] Judging from the epic's content, it is clear that those who were not familiar with bread were regarded as savages.

In professional literature it is assumed that bread dough fermentation is an Egyptian discovery. However in view of the latest research, it is not out of the question that the inhabitants of ancient Mesopotamia had been familiar with this process one thousand years earlier.[4] They may be responsible for introducing beer-yeast to leaven some kinds of bread, for example beer-bread.

Bread today among Assyrian peasants in the Middle East

The original bread shape of a rounded cake was the same everywhere and resembled the sun or the full moon. This shape has been preserved until today not only among the Assyrians in the Middle East. Rounded flat bread is still eaten by almost half of the population of the globe.[5] Its shape may be close to round, sometimes oval or elongated. It varies in thickness (0.2–2.5 cm) and size (diameter from 20 cm to 1 meter). Bread baked in country ovens looks a bit different from that produced in workshop or industrial bakeries. There are also round ones with a small hole in the middle. Such bread, which is baked from left-over dough, is called by Assyrians *qelluro*.[6] It is used as a snack for impatient children. Attracted by the smell of bread, they gather round the oven. Depending on the country and region the same kind of bread can be called by different names. It is always made of wheat flour.

The evidence that bread is the essential component of the Assyrians' diet is that in the country bread provides about 65 per cent of all food demand. It is the main source of protein and energy, and almost the only product consumed by the young ones to fill their stomachs between meals. It is generously spread with a layer of home-made tomato paste whose surface is usually highly seasoned with dried leaves of peppermint. It is also frequently rubbed with a garlic clove spread with salt. In towns bread is served with all meals and dishes. It is eaten with rice, groats and potato chips. Without bread one cannot reach the feeling of satiety. It is said to *kosoned u lebo* – support one's heart.[7]

The only kind of bread consumed in Assyrian villages is the type called *tanuro* (*tanura*).[8] The dough is prepared with a starter in an aluminium bowl called *tst* or *lagan*. The sign of a cross is pressed out on the dough with widely spread fingers: thumb and index finger. The disappearance of the sign indicates the end of the fermentation, which normally lasts for about 1 1/2 to 2 1/2 hours. Baking bread is performed solely by women.

The oven, also called *tanuro*, is constructed from brown clay mixed with finely cut chaff, which reinforces the oven's construction like cement. This work, which requires a lot of precision and patience, is mainly performed by women. In shape the oven resembles a big bell or a barrel cut in half crossways. It is built gradually, starting from the base with a diameter of about 80-100 cm. Next, further levels of several centimeters are added, always after the previous one has well dried out. The higher they go, the smaller the diameter of each layer. The wall thickness is always the same at about 2cm; the height of the whole oven reaches about 1.2 meters. Next the oven is 'burnt out' at a high temperature generated by burning bones which turn to ash. It happens that during the 'burning out' some ovens crack, so several ovens, and amphoras, are made by the inhabitants of a village. There is a hole at the bottom of the oven, which is a ventilation channel, allowing also the removal of ashes with a metal stick (*bst*, *maqeblana*). The top hole is used to load fuel, which is usually dried animal excrement, the most available and efficient calorifacient material in Middle Eastern villages.[9]

When it is being constructed the oven tilts forward slightly on the side of the hole. The sides and back are protected with a casing about 40 cm thick. This serves three purposes: it is a good insulation, it protects from physical damage, and a bowl with dough and a wooden board for hand

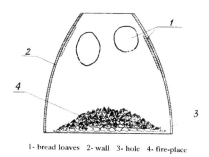

1- bread loaves   2- wall   3- hole   4- fire-place

An Assyrian oven or tanuro.

forming and flattening the dough can be placed on it. It is also there that freshly baked loaves are left in a separate bowl covered with a cloth. Such an oven can last for ten years or more. It is located in the vicinity of the house, often against a low clay wall. Sometimes it can belong to two or more neighbouring households.

After adequate heating the walls of the oven change colour to a lighter shade. Then formed bread cakes (about 2 cm thick with a diameter of 20-30 cm) are stuck on – with the help of a special cushion – to the interior wall above the fire. At that stage the lower hole should be closed. After the cakes have been attached to the walls, the top hole is closed. The baking takes about 20-30 minutes. After they have been taken out the loaves are cooled down outdoors. Women place the bowl with the bread on their heads and, holding it with both hands, they take them into the house. Passers-by, who are usually invited to taste fresh bread, thank them for the gesture or help themselves to a small morsel, wishing the hostess that neither she nor anyone else may ever be short of that gift.

The oven is also used to prepare special cakes, *kilicha*, and hot ash is used to bake potatoes and eggs without fat or water. A clay vessel containing sheep's legs, stomachs and head is also placed in the oven so that throughout Saturday and Sunday night they can be slowly cooked. This rational use of the heat after Saturday bread making allows the housewife rest on Sunday.[10] This is how bread is baked in the Middle Eastern homelands, which many Assyrians were forced to leave for ever.

Bread among the Assyrian immigrants to Sweden

More than 50,000 Assyrians reached Sweden. The majority of them came from Turkey, which they left at the beginning of the 1960s. Their biggest centre is in Södertälje, south of Stockholm. To find out about their attachment to their national cuisine, I prepared in the summer of 1995 a question-naire and distributed it among those who were willing to complete it. The questionnaire was quite extensive. Part of it dealt with bread. Out of 300 forms distributed, I received back 118.[11]

Assyrian expatriates started a large bakery in Södertälje with partially automated technology designed according to the methods of world famous companies (Winkler from Germany and Babb from USA). Daily, using a constant quality Swedish flour, it bakes a few tons of flat bread with a hollow inside, ideally with both layers of equal thickness and with a diameter bigger than in the Middle East. The whole technological process lasts about one hour and the actual baking takes from 2 to 6 seconds. Automatically packed in plastic foil, the bread reaches many Swedish cities, where it is also purchased by the Swedes.

An analysis of the survey allows one to conclude that a majority of Assyrian families bake their bread at home. They explain that they prefer to prepare this fundamental food themselves. Being a frequent guest of Assyrian emigrants in Sweden, I had a chance to observe the complicated process of dough preparation, its fermentation, shaping and baking. Although some housewives have electric mixers, they prefer to 'box' the dough with their hands. Many of them can count on support from their children.[12] Pieces of dough, flattened after the first fermentation, are placed on a table on a piece of cloth and covered with another piece of cloth.

Beside the emotional elements which lead housewives to make the effort of baking 'their own' flat bread, it is also worth stressing that it constitutes an important financial factor for the family budget. Typical Swedish bread does not only look and taste differently, but is also considerably more expensive. One should also add that an average kitchen in a Swedish apartment – big and conveniently equipped with a regulated electric stove with glass door and a freezer for storing baked bread – facilitates bread baking at home. An available microwave oven allows for quick bread defrosting and warming up for current needs.

Eighty-six per cent of the respondents who live in families bake bread at home. It is also a practice of some people who live alone. These families number 412 people and buy 408 kilograms of flour a week, so one person consumes about 1 kg of flour which is approximately equivalent to 1.6 kg of bread (see table below). Sixty-one per cent of families bake bread once a week, twenty-two per cent twice a week and seventeen per cent two or three times a week. Fifty-nine per cent of those surveyed season bread with fennel or sesame seeds, especially during seasonal celebrations. Others add some bran and cereal seeds or prepare the dough with some whole-wheat flour. This innovation is introduced by the young ones who learn about health food. The consumption of dark bread is higher among young people than among adults.

Sixty-six per cent of those surveyed purchased perfectly round flat bread from a large private bakery in Södertälje. Professionally baked bread is distributed in numerous Swedish centres. Slightly fewer people (sixty-one per cent) also buy Swedish bread. However, it should be noticed that these two are only occasional sources of bread, supplementing home-made bread in an amount not bigger than 0.8 kg per person per week. Taking into consideration that children have their first meal of the day at school and that many people work at pizzerias where they not only eat their meals but also take some food home with them, one can surmise that the average bread consumption of an Assyrian in Sweden is larger than might appear from the above calculations. It may amount to as much as 0.5 kg per day. Children constitute half the family of those who bake bread at home. On the lists of products of reduced, increased or unaltered consumption in comparison with that in the previous country of residence, bread was placed in the third group along with pumpkin and watermelon seeds, pickled vegetables, burghul, legume seeds (without lentils), salt and onions.

Among the routine activities of an Assyrian housewife, dough preparation is almost a daily practice. This is also true for some men. Some of them can evaluate a flour's quality and usefulness for a specific kind of bread by merely taking a handful of it. That explains, among other things, the great number of Assyrian immigrants in Sweden (as well as in the Netherlands)[13] who work in pizzerias. Moreover it should be added that pizza is not a new dish for the Assyrians. They have been familiar with slightly tastier versions for ages. Most frequently one variety is served, prepared according to a specific recipe which in Arabic is called *lahm b 'agin*. A thin cake of dough (thinner than for an Italian pizza) is spread with tomato paste and then covered with a layer of slightly fried minced meat, seasoned with onion and parsley. It is baked in an oven with a horizontal stone base. Electric stoves are ideal for this purpose. Though *lahm b 'agin* is known in the whole Middle East, especially among city people, many Assyrians consider it to be their national dish. It is classified as a festive dish, served on special occasions. Although pizzas are available everywhere in Sweden, the consumption of *lahm b 'agin* is still very high among the Assyrians.

It is not known if in other West European countries (e.g. Germany) the Assyrian immigrants bake bread at home as much as they do in Sweden. I guess that the proportion of those who do is slightly smaller, maybe due to worse standards of accommodation in comparison with Sweden. However flat bread is available on the West European market. It is difficult to foresee if the same level of bread consumption will be maintained in the future. From the survey data one may draw a conclusion that fewer and fewer Assyrians observe fasting periods, when bread consumption is higher than on festive days.

NOTES

[1] Diringer, D. *The Alphabet, A Key to the History of Mankind*. Polish edition: *Alfabet, czyli klucz do dziejów ludzkosci*, tr. Wojciech Hensel, PIW, Warszawa 1972, chart 13.

[2] In the folk habits of Assyrians and related groups, Yezidis and Sabaeans, one may find many practices referring to the importance of April 1st. On that day 'soil reproduces itself'. Some believe that dew which appears on grass at night can start yoghurt fermentation of milk.

[3] A famous piece of writing, translated into many languages. The original quotation comes from a Polish translation, which was reconstructed with a foreword by Robert Stiller, Bibliotheca Mundi, PIW, Warszawa 1982, 100-1.

[4] It has not yet been established where and when the dough fermentation process was applied for the first time. It is assumed that its popularisation became possible only after the Hebrews left Egypt.

[5] For more information on the role of flat bread in diets on various continents see: H. Gasiorowski, M. Abdalla, 'Fladenbrot in der Welt', *Getreide Mehl und Brot*, vol. 44, no 9, 1990, 281-3, Detmold.

[6] The term *qelluro* appears, among others, in an Assyrian fable about a greedy bird. The hole allows for hanging the loaf on the neck of children who cannot part with bread. Such a child was sometimes laughed at by its peers, who called him or her *talmono* or *talmonito* (the one of the loaf of bread). My sister, who lives in Sweden, told me that one day her youngest son had asked her why she did not bake him this kind of bread with a hole, which he missed a lot.

[7] In this case, as on many other occasions, heart stands for stomach.

[8] Various forms of this name, derivatives from an Assyrian original, can be found in all countries of the Middle East, where they mean oven.

[9] Animal excrement is collected at dawn, after the animals are let out to pasture. It is formed into round blocks and dried in a sunny place, next to a farm. Later they are stored in a special room and used as the only source of heating fuel. They burn slowly, generating a high temperature.

[10] Abdalla, M. 'Cooking Pots Used in Present Day Assyrian Village Kitchens in the Middle East', *The Cooking Pot*, ed. Tom Jaine, 7-11, Prospect Books Ltd, London 1989.

[11] An extensive evaluation of the survey results was presented at the 11th International Ethnological Food Research Conference, Cyprus, 2-8 June, 1996.

[12] When I visited my sister in Sweden in the summer of 1995, I offered help to my nephew (a student at Stockholm University), since his mother asked him to prepare dough and bake bread. However my nephew refused to accept my help explaining that my chest hair might fall into the dough.

[13] Abdalla, M. 'A few Words about Assyrian Immigrants and Public Eating Houses run by them in Holland', *Ethnologia Polona*, vol 19, 24-31, 1996, Polish Academy of Sciences, Institute of Archaeology and Ethnology, Poznan.

Chart showing sources of bread supplies and levels of consumption per person.

Home made	From the oriental bakery at Södertälje	Swedish bread	Average weekly consumption (kg)	
			Home made	Purchased
86%	66%	61%	1.6	0.8

'God sends meat, but the Devil sends cooks',
or
'A solitary pleasure': the travels of the Honourable John Byng through England and Wales in the late 18th century

Joan P. Alcock

The Honourable John Byng

The Honourable John Byng (1742-1813) may be considered both unfortunate and fortunate; unfortunate in that, as the brother of the 4th Viscount Torrington, he died a few weeks after inheriting the title, fortunate in that his love of travel and his habit of keeping a diary has ensured that his name has been kept before posterity. The diaries, covering journeys in England and Wales between 1781 and 1793, were written with this in mind: 'I will now indulge in a little hasty vanity and satisfaction, in thinking how pleasant my tours will be to readers, an hundred years hence; if they or the ink of them shall abide. Tour writing is yet a novelty, our ancestors never thought of such a thing' (Vol.II, 28). He was wrong in this last view, but his detailed descriptions of the countryside, weather, inns and antiquities, vividly recall the moment of change from an agricultural country to one beginning an industrial revolution. Industry was still a curiosity. The iron bridge at Coalbrookdale Byng saw as one of the wonders of the world; he visited and marvelled at the 'magnificent cotton mills', which Sir Richard Arkwright had created at Cromford.

He wrote thirty-one manuscript volumes, illustrated with his own drawings, which after his death were kept at Yates Court in Kent, until the estate was sold in the 1920s. They were then auctioned and scattered to a variety of places including the Bodleian Library, Oxford, Cardiff Public Library and a draper's shop in Blackburn. Finally, in the 1930s, twenty-four volumes were tracked down and published by C. Bruyn Andrews, who thus ensured Byng's fame.

Byng's early life in the army gave him a taste for travel. Having started as a Cornet in the Royal Horse Guards, he progressed through a series of army purchases – Captain in the 58th Foot, Lieutenant, then Captain, in the First Foot Guards – before retiring with the rank of Lieutenant Colonel in 1780. He then obtained the position of Commissioner of Stamps, wending his way daily from his house in Duke Street near Manchester Square to Somerset House. He neatly summed up his career (Vol.II, 237) as:

> His early days were spent in camps
> His latter days were passed in stamps.

He makes it very plain why he travels:

> I seek not company and noise; I turn not my head to look at a woman; for I leave London to look at nature in her most becoming attire...I come abroad to view old castles, old manors and old religious houses, before they be quite gone...I enjoy a grove of venerable old oaks; feel transported at the sound or the sight of a wild waterfall; and taste the animation of a fox hunter at the unkennelling of a fox when I discover a castle, or a ruin (Vol. II, 39).

He sought out local people for information, but was often disappointed when they replied that there was nothing of interest to see, even if there was a ruined building nearby. Sometimes their indifference could assume a strange ignorance. When at Caerleon on July 30 1789, Mr Osborn, Byng's travelling companion, asked some inhabitants where were the remains of the Roman amphitheatre, he received the reply, 'that they knew no such person'. In spite of the increased number of travellers on the improved roads, much of the population of England and Wales remained unconcerned about what was beyond their immediate vicinity.

Byng liked to ride in company and with friends, but was hostile to strangers. At the Black Dog in Cromford, Derbyshire (July 29, 1793), an old lady, a young man and two young women tried to join Byng and his friend for supper. He flatly stated that he had urgent business with his friend and blamed the other party for their 'strange request' which he put down to their being unused to travelling. Even at Blyth (June 2, 1792), when he was feeling ill with a sore chest, which he cured with copious draughts of snail tea, and bemoaning how wretched a single person is who cannot communicate with a friend, he still muses that travelling is 'a solitary pleasure'. Yet in spite of this, when he does not have a companion 'to partake and encourage' he states that this forfeits his title as 'an active and zealous tourist'.

On some of his early tours, Tom Bush, his ex-groom, went with him. Byng had got a place for Bush in the Stamp Office but he was always available to look after Byng's horse and luggage. After Bush's untimely death in 1790, his replacement, Garwood, was not so attentive. A third servant, whom he does not name, followed Garwood; Byng suspected him of being a rogue, careless of the comfort of himself and his horses.

Travelling arrangements

The mail coach service for passengers, begun in 1784, established itself rapidly as a means by which the country could be traversed more easily. Byng wrote at the time when it was becoming a popular form of transport, because of good timekeeping and because coaches were built to more exacting specifications, which made them comfortable. Not that Byng approved. In spite of using them, he asked rhetorically, 'why is every part of the kingdom to be overcome by mail coaches, where formerly the little post was quietly run and regulars serviced by the post boy' (Vol.11, 273)? He notes that the coming of the mail coaches to a town put up the price of food: fowls rose from 3d to 4d, butcher's meat rose 4 or 5 farthings a pound to 4d (Vol.I, 300).

Byng commented that 'I am just old enough to remember turnpike roads few, and those bad; and when travelling was slow, difficult, and, in carriages, somewhat dangerous (Vol.II, 149). The development of the turnpike system (Albert, 1972) made all the difference to the comfort and speed of travel, so much so that Byng thought 'speed had reached its summit'. By this time it was possible to get from London to Edinburgh in three days instead of two weeks and the Exeter to London run was reduced from two days to 32 hours (Copeland 1968, 85). Byng himself caught the coach from Manchester early in the morning on June 12, 1790 arriving in London at 6 pm.

Byng preferred to travel on horseback and used four horses during his years in travel, always checking that Spot, Poney, Blacky or Bumper were settled for the night before he had supper. He hated 'being box'd up in a stinking coach dependent on the hours and guidance of others, submitting to miserable associates and obliged to hear their great nonsense'. This happened in June 1790 when he left London at 7 am to travel north to join his servant, Tom Bush, who had gone ahead with the horses. Three women, including 'a fat creature like a cook', were his companions, but two other ladies got in at Islington, although the coach interior could only hold four. Byng 'skulk'd at a corner and endured'. There were frequent changes of horses, and a longer stop for dinner, at which Byng 'ordered at my own charge, a pint of red wine to entertain the ladies', before Northampton was reached at about 8 pm, when the company had tea. Byng felt overwhelmed by views on ladies' fashions, and 'servants' hall ribaldry'. It was 1.30 am when they reached Leicester, where Byng emerged, bored beyond belief, and with cramped legs and a sore hip.

He was not alone in disliking such journeys. Thackeray describes Major Pendennis' dreary night passed in the mail-coach with a stout passenger snoring loudly, a widow lady cutting out all fresh air by closing the windows, and sipping rum and water perpetually, and the major being started awake by the twanging of the horn at every turnpike gate. And this went on for twenty-four hours while the coach swayed on at eight miles an hour (Thackeray, (1848), 1958, 68). A correspondent to a Sheffield local newspaper detailed the profanities of the outside passengers, the smell of putrid game and fish, the long chilly wait for connecting coaches and the immense loads of luggage carried on the roof to the danger of passengers (Burne 1922, 54). On arrival at the Greyhound, Hatfield (May 29, 1789), Byng found a friend recovering from bruises and a cut head. His coach had broken down causing him to fall under five female passengers and then being hit by the luggage falling through the cracked roof.

Sometimes Byng went on long walks, especially in North Wales. At the end of his tour of Bedfordshire in August 1790, he walked the 45 miles back to London. Byng seems to have kept remarkably fit in spite of travelling through some atrocious weather. There are mentions of lung complaints and feverish colds, not helped by being in inns where the windows were broken. If he got very wet, in order to prevent a cold, he would strip by a good fire and rub himself with brandy. At the Bull Inn at Bala (August 5, 1793) when the rain had 'fallen in buckets', brandy was not available, so he used gin and then calling for candles sat by a great fire having supper, while listening to a Welsh harper and drinking 'tolerable' port wine.

If he was feeling very ill, he drank snail tea. This was a noted remedy in the late eighteenth century for colds, lung congestion and consumption, and indeed one which continued into the twentieth century. A recipe from Ireland comments that the snails, the common garden variety, are placed on a large dish and liberally sprinkled with dark sugar. A dish is placed over them to prevent them getting away and the next morning the syrup which has been made is drained off, bottled and a spoonful taken three times a day. A little lemon juice could be added for flavour. (Another recipe from Co. Tipperary commented that after surviving this treatment the snails were boiled in veal broth, before being consumed.) 'Bruised' snails were also used to froth up milk (Smollett, (1771) 1966, 122). At the Spread Eagle, Settle (June 20, 1792), 'a bad dismal inn, on a black dismal raining evening', with mice running behind the wainscotting, he felt, not surprisingly, distinctly unwell, so he swallowed Dr James' pills and sweated profusely in 'a great floundering feather bed'. Next day his valet, Garwood, brought him a hot shirt to put on and an early dinner of beef steak, lamb chops, pickled salmon and tarts put him in a cheerful mood, especially as his dinner was only 9d.

Once only does he complain of stomach upset (May 31, 1789), when a supper of port and pigeon made his stomach 'much abused'. After a disturbed night, he was driven to visit the apothecary (who went by the appropriate name of Mr Gall). That night he let the apothecary have his port, one of the few occasions when he could not face his drink, and the next morning reverted to buttermilk and fresh strawberries, which caused him further spasms later. He vowed to take much more care with his diet and to observe certain rules, but a glance at the remainder of his journals does not indicate a great change in his eating habits. Hearty eating was indulged in by all ranks of society. The poor gorged when they could; the rich as a matter of course. Four or five dishes could easily be devoured; wine, ale, port and brandy were downed in great quantities. 'As a solace of the flesh, gluttony shared the honours with drinking' (Porter 1990, 20).

Travelling light

Byng arranged to collect his letters and draw money at the towns through which he passed, but was not averse to borrowing funds. He always travelled light. On some tours he sent his luggage from one inn to the next by post boy or carrier, expecting it to arrive before he did, although sometimes, as at Buxton, he was forced to wait several days for its arrival. Tom Bush, and later his successor, Garwood, would take their master's small portmanteau containing two shirts, a pair of 'articles', two neckcloths, two pairs of stockings, a pair of shoes and a waistcoat. On his tour north in 1789, Byng and his companions sent their baggage on ahead by stagecoach until after Newark their servants joined them to carry the luggage. Byng himself carried a small cloak bag in which was his hair powder in a powder bag with puff, and, by 1793, some medicines. His thick cotton nightcap always travelled with him in his pocket and was worn whenever he slept, even in a coach. At the Bulls Head, Aber (August 3, 1793), when he found that he had lost it, he was unable to sleep until his landlady lent him a square of flannel.

In 1792 there is mention of a second pair of breeches, which came in useful at Marsham (June 8), when, drenched by lashing rain, he was forced to change and have 'a grand ablution' of brandy: 'It feels November, I must creep to bed and pray for summer'. Five days later at Middleton he was again soaked, so he stripped off his wet stockings and followed his usual routine of rubbing with brandy and eating a good meal, this time trout and Scotch collops. Later he purchased an extra pair of worsted hose, which were warm and found to be very comfortable. There is no mention of a hat, but for a gentleman not to have had a hat would be tantamount to appearing naked. His greatcoat usually protected him from the worst of the weather.

His washing was done on route. He came down early to breakfast at the Swan Inn, Atherstone (June 27, 1784), to find the maid washing his upper and under waistcoats, so talked very civilly to her until they were dry, having been put either in, or in front of, the great ovens. He always took his own sheets with him, which being aired before they were put on the bed, gave him great comfort when he slipped between them. He feared finding wet sheets and having to sleep in filthy blankets; sometimes he slept on the floor to avoid this, but if needs be dirt was better than death caused by wet sheets. He had his own method of coping with these kind of blankets as at the Green Dragon, Montgomery (July 2, 1784) and the Bear and Ragged Staff, Rugby (June 30, 1789), where 'the sheets stank and the blankets were dirty and stinking'. He was forced to take off the sheets and use a pint of brandy to purify the room, sprinkling it, as well, over the blankets.

He was probably quite right about the problem relating to wet sheets. In 1732, the painter, William Hogarth, and four friends, when staying at an inn in Kent, had found the sheets so damp that they were forced to sleep fully clothed on the floor (Jarrett 1974, 148). On Byng's South Wales tour, his friend, Mr Osborn, caught a chill as a result of sleeping in wet sheets at Cardiff, while his own were in the wash. He was so unwell for the rest of the tour that several times Byng had to call a doctor. At Hereford, Byng urged him not to lose time, but instantly to seek his own physician; this Osborn was only too willing to do. By that time Byng had been alarmed by Osborn's poor appetite – a crust and tea for breakfast, a slice of mutton and a little glass of wine and water for dinner and another crust of bread for supper.

Given the choice Byng preferred a hard, smooth bed with his own sheets, aired before a roaring fire, and a well-filled bolster, pillow and mattress. Innkeepers often did not stuff the latter three items sufficiently or ignored them when they began to split. Cold sheets he hated, as they gave him cold feet, which he had to rub hard to get warm.

Rather surprisingly, he was never robbed, 'but I do not attribute this so much to luck, as to my observance of early hours'. By arriving early at an inn he got the best bed and the best horse stalls.

> I see neither the use, nor take the pleasure, of travelling in the dark. Not like young
> men who think it polite to travel in the dark and knock up inns…demanding applause
> or pity and for being encouragers of roguery.

Such travellers were the prey of highwaymen. Hence he avoids such menaces as those men who
infested the Essex roads (Copeland 1968, 99) or who robbed the Macclesfield mail, when a spirited
counter-attack left two bloody fingers on the ground, which, not surprisingly, no one came forward
to claim (Alcock 1972, 17).

Only once (June 20, 1789) is a night ride mentioned. P (his unidentified companion) ignored
Byng's arguments that he loved roosting like a turkey in the evening, could not see the view, nor
the bad track, that it made him and his horse too tired for the next day and that there were no aired
sheets, and forced him to ride from Swanton, Derbyshire, to Ashby de la Zouch in Leicestershire.
His companion rode on ahead, Byng lost his way and entering the Queen's Head just before midnight found Mr P seated at table, but no supper ordered. Eventually cold meat and liquor were
produced. As a result of this late arrival, Byng did not wind his watch and woke at what he thought
was 7 am, only to find that it was two hours later. He was furious at 'the consequences of our
unpleasant night ride.'

Byng was also shrewd, for when setting off on a tour of Bedfordshire in 1790, he ordered his
companion, Mr Colman, to conceal his pistols and not invite trouble 'for hazards and bloodshed are
clearly avoided by payment of five guineas'. Colman, shocked by this, said that he grieved to see
Byng's cowardice in forcing him to hide his pistols but, unperturbed, Byng would not have these
'instruments of valour and revenge on view'.

Cost of food

Byng was meticulous in recording details of inns, the food and drink together with their costs,
which appear to stay roughly the same over ten years. Sometimes the food was remarkably cheap.
At the Blackamoor's Head in Ashbourne in June 1779, his supper was cold ham, boiled fowl, trout,
bacon, tart and roasted bullock's heart washed down with wine and brandy, all at a cost of 2s 11d.
But at Maske, a small village near Richmond in Yorkshire, on June 12, 1792, he had a boiled fowl,
cold ham, Yorkshire pudding, roast loin of mutton, gooseberry pie and cheese at what he thought
was to be a heavy charge – 1s 6d but he was pleasantly surprised to find it was only 1s 3d. His
horse's hay and corn cost much more.

Usually the cost of his servant's food was included in the overall bill, but a four day stay at the
Three Cranes, Leicester, (June 23-26, 1790) cost him, his companion and three horses £2 9s 7d,
with an extra 14s for Tom Bush. In view of the fact that this covered all food, drink, rushlights and
hay and corn for the horses, even Byng was constrained to say that such a bill cannot make the
fortunes of an innkeeper. At the Golden Lion, Dolgelly, 'very civil, very cheap', where he, his friend,
Mr Palmer, and their two servants, stayed three nights in August 1784, he details his bill for twelve
meals as: eating 13s, brandy 6s 2d, ale 1s 8d, wine 2s 6d, porter 2s 9d, tobacco 6d, servant's eating
and ale 2s 10d, and horses' hay and corn 15s 9d. At the end of the thirty day tour of North Wales, the
overall cost was £40 including all expenses for the men and four horses and eating four meals a day:
'we saw many places and tipped generously'.

At the end of that tour his spirits were so high that he regrets not having stayed longer in Wales,
expressing a wish to visit it again soon, health and fortune permitting. But it was nine years before
he was to take the same route and it was a case, as so many travellers find, that expectation is
greater than realisation. In July and August 1793 the weather was sometimes very wet, he missed
his friend and the inns seemed worse than he remembered them.

The inn at Festiniog (July 30, 1793), which nine years previously had been a 'civil, clean and accommodating inn, a place which had a relish beyond the sauces of Mannheim and an invention of French cookery', and where Mr Palmer and he had met a very hospitable doctor, now appeared gloomy, with a wretched parlour and a horrid bedroom. His dog was fed 'oatmeal mess', and even a dinner of freshly caught salmon, hot salted roast beef, tart, cheese and port depressed him. He cheered up at supper when a hot roasted leveret was set before him and was thought so delicious that he would not allow any of it to be taken back. For both these feasts he paid 8d a meal and the same price for his breakfast the next morning – whey, coffee, bread and newly churned butter. In 1760 James Boswell described himself entering a London inn and taking the first empty place, and getting good food – beef, bread and beer – and this together with a penny tip for the waiter, cost him a shilling.

Costs are difficult to estimate in relation to the present time; at a rough estimate for a parallel with 1996, a multiplier of 80 can be suggested. In the later eighteenth century, manual wages were about one shilling a day and a labourer earned about £20 a year. It was impossible to keep a family on this, so supplements in kind were often available. The middle classes could exist on £80–£100 a year and in *Pride and Prejudice* Lydia and Wickham get by on £300, although they often appeal to Elizabeth for a share of Mr Darcy's £10,000, which was ample to keep up Pemberley. It is difficult to calculate Byng's income, but as he probably relied on half pay and his salary from the Stamp Office, it would not be less than £1,000. A truer estimate of costs comes from noting the price of a 4 lb (1.8 kg) loaf, one of the staple foods of the time. At the beginning of the century it cost 4d, at the end it cost 8d (Porter 1990, xv).

Landlords

Although in one sense travellers might expect conditions at an inn to be primitive, nevertheless, rising standards of living throughout the century led to greater expectations of comfort and cleanliness, which were not always met. Byng was continually exasperated and angry about the state of the inns and did not mince his words:

> I look upon an inn as a seat of all roguery, profaneness and debauchery, and sicken of them every day, by hearing nothing but oaths and abuse of each other (Vol.I, 105).

A bad inn, one suspects, could affect his view of the food. When staying at the White Hart and Star, Andover, in August 1782, the stable was bad and the inn intolerable: 'I never dined worse or was in a crosser humour about it; a miserably stale trout, some raw, rank mutton chops and some cold, hard potatoes'. At times he could be judicious in blame and praise., On his ride back from Wales in July 1784, he noted that while the White Lion, Shrewsbury, was a noisy, dirty, cold hotel, it also provided good port wine. The Hop Pole at Worcester was a noisy, dear inn, but fed a traveller hot rolls for breakfast. The Swan Inn at Warwick (July 11, 1785) had excellent wine and ale, but bad beds.

Sometimes he experienced the same feeling as those of modern travellers who find their views of inns change from year to year. On a visit to Bakewell in 1789 (June 15), he had found the White Horse to be a very tolerable inn, where he had an excellent dinner of cold lamb, a cold duck, 'sallad', tarts and jellies – 'nothing so pleasant after fatigue (at a certain age too), as eating and drinking'. The charge was 'exceedingly cheap and think what a service I had'. But the next year, when he stayed overnight, it was a different experience. As he left the White Horse on June 18, 1790, he noted acidly that he 'never was in a nastier house' or a more gloomy place, 'everything dirty and offensive to the smell', so he was eager to get away even in the rain, as 'the master and mistress – not to be seen, having probably been drunk over-night'. But he does admit that during a short stay on a hot summer's day, 'the inn appear'd more agreeable to me, than now, in a gloomy long stay.' The weather affects views of travel whatever the century.

Yet it was landlords and landladies who made or destroyed the reputation of an inn. The Red Lion at Worksop, where the 'conceited fool' of a landlord did nothing about the stinking feather beds, produced a 'very bad' dinner. The Talbot at Shifnal, Shropshire (June 30, 1792) was run by a drunken ostler and a mincing fine landlady, but still produced a hearty supper of cold meats and hot peas. J.G. Hohman, the landlord of the Crown Inn at Rotherham, was selling up in June 1789 because he could gain more money by making marbles for children. It was not surprising that Byng noted that a

> more dreary, tumbledown, blacker, old castlemented ruin cou'd not be found. In a front room upstairs, uneven as a plough'd field, we drank tea, and then with melancholy faces survey'd our shatter'd beds, windows broken, paper hanging down, blankets and curtains torn.

The general view of the inadequacy of certain inns can be complemented by the description in *Tom Jones* of the inn at Upton, where Tom stays on his journey to London (Fielding (1749), 1985, 336). The landlord begged Tom to excuse the poor accommodation as his wife had gone off with half the furniture and locked up the rest; Tom was forced to sleep in a rush chair.

Overall, Byng's view of landlords was somewhat jaundiced. They were insolent, 'the ostlers sulky, the chambermaids pert and the waiters are impertinent; the meat is tough, the wine is foul, the beer is hard, the sheets are wet, the linen is dirty and the knives are never cleaned'. Ostlers seem to be drunk constantly. What story lies behind the sight which met his eyes at the Rose and Crown, Wisbech (July 4, 1790), where he was greeted by a 'conceited dressed-out' landlady and an ostler with two black eyes? It was inevitable that here the dinner was bad and the charges dear. Ostlers were a suspect group. The name derived from the French 'hostelier', but the English nickname was 'oat-stealer', which was one reason why careful travellers checked on their horses before they attended to their own comfort. Ostlers were also notorious for running their hands over and in to saddlebags, as they helped gentlemen to dismount, to see if there was anything worth stealing (Haydon 1994, 150).

At 'Newcastle-under-Lime' on June 28, 1792 Byng was in despair: 'one of the most savage, dirty ale houses I ever enter'd (Traveller beware the Roe Buck in Newcastle)'. Cold meat could not be touched, the bread was oniony: 'I could not stay and was loth to go; despair forced me to order my horses; (an hungry man does not do this without due provocation)'. The weather might have affected him; it had rained constantly and June 29 was like a November evening.

In some inns he made the best of a bad job. On his way back from Wales in August 1793 he was forced to put up for two days at the Flower-de-Luce Alehouse near Weston (Staffordshire), because of the bad weather. Although alehouses had been debarred from selling wine by the Vintners Company, the monopoly was falling into some disuse but it was up to the innkeeper to apply for a licence from the magistrates. At this inn the landlord was not in attendance, seemingly because he was farming elsewhere. Byng's moroseness, a result of not getting any wine, was intensified by a visit to the stables, where he found that a pin had been driven through the saddle just missing his horse's backbone. He suspected his new valet, 'such a mixture of roguery and folly'. When he returned to the inn he noted miserably that the kitchen was full of cradles and squalling children. Even so, the maids waited on him assiduously and the ostler was very civil; there was a quarter of lamb roasted with potatoes and good cheese, and his sheets were dry.

When it was a bad inn, Byng, like so many people, took the line of least resistance, while silently vowing never to return. He was scathing about the Black Bull at Cambridge (July 5, 1790):

> I never was in a worse or dirtier inn for all Cambridge is in comparison of Oxford about 100 years behindhand – dirty glasses, bad wine, vile cooking but I answer to any question with, 'Oh, it is excellent' and why shall I not. Now Colonel Bertie [his travelling

companion] takes another plan; and roundly reproves them; but I, resolved never to come again, don't like to vex myself, and so I say, 'It is all very good'. Tho' here it went much against the grain.

After walking in 'desperate rain' and sleeping in a tent bed in a dark room, opening from an old gallery, he wrote in despair, 'This wretched inn with most of this wretched town ought to be burned down'. His temper was not improved by finding that brandy was 7s a quart, whereas he usually paid 1s a pint.

Good inns

But there were good inns. The Talbot at Hartlebury on July 21, 1784 met with his total approval, 'quiet, cheap and pleasant, ...Just such a one as a horse traveller shou'd stop at, and what I allways seek; where the whole family are employed in your service, for the boy is despatched to the butcher and baker and the mistress acts as cook'. He visited the Ram's Head at Disley in Cheshire twice, 'a neater and more cheerfully situated inn I never saw. The stables are excellent, the brown bread and cheese so good; the water so cold; the decanters so clean and the bedrooms so nice'. Its larder was 'wonderful' – salmon, pigeons, mutton, veal, cold ham: 'Take it all in all', he sighed on June 13, 1790, 'I may ne're look upon such an inn again'. Staple Hall, Witney, on June 25, 1784 was approved as one of the best and cleanest that he had found. The Sun at Biggleswade always welcomed him. On August 20, 1791 he was happily settled with a well roasted fowl, nice apricot tart, good bread, good cheese, fruit and a decent pint of port wine 'with no headache following'.

At the Haycocks Inn at Wansford Bridge he stayed so often that he was received as almost one of the family. If he went fishing, the landlady, Mrs Norton, was happy to cook the bream he caught. In July 1790 he stayed a week with his family and the next year he returned from his tour of the north to where it was 'all neat and comfortable' and he was at home. Mrs Norton greeted him with, 'Pray Sir, walk into your *own* room', and he was soon settled with pens and papers while the waiter fussed round him with the assurance that roast beef, potatoes and fresh tart would be ready by half past one. It then suited him to follow his own advice: 'After dinner, Sir, rest awhile'.

At the end of a tour, he also felt at home at the Bear at Woodstock, 'a charming inn with a good stable', though he sometimes had damp sheets. He liked to walk in Blenheim Park and one year bought a spaniel puppy, 'such a love and exactly like animated china', but soon had second thoughts, realising its incompatibility with his London dog, Jock, so gave it back. He was often accompanied by one of his dogs. On the North Wales tour in 1793, it was Flora, who had to be left at the Bulls Head, Conway, for some days to recuperate from lameness. On his northern tour in 1790, a dog attached itself to him at Stamford (June 20) and 'Sancho' accompanied him for the next two weeks until finally, when back at his comfortable Haycocks, he saw an advertisement in a Stamford newspaper for the lost dog. Byng wrote hastily that 'Sancho' should be sent for, commenting on the one hand that he was an incessant plague and on the other that on occasions he was amused by him and glad to have him.

Breakfast

Byng's usual plan was to pay his bill the night before departure (or get his companion to pay it in the morning), get up early, eat a slice of bread and butter and swallow some milk, which he had taken to his room the night before (according to his old hunting custom). The butter was probably better than that obtained in London which was often mixed with candle grease. Then, after shaving himself with cold water, 'without much delay I must go early and ride gently' and 'by this means you get forward on the day, enjoy the morning air and go to breakfast with true relish'. When he reached a suitable inn, he would have coffee and a hot roll, bread and butter, or perhaps buttermilk, which always did him good. While he was eating he would sometimes see his servant, Garwood, ride by, 'who would be an hour at breakfast and then make up his time by riding hard'. Byng could not cure him of 'loitering every morning with the maids or the mistress over a tea board; sip, sip, sip, by the hour (which makes one sick) and complimenting about lumps of sugar'.

When staying for longer in certain towns, he made a more leisurely meal. At the King's Arms at Holywell, Oxford (July 16, 1792), he had 'Brown George' as part of his breakfast, a nickname given to a coarse brown loaf, the content of which was the result of the government strategy over bread prices. When the price of bread rose in Oxford, it was decreed that no white bread should be sold, only that made with mixed flour.

Dinner

Dinner was taken any time between 2.30 pm and 4.30 pm. The food he ate would be local, which pleased Byng who believed 'get what is best in every county', but sometimes he ate in abundance of one commodity. On his tour of South Wales in 1787, he was treated constantly to salmon and sewen, a young form of salmon, which being less firm, he thought not equal to either salmon or trout. So common was salmon that Mr James, the Custom Sub-collector at Chepstow, told Byng (July 29, 1787) that a clause was included in indentures at Gloucester that the apprentices should not 'be obliged to dine on salmon off'ner than twice a week'. Trout, Byng thought, should be served boiled, accompanied by anchovy sauce, rather than fried in butter with fennel and parsley. He was willing to try grey mullet at the Crown, Ringwood (August 24, 1782) but seems to have been disappointed with this 'strong and oily' fish, which 'was not much superior to chub, nor would any dressing render him palatable'.

On July 28, 1787, during the South Wales tour, he and his companion, Mr Osborn, hired a boat from Raglan to visit Tintern Abbey. 'This river', said the boatman, 'is call'd Wye, Sir'. 'Yes', answered Byng, 'But my voyage on it will not make me wiser'. Before leaving they purchased a botcher (young salmon) of 3-4 pounds weight. This, together with the other provisions they had brought with them, was cooked by the landlady at the inn at Tintern. Byng's concern was that the landlady would be dissatisfied with the arrangement, especially as they brought with them their own wine, but she 'attended to them with assiduity and cheerfully brought of her ale before us'. No doubt she was amply recompensed, because, although Byng demanded value for money, he does not appear to have been mean.

Dinner could be a plain snack of bread, cheese, brandy or ale. He liked sage cheese and Derbyshire cheese, which he thought was a medium between Cheshire and Stilton. He enjoyed excellent local cheese at Cotherstone (July 13, 1792) and the blue cheese, which he was given at Cowbridge near Cardiff (July 12, 1987), resembled, both in colour and taste, the blue mould Cheshire cheese. He was not always so complimentary about Cheshire cheese. Some eaten at the George in Knutsford (June 13, 1790) was considered to be most unsatisfactory and he lamented that the best had been sent to London. In this he was probably right because cheese was often shipped there from the ports of Chester and Liverpool in coastal vessels. A good Cheshire cheese was judged by jumping on the huge round; if it collapsed it was full of maggots (personal communication). Byng was more fortunate than George Borrow, who visited Chester in 1862 on his way to Wales. Having described Chester as the capital of the cheese country, he looked forward to having some cheese in its prime. To his horror this had much the appearance of 'soap of the commonest kind', which he found it also resembled in taste, so he 'spat the half-masticated morsel into the street' and followed it with a mouthful of very bad ale (Borrow, 1862, 27).

A more robust dinner was eaten when Byng and his companion called at the Peacock Inn near Belvoir Castle in June 1789. Having been assured that a leg of mutton would be ready for them in an hour, they decided to visit the castle but were dismayed to find the rooms in a state of neglect, not surprisingly as the housekeeper was 'of a very drunk, dawdling appearance'. On their return, they were told bluntly that the mutton was for the lodgers and not for them: 'If so, Madam, get us anything you please, and we will give up the mutton'. Possibly unwilling to lose custom, or pacified by Byng's comment, the landlady set before them a round of boiled beef, the roasted leg of mutton, and greens, and a rice pudding and gooseberry tart, 'all served up with smiles'. This feast was fairly priced at 2s, with brandy for 1s and wine 1s 9d.

Another hearty meal was provided by the Golden Lion at Brecon (August 8, 1787), where he dined on a large piece of salmon and roasted sirloin of beef, 'of which I ate 2 pounds', washed down with a bottle of port. The Bear Inn at Newnham, Gloucestershire, on July 17, 1781, provided him with a round of beef, just taken from the pot, and a gooseberry tart. Often he had bacon and eggs and never more enjoyed it, with the addition of bread and cheese, than when sheltering from a thunderstorm, 'the clatter of clouds' (July 25, 1787) at an alehouse on Birdlip Hill, Gloucestershire. During his tour of South Wales, he remarked that, in summer, beans, eggs and bacon, 'which are to be eaten with true relish', were to be met with in every ale house.

Roasted bullock's heart was served at the Blackamoor's Head, Ashbourne (Derbyshire); at the Angel, Macclesfield (June 12, 1790) he ate 'boil'd buttock of a bull', but indicates that it was a nondescript dish such as was to be found in 'Porridge Island', an alley in London, where indifferent butchers cut off ready dressed meat from every part of the animal (Partridge 1931, 267). He was moved to comment, slightly unfairly, that London was the only place for fruit, wine, fish, venison and turtle: 'A London gentleman slips into a coffee house, orders venison and turtle, at the instant, and a delicious bottle of port or claret, upon a clean cloth, without form; he dines at the moment of appetite'.

As may be noted, on the tours, roasts were common – loin, shoulder and saddle of lamb, neck of mutton, often with caper sauce; cold meats were also frequent. There is little mention of pork, and few references to game; venison, for example, was served at the Bear Inn, Woodstock, no doubt supplied from Blenheim Park. Roasted rabbit was mentioned once. This emphasis on meat is confirmed by a menu for coach passengers, still surviving at the Sugarloaf, Dunstable – boiled round of beef, roast loin of pork, roast aitchbone of beef, boiled hand of pork with pease pudding and parsnips, roast goose, boiled leg of mutton (Gould 1968, 18). Beef was very popular. Hogarth's painting of *The Roast Beef of England (Calais Gate)* 1748 (Tate Gallery), with its monstrous sirloin of beef, deliberately emphasised the true Englishman's devotion to it and by the end of the century beef eating was part of patriotic fervour competing against the French tradition of using spices and other flavourings in meat stews or ragouts.

M. Misson, on his travels in England in the 1690s marvelled at the English being great flesh eaters, having little bread but devouring meat in huge mouthfuls. Fielding likewise extols the capacity for consuming huge amounts of meat. As he put it, before Tom Jones bedded Mrs Waters, 'three pounds, at least, of that flesh which formerly had contributed to the composition of an ox was now honoured by becoming part of the individual Mr Jones' (Fielding (1749) 1985, 453). Even when Parson Woodforde was very ill, the last entry in his diary on 17 October, 1802 reads: 'Very weak this Morning, scarce able to put on my cloaths and with great difficulty, get down Stairs with help...Dinner today Rost beef etc' (Woodforde 1947, 619).

Byng's appetite also rarely faltered. Even when ill and feverish, while staying at the Greyhound at Folkingham on June 22, 1789, he managed a dinner of boiled fowl, roast beef and young potatoes, 'a family meal'. In this he followed his fellow countrymen who consumed large meals, taking their time to eat well and often following it with some hard exercise. His friend, Mr Colman, thought nothing of eating twelve chops at one sitting. He confessed that he always thought of dinner for half an hour before arrival at an inn, which gave him an appetite, and a hurry for eating. Then, if he could have his meal quickly, he found that 'both body and mind are instantly refreshed and recovered'.

Supper

His supper, usually taken after an evening walk, could be as hearty a meal as dinner. Supper at the Cross Foxes, Llanvair (July 3, 1784), consisted of six dishes – cold veal, cold tongue, eggs, tart, cream, toasted cheese and butter. If meals of this standard could seem a little heavy, as he confessed was the case at Neath (August 6, 1787), he might go for a walk before supper as long as the twilight lasted and follow this merely by a slice of meat and brandy and water. With the remainder of the half pint of brandy, he could 'retire in safety from spasms to bed'.

Very occasionally, there is something out of the ordinary: 'spitch-cocked eels', potted trout, tripe and onions, kid or a young roasted leveret. At Dolgelly (July 7, 1784) he ate sand eels, which, when fried, tasted like whitebait; it was here also that he had his only lobster. At Neath (August 4, 1787), he supped on 'magnificent flounders, but not so well drest, as they wou'd have been at Greenwich or Blackwall'. A fisherman waiting at the door of the Crown Inn, Faringdon, near Oxford (July 23, 1787), sold him an eel weighing 3 lb (1.3 kg), which the landlady cooked for his breakfast the next day. He was disappointed later that day, when he visited the garden of a house at Fairford. Grapes, nectarines and pineapples were growing in the greenhouse, but the gardener did not offer him any. 'Suppose a woman had been with me', was his cryptic comment.

At Hastings (August 17, 1788) he ate wheatears, after plucking them himself. These had been caught in traps on the hillside below the castle and it was the custom to leave a penny in the trap if the wheatear was removed. Dinner that night at the Swan Inn consisted of roast duck, cold beef, plum pie and three and a half wheatears each for himself and his friend, I(saac) D(alby), a teacher of mathematics. When he moved to Lewes, the White Hart gave him potted wheatears.

Bread

Bread seems to have been included in the price of the meal, because once Byng was surprised to find it charged to his bill. Bread and cheese, he comments, are to be found everywhere in Wales, although once his bread was soft and tough through being baked in cabbage leaves. He often had bread and butter for breakfast and sometimes mentions that he ate excellent brown bread, for example at the New George at Tideswell (June 12, 1790) and at the Kings Arms, Askrigg, in Yorkshire (July 15, 1791). At Lewes (August 21, 1788) he moans 'I have sometimes seen wholesome, comfortable-looking brown bread under a cottager's arm', yet he had been obliged to eat white tasteless bread. The year after (May 30, 1789) at Silsoe, he had excellent brown bread – 'white I allways discard'. In this he probably differed from his contemporaries, because not only was white bread in demand during the late eighteenth century as a sign of status, but as Arthur Young commented in 1767 'rye and barley bread are looked on with horror even with poor cottagers' (Williams 1962, 114). In Wales Byng was given good oaten cakes with a slice of ham, but he had soft, bad ones with cheese and ale at the Dog and Partridge near Ashbourne in 1790.

This view of status is exemplified by Thomas Smollett in his novel *Humphry Clinker* (Smollett (1771), 1966, 122). In a letter written to Dr Lewis, Matt Bramble comments that the bread he eats in London is a

> deleterious paste, mixed up with chalk, alum and bone-ashes, insipid to the taste and destructive to the constitution. The good people are not ignorant of this adulteration; but they prefer it to wholemeal bread because it is whiter than the meal of corn.

Vegetables

Vegetables are mentioned rarely, possibly because he had the same prejudices as the rest of society against them, or because they figured little in his diet, meat being the main component. Pastor Moritz[2] in 1782 noted that the midday meal in England consisted of a piece of half boiled or half roasted meat and a few cabbage leaves boiled in plain water, on which they pour a sauce made of flour and butter, the usual method of dressing vegetables in England. As vegetables were seasonable, they could be expensive. But Byng liked peas in season. Beans are often eaten with bacon; turnips, boiled cabbage and potatoes are also offered. Several times he has 'sallet' or 'sallud', and asparagus; the Bulls Head, Bosworth in Leicestershire (June 26, 1789), provided him with 'two stacks of it, each one foot in height'.

Poultry

Both at dinner and supper fowl or duck was a popular dish. Tom Bush warned him at the Bull Inn, Dunstable (July 3, 1789), not to eat duck as he had seen dead and dying birds in all parts of the garden. Byng was convinced that 'fowls are the only thing to bespeak at an inn, as every other dish is either ill-dressed, or the leavings of other companies'. The landlord of the New Inn, Winchelsea (August 18, 1788) told him that the tough fowl had just been killed for him, but Byng preferred the one which he had five days later at the White Hart, Godstone, where he knew its parentage and education. That fowls were often on the menu can be confirmed by Mr Jingle's comment to the Pickwick party at the Bull Inn, Rochester, that broiled fowl and mushrooms were a capital dish (Dickens (1836-7), 23). Tom Jones at the inn at Upton ate a 'large mess of chicken or rather cock broth, with a very good appetite, as indeed he would have done the cock it was made of, with a pound of bacon into the bargain'. Pigeons were part of Byng's diet; tolerable pigeon pie was obtained at the Royal George, Grantham.

Desserts

Desserts seem to have been mainly tarts or 'pyes' – apricot, gooseberry, plum, apple, morello cherries – with the occasional custard. Occasionally he buys strawberries in certain towns and it is to be hoped that they were better than the 'pallid, contaminated mash' which was 'soiled and tossed by greasy paws through twenty baskets crusted with dirt' (Smollett (1771), 1966, 122).

Only once is plum pudding mentioned. The lack of puddings seems to contradict the oft-quoted statement of Henri Misson, extolling puddings. The English 'bake them in the oven, boil them with meat, they make them fifty different ways: blessed be he that invented pudding…Give an English man a pudding and he shall think it a noble treat in any part of the world' (Wilson 1973, 321). Once, at the Unicorn, Altrincham (June 13, 1790), he was offered cheesecake, but a most unusual dessert was served at the Kings Arms, Askrigg (June 15, 1792), when he was offered radishes, 'much as they serve up turnips in Scotland'.

Drink

Drinking was on as hearty a scale as eating. He drank mainly port and brandy, although in Wales he drank greedily of the ale when it was good or when nothing else was available, and even more occasionally, porter, which had been first brewed in England in the early eighteenth century, but usually he could finish off two bottles of claret or a pint of port and a bottle of brandy with ease. As he said, 'I gave sufficient encouragement to the French by the consumption of their brandy, which I commonly call for a pint per diem'.

In his drinking, he was no different from his contemporaries; three or four bottle men were not uncommon and both Richard Brindsley Sheridan and the Prime Minister, William Pitt, were six bottle men (Porter 1990, 19). The bulbous, upright bottle, however, held about a pint. Byng often refers to a pint of port, which makes the six bottles consumed seem less remarkable. Port had become very popular in England as a result of the Methuen Treaty of 1703, which enabled Portugal, as England's oldest ally, to import port without paying much duty. By the end of the century it was considered patriotic to drink port instead of claret because of the deteriorating relations with France. Dr Johnson, however, declared that claret was a drink for boys and port for men. The port was not heavy fortified wine, but a lighter kind, which had absorbed brandy for, at most, four years instead of the ten or fifteen years which would become common in the next century. Byng boasted that no one understood port better than he did and no one else would go to more effort to procure it. He certainly knew when he was being offered 'puckering port' as happened at Sevenoaks on his Sussex tour of 1788. Port and his writings were his greatest support when travelling.

On his Lincolnshire tour, he confessed that he had become more addicted to gin, downing 'Hollands' very plentifully, but his heart was not in it as he complained that gin and water did not agree with him. The middle and upper classes on the whole preferred not to drink gin (Haydon 1994, 100). Even so, at the Red Lion, Worksop (June 10, 1789), Byng mentions that he and his companions 'ginned themselves without being strangled'. This refers to the notorious custom of nurses throwing a spoonful of gin down children's throats to keep them quiet, but which usually killed them (George 1930). When asked the cause of death, the nurses replied, 'consumption'.

If he had made his tours at the beginning of the century he would probably have been more addicted to gin. Until the Gin Act of 1751, which began the process of placing an additional duty on gin, the spirit had been the normal tipple in England, with gin shops proclaiming 'drunk for a penny, dead drunk for tuppence, clean straw provided'. In 1783 the raising of the duty on home-made spirits to £61 19s 9d intensified the decline of the trade and led to a greater consumption of ale or, if it could be afforded, wine.

The only time punch is mentioned was at the Crown Inn, Slough (July 22, 1787), when he made an excellent cold punch for himself, his wife and his mother-in-law, commenting that from the pleasure of the taste and their ignorance of the mixture, women are often 'induced to drink a great deal and be jovial'. This is borne out also by Mrs Honour's behaviour in *Tom Jones*, when, as she drank from a huge bowl of punch, her anger was exaggerated by 'pouring liquid fire' down her throat (Fielding (1749) 1986, 539). Byng's punch was better than that which he had the next night at the Black Bear, Reading. He sighed that it was sour and weak, and to add to his discomfort, when he went to bed, he feared his sheets were damp. Punch had become popular because of large quantities of rum imported from the West Indies.

Byng also likes the more sober drinks of tea and coffee, tea often being served with cream and accompanied as was the custom of the time by dry toast. Once for breakfast he drank a pint of cream with his tea. The duty on tea was lowered in 1784, thus allowing the East India Company to increase imports and making it a more popular drink. Milk and sugar were added, the former to prevent the tea tannin staining the cups, the latter to assuage the English liking for sweet drinks. Tea was the drink of all classes, but coffee was the drink of the gentry, who expected it to be provided by the inns; once the duties on imported West Indian coffee were reduced, then coffee consumption increased (Wilson 1973, 407), especially as it was regarded as being less adulterated than tea. Byng expected to have tea in the afternoon and coffee in the morning at the inns.

Service

Byng always believed in trying out the family fare, saying that the meal was often better and cost half as much as that of an ordered dinner. He was annoyed with his companion, Colonel Bertie, on the Lincolnshire tour as the Colonel ordered 'this and that', thereby delaying the meal so that the dishes were served cold. Byng preferred to run into the kitchen and 'see what is going on and likely to be ready; there is leg of mutton roasting, and a veal pye, did you say. Bring them in. So I dine quickly, cheaply and at the moment of appetite.' It also enabled him to check on the state of the kitchen: at Skegness (July 7, 1791), the kitchen stank of strong mutton and 'roasting hog'. It was inevitable that he was served only miserable smelts and rank raw beef for supper.

He also disliked the Colonel's method of continually ringing the bell to summon the waiter, preferring to have everything laid out and to get what he wanted from a side table. He told the Colonel to determine what he wanted beforehand and not to keep the waiter in the room 'questioning about brewing and baking'. He was equally exasperated by the bantering which his two younger companions had with the maids on a tour of the Midlands in 1789. If it went on too long he sulked, wanting his food and drink served first without any chatter. To their mocking that he was 'an old fellow', he replied, 'Aye, so I am and know how much better it is to be well waited upon than to make the servants impertinent by familiarity.'

He remarked on the difference between Mr P and himself. P was like Colonel Bertie ordering the waiter to stand behind his chair and hand him everything he wants. Byng was uneasy when the waiters were watching him, taking away his plate too soon and winking at the others. There might also be a 'nasty dirty wench watching you all the time, picking her nails, blowing her nose on her apron and then wiping the knives and glasses with it; or spitting and blowing upon the plates.' He preferred to have everything necessary laid on the table before him, so that he could tell the servants not to stay, then he could talk and eat at leisure; if he wanted them he would ring. He remarked shrewdly that when people come in tired, 'they are as greedy of food, as of venting their minds to each other of past travells and future intentions; and this they cannot do before attendants.' As many people, however, in the eighteenth century, hardly noticed servants, he may, perhaps, have been too sensitive on this issue.

But it was the waiters in Wales in 1787 (Vol.II, 303) for whom he reserved the most spleen; they are

> sulkey, insolent and uncomb'd; and idle fellows are seen basking in the sun – if a waiter, here, brings a cup, he forgets the spoon, and eternally leaves the door open and when you speak to him, appears not to hear, for you get no answer – what you require they never bring, but when you are quiet, they force in, with, 'did you call?'

Bad meals

Occasionally he was defeated by his meals. At the Kings Head, Richmond, Yorkshire, (June 11, 1792), he was faced with buttered chops, 'which did not make my chops water'. When passing through Manchester, the stale salmon and the thick, raw fried chops served at the Bulls Head (June 25, 1792) made him moan, 'God sends meat, but the Devil sends cooks. I could not eat; I try'd to drink of the port wine but could not; the bread was intolerable and the cheese was in remnants; – I said take it away; I cannot eat.' To add to his misery it began to rain, the landlord would not change a £10 note and implied that he had left a counterfeit half guinea. He left the waiter 1s 'for his non-attendance' and for this badly served badly cooked feast he was charged 2s with dear wine at 2s 6d, but he was let off lightly for his horses' hay and corn at 1s 6d.

He could be defeated in another way by sheer greed. After a hearty dinner at the White Hart, Broadway (August 12, 1787), where he attacked a loin of veal 'in ample measure', then had a 'superabundant temptation by an apricot tart', he set off, but before he had gone forty yards he cried to his servant, Tom Bush, 'I must return – I am tired – I am too full – and can't ride'. So he went back to the inn, and returned to a clean parlour in which, by reading and writing, supping on chicken, thinking and drinking, he occupied himself until bed about 11 pm, his usual time for retiring. The next day, still disinclined to ride, he decided to take the Worcester coach, when it overtook him at Moreton in Marsh, leaving Tom Bush to follow with the horses, and continued to Woodstock where he was put up at his favourite Bear Inn.

Bush arrived with the horses only half an hour after the coach, which had stopped for the midday meal at Enstone. Byng was not hungry enough to take the coach dinner but contented himself with bread and cheese and a glass of wine. By evening his appetite had returned and he did justice to venison pasty, duck and peas and 'was full of content'.

Modern attitudes

Enough has been said to give a good indication of this indefatigable character, whose ideas are akin to those of today. Like many modern travellers, he went abroad to be busy and active and not to lose time, especially in good weather, and like them, he can be disaffected when places do not live up to his expectations; but he accepts this and warns that tourists should think for themselves and forget what they have read, for 'sadly do Recollection and Invention clash'. Modern travellers have a variety of country houses to visit and have to pay for this pleasure. Byng visits any he wishes by the simple expedient of asking the owner or the housekeeper to show him around.

He laments that he was born fifty years too late as the new turnpike roads have introduced contemptuous insolence, towns were growing quickly, antiquities were being destroyed and a dreadful sameness was pervading the countryside: 'I am one of the very few who regret the times when England afforded to the observant traveller a variety of manners, dress and dialect'. Modern travellers have this sense of sameness which affects present day Britain, as well as fearing that the heritage is being destroyed.

Perhaps modern travellers also suspect that they are neglected for the large tour party. Byng had already sensed this. Most good inns, he noted, were kept by, and for, a change of post horses; fine gentlemen never step out of their chaises on the longest journeys. Others travelled by mail coach so that the tourist who wants only supper or a bed, is considered a troublesome, unprofitable intruder; nor was it necessary to tempt him with good drink and civility. The parallel might be drawn today of the single traveller forced to pay the single supplement in a hotel and failing to get a drink because he or she is elbowed out by the tour parties and the business clientele.

A sense of continually moving on, rarely staying more than one night at an inn, is also present. On July 19, 1784 at the White Lion, Shrewsbury, he was vexed in regard to 'a daily worry or a nightly change of beds; in consequence my nerves shatter and my spirits tire.' Sometimes it is almost as though he experienced a psychological pain at getting back to work. In July 1790, while he was staying at Wansford Bridge, the thought of a return to London, trudging every day to Somerset Place brought on such 'crickish pain' at the back of the neck and rheumatism in his shoulder and chest, that two days later he had to retire to bed and regale himself with 'liberal libations of warm wine and brandy'. Just so can a modern traveller experience the 'today's Tuesday, it must be Belgium' syndrome, or have withdrawal symptoms at the thought of a return to work.

Dining at inns

Innkeepers were quick to cater for a captive clientele, for when the coach rolled up to the door, where would travellers dine but in the coaching inn? A timetable still displayed on the wall of the Cock Inn, Stony Stratford, notes that the Manchester coach arrived at 1.47 pm and left at 2.12 pm. This proprietor was shrewd enough to own the inns of the preceding and succeeding stages, for where the coach did not stop long enough for travellers to have a meal, there had to be change of horses at each stage, usually every 7 to 10 miles (Haydon 1994, 90).

Thomas Hughes in describing Tom Brown's journey to Rugby (Hughes, Chapter 2) allowed one and a half minutes for a change of horses and twenty minutes for breakfast, a far more substantial feast than Byng had – a table, covered with the whitest of cloths and china and loaded with pigeon pie, a round of cold boiled beef, cut from a mammoth ox, a ham, and a great loaf of household bread placed on a wooden trencher. Then the waiter appeared with a tray of kidneys, steak, bacon, poached eggs, buttered toast and muffins, tea and coffee; cold meats were on the side tables. The coachman ate cold beef, rather than the hot dishes, and drank a tankard of ale. When Tom has 'imbibed muffins, kidneys, pigeon pie and coffee, till his skin is tight as a drum', he is lifted up on the coach again which is off again at the exciting speed of 11 miles an hour, an increase from the average speed of 7 1/2 miles at the beginning of the century (Gould 1968, 6).

Diners had to eat quickly. Disraeli indicates the huge spread available for travellers in a passage in *Tancred* (quoted in Richardson 1934, 94), which they must consume in half an hour. 'What a dinner! What a profusion of substantial delicacies! What mighty and iris-tinted rounds of beef! What vast and marble-veined ribs! What gelatinous veal pies! What colossal hams! Those are evidently prize cheeses! And how invigorating is the perfume of those various and variegated pickles!' There is an 'all-pervading feeling of omnipotence from the guests who order what they please to the landlord, who can produce and execute everything they can desire. 'Tis a wondrous sight!'

Byng travelled in summer but in winter passengers went in danger of their lives. When the Bath coach reached Chippenham on a bitterly cold day in March 1812, the inn folk were very surprised to see three inert outside passengers, but their 'surprise was converted to horror when they perceived that vitality had been extinct in two of them for some time, the bodies being properly cold' (Copeland 1968, 98). Even in summer, however, Byng's weather was often so bad that a good fire was necessary. How much more welcome would that fire have been in winter. Washington Irving in *Travelling at Christmas* noted the roaring kitchen fire through the windows as soon as the coach rolled into the inn yard. As he entered the inn he 'admired for the hundredth time, that picture of convenience, neatness, and broad honest enjoyment, the kitchen of an English inn. It was of spacious dimensions; hung round by copper and tin vessels...hams, tongues and flitches of bacon were suspended from the ceiling...A well-scoured deal table extended along one side of the kitchen, with a cold round of beef, and other hearty viands upon it, over which two foaming tankards of ale seemed mounting guard' (quoted in Richardson 1934, 85).

Such warmth was fully appreciated by travellers, who staggered in, rigid with cold. Coachmen, recognisable by their hands, claw-shaped and broken-fingered from clutching the lead reins thirty feet long, often had to be lifted down and set by the fire to thaw. At Hereford, outside passengers who had paid 25 shillings for the 36 hour journey to London, fortified themselves before setting out with an 'early pearl', a pick-me-up consisting of half a pint of boiled ale, a 'joey' (half a pennyworth) of gin, a little sugar and a pinch of ginger. Ladies could have a hot rum and coffee (Howse 1946-48, 39). Even when the coach set off, the dangers were not yet over. One passenger wrote, with deep feeling, 'Give me a collision, a broken axle and an overturn, a runaway team, a drunken coachman, snowstorms, howling tempests: but Heaven preserve us from floods!'(Alcock 1972, 11).

Some of Byng's comments about the weather strike a chord with modern travellers. In June 1792, with the rain pouring day after day, he moaned: 'Here is winter coming; and my flannell under-waistcoat not yet changed for a callico one'. When it was cold and wet, Byng loathed the inns, the food and his fellow travellers, so that at times he vowed never to travel again. But when, in 1791, he came into hot, dusty London his thoughts turned to the following year, 'In my way planning future tours – and if – and how, to be managed'. His ideal tour was 'a passage through new country, upon a safe horse, in a charming summer morning' (Vol. II, 219), followed by 'a good dinner, a good parlour and good attendance.' such as he stated he had at the Red Cow, Dunnington on July 3, 1791. This was not his experience in Ashby de la Zouche on June 21, 1789: 'What can exceed the dullness of a country town on a Sunday evening in heavy rain,' a heartfelt comment often invoked today.

In July 1793, when he returned from his somewhat depressing trip to North Wales, he was in a more subdued mood: 'Thus ends this eventful history of 1793. May it serve to warn posterity from a love of rambling; and may it instruct them to keep (*quietly if they can*) at home.' But, if this energetic man had stayed at home, we would not have had this illuminating glimpse of dining in the inns of eighteenth-century England and Wales. He may be excused his self-satisfied remark that 'of all the tours he reads he likes his own the best', because of the pleasure which he gives to the reader two hundred years later. The reader can wholeheartedly agree with Byng that 'a tour can be enjoyed three times over, viz by anticipation, by the present enjoyment and by a record of the past'.

ACKNOWLEDGEMENT

I am most grateful to Regina Sexton of Vicarstown, Co. Cork for supplying me with the information on snail syrup.

BIBLIOGRAPHY

Albert, W. *The Turnpike Road System in England 1663-1840*, Cambridge: Cambridge University Press, 1972.
Alcock, Joan P., *The Industrial Scene*, Congleton: Congleton History Society, 1972.
Andrews, C. Bruyn, *The Torrington Diaries containing the Tours through England and Wales of the Hon. John Byng (later Fifth Viscount Torrington) between the years 1781 and 1794*, 4 vols, London: Eyre and Spottiswood, 1934-1938.
Andrews, C. Bruyn, *Clouds and Sunshine by an English Tourist of the Eighteenth Century being the first part of the tour of 1789*, Marlow: Roy Patrick Smith Press, nd.
Baker, Margaret, *Discovering the Bath Road*, Princes Risborough: Shire Publications, 1968.
Borrow, George, *Wild Wales, its People, Language and Scenery* (1862), London: Collins, 1967.
Burne, S.A.H. 'The Coaching Age in Staffordshire', *Transactions of the North Staffordshire Field Club*, 56, 1922, 46-74.
Copeland, John, *Roads and their Traffic 1750-1850*, Newton Abbot: David and Charles, 1968.
Dickens, Charles, *The Pickwick Papers* (1836-7), London: Hazell, Watson and Viney, nd.
Fielding, Henry, *Tom Jones* (1749), London: Penguin Classics, 1985.
George, M.D. *London Life in the Eighteenth Century*, Oxford: Oxford University Press, 1930.
Gould, Jack, *Discovering the Birmingham Road,* Princes Risborough: Shire Publications, 1968.
Haydon, P., *The English Pub: a History*, London: Robert Hale, 1994.
Howse, W.H. 'The Coaching Era at Hereford', *Transactions of the Woolhope Naturalists' Field Club*, 32, 1946-1948, 38-40.
Hughes, Thomas, *Tom Brown's Schooldays* (1857), London: The Heirloom Library, 1957.
Jarrett D., *England in the Age of Hogarth*, Yale: Yale University Press, 1974.
Partridge, Eric (Edit), *Dictionary of the Vulgar Tongue by Captain Francis Grosse*, London: Scholastic Press, 1931.

Porter, Roy, *English Society in the Eighteenth Century*, Revised Edition, London: Penguin, 1990.

Richardson, Albert E., *The Old Inns of England*, London: Batsford, 1934.

Smollett, Tobias, *The Expedition of Humphry Clinker* (1771), edited by Lewis M. Knapp, Oxford: Oxford University Press, 1966.

Thackeray, W.M., *Pendennis* (1848), London: Dent, Everyman's Library, 1958.

Williams, Eric, *Life in Georgian England*, London: Batsford, 1962.

Wilson, C. Anne, *Food and Drink in Britain*, London: Constable, 1962.

Woodforde, James, *The Diary of a Country Parson 1758-1802*, edited by James Beresford, Oxford: Oxford University Press, 1949.

A Meal in a Piece of Pasta

Josephine Bacon

There is no food so redolent of the thundering hooves of the Golden Horde dashing over the steppes of Asia and Russia and the plains of central Europe, conquering all in their path, as the fermented, dried pasta, known variously as *tarana, tarbonya* and *trahanas*. Wherever the Magyars and the Seljuk Turks and their descendants, the Ottoman Turks, made their home, you will find this complete meal-in-a-pasta.

Pasta has always been the most obvious portable food, compact and nutritious. Wheat is easier to grow than rice, it almost cultivates itself. When the wheat berries are ground, they can be dried more successfully than a whole grain or berry which has a tendency to rot. The earliest versions of the fermented pasta may well have been produced from such wild grains as barley, rye and buckwheat, but it was soon discovered that the leavening properties of wheat and the enzyme known as phytase which softens dough naturally made it the tastiest grain to use for making this portable food. However, grain and water hardly constitutes a whole food, and raw dough is neither palatable nor digestible. Thus unleavened pasta was born, a pasta enriched, usually with dried fermented milk and vegetables.

As with most traditional foods, there is no definitive recipe. The mixture varies from country to country, from village to village, even from household to household. Sometimes *tarbonya* looks like yellow lumps, sometimes it is like little grey-brown sheets, sometimes it is thick with whole sesame seeds, sometimes it is ground into small pellets that look like All-Bran.

The most authentic versions of *tarbonya* (I will call it that for the sake of brevity) I have found are from Cyprus and the least authentic in Hungary and Bulgaria, where the product has been commercialised. In fact, in Hungary, *tarbonya* has lost so many of its traditional ingredients that it is now nothing more than an egg soup pasta. In *The Cuisine of Hungary*, George Lang's recipe for *tarbonya* contains nothing but 900g/2lbs (8 cups) flour, seven eggs and water. The resulting *tarbonya* are small rice-like grains, a little like the Jewish soup pasta known as farfel. Josef Venesz, in *Hungarian Cuisine*, describes *tarbonya* as a granulated, dried pasta made of flour and eggs, the use of which, according to some authors, had been introduced by our nomad forbears in the distant past. '*Tarbonya* consists of pasta kneaded from eggs and flour, granulated in a special way into small pellets and dried...'. *Tarbonya* may be kept in dried condition for a long time. This is how modern Hungarian housewives tend to make *tarbonya* – if they make it at all.

In Bulgaria and Macedonia, *tarana* still contains dried fermented milk, even when packaged and sold commercially but they are very different from the traditional versions of *tarbonya* still found in Bulgaria and Cyprus. To quote from Maria Johnson, who wrote the introduction to a *trahana* recipe in *Grains, Pasta and Pulses* (simply *Pasta*, in the American version), in the Time-Life Good Cook series:

> '*Trahana*, a leavened pasta with a pleasantly sour flavour, is one of the most ancient grain products. It is served as an accompaniment to meat, fish or cheese throughout the Balkans and the countries of the former Ottoman Empire. *Trahana* takes at least two weeks to prepare. A purée is made from such vegetables as courgettes (zucchini), green peppers and sometimes hot chillies. It is mixed with flour to form a dough. Ground sesame seeds and sourdough (flour and water left for a few days in a warm place to ferment naturally) are added. The dough is then set in a warm place for a few days. When doubled in bulk, the dough is sieved or chopped into small pieces the size of peas and left to dry out completely for at least a week.'

This is the *trahanas* I remember from Cyprus. One would often pass through a village on a sunny day in Spring and see bedsheets laid out on the pavement outside houses on which pieces of the dough had been spread out to dry. However, it is not necessary to dry *tarhonya* in the sun. The Albanians, who call it a wind-dried pasta, place it in linen bags and hang them in a well-aired place. In the old days, the bags were attached to the horseman's saddle and the rider would 'gallop the pasta dry'.

In Cyprus, yogurt is often added to the mixture, to help the fermentation process and give the dough a pleasantly tangy taste. Chillies are never used, peppery food is not popular in Cyprus, and I do not remember the use of green peppers either. Tiny pieces of tomato and courgette are sometimes used but in all cases, the vegetables needed to have dried out by themselves first. *Trahanas* must be white or yellow, though some versions are almost greyish and vegetables must not be allowed to spoil the colour.

Although *tarhonya*, *trahanas*, etc. would seem to be an excellent accompaniment for soup, it does not seem to be used in that way, but rather as a side dish to be eaten with the main course, like pasta or potatoes. In the days when potatoes were unknown, root vegetables available only in season, and the rather tasteless colocassia the only bulky staple known to the ancient world (and it could only be grown in hot climates), the only cheap filling food available was grain. Thus *tarhonya*, like porridge, was a main course, and it is still eaten as such though nowadays it tends to accompany chicken, a meat stew, or cheese. Josef Venesz says *tarhonya* 'can be used just like rice, fried lightly in lard, then cooked in water until tender and served chiefly as an accompaniment to meat dishes, served with plenty of gravy.' His recipe advises adding water sparingly. So while small pasta is mostly associated with soups, *tarhonya*, *trahanas* etc., is very definitely associated with the main course. In Bulgaria, it is eaten with the salty white cheese known as *sirene*.

Tarhonya is now available commercially and can be found at Greek Cypriot and Turkish Cypriot grocers in Britain, and wherever there is a sizeable Greek or Turkish community. Fortunately, it is still made only by small manufacturers. I have even found it in Sainsbury's in a neighbourhood where there is a large Greek population, but as far as I am aware it is a speciality of northern mainland Greece, the province of Macedonia.

Perhaps the most fascinating aspect of *tarhonya*, *trahanas*, *tarana*, etc., is that it proves that the ancient nomads had an instinctive grasp of nutritional principles. Clearly, the original version of the product contained fermented wheat, easily digestible and containing vitamin B12 from the yeast or yeast-like organisms used in the fermentation, milk or a milk product (calcium, fat, trace elements), and, above all, vegetables to provide vitamin C (this vitamin would also be present in the grain). All this at least 1,000 years before doctors in Western Europe ever studied nutritional deficiencies in professional travellers such as sailors.

Perhaps rather than being likened to a pasta, *tarhonya*, etc. has a closer relationship to the Cornish pasty and other whole, portable meals popular with working people throughout the centuries. Manual workers knew instinctively what foods did them good, what a pity their 'superiors' never took any notice of their practises, it would have saved many lives and much suffering due to scurvy, beri-beri, etc.

The Most Travelled Food in the World, the Peanut

A. Blake

Arachis hypogaea has been known by many names since man first discovered its value as a food. *Mani, Ynchic, Mandubi, Tlalcacauatl, Chocopa, Nguba, Erdnuss, Cacahuète* are a few of the alternatives to the Peanut or the Groundnut which has been spread across the globe from its initial home. Spread so far and so well known everywhere that most people are unaware of where its origin was.

As with many of the commonplace foods we eat today the peanut first came to Europe with the discovery of the Americas, but before this time it was known and grown widely throughout the tropical and subtropical regions of South America, so there has been much speculation as to precisely where peanuts were first eaten by man. The wild species of the plant are found exclusively in this continent from north-eastern Brazil to north-western Argentina and from the south coast of Uruguay to the north-western Mato Grosso; Gregory and others have suggested the Pantanal in Brazil as the centre of the area from which the peanut originated.

The peanut is of course not a nut but a member of the legume family; the flowers of the plant are pollinated above ground but afterwards the fertilised ovary grows down into the ground on a 'peg' where the seedpod develops. The earliest archaeological evidence of peanut consumption has come from the coastal region of Peru at a latitude of about 8°S and at the time when ceramic pottery was first developed in this region about 1200 to 1500 BC. This dates the appearance of peanuts as a food somewhat before that of maize. Since that time peanuts appeared in most of the early South American civilisations but did not get to Mexico until much later and was probably introduced there by the Spanish. Most of the early European descriptions of the plants of the New World make some reference to peanuts and their cultivation. The Portuguese naturalist, Soares de Souza, gave one of the first descriptions of the plant and its cultivation. He also added an 'essential' aspect relating to this : 'The plants are grown in a loose humid soil the preparation of which has not involved any male human being, only the female Indians plant them and their husbands know nothing about these labours. If the husbands or their male slaves were to plant them they would not sprout; the females also harvest them.' It is presumed that this inability of the males towards growing the crops did not extend to eating them! The origin of the name 'Arachide' is generally credited to the French naturalist Plumier (1693) and some three years later the British physician Sir Hans Sloane used this name in a catalogue of plants he compiled in the West Indies.

Subsequent to its discovery by Europeans they transferred the plant to other parts of the world. The Spanish took it to Mexico, the Dutch to the Dutch East Indies, the Portuguese to Africa and India; Peruvian varieties were also transported to China via the Pacific and to Java and Madagascar. It is known too that peanuts moved up the west coast of Peru to Mexico and thence across the Pacific on the Acapulco-Manila galleon line, which had scheduled crossings from 1565 to 1815. Today India and China are the main peanut producing countries in the world and account for about half the total annual production.

In present-day Indonesia the peanut is considered a local crop and is hawked around the streets of Jakarta and Surabaya. The locals who eat them everyday and prepare satay sauce from them are for the most part quite surprised to learn that this staple of their diet originated on the other side of the Pacific.

Spain also played an important part in the spread of the peanut within Europe; Talvares de Ulloa took the peanut to Valencia in 1798 and from there it was taken to the south of France by

Lucien Bonaparte in 1801. It was the Spanish too who first extracted peanut oil and the Bishop of Valencia, Tabores, is credited with inventing the first machine for shelling the nuts.

It is not known when the peanut made the first journey to North America but it is generally accepted that this was not by the most obvious land route from South America via Mexico. One explanation is linked to the transport of slaves from Africa to the new colonies and that the peanut, which was by now well accepted in Africa, was taken along as food for the voyage, though direct introduction from the Caribbean to North America is also a possibility. In truth there were probably several introductions of peanuts into America over the Colonial period and it is recorded that Spanish peanuts were introduced into the US from Malaga in Spain in 1871 where the crop was by now being used for the extraction of its oil. The realisation of the utility of peanut oil was now to drive the cultivation of this crop in many parts of the world on a large scale at a time when there was a world shortage of oil for food and other uses such as soap making. It was a French trader Jaubert who had sent a sample of peanut oil to Marseilles in 1833 and is credited with initiating this process with a shipment of 722 kg in 1840, the year when France reduced its import tariffs on peanuts. The first large shipments came from the Cape Verde islands to Marseilles in 1848. Similarly Britain was looking for new sources of oils and fats for its emerging industrial society and the Gambia became a major source of supply; records show that 213 baskets of peanuts were imported in 1834 which by the 1840's had risen into several thousand tonnes. In the USA the Civil War created its own demand for oil products and whereas peanuts had been grown as a garden crop up to 1865, the crop was commercialised on a larger scale in the years up to the end of the century.

George Washington Carver is credited with being one of the key pioneers in the American development of the peanut industry; he promoted the planting of peanuts in the southern states and encouraged the use of the plant as a foodstuff and forage crop. The cotton crop of America was seriously threatened by the boll weevil at the start of this century and many farmers in the southern states of the USA turned to peanuts as an alternative source of income since disused cottonseed mills could be converted to the processing of peanuts instead. In 1919 the business community of Coffee County Alabama erected a monument to the boll weevil for the role it played in diversifying the agriculture of the region.

Although the need for peanut oil was the driving force behind the industrialisation of the crop, the nut was also being more widely accepted as a foodstuff in its own right and it was cheap; we still use the expression 'working for peanuts'. Roasted peanuts cooked in their shells became popular throughout the USA during the nineteenth century. In the 1890's Dr. J. H. Kellogg, famous for the cornflakes which his brother introduced to the world, took out the first patents for peanut butter which he promoted at the Western Health Reform Institute at Battle Creek, Michigan. It was an employee at his Sanatorium, Joseph Lambert, who later began to manufacture and sell the equipment for making peanut butter which soon became part of the American diet.

The activities of Dr. Kellog sent the peanut on another long voyage, this time to Australia. The small but thriving Seventh Day Adventist church in Australia was impressed with the dietary teachings of Dr. Kellog and made contact with him to organise the importation of his health foods for their growing band of converts. Peanut butter was one of the new foods introduced in this way and eventually it came to be produced locally by the manufacturing facilities set up by the Adventist Church in Australia and New Zealand at the end of the nineteenth century. It is still today an important product made by the Sanitarium Food Company based in New South Wales.

Other American innovators began to see the possibilities of using peanuts as a cheap ingredient in confectionery and the sale of this was boosted in the USA by the invention of slot vending machines. Started initially in Chicago in 1901 by two brothers called Mills, the slot machine craze caught on rapidly and by the end of that decade some 30,000 machines were dispensing peanut candy. The company that was to make its name synonymous with peanuts was launched by two

Italian immigrants to the USA; Amedeo Obici and Mario Peruzzi who founded the Planters Nut and Chocolate company in Wilkes Barre, Pennsylvania; in 1912 they introduced a schoolboy's drawing of an animated peanut as the company logo and Mr. Peanut was born.

We have already commented on the use by the French soap and candle making industry of African peanut oil; the trading links which France developed with Africa were to compete with those of Britain and substantially change the European relationship with West Africa. Up until the early nineteenth Century, European traders visiting the West African coast were only vaguely aware of a vast trading complex stretching into the interior of Africa which brought slaves, gold and ivory to the coast via many and varied exchanges for commodity products on the way. The peanut trade was destined to change this pattern of commerce as the cultivation of the plant on the upper Guinea coast revolutionized the trading contacts with Europe and to a lesser extent the United States. Although grown as a local crop for several centuries after introduction into Africa by the Portuguese, the first exports of peanuts are thought to be from the Gambia between 1829 and 1830 to the West Indies. The first small quantities of peanuts to come to Britain from Africa arrived soon after this date and were organised by the trading house of Forster & Smith whose directors had become interested in the importation of oil-producing nuts. Those early samples clearly proved interesting and the table below shows the exports recorded from the Gambia in subsequent years.

Year	Volume (Unshelled nuts)	Total value	Britain	USA	Foreign
1834	213 baskets	£23	£2		£21
1839	810 tons	£9,795	£2,617	£7,139	£39
1841	2,304 tons	£26,325	£15,829	£8,127	£2,369
1847	8,100 tons	£95,659	£3,858	£9,463	£82,338
1851	11,095 tons	£133,133	£9,773	£8,994	£114,366

Source: *Gambia Blue Books*, 1834-51.

In this period of less than twenty years the export of peanuts from West Africa was to change history and there are several interesting facts behind these figures. The first is the enormous local effort which was needed to change a minor food crop into a major export product with all the associated effects on agriculture, labour and local society. Although the American traders were rapidly on the scene their imports were in competition with locally produced peanuts from the southern states; from 1842 new import tariffs into the USA favoured the local produce and this eventually stopped the African trade.

In Europe things were different. Although the British were first on the scene the table shows the rapid growth of exports to 'Foreign' states; this means essentially France, because it was the French and Senegalese traders who successfully bypassed the local British interests and came to dominate the trade in peanuts by the 1860's. This trading success was eventually to lead to the French domination of this part of Africa in the colonial era which followed.

Although Britain turned largely to the oil palm as a source of vegetable oil it did not entirely forget peanuts, and the topic was to reappear significantly some seventy years later. In 1947 the Minister of Food presented to Parliament a plan for the mechanised production of groundnuts in East and Central Africa. The well-intentioned plan to help alleviate the world's chronic shortage of edible fats in the aftermath of World War 2 by the cultivation of a planned 800,000 tons of peanuts per annum was known as the Ground Nut Scheme. Unfortunately this grand plan was to be a major disaster and was abandoned after an investment of some £36m. The chief reason for failure was the planting of the crop on heavy clay soil which baked so hard in the African sun that the immature fruit could not get underground to ripen as it does on friable soil. It is interesting that so many years later, although the reports discussing the early optimism on the scheme are available, the later reports of failure seem to have 'disappeared' from the library in the Ministry of Agriculture, Fisheries and Foods.

The groundnut has travelled from South America, made its way with the Portuguese to Africa, and the Spanish to Europe and S.E. Asia. It returned again to America, this time the North and has become a world wide food item through its oil and as roasted peanuts, peanut candy and peanut butter. But it hasn't always been without problems. For some it has been the source to new businesses and considerable wealth; for others it created political disasters and governmental headaches. It has carried in its wake other unexpected hazards; in the 1960s we heard for the first time about aflatoxin poisoning caused by moulds growing on peanuts and now in the '90s the new fear is Peanut Allergy. Sadly a significant part of the human population appear to have become sensitized to certain proteins in the peanut and in extreme cases such allergic responses can lead to fatal anaphylactic shock. Only from recent studies is the extent of this problem now being appreciated.

My claim that the peanut is the most travelled food in the world is based on the fact that until recently most airlines served roasted peanuts with their drinks trolley. At a conservative estimate this gives a collective 2.8×10^{13} peanut-miles per year. But with the growing awareness of peanut allergies this might become a thing of the past. Whatever else, researching the background about peanuts in order to write a paper on them teaches a great deal about geography, history and travel – *Quo Vadis, Arachis?*

BIBLIOGRAPHY

Krapovickas, A., 'The Origin, Variability and Spread of the Groundnut (*Arachis hypogaea*)', *The Domestication and Exploitation of Plants & Animals*, Eds Ucko J. & Falk I.S., Gerald Duckworth Co., London, 427-441, 1969.

Brooks, G. E., 'Peanuts & Colonialisation: Consequences of the Commercialisation of Peanuts in West Africa 1830–70', *Journal of African History* 16, 29-54 (1975).

Hammons R. O., 'Origin and Early History of the Peanut', *Peanut Science & Technology*, Eds. Pattee H.E. & Young C.T., American Peanut Research Education Society, Yoakum Texas, 1-20, 1982.

'Le Marché Mondial des Arachides', Anon, *Etudes et Conjoncture* 8ème année (1953), No.10 (Octobre). Presses Universitaires de France, St. Germain, Paris, 1059-1105, 1953.

'A Plan for the Mechanized Production of Groundnuts in East & Central Africa.' Paper presented to Parliament, Feb. 1947, HMSO London, Cmd 7030.

East Africa Groundnuts Scheme: Review of Progress to the End of November 1947. Jan. 1948, HMSO London, Cmd. 7314.

What Hath God Wrought: The Sanitarium Health Food Co., Parr R. & Litster G., 1996. Pub. by The Sanitarium Health Food Co. Berkely Vale, NSW 2261, Australia.

Travelers' Diarrhea,
the Science of 'Montezuma's Revenge'

Fritz Blank

It is reasonable to assume that travelers and diarrhea have been partners throughout mankind's existence. Yet few of us involved with food really concern ourselves with those diseases associated with food and drink. Approaching the twenty-first century, we in fact relegate this 'speciality' to the medical profession, government health agencies and the media, each of which occasionally create unnecessary havoc by using scare tactics. Nonetheless, food handlers who give this subject short shrift are the very persons who need to be the most informed and who need to most diligently practise preventive methods.

It has been said that 'travel expands the mind and loosens the bowels', and many pleasant journeys – especially junkets to tropical areas – have been interrupted by the intestinal agonies of Travelers' Diarrhea, the official medical name for this affliction. It infiltrates all ranks and ignores social status; armies on the march have been totally incapacitated by this plague, and embarrassing moments often reign. Worldwide in scope, and as a target for earthy humor, an entire lexicon of pseudonyms have developed. Familiar names include: 'the G.I. trots,' 'Delhi belly,' 'the runs,' 'Casablanca crud,' 'Aden gut,' 'the green apple two-step,' 'the Hong Kong dog,' 'gippy tummy,' 'the Turkey trots,' 'Bali belly,' 'the Aztec two-step,' 'the scours,' plus the title of this paper, tourista and 'Montezuma's revenge.' Apropos from Russia we find 'the Trotskys,' and last but not least and probably the most un-euphemistically descriptive and universally understood: 'the shits!'

It is estimated that each year well over 300 million people participate in international travel. Of this number at least 16 million persons from industrialized countries travel to 'developing' or so called 'third world' countries, and 30 per cent of those become ill from diarrhea. Three million North Americans travel to Mexico per year with an attack rate ranging from 25 to 50 per cent, this means that over one million are affected by diarrheal disease.

Of those infected, close to 30 per cent will be ill enough to require confinement to bed and another 40 per cent will need to alter their scheduled activities. Public concern for and fear of this illness has led to a wide variety of nostrums for prevention and treatment. Some remedies are comforting, some totally ineffective, while still others may actually cause harm, in addition to being ineffective.

The clinical definition of travelers' diarrhea (TD) is a syndrome which exhibits a two-fold or greater increase in the frequency of bowel movements – usually unformed – within a 24-hour period. TD is commonly associated with other symptoms including abdominal cramps, nausea, bloating, and urgency. In most cases, the average number of stools per day is four or five. It also should be noted that as a 'working definition,' diarrhea is, in fact, any bowel movement which fits the shape of the container into which it is discharged.

Travelers-at-risk are persons from industrialized countries visiting a region or country where there is a known penchant for developing the disease. Thus, the major determinant of risk is the destination of the traveler. 'High-risk' destinations, with TD infection rates of 20 to 50 per cent include Latin America (including Mexico), Africa, the Middle East, the subcontinent of India, and Asia. 'Intermediate-risk' destinations include most southern European countries and a few of the Caribbean islands. 'Low-risk' areas include Canada, Japan, Singapore, northern Europe, Australia, New Zealand, the United States, and a majority of the Caribbean islands.

It is interesting, that the national origin of the traveler is also an important liability factor. For example, at international meetings held in Teheran, Iran and Mexico City, Mexico, 40 to 50 per cent of all reported TD occurred among North Americans, South Africans, and western Europeans. This compares with only a one to eight per cent incidence among visitors from Asia, South America, and southern Europe. This 'protection' is probably due to an acquired immunity resulting from frequent encounters with the infecting organisms in those countries. This altered host/parasite relationship is probably the result of colonization of the host with pathogenic microorganisms which then become autochthinous or commensal flora, thus achieving a carrier state, rather than a disease state.

It is perhaps not surprising that the purpose of travel and how and where consumption of food occurs also play a significant epidemiological role regarding TD. For example, students and casual vacationers are the group most likely to develop TD, while those persons visiting relatives are least at risk. Intermediate risk is associated with those who frequently travel for business purposes. Most cases of diarrhea occur in people who eat in school or industrial cafeterias and restaurants – with an especially high risk for those eating the wares of street vendors. [In the United States outbreaks of foodborne illnesses are most commonly associated with summertime social functions – community suppers, picnics and the like – whereby food is prepared and/or stored in church kitchens, for instance – kitchens which just happen to be exempt from US state and local food licensing and inspection laws. Those of us who are older might appreciate the statistical finding that advancing age for some unknown reason seems also to lower the probability of contracting Travelers' Diarrhea.]

Travelers' Diarrhea is almost universally acquired by the ingestion of fecally contaminated food or beverages. This mode of infection is called 'fecal-hand-mouth' (FHM) transmission by epidemiologists, and certainly conjures up disgusting thoughts. It is the most culpable infectious method for any of the food-associated and/or so-called 'hospital acquired' infections. Infections brought about this way are, in fact, the easiest and cheapest to prevent, and would be totally effective but for the fact that total participation is required by all. For decades, the simple act of frequent hand washing has been demonstrated to be the most efficacious means for preventing these types of diseases. Hand washing – not hand 'disinfection' or the wearing of rubber gloves – but hand washing, with plain soap and water by any and all persons who handle food (or patients with infectious diseases) has repeatedly been shown beyond any reasonable doubt to virtually eliminate those diseases transmitted via the FHM route!

Both cooked and uncooked foods may be implicated – proper handling being more important than the state of the product per se. Risky foods include raw vegetables, raw meat and raw seafood and sometimes shellfish harvested from fecally contaminated waters. Especially culpable are salad greens, and of recent concern in the United States, ground meats – in particular hamburgers of the fast food type. Although cooked foods are usually rendered safe, contamination often occurs by improper handling and storage – unwashed hands, dirty containers and/or improper hold temperatures – or for ground meat by insufficient cooking. Tap water, ice, unpasteurized milk and milk products, as well as unpeeled fruit have also been associated with high risk; however, and perhaps unsurprisingly, raw salads always seem to head the list. Beer, wine, hot coffee or tea, water which has been boiled or treated with iodine or chlorine and bottled carbonated beverages are generally considered safe to consume.

Travelers' Diarrhea usually is a mild, self limiting disorder – more of a nuisance than a disease. Even untreated, the average duration is three to four days, although 10 per cent may persist for a week or more. Prolonged untreated cases are uncommon with only two per cent lasting longer than a month, and less than one per cent lasting more than three months. These benign figures do not necessarily succor suffering patients; indeed, non-treatment is not especially recommended.

Typically, onset of Travelers' Diarrhea begins any time past the second or third day after arrival at a new destination. Watery, loose stools is the most common complaint. Some people also experience vomiting and between two and ten per cent will present with bloody stools and fever – technically then called dysentery. Associated sequellae such as abdominal pain, cramps, gas, fever, fatigue, headache, and loss of appetite are often more bothersome. Despite this panoply of symptoms, TD is rarely life threatening.

The microorganisms most often identified with TD, in order of frequency are:

EPEC (Enteropathogenic *Escherichia coli*) – including invasive and toxogenic strains
Salmonella enteritidis – various non-typhoid serotypes
Shigella species
Campylobacter jejuni
Aeromonas hydrophila
Giardia lamblia
Entamoeba histolytica
Cryptosporidium species

As an aside, it should be pointed out that the severe dysentery type enteritidies are usually grouped and codified separately from 'travelers' diarrhea.' These non-TD diseases include cholera (*Vibrio cholerae*), typhoid fever (*Salmonella typhi*), and endemic food-borne outbreaks due to *Shigella dysenteriae*, certain serotypes of *Escherichia coli*, and *Salmonella enteritidis*, and/or other enteric organisms that produce so-called Shiga toxins – especially *E. coli* serotype O157:H7 – or other endo- or exo-toxins all of which may or may not be associated with food, drink or travel. By and large, these more severe gastrointestinal illnesses are more debilitating and are often complicated by high fever, massive fluid loss, and life-threatening septicemia.

The symptoms, management and treatment of these two gastrointestinal syndromes are quite different and as such must be clinically differentiated from each other, even though the causative microbial agents may be the same.

For the record, public health authorities characterize a non-TD food borne disease outbreak as being two or more persons experiencing a similar illness, usually gastrointestinal, after ingestion of a common food, and that epidemiological analysis implicates food as the source of infection. Pathogens included as etiological agents in this classification include *Staphylococcus aureus*, *Bacillus cereus*, certain non-cholera *Vibrios*, and both *Clostridium botulinum* and *Clostridium perfingens* – all of which are not usually associated with travel.

Harmful chemical contaminants, ingested sharp objects (such as broken glass, ceramic shards, pieces of plastic and metal, paperclips, nails, tacks and the like as well as seeming innocent objects like bay leaves), and/or noxious and poisonous plants – such as certain mushrooms – are also included in the list of agents responsible for food poisoning but are not particularly included within the definition of TD.

Suffice it to mention that of particular public concern in the United States are recent sporadic outbreaks of serious illness and some deaths attributed to undercooked hamburger tainted with *E. coli* – serotype O157:H7. The prime source of these infections is thought to be beef which has been contaminated with cattle feces or intestinal fluids during slaughterhouse operations. How the animals have become colonized with these human pathogens is not fully understood.

Because Travelers' Diarrhea is such a commonly encountered disease, much home-spun wisdom and folklore exist. Theories abound regarding cause, prevention and cure. Spicy foods, too much sun, jet lag, and the mineral content of water have all been listed as prima facie causes as testified by 'expert', often first-time, tourists. Scientific investigations, however, continue to show that the major cause of TD is pathogenic enteric microorganisms. The failure of ten per cent or more of cases to be associated with a specific etiological agent is most likely due to improper specimen collection methods, poor laboratory techniques, and/or microbiological isolation procedures rather than to yet undiscovered causes.

It is also curious to report a high frequency of asymptomatic infections. For example, 15 per cent of healthy travelers acquire toxogenic *Echerichia coli* and another 15 per cent *Shigella*, and yet these individuals do not get sick. The reasons for this type of resistance and/or the existence of carriers (e.g. 'Typhoid Mary') is not fully understood. The major reasons standing in the way of such studies are matters of cost and experimental design since so many variables would need to be included. Using humans as experimental models is touchy as well – the ethics of feeding fecal organisms to unsuspecting volunteers always has been a questionable act, even in the name of scientific study.

Methods to prevent Travelers' Diarrhea can be grouped into three major approaches:

#1 the practice of 'safe' food and beverage consumption
#2 use of prophylactic antimicrobial drugs
#3 the prophylactic use of non-antibiotic medications.
[Immunization as a fourth method of prevention has certainly been considered. However, the cost and technical difficulties associated with developing a multivalent vaccine have rendered this avenue prohibitive.]

Although prescribed by many physicians, the universal use of antibiotic drugs (principally sulfa drugs) as a safeguard when traveling to ward-off Travelers' Diarrhea is generally discouraged by those physicians, clinical microbiologists, epidemiologists, and others who are infectious disease specialists. This caution is due to concerns regarding the overuse of antibiotics and the subsequent effects upon the development of resistant organisms within the endogenous normal flora of the host, as well as the environment. There is also an increased risk by subjecting patients unnecessarily to harmful side effects from the antimicrobial agents themselves.

Of the non-antimicrobial prophylactic medicines available in the United States, three have received the most attention, those being Lomotile®, Pepto Bismol® and a Mexican product called Enterovioform (which is not yet licensed in the U.S.). In a series of well designed, double blind clinical trials, only Pepto Bismol® demonstrated any statistical efficacy. However the dosage of bismuth subsalicylate required to induce protection is very large, which logistically can be more of a problem than contracting the disease itself. Also of some question is the unknown effects of long-term bismuth intake not to mention those people who have a known intolerance for salicates. Nevertheless, Pepto Bismol ® is the only medication which is licensed by the FDA to advertise itself as a preventative for TD.

By far the safest and most effective method for the control and prevention of Travelers' Diarrhea is the careful restriction and attention regarding the intake of food, water and other beverages.

When TD does strike, as uncomfortable and as inconvenient as it can be, the disease is still usually defined (probably by people who are not or have never been inflicted) as a self-limiting disorder, with complete recovery occurring even in the absence of therapy. Thus, treatment is generally directed towards relieving the discomfort and symptoms of the disorder rather than 'a cure'. To this end, many supportive therapeutic remedies have been proposed and prescribed by physicians and laymen alike. Sadly, the fact is that all but a few are truly ineffective.

Three basic routes of treatment are available to manage Travelers' Diarrhea. With the exception of attempting to exterminate the causative pathogen, these methods can be characterized as palliative and, in fact, succor rather than cure the suffering patient. Be that as it may, the psychology of taking medicine, in and of itself, can indeed provide a feeling of well-being – the so-called 'placebo effect' – and should not be overlooked.

#1 Rehydration and the reversal of the physiological effects – including electrolyte imbalance – of fluid loss and associated dehydration.

#2 Symptomatic relief of cramps, abdominal pain, urgency and frequent bowel evacuation.

#3 Removal of the pathogen by antimicrobial agents.

Although severe fluid loss can occur in certain enteric diseases – cholera for example – serious dehydration is rarely a problem with individuals who suffer from TD. Fluid replacement by ingestion of bottled water, fruit drinks, caffeine-free soft drinks, along with salted crackers is usually sufficient to restore mild to moderate fluid imbalance. Alcoholic and carbonated beverages are not recommended. Bottled aqueous commercial products, such as Gaiter Aid®, which are based upon the formulation for Ringer's lactate solution are especially recommended. These products, which were originally developed for use by professional athletes, are sanctioned for use by the World Health Organization.

Certain commercial anti-diarrheal medications are available and have received good reports by users and in rigorous clinical trials as well. Loperamide hydrochloride (Imodium A-D®), attapulgite (Kaopectate®), and bismuth subsalicate (Pepto Bismol®) top the list of highly recommended over-the-counter remedies.

The use of prescription-only antimicrobial agents for Travelers' Diarrhea remains a subject of debate among practitioners. Weighing the side effects – both to the environment and to the patient – against the benefits of a cure for a disease known to be essentially self-limiting is judgmental. The argument is compounded by the income and economy generated by this lucrative market and by the pressures brought to bear by the multitudes of persons seeking relief from this nasty, nuisance-of-a-disease. Again, as in the prophylactic use of antibiotics, sulfa drugs – especially trimethoprim-sulfamethoxazole – and doxycycline, are the current agents of choice.

Note well that children, pregnant women, 'the elderly' [not yet defined] and persons with underlying conditions such as cardiovascular disease, diabetes and hyper- or hypotension, and/or persons who present prolonged symptoms and/or high fevers should consult a physician rather than relying on self treatment.

ACKNOWLEDGEMENTS

Dr. Kenneth R. Cundy, Professor Emeritus, Department of Microbiology, Temple University School of Medicine, Philadelphia, Pennsylvania.

Dr. Harry Smith, Professor Emeritus, Department of Microbiology, Thomas Jefferson University School of Medicine, Philadelphia, Pennsylvania and Cholera Consultant, World Health Organization, Geneva, Switzerland.

Mr. Jonathan Tan, C.H., a traveler from Singapore.

BIBLIOGRAPHY

Sherwood L. Gorbach (Editor), *Infectious Diarrhea*, 1986

Emamuel Lebenthal and Michael E. Duffey (Editors), *Textbook of secretory diarrhea*, 1990

Michael Field (Editor), *Diarrheal diseases*, Elsevier Publisher (NYC) 1991

Readings on Diarrhoea – A student manual. The World Health Organization (Geneva) 1992

The Management and Prevention of Diarrhoea: practical guidelines. 3rd Edition., The World Health
  Organization (Geneva) 1993

Mislkovitz, Paul F., *The Evaluation and Treatment of the Patient with Diahrea*. Andover Medical
  Publishers (Boston) 1993

Meyer, Kathleen., *How to Shit in the Woods: An environmentally sound approach to a lost art*. Ten Speed
  Press, 1989

Ewald, Paul W., *Evolution of Infectious Disease*. Oxford University Press, 1994

U.S. Department of Health and Human Services, *Health Information for International Travel*, HHS
  Publication # (CDC) 94-8280. U.S. Government Printing Office.

Weinhouse, B., *The Healthy Traveler*. Pocket Books, New York 1987

Dawood, R., *Travelers' Health: How to Stay Healthy Abroad*, 3rd Edition. Oxford University Press 1992

Rose, S. R., *International Travel Health Guide*, Travel Medicine Inc. 1995

Losos, J. et al., *Children Abroad: A Guide for Families Traveling Overseas*. Deneau Publishers Ltd.,
  Toronto 1986

Wheeler, M., *Travel with Children: a survival guide kit for travel in Asia*. Lonely Planet Publication, 1985

Keystone, J. S. (Editor)., *Don't Drink the Water* ... The Canadian Public Health Association and the
  Canadian Society for International Health, Ottawa, 1994

Gardner, P. (Editor)., 'Health Issues of International Travelers.' *Infectious Disease Clinics of North
  America* 6: (2) 275-510. W. B. Saunders, Philadelphia, 1992

Jong, E. and McMullen, R., *The Travel and Tropical Medicine Manual*, 2nd Edition, W. B. Saunders,
  Philadelphia 1995

William Bartram's Travels in Lands of Amerindian Tobacco and Caffeine: Foodways of Seminoles, Creeks and Cherokees

Phyllis Pray Bober

Perhaps less well-known than his father John Bartram (1699-1777), the 'greatest natural botanist in the world,' – in the opinion of Linnaeus – William Bartram (1739-1823) captures one's interest more readily today because with objective science he cultivated equally a subjective rapport with nature and fellow creatures, among them native Americans. The fervor of his engagement with the wilderness of the south-east frontier from northern Florida to the Carolinas and west to the Mississippi, as effectively recreated in his writings, had a significant influence on Wordsworth and Coleridge as well as on certain continental writers of the Romantic movement.[1] Adding to the relevance of his achievements for those who live in Britain is the presence in England of much of the documentation for them including, in London's Museum of Natural History, both his field notes and drawings of flora and fauna discovered on his travels.[2]

The travels in question occupied the years from 1773 to 1777 in the southern reaches of yet colonial America and afford my starting point to consider some aspects of Amerindian cookery in order to convince you that it deserves the name of 'cuisine'. Bartram's account, published as *Travels through North and South Carolina, Georgia, East & West Florida, the Cherokee Country, the Extensive Territories of the Muscogules, or Creek Confederacy, and the Country of the Choctaws, containing an Account of the Soil and Natural Productions of those Regions, together with Observations on the Manners of the Indians*, Philadelphia, 1791, is supplemented by an interview which took place in 1789 but did not see the light until its record was rediscovered much later: *Observations on the Creek and Cherokee Indians* (Transactions of the American Ethnological Society, volume III, part 1, 1853; re-issued 1900). Earlier William accompanied his father on explorations in Florida and the Southeast, where the British crown still needed to assess unknown resources hidden in lands wrested from Spanish domination.[3]

William's account of his more solitary treks among the natural wonders of what continued to seem to Europeans a prelapsarian paradise are imbued with his Quaker reverence for that divinely created 'Great Chain of Being' perceived by human intellects of the Renaissance and Enlightenment. His observations share with those of his father the rapture of a deist's communion with Nature joined with an eighteenth-century concern for encyclopaedic documentation (especially of plants, of birds, and of topography). But, strongly differing from John's somewhat jaundiced view of 'savage' native Americans, who may, indeed, have massacred his own father, William's attitude towards the Indians reveals an ethnographic acumen remarkable for its breadth and open-mindedness.

If his vision of sending government commissions of friendly researchers to systematically investigate language, customs, laws and traditions of the 'red men' had ever borne fruit, the United States might have been spared the shame of subsequent outrage to human rights that, from 1832, saw the bulk of south-eastern tribes forcefully exiled to Oklahoma.[4] As N.B. Fagin expresses Bertram's motivation, 'Knowledge, then, he believed, is the first step towards justice.'[5]

Bartram's open, Quaker lack of guile and genuine interest in the history of different tribes, both recent and remote, made correspondingly for hospitality almost everywhere he ventured. Some called him Puc Puggy, the 'Flower Hunter;' almost all recognized, without being able to name the concept, his reverence for every least form of life. Because it entails relish for an *al fresco* meal enjoyed when he fell in with some traders who shot a Florida sandhill crane, I cannot resist quoting his bemused comments: 'We had this fowl dressed for supper, and it made an excellent soup; nevertheless, as long as I can get any other necessary food I shall prefer their seraphic music in the ethereal skies, and my eyes and understanding gratified in observing their economy and social communities, in the expansive green savannas of Florida.'[6] E. Earnest found a manuscript among Bartram papers at the Historical Society of Pennsylvania that expounds upon the faculties and powers of reasoning possessed by animals, their universal language within the given orders, to conclude '…it's self-evident that they have intelligence and understanding.'[7]

Throughout the region he carefully recorded traces of the burial and temple mounds with associated structures such as ball courts and chunkey yards which, together with the cultivation of maize, stand out as the most tangible evidence of Meso-American practices reflected in the cultures of south-eastern tribes during their Woodland stage (*ca.* 1000 BC–1000 AD). Eighteenth-century Indians – federated as Cherokees, Creeks, Chickasaws, Choctaws and Natchez, for example – had lost the memory of the ancestors who had constructed the huge mounds, (often still with traces of broad avenues and sacred lakes)[8] that they could utilize to structure civic and religious life in many of their 'modern' towns.

As drawings by John White and Jacques LeMoyne document for us an earlier stage of aboriginal life and agriculture in their settlements, so William Bartram vividly pictures in words their accomplishments in his own day. Major changes affecting sustenance and cookery may be summarized at this point. Bison that had once roamed east of the Mississippi are now few and far between, but in recompense domestic animals from European stock have been added to ancestral dogs and sporadic tamings of wild fowl chicks and the young of other species;[9] chickens and even cattle are raised by enterprising types and pigs escaped from Spanish outposts have reverted to wild boars. Still the norm for all south-eastern Indians is dual reliance on hunting and gathering combined with as much agriculture as tribal geography might permit. Areas of good topsoil such as the food plains of rivers make for large, planned towns and organized farming.

Aside from tobacco, major crops include maize (*Zea mays*, 'corn' to Americans), beans (*Phaseolus* species absent in the Old World), cucurbits ('pumpkins' or 'pompions', squashes – and watermelons welcomed from the Europeans), gourds (*Lagenaria*, including *L. siceraria*, the bottle gourd for water vessels and an entire range of implements), sweet potatoes (*Ipomoea batata* which Bartram calls *Convolvulus batata*), and sunflowers (*Helianthus tuberosus* and *lenticularis*, the former for the tubers or 'Jerusalem artichokes', the latter for seeds and oil).[10]

From about 800 AD, in what is termed by anthropologists the 'Mississippian transformation,' intensive horticulture raised corn that had been cultivated for centuries to the status of veritable 'staff of life.'[11] A Scot, Thomas Campbell, who visited the Creek Nation in 1764-65, puts the reliance very well:

> When they have a bad crop they must be in great distress, as Indian corn is their chief food all summer which they use in many different ways; by beating to a fine flower in a large wooden mortar they make bread of it; by parching before it is made into flower they make homeny or potage; and by preparing it not quite so small, and boiling it with oak or hickory ashes, they make their drink, which is mostly used all summer, the salts which is [*sic*] in the ashes makes it ferment after boiling which gives it an agreeable taste, makes it cool, refreshing, wholesome and fit for that hott season.[12]

He may be excused for not realizing that liming the corn with alkaline wood ashes was necessary both to remove the hard outer shell of the kernels and to enhance the nutritional value of hominy or cornmeal by making its niacin more accessible.[13]

Appreciation for the culinary skills of the Indians arises when one learns that two observers speak of as many as forty and forty-two different dishes created from corn. Even if some of these 'styles' as Dumont de Montigny calls them, resulted from, say, adding some berries or another ingredient to cornbread, this testimony reflects considerable artistry with a staple foodstuff.[14] Bartram merely mentions eating hot corn cakes on several occasions, as well as enjoying a 'pleasant cooling liquor made of hommony [sic] well boiled, mixed afterwards with milk [perhaps still nut milk, since William mentions no cattle at the seat of the host, chief of Whatoga]...served in a large bowl with a very large spoon or ladle to sup it with.'[15]

Others write of pounded chestnuts or sweet acorns, or again sunflower seeds added to cornmeal for bread that might be boiled, wrapped and tied in corn husks like tamales we know from Mexico. Bread was also baked as in the ancient Old World, on a stone at the edge of the fire, set under an inverted earthenware bowl with coals heaped over its top. But the favored bread seems surely the flat cake baked in ashes or on a stone like Scottish oat cakes; it is the direct ancestor of our southern corn pone and skillet corn bread.

According to several specialists, south-eastern Indians also cultivated a number of the plants they gathered in the wild, namely chenopodium or green amaranth, and lamb's quarters.[16] They cultivated as well certain fruit trees that had been naturalized from European imports: Seville oranges in Florida, peaches and figs to supplement native wildlings, among them cherries, plums, mulberries, crab-apples, grapes (muscadines and scuppernongs of the American species *labrusca*), papaws (*Asimena triloba*) and maypops (passion flower plant, *Passiflora incarnata*). But the most important fruit for the entire region before the introduction of the peach was the persimmon (*Diospyros virginiana*) which loses its fabled sourness when fully ripened in autumn; this they not only dried like a prune, but made up into a kind of 'bread' noted by chroniclers of De Soto's expeditions and later visitors.[17]

In addition to nature's bounty in the matter of game animals (white-tailed deer, bear, wild turkeys, rabbits, racoons, oppossums and squirrels heading the list), fish and favored box turtles or terrapins, merely to cite quadrupeds in neglect of avian and reptilian rewards, Indian exploitation of wild resources provided everything required for cooking well. Forest trees gave up their nuts in autumn harvests – shag or shell-bark hickory, chestnut, chinquapin (*Castanea pumila*), beech, pecan, hazel (*Corylus americana* not *avellana*), and walnut, white or black, plus the versatile fruit of the sweet oak, acorns. Bartram notes signs of ancient plantations of some of these precious sources for both oils and 'dairy' products as well as seasonings. He singles out the shell-bark hickory nuts: '...the Creeks store up the latter in their towns. I have seen above an hundred bushels of these nuts belonging to one family. They pound them to pieces, and then cast them into boiling water, which, after passing through fine strainers, preserves the most oily part of the liquid: this they call by a name which signifies Hiccory milk; it is as sweet and rich as fresh cream, and is an ingredient in most of their cookery, especially homony [sic] and corn cakes.'[18]

Bartram describes other 'nuts' of which we would deny the name: the groundnut (*Apios americana*) he calls *Glycine apios* that served as another tuber and the 'tallow nut,' as his father dubbed *Ximenia americana*, the tropical wild lime of Florida with plum-like yellow fruit concealing a kernel inside its stone 'somewhat of the consistence and taste of the sweet Almond, but more oily and very much like hard tallow...'[19]

Another tree receives extended attention from Bartram because of its ceremonial value to the Indians; it may claim ours also as a marker still for regionalism in American foodways. This is yaupon (*Ilex cassine* Walt. or *Ilex vomitoria* Ait.), a variety of holly 'held in sacred veneration by the ...Creeks, & by all the Indians of Florida & Louisiana.'[20] Its roasted leaves, young shoots and twigs made a potent brew called the 'Black Drink,' known to present-day Carolinians in a milder form as 'cassina tea'. For Indian men – and solely men, the leaders – it was a purifying drink served in conch shells to welcome visitors to formal assemblies where tobacco also circulated in ritual order. One shared it as well when treaties were to be ratified and, with either induced or involuntary vomiting that gives it one name, on other solemn occasions such as preparations for war.[21] We are less surprised at esteem gathered by yaupon on learning that a major constituent is caffeine – perfect accompaniment to the pipe of peace. It is engaging to find that among the south-eastern tribes one stirred up a head of froth when imbibing *assi*, just as Indians of South America consume chocolate, as well as *maté* from a related holly, *Ilex paraguensis* or *Yerba de maté*.

Such a host of wild seeds and greens are encountered in Bartram's pages – all of importance to Indian cookery and most still relished by foragers – that it would abuse my share of space in these *Proceedings* to consider more than a few of exceptional interest. Historians of ancient culinary arts will be startled at Bartram's references to 'silphium', which raises images of a supposedly extinct plant dear to Greek and Roman cooks. According to Harper, our botanist means a genus of *compositae*, comprising the rosin-weeds, including a tall species, *S. terebinthinaceum Jacq.* and possibly one today commonly appearing in the prairies of Alabama, *S. laciniatum*;[22] the tuberous roots of these would have been exploited by the Indians.

Another plant that must not be overlooked is a quite unprepossessing cat-briar, *Smilax pseudo-China*, growing in entangled and spiny thickets, but yielding up its roots to Indian ingenuity by providing *kunti* (anglicized as contee). Here is Bartram on use of this product. He is reporting a feast offered him by a chief at Talahasochte, Florida,

> consisting of bear's ribs, venison, varieties of fish, roasted turkeys (which they call the white man's dish), hot corn cakes, and a very agreeable, cooling sort of jelly, which they call conte which they prepare from the root of the China brier;...they chop the roots in pieces, which are afterwards well pounded in a wooden mortar, then being mixed with clean water, in a tray or trough, they strain it through baskets, the sediment, which settles to the bottom of the second vessel, is afterwards dried in the open air, and is then mixed with warm water and sweetened with honey, when cool becomes a beautiful, delicious jelly, very nourishing and wholesome; they also mix it with fine Corn flour, which being fried in fresh bear's oil makes very good hot cakes or fritters.[23] [It is worth adding that young shoots of the China brier were and are still eaten like asparagus in the spring. It is also of note that one variety of smilax makes sarsaparilla beer, a thirst-quencher for Confederate soldiers during the Civil War.[24]]

Mention of honey in Bartram's paragraph above leads to consideration of a few flavorings characteristic of Indian foods. Some sources insist that there were no honey bees in North America until the Spaniards introduced them;[25] Indians tapped maple and other trees such as birch for sap to make syrup sweeteners. They recognized the sweetening power of corn, since they apparently sucked on the stalks just as they would later chew on sugar cane once it was imported from the West Indies, but, fortunately for their health, did not anticipate modern corn syrup additives to our daily fare.

With chile peppers they did not feel the lack of pepper and other oriental spices. But certain berries did serve them almost as well: for example, those of (*Lindera benzoin*) the 'spice-bush', as the colonists would dub it, which substituted for Jamaican allspice during the Revolutionary War.[26] Other flavorings abounded among roots, seeds and herbs gathered for medicinal purposes. An Indian febrifuge tried by Bartram when taken ill – which he called Collinsonia after a London friend of his father – is evidently a stone-root, *Micheliella anisata*, judging by his description:

> ...It is diuretic and carminative...an infusion of its tops is ordinarily drunk at breakfast, and is of an exceeding pleasant taste and flavor; when in flower; which is the time the inhabitants gather it for preservation and use; it possesses a lively aromatic scent, partaking of lemon and aniseed.[27]

As the ancients well knew, the savor of lemon also effuses from sumac (*Rhus glabra*, not to be confused with poison sumac); from Indian usage it was adapted by settlers and remains today a favorite source of 'Appalachian tea,' or 'lemonade'.

Bartram waxes poetic on topics such as landscape, birds and flowers, but dwells very little on pleasures of food and drink. Probably gastronomic reaction to meals he mentions would have struck him as self-indulgent materialism. One is able to read his satisfaction on a few occasions. Notable is his appreciation in Florida of being able to spice up his camp cookery with wild bitter orange juice. After fighting off an attack by alligators and surviving a hurricane, William's relish is palpable, if expressed in one adjective, when he grills some trout at his campfire: 'their heads I stewed in the juice of Oranges, which, with boiled rice, afforded me a wholesome and delicious supper.'[28]

He can be more reactive on occasion, as his negative response to one dish at an Alachua banquet:

> ...a very singular dish, the traders call it tripe soup; it is made of the belly or paunch of the beef, [this tribe did herd cattle] not overcleansed of its contents, cut and minced pretty fine, and then made into a thin soup, seasoned well with salt and aromatic herbs; but the seasoning not quite strong enough to extinguish its original savour and scent. This dish is greatly esteemed by the Indians, but is, in my judgement, the least agreeable they have amongst them.'[29]

RECIPES

Succotash

In 2 tablespoons sunflower oil, sauté 1 medium onion, chopped and 1 green pepper, also chopped, until wilted but not browned. Combine with 2 cups corn (either kernels cut from the cobs or 1 package frozen if you cannot find green corn) and approximately the same quantity of lima beans (fresh ones shelled and blanched, or frozen). Add water to barely cover, and whole small salt fish (1 salted sardine or 2 or 3 dried salt fish, either available in Chinese groceries). Simmer about 20 minutes or until water evaporates; dress with 2 tablespoons nut or sunflower seed butter (made by crushing in a mortar). If you miss seasoning with salt and pepper, remember that the Indians did have salt, evaporated from salt licks primarily, but pepper must be replaced by ground dried chiles or sumac (*Rhus glabra*).

Jerky

Cut venison (or beef flank steak) with the grain, not across it, into long strips as thinly as possible; it helps to flash freeze the meat first to firm it. Dip strips in hot brine (salt should be added until no more will dissolve) to eliminate blood if need be. Drain thoroughly and coat well with a mixture of salt and ground red pepper (cayenne). Dry in the sun where air can freely circulate (a clean wire screen is good and strips may be covered with cheesecloth in a single layer if needed to keep off windblown dust and insects). Depending on wind and temperature, to dry the strips may take a day or two or much longer. Store in a container with holes in its cover so air may continue to circulate, or in a porous cloth bag hanging in a dry, cool place.

Alternatively, smoke the strips following directions for your smoker.

Stove method: toss strips with 1/2 cup soy sauce, a crushed clove of wild garlic or ramps, and cayenne pepper. Place in a single layer on a rack over a baking sheet. Bake in a very slow oven (150°F) for 10 to 12 hours until thoroughly dried. Store in an air-tight container in this case.

This makes a chewy snack, and jerked meat may be added to stews, soups and the like. When ground and pressed with additional nutrients (seeds, crushed nuts, bear fat etc.) this made *pemmican*, a food to sustain one on long treks.

Corn bread

For an authentic flat bread, blend 2 cups cornmeal (yellow or white) with 1 cup hot water in which ashes of juniper or another redolent wood have been added, then strained, and 1 tablespoon drippings (of bacon fat in lieu of bear's fat), plus 1/2 teaspoon salt. Shape this stiff dough into 3 flat cakes and cook in a fireplace or barbecue on a layer of hot ashes, covered with more ash and a few coals. After 45 to 50 minutes, check the cakes, turning them over if they are not quite done; re-cover with ash and coals for about 10 or 15 more minutes. When done, pour water over them in a basket to wash off lingering ash.

For a modernized but still Indian corn spoonbread, grease a 2 quart earthenware casserole. Sift 2 cups cornmeal with 1 teaspoon each of salt and baking soda; make a stiff dough with up to 2 cups boiling water. To this dough add 1 tablespoon drippings, 2 beaten egg yolks, 2 cups buttermilk (the Indians would have used milk from hickory nuts much as medieval and renaissance cooks made almond milk for fast-day cookery). Finally, fold in the 2 egg whites beaten stiff but not dry. Pour into the prepared casserole and bake in a moderate oven (350–375°F) until a knife inserted comes out clean.

Sumac Lemonade

Staghorn sumac, Dwarf sumac as well as Smooth sumac (*Rhus glabra*) may all be used. However, be certain that you are gathering densely clustered berry-like RED fruits, not the white ones of poison sumac. Make this drink in late summer when the fruits ripen; they will remain ripe on the shrub or tree into winter, although you may also dry any remaining 'heads' of fruit as the Indians did. The advantage is in not allowing autumn rain or winter snow to dilute the acid which is primarily found in little hairs on the surface of the fruit. Bruise the berries and soak in water until it turns pink. Alternatively, submerge a slightly crushed cluster of berries in a clear glass pitcher of water and allow to steep in the sun for a few hours. Strain through muslin or several layers of cheesecloth to remove berries and the little hairs. Sweeten with honey and serve chilled (or hot as a tea).

NOTES

[1] By now a commonplace, discussed among others by N.B. Fagin, *William Bartram, Interpreter of the American Landscape*, Baltimore, 1933; Lane Cooper, *Methods and Aims in the Study of Literature*, Ithaca NY, 1912; Ithaca, Cornell University Press/London, Oxford University Press, 1940.

[2] The patron who underwrote Bartram's explorations of the interior was the learned London physician Dr. John Fothergill, originally his father's friend and correspondent (as with many of the colonial natural scientists, including Franklin) who sought plants and seeds for his botanic garden of some 3,400 species of exotics from all parts of the world. On the garden, at Upton in Essex: Brooke Hindle, *The Pursuit of Science in Revolutionary America 1735-1789*, Chapel Hill NC, University of North Carolina Press, 1956, p.14; on Fothergill's support and detailed instructions: Frances Harper, *The Travels of William Bartram*, New Haven, Yale University Press, 1958, p.xix, p.510 (with bibliography).

In addition to the materials sent to Fothergill and other avid British collectors of new trees and plants from North America, much resides in the American Philosophical Society's archives in Philadelphia, as well as scattered in other U.S. collections.

[3] The treaty of 1763 which closed the French and Indian wars, brought Britain St. Augustine and dependen-

cies, but Florida as a whole was not purchased from Spain until 1821, manifestly by the US. John Bartram's *Travels* were published from a report for Peter Collinson as *An Account of East Florida, with a Journal kept by John Bartram upon a Journey from St. Augustine up the River St. John's*, in William Stork, *An Account of East Florida*, London 1766 [subsequent eds. 1767, 1769, 1774; reimpression of 1767, 1881]; also 'Diary of a Journey through the Carolinas, Georgia and Florida from July 1, 1765 to April 10, 1766,' annotated by Francis Harper, *Transactions of the American Philosophical Society*, n.s. 33, pt.1 (1942), pp.1-120; 2 (1943), 121-242. Billy, as his father called him, even remained for a time on the St. John's attempting unsuccessfully to develop a plantation to raise indigo and rice.

[4] See his *Observations on the Creek and Cherokee Indians*, 1789 interview, [T.P. Slaughter], *William Bartram, Travels and Other Writings* (The Library of America), 1996, pp.527-567.

[5] N. Bryllion Fagin, *op.cit*, p.65 in a chapter on William's studies of the American Indian.

[6] E. Earnest, *John and William Bartram, Botanists and Explorers, 1699-1777, 1739-1823*, Philadelphia, University of Pennsylvania Press, 1940, p.144, on the 'Dignity of Animal Nature'.

[7] Earnest, *op.cit*, p.144, on the 'Dignity of Animal Nature.'

[8] See the description of Mount Royal, Florida, *Travels*, 1791, pp.99-100 (Harper, *op.cit*, p.64f., fig.9 for Bartram's sketch). At *Travels*, pp.54-55, Bartram mentions the impressive Ocmulgee mounds, terraces and fields near Macon, Georgia, where Creeks claimed to have made their first settlement when they came as immigrants from west of the Mississipi. Today remains of the town are part of the Ocmulgee National Monument; Harper, fig. 26, p.579. For the successive levels of occupation, beginning about 900 AD, see Charles M. Hudson, *The Southeastern Indians*, Knoxville, University of Tennessee Press, 1976, pp.83-84.

[9] For examples gleaned from various sources, see John R. Swanton, *The Indians of Southeastern United States* (Bulletin, Bureau of American Ethnology, no.137), Washington, D.C., 1946, p.346. He queries one report that would indicate it is possible to raise wild turkeys from stolen eggs, but Indian cultures of Central America succeeded in raising turkeys, ducks and pigeons. The clouds of passenger pigeons (*Ectopistes migratorius*), before they were hunted to extinction, must also have been raised on occasion. Of course, the most important domestic animal acquired through the newcomers from the Old World was the horse – too prized to ever be exploited for food.

[10] Hudson, *op.cit.*, pp. 289-99 gives an excellent summation of agricultural practice, explaining its 'riverine' character and how, without fertilization, it was still possible to develop permanent fields and towns rather than 'swidden' farming when fields must lie fallow for a time to be renewed, especially when corn quickly exhausts soil; the answer lies in frequent flooding of the bottom lands, cultivation of root vegetables that make less demand on the soil and the importance of bean culture which add nitrogen to it, all this in addition to a significant contribution to sustenance from hunting and gathering. See also Swanton, *op.cit.*, pp.256, 372ff. (preservation of foods).

[11] Hudson, *The Juan Pardo Expeditions: Exploration of the Carolinas and Tennessee, 1566-1568*, Washington, D.C., 1990, pp.52f.

[12] Quoted from papers at the University of Aberdeen by David H. Corkran, *The Creek Frontier 1540-1783*, Norman, University of Oklahoma Press, 1967, pp.9f. His error is to ascribe reliance on corn only to the summer months; it was dried and put away in granaries or corncribs, while both hominy and cornmeal were also preserved for use throughout the year.

[13] For a scientific explanation of how the Indians' process contributed to nutrition and why pellagra stalked – and still threatens some third-world peoples today – see Harold McGee, *On Food and Cooking*, New York, 1984, p.242-45. The Indians' consumption of corn with varieties of beans, which they often grew symbiotically to climb up the corn stalk, proved an additional protein enhancement.

Varieties of corn grown by south-eastern Indians starting about 200 BC were a tropical Flint and its descendant that makes popcorn and, from 800-1000 AD, Eastern Flint better adapted to germinate in a relatively cool, moist climate, which tribes of the plains and the northeast developed into hard Northern Flint for their short growing season. Dent corn is documented for the southeast by the early eighteenth century, but its date of introduction is not certain. Sweet corn was grown in a number of areas, but its advantage for eating fresh would have been lost when the ears were simply roasted before a fire.

[14] De Montigny (in his 1753 volumes on Louisiana) cites merely specific 'styles' or processes: bread, porridge, 'cold meal', and ground corn or grits, smoke-dried meal ('which has the same taste as our small peas and is as sugary'), gruel and hominy cooked with oil or meat. For a rich gathering of this and other early testimony, see Swanton, *op.cit*, pp.351-60 in his section on 'The Preparation of Vegetable Foods.'

[15] Hudson, *Travels*, p.222 [351]; Dover ed. p.285. His impression of the 'noble savage' is shaped by 'perfect and agreeable hospitality…by these happy people; I mean happy in their dispositions, in their apprehensions of rectitude with regard to our social or moral conduct: O divine simplicity and truth, friendship without fallacy or guile, hospitality disinterested, native, undefiled, unmodified by artificial refinements.'

[16] Hudson, *Southeastern Indians*, p.294 and notes.

[17] Swanton, p.363 quotes from Le Page Du Pratz's history of La Louisiane on the persimmon loaves 1 and 1/2 feet long, 1 foot broad, and the thickness of a finger, which are very long-keeping. Clearly the result is akin to quince paste (*cotognata*); they did the same with peaches.

[18] *Travels*, p.38; Harper, p.25 and note p.545.

[19] *Travels*, p.115; Harper, p.73 and note p.641.

[20] Bartram in a letter to Henry Muhlenberg, quoted by Harper, *Travels*, note p.466; see Bartram pp.359, 476, a ceremony described pp.450-453.

[21] Its Creek name was *assi*. For detailed study of this drink, see Charles M. Hudson, ed., *Black Drink: A Native American Tea*, Athens GA, University of Georgia Press, 1979, including among its articles Charles H. Fairbanks, 'The Function of Black Drink Among the Creeks,' pp.120-149 and William C. Sturtevant, 'Black Drink and Other Caffeine-containing Beverages among Non-Indians' (on Spanish addiction to it at St. Augustine and spread of use among whites).

[22] *Travels*, notes p.626 and references.

[23] *Travels*, p.241; Harper, p.152, notes pp.480, 628. Our wild food guru, Euell Gibbons (*Stalking the Healthful Herbs*), [1966], Field Guide ed., 1970, pp.240-245) discusses various smilax species and his labor-intensive efforts to make the jelly of 2 tablespoons meal boiled 10 minutes in 2 cups of water, then cooled; he preferred the batter cakes made 1/2 and 1/2 red meal and ordinary flour, topped with wild fruit jam. Other roots of *Zamia integrifolia* or *Z. pumila* in Florida were similarly used to make white coontie, called Florida arrowroot, a staple among the Seminoles. See John R. Swanton, 'Coonti,' *American Anthropologist*, 15 (1913), pp.141-2; Harold D. Cardwell, Sr., 'Coontie Root: The Dangerous Blessing,' *Florida Anthropologist*, 40 (1987), 333-35; [Alan Hall], *The Wild Food Trail Guide*, 1973, p.52.

[24] Sturtevant, *Edible Plants*, p.538.

[25] See especially Swanton's work for the U.S. Bureau of Ethnology, *op.cit.*, p.268, noting that alleged reference for 'honey' in a report of 1564-65 by the Frenchman Laudonnière on Florida Indians carrying it with them on travels is actually a mistranslation of his '*mil*,' meaning 'millet' or rather cornmeal, taken for '*miel*.' On the other hand, it is difficult to believe that in no case did honey bees penetrate north of Mexico in their wild state.

[26] Sturtevant, *Edible Plants*, p.337; Harper, p.549. Settlers moving West and Confederate soldiers made an aromatic tea from leaves and twigs of this plant.

[27] *Travels*, p.412; Harper, pp.260-61, note p.477.

[28] *Travels*, p.158; Harper, p.100 and note, pp.582f. quoting Harold H. Hume (*The Cultivation of Citrus Fruits*, New York, 1926) on naturalization of the bigarade or bitter-sweet orange in Florida from seeds dropped by wandering Indians who had been offered some to eat by Spaniards, while the sweet orange, proving less hardy, did not succeed in being so abundant among native trees.

[29] *Travels*, p.191; Harper, p.122.

Patents for Portability,
Cooking Aboard Ship 1650 –1850

Helen Clifford

Summary

In this paper I want to explore how problems inherent in cooking *in transit*, and most notably at sea, were solved; and how these solutions contributed to some of the advances in cooking stoves and ovens for use in domestic kitchens at a later date. The sources will be described and explained in the appendices. The main text will identify the specific problems posed by cooking on board ship, and how inventors attempted to overcome the technical challenges. The final section will look beyond the confines of the cook's cabin to show what impact the inventions made on more conventional arenas of food preparation.

Introduction

The problems of preparing and cooking food beyond the stable confines of a permanent kitchen might seem a minor issue to the majority of us. For some it was of paramount importance, particularly for those involved in sea-faring. How do you cook for sixty or more men (and sometimes women) aboard ship, without setting light to the vessel, in a cramped space with concern for any additional weight, and with the possibility of being attacked by foreign ships or being caught in a storm? That these issues needed addressing, and that considerable time, effort and money was spent in overcoming them is evident from the letters patent which included inventions related to exactly these problems. As it cost up to £300 to register a patent it was no mean decision to embark on the lengthy process of application.

Cooking in transit, the problems addressed

A reading of the patents of invention connected with 'machines' made for cooking at sea reveal four major issues which taxed the inventors' ingenuity. Perhaps the most urgent factor to be addressed was the need for fire safety. The very first patent connected with 'portable' cooking equipment was Castle and Ewbank's patent of 1676 'for makeing certaine secure & commodious fire hearthes ffor ships made of iron ... by means whereof shipps & other vessels may be the better preserved from burning'.

A second major factor was the need to reduce fuel consumption, not only because it was more economical, but also because it reduced the weight on board. This was one of the key advantages of Stephen Beck's invention of 1785. His 'new invented machine or ships' hearth', 'not only more commodiously dressed' the victuals, but required much less fuel than the ordinary mode of dressing'. Rutherford's early nineteenth-century trade card for their Patent Ships Fire Hearth stressed that it was 'For lessening the consumption of Fuel'.[1] A result of having less fuel burning at a higher temperature meant that the food was cooked more quickly. As Rutherford's trade card hastens to point out, the Patent Ships Fire Hearth 'will cook the Ships Provisions in about one half the Time of the Fire Hearths in general'.[2] In Joseph Collier's ships' stove of 1807 a moveable plate by which more air could be introduced acted 'as a blower to cause the fire to burn more briskly', and as a result cook more quickly. The notification and description published in the *Transactions of the Royal Society of Arts* also mentions the price. For a stove twelve inches in diameter the cost was about eight pounds.

The concern to save fuel was not restricted to primarily sea-faring equipment. John Joseph Merlin, perhaps one of the most well-known and prolific of eighteenth-century inventors worked on at least two fuel-saving cooking inventions. The first a 'new invented ... spring jack ... having a reflector to increase the heat', was enrolled in April 1773. In the same year he produced a 'Dutch oven or machine for roasting meat'. Merlin explained that as well as roasting meat, game and poultry it could double as an oven for baking puddings and as a plate warmer. Merlin stresses exactly the qualities we would expect to find enumerated today; the oven's saving on fuel, its ability to cook in two-thirds of the usual time, and its reliability. He also pointed out that its lightness (it was constructed of tin) made it ideal for use in camps or on board ship.[3] The advertisement states that these *rotisseurs* cost between two to six guineas depending on size.

Ships' stoves, unlike those for ordinary use, had a dual role to fulfil. Not only did they have to cook food, they also had to supply fresh water. Lamb's Patent Ships Firehearth rendered

> Salt Water fresh ... The Patentees beg to assure the Public that these improvements are such as will afford a constant supply of Pure Wholesome Fresh Water for the Ships Company from the Water of the Ocean without any Additional expence. They are adopted in His Majesty's Navy and meet with universal approbation. Orders received by John Lamb & Co., 20 Pavement, Moorfields and at the Manufactory of S. Rutherford No.2 East Smithfield.[4]

The food: where and what prepared?

By looking at ships' inventories it is possible to reconstruct in what conditions the ship's cook prepared the food. An Inventory of the Sundry Stores on Board the 'Bonita' dated 1712/13 reveals the limited extent of the cook's equipment, which comprised[5]:

Cooks Stores	
2 large Potts	1 Frying Pan
2 Fish Kettles	1 Gride Iron
3 Sashpans of Different Sizes	2 Ladles
2 Pudding pans	9 Patty pans
1 Stew Pann	3 Spitts
2 Cutcherree pans	1 Bakeing pan
	2 large Knives

We also know the sort of food that was loaded on board the same boat in 1717, an invoice from 'Capt. John Hardy Dr to John detailing Beef and Pork Delivered Aboard the Boneta' survives:

Dec 4, 1717	£	s	d
To: 29:02:26 of harbor Beef att 20s per cwt	29:	14:	07
To: 153:03:13 of Sea Beef and pork att 23s per cwt	176:	18:	11
To: 00:02:09 of Sewitt att [4d per lb]	01:	01:	08
Jan 22, 1718			
To: Literidge abord att 3 times	00:	12:	00
To: Salting ye Beef and pork	01:	08:	08
To: new salting ye Beef and pork and pickling	01:	02:	00
To: Bred and Bear for ye Men att 3 saltings	01:	01:	03
	211:	19:	01

A series of inventories survive for the eighteenth century with the papers of a ships' broker, William Panter. Panter, by coincidence, was also a keen inventor. All the ships, which were prizes, had an iron hearth with a greater or lesser array of equipment. The cabin stores help to create a picture of what it must have been like to eat on board in the eighteenth century. The good ship 'Nancy' provided quite a refined interior, with a mahogany table, four chairs, plates, dishes, knives and fork and two brass candlesticks (see Appendix 2). The diaries of the Wynne sisters reveal that even at sea during the Napoleonic Wars refined dining and entertainment was possible.[6]

Elizabeth Wynne writes of Friday July 15th, 1796, 'We lead a very regular life here. Breakfast at 8 dine at half past two sup before 9 and go to bed at ten. Captain Foley keeps an excellent good table his ship is a little Town - you get All your desire in it.' On August 7th, 'The whole Fleet has been exceedingly busy these two days to get all the stores out of the transports, we had fresh beef and a great many other provisions.'

Beyond the cook's cabin

Many of the inventions discussed above were used on dry land, the advantages which they offered being too useful to restrict to ships' use. Joseph Collier's ships' stove for example was also 'employed in drying houses, &c with more safety than those in present use'.

In 1855 the *Journal of the Society of Arts* advertised a portable heating and cooking stove developed by Price's Candle Company.[7] It was proposed by them as suitable for the use of the army in the Crimea, and used a light and cheap fuel:

> It is simple and compact in its arrangement. The fuel used is cocoa-nut stearine, in cakes, burnt by means of six wickes introduced into each cake. No smoke is produced, and the stove is capable of boiling, baking, and broiling, and the whole is comprised in a cube of about sixteen inches. The cost of the fuel burnt is at the rate of one penny per hour, a cake lasting eight hours.

One of the stoves was placed on a table during the R.S.A. meeting, and remained efficently in action throughout. So keen in fact were the R.S.A. to develop and test stoves that nineteen years later they initiated a series of stove trials, prizes being awarded for 'stoves which could use coal economically for both heating and cooking'. The resulting entries were tested in a specially erected building.

The next set of developments, in the second half of the nineteenth century, would, as someone suggested at the Symposium, relate to preparing food on 'track'. Cooking for the great railway age is a much under-explored area.

Introduction to appendices. an explanation of the sources

1. Inventions
a) Letters Patent

The Crown has since the late sixteenth century granted inventors letters patent protecting for a limited period their exclusive right to manufacture their inventions. Two principal types of document resulted: letters patent, constituting legal protection, and specifications describing the invention in more detail, often with an explanatory drawing. Other subsidiary documents, such as petitions and reports, were also produced.[8] Until 1853 patents and specifications for inventions were recorded in one of the three Chancery offices, and thereafter at the Patent Office. The Public Record Office holds patents and specifications of inventions to 1853. The procedures for obtaining a patent are discussed in detail by A.A. Gomme, *Patents of Invention*, (1946). The inventor began by preparing a petition to the Crown. This he took to one of the secretaries of state, or from 1782, to the Home Office. Then it was endorsed and referred to one of the law officers (either the attorney general or the solicitor general) who examined the petition and produced a report. In some cases the law officer had to adjudicate between rival inventors. Once the inventor had obtained a favourable report from the law officer, he took it with his petition to the secretary of state or to the Home Office. A warrant was then made out instructing the law officer to prepare a bill which would in its turn – after complex formal procedures had been completed – result in the grant of letters patent. A specification giving fuller details of the invention, was later enrolled at one of the three Chancery offices.[9] Specifications are the most informative records about inventions; in many cases they include plans or drawings. Introduced in 1711, they became mandatory from 1734. Letters patent record the name and the date of registering the patent, the number (in sequence from 1617), the name of the patentee, and often his or her occupation and place of residence, and a description of the invention. A multiple index to patents was compiled by Bennett Woodcroft which was published in 1853.[10] The *Subject Matter Index* reveals a large section connected with cooking equipment, including vessels and ovens. For a transcription of Stephen Beck's specification for a ship's hearth or stove see Appendix 3.

b) Royal Society of Arts.[11]

Founded in 1754 as the Society for the Encouragement of Arts, Manufactures and Commerce, it awarded from 1758 monetary prizes, (called premiums), and medals for developments in Agriculture, Chemistry, Colonies & Trade, Manufactures, Mechanics and the Polite Arts. To be awarded a Society premium, the competitor was required not to have pursued a patent.

2. Trade and advertising cards

How individual businesses chose to sell themselves, both in words and pictures, tells us a great deal about what they regarded as important. There are many collections of trade cards in Britain, one of the largest being the Banks and Heal Collection in the Department of Prints and Drawings in the British Museum, in the Guildhall Library (part of the Corporation of London), and in the John Johnson Collection in the Bodleian Library, Oxford. A survey of a large selection of trade cards reveals that those enterprises dealing with ovens and carriages seemed keen to exploit the advertising value of patents, and included illustrations of their patents within the trade card format.

Appendix 1

Inventions Associated with Portable Cooking.
Source: Bennett Woodcroft, *Titles of Patents of Invention*, Part 1, (London), 1853

Date	March 1677
Patent No.	197
Name of Patentee(s)	William Castle & Collowell Henry Ewbank
Occupation of Patentee(s)	Esquires
Place of Residence	Not stated
Description of Invention	'for makeing certaine secure & commodious fire hearthes for shipps made of iron, copper & other metals, by means whereof shipps & other vessels may be the better preserved from burning'.

Date	January 1754
Patent No.	688
Name of Patentee(s)	William Johnson
Occupation of Patentee(s)	Brazier
Place of Residence	Rotherhithe
Description of Invention	'double and single kettles and boilers of wrought iron plate instead of copper for the navy'.

Date	February 1769
Patent No.	917
Name of Patentee(s)	George Scott
Occupation of Patentee(s)	Gentleman
Place of Residence	Knightsbridge, Middlesex
Description of Invention	'Boiler, pot, or utensil of metal, for dressing ships' provisions with sea water or other water and purifying the same; also extracting broths or soups'.

Date	July 1770
Patent No.	964
Name of Patentee(s)	Jedediah Strutt & Joseph Strutt
Occupation of Patentee(s)	Glass Seller & Hosier
Place of Residence	Prescott Street, St Mary, Whitechapel, London & St Peter, Derby
Description of Invention	'new invented machine for roasting, boiling and baking, consisting of a portable fire stove, an air jack, & a meat skreen, contrived to move from place to place & to be used in the field, and houses where the stove, jack & skreen may be separately used'.

Date	June 1780
Patent No.	1261
Name of Patentee(s)	William Redman
Occupation of Patentee(s)	Tin Plate Worker
Place of Residence	Salisbury, Wiltshire
Description of Invention	'the Salisbury portable kitchen, for roasting boiling or baking any kind of provision in any room, or in the open air, without the assistance of a common fireplace, and which may be removed from place to place at pleasure'.

Date	December 1780
Patent No.	1271
Name of Patentee(s)	Alexander Brodie
Occupation of Patentee(s)	Whitesmith
Place of Residence	Carey Street, Chancery Lane, Middlesex
Description of Invention	'New ship stove, kitchen or hearth with a smoke-jack'.

Date	January 1784
Patent No.	1413
Name of Patentee(s)	Stephen Beck
Occupation of Patentee(s)	Brazier
Place of Residence	Bell Dock, Wapping, Middlesex
Description of Invention	'New invented machine or ships' hearth or stove with kettles, for the dressing of victuals on board of ships, whereby such victuals are not only more commodiously dressed, but much less fuel is necessary than is consumed in the ordinary mode of dressing the like victuals'.

Date	August 1788
Patent No.	1666
Name of Patentee(s)	William Hanscombe
Occupation of Patentee(s)	Unknown
Place of Residence	Unknown
Description of Invention	'New invented Machine for roasting many joints of meat, on a mathematical principle, horizontally & vertically, at the same time or separately, and to the weight of one hundred pounds or more, in such manner that several joints may be ready at one time, or progressively one after another, which said machine will be of great utility for any nobleman or gentleman's kitchen, where there is a large family, or for large taverns, inns or large ships of war, India ships & when in harbour or when fresh provisions are used'.

Date	May 1794
Patent No.	1986
Name of Patentee(s)	William Whittington
Occupation of Patentee(s)	Wheelwright
Place of Residence	Whittington, Sheffield
Description of Invention	'machine for roasting meat or other food, will be of great & universal utility, as well as in private and other families, as in camps, and on board ships'.

Date	June 1796
Patent No.	2118
Name of Patentee(s)	William Whittington
Occupation of Patentee(s)	Wheelwright
Place of Residence	Whittington, Sheffield
Description of Invention	'portable baking stove'.

Date	May 1810
Patent No.	2500
Name of Patentee(s)	Edward Walker
Occupation of Patentee(s)	Vintner
Place of Residence	Rathbone Place, St Mary-le-Bone
Description of Invention	'portable stove or kitchen for dressing and cooking victuals'.

Date	April 1812
Patent No.	3556
Name of Patentee(s)	Charles Fly Blount
Occupation of Patentee(s)	Engineer draughtsman
Place of Residence	Prujean Square, Old Bailey, City of London
Description of Invention	'Arrangements of machinery for improvements of ships' firehearths, and for other purposes'.

Date	April 1815
Patent No.	3890
Name of Patentee(s)	Thomas Deakin
Occupation of Patentee(s)	Formerly Ironmonger
Place of Residence	Ludgate Hill, City of London
Description of Invention	'portable kitchen'.

Date	January 1818
Patent No.	4201
Name of Patentee(s)	James Fraser
Occupation of Patentee(s)	Engineer
Place of Residence	Long Acre, St Martins-in-the-Fields, Middlesex
Description of Invention	'Cooking machine, useful for decomposing salt water, and rendering the same useful for the general purpose of a ships' crew at sea, without any extra apparatus except the cooking machine or, in other words, its structure will answer the end of a worm or condenser and worm tub'.

Date	September 1822
Patent No.	4706
Name of Patentee(s)	John Dowell Moxon & James Frazer
Occupation of Patentee(s)	Merchant & Ship Owner
Place of Residence	Liverpool, Lancashire
Description of Invention	'ships' cabooses or hearths, and also apparatus to be ocassionally connected therewith for the purposes of evaporating and condensing water'.

Date	April 1826
Patent No.	5352
Name of Patentee(s)	John Williams
Occupation of Patentee(s)	Ironmonger
Place of Residence	Commercial Road, Middlesex
Description of Invention	'ships' hearths, and apparatus for cooking by steam'.

Date	December 1834
Patent No.	6736
Name of Patentee(s)	Henry Stothert
Occupation of Patentee(s)	Founder
Place of Residence	City of Bath
Description of Invention	'ships' hearth or cabooses'.

Date	March 1845
Patent No.	10,576
Name of Patentee(s)	William Bowser & William Bowser Junior
Occupation of Patentee(s)	Engineers
Place of Residence	Parsons Street, St George's-in-the-Fields, Middlesex
Description of Invention	'ships' hearth'.

Appendix 2

Portable Stoves in Context. Inventories of Cooks' Stores.
Source: Chancery Masters' Exhibits, Public Record Office

C.112/61 [Printed Advertisement]

Taken from the bankruptcy papers of William Panter Esquire, Broker.

For SALE by the CANDLE,
AT NEW LLOYD'S Coffee-House over the Royal-Exchange, on
Tuesday the 22d January, 1782, at One o'Clock,
The good Ship NANCY,
WILLIAM COOK, master
Taken by the FRENCH on her Passage from JAMAICA, and re-captured
by the JUPITER Private Ship of War, of BRISTOL;

Square Stern, Plantation built, Burthen Two Hundred and Sixty Tons, more or less, shifts without
Ballast, a prime Sailer, is well found, and well known in the WEST-INDIA Trade; now lying near
EAST-LANE, ROTHERHITH

The INVENTORY

Cook's STORES

1 copper kettle
1 tin ditto
1 gridiron
1 iron hearth and copper
1 wood caboose

Cabin STORES

1 glass
1 stove with shovel, tongs and poker
4 chairs

1 mahogany table
some plates and dishes
knives and forks
2 brass candlesticks
a water stome
1 brass compass
3 wood ditto
1 hanging ditto

C.112/61 [Printed Advertisement]

FOR SALE
BY THE CANDLE
NEW LLOYD'S Coffee-House, over the North West
Part of the *Royal Exchange*;
On FRIDAY the 11th of JANUARY, 1782, at One o'Clock,
THE GOOD SHIP
Jonge Vrouw Anna Maria Elizabeth,
A Dutch Prize, from *Surinam*, taken by His Majesty's Ship the Hyena,
Edward Thompson, Esq. Commander

Frigate built, burthen 600 Tons more or less, is an exceeding strong well
built Vessel, about four Years old, pierced for 14 guns, and capable of
mounting 20; shifts without Ballast; is a very roomy Ship, well calculated
for a Letter of Marque, an Ordinance Store Ship, West-Indiaman, or any
other Trade where Room and Burthen are required; now lying off Wapping
Old Stairs.
The INVENTORY
Cook and Cabbin Stores

1 Large iron hearth
1 Pair of Iron dogs for ditto
1 Iron pot
1 Cabbin tables

C.112/61 [Printed Advertisement]

FOR SALE
BY THE CANDLE
New Lloyd's Coffee-House, over the
North West Part of the *Royal -Exchange*,
On *Tuesday* the 29th of *May* 1781, at One o'Clock at Noon,
The good Galliot DRIE GESUSTERS,

Dutch built in 1780, Round Stern, Burthen about 190 Tons, well sound with all necessary Stores,
taken by His Majesty's Cutter of War *Repulse*, *Edward Byam*,
Esq. Commander, now lying at *Union-Stairs, Wapping*

The INVENTORY
Cook and Cabin STORES

1 brass kettle	1 pair bellows
1 copper ditto	6 chairs
1 tea kettle	a writing desk and drawers
1 trevet with bars in the cook room	1 cabin bell
1 gridiron	1 table
2 pair tongs	

Appendix 3

Full Patent Specification of Stephen Beck's Invention, with Drawing.
Source: Patent Rolls, Public Record Office, C.210.27

Stephen Beck of Bell Dock in Wapping, Brazier invented a ships hearth or stove with copper and iron kettles for the dressing of victuals on board of ships whereby such victuals are not only more commodiously dressed but with much less fuel is consumed than in the comon mode of dressing the like victuals. January 16, 1784 (patent no. 1413): '– stove of hexagonal form two thirds of the sides whereof are made of cast iron the other part or tops with raising of copper or rolled iron plates and covered with wrought iron plate-pipe... with an elbow or bend ... (by which a considerable space is saved) ... in front of the machine or range with four or five iron Bars with spit racks to put on and take off occassionally ... designed to roast, boil and bake at the same time and by one and the same fire by which a great saving is made:

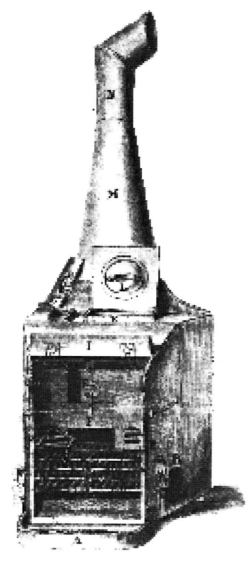

A- pan for ashes
B- front of range 4-5 bars
D- trivet/s on top bar
EE- opening to convey smoke from range
F- sliding door
G- hook to hold up sliding door
H- cross-bar - hooks to hang tea or other kettles on
I- flaps to lift up
KK- hang square kettles or boilers
LL- covers for Do
M- Chimney
N- elbow to turn or sway as the wind sets
OO-hooks to hang on folding doors
P- spit racks
QQ-rings to lash the machine or hearth to the decks
R- entrance or mouth of the oven that goes under the grate

Appendix 4

Mr. Collier's Ship Stove.

Transactions of the Society for Arts, Manufactures and Commerces, vol.XXV (1807) pp 93-5.
I acknowledge and thank the RSA for permission to reproduce this item.

The Sum of FIFTEEN GUINEAS was this Session voted to Mr. JOSEPH COLLIER, No. 11, *Crown Street, Soho*, for an improved Ship Stove.

The following Communication was received from him, and an Engraving is annexed.

A complete Model is placed in the Society's Repository.

SIR,

I HEREWITH send you a model of an improved ship stove, which may also be employed in drying houses, &c. with more safety than those in present use.

I submit it to the inspection of the Members of the Society, who, I make no doubt, will see its advantages, and am, Sir,

Your humble Servant,
JOSEPH COLLIER.

P. S. The expence of one twelve inches diameter will be about eight pounds.

Reference to the Engraving of Mr. Collier's Ship Stove, Plate VII. Fig. 1, 2, 3, 4.

Fig. 1. The stove, with the front partly closed by the circular slide A, which is moved from the back by the brass handle B. C a moveable plate attached to the slide A, now supported by the latch catching a pin, by which means it acts as a blower to cause the fire to burn more briskly, but which slides down also to shut the fire up.

D another plate, now hanging on its latch, but which can be let down to shut up the ash pit or dish I, which can be drawn out when the side facings FF are pulled up. G a circular plate or cap, which slides so as to shut the chimney up close.

Fig. 2. The body of the stove with the slider A moved round to the back, and thus leaving the fire-place completely open.

Fig. 3. The ash-dish shown separate.

Fig. 4. One of the side facings taken out to show the figure H, which slides into a hole made in the corner of the stove to hold it.

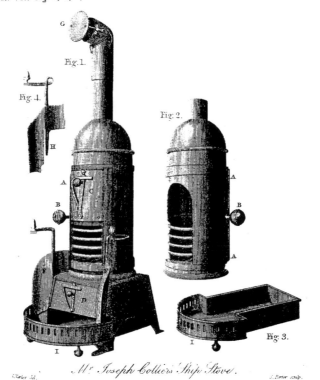

Mr. Joseph Collier's Ship Stove.

REFERENCES

[1]Trade Cards, John Johnson Collection, Bodleian Library, Oxford.

[2]Ibid.

[3]*John Joseph Merlin The Ingenious Mechanick*, (London 1985), pp.66-67.

[4]Trade Cards, John Johnson Collection, Bodleian Library, Oxford.

[5]Public Record Office, Chancery Masters Exhibit, C.108/133.

[6]Anne Fremantle (ed.) *The Wynne Diaries. The Adventures of Two Sisters in Napoleonic Europe*, 1935, (Oxford 1982), p.207.

[7]*Journal of the Society of Arts*, vol.iii (1855), p.113, proceedings of a meeting held January 17, 1855.

[8]Christine MacLeod, *Inventing the Industrial Revolution.The English patent system 1660-1800*, (Cambridge, 1988), p.1.

[9]Enrolment Office (C 54), Rolls Chapel (C 73) and Petty Bag Office (C 210), held in the Public Record Office, from November 1996 at Kew.

[10]Bennett Woodcroft, *Subject Matter Index of Patents of Invention*, 2 vols, (1855) arranged by subject; *Titles of Patents of Invention*, 2 vols (1854) arranged chronologically; *Alphabetical Index of Patentees of Invention*, (1854) arranged by patentee.

[11]My thanks to Susan Bennett, the Librarian and Archivist of the Royal Society of Arts for her advice and guidance.

Domesticating Western Food in Japan, a Comparative View

Katarzyna Cwiertka

Introduction

The Japanese are known to themselves and to others as an imitative people, unable or unwilling to create. It is often stated that the genius of the Japanese lies not in invention but in adaptation. Some researchers of Japanese culture view this Japanese adaptation in a less simplistic manner, describing it as a creative synthesis of the exotic with the familiar, the foreign with the domestic, or the progressive with the traditional.[1]

In this essay, I intend to explain this 'creative synthesis' in the context of food, demonstrating how the Japanese and Western culinary traits were, and still are, deliberately mixed in Japan. I will investigate in detail the way the Japanese domesticated Western dishes in their homes and restaurants in the early twentieth century, and how the food industry followed this tendency in recent decades. However, I will refrain from examining the incorporation of Western foodstuffs, such as onions, cabbage, pork and beef, into Japanese cuisine.

Excluding foodstuffs from the discussion on domesticating foreign culture is based on my judgement of their cultural notion. In my view, foodstuffs are very flexible, and can be very easily accommodated to new circumstances. Originally, foodstuffs have no cultural content,[2] although they can easily acquire one in a certain cultural context. A cultural meaning acquired in certain circumstances may be adopted together with the foodstuff while it migrates, but close examination of their migration leads to the conclusion that this cultural connotation is usually dropped.[3] For example, potatoes and maize were nothing more than exotic foreign foodstuffs at the moment they were brought to Europe. As time passed, potatoes came to be perceived in many European societies as a necessary item of a proper meal, and maize lost the sacred meaning it once had in its original cultural setting.

Contrary to foodstuffs, the category which I called dishes (see figure 1) is a product of the cultural process of transformation. The same foodstuffs may be combined and prepared differently in different societies, and based on this argument, I believe that dishes have stronger cultural connotations than foodstuffs. For example, rice is less representative of Japanese cuisine than sushi.[4]

A third category in my model – cuisines – is even more imbued with cultural symbolism. Cuisine consists of a set of dishes to be consumed with the use of certain eating utensils according to a certain table etiquette etc., all characteristic of a certain society. For example, sushi eaten with chopsticks in a Japanese setting gives a stronger Japanese image than one consumed at the table with a knife and a fork. Similarly, the same sushi will partly lose its cultural notion when served together with tomato soup, even if chopsticks are used.

Consequently, the different cultural connotations of foodstuffs, dishes, and cuisines, behave differently in alien culinary contexts. Migrating foodstuffs become relatively easily domesticated as they carry minimal cultural messages, while cuisines remain in a very loose contact with a recipient culture because they are already too culturally inclined. Preparing a foreign foodstuff according to domestic cooking techniques is a widely practised and relatively well-documented phenomenon.[5] Cuisines, in turn, function abroad as representatives of the culture of their origin.[6]

Dishes seem to be much less suited for adoption than foodstuffs, but they are not able to function independently as cuisines. Therefore, domesticating foreign dishes is a highly complicated process, taking place less often than domesticating foodstuffs. A discourse between two culinary cultures is much stronger in the case of dishes, as more cultural elements are involved in this phenomenon.

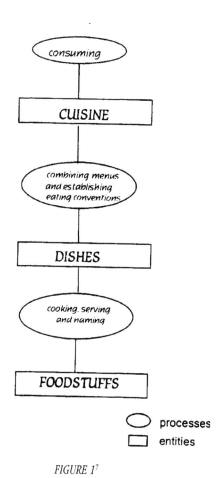

FIGURE 1[7]

In relation to foodstuffs and dishes within the framework of my classification, it needs to be kept in mind that these two categories overlap each other (see figure 2).

It is possible to classify prepared foodstuffs, such as soy sauce and margarine, as both foodstuffs

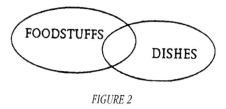

FIGURE 2

and dishes. Moreover, foods that will be treated as foodstuffs in one culture may be treated as dishes by another (for example raw fish vs. sashimi[8]).

For these reasons, my model should not be treated as an attempt to structure a cuisine, a meal, or a food culture. It is rather a useful tool for discussion of the adoption of foreign food.

If we assume that dishes are more 'cultural' than foodstuffs, examination of Western dishes in Japan should reveal how their cultural connotation of being Western was transformed into a new cultural form. Moreover, a comparison with the domesticating of Indian dishes in the United Kingdom should enable us to evaluate in a broader perspective the stereotype of the Japanese manner of creation through adaptation.

Domesticating Western dishes in Japan
Seasonings, ingredients, and cooking techniques

In the early stage of their presence in Japan, Western dishes were domesticated in the first place by adding Japanese ingredients, or replacing original ingredients with the Japanese ingredients. For example, adding taros into Western-style stews, or replacing macaroni or spaghetti with Japanese noodles was widely practised. Early twentieth-century Japanese household literature was full of experimental recipes such as sandwiches with marinated dried abalone and chopped seaweed,[9] and spinach and soybean curd in mayonnaise sauce.[10]

Flavouring Western dishes with Japanese seasonings was common as well. In 1916, the magazine *Katei Shûho* (Home Weekly) introduced a recipe for 'French Salad' made of leek, potatoes and burdock root dressed in a mixture of salt, vinegar, and sesame oil.[11] In this recipe, Western style salad had been domesticated by adding burdock root - a vegetable widely used in Japanese cuisine, but unknown in the West. The familiar taste of sesame made this dish more acceptable. However, the example most often found in the early twentieth-century recipes was soy sauce or fish stock added to Western soups, sauces, and stews. According to a 1909 recipe from the magazine *Katei Shûho*, hamburger was not supposed to be fried, but simmered in fish stock with sugar and soy sauce.[12]

Nowadays as well, Japanese ingredients are added to Western dishes consumed in Japan. Pizzas are topped with octopus, squid and fermented soybeans (*natto*); spaghetti is mixed with cod roe sauce and seaweed; and hamburgers garnished with shredded burdock root. As a typical example of domesticating the flavour of modern Western foods, I should also mention potato chips flavoured with dried bonito, ice-cream with a green tea flavour, and milk pudding with sweet azuki bean paste.

As far as domesticating Western dishes by changing cooking techniques is concerned, the most common was steaming instead of baking. In pre-war Japan only a limited number of élite and middle-class households possessed an oven, and even nowadays a microwave is a far more popular device than an oven. *Mushi pan* (steamed bread) was recommended in the first decades of the twentieth century as a cheap and simple snack bringing variety to a monotonous diet.[13] During World War II, steamed bread dough mixed with various vegetables helped many Japanese to escape starvation.[14] Although nowadays steaming bread at home is not popular any longer, a great variety of steamed rolls and cakes are available in stores.

Combined display

Another method of making Western dishes in Japan appear less alien was serving Western dishes on Japanese tableware. For example, displaying Western dishes in the traditional Japanese New Year boxes was suggested in 1914 by the magazine *Ryôri no tomo* (Cook's Friend).[15] The first box of this experimental meal was supposed to contain chicken and egg sandwiches; the second box, baked beef, jellied ham and roast chicken; and the third box, potato salad and lettuce salad.

With or without modifications in the flavouring, ingredients and preparation methods, the foreign character of Western dishes was diminished when served in Japanese tableware. They became more acceptable to the Japanese than when served on Western plates. Similarly, Western dishes seemed to have been more easily accepted when served with rice – the staple food of the Japanese.[16] For example, one of the reasons why English curries gained extreme popularity in Japan a century ago was the fact that they were to be consumed with rice. Owners of Western-style restaurants, in order to encourage Japanese clientele to try Western dishes during the last decades of the nineteenth century, began to serve them with rice placed on a separate small plate (see figure 3). The entire gastronomic web of contemporary Japan, from factory and university canteens, to the American-style family restaurants offer customers rice, or a choice between bread and rice, to accompany any dish.

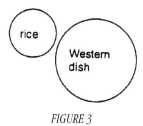

FIGURE 3

From the early twentieth century onwards, reformers of Japanese home cookery began to advocate including Western dishes in Japanese-style home meals. Examples of menus containing Western-style side dishes were published in women's magazines or domestic science textbooks in order to provide middle-class housewives with proper inspiration. These examples are translated from the compilation of cooking lectures at the Women's University of Japan, published in 1909.[17]

Dinner from menu no. 6

Vegetable soup
Beef grilled *Japanese style* (with *soy sauce* and *ginger root*)
Cucumber and horse mackerel dressed in sake-lees sauce
Strawberry cottage pudding

Dinner from menu no. 15

Clam chowder
Grilled fish in butter sauce
Boiled onions in *miso sauce*
Vinegared grated yam
Chakin kuri[18]

Dinner from menu no. 21

Miso soup with bean sprouts
Beef steak with onions
Arrowhead bulb boiled in soy sauce
Sour octopus with turnips
Rice pudding

All these dishes, excluding desserts, were served with plain boiled rice. Rice was supposed to indigenise Western dishes in order to make them more easily accepted in Japanese homes. In the first decades of the twentieth century, some restaurants went even further and began to serve Western dishes on the top of rice in a large bowl (see figure 4). For example, a *katsudon* (an abbreviation of *katsu[retsu]* + *don[buri]*), was the result of placing a Western cutlet (*katsuretsu*) on the top of a large bowl of rice (*donburi*), and *karêkatsudon* (an abbreviation of *karê* + *katsudon*) was a *katsudon* with curry (*karê*) poured over it.

FIGURE 4

Serving boiled rice and a Western dish in one Japanese-style container seemed to remove the Western connotation of the dish, and transform it into a hybrid form which over time would come to be perceived as Japanese.

The interaction between Western dishes and the Japanese culinary context was accelerated by the economic growth of the 1960s which opened up the possibility for a wide fraction of society to experiment with food. Old and new culinary imports from the West continued to lose their Western character. Combining them with rice was still a very important means of domestication. For example, a salad which is one of the most popular dishes in Japan, was turned into a 'Salad-roll' (*sarada-maki*), in which it is used as a core surrounded by rice and wrapped in dried *nori* seaweed (see figure 5).

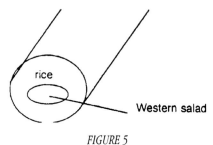

FIGURE 5

Another example of Japanising Western dishes by serving them with rice is the so-called 'Rice burger' (*raisu bâgâ*). Rice Burgers appeared in many Japanese fast food chains specialising in hamburgers started in the 1980's. In a Rice Burger, hamburger steak is put between bun-shaped wedges of pressed rice, and not, as usually, on a bun (see figure 6).

FIGURE 6

These are only some of the Japanese culinary experiments in which rice plays an important role of mediator between Japanese and Western culinary cultures.

Domesticating Indian dishes in England

Indian food was brought to England in the eighteenth century, becoming fashionable at the highest social levels.[19] Early Indian recipes printed in England were 'To make a Currey the India way' and 'To make a Pellow the India way' included in Hannah Glasse's *The Art of Cookery made plain and easy*, published in 1747.

To make a Currey *the* India *way*

> Take two Fowls or Rabbits, cut them into small pieces, and three or four small Onions, peeled and cut very small, thirty Pepper Corns, and a large Spoonful of Rice. Brown some Coriander Seeds over the Fire in a clear Shovel, and beat them to Powder, take a Tea Spoonful of Salt, and mix all well together with the meat, put all together into a Sauce-pan or Stew-pan, with a pint of Water let it stew softly till the Meat is enough, then put in a Piece of fresh Butter, about as big as large Walnut, shake it well together, and when it is smooth and of a fine Thickness, dish it up, and send it to Table; if the Sauce be too thick, add a little more water before it is done, and more Salt if it wants it. You are to observe the Sauce must be pretty thick.[20]

This recipe already shows several English modifications, such as omitting chillies, using fresh butter, and cooking meat with the addition of rice. Nevertheless, still no flour is used for the thickening of the sauce, and mixed spices are not yet replaced by curry powder – invented for the British market.

By the mid-nineteenth century, curries and chutneys began to spread down the social ladder, which was a reason for the élite to abandon the Indian fashion. The author of *Culinary Jottings for Madras* – a cookery book for English housewives residing in India – wrote the following words in 1885:

> [T]here can be no doubt that modern improvements in our cuisine, and modern good taste, have assisted in a measure in elbowing off the once delectable *plats* of Indian origin. … Having thus lost 'caste,' so to speak, it ought hardly to surprise us that curries have deteriorated in quality.[21]

Nevertheless, curries and chutneys did not disappear in England. Their career took a different path, and they became a mainstay of every middle-class oriented cookery book. Eliza Acton, for example, devoted an entire chapter of her *Modern Cookery for Private Families* to curries and potted meats. There we find a recipe for 'Mr. Arnott's Currie-powder,' and she advises the use of curry powder in recipes for curries.[22] She also gave recipes for 'Chetney Sauce,' 'Mushroom Catsup,' and 'Real Indian Pilaw.'

Seasonings, ingredients, and cooking techniques

Incorporating Indian dishes into the menus of the middle-classes in England in the late nineteenth and the first half of the twentieth centuries, was based on very similar methods to those used in Japan.

First, Indian ingredients which could not be easily obtained were omitted or replaced. For example, coconut juice was omitted in most recipes for curries, or replaced by grated coconut. Moreover, *ghee*, or clarified butter, was always replaced with fresh butter or lard[23], and later margarine.[24]

Culinary publications from the first half of the twentieth century advised English housewives to substitute Indian green mangoes and guava by green apples, rhubarb and tomatoes.[25] By the 1930s, home-made chutneys and ketchups were part of the skills that a country housewife was supposed to have under control. In 1934, there was an article on pickling in the magazine *Good Housekeeping* which gave many recipes for different chutneys: two recipes for 'Green Tomato Chutney'; one for

'Old Dower House Chutney' made of plums, apples and tomatoes; three recipes for 'Apple Chutney'; one for 'Red Tomato Chutney'; and two for 'Gooseberry Chutney'. Lucy H. Yates gave six suggestions for chutneys and four recipes for ketchups in her book published in the same year, entitled *The country housewife's book*.

European vegetables, such as cabbage, peas, carrots, turnips, tomatoes, potatoes and beans were added to curries. For example, *Home Chat* gave in 1898 a recipe for 'Curried Mushrooms':[26]

> Trim, peel, and carefully clean one dozen good-sized mushrooms. Make some good curry sauce. Lay the mushrooms in this sauce, and gently simmer for half an hour. Turn all into a china basin for the night, and re-warm in a saucepan in the morning, but do let it really boil. Serve in a very hot dish. Make a thick border of the rice round the dish first of all, and then pour the mushrooms into the centre.

However not only vegetables, but other English ingredients were added to curries. A recipe for 'Curried Salt Fish' appeared in the magazine *Home Chat* in 1905,[27] and Eliza Acton's *Modern Cookery for Private Families* included a recipe for 'Curried Sweetbreads':

> Wash and soak them as usual, then throw them into boiling water with a little salt in it, and a whole onion, and let them simmer for ten minutes; or, if at hand, substitute weak veal broth for the water. Lift them out, place them on a drainer, and leave them until they are perfectly cold; then cut them into half-inch slices, and either flour and fry them lightly in butter, or put them, without this, into as much curried gravy as will just cover them; stew them in it very gently, from twenty to thirty minutes; add as much lemon-juice or chili vinegar as will acidulate the sauce agreeably,* and serve the currie very hot. As we have already stated in two or three previous recipes, an ounce or more of sweet freshly-grated cocos-nut, stewed tender in the gravy, and strained from it, before the sweetbreads are added, will give a peculiarly pleasant flavour to all curries.

> *We find that a small portion of Indian pickled mango, or of its liquor, is an agreeable addition to a currie as well as to mullagatawny soup. [28]

Reduction of the use of spices seems to have been a major modification as far as the flavouring of curries and chutneys by English standards is concerned. The author of *Culinary Jottings for Madras* warns readers that in India 'cooks are inclined to over-flavour everything' and advises that 'spice, if necessary, should be doled out in atoms, the cook ought never have it under his control.'[29]

Addition of flour in order to thicken the curry sauce was generally practised in recipes written by Eliza Acton, Mrs. Beeton, and other cookery writers of the nineteenth and the early twentieth centuries. Addition of flour was a major modification of the technique of cooking curries. However, curries were also transformed further into more domestic forms. For example, 'Curry Cakes' introduced by *Home Chat*[30] were deep-fried cakes made of curry and boiled rice covered with bread crumbs:

> Required: half a pound cold curry and sauce, 4 ounces cooked rice, 1 egg, crumbs, and fat for frying.

> Overnight mince the meat from the curry finely, and during this process be careful not to waste the thick, cold curry sauce that will be coating it, otherwise you will find the mixture will be too dry. Next, well mix and heat the minced meat, sauce and rice. Add seasoning if necessary. Leave till cold, then form into cakes, like fish-cakes. Brush these over with beaten egg. Cover with crumbs, or medium oatmeal, and next morning fry a crisp brown in smoking fat.

Combining with the domestic

Similarly to what happened in Japan, Indian dishes were incorporated into English home menus. For example the recipe for 'Bengal Curry' appeared in a luncheon menu in *Home Chat* in 1895.[31] The menu included:

> Fish cakes
> Bengal curry (from cold veal)
> Stuffed tomatoes, cucumber
> Chocolate tartlets
> Baked semolina pudding
> Stewed cherries
> Cheese, biscuits

A vegetarian lunch introduced by *Home Chat* several years later was also assimilating an Anglo-Indian dish into an English menu:[32]

> Carrot and Lentil Soup
> Curried Cauliflower.
> Macaroni Cutlets.
> Savoury Eggs and Salad
> Savarin à la Chantilly

In the early twentieth century, cooking writers employed their creativity in order to bring Indian dishes to the reality of English middle-class kitchens. The cookery column of the magazine *Home Chat*, introduced several experimental curries and chutneys. *Home Chat* advised in 1911[33] that 'quite one of the most useful things to make is chutney. It is delicious to serve with cold meat of any kind, and a little added to stews or hashes improves the flavour tremendously.' On the advertisement for Sharwood's 'Green Label' Chutney, from 1948,[34] we read: 'It is the perfect addition to all cold meats, curries, stews, etc.'

Similarly to the Japanese tendency to combine Western dishes with rice, in the United Kingdom curries and chutneys were combined with the English staple – bread. This tendency could be observed in the English household literature of the first decades of the twentieth century. For example, the week-end house party menu introduced by *Good Housekeeping* in 1932[35] included a snack called 'Cheese, chutney and cress':

> Season cream cheese. Spread rolls or bread and butter with cheese – put on this a layer of tomato or other chutney. Cover with a little cress.

A booklet of curry recipes published by The Wine and Food Society in 1938 advised curry paste 'for use on biscuits, fried bread or as sandwiches.' Here, I quote the recipe for 'Toast Curry' which if left to get cold could be spread on biscuits:[36]

> Cut up an onion into very thin rings; chop two heads of garlic, two bay leaves, and fry all these in 2 oz. of butter with 12 cloves until nicely browned. Then add one tablespoonful of curry powder and stir. Then put in one large cupful of good tomato ketchup, a teaspoonful of tarragon vinegar and the seeds of 8 cardamoms; simmer gently for about fifteen minutes until the mixture is thick. Spread generously on rounds of fried bread. Garnish with parsley and serve hot.

A dish with the name 'Canapés Indian'[37] was very similar to 'Toast Curry,' but it was browned for a few minutes under the grill:

> Required: the remains of curry of any kind, a little butter, a little cooked tomato, rounds of toast, a little chopped parsley.

Chop up the curry. Melt a small piece of butter in a saucepan, add the curry and a little cooked tomato. Make it thoroughly hot. Have ready some meat, small rounds of toast about the size of a five-shilling piece, spread some of the mixture on each, heaping it up slightly, put the canapés under the grill for a few minutes to brown them nicely. Sprinkle a little chopped parsley on them, and serve.

In 1906 *Home Chat* printed a recipe for 'Chutney Croutons':[38]

Required: 2-3 tablespoonfuls of chutney, 2 tablespoonfuls of grated Parmesan cheese, a little made mustard.

Cut some very thin slices of bread, stamp out some rounds about the size of a two-shilling piece, and fry these a very light brown. The chutney should be heated and mixed with enough cheese to well stiffen it, and rendered still hotter by the addition of a little mustard. Spread this mixture, as hot as possible, on some of the croutons, while another one should be placed on the top of each other – like sandwiches. Dust a little cheese on the top of each one, and they are ready.

I intentionally chose to close this list of the early twentieth century's English culinary experiments with Indian dishes with the recipe for 'Indian Eggs' included in one of the 1895 editions of the magazine *Home Chat*.[39] This recipe in a very symbolic way shows how in the process of domesticating Indian curries in England, rice was degraded from the position of the core of the meal into that of a garnish, while British toast became the basis of the dish (see figure 7):

Neatly poach an egg for each person, and lay them on squares of buttered toast. Have ready some curry sauce, so thick that it will coat the back of the spoon. And when very hot, pour it over the eggs.... Garnish the top of each egg with a little heap of rice boiled as for curry.

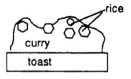

FIGURE 7

Conclusion

The world of the late twentieth century is increasingly cosmopolitan, and as Arjun Appadurai formulates it: 'the central problem of today's global interaction is the tension between cultural homogenisation and cultural heterogenisation.'[40] In the context of culinary culture, on the one hand, a global spread of foodstuffs, dishes, and cooking techniques can be observed, while at the same time culinary elements brought into new societies tend to become indigenised.

In this essay I focused on the early twentieth century, when this contemporary phenomenon often described as a 'melting pot' was not yet fully developed.[41] Nevertheless, similar tendencies could be observed in the process of domesticating foreign dishes in two different societies, the examples of Japan and England.

Both cultures developed in different historical circumstances, and their attitudes towards the cultures from which they were adopting varied remarkably. England imported Indian dishes from the position of the coloniser, with the ignorant assumption of cultural superiority. The attitude of Japan was quite the opposite. Japanese adoptions from the West were conditioned by the inferiority complex towards Western civilisation. At any rate, the process of adoption of foreign food in both societies showed several similarities.

From the 1860s onwards, British, French, and American cuisines consistently influenced Japanese eating habits, initiating several processes that led to the transformation of Japanese food culture. Within a hundred years, many of the once exotic Western foods have blended with Japanese foods and melted into the Japanese reality. Some of the eclectic Japanese-Western combinations were transformed to such a degree that their original form is almost impossible to trace.

Curries and chutneys brought to England in the eighteenth century, within a hundred years established a firm position in élite and middle-class meals. Several decades later, some modified Indian dishes, or dishes created in England under the Indian influence, have become a part of British culinary tradition.

Both, in the United Kingdom and Japan, methods of domesticating foreign dishes were similar. Along with mixing ingredients, flavourings, and cooking techniques, neutralising an exotic connotation of foreign dishes by combining them with the domestic staple food were the most common modifications. I presume that incorporating foreign dishes into a new culinary context was, and continues to be, based generally on a set of universal domesticating techniques.[42]

The question remains whether any preference for one or another technique can be observed in different societies. Another problem that needs to be extensively and comparatively examined is the process of the spread of foreign and hybrid dishes. Without a doubt, economic, social, and technical factors play an essential role in this process, together with the taste preference and the meal structure characteristic for each society.

The question whether the recipes with a Western influence in Japan, and the recipes with Indian influence in England are representative for the Japanese, or respectively English, cookery was not my main concern here. Nevertheless, the consistent appearance of the experimental Anglo-Indian recipes in English household literature proves that the creative synthesis of the exotic with the familiar, the foreign with the domestic, and the progressive with the traditional is not an exclusively Japanese phenomenon.

NOTES

[1] For an extensive study of Japanese adaptation see J. J. Tobin, ed., *Re-made in Japan* (Yale UP 1992).

[2] Of course, the simple fact of consuming certain foodstuffs that are not consumed by others may be characteristic for a culture, but this characteristic disappears once they are adopted elsewhere.

[3] A cultural meaning of foodstuffs often alters even without migrating, due to the change of the historical setting. For example, sugar has been extensively studied in this context by S. Mintz in *Sweetness and Power*. (Penguin Books 1985).

[4] *Sushi*: vinegared boiled rice mixed with various vegetables and/or seafood. A version most widely known outside Japan is the so-called '*nigiri zushi*' - small oval-shaped vinegared rice balls topped with sliced fillet of a variety of fish and shellfish (mostly raw but sometimes cooked).

[5] For example, potatoes in the Netherlands. See J. Witteveen, 'Potato recipes in Holland from 1600 until 1850.' in A. Davidson, ed., *Food in motion* (Prospect Books 1983), pp. 41-58. Assimilating pork into Japanese cuisine is referred to in my article on 'Minekichi Akabori and his role in the development of modern Japanese cuisine.' in H. Walker, ed., *Cooks and other people* (Prospect Books 1996), pp. 68-80. Indigenisation of tomatoes in Italy and Spain, chillies in Hungary, and turkey in England is also covered by R. Sokolov, *Why we eat what we eat* (Summit Books 1991).

[6] Ethnic food links immigrants to the culture left behind, and ethnic restaurants emphasise their cultural symbolism (as part of marketing) with additional elements such as music or interior.

[7] Figure 1 demonstrates a very simplified model of a 'food system' (defined after J. Goody, *Cooking, cuisine, and class* Cambridge UP 1982) with the phase of production excluded. A combination of

foodstuffs is prepared according to certain techniques, displayed in a certain manner and given a certain name. In this way foodstuffs become dishes. A set of dishes together with eating utensils, table setting, etiquette etc. form a cuisine. The sequence: 'foodstuffs, dishes, cuisines' seemed most proper to me, but 'ingredients, prepared foods, meals' could be appropriate as well.

[8] *Sashimi*: slices of raw sea food consumed with soy sauce with grated Japanese horseradish (*wasabi*).

[9] Editorial, 'Issun shita himono no ryôri' in *Katei Shûhô* no. 401 (1917), p. 6.

[10] Editorial, 'Montô ran' in *Katei Shûhô* no. 252 (1913), p. 7.

[11] Editorial, 'Sôsai seiyô ryôri' in *Katei Shûhô* no. 357 (1916), p. 6.

[12] Editorial, 'Montô' in *Katei Shûhô* no. 177 (1909), p. 7.

[13] M. Mitsuta, 'Mushipan no tsukurikata' in *Ie no Hikari* 1930 no. 12, pp. 132-134.

[14] *Kokumin hokenshoku no shiori.* (Zenkoku jogakkôchô kyôkai 1941).

[15] Dainihon ryôri kenkyûkai, 'Shin'an no yôshoku jûzume.' in *Ryôri no Tomo* 1914 no. 1, pp. 44-54.

[16] Such a pattern established itself in the diet of urban citizens of various degrees of wealth, and among landlords. Peasants could not afford consuming rice on a daily basis, and generally speaking the entire Japanese population reached the same standard around the 1950s. Nevertheless, the pattern: rice, miso soup, side dishes was representative for the diet of the part of that population which could afford to dine Western-style.

[17] *Kôgiroku 14: Ryôri.* (Nihon joshi daigakkô 1909). Japanese dishes and Japanese elements in Western dishes are in italics.

[18] *Chakin kuri*: a category of traditional Japanese sweets made of sugar, azuki beans, and chestnuts.

[19] I thank Harlan Walker for his valuable comments and information concerning Indian food in England.

[20] H. Glasse, *The Art of Cookery made plain and easy* (Prospect Books 1995, a facsimile edition of the 1747 edition).

[21] Wyvern (Colonel Arthur Robert Kenney-Herbert), *Culinary Jottings for Madras* (Prospect Books 1994, a facsimile of the 1885 [fifth] edition originally by Higginbotham of Madras), p. 286-7.

[22] E. Acton, *Modern Cookery for Private Families* (Elek: London 1966, a reprint of the 1865 edition).

[23] Editorial, 'Indian Cookery. For use in all countries.' in *Times Literary Supplement* October 3, 1936.

[24] As used in the recipe for Mild Curry by G. Owen, 'Hungry as hunters' in *Home Chat* no. 3163 (1955), p. 39.

[25] *Curry Recipes. Selected from the Unpublished Collection of Sir Ronald Martin by Mrs. Jessop Hulton* (The Wine and Food Society 1938), introduction.

[26] Editorial, 'Our weekly cookery chat' in *Home Chat* no. 182, p. 611.

[27] Editorial, '– are cheap today!' in *Home Chat* no. 523, 1905, p.57.

[28] E. Acton, pp. 301-2.

[29] Wyvern, p. 16.

[30] G. Owen, 'Breakfasts' in *Home Chat* no. 1384 (1921), p. 506.

[31] E. Beeton, 'Weekly menus for tired housekeepers' in *Home Chat* no. 14 (1895), p.31-32.

[32] Editorial, 'A seasonable lunch' in *Home Chat* no. 577 (1906), p. 163-164.

[33] G. Owen, 'For the store cupboard' in *Home Chat* no. 851 (1911), p. 179.

[34] Included in *Good Housekeeping's Cookery Book.* (1948).

[35] Quoted in Braithwaite, B. and N. Walsh, eds., *Food Glorious Food* (Leopard Books 1995), p.127.

[36] *Curry Recipes*, pp. 7, 14.

[37] Editorial, 'Savouries, the ingredients for which cost next to nothing.' in *Home Chat* no. 538 (1905), p. 163.

[38] Editorial, 'A little dinner' in *Home Chat* no. 568 (1906), p. 324.

[39] Editorial, 'Our weekly menu for tired housekeepers' in *Home Chat* no. 33 (1895), p. 294.

[40] Appadurai, Arjun, 'Disjuncture and difference in the global cultural economy' in *Public Culture* Vol. 2, no. 2: (Spring 1990), pp. 1-24.

[41] For the account of domesticating ethnic foods in the US see Belasco, Warren J., 'Ethnic fast foods: The corporate melting pot' in *Food and Foodways* 1987 vol. 2, pp. 1-30.

[42] It should be mentioned at this point that reducing the number of courses in English meals after World War II, has made it difficult to assimilate foreign dishes. The construction of the middle-class meal in the early twentieth-century England, consisting of several courses, was more suited for domesticating foreign dishes by incorporating them into an English menu. The structure of a contemporary Japanese meal, which consists usually of small quantities of several dishes consumed at the same time with rice, soup, and pickles, is a favourable factor for assimilating foreign dishes, and might be a reason for incorporating various foreign dishes in Japanese cuisine.

Christmas Dinner in Byzantium

Andrew Dalby

Constantinople, capital of the Roman Empire for a thousand years, was a city of magic and mystery to Christians of the West and of Russia. A few might hope to visit it ... once in a lifetime.

Some of the medieval texts that follow are historical, some are legendary: the two blend together. They are put together in this way to bring back to life the magic of real and imagined voyages to medieval Constantinople — a city more than half way to the edge of the world.

In particular, I want to show a little of how the tastes and smells of Byzantium can be reconstructed through travellers' reports. Naturally, the imagination has to be given full play. I quote, for example, from several French romances of the thirteenth and fourteenth centuries. In these, fantasy shades smoothly into reality: whether or not their authors had ever travelled, actual knowledge of the East, and of Constantinople in particular, was brought back from pilgrimages, embassies, trade and Crusade.

> They steered their galley before the Isle of Bogie, where no man goes, and there are none but apes. They passed the land of Persie, and that of Femenie; they left Coine to their left, and the land of Babiloine; they saw the tower of Marroc, where King Rabaot was, and the land of Jerusalem, and they navigated the River Jordan. They coasted Costantinoble and left behind them the land of the Griffins, and sailed on till they saw nothing but sea and sky.
>
> *Blancandin et l'Orgueilleuse d'Amour* 2785-2800.

The way there

On the way to Constantinople there were strange sights to see. The oldest narrative used in this paper narrates, quite factually, the pilgrimage of an Anglo-Saxon backpacker of the eighth century. St Willibald travelled simply. He was a young Englishman who had gone to Germany as a missionary, and he was to end his career as a bishop of a German see, but meanwhile he had persuaded his brother Wunebald, his sister Walpurga and their father Richard all to set out on pilgrimage together.

> They walked to the place where the Seven Sleepers lie, and on to a church of St John the Evangelist at a beautiful spot not far from Ephesus. From there they walked for two miles beside the sea to a large town called Figila. They stayed there a day, and got some bread and went to a spring in the middle of the town and sat on the bank and dipped their bread in the water and ate it.
>
> *Journey of St Willibald.*

Much later, Crusader experiences were incorporated into medieval retellings of classical mythology. In the next quotation, the old legend cycle of Thebes and Oedipus, retold in thirteenth-century France, somehow involves a journey through Bulgaria — just such a journey as, not many years before, the hard-pressed mass army of the Second Crusade had had to make, on its way to catastrophe in Asia Minor. Thus Bulgaria was in the news.

> Far off, said [the Bulgars], near Russia, along the bank of the Danube, there is a fertile country, but there is a high mountain in our way. Beyond its summit is a wide plain, well worked, farmed, levelled. There is strong Theleis wine, good meadow grain, strong

big grain, and there are wide fields of vines, and orchards enough that we might all live off fruit. There are wide ploughlands and big herds of swine: pigs, sheep, fat deer in the woods, deer and stags, goats and wild boar, and plenty of cattle in the fields ...

There was terrible famine in the army, a dearth of flour. Bread was sold for pure gold, a bit of bread for a maravedi. They lived in agony, some had lost their colour: the poor, in their hunger, were sick, sallow and pale.

Roman de Thèbes 7908-25, 8231-8.

Individual travellers, too, even diplomats, suffered hardships on the long journey. Liutprand travelled as ambassador of Lombardy in 949 and again on behalf of the Holy Roman Emperor Otto I in 969.

On the sixth of December we came to Leucas, where, just as by all the other bishops, we were most unkindly received and treated by the bishop of Leucas, who is a eunuch. In all Greece — I speak the truth and do not lie — I found not one hospitable bishop. They are both poor and rich: rich in gold coins wherewith they gamble recklessly; poor in servants and utensils. They sit by themselves at a bare little table, with a ship's biscuit in front of them, and drink their own bath water, or rather, sip it from a tiny glass. They do their own buying and selling; they close and open their doors themselves; they are their own stewards, their own donkey-men, their own *capones* ... I meant to say *caupones*, 'innkeepers', but I wrote *capones*, 'eunuchs', and that is all too true, and against canon law — and the other is against canon law as well. True it is of these bishops:

Of old a lettuce ended the repast:
Today it is the first course and the last.

Liutprand, *Embassy* 63 [with acknowledgements to F. A. Wright's translation].

Liutprand's complaints remind one of the similar irritation of a nineteenth-century traveller, Edward Dodwell, who benefited from the hospitality of a Greek bishop: 'there was nothing to eat,' he wrote in exasperation, 'except rice and bad cheese; the wine was execrable, and so impregnated with rosin, that it almost took the skin from our lips! ... The Bishop insisted upon my Greek servant sitting at table with us; and on my observing that it was contrary to our customs, he answered, that he could not bear such ridiculous distinctions in his house.'

The city and its markets

In the centuries before 1204, when Constantinople was surprised and captured and sacked by the adventurers of the Fourth Crusade, it had been probably the largest city in Europe. Though it took a long time to recover from this disaster, Constantinople remained a great city and a metropolis of world trade. In different ways, all travellers expressed astonishment at its size, its wealth and its markets.

The citizens are continually supplied with all their needs by busy seaborne trade. Cyprus, Rhodes, Mytilene, Corinth and many islands minister to the city; Achaea, Bulgaria and Greece labour to satisfy it, and send it all their finest produce. The cities of Romania [the Roman Empire], in Asia and Europe and Africa, never cease to send it their gifts. In it are Greeks, Bulgarians, Alans, Comans, Pigmaticans, Italians, Venetians, Romanians, Dacians, Angles, Amalfitans, even Turks. Many heathen peoples, Jews and proselytes, Cretans and Arabs and people of all nations come together there.

Bartolf of Nangis, *History of the Franks who Stormed Jerusalem*.

That twelfth-century view may be compared with a fifteenth-century report:

Outside St Sophia are great squares with houses where they are accustomed to sell wine and bread and fish, and more shellfish than anything else, since the Greeks are in the habit of eating these. At certain times of fasting during the year they do not merely confine themselves to fish, but to fish without blood, that is, shellfish. Here they have great tables of stone where they eat, both rulers and common people, together.

Pero Tafur, *Travels and voyages*.

It would be wrong to suppose that only Christians were impressed. There was already a mosque and a settled Muslim community in twelfth-century Constantinople, and regular diplomatic exchanges with the Muslim world. The traveller Ibn Battuta fulfilled a lifelong ambition when he was able to visit the great city around 1330. He arrived from Astrakhan, where he had been engaged on a diplomatic mission. It happened that the Byzantine emperor's daughter had been married to the Khan at Astrakhan: she was pregnant, and wanted to go home to Constantinople to have her baby. Ibn Battuta begged to accompany the party. The 'Sultan' of the following text is the 'Emperor' of Western reports.

It is their custom that anyone who wears the king's robe of honour and rides on his horse is paraded through the city bazaars with trumpets, fifes and drums, so that the people may see him. This is most frequently done with the Turks who come from the territories of the sultan Uzbak [i.e. of the Golden Horde], so that they will not be molested. So it was that they paraded me through the bazaars ...

One of the two parts of the city is called Astanbul: it is on the eastern bank of the river [i.e. of the Golden Horn, whose mouth points north-eastwards] and includes the places of residence of the Sultan, his officers of state, and the rest of the population. Its markets and streets are spacious and paved with flagstones, and the members of each craft have a separate place, no others sharing it with them. Each market has gates which are closed upon it at night, and the majority of the artisans and salespeople in them are women.

Ibn Battuta, *Travels*.

Constantinople was famous not only for its exotic luxuries but also for its water supplies, its aqueducts and tanks and fountains, here noticed by a Russian pilgrim and a Muslim prisoner of war:

In the precinct of St Sophia there are wells, and the Patriarch's garden, and many chapels. All kinds of fruit for the Patriarch: melons, apples and pears, are kept there in a well: they are placed in a basket on the end of a long rope, and when the Patriarch is to eat they pull them out, quite chilled. The Emperor eats in this way too.

Anthony of Novgorod (pp. 58-9 Ehrhard).

In Constantinople there is an aqueduct that brings water from the country called Bulgaria. This water flows for a distance equal to twenty days' journey. When it reaches the city, it is divided into three channels, one to the Royal Palace, one to the prison in which the Muslims were, and a third to the baths of the nobility, and the population of the city also drinks from this water, which has a slightly salty taste.

Ahmad Ibn Rustih, *Kitab al-a'lah al-nafisa*.

... a tank from which water is piped to the statues at the top of the columns. On the festival day this tank is filled with ten thousand jars of wine and a thousand jars of white honey, and the whole is spiced with a camel's load of nard, cloves and cinnamon. The tank is covered so that no one can see inside. When the Emperor leaves the Palace and enters the church, he sees the statues and the spiced wine that flows from their mouths and their ears, gathering in the basin below until it is full. And each person in his procession, as they go towards the festival, gets a brimming cup of this wine.

Ahmad Ibn Rustih, *Kitab al-a'lah al-nafisa*.

So much vaster than most visitors had ever experienced before, such a city had its terrors, as hinted here by a Russian pilgrim (obviously short of pocket money) and a chronicler of the Second Crusade:

> Entering Constantinople is as if you were in a vast forest, and you cannot find your way without a good guide. If you try to find your way cheaply or stingily, you will not be able to see or kiss a single saint, except, perhaps, that you can do so if it is that saint's feast day.

Stephen of Novgorod, *The Wanderer*.

> Constantinople itself is squalid and fetid and in many places afflicted by permanent darkness, for the wealthy overshadow the streets with buildings and leave these dirty, dark places to the poor and to travellers. There murders and robberies and other crimes of the night are committed. People live untouched by the law in this city, for all its rich men are bullies and many of its poor men are thieves: a criminal knows neither fear nor shame, for crime is not punished by law and never comes entirely to light. Constantinople is a city of extremes. She surpasses other cities in wealth, and she surpasses them in vice.

Odo of Deuil, *The Pilgrimage of Louis VII*.

The pilgrims' ultimate objectives were Jerusalem and the holy places of Palestine. But there were so many relics and sacred sites in Constantinople that most pilgrims stopped there too, found a guide, and wrote down the various wild stories that the guides told. Just a few are chosen here – a few that in one way or another have to do with the theme of food and drink – and there is not room to show, as would be all too easy, how travellers were shown 'the same' relic in different places and how they were told contradictory tales of the same place! All who follow modern guided tours in foreign countries know very well that pure ignorance, desire to tell a good story, and linguistic incompetence (in guide and tourist) all contribute to the growth of tales such as these. Some, however, have a respectable pedigree.

> As you go by the covered market on the way to the Hippodrome, on the left, is a church of the Virgin. In this is the Lord's table, made of marble, at which he dined on Holy Thursday with his disciples.

Anthony of Novgorod, *Pilgrimage*.

> There are so many sights [in the Studite Monastery] that it is impossible to describe it. We kissed the body of St Sabas the cook (for forty years he cooked for the brotherhood) ... Here there is a kneading trough on which the Holy Mother of God appeared with Christ. The baker of the communion bread sifted the flour on to a board, and poured on water, and the child in the flour on the board cried out. The communion baker was terrified and ran to the brothers. The prior and brothers came, and saw the image of the Holy Mother of God with the infant Christ on the board ... The refectory where the brothers eat is more wonderful than that of other monasteries.

Stephen of Novgorod, *The Wanderer*.

> In the town of Is Pigas [Pera], in the Church of the Mother of God, St John is painted on a wall. From his forehead, in the week of Quinquagesima, a rose grew, as white as cheese. All the people of the town came to see it and venerate it.

Anthony of Novgorod, *Pilgrimage*.

A thousand years was a long time. It was inevitable that stories would be told of the decline of Constantinople. In the fifteenth century, when Turkish territory surrounded the magic city on all sides, it was inevitable that prophecies would begin to hint at its coming destruction.

There was another palace below the Imperial Palace, and in this palace there is a cup that used to be full of water. Christians and Franks came and took water from the cup, yet it always stayed full and the water never went down, and this water cured sicknesses. But now this cup stands empty ...

In the monastery of Mangana, on your right as you come out of the church, in the narthex, are two paintings by Leo the Wise. One represents the patriarchs, the other the emperors who will reign over Constantinople. From his own reign to the end of Constantinople Leo painted eighty emperors and one hundred patriarchs, and the last emperor will be the son of Kalojan, who now reigns. Afterwards, God knows.

Russian pilgrim's description of Constantinople, about 1425.

The royal palace

The traveller's troubles and fears were surely all forgotten if he was privileged to be a guest at the Palace, whose wonders were themselves the stuff of legend. The next three quotations are from *chansons de geste*, the epic poetry of medieval France, dating from the eleventh and twelfth centuries. The events are completely fictional. Charlemagne never visited Constantinople. There was no Emperor Hugh to entertain him, and (we believe) no palace that turned when the wind blew.

Charlemagne saw the palace lightly turning: the French covered their heads, they dared not look. The Emperor Hugh the Brave came and said to the French:
'Don't be afraid.'
'Sire,' said Charlemagne, 'will it never stand still?'
Hugh the Brave said:
'Wait a little longer.'
Evening approached; the storm subsided, and the French got to their feet. Supper was ready. Charlemagne sat at table, his brave nobles sat, and Emperor Hugh the Brave and his wife at his side, and his blonde daughter, her face beautiful and pale, her skin as white as a summer flower. Oliver looked at her and fell in love:
'May the glorious heavenly king grant me to take her home to my fortress, where I could do all I wished with her!'
He said it between his teeth, so that no one could hear.
Nothing that they wanted was denied them. They had plenty of game, venison and boar, cranes and wild geese and peppered peacocks. Wine and *clarez* was served liberally, and the *jongleurs* sang and played their viols and their rotes, and the French had a fine time.

Voyage de Charlemagne 392-414.

In the quarter of St Sophia, near the cathedral, the Emperor lodged each French prince in a noble house. There you would have seen new silk strewn underfoot, you would have scented many a spice, for he had balsam burning everywhere. No other king matched his wealth.

He gave them all they wished at night, and next day he sat them down in his palace, and they began to talk of their business. But he showed them his strange games, and had his necromancers make a storm of rain and create powerful illusions. When he had fed them with fear, he set up more magic tricks and pleasant games, enjoyable to watch, so that they were distracted until the evening of the next day.

Chanson de Girart de Roussillon 203-218.

Then they wanted to cross the Arm of St George [the Golden Horn], but he loaded them with costly spices and mandragora. And when he had shown them the grandchildren of God [the relics of the Apostles], he took them to his vaulted chamber, its floor strewn with many-coloured gems. He said to each:

'Take all you want.'

He wrapped black sable pelts around their necks, he gave them rings, brooches and cups, new silk and purple and samite, and vases full of theriac and balsam.

Chanson de Girart de Roussillon 279-288.

The Christmas dinners

The magic tricks with which the Emperor distracted his guests in the *Chanson de Girart de Roussillon* do have a link with reality. The Emperors' guests really were astonished by some of the feats of conjuring, or technology, that were employed at Palace festivity. In fact, the legends were hardly more wonderful than the truth: and that is described in the two texts which now follow.

Harun Ibn Yahya was a Syrian prisoner of war who was held in Byzantium in 911/912. The hostages were treated to Christmas dinner at the Palace:

If you lift the curtain and enter the Palace, you will see a vast courtyard, four hundred paces square, paved with green marble. Its walls are decorated with various mosaics and paintings. ... To the left of the entrance is a room two hundred paces long and fifty wide. In this room are a a wooden table, an ivory table, and, facing the door, a gold table. After the festivities, when the Emperor leaves the church, he enters this room and sits at the gold table.This is what happens at Christmas. He sends for the Muslim captives and they are seated at these tables. When the emperor is seated at his gold table, they bring him four gold dishes, each of which is brought on its own little chariot.

One of these dishes, encrusted with pearls and rubies, they say belonged to Solomon son of David (peace be upon him); the second, similarly encrusted, to David (peace be upon him); the third to Alexander; and the fourth to Constantine. They are placed before the Emperor, and none may eat from them. They remain there while the Emperor is at table: when he rises, they are taken away. Then, for the Muslims, many hot and cold dishes are placed on the other tables, and the imperial herald announces: 'I swear on the Emperor's head that there is no pork at all in these dishes!' The dishes, on large silver and gold platters, are then served to the Emperor's guests.

Then they bring what is called an organ. It is a remarkable wooden object like an oil-press, and covered with solid leather. Sixty copper pipes are placed in it, so that they project above the leather, and where they are visible above the leather they are gilded. You can only see a small part of some of them, as they are of different lengths. On one side of this structure there is a slot in which they place a bellows like a blacksmith's. Three crosses are placed at the two extremities and in the middle of the organ. Two men come in to work the bellows, and the master stands and begins to press on the pipes, and each pipe, according to its tuning and the master's playing, sounds the praise of the Emperor. The guests are meanwhile seated at their tables, and twenty men enter with cymbals in their hands. The music continues while the guests enjoy their meal.

Such festivities continue for twelve days. On the last day, each Muslim captive receives two *dinars* and three *dirhams*.

Ahmad Ibn Rustih, *Kitab al-a'lah al-nafisa*.

That was a Muslim view. Fifty years or so later, the Christian ambassador Liutprand was also treated to Christmas dinner at the Palace.

> There is a hall near the Hippodrome looking northwards, wonderfully lofty and beautiful, which is called *Decanneacubita*, the House of the Nineteen Couches. The reason for its name is obvious: *deca* is Greek for 'ten', *ennea* for 'nine', and *cubita* are couches with curved ends, and on the day when our Lord Jesus Christ was born in the flesh, nineteen covers are always laid here at the table. The emperor and his guests on this occasion do not sit at table, as they usually do, but recline on couches: and everything is served in vessels, not of silver, but of gold. After the solid food, fruit is brought on in three golden bowls, which are too heavy for men to lift and come in on carriers covered over with purple cloth. Two of them are put on the table in the following way. Through openings in the ceiling hang three ropes covered with gilded leather and furnished with golden rings. These rings are attached to the handles projecting from the bowls, and with four or five men helping from below, they are swung on to the table by means of a movable device in the ceiling and removed again in the same fashion. As for the various entertainments I saw there, it would be too long a task to describe them all, and so for the moment I pass them by. One, however, was so remarkable that it will not be out of place to insert an account of it here.
>
> A man came in carrying on his head, without using his hands, a wooden pole twenty-four feet or more long, which, a foot and a half from the top, had a cross piece three feet wide. Then two boys appeared, naked except for loincloths around their middles, who went up the pole, did various tricks on it, and then came down head first, keeping the pole all the time as steady as though it were rooted in the earth. When one had come down, the other remained on the pole and performed by himself, which filled me with even greater astonishment and admiration. While they were both performing their feat seemed just about possible, wonderful as it was, for the evenness of their weights helped to balance the pole up which they climbed. But when one remained at the top and kept his balance so accurately that he could both do his tricks and come down again without mishap, I was so amazed that the Emperor himself noticed my astonishment. He therefore called an interpreter, and asked me which seemed the more wonderful, the boy who had moved so carefully that the pole remained firm, or the man who had so deftly balanced it on his head that neither the boys' weight nor their performance had disturbed it in the least. I replied that I did not know which I thought more wonderful. The Emperor burst into a loud laugh and said that he was in the same case: he did not know either.

> Liutprand, *Antapodosis* 6.8-9.

The Christmas menu

Sadly, neither guest specifies what was served in those great gold dishes that were brought into the room and transferred to the tables in an effortless demonstration of the high technology of tenth-century Constantinople. And although there is a very full description, in a Byzantine manual of Court ceremonial, of the timetable, the service, the rituals and the courtesies of Christmas dinner at the Palace (Constantine Porphyrogenitus: *Book of Ceremonies*) this is the one question that remains unanswered. What was on the menu?

We can at least say what an upper-class Byzantine expected to get for his Christmas dinner. This comes from an unexpected source. According to the theory of humours, accepted without question by Byzantine doctors and set out in popular medical manuals in medieval Greek, foods had to be judged and balanced for their effects on the bodily humours, month by month, hour by hour and according to individual constitution.

Theodore Prodromus, prolific poet of the twelfth century, is claimed as the author of a set of doggerel verses about foods and a healthy life style month by month. Among the scraps of advice: in March, sweet food and aromatic wine; in April, keep off radish; in May, no sausages; in July, no sex (much too heating); in August, eat fruit; in September, drink milk; in October, poultry and leeks. In November, don't have any baths. In December, uniquely, Theodore Prodromus mentions a special occasion.

> December: I hunt hares, festival food from the wild; I fill my dishes with tasty partridges, and I celebrate the Feast of the Nativity, the greatest feast of the Word of God. Take generously of all foods, I say, and reject the melancholy cabbage.
>
> Theodore Prodromus, *Verses on dietary rules* (Ideler 1841-2 vol. 1 pp. 418-420).

This is the only dietary manual that drags in the festival of Christmas – but all the doctors agree that Theodore Prodromus's prescription would be ideal for a December banquet. Venison, beef, hare, kid, wild boar, wild goat and gazelle and all game birds, said Hierophilus the Sophist in the tenth century. Eat lean meat, well cooked, hot, with a spicy sauce, and you can have suckling animals if you like; and any fish except the wet ones (wet in terms of the theory of humours); pungent flavours, including pepper, leeks and mallow; among pulses, not beans or chickpeas or lupins; among fruits you must keep off dates and bay berries, but plenty of others remain. You can have eight baths in the course of the month so long as you soap yourself with aloe vera and a touch of myrrh. Finally, drink lime tea from time to time – a decoction, that is, of the flowers of the lime or linden tree.

I think it is now almost legitimate to speculate what might have been served to the Emperor, his guests and his hostages in the Nineteen-Couch Room on Christmas Day. To begin with, surely a spiced wine as apéritif: *Conditum*, a Latin name for a traditional liquid delicacy. The Byzantines adjusted their *conditum*, under medical advice, incorporating different spices and herbs for each season. In winter you might add spikenard, pepper, cinnamon, cloves, benzoin and honey. Then the meal proper might begin with some fish dishes, in the classical way: but 'not wet', so perhaps tuna, swordfish, bream, bass, red mullet; fried fish was recommended in winter, coated in flour and with a hint of mustard. Now the pièces de résistance: Theodore Prodromus has told us this, hare and partridge. It's clear from Hierophilus that other game might be substituted as far as the dieticians were concerned, but wild boar would have offended Muslim guests. The Imperial table might have had venison and gazelle, the latter a real delicacy of medieval Byzantium, to set beside the traditional hare and partridge. The game was to be served hot with a spicy sauce – but what spices? Winter instructions are given by Hierophilus under January. The partridge might be best served with mustard, cumin-salt, and a dip of wine and fish sauce. Other spices to be used in winter were pepper, caraway (Anatolian caraway, according to the text), cinnamon, and (even more exotic) spikenard. On the side I seem to see pea or lentil soup (flavoured with salt, olive oil and cumin). Among vegetables, leeks, carrots and perhaps wild asparagus (vegetables might sometimes be cooked or dressed with honey); and a little dish of roasted garlic to rub on to your bread, the fine bread of the palace bakery. Mallow, also recommended, might serve (as in Rome) as a garnish for the serving dishes.

We know that fruit was served – and we know that fruit for the Emperor's table was kept chilled, in an underground cistern, till the moment it appeared in the dining room. The wine would be mixed fairly strong – that is, half-and-half – for winter. The Muslim hostages would have had to ignore the doctors' advice, which was: 'Never drink unmixed water, except in summer', or, in other words, always add wine! The wine that came to Byzantium was world-famous (famous as far away as Anglo-Saxon England, at any rate) and on a feast day the sweet wines of Crete and Samos would be much in evidence.

The problem with the twelve days of Christmas, in Byzantium as in some other societies, is that they leave you overfull, heavy-eyed, and a little stale. This is surely why one Byzantine medical writer begins his dietary advice for January with the significant phrase 'After excess ...'

After excess of any kind, this anonymous author instructs, early in the morning you must take three doses of fine wine with a good bouquet, and no food until midday, when, according to Hierophilus the Sophist, a little quince marmalade might be in order. And in general the dietary advice for January is particularly full and detailed in all the manuals, as if there was a good deal of remedial work to be done.

BIBLIOGRAPHY

Ahmad Ibn Rustih, *Kitab al-a'lah al-nafisa*. French tr. Izeddin. 1948.

Anthony of Novgorod, *Livre du pèlerin*. French tr. M. Ehrhard in *Romania* vol. 58 (1932) pp. 44-65.

Bartolf of Nangis, *History of the Franks who Stormed Jerusalem*. Ed. and French tr. in *Recueil des historiens des Croisades* vol. 3 p. 490 ff.

Blancandin et l'Orgueilleuse d'Amour: roman d'aventures du XIIIe siècle. Ed. Franklin P. Sweetser. Geneva: Droz, 1964.

Chanson de Girart de Roussillon. Ed. W. Mary Hackett with modern French tr. Micheline de Combarieu du Grès and Gérard Gouiran. Paris: Livre de Poche, 1993.

Constantine Porphyrogenitus: *Book of Ceremonies*. In Migne, *Patrologia Graeco-Latina*.

Edward Dodwell, *A classical tour through Greece*. London: Rodwell and Martin, 1819.

Hierophilus the Sophist, *Dietary Rules*; Theodore Prodromus, *Verses on dietary rules*. Both texts in *Physici et medici graeci minores*. Ed. I. L. Ideler. Berlin: Reimer, 1841-2.

The travels of Ibn Battuta A.D. 1325-1354 tr. H. A. R. Gibb. 3 vols. Cambridge, 1958-71.

Journey of St Willibald. Ed. Tobler and Miolinier.

Liudprandi opera. Ed. J. Becker, Hanover 1915; *The works of Liudprand of Cremona*. Tr. F. A. Wright. London: Routledge, 1930.

Odo of Deuil, *De profectione Ludovici VII in Orientem*. Ed. and tr. V. G. Berry. New York: Columbia University Press, 1948.

Pero Tafur, *Travels and adventures 1435-1439*. Tr. Malcolm Letts. London: Routledge, 1926.

Roman de Thèbes. Ed. with modern French tr. Francine Mora-Lebrun. Paris: Livre de Poche, 1995.

Russian pilgrim's description of Constantinople, about 1425; and Stephen of Novgorod, *The Wanderer*. Both texts, with English translation, in George P. Majeska, *Russian travelers to Constantinople in the fourteenth and fifteenth centuries*. Washington: Dumbarton Oaks, 1984.

Voyage de Charlemagne à Jérusalem et à Constantinople. Ed. Paul Aebischer. Geneva, 1965.

Food and the Roman Army:
Travel, Transport, and Transmission
(with Particular Reference to the Province of Britannia)

Carol A. Déry

Introduction

'An army marches on its stomach' is a maxim of universal application attributed to Napoleon, which evokes the importance of ensuring an adequate supply of food for the troops at all times. Indeed Vegetius, the fourth-century AD writer on military affairs, observed that 'Starvation destroys an army more often than does battle, and hunger is more savage than the sword' (*On Military Science*, 3.3). The Roman army was one of the most widely-travelled bodies in the ancient world, responsible for policing a vast empire, which at its height embraced the whole of the Mediterranean basin, encompassing much of Europe (from Britain at its furthest north-western outreach to the area of the Black Sea at its easternmost terminus), Asia Minor, Syria, and North Africa, so that the logistics of supply were often complex. The army was not only an important mechanism in the transmission of Roman culture in general to the provinces, but also made a significant contribution to the transference of foodstuffs around the Empire, for the Romans brought back with them many of the new foods they encountered on their travels, and attempted to acclimatize useful foodplants wherever they went.[1] It is the intention of this paper to examine the legacy of the Roman occupation of Britain regarding the introduction of new forms of flora to the province, alongside a survey of the diet of the army on active service, with especial reference to the military impetus for long-distance trade in foodstuffs.

Feeding the troops: the Roman military diet, basic rations and supplies

The basic iron rations carried by the Roman army on expedition are mentioned in connection with the reforms of two second-century AD generals, who sought to maintain discipline on campaign by removing superfluities from the soldiers' diet:

> [Avidius Cassius] forbade the soldiers to carry anything except *laridum* (bacon), *bucellatum* (biscuit), and *acetum* (sour wine) on campaign, and if he discovered any fancy foods, he inflicted severe punishment. (*Augustan Histories: Avidius Cassius*, 5.3).

> [Pescennius Niger] forbade anyone to drink *vinum* (wine) on campaign, but all were to be content with *acetum*. He forbade pastry-cooks (*pistores*) to follow expeditions, ordering all soldiers to be content with *bucellatum*. (*Augustan Histories: Pescennius Niger*, 10.3-4).

Bucellatum or 'hard tack' was a sort of biscuit that had been cooked twice in order to prolong its 'shelf-life'. It formed part of a soldier's regular corn ration, but prepared in a form that would keep for a longer period on the march, and which was easily transportable by back-pack.[2] *Acetum*, often mixed with water to make *posca*[3], a popular military beverage, was a low quality wine, and was inferior to *vinum*, which was better quality wine.

The ancient authorities indicate that these rations regularly formed part of the soldiers' basic diet in peace-time also, for example:

[The emperor] Hadrian himself also used to live a soldier's life amongst the other ranks, following the example of Scipio Aemilianus, Metellus, and Trajan, and cheerfully ate in the open such camp fare as bacon, cheese, and *posca*.' (*Augustan Histories: Hadrian*, 10.2).[4]

The literary sources generally maintain that it was regular practice for the legionaries to carry sufficient rations for about 17 days, though Josephus asserts that it was only enough for 3 days.[5] Supplies could often be replenished at halting-places (*mansiones/stationes*) along the route of a march in occupied territory,[6] but in enemy territory the soldiers might have to forage in the surrounding countryside, or perhaps requisition supplies from a subdued local populace. Josephus tells us that sickles with which to reap the crops in nearby fields were carried as part of the standard tool-kit (*Jewish War*, 3.95), but the soldiers would also gather whatever fruit, nuts, berries, or plants they could find growing in the vicinity, as well as driving off animals. Indeed the war records of Julius Caesar suggest that foraging was a necessary commonplace in his day.[7]

The legionaries did their own cooking, and each had as part of his campaign kit such items as a string-bag for foraging, a spit, a metal cooking pot, a *patera* (shallow skillet) that served a dual function as a pan for cooking and a plate for eating, and a cup. These items were usually carried in bundles on poles slung over the shoulders,[8] and indeed reliefs from Trajan's Column in Rome clearly show collections of mess tins being carried in this manner by the troops.[9] When preparing to encamp for the night, responsibility for the procurement of food and water, along with firewood for cooking, was meted out to various contingents, whilst others were given the task of securing the temporary lodging-place against potential enemy attack.[10]

Grain was the most important staple food, both for the mobile forces and for those stationed in the provinces, so that great care was taken to try to ensure a good reserve. Indeed Vegetius commented that 'he who does not prepare a supply of grain and other essentials is conquered without a blow' (*On Military Science*, 3.26). The supply of corn to the army under the early Empire was regulated by the *procurator* of each province,[11] but by the late Empire the organization of supplies had fallen to the *primipilares* (commissary officers), who were mainly responsible for provisioning the frontier garrisons.[12] Corn was frequently requisitioned in the forms of tithes on provinces, or sometimes it was voluntarily donated for the upkeep of the army,[13] but *frumentum emptum*, or compulsory purchase at a fixed price by the state, could also be enforced to supply the troops. In the *Agricola*, Tacitus describes how the native Britons were forced to sit outside the doors of closed granaries waiting to buy back their own corn at inflated prices after it had been requisitioned in this manner (19.4).[14] It was not until about the end of the third century or beginning of the fourth century AD that the *Anonna Militaris* came into effect, which was a regular tax in kind imposed upon the provinces for the support of the army.[15]

On expedition bulk supplies of grain for the troops would normally be carried in sacks in the baggage train using pack-animals or wagons; Corbulo, en route to Armenia, carried his corn by camel caravan, which choice was largely dictated by the nature of the terrain (Tacitus, *Annals*, 15.12). In the provinces grain would be stored in large warehouses or granaries (*horrea*), and each Roman fort or fortress was equipped with at least one granary to house its garrison's supply. Some forts, such as South Shields on Hadrian's Wall (the vast stone barrier, built in the early second century AD, which spans the Tyne-Solway isthmus for a distance of some 80 miles), possessed an inordinately large number of granaries, and evidently functioned as supply-depots from which other forts in the vicinity could be provisioned. The basic granary design was of a large rectangular building with thick walls, often buttressed, and raised floors to allow air to circulate underneath the stored grain to prevent it becoming damp. Tacitus' statement (*Agricola*, 22.2) that every fort in Britain held sufficient supplies to last a year under Agricola's (his father-in-law) governorship seems to be borne out by modern calculations based upon the dimensions of these buildings, and the estimated quantities of grain that would be required to meet a daily allowance of about 3 lbs per man per day.[16] It seems probable that granaries were also used to store other foodstuffs in addition to grain, such as wine, cheese, pulses, fruit, and vegetables, perhaps in the loft-space above. *Carnaria* (meat-racks), wicker frames hung from the ceiling, may also have been used to suspend cured meats and other foods, thus making optimum use of an otherwise redundant roof space.[17]

Army corn rations normally comprised wheat, the preferred grain of the Romans; barley was only issued to the troops in times of hardship, or as a punishment for misdemeanours.[18] The soldiers each had their own hand-mill or rotary quern with which to grind their corn allowance, and the resulting meal could be made into porridge[19] or baked into bread.[20] Military bread (*panis militaris*) was of the wholemeal variety,[21] and there were apparently two grades: *panis militaris castrensis* (ordinary standard) and *panis militaris mundus* (a better quality bread, probably made from a more finely refined flour, perhaps for the officers).[22] Domed ovens for the baking of bread are frequently found tucked into the interior flank of fort ramparts opposite the end of each barrack block, suggesting that the production and supply of bread was not managed centrally within the fort, but was operated amongst smaller companies within the garrison, perhaps based on the *centuria* or smaller unit.[23] Bread stamps provide further evidence for cooking arrangements based upon company divisions.[24] The presence of hearths within the individual rooms (*contubernia*)[25] of the standard barrack-block suggest that some cooking also probably took place within the barracks themselves, and graffiti discovered on potsherds indicate that each *contubernium* had its own cooking equipment and mess utensils.[26] It seems likely that there would have been a rota system in operation, whereby individuals or small groups of solidiers took it in turns to cook and bake bread for themselves and the rest of their outfit.

Life was rather different for the commanding officer of a fort or fortress however, who was often able to take his family and household staff with him when he received a foreign posting of any length. His official residence (*praetorium*) had its own permanent kitchen, and his meals were prepared for him by his domestic servants. He typically enjoyed a high standard of living within the *praetorium*, with many of his customary home-comforts, which is evidenced in part by the remains of fine tablewares that have been recovered from officers' quarters at numerous military sites, and the occasional chance survival of documents listing foodstuffs which were probably destined for the *praetorium*.[27] Four fragments of a writing tablet discovered at the Roman fort of Vindolanda near Hadrian's Wall together form part of an inventory of household equipment relating to the *praetorium*, which lists part of a dinner service, including *scutulae* (plates or dishes), *paropsides* (side-plates), *acetabula* (vinegar-cups), *ovaria* (egg-cups), *lanx* (platter), *panaria* (bread-baskets), *calices* (cups), and *trullae* (ladles) amongst other items (*Vindolanda Tablet*, 2.196). A particularly fine example of a *praetorium* from the double legionary fortress at Vetera possessed a large dining-room (*triclinium*) for entertaining guests, where such a dinner-service would have been quite appropriate, with a suite of rooms close by which may have been used for receiving visitors.[28]

A deduction was made at source from the soldiers' salaries to cover the cost of basic rations, though additional stoppages might be made on the occasion of special camp-dinners, such as at the *Saturnalia*[29] or some other festival. A document from Vindolanda records quantities of unspecified foods being brought in during the month of June (year uncertain) for a festival, in addition to a *modius*[30] of wine 'for a festival of the Goddess' (identity unknown) (*Vindolanda Tablet*, 2.190).

Supplementary foods in the military diet

A great many other foods are known to have been eaten by the troops when available, in addition to the basic rations already outlined. The osteological record from fort and fortress sites throughout the Empire indicates that a wide variety of animals were regularly consumed by the soldiers. The ox appears to have been the most frequently eaten animal, but pigs, sheep, goats, and deer were also consumed in large quantities, supplemented by hares and wild boar, and many of the animals were found to be immature at time of butchery. In several cases large quantities of bones had been purposely split to extract the marrow for use in soups and stews. The bones of other less commonly eaten animals such as the fox, elk, wolf, badger, bear and beaver, to mention but a few, have also been discovered at a number of Roman military sites throughout Europe, but it is uncertain whether these animals served as food or were merely hunted for sport. Foxes and bears are however mentioned as foods by the second century AD by the medical writer, Galen,[31] and the Roman army comprised numerous foreign contingents who may have been partial to the more unusual types of meat.

Seafood was also eaten by the soldiers, and not merely in coastal locations where they would have been readily obtainable, for there is ample evidence, mainly in the form of shell debris, that they were regularly transported into inland sites. The remains demonstrate that a wide variety of shellfish were enjoyed, including cockles, mussels, whelks, limpets, and even some species of edible small snail, but finds of oyster shells are particularly widespread on military sites, indicating that their consumption was not restricted to civilian gastronomic circles. A writing-tablet discovered at Vindolanda records a letter written to a certain Lucius, *decurion*, by an unknown soldier, and reads: 'A friend sent me 50 oysters from Cordonovi' (*Vindolanda Tablet*, 2.299). Cordonovi has not yet been identified with any certainty, but is thought to have been located somewhere in the Kent area.[32]

Freshwater and sea-fish were also eaten when available, and fish bones and fish hooks were found at the legionary fortress of Vindonissa in Switzerland. The troops would often fish for themselves, as much for sport as for the procurement of food, but dried salt-fish was also transported over long distances to supply the military; indeed inscribed amphorae still containing the remains of fish were found at the Roman military encampment at Masada in Judaea. Food-poisoning from fish was a potential hazard however, and an incident of this is attested in a letter written by a legionary named Terentianus stationed at Alexandria in Egypt in the second century AD, to his father explaining why he had failed to meet with him:

> For it was at that time that so violent and awful an attack of fish-poisoning made me ill, that for five days I could not even drop you a line, never mind go out to meet you. None of us could even leave the camp gate.[33]

Other types of animal food that were eaten by the troops include chickens, ducks and geese, which comprised a ready source of eggs as well as meat. Bone assemblages from numerous other species of bird, including pheasants, swans, and pigeons, have been recovered from a number of military sites, and a document from Vindolanda mentions hunting-nets for catching thrushes and a larger dragnet for ensnaring swans.

Beans and lentils constituted other staple fare for the troops, and were probably consumed mostly in the forms of soups and stews, though some pulses could also be ground into flour and used to make bread. The basic diet was further supplemented by a wide variety of fruit, vegetables, nuts, and berries, many of which would have been grown or gathered from the wild locally, though shipments of preserved fruits and vegetables are well known. Cheese is attested by finds of cheese-making equipment at a number of military sites such as Corbridge on Hadrian's Wall, which demonstrates that at least some of the cheese consumed by the soldiers was home-produced. Hard cheeses however can be easily stored for long periods, and will readily withstand long-distance transportation, hence the possibility of imported cheeses should not be precluded.

Despite the testimony of the authors of the Augustan Histories cited earlier, it appears that the troops customarily drank *vinum* alongside *acetum*. Vegetius, for instance, recommended that a reasonable supply of corn, *acetum*, *vinum*, and salt should be maintained at all times (*On Military Science*, 3.3), and when siege threatened, *vinum*, *acetum*, grain and fruit should be taken into the fort, along with fodder for the horses (*On Military Science*, 4.7). Appian, relating an incident in the *Spanish Wars* in which food shortages were experienced by the army, gives no indication that wine was an uncommon ration:

The soldiers had no salt, *vinum*, *acetum* or oil, but lived on barley and wheat, and venison and rabbit boiled without salt, which caused dysentery, and many died (9.54).

Cervesa (Celtic beer) was also a favourite military beverage, particularly amongst the non-Italian contingents in the army.[34] *Vindolanda Tablet* 2.190 records the receipt of quantities of *cervesa* at the fort on several days in June, testifying to its popularity, while sprouted grains noted at several Roman sites may constitute possible indications of brewing activity.[35]

The sources from which such a variety of foods could be obtained were themselves numerous. In areas of political and economic stability, the soldiers could purchase food at their own personal expense from the local civilian population, often from the shops and inns in the settlements (*vici*) that regularly grew up around forts. The military land (*territorium/prata*) surrounding each fort might also be farmed by the soldiers themselves, or leased out to civilians for the purpose. Hunting or fishing in the surrounding locale often provided an additional source of food as well as sport, though hunting trips seem to have been subject to official military regulation.[36] A letter written by a soldier stationed at Wâdi Fawâkhir near Thebes in Egypt, and preserved on a potsherd, reads:

> Antonius Proculus to Valerianus. Write the note to say that from the month of Agrippina until now we have been hunting all species of wild animals and birds for a year under the order of the prefects. We have given what we caught to Cerealis, and he sent them and all the equipment to you...[37]

Vegetius recommended that hunters of deer and wild boar be recruited into the army (*On Military Science*, 1.7), and some forts had *vivaria* or parks attached to them, in which semi-wild animals such as deer, hares, and wild boar were frequently kept. A *custos vivari* (game-warden) is mentioned in an inscription.[38] Extortion provided a further, though unlawful, means of procuring food, instances of which are often attested in the form of edicts banning such practices.[39] One governor forced a group of soldiers who had stolen a chicken from a provincial to make redress with a sum ten times the bird's worth (*Augustan Histories: Pescennius Niger*, 10.5-6).

Another common source of supply were food parcels sent to legionaries stationed a long way from home by family and friends. Egypt has produced a great many letters written by soldiers requesting that items be sent, and many indicate that the traffic in food went both ways, with the soldiers reciprocating the favour and sending foodstuffs back home. A letter written by the same Terentianus mentioned earlier to his sister reads:

> Take every step to provide me with two *ceramons* of the biggest size of *olyra* and an *artab*[40] of radish oil. I have sent you the marjoram with the oil.

Olyra was a type of grain (emmer wheat), while radish oil, highly esteemed in Egypt, was pressed from the seeds of the plant, and used as an alternative to olive oil.[41] One of Terentianus' other letters requests that fresh asparagus be sent to him, whilst another indicates that he had sent to his father two *amphorae* of olives, twenty Alexandrian loaves (a local speciality, flavoured with cumin), and some apples.[42]

A large quantity of letters discovered at Wâdi Fawâkhir are concerned with food, as are the following two examples, taken from a collection of five, which were written by one Rustius Barbarus to his friend Pompeius.[43]

> ...I have received the bunches of cabbages and one cheese. I have sent you, by Arranius the trooper, a box, inside which is a cake and a *denarius*[44] (?)wrapped in a small cloth. Please buy me a *matium* of salt and send it to me without delay, for I want to bake some bread.

> ...I have received a bunch of beetroot, and you write to me about ( ) and salt, if I need any...I need it on a holiday and I have sent you an oil jar to send me 6 *cotyli* of oil, either castor-oil or radish-oil. Take care to write and tell me the cost to you, so that I can pay you like a friend...[45]

Trade and transport

Thus even when far from home the Roman soldier was able to enjoy many of his customary foods. Olives and olive oil were considered essential commodities and were transported even to the furthest reaches of the Empire.[46] An amphora of Spanish origin containing olives was found upon a sandbank in the Thames estuary, and olive stones have been found on a number of Roman sites in Britain including York, Colchester, Caerleon in Wales, and several fort sites in Scotland. Olives could be preserved in a variety of ways which would enable them to withstand long-distance transport; the literary sources mention olives preserved in their own oil, sometimes with added fennel, mastic seeds and toasted salt, *amurca* (oil-lees), *muria* (fish-pickle), perhaps with added vinegar, *acetum*, *sapa* or *defrutum* (wine-must reduced to varying consistencies), and *passum* (raisin wine).[47]

Nor was the Roman passion for fish-sauce neglected by the military, who made great use of *muria*, a less expensive and slightly inferior form than *garum*. *Hydrogarum* (fish-sauce mixed with water) had long been in use in army camps before the emperor Elegabulus became the first to serve it at public banquets (*Augustan Histories: Elegabulus*, 29.5). Amphorae containing Spanish salted-fish products (notably varying grades of fish-sauce, including *garum*, *liquamen*, and *muria*) have been recovered from shipwrecks in the English Channel, evidently lost in transit to Britain, and they have also been found as far north as the fort at Vindolanda in Britain, and along the frontier zones of Gaul and Germany.[48]

Finds of inscribed amphorae provide a useful source of evidence for foodstuffs imported for the military market, whose painted labels (*tituli picti*), identifying the contents and their place of origin, give precise indications of the large distances over which they were transported. For example, an amphora found at the military stores depot at Richborough on the south coast of Britain inscribed *LYMP[A]*, indicated that it had once held Italian wine imported from the area around Mt. Vesuvius. Italian wines are known at many Roman sites throughout Britain; Aminean wine (*AMINE*) was exported to Caerleon in south Wales, while Massic, another esteemed Italian wine was shipped to Vindolanda in northern England, though it seems doubtful that it was destined for consumption by ordinary soldiers; perhaps it was intended for the governor's household (*Vindolanda Tablet*, 2.190). The Roman fortress at Vindonissa in Switzerland imported a number of Mediterranean wines including a very mature wine from Surrentum in Southern Italy (*Surre[ntinum]) perv[etus]*), and wines from Messina in Sicily (*Mes[sanium] [amphora]XIII*), in addition to other varieties from Spain and southern Gaul.[49] A number of Spanish and Italian amphorae used to transport wine and oil were also found at Roman sites in London.

A great many other products were transported empire-wide by amphora. One amphora found at Brough-on-Noe on Hadrian's Wall contained plums (*PRVN[A]*), while another discovered at Tower 16b on the Cumberland Coast contained an unsalted product, possibly olives (*INSVLSAI[I]*). Eleven amphorae containing beans were discovered at Vindonissa (*fab[ae] [amphora]XI*), as well as a vessel that held 176 lbs of honey (*mel[...]p[condo] CLXXVI*), the principal Roman sweetener. The remains of a jar inscribed *SCO.FLOS SCOM[BRI]* indicates that prime extract of mackerel was imported into Alcester, probably from Spain. Preserved or dried fruits such as figs, dates, grapes, plums, apples, pears, peaches, cherries, and doubtless others besides, were habitually transported to military and cirilian sites.[50] A number of exotic foreign foodstuffs have been identified at Roman sites in London, including lentils, cucumbers, figs, peaches, and olives, which provide further evidence of importation to meet demand. Rice, which was usually eaten for medical reasons in this period, has also been found on a number of Roman sites in Europe, including Britain and Germany, where it represents an indubitable import from the East. Some foodplants however leave little or no trace in the archaeological record, so that the remains of plants and other foodstuffs recovered from sites may represent but a small sample of the total actually consumed.

Evidence for the Roman diet from Bearsden

The Roman fort at Bearsden has been the subject of recent intensive archaeological investigation and botanical analysis, furnishing much useful information concerning the dietary habits of its garrison. The fort itself is located on the Antonine Wall, a turf-on-stone rampart 40 miles long, which was built in the second century AD, and ran from Bowness on the River Forth to Old Kilpatrick on the Clyde. Sewage deposits from the latrine building, which had drained into the ditch in the eastern annexe of the fort, yielded large quantities of cereal bran, identified as predominantly emmer wheat (*Triticum dicoccum*) and spelt (*Triticum spelta*), and indicating the consumption of wholemeal bread. Evidence of foreign grain pests suggested that much of the wheat had been imported into the site from abroad, though a certain amount may have been obtained locally.[51] Some degraded fragments of barley, presumably produced by pulverizing the grains in a mortar during the manufacture of pearl barley for use in soups and stews, were also found, though pearl barley had a significant medical as well as culinary usage in antiquity.[52]

Seeds from a small number of spice plants were also recovered including opium poppy (*Papaver somniferum*), wild celery (*Apium graveolens*), coriander (*Coriandrum sativum*), and dill (*Anethum graveolens*). All these spices were much used as flavourings in Roman cookery; Pliny for example, tells us that poppy seeds were often sprinkled onto the top crust of country loaves, whilst celery was placed under the bottom crust to impart a 'festival flavour' to the bread (Pliny, *Natural History*, 19.53.168).[53] Linseed (*Linum usitatissimum*) was also present, which may have had either a culinary or medicinal purpose. However the opium poppy is not a member of the native British flora, and both coriander and dill belong to the Umbelliferae family which is indigenous to the Mediterranean area and south-west Asia. The finds of these plants in Scotland thus indicate possible Roman introductions of these plants on to British soil, or otherwise importation of the dried seeds for culinary or medical usage.

The evidence for legumes in the soldiers' diet at Bearsden included fragments identified as field beans (*Vicia faba*) and lentils (*Lens esculenta*). Documentary evidence suggests that beans and lentils were the most commonly consumed pulses in the Roman army diet. The field bean is thus far not known from pre-Roman sites in Scotland, and its presence at the fort may suggest the possibility that it was brought into cultivation by the Romans from the south, but inscribed amphorae discovered at numerous Roman sites throughout the Empire indicate that beans were customarily shipped abroad to meet the demand for them, and that could equally be the case here. Lentils however are difficult to propagate in Britain, and their presence in Bearsden as imports despatched from the Mediterranean seems more certain.

Fragments of hazelnuts were also recovered from the sewage deposits, along with the seeds of several soft fruits including raspberry, strawberry, blackberry and bilberry, which were probably gathered locally from the wild as welcome supplements to the basic diet. The presence of fig-seeds however provides further evidence of the importation of foods to supply the military market; figs would have been very unlikely to have set seed successfully in the cold and damp conditions of the Scottish climate, but in their dried form, the fruits would have easily withstood long-distance transport from the Mediterranean area.

Desperate times and desperate measures

War was a hazardous occupation which could disrupt even the most well-prepared supply-routes. During the civil war between Caesar and Pompey, whilst engaged in a siege at Dyrrachium (modern Durazzo in Albania) in 48 BC,[54] Caesar's supply of wheat ran out. The soldiers turned to barley and legumes as a substitute, but when these begain to fail also, the troops discovered a new kind of root growing in abundance in that locale called *chara*,[55] which could be eaten mixed with milk or made into bread. Furthermore, in order to demonstrate that they had no intention of surrendering whilst they still had food of some sort, the soldiers threw some of these loaves into Pompey's camp, and swore that they would eat even the bark of trees before contemplating surrender. Lucan vividly describes Caesar's men lying on the ground to eat the food of wild beasts, plucking the leaves from bushes and rifling the trees, beset by the potential hazard of poisoning from unfamiliar plants. Nevertheless they were able to withstand their food shortages.

Antony's army was less fortunate however when troubled by famine during the war against the Parthians in the first century BC. Hardly any grain could be obtained, but the soldiers had in any case abandoned most of their grinding implements as excess baggage, when the loss of many of the pack-animals forced them to carry the sick and wounded themselves. It is said that at that time barley loaves sold for their weight in silver, which, considering the usual Roman distaste for barley, gives some indication of the extent of their plight. The troops were thus forced to forage for whatever roots they could find, risking their health in eating plants never before tasted. Unfortunately it transpired that some of them were poisonous, causing a variety of symptoms such as memory loss, vomiting, and even death, so that many of the soldiers were wiped out (Plutarch, *Antony*, 45). A similar calamity befell Septimius Severus' army, incidentally also campaigning in Parthia, who were reduced to grubbing up roots, and contracted diarrhoea and various other ailments as a result (*Augustan Histories: Septimius Severus*, 16.2).[56]

The 'scorched earth' policy adopted by some generals could cause enormous problems, devastating the countryside for miles around. Maximinus' army, laying siege to Aquilea in northern Italy, could find no crops or fruit trees still standing to turn to when their food supply broke down (Herodian, *History of the Empire*, 8.5.3-4),[57] while Germanicus' troops, shipwrecked off the coast of Germany in AD 16, found themselves with no alternative source of food to horseflesh (Tacitus, *Annals*, 2.24).

Some Roman plant introductions into Britain

Archaeological excavation of numerous Roman sites in Britain has revealed evidence for the presence of a number of food-plants which are not indigenous to Britain. These may be identified from seeds, pollen grains, or other plant material that has survived, perhaps in water-logged deposits or as carbonized plant matter, but in certain cases it can be difficult to determine whether the remains are indicative of introductions or importations. While we may be quite confident that finds of rice or date- or olive-stones in Britain are representative of long-distance trade, since these plants are not cultivable in this country, other finds are implicative of actual introductions from abroad into our native flora. Discovery of the remains of perishable food-plants such as mulberries, which are indigenous to Asia, may represent introductions rather than importations, since it is doubtful whether the soft fruit would travel well over long distances. Nevertheless even when instances of plant introductions are confirmed, they do not necessarily preclude the continuance of trade in these products as well.

Alexanders, balm, balsam, coriander, dill, fennel, garden leek, garlic, hyssop, marjoram, mint, mustard, onion, opium poppy, parsley, rosemary, rue, sage, savory, and thyme, are strong candidates for being Roman introductions into Britain along with garden varieties of beet, cabbage, carrot, cucumber, endive, lettuce, mallow, orache, parsnip, radish and turnip.[58] Some wild varieties of these plants were already in use at this time, so that the new cultivated types would have been easily accepted.

Pliny furnishes useful testimony concerning the transference of the cultivated cherry (the sour or morello cherry, *Prunus cerasus*) to Britain via the Mediterranean.

> Before the victory of Lucius Lucullus in the war against Mithridates, until the 608th year of the city (74 BC), there were no cherry trees in Italy. Lucullus first imported them

from Pontus and in 120 years they have crossed the ocean and got as far as Britain; but they have not been able to be grown in Egypt. (Pliny, *Natural History*, 15.30.102).

Large quantities of cherry stones have been found in Roman contexts in Germany and several central European countries also, indicating further areas of introduction.[59] The plum tree (*Prunus domestica*) is also considered to be a Roman introduction into Britain.

Vines were introduced into southern England soon after the Roman conquest of AD 43, where the warmer conditions allowed them to be grown successfully. Viticulture in Britain was temporarily halted by Imperial edict for a time when vine-growing in the provinces was prohibited by Domitian, but whether the restrictions were lifted or were never properly enforced, the planting of vines in Britain, as also in Gaul and Spain, was encouraged by the emperor Probus in the third century AD (*Augustan Histories: Probus*, 18.8)[60] However, the scale of wine production in southern England was never sufficient to meet the demand created by both military and civilian markets, and vast quantities of wine continued to be imported, principally from Italy, Spain and Gaul.

Rye was perhaps brought to Britain by the Romans from Germany or northern Gaul, which provinces, with their cooler climates, excelled in its production. They may also have been the agents of rye's transfer to Sicily and Anatolia. Club or Bread wheat (*Triticum vulgare*) was brought to Britain as a cultivated crop, and oats continued to be grown under Roman occupation.

Thus many new plants were introduced into Britain during the Roman occupation, which were soon established and cultivated on British soil. The Romans also brought with them the mortar and pestle for pounding herbs and spices for use in cookery, and under their influence, use of the rotary quern became widespread, replacing, to a large extent, the earlier saddle-quern.

APPENDIX
The Vindolanda writing-tablets

The collection of documents discovered at the Roman fort at Vindolanda, which comprises a number of personal letters, military records, household receipts, and administrative accounts, affords a unique insight into Roman life in a frontier province. A number of the tablets thus far recovered mention foodstuffs which include:

acetum	sour wine	*(h)alica*	semolina
alium	garlic	*(caro) hircina*	goat meat
alliatum	garlic paste	*hordeum*	barley
amulum	wheat starch	*lardum*	bacon
apua	small fish	*lens*	lentil
avena	oats	*ligusticum*	lovage
axungia	pork-fat	*malum*	apple
bracis	cereal used for brewing beer	*mel*	honey
buturum	butter	*mulsum*	honeyed wine
callum	pork-crackling	*muria*	fish-sauce
caprea	roe deer	*offella*	pork cutlet
cervesa	Celtic beer	*oleum*	olive oil
cervina	venison	*olivae*	olives
condimenta	spices	*ostria*	oysters
conditum	liquor for pickling	*ova*	eggs
fabae	beans	*panis*	bread
faex	wine lees	*perna*	ham
frumentum	wheat	*piper*	pepper

porcellum	piglet	*spica*	cereal
prunolum	plum	*turta*	twisted loaf
pullus	chicken	*ungella*	pig's trotters
radices	radishes	*vinum*	wine
sal	salt		

Most of these foods probably represent supplies for the *praetorium* rather than the ordinary soldier. The majority would have been obtained locally, but some are obviously imports, such as the spices, pepper, fish-sauce, olive-oil, olives, wine of varying qualities, lentils, and probably the beans too. The presence of pepper is particularly interesting since it was an expensive luxury imported from India, but also an indispensable ingredient in sophisticated Roman cookery, as the recipes of Apicius suggest. So too the spices, which are not individually identified but which were imported from the East at considerable cost. The remainder represent essential commodities, rather than luxury items, which were habitually transported to Roman sites around the Empire.

A few examples of the texts

* *Vindolanda Tablet*, 2.301 is a letter from Severus to his brother, Candidus: 'Greetings. Regarding the... (item of food is missing)... for the *Saturnalia*, I ask you, brother, to see to them at a price of 4 to 6 *asses*, and radishes to the value of not less than half a *denarius*.[61] Farewell, brother.'
* *Vindolanda Tablet*, 2.302 addressed to a slave of Verecundus, seems to be a shopping list and reads: '...2 *modii* of bruised beans, 20 chickens, 100 apples, if you can find nice ones, 100 or 200 eggs, if they are for sale at a fair price...8 *sextarii*[62] of fish-sauce...a *modius* of olives...' (The quantities mentioned are large, and may have been intended for use in the *praetorium*).
* *Vindolanda Tablet*, 2.191 is an account of meat and other foodstuffs: '*denarii*...spices...,roe-deer..., of salt..., piglet..., ham..., of wheat..., venison..., for pickling(?)..., roe-deer...,(total, *denarii*...),total denarii 20+, of *bracis*...'
* *Vindolanda Tablet*, 2.180 is an account of the distribution of measures of wheat to named recipients, some of which was to be used for making twisted loaves (*turta*).
* *Vindolanda Tablet*, 2.182 is an account of sums received for various items including bacon, ham, and pork-fat.
* *Vindolanda Tablet*, 2.192 is an account of foodstuffs and textiles, and mentions 55 *modii* of beans and ? *modii* of honey.

BIBLIOGRAPHY

Bowman, A.K. and Thomas, J.D. (1983) *Vindolanda: The Latin Writing-Tablets*, (London).
Bowman, A.K., (1994) *Life and Letters on the Roman Frontier: Vindolanda and its People*, (London).
Bulmer, W., (1969) 'The Provisioning of Roman Forts: A Reappraisal of Ration Storage', *Archaeologia Aeliana*, 47, 7-13.
Curtis, R.I., (1988) 'Spanish Trade in Salted Fish Products in the 1st and 2nd Centuries AD', *The International Journal of Nautical Archaeology and Underwater Exploration*, 17, 205-10.
Davies, R.W., (1971) 'The Roman Military Diet', *Britannia*, 2, 122-42.
Davison, D.P., (1996) 'Military Housing', in I.M. Barton (ed.) *Roman Domestic Buildings*, (Exeter), 153-81.
Deutsch, M.E., (1917/8) 'Roman War Bread', *Classical Journal*, 13, 527-8.
Dickson, C., (1989) 'The Roman Army Diet in Britain and Germany', *Archäobotanik Dissertationes Botanicae*, 133, 135-54.
Dickson, C. and J., (1988) 'The Diet of the Roman Army in Deforested Central Scotland', *Plants Today*, July/August, 121-6.
Dickson, J.H., (1979) 'Exotic Food and Drink in Ancient Scotland', *Glasgow Naturalist*, 19, 437-42.

Dickson, J.H., Dickson C.A., and Breeze, D.J., (1979) 'Flour or Bread in a Roman Military Ditch at Bearsden, Scotland', *Antiquity*, 53, 47-51.

Gentry, A.P., (1976) *Roman Military Stone-Built Granaries in Britain*, (Oxford). (B.A.R. 32).

Grant, M., (1974) *The Army of the Caesars*, (London).

Greig, J., (1983) 'Plant Foods in the Past: A Review of the Evidence from Northern Europe', *Journal of Plant Foods*, 5, 179-214.

Helbaek, H., (1952) 'Early Crops in Southern England', *Proceedings of the Prehistoric Society*, 18, 194-233.

Helbaek, H., (1964) 'The Isca Grain: A Roman Plant Introduction in Britain', *The New Phytologist*, 63, 158-64.

Jones, M., (1991) 'Food Production and Consumption – Plants', in R.F.J. Jones (ed.) *Britain in the Roman Period: Recent Trends*, (Sheffield), 21-7.

King, A.C., (1984) 'Animal Bones and the Dietary Identity of Military and Civilian Groups in Roman Britain, Germany, and Gaul', in T.F.C. Blagg and A.C. King (eds.) *Military and Civilian in Roman Britain: Cultural Relationships in a Frontier Province*, (Oxford), 187-218. (B.A.R. 136).

King A.C., (1991) 'Food Production and Consumption – Meat', in R.F.J. Jones (ed.) *Britain in the Roman Period: Recent Trends*, (Sheffield), 15-20.

Knights, B.A., Dickson, C.A., Dickson, J.H., and Breeze, D.J., (1983) 'Evidence Concerning the Roman Military Diet at Bearsden, Scotland, in the 2nd Century AD', *Journal of Archaeological Science*, 10, 139-52.

Körber-Grohne, U., (1988) *Nutzpflantzen in Deutschland*, (Stuttgart).

Lauwerier, R.C.G.M., (1986) 'The Role of Meat in the Roman Diet', *Endeavour*, 10, 208-12.

Middleton, P., (1979) 'Army Supply in Roman Gaul: A Hypothesis for Roman Britain', in B.C. Burnham and H.B. Johnson (eds.) *Invasion and Response: The Case of Roman Britain*, (Oxford). (B.A.R. 73).

Middleton, P., (1983) 'Roman Army and Long Distance Trade', in P. Garnsey and C.R. Whittaker (eds.) *Trade and Famine in Classical Antiquity*, (Cambridge), 75-83.

Rickman, G.E., (1971) *Roman Granaries and Store Buildings*, (Cambridge).

Sealey, P.R., and Tyers, P.A., (1989) 'Olives from Roman Spain: A Unique Amphora Find in British Waters', *Antiquaries Journal*, 69, 53-72.

Straker, V., (1984) 'First and Second Century Carbonized Cereal Grain from Roman London', in W. Van Zeist and W.A. Casparie (eds.) *Plants and Ancient Man: Studies in Palaeoethnobotany*, (Rotterdam), 323-9.

Watson, G.R., (1969) *The Roman Soldier*, (London).

Wilcox, G.H., (1977) 'Exotic Plants from Roman Waterlogged Sites in London', *Journal of Archaeological Science*, 4, 269-82.

Wilson, C.A., (1973) *Food and Drink in Britain*, (London).

Zohary, D. and Hopf, M., (1988) *Domestication of Plants in the Old World*, (Oxford).

NOTES

[1] Smoked Lucanian sausages, first discovered by soldiers serving in southern Italy during the Late Republic, were brought back to Rome by the returning troops; likewise, the army was responsible for introducing the Faliscan haggis into the city, which they had encountered whilst on active service in Etruria (Varro, *On the Latin Language*, 5.111; Martial, *Epigrams*, 4.46.8, 13.55). Lucanian sausages became popular as an hors d'oeuvres at dinner parties (Cicero, *Letters to his Friends*, 9.16.8), and a recipe in Apicius tells us they were made from pork mixed with pine-nuts and peppercorns, and flavoured with cumin, savory, rue, rock parsley, mixed spice, laurel-berries, and *liquamen* (fish-sauce) (*Roman Cookery*, 2.4).

[2] Ammianus Marcellinus, *Roman History*, 17.8.2.

[3] *Posca* was the 'vinegar' offered by the soldier to Jesus on the cross, as related in the Gospels (*Mark*, 15.36; *Luke*, 23.36; *John*, 19.29).

[4] *Augustan Histories: Severus Alexander*, 51.5, 61.2, *Pescennius Niger*, 11.1; Herodian, *History of the Empire*, 2.11.2, 4.12.2; Ammianus Marcellinus, *Roman History*, 25.2.1. For the emperor or general to dine in company with the troops and to eat the same food as they did served to boost the soldiers' morale.

[5] *Augustan Histories: Severus Alexander*, 47.1; Ammianus Marcellinus, *Roman History*, 17.9.2; Cicero, *Tusculan Disputations*, 2.16.37; Josephus, *Jewish War*, 3.95.

[6] *Augustan Histories: Severus Alexander*, 47.1.

[7] Caesar, *Gallic War*, 4.32, 5.17, 7.17, 7.56, *African War*, 67, 68, *Civil War*, 1.48, 1.52; Josephus, *Jewish*

War, 2.58; Appian, *Spanish Wars*, 9.54, 13.78, *Punic Wars*, 3.18; Polybius, *History*, 1.17.9. An ancient oath that soldiers were once required to take was recorded in Cincius' book *On Military Science* (now lost, save for this single citation by Aulus Gellius), and permitted the carrying off of fruit (*poma*) and fodder for the animals (*pabulum*) amongst other things (Aulus Gellius, *Attic Nights*, 16.4.2).

[8] Frontinus, *Stratagems*, 4.1.7 says this practice was instituted by Gaius Marius, for the purpose of reducing the number of pack-animals required on expedition; the soldiers were thereafter nicknamed 'Marius' mules'. See also Plutarch, *Marius*, 13; Appian, *Spanish Wars*, 14.85; Polyaenus, *Stratagems*, 8.16.2.

[9] See pl.1 in Richmond, I., (1982) *Trajan's Army on Trajan's Column*, (London).

[10] Josephus, *Jewish War*, 3.85.

[11] Strabo, *Geography*, 3.4.20; Vegetius, *On Military Science*, 3.8; *Oxyrhyncus Papyrus*, 735.

[12] *Codex Theodosianus*, 8.4.6.

[13] E.g. Livy, *History of Rome*, 31.19.4, 32.27.2,36.4.8, 43.6.11; Plutarch, *Caesar*, 55. An inscription from Lete in Macedonia provides another example of private benefaction towards the army: 'the city celebrates Manius Salarius Sabinus...who, when the emperor's (Hadrian) army was passing through, provided for the *annona* 400 *medimnoi* of wheat, 100 of barley, and 60 of beans, plus 100 *metretae* of wine at a much cheaper rate than the current price.' (A *medimnos* was the equivalent of 6 *modii*, where a *modius*, the principal Roman measurement of capacity was approximately 9 litres or 1 peck).

[14] Cf. Cassius Dio, *Roman History*, 62.3.

[15] See Berchem, D.Van, (1937) *L'Annone Militaire dans l'Empire Romain au IIIème Siècle*, (Paris), and Rickman's critique of Van Bercham's conclusions in Rickman (1971).

[16] The fourth century AD is the only period for which specific quantities are known: 3lbs of bread, 2lbs of meat, 2 pints of wine, and one-eighth of a pint of oil per man per day were provided, but it seems unlikely that there would have been much variation from these amounts in earlier periods.

[17] For *carnaria* see Plautus, *Captives*, 915; Cato, *On Agriculture*, 162.3; Varro, *On Agriculture*, 2.4.3; Pliny, *Natural History*, 19.19.57.

[18] Frontinus, *Stratagems*, 4.1.25, 4.1.37; Suetonius, *Augustus*, 24.2; Cassius Dio, *Roman History*, 49.38.4; Plutarch, *Antony*, 39.7, *Marcellus*, 25; Vegetius, *On Military Science*, 1.13.

[19] Ammianus Marcellinus seems to imply that porridge was disdained by the soldiers (*Roman History*, 25.2), but porridge (*puls*) was a staple food of the Romans, and in early times it was practically the national dish.

[20] It is even noted of some emperor-generals that they were not beneath personally grinding their own corn ration and baking their own bread (Herodian, *History of the Empire*, 4.7.5 of Caracalla).

[21] Pliny, *Natural History*, 18.12.67; Moritz, L.A., (1958) *Grain Mills and Flour in Classical Antiquity*, (Oxford), 195ff.

[22] *Augustan Histories, Aurelian*, 9.6.

[23] The century (*centuria*) was a group of originally 100 soldiers, but later usually 80.

[24] *CIL* 13.6935 = bread stamp from Mainz.

[25] The *contubernium* was essentially a tent-group comprising eight men, but the same name was also applied to the lodgings within the army barrack building which accommodated each tent-group in fixed quarters.

[26] Davison (1996), 179.

[27] *Vindolanda Tablet*, 2.302.

[28] See figure 61 in Davison (1996), 159.

[29] The midwinter festival in December; the Roman equivalent of our Christmas.

[30] For the *modius* see n.13.

[31] Galen, *On the Properties of Foods*, 3.1.10-11; cf. Athenaeus, *Dinner of the Sophists*, 282b. Foxes, moles, weasels, hedgehogs, and badgers are mentioned as edible foods in Aristophanes, *Acharnians*, 878-80.

[32] British oysters were well known in Imperial times, and were exported from Richborough in Kent to Italy for the Roman gastronomic market. See Tacitus, *Agricola*, 12.6; Pliny, *Natural History*, 9.79.169, 32.21.62; Juvenal, *Satires*, 4.141; Ausonius, *Epistles*, 5.37.

[33] No. 478.8-13 in Edgar, C.C., Boak, A.E.R., Winter, J.G. et al. (1931-) *Papyri in the University of Michigan Collection* (Ann Arbor).

[34] Pliny, *Natural History*, 22.82.164.

[35] Helbaek (1964).

[36] *Digest*, 49.16.12; Suetonius, *Tiberius*, 19.

[37] No.14 in O. Guéraud (1942) 'Ostraca Grecs et Latins de l'Wâdi Fawâkhir', *BIFAO*, 41, 141-96.

[38] CIL, 13.8174.

[39] *Augustan Histories: Avidius Cassius*, 4.2, *Pescennius Niger*, 10.5-6; *Luke*, 3.12-4.

[40] The principal Egyptian dry measure.

[41] Pliny, *Natural History*, 19.26.79.

[42] *Michigan Papyri*, 467, 468, 476, 478, 481.

[43] *Corpus of Latin Papyri*, 303-7.

[44] The *denarius* was the basic denomination of Roman currency.

[45] For other examples, see Davies (1971).

[46] Not all olive oil was for cooking and eating. Oil was also the primary source of fuel for lighting in the ancient world, and it had a further usage as a toiletry.

[47] Columella, *On Agriculture*, 12.49.1-11; Pliny, *Natural History*, 15.4.16. The olives would also take on the additional flavours of the liquors used to preserve them.

[48] Curtis (1988). For the importation of fish-sauce into Britain, see also Bateman, N. and Locker, A. (1982) 'The Sauce of the Thames', *London Archaeologist*, 4, 204-7.

[49] For references see Davies (1971); *Journal of Roman Studies*, 56, (1966), 224, no.52..

[50] Callender, M.H., (1965) *Roman Amphorae*, (Oxford); *Journal of Roman Studies*, 45, (1955), 148, no.2, & 56, (1966), 224, no.52.

[51] Finds of foreign weed contaminents such as lentils among grain fragments from Roman London point towards the conclusion that much of the corn was imported from abroad. See Straker (1984), 327.

[52] Pliny, *Natural History*, 22.66.136.

[53] See also Andrews, A.C., (1949) 'Celery and Parsley as Foods in the Greco-Roman Period', *Classical Philolgy*, 44, 91-9, and id. (1952) 'The Opium Poppy as a Food and Spice in the Classical Period', *Agricultural History*, 26, 152-5.

[54] Caesar, *Civil War*, 3.48; Lucan, *Civil War*, 6.109-17; Suetonius, *Julius Caesar*, 68.2; Pliny, *Natural History*, 19.41.144; Appian, *Civil War*, 2.61; Plutarch, *Caesar*, 39; Polyaenus, *Stratagems*, 8.23.24.

[55] A.C. Andrews identifies *chara* as the Tartar bread-plant (*Crambe tatarica* Jacq.). Pliny however says the plant on which the soldiers fed was called *lapsana*, which he describes as being a sort of wild sprout similar to broccoli (*Natural History*, 19.41.144; 20.37.96), which Andrews identifies as hoary mustard (*Sinapis incana* L.). See Andrews, A.C., (1942) 'Alimentary Use of Hoary Mustard in the Classical Period', *Isis*, 34, 161-2.

[56] Cf. Seneca, *Epistles*, 17.7: 'Armies have endured all manner of want, have lived on roots, and have resisted hunger by means of food too revolting to mention.' See also Seneca, *On Anger*, 3.20.2-4.

[57] Cf. Ammianus Marcellinus, *Roman History*, 25.2.

[58] Wilson (1973).

[59] Zohary and Hopf (1988), 159.

[60] Suetonius, *Domitian*, 7.2; Statius, *Silvae*, 4.3.11-12. See also Levick, B., (1982) 'Domitian and the Provinces', *Latomus*, 41,50-73.

[61] An *as* was worth one-sixteenth of a *denarius*.

[62] The *sextarius* was a measure, equivalent to one-sixteenth of a *modius*.

I would like to thank fellow symposiasts Andrew Dalby and William Woys Weaver for supplying the Greig and Körber-Grohne bibliographic references respectively.

Queen Christina of Sweden and the Triumph of the Baroque Banquet in Italy

June di Schino

Triumphant is the expression which always heralds the entry of Christina of Sweden into Italy. 'Elle parut comme une Impératrice victorieuse et conquérante, marchant en triomphe d'une manière glorieuse et superbe'.[1] The baroque banquet described in all its pomp and splendour is equally triumphant. 'Even if knives became pens and sauces were transformed into ink, …five reams of paper would not suffice to recount of the "superbissimo" and princely magnificence of the table.'[2]

Cardinal Sforza Pallavicini, confessor to Alexander VII, proclaimed her arrival 'one of the most memorable events, and one of the most glorious for our faith, which may be read in the histories.'[3] In a detailed account he described the event as 'more captivating than any romance'. Another chronicler of the times declared: 'There was no lack of those foods which, being dressed with the most precious trappings of luxury, give further splendour to an already admirable appearance.' Never was more imaginative genius lavished upon royal feasts.

Upon the arrival of the queen, continues Sforza Pallavicini, 'the walls themselves exulted…now that all is embellished and adorned'. And the chronicler added, 'There was no shortage of *Pièces Montées* on the table, or Arches, Games, and Colossi so marvellously carved with Art that they put Nature to shame'. The banquet table too, was the most glittering display of every imaginable decoration and adornment.

Cities and cardinals vied with one another to offer the Queen the most artful and splendid reception, as is attested by the lengthy list of 'Relations of the severall entertainments and recreations given to her Majesty by divers Princes in her journey to Rome.'[4] Theatrical performances, concerts, jousting, *intermezzi*, balls and pyrotechnics were some of the exceptional events that formed part of the galaxy of pleasurable divertissements. Certainly, of all the feasts in the Baroque world, the banquet created the greatest expectation. It represented the culminating ceremony, the most spectacular event, the triumphant apex.

The passage of Christina, begun on 20 November 1655, was marked by fabulous banquets: Mantova, Forlì, Imola, Foligno and Assisi were among the hosts of feasts honoured by Christina's attendance before her majestic entry into Rome where the Pope had gone to prodigious lengths to procure every possible approval of the Queen. Alexander VII personally supervised the preparations of the Vatican Palace, and the extensive scale of the work involved in fabricating the host of gorgeous gifts such as a carriage, a sedan chair and a litter all embroidered in heavy bullion.[5]

A revealing example of the assiduous attention invested in minor details emerges from the silversmith's accounts in the Vatican treasury. Christina's heraldic sheaf of corn and lions were incised on the heads of 4,370 nails destined to decorate her sumptuous transportation.

Contrary to the opinion of most Christinologists who have confirmed a lacuna in historical documentation concerning the Queen's presence at the banquets, we have a complete account of one of the very first great dinners prepared for her Majesty on 27 November 1655. It follows a text considered a jewel of seventeenth-century Italian gastronomic literature – *L'Arte di ben Cucinare*.[6]

Until now, the names of the great magicians of the kitchens, the artificers of the *ars magirica*, who prepared these exceptional events were thought to be unknown. In this case, however, the author was our very own cook, Bartolomeo Stefani, who refers to three banquets offered to Christina; the first at Revere on the banks of the river Po, the second in the town of Casale Monferrato and at the third in Mantua, she made her first public appearance. As he expains, 'I myself served her in the *trionfi, refreddi* and other dishes.' We can even admire his likeness in an engraving of the time, and read the sonnets written in praise of his virtuosity.

The Duke of Gonzaga, *Sua Altezza Serenissima* offered this memorable *banchetto* in the opulently decorated Hall of Virtues. The sideboard was 'rich in bowls and gilded vases and bottle stands laden with vases of crystal and tied in gold. These were made with such mastery that those who saw them were filled with wonder.'

Six services totalling fifty-seven different dishes were served, followed by sixteen desserts. The first service from the sideboard was composed of ten dishes beginning with hulled strawberries in shells made of sugar surrounded by marzipan birds pecking at them. To follow, 'a pheasant *pasticcio*' was served, 'made naturally (carefully larded, marinated in spices and roasted on a spit), which was entirely made of marzipan'. On the edge of the plate decorated with gilded quince jelly flowers, sat two sugar *putti*. One held the pheasant's head, while the other fed it with grapes. In the essentially Baroque tension between nature and artifice, artifice was rendered more natural than nature itself.

The first service from the kitchen was composed of eight elaborate dishes among which royal pheasant soup with rich cheese, slices of capon breast and pumpkin and stuffed calves' eyes covered over with a thin layer of pastry lattice work. Even more elaborate was the highly acclaimed *Bisca* or bisque, a layered dish of a myriad ingredients among which pigeons, mushroom ragout, brains, cocks' combs and truffles braised in a succulent sauce and served with style on slices of toasted bread.

Allegorical forms abounded on the table, being an integral part of the presentation. Here the magic of metamorphosis and marvel reigned supreme. 'Wild fowl with their wings outspread with heads, tails, and claws so natural they appeared to be alive, all made of flaky pastry.' Dead animals were revived into their feathers and plumes, to live a new, 'realistic' life on the banquet table, only to be confronted, once again, with a second death to die triumphantly on the guest's plate. Cavaliers with lances, menacing hunters, and 'a butcher carved out of cheese from Lodi, in the act of scalping the heads of the beasts, and from their wounds red pomegranate juice seeped.'

In his account of the 'feast as a project' Maurizio Fagiolo dell'Arco illustrates how the occasion 'can also be a chance to penetrate into the Baroque workshop: that highly articulated and complex chorus of arts, the memory of which is now lost.'[7] During the inauguration of the church of Sant'Ignazio, Cardinal Ludovisi discussed a series of images representing the various stages of construction. He dwelled on several aspects including: 'Building, Architecture, Music, Tapestry, Statuary, Inlaying, Enamelling…and the sublime presence of Fragrance.'

All these forms take life on the table. The ephemeral architecture of the baroque festivities, with its animated complexity and minute attention to detail, is perfectly reflected in the presentation of the banquet. The monumentality of the Baroque machine, for example, finds an eloquent form of communication on the banquet table prepared in Christina's honour at the court of Mantua.

> In the center of the table rose a centerpiece made of sugar, and it was Mount Olympus with the altar of faith. At the summit, two *putti* held up a royal crown above the coat of arms of Her Majesty. On either side of the table were distributed four vases of oranges with their tree – their fruit and fronds made of gelatine – whose appearance was quite natural. Between each vase was a gallery made entirely of sugar, in a good architectural design. On one side were twelve corinthian columns and on the other twelve ionic. In one of these galleries stood statues of the first warriors, who in the art of war had performed marvellous feats. There were also various fantastic animals, as one is wont to see in such galleries. In the other gallery were the most virtuous men the world had ever seen, and both galleries were similar in architecture.[6]

In view of this carefully choreographed construction, we can appreciate Michele Rak's fitting definition of the 'combination of practices of communication, set to work in order to construct, package and stabilize the identity', expressed even in refined details such as the 'Pastries made with partridge breast, veal brains, marrow, small birds from Cyprus, capon cutlets, truffles, sauces and spices. The pies were octagonal, and on each side was the coat of arms of Her Majesty decorated on top with dancing *putti*'.[6]

This grandiose spectacle, in all its complexity, took place within a well-defined architecture with a carefully articulated choreography of its own. Bernini's admirable *composto* and the fusion of art and technique, found its ideal expression in the culinary world of the times. 'On the table stood transparent works in gelatine, and sugar statues so beautifully designed, so mysterious and admirable, that they gave pleasant nourishment to both body and soul.'[8]

The complex ceremony required considerable technical structures and highly specialized services such as the *offizi della bocca* (offices of the palate). The *scalco* – the high supervisor, the *credenziere* – in charge of the table and sidetable, and the *coppiere* – cup master, all had precise functions; but perhaps pre-eminence should go to the extraordinary figure of the professional *trinciante* – carver. With an acrobatic flight of knives he would 'cut every food in the air,' such as artichoke, roast suckling pig, *melarosa*, shrimp and so on. As Emilio Faccioli put it, 'his every movement carried a power of allusion and a significance through gesture.'[9] Even the most modest operation was invested with such detailed ritual.

Table napkins, folded into innumerable meticulously tight pleats, were transformed into splendid animals and castles with pennants. 'The golden bread holders...were covered with a covering of very fine pleats. Her Majesty's was shaped like a beautiful lily and that of our *serenissimo* was in the shape of a helmet, with plumes formed by the same pleating.'[6]

Countless modes were invented to artfully fashion a very particular substance – sugar – into veritable majestic sculptures representing allegories of gods, as well as metaphors of Christian symbolism. The sugar *trionfo* is perhaps the highest expression of Baroque ephemeral art. Christina had met Luigi Fedele, the foremost expert of this refined art, in Ferrara. His works of art were so well-known that we have a book dedicated to his achievements: 'the superb *trionfi* and works in sugar made by him during the passage of her Majesty, Queen of Sweden.' A madrigal was written expressly in order to proclaim the beauty of the *trionfi* created in her honour.

At Imola, Christina was seated between Cardinal Donghi and Mons. Servanze, her spiritual guide. The first of the courses offered was

> Religion, a beautiful statue in marzipan. She trampled heresy underfoot, and struck serpents and devils by lightning. Before her stood a *putto* and the tablets of the law. During the second course, Pallas Athena was brought in upon a superb and triumphant chariot and, after several dishes, a platter with six angels atop a festoon made of pastry, topped by a large sugar crown above the coat of arms of Her Majesty. Then, in the center of the table, stood a very tall temple upheld by six columns and surrounded by six steps, all made of amber-coloured gelatine which enraptured the eyes.

For dessert, they served,

> ten enormous bowls for Her Majesty, girded with balustrades made of sugar, in the likeness of theatres. In the centre stood lions, elephants and cupids riding horses and holding crowns, gifts and all kinds of things made of sugar.[10]

One might surmise what Christina's reaction to these marvels might perhaps have been, and we may have an answer. At Assisi, on 13 December, Cardinal Paolo Emilio 'received Christina, Queen of Sweden, with regal splendour' at a public banquet where, 'in order to express the sumptuousness and the exquisiteness of the foods, suffice it to say that there was all that is excellent and born of the earth, all that is precious and flies in the air, and all that is good and hides in the water.'

A fabulous array of sugar statues and *trionfi* of high artistic mastery were presented as tributes: 'The four cardinal virtues atop a pilaster adorned with gilded bas reliefs, Pallas Athena standing in the reverent pose of offering a crown to the Queen, the chariot of the Sun driven by Apollo[4] were among the superlative works which adorned her table. At the end of the meal, Christina retired to her rooms.

She was truly struck by the exceptional quality of the works and asked for all the *trionfi* to be brought to her room so that she might admire in private such 'talent and inventiveness'. There were gods, virtues and heroes, and Christina, having observed them carefully one by one, realized that one allegory – perhaps the most important – was missing: Immortality. Perturbed, she immediately requested it, and Immortality arrived with a medal bearing the seal of Her Majesty. Together with Painting, Sculpture and History, he was intent 'upon immortalizing the name of Her Majesty 'among golden ears of wheat and vases sprouting sugar flowers of admirable artifice, and the entire work rested upon a candied fruit.' Perhaps she worried unduly…

The master organizer of the luxurious and splendid decorations of Alexander VII's banquet was Gian Lorenzo Bernini. Some of the *trionfi*, among which Mercury and Pegasus, have been attributed to him and to G.P. Schorr. Among these was the Sun, an emblem favoured by the Queen. It was often associated with the phoenix – a symbol of Christian resurrection and a sign pertaining to alchemy. This symbol so pleased Christina that she had a medal made with her profile on the recto and a sun with a human face on the verso.

Until this period, sugar was new, rare and expensive, used mainly as a vehicle for medicinal substances, and considered more as a spice. Now the rich and powerful highly appreciated all sweet things, drawing intense pleasure from every contact with sugar. Sugar was also associated with a precise hierarchy. Pope Alexander VII regularly sent bowls of sweets as gifts to placate Christina. 'On the day of Tuesday 28, Our Lord sent a gift of various bowls with candies, *trionfi*, twelve in number, upon the heads of carriers.'[4]

No event was complete without the presence of elaborate confections.

> Being come to the vineyard of Pope Julius…(a palace with a vineyard, Gardens, Courts,
> Fountains, Walkes). 'Twas past 18 hours when Her Majesty arrived alighting out of the
> Pope's sumptuous coach of rich velvet and gold, she went into the higher rooms where
> a table was nobly furnished with a variety of meats, wines, waters and a great store of
> sweetmeats.[4]

Sugar paid an important role in the festivities surrounding Christina's arrival – we need only mention the regal 'repasts of sweetmeats' offered to Her Majesty. For example, after the spectacular performance at the Palazzo Barberini of *Humane Vitae* written and dedicated to her by Giulio Rospigliosi (Clement IX), an even more spectacular assortment of confectionery followed. It included no less than seventy different types of sweets, among which were candied fruits and vegetables, *confetti*, gelatines, preserves and biscuits. The accounts justifying these very expensive delicacies give us an idea of their enormous price: 528 *scudi* and 81 *baiocchi*. We note that for this same feast, Grimaldi received 80 *scudi* short of his promised fee, while no reductions were made in the expenditures on these so socially significant sweetmeats.[5]

'One might almost say that Christina had left Sweden for no other reason than to reign over the Land of Cockaigne'. Baron de Bildt's words remind us that the rite of the banquet and the domain of the table were always associated with the principal expressions of fantasy and imagination.

The effect of the ephemeral baroque feast is exceedingly potent, dazzling. The pleasures of the eye and the pleasures of the palate alternate at such a rhythm that one is left suspended in time, stupified and enraptured by the enchantment of the spectacle, overwhelmed with hyperbolic admiration.

The banquet, the highest symbolic expression of all the Baroque feasts is rich in cultural meanings, a true mirror of the social fabric of the era. Entry into this universe allows an excitingly new and significant reading of history.

BIBLIOGRAPHY

A.A.V.V. *Bildtiana Kristina miscellanea*, ed. C. De Bildt, Svenska Institutet, Rome n.d.

C. de Bildt, 'Un Banchetto al Quirinale nel Seicento' in *Nuova Antologia di Lettere e Scienze*, ed. Arti, Rome 1901.

P. Bjustrom, 'Banquets Arranged for Christina and other Dignitaries', in A.A.V.V. *Analecta Reginensia*, Stocholm 1966.

G. Castelvetro, *Brieve racconto di tutte le radice di tutte l'erbe e di tutti i frutti che crudi o cotti in Italia si mangiano*, 1604, ed. Emilio Faccioli, Mantua 1988.

Christina Queen of Sweden – a personality of European civilisation, Nationalmuseum, Stockholm 1966.

V. Cervio, *Il Trinciante*, 1593.

G. Claretta, *La Regina Christina di Svezia in Italia*, Turin 1892.

Di Costanzo, Cristafani, *Chronicle of the reception offered by Cardinal Paolo Emilio Rondanini for Christina Allessandra in Assisi*, 1656.

C. D'Onofrio, *Roma vale bene un abiura*, Rome 1986.

E. Faccioli, *L'arte della cucina in Italia*, Turin 1987.

M. Fagiolo dell'Arco and S. Carandini, *L'Effimero Barocco*, Rome 1978.

C. Festini, *I Trionfi della Magnificienza Pontificia nello Stato Ecclesiastico e in Roma per Maestà della Regina di Svetia*, Rome 1656.

G. Fusconi, *Disegni del Barocco Romano*, Rome 1978.

R. Galli, 'Cristina di Svezia a Imola' in *Bildtiana Kristina miscellanea* q.v.

A. Latini, *Lo scalco alla moderna* Naples 1690.

A. Latini, *Autobiografia (1642-1692) La Vita di uno Scalco*, ed. Furio Luccichenti, Rome 1990.

F. Lissarague, *Un flot d'images. Une est étique du banquet grec*, Paris 1987.

D.A. Lupis, *Mastro di Casa Universale di Corte*, Venice 1657.

G. Masson, 'Papal Gifts and Roman Entertainment in Honour of Queen Christina's Arrival' in A.A.V.V. *Analecta Reginensia*, Stockholm 1966.

G. Lunadoro, *Relatione delle Corti di Roma e dei riti da osservarsi in essa e dei suoi magistrati e offici, con la loro distinta giurisdittione*, Venice 1671.

R. Morelli, 'Protocollo e cerimoniale presso le corti romane del 600', in *Appunti di Gastronomia*, n. 19, Milan 1996.

C. Panepuccia and R. Clementi, *Castelnuovo di Porto – Città e territorio*, Rome 1990.

G.G. Priorato, *Historia della Sua reale Maestà Cristina Alessandra Regina di Svezia*, Rome 1656.

F. Ratta, *Disegni del Convito*, Bologna 1693.

C. Ricci, 'Cristina di Svenzia in Italia' in *Nuova Antologia*, Vol. XLI Serie III, Rome 1892.

G. Rosetti, *Dello Scalco*, Ferrara 1634.

G. Roversi, *La tavola imbandita da Giuseppe Lamma. Il ricettario di un cuoco Bolognese del 600*, Bologna 1988.

B. Scappi, *Opera*, Venice 1570.

P. Sforza Pallavicini, *Descrizione del primo viaggio fatto a Roma dalla Regina di Svezia Christina Maria...*, Rome 1838.

B. Stefani, *L'arte di benm Cucinare, et Instruire I men Periti in questa Lodeuole Professione*, Mantua 1662.

REFERENCES

[1] Ricci
[2] Claretta
[3] Sforza Pallavicini
[4] Priorato
[5] Masson
[6] Stefani
[7] Fagiolo dell'Arco and Carandini
[8] Di Costanzo
[9] Faccioli
[10] Galli

Salmon, the Food that Travels

John Doerper

Great blue herons are staking out perches on top of weathered snags rising above Padden Creek from the dense brush of the shore. Bald eagles patrol the creek on limber wings, following every twist and turn of the stream's course, circling above riffles and cataracts. River otters patrol the banks and have been seen playing above the bluff in the vacant lot where John Moceri keeps scrap lumber.

These are the unmistakable signs that the salmon are returning from their long sojourn in the Pacific Ocean, where they grew from smolt into adult fish, to the stream of their birth, where they will spawn and die. The herons, eagles, and otters are assembling to feed on the spent carcasses.

What makes Padden Creek unique is that it supports a viable run of wild salmon which are spawned in its waters, roam the Northern Pacific for several years while they grow to adulthood, and then return to this very urban creek – all of it flowing within Bellingham city limits. While the creek is shaded by the trees of a greenway, it is rarely out of sight of urban homes. It is only a short walk from my home, but several of my neighbors can look right out of their living room windows to watch salmon spawn in the creek below.

West coast species of salmon stop feeding when they leave saltwater and begin ascending freshwater streams and rivers to their spawning sites. Spawning under these conditions is so exhausting that the salmon die soon afterwards, their flaccid bodies lining the shores or drifting downstream, providing a seasonal feast for the denizens of the shore. It has been repeated countless times, we may assume, for the millions of years that have passed since both creek and salmon evolved together.

Salmon seem to know instinctively how much energy they need to store in their bodies to reach their home streams and spawn. That's why fish traveling up the longest and fastest rivers – like the Yukon or Fraser – are also the fattest, while chum salmon, who, at the most, travel only a few kilometers above tidewater, are rather lean.

Because salmon don't feed as they ascend the rivers, they do not take lures – which has disgusted a great number of serious anglers. One of the earliest accounts comes from Captain the Honorable John Gordon, commander of the British frigate *America*, who visited the Hudson's Bay Company's Fort Victoria in September of 1845. According to an account handed down by Roderick Finlayson, Officer-in-charge at Fort Victoria, Gordon was not at all enamored by the Northwest and its plentiful fish:

> Gordon claimed he would not exchange 'one acre of the barren hills of Scotland for all he saw around him.' What especially disgusted Gordon was that the salmon were caught by baits [sic] or nets, and not by the fly as in his beloved Scotland. '*What a country*,' he is reported to have exclaimed, '*where the salmon will not take to the fly*.' [emph. mine] His negative reactions were not shared by all the naval officers on the coast... [1]

Since Gordon was the brother of the Earl of Aberdeen, the British foreign secretary, we can assume that his low opinion of the Northwest may have influenced the way the latter appraised the Northwest and may have eased the final partition of the Oregon Territory between Britain and the United States in 1846. The value of the salmon harvest was not considered during the negotiations, since as yet this resource was exploited mostly by native Americans using traditional methods.

Unlike other fisheries, fishing for salmon follows a set seasonal pattern because the pilgrimage of the salmon to their place of origin happens every fall. It was the paramount event for native Americans who depended on salmon – primarily chum – for their sustenance during the long, lean days and nights of winter. Chum, also called 'dog salmon' in the Northwest because they were fed to sled dogs in the far north, are among the latest of salmon to spawn, often waiting until November and December before ascending their native creeks. This was of the greatest importance to the native people, since the weather is stormy at this time of the year, making fishing in the ocean or bays too dangerous from canoes. (Even twentieth-century fishermen, their boats equipped with powerful engines and the latest electronic gadgets, prefer to stay in port at such times.) Because chums spawn in shallow streams they are very easy to catch even by primitive methods such as spearing or gaffing. This meant that in years when the fish were plentiful, the fishermen could catch them even during inclement weather.

> The gaff was used like the harpoon from canoes in deeper water or from the banks of smaller streams.
>
> Salmon could be taken in the smaller streams with even simpler gear. If a man wanted to fish for immediate use while passing a small creek during the salmon run, he might merely sharpen a vine-maple or hazel stick to make a spear that he could discard after using.[2]

But catching salmon should never be done frivolously. As Lummi Reservation resident Lucy Lane Handyside recalled,

> ...we'd walk in the river and grab the fish. Their backs would be sticking up in the water and they'd be going up in the water to spawn. We'd grab them and throw them on the beach. We'd have a lot of fun. And Mama would get after us. She'd say, 'You can't do that. You're murdering them. They want to make babies.'[3]

Catching salmon was a serious – even sacred – business for native Americans, who thought of salmon as undersea people who put on salmon skins to swim ashore and offer themselves as food to the hungry land people who might otherwise starve.

Oral tradition records that when Captain James Cook's ships first touched on the Northwest Coast at Nootka, the local natives took the unfamiliar white-skinned British sailors for salmon people coming to visit. They even thought they could pick out the different species:

> One white man had a real hooked nose, you know. And one of the men was saying to this other guy, 'See, see...he must have been a dog salmon, that guy there, he's got a hooked nose.' The other guy was looking at him and a man came out of the galley and the other one said, 'Yes! We're right, we're right. Those people must have been fish. They've come alive into people. Look at that one, he's a humpback. He's a humpback!' [that is 'humpie,' spawning pink salmon]...So they went ashore and they told the big Chief: 'You know what we saw? They've got white skin. But we're pretty sure that those people on the floating thing there, that they must have been fish. But they've come here as people.'[4]

Swaneset, a culture hero of the Katzie people who lived on the lower Fraser River in British Columbia, was given the task of finishing the work 'He Who Dwells Above' left unfinished. During his travels, he visited the villages of the different people:

> The next village he approached was the home of the Dog Salmon, who at that time possessed the shapes of human beings, as did all other fish and animals and birds, except the eulachon he had brought back from the sky. He remarked the houses of the Dog Salmon, painted with red stripes. He saw, too, that some of the villages wore red-striped blankets, others black-striped; whence the dog salmon that enter the Fraser River to-day bear similar stripes on their bodies.[5]

Swaneset did not linger, but traveled to the village of the sockeye people, where he married the daughter of the chief, signifying that the sockeye played a more important role in the diet of the

Katzie than the dog [chum] salmon, perhaps because the Katzie lived near lakes that remained open for fishing all winter long. Yet the Katzie asserted that the chum salmon people occupied themselves during the off-season by chanting the songs they had learned during their brief sojourn in the Katzie's longhouses.

The belief that salmon lived in houses during the off-season was common among native tribes of the Northwest Coast, as we also learn from a myth of the West Coast (Nootka) People who live in the fjords on the west coast of Vancouver Island:

> Under the sea, not far offshore, was a great house with the Salmon people in one half and the Herring people in the other, representing the main food sources of the West Coasters. Rites were performed to honour them. If these were neglected, the Salmon and Herring People would become angry and dangerous...[6]

To placate the salmon, natives observed a first salmon ceremony. It might be as simple as the one recorded by Dora Williams Solomon for the Lummis:

> When the first netload of salmon was caught in season, each child would carry one fish, with it laying across his arms. Each child would bite the fin on the back as he carried it to the beach. This was the first salmon ceremony to show respect for the salmon. The fish were then butchered and cooked and eaten as part of the ceremony.[7]

The bones of the salmon were gathered up and returned to the river or creek. Otherwise, it was believed, the salmon people could not be reborn and the cycle of regeneration would be interrupted. Because of this other salmon people would be angry and not come back the next year.

Swaneset's father-in-law, the chief of the sockeye salmon people, said to him as he was leaving:

> My son-in-law, you are taking my daughter away with you. At a certain time of the year all her relatives shall visit you. You may eat them, but of the first ones you catch you must throw back into the water the bones, the skin, and the intestines. Then their souls will return hither and take on new bodies.[8]

When Christian missionaries began to convert natives, they did their best to replace local customs and beliefs with Christian ones. One of the most detailed accounts comes from Father Augustin Joseph Brabant, a Catholic missionary laboring at Hesquiat village on the West Coast of Vancouver Island. Father Brabant was not at all in sympathy with native customs:

> As this is the salmon season, the old people are as usual preaching to the tribe the propriety of conforming with the old established regulations, lest this great article of food should leave the neighbourhood and not come back again. For instance, salmon should not be cut open with a knife. They should not be boiled in an iron pot and not be given as food to dogs or cats. Under no consideration must salmon be given to any white man, including the priest, lest he prepare it in lard or in a frying pan. It should not be taken to the houses in baskets, but carried carefully one in each hand.[9]

Brabant called these customs 'absurdities' and railed against them in a sermon, which created quite a disturbance in the camp and made the natives regret they let a Catholic priest settle among them. The fishermen refuse to give or sell any salmon to Brabant, ' for fear that I might fry it in lard, or boil it in an iron pot!'[10]

The priest decided to go fishing himself and to treat any salmon he caught in the white man's fashion, to prove that the native myths are based on false beliefs:

> November 11. — I asked a couple of boys to come with me and have a canoe ride on the bay. I took along a line and a spoon bait.... As soon as I got away from the shore with my boys, I threw out a line and spoon bait. After a few minutes we caught a fine, large salmon. Upon landing, I called the dog and put the salmon in a basket, which was against

the rules. The brute took the basket and preceded me home. Of course no Indian would attempt to molest the large, faithful animal. Quite a number of men and chiefs assembled at my house, and protested against my using a knife or frying pan. I took no notice and proceeded with my work. My aim was to show them that their superstitions were absurd and to try by all and every means to get them to give them up.[11]

After this incident, several young men agreed to sell salmon to the priest, but when the fish are brought in, Brabant notes that 'the head is cut off and the fish split open – perhaps too the fish are not fresh' Brabant rejects the fish, for he has been told that 'the superstitious observances are only applied in the case of fresh salmon not yet beheaded or cut open.'[12]

A week later, a young man brought him a supply of fresh salmon – over the opposition of the tribe: 'It is easy to notice the feelings of indignation of the old people. But they are afraid to do more than make a few remarks of remonstrance, owing to the presence of seven white men, who have just arrived...At a meeting of the tribe, the chief speakers predict famine for the rest of the winter.'[13]

But two weeks later the chiefs met and agreed to give up the old customs to 'make peace with the priest.' Brabant recorded that by the next spring, the natives were carrying salmon from their canoes to their houses in baskets. The villagers stuck to the new customs during a food shortage, because other tribes were faring worse, even though they were holding on to the old traditions: 'A canoe arrives from Clayoquot and reports the Indians of those parts are in very great distress, owing to lack of food.... put the blame on one vicious fellow who last year had crushed the head of a fresh herring with a stone.'[14]

Culture change would have taken place even without the priest's insistence, since the natives were quick to recognize the superiority of European technology:

> The Indians soon learned that some of the European implements were more efficient than their own and quickly obtained tools and firearms from the early explorers and fur traders. It was very evident that rifles were very effective at killing game without any special blessing, although the Indians undoubtedly relied on their ritual training to entice the animals within range. West Coast whalers used iron and steel harpoon heads when available instead of the traditionally prescribed and supernaturally potent bone and mussel shell head whose design had been dictated by a spirit being. The successful performance of implements lacking supernatural endowment could have led to questioning of the need for spiritually superior implements. However, until relatively recent times, the Moachat still would cut salmon with nothing but mussel shell knives during the dog salmon season for fear of angering the Salmon (Drucker, 1951). Thus, although the early use of European tools and weapons undermined some of the traditional supernaturally endowed hunting techniques, many hunters relied on their own spiritual power to entice animals within range and were very careful to honor the game that they caught.[15]

But while technological changes came quickly, the basic food did not. Smoked or dried chum salmon remained the staple food for the wet and cold days and nights of winter.[16] If the chum runs failed, and the winter was harsh, whole villages might starve.

> Fish, especially salmon, was the mainstay of life and was dried and smoked in huge quantities and stored for the lean times. Without this important food asset there would have been hunger at times when hunting conditions were not good.[17]

Because chum salmon are low in fat, they were the ideal fish for preserving by the Indian no-salt smoking and drying methods, an inadequate process at best, that will not keep fat from turning rancid and spoiling. Other, fattier, salmon species were eaten fresh. At least one tribe observed a prohibition about keeping chinook salmon – a very fatty fish – in the house overnight. It had to be eaten fresh the day it was caught.

After the arrival of the British and Americans, the natives adopted the salt-brine method of marinating salmon before smoking, because it greatly improves the keeping qualities of the fish. This meant that fattier species of salmon began to play a larger role in the native diet – because they could now be preserved. It also removed fishing pressure from the chums, since the white settlers who built the first canneries, were more interested in the oilier – and thus richer-tasting – chinook and sockeye salmon.

The method employed for processing the fish after contact was a hybrid of Anglo and Indian ways. Ronomus 'Toddy' Lear of the Lummi tribe recalled:

> They dried their fish in a smokehouse. They didn't wash their fish. They got these ferns from big fern patches up where Baker's is now. [A grocery store in Marietta, Washington.] You'd see all the people come back with great big bundles of ferns. They'd carry them down the hill here. Then they'd have big beds of ferns six to eight inches thick. All these dog salmon would be laying there. Then the women, or whoever it may be, would butcher them. Then they'd take a handful of ferns and they'd wipe all this slime off them. Ferns were really sharp. They would clean the fish right off. The fish would be cut open. They sprinkled salt over them and then folded them back up. Then they let them set overnight. The next day, they'd hang them up on top of the smokehouse and smoke them.
>
> They had a reason for not washing their salmon. They said that when you hung them up they would be too moist and the flesh would tear and drop off. It would create steam and they would be too steamy. The salt too would draw moisture out. They'd drip a little bit.
>
> They would flop the row of salmon eggs over a group of sticks and they'd dry them too just like the salmon. I liked eating the eggs but they would stick to my teeth, so I didn't eat very much of them.[18]

Salmon might be smoked so long until, in the words of Herman Olsen, it became 'dry as a board.'[19] Hard-smoked salmon is no longer a staple food of local tribes, though a few fishermen still preserve salmon in this fashion, for ritual feasting and for sale.

Though no village of the local Lummi tribe of Salish-speaking Indians rose above the banks of Padden Creek in recent history, this creek was – like all salmon-bearing streams – an important link in the native food chain. Archaeologists have found shell middens, stone knives and scrapers, arrowheads, and harpoon points dating back to the times of the Clovis culture, one of the earliest of America's civilizations, about 13,000 years ago. A village site on the low bluff above Padden Creek Marsh has been particularly rich in these prehistoric remnants. Which makes Padden Creek not only a pleasant place for a shady walk, but provides a link to the pre-Columbian history of the region. You know that you are walking into history as you stroll along the banks and watch the salmon struggle upstream through the riffles. Where heron now wait, hoping to spear a fish, you can imagine a Clovis man or proto-Salish fisherman standing, salmon spear in hand, poised to snag a fish for dinner.

Padden Creek is short for a salmon stream. Just a few kilometers long, it rises on a ridge within sight of Bellingham Bay, trickles into Padden Lake and meanders through a marshy valley flanked by the suburban housing developments of Happy Valley. After flowing through the tree-shaded meadows of Fairhaven Park and skirting the bluffs of a narrow, wooded canyon, it lingers among the alders and willows of Padden Creek Marsh before crossing under Harris Avenue in a culvert and dropping over a low waterfall into Padden Lagoon. This tidal lagoon is separated from Bellingham Bay by a narrow spit. Inflowing and outflowing waters pass under a low railroad trestle which dams the lagoon at the very highest spring tides. The waterfall is evident only at low tide. The salty floodwaters of high tide drown the fall and push a hundred meters upstream to the base of the lagoon. Very high tides penetrate deep into the lagoon. At low tide, Padden Lagoon turns into mudflats. Gulls and crows take the opportunity to bathe in the fresh water of the meandering streambed.

Salmon returning to the creek to spawn linger in the lagoon before ascending the creek, swimming into and out of the lagoon with the rise and fall of the tide, and may be entrapped in the set nets of gillnet fishermen. While the salmon wait for the creek to reach the proper water temperature, depth, and clarity, their skin changes from silvery blue into its dark olive green to dusky black spawning colors. The males aquire reddish purple vertical bars and splotches across their backs that look as though someone had splashed them with blood or flames.

The colors of the spawning chum salmon make perfect sense in the environment of the creek, when we consider that – despite their brightness – they are meant to camouflage the fish from predators. While both chums and cohos spawn in creeks, the cohos tend to prefer the deeper water of the lower reaches, just above tidewater and they hide in deep pools where their dark red colors blend into the dusky water. Chums, on the other hand, ascend creeks so shallow that their backs often stick from the water. Yet they are difficult to spot, unless they move, which they do with a great deal of splashing. Their progress across the riffles is very slow and they may make more than one attempt, drifting back to the safety of a pool after each try.

The speed with which the salmon ascend the stream varies with the difficulty of the water. Each strenuous effort is followed by a prolonged period of rest (which can severely try the patience of anyone watching the fish). As chum salmon ascend the creeks, they try to expend a minimum of energy: they'll try to wriggle under a waterfall before they jump it.

Salmon ascending Padden Creek have a clean run, at high tide, from the lagoon through the first culvert and the tidewater reach of the creek to the base of the marsh, where they encounter the first riffles. Almost the entire length of Padden Creek is marked by riffles of variable height and velocity. One reason salmon spawn late in this creek, is that for most of the year the water is too low to allow the large fish to travel upstream. (A mature chum salmon may reach a length of 102 cm and a weight of 15 kg, though a weight of 4.5 to 7 kg is more common.)

The natural configuration of Padden Creek and its banks was disturbed in the mid-nineteenth century when American settlers felled the large trees and built first a road, then a railroad through the canyon. Today the trees have grown back and the road is an unpaved greenways trail. To make the creek accessible to salmon, its waters have been impounded in several places behind artificial gravel and log barriers. Some of these are only a few centimeters high, but dam enough water to create pools where salmon can rest.

Where the high embankment of the trail crosses the creek, concrete fish ladders enable the salmon to continue their upstream journey. These 'ladders' consist of a series of water-filled boxes ascending from the creek to the mouth of the culvert. Water from the culvert cascades into the highest box and pours from here into the next lower box, until the lowest of the artificial cascades splashes into the creek. A salmon leaping the lowest 'fall,' can rest in the calm waters at the bottom of the box while gathering strength for the next leap. A final vault will take the salmon straight into the mouth of the culvert.

Between the impoundments and fishladders, the creek runs over gravel beds where the salmon spawn. A few fish spawn on the first gravel beds, just above tidewater, between Padden Creek Marsh and the second culvert, about three hundred meters above the mouth of the creek.

This culvert is a formidable obstacle. Two concrete pipes – each about a meter in diameter – carry the creek below a road intersection for a length of some sixty meters. It is the longest tunnel the salmon traverse on their upstream journey. Before leaping the low cataract flowing from the pipes, the salmon rest in a shallow, gravelly pool. Above the culvert, the creek runs over a series of gravelly riffles where more of the chum salmon spawn.

Salmon travelling further upstream encounter the first fish ladder. The culvert above the fish ladder also has two concrete pipes, but these are only twenty meters long. Only one of these pipes is connected to the pools of the fish ladder; water from the other pipe gushes straight into the creek. Above this culvert are more gravelly riffles where the salmon may spawn and another fish ladder – this one consisting of two shallow basins not much higher than the gravelly pools – and another culvert. For the next several hundred meters, the creek runs over gravelly riffles that skirt the meadows of a popular park. Here you can sit at a waterside picnic table and watch the salmon rest above the spawning riffles just a few meters away. The salmon may wait as much as a week or two for their roe and milt to 'ripen.' When a female is ready to spawn, she scratches a 'redd' from the gravel and sticks her tail down, the signal for the accompanying male(s) to spring to action. After eggs have been deposited and sprayed with milt, she covers them with gravel from the upstream side of the redd. The process continues until the salmon are spent. Both females and males die a short time later, from sheer exhaustion.

The next culvert also has a fish ladder leading to a twenty-meter-long pipe. Above here the creek narrows, but few salmon spawn in the constricted channel. In another hundred meters, about 2 kilometers above tidewater, an exceptionally long culvert blocks the further ascent of the salmon. Here the natural flow of the stream has been interrupted by a several-hundred-meter-long pipe. While the second, the sixty-meter-long, culvert under the street intersection does not appear to slow down the salmon, this one stops them. Perhaps the salmon do not continue their upstream journey because the pipe does not run in a straight line and the salmon can, quite literally, see no light at the end of the tunnel.

Thus only salmon who spawn close to tidewater come to Padden Creek to lay their eggs. The long culvert keeps sockeye salmon from running in Padden Creek because it blocks their access to Padden Lake: sockeyes spawn in creeks flowing into lakes and spend part of their youth in a lake before descending to the ocean and adulthood. Chinook salmon do not spawn in Padden Creek, because they need deeper water. A few coho salmon do spawn here with the chums. They are easy to tell apart by their different breeding colors: coho salmon turn bright red to deeply purple and can also be distinguished from the chums by the depth of their colors. The sexually mature coho males grow humped backs. As male cohos get ready to spawn, their upper jaw hooks downward – the reason they are called 'hooknose' by fishermen. The chums jaws curve only slightly, but the males front teeth grow menacingly large.

One reason chum salmon thrive in Padden Creek and in other urban waterways is that the young fry do not spend much time in the creek after they hatch but head for the ocean as soon as they wiggle their way from the natal gravels. Even in longer streams, the young stay in freshwater for only a few days, and they rarely feed on their short downstream journey. That way, they escape the havoc pollution by pesticides, household chemicals, and other noxious substances afflicting urban creeks. The greatest danger to their early existence is waterborne silt – from construction sites, logging operations, or backyard erosion – which may cover the gravel redds and suffocate the as yet unborn fry by keeping oxygen from reaching the eggs. Once the young chum salmon reach the ocean, they travel far out to sea, feeding voraciously until they return as adults in as little as six months or as much as four years. This staggered return helps preserve the species, since it makes up for years in which the entire spawn may have been washed downstream by floods or smothered in silt.

Coho salmon, which also spawn in Padden Creek, do not fare as well, since their young may live in freshwater for a year before swimming downstream to the ocean. They are thus threatened by the pollution the young chum avoid. Which makes it seem almost a miracle that any coho survive long enough in this small creek to eventually reach the ocean, mature for two to three years and return to the creek to spawn. Unlike chums, cohos take lures and are caught at sea by trollers – another hazard to the survival of the species. The chums quite definitely have the edge and are thus – not at all surprisingly – more plentiful.

Other local creeks also support runs of chum salmon. Perhaps the most spectacular of these is Oyster Creek, some 15 kilometers south of Padden Creek. Oyster Creek has no fish ladders but drops through a series of rocky pools from a high mountain ridge to the ocean. A hundred meters upstream, you can sit in the dining room of the Oyster Creek Inn, a popular restaurant, and watch the salmon rest in the pools below and leap the low falls. Oyster Creek chums face bigger obstacles in their upstream journey than Padden Creek chums, and are correspondingly more active. At least some of them are. There is one special population which, by a fluke, always spawns just above tidewater. Here the salmon are packed so tightly into the creek in spawning season that you could, as early pioneers claimed, 'walk across the stream on the backs of the salmon.'

This local abundance has unnatural roots: In the 1930s, when fisheries managers just began to learn about raising salmon in hatcheries, workers of a salmon restoration program dumped fingerlings near tidewater, where a road crosses the stream. These salmon never learned to ascend the creek; nor have their offspring. They return to the riffles where their ancestors were dumped year after year, even though there's hardly enough room for all of the fish to squeeze in.

Yet the wild upstream chum salmon still leap the rapids to return to their native haunts, as they have done for millions of years. It's humbling to realize that there were salmon in these streams long before the first man arrived to fish for them, and that there may be salmon in them long after the last man has vanished.

The bounty of salmon in Padden and Oyster Creek is somewhat deceiving, and is enhanced by a prohibition on fishing above tidewater. Throughout the Pacific Northwest, populations of native salmon are fighting for their survival. Several races have been placed on the threatened or endangered species lists. Even the coho, once thought to be inexhaustible, has been sufficiently threatened by loss of habitat and overfishing to have its seasons drastically curtailed. In British Columbia, there will be no fishing season in 1996 for the once plentiful Fraser River sockeye salmon, the most luscious of all the salmon for smoking and grilling. Only in Alaska are salmon still plentiful, due to strict conservation measures taken several decades ago. But, curiously, while fishermen keep catching these fish in record numbers, the surplus catch piles up in warehouse freezers, because farm-raised salmon, which can be produced at a much lower cost, are taking an increasing market share. In 1996 almost half the salmon served in U.S. restaurants or sold in fish markets were farm-raised. So why do fishermen keep fishing? It's the only skill many of them have. There's nothing else for them to do.

Which may also be the reason why Bellingham fishermen continue to pursue the local chum salmon, ultimately threatening the Padden and Oyster Creek populations of fish. But these salmon are also endangered by other factors, ranging from a thoughtless city engineer who paved over more than a hundred meters of their spawning creek to city crews clearing ditches of debris during spawning season and flushing the silt-laden waters into the creek where the silt may suffocate the eggs freshly deposited in clean gravels. Even such 'minor' disturbances as inconsiderate folk letting their dogs splash through, shallow the creek, upsetting the spawning salmon, as well as little boys trying to catch the fish with their bare hands, contribute to a loss of eggs – and thus of salmon who will return to the creek in the future.

On the other hand, these salmon have survived the onslaught of herons, otters, eagles, bears, and native American fishermen. We suspect that their descendents will be running up these creeks to spawn and die a million years from now, when the last traces of human civilization have been swallowed by the forest.

REFERENCES

[1] Gough, Barry M., *The Royal Navy and the Northwest Coast of North America, 1810-1914: A Study of British Marine Ascendancy*. Vancouver, B. C.: University of British Columbia Press; p. 73.

[2] Suttles, Wayne, Katzie Ethnographic Notes. *Anthropology in British Columbia*. Memoir No. 2. Victoria, B. C.: The British Columbia Provincial Museum, 1955.

[3] In Nugent, Ann, ed., with special assistance from Eva Kinley, *Lummi Elders Speak*. Lynden, Washington: Lynden Tribune, 1982, p. 32.

[4] Efrat, B.S. and W.J. Langlois, 'The Contact Period as Recorded by Indian Oral Tradition', *nut•ka• Captain Cook and The Spanish Explorers on the Coast*, eds. Efrat and Langlois, Victoria, B. C.: British Columbia Provincial Museum, 1978, p. 54ff.

[5] Jenness, Diamond, 'The Faith of a Coast Salish Indian', *Anthropology in British Columbia*. Memoir No. 3. Victoria, B. C.: The British Columbia Provincial Museum, 1955, p. 18.

[6] Arima, E. Y., *The West Coast (Nootka) People*. British Columbia Provincial Museum Special Publication No. 6. Victoria, B.C.: British Columbia Provincial Museum, 1983, p. 8f

[7] Nugent, p. 19.

[8] Jennes, p. 35.

[9] Lillard, Charles, ed.; *Mission to Nootka, 1974-1900. Reminiscences of the West Coast of Vancouver Island* [of Father Augustin Joseph Brabant]. Sidney, B.C., Canada: Gray's Publishing Ltd, 1977, p. 61.

[10] ibid, pp. 64f. Before setting out to fish on his own, Brabant tried to buy salmon from the natives: 'I must first mention that yesterday I had sent a young man for a salmon and had paid three fish hooks for it. The owner of the salmon was out at the time, so the messenger simply told the woman in the house that he was taking one of the "sacred" fish for the priest and in due time he gave it to me. When the owner of the salmon came home, he was told that one was missing. He at once called three friends to accompany him to my house. Seeing the now-famous salmon about to pass under the knife, he sprang forward and took it away. Throwing me the three fish hooks, he went on his way growling. This upset me so much that I resolved to go out fishing myself.'

[11] ibid.

[12] ibid.

[13] ibid.

[14] ibid, p. 74.

[15] Moon, Barbara J., 'Vanished Companions: The Changing Relationship of the West Coast People to the Animal World.', *Nu•tka•*, p. 76.

[16] Arima, p. 57: 'One reason for the particular importance of dog salmon, besides its abundance, was that it was not overly fat so that it could be dried easily.'

[17] Sampson, Chief Martin, *Indians of Skagit County*. Skagit County Historical Series No. 2. Mount Vernon, Washington: Skagit County Historical Society, 1972.

[18] Nugent, pp. 52f.

[19] ibid, p. 57.

Three Lunches:
some Culinary Reminiscences of the Aptly Named Cook Islands

Hugo Dunn-Meynell

The traditional diet of the Pacific islanders consists of root crops and fruit, plus lagoon fish and the occasional pig. The vegetables include taro, yams, cassava (manioc), breadfruit, and sweet potatoes. The sweet potato (*kumara*) is something of an anomaly – it's the only Pacific food plant with a South American origin...

The ancient Polynesians stopped making pottery over a millennium ago and instead developed an ingenious way of cooking in an underground earth oven known as an *umu* or *lovo*. First a stack of dry coconut husks is burned in a pit. Once the fire is going well, coral stones are heaped on top, and when most of the husks have burnt away the food is wrapped in banana leaves and placed on the hot stones – fish and meat below, vegetables above.

South Pacific Handbook by David Stanley, 1994.

As a result of what the airlines call 'an operational problem', I spent a recent week on a delightful Pacific island named Rarotonga, an oyster-shaped hundred square miles about halfway between Fiji and Tahiti. This is the story of three meals, which between them, are a telling illustration of how a tourist industry can affect ethnic food – whether for better or worse. (To get rid of an uncomfortable subject I will inject a historical note: before the islanders' conversion to Christianity in the nineteenth century, many visitors – pirates and so on – made a periodic contribution to the local culinary skills. Cannibalism, however, is now in the past).

My hotel

I stayed at a 'holiday complex'. Geared to packaged visitors, mainly from New Zealand, it provides what most of them surely expect. The place is comfortable, efficiently run, with tennis courts, a handsome swimming pool (a few feet from the beach), excellent plumbing and traditional folk dancing in the evenings (the famous Cook Islands eroticism heavily censored). I would recommend the Edgewater – or any of its few competitors – as a place which provides everything it promises, staffed by smiling people who give prompt service, with a cheerful bar and efficient laundry – but with an almost total insulation from the true, vibrant life a few hundred yards inland.

In the Edgewater's menu, lurking here and there, are some natural Polynesian foods. *Ika mata* is – and, to the great credit of the chef, it was – a superb marinade, and the anonymous raw 'fish' was indeed fresh. Apart from that and the 'fruit platter' and paw paw crumble, the bill of fare might just as well have propped up the cruet at any Marriott, Hilton, Sheraton or Forum.

Most of my fellow lunchers were tucking into the beef burgers which the couple at the next table told me were very nice; or the lamb chops, which evidently had survived the journey from New Zealand with less jet-lag than I; or the *crêpes*, though why 'de Paris' when a *crêpe* is traditionally Breton and Cointreau comes from Anjou, no one could tell me. But, make no mistake about it, the customers were all having fun, and the service was fine – as well the excellent Captain Cook lager, from Rarotonga's own tiny brewery. If I had been homesick for Europe and *la dolce vita*, I could also have chosen to eat at the 'Spaghetti House' (no relation to Britain's homonymous catering chain) in the hotel's grounds.

On special nights, the agreeable hotel also offered its version of an *umu-kai* (*Umu* = underground oven; *Kai* = food), but I did not find this compared too favourably with that of Pa, a grass-skirted native who lived not far away, but on the inland side of the *aru tapu*, the island's ancient road which runs round the whole perimeter. I had quickly discovered that the hotels lived on the sea side of this, and Rarotongans not involved in running them, on the inland side: a thousand yards inland is where civilisation ends (or in the Rarotongans' opinion, begins).

Pa

Pa is a mountain guide and fisherman. When I questioned him about present-day culinary standards, he generously invited me home to sample some of his own *umu-kai*. My host lives in the hills with his New Zealander wife (an accomplished artist). Once they had hung an *ei kaki* of threaded flowers around my neck and we had rubbed cheeks (which the islanders apparently prefer to the nasal greetings of the New Zealand Maoris), they explained the subtleties of *umu-kai*. Not complicated:

1. Dig a hole in the ground. Or use yesterday's hole – which was probably made 150 years ago by one of the family.
2. Fill it with the husks of coconuts, which obligingly keep falling off the palm trees (the dented roofs of many vintage Volkswagons testify to the unwisdom of parking beneath one).
3. Light the fire. No point in wasting a match. You rub together two bits of dry banana wood till they ignite. When all's aglow, you place on top a few of the pumice stones which are lying about everywhere (not $5 a-piece like they are at the Body Shop).
4. Cut some banana leaves. With these you wrap parcels: perhaps some sliced *manioc*, arrowroot to you; breadfruit (*kuru*); an *eke*, that's octopus; *kumaras*, sweet potatoes; a huge hunk of *puaka*, suckling pig; and a colourful parrot-fish (*u'u*) or ten; a chicken [Pigs and chickens run freely all over the island, causing traffic mayhem at what Rarotongans call the rush hour – which means two cars passing each other on the same road. How any owner recognises his own porkers or chookies, I could not fathom. There are also a lot of wild chickens which nobody owns – delicious after marinating in guava juice.]; some *taro* root, and – in a separate package – its leaves, which taste like excellent spinach. You place these on top of the stones.
5. Put some oil in a pot, and (when it's hot) add slices of *kara*, which looks like an outsize grapefruit and makes super chips.

We then sat around with glasses of coconut milk and ate and ate. Pa, who was strong on enthusiasm but weak on conceit, then told me that as a member of the Guild of Food Writers, I would enjoy an encounter with another exponent of the island's culinary riches.

The Flame Tree Restaurant

My third, and no less memorable meal, was eaten on a beautiful lagoon, at a restaurant owned by a lady named Sue Carruthers – which the locals must consider an eccentric appellation, since the telephone book for the most part lists subscribers like Papa-Mama Pokino, Ah Young Enjoy, Panapa Nganoo Katuke and Numangatani Ukanrangi - with not a Jones or a Robinson in sight, and only four Smiths.

Sue, Kenyan by birth, a restaurateur by profession, had visited Rarotonga in 1986 and had been so struck by the abundance of natural food that she decided to show the world what a trained chef could do with such magical ingredients. She named her establishment after the main feature in its garden – the same tree as inspired Elspeth Huxley's *The Flame Trees of Thika*.

Using locally grown produce and fish, Sue's menu reflected in a most intriguing way what she calls 'the culinary melting pot that is the Pacific'. I mentioned earlier that Rarotonga is oyster-shaped; I found that The Flame Tree is its pearl. Every day Sue offers a new menu to those visitors who appreciate her skills as much as she enjoys exercising them. Her range is wide. When I ate there, the choice of seafood included *koura tai* (blue-spot lobster), scallops, oysters, tuna, parrot-fish and octopus. Alas, that curious beast, the sea cucumber, was out of season; and *unga patua* – the chocolate hermit crab – stays obstinately in its shell when not laying eggs, and it had evidently decided to abstain from procreation during my visit.

I ordered marlin, smoked on the premises to a gentle pink, with sliced mangos and a mustard sauce that would not have disgraced the late Simone Prunier. Then a fried *mahi-mahi* fish, served with a rich wine sauce and that amazingly versatile vegetable, the *taro*. On came an aromatic potful of Pacific pork stew – with an orange and coriander sauce – followed by an artful upside-down pineapple pudding with hot butterscotch. My neighbours at other tables were wolfing down huge helpings of the house's other specialities – a leg of lamb stuffed with tropical fruits, honey-roast duck with paw-paw and ginger, Sue's famed Flame Tree seafood curry, and so on. In short, here were the same raw materials as I had eaten chez Pa, but touched by the hand of a master cook who knows (as few chefs do) the amazing quality of sea slug caviar, the tenderizing properties of various tropical juices, and the astonishingly rich flavour of a banana which has had the pleasure of ripening in the sun rather than in the hold of a ship.

Take, for example, the *taro* root, which Pa had simply roasted on stones (and very good it was); in Sue's hands it was steamed in coconut cream, with its leaves prepared in an egg-enriched *gratin*. At The Flame Tree, an octopus became a curry, pork a roast with paw-paw and cumin; and the ice-creams – guava, coconut and avocado flavours – out-Dayvilled the maestros.

One really should hesitate to draw too many conclusions from all this. Food is God's gift to nourish us, to give us pleasure and to bring us together with our kin and peers in a relaxed and happy atmosphere. Sad though some of us may consider it to be, there are a lot of people in the world who find these criteria well met in a hamburger with Caesar salad on the side, and would approach Pa's pumice-filled pit or Sue's poached wahoo fillets or soursop jelly rather gingerly. I simply submit my traveller's tale as one might discuss a box of eggs – which English breakfasters would probably fry, Algerian camel drivers will munch as a *brique* and Paul Bocuse might dazzle his customers with as a spectacular Soufflé Rothschild. If my story illustrates anything, it is a synergy in which I profoundly believe – that the excitement of travel is hugely enhanced by availing oneself of its culinary opportunities; and that good food tastes best within a sympathetic environment. And so say all of us.

BIBLIOGRAPHY AND NOTES OF ADDRESSES

Cook Islands Tourist Authority, P.O. Box 14, Rarotonga, Cook Islands.
The Tourist Council of the South Pacific, 375 Upper Richmond Road, London SW14.
The Edgewater Resort, P.O. Box 121, Arorangi, Cook Islands.
Pa – Just ask anyone on Rarotonga where he is today.
The Flame Tree Restaurant, Muri Beach, Rarotonga, Cook Islands.
David Stanley, *South Pacific Handbook*, Moon Publications Inc. of California
Tony Wheeler and Nancy Keller, *Rarotonga & The Cook Islands*, Lonely Planet
Sue Carruthers, *The Flame Tree Cookbook*, G.P. Publications of New Zealand
Judith Künzlé, *Cook Islands Heritage Project*, P.O. Box 781, Rarotonga, Cook Islands.

An Englishman Civilizes the American West:
Fred Harvey and the Harvey Girls
Feed the Hungry Traveller

Barbara Haber

In 1850, a fifteen-year-old left his home in London for Liverpool where he boarded a sailing ship and emigrated to the United States. This budding entrepreneur would later change the nature of food service throughout the American Southwest, winning the respect and gratitude of generations of hungry travellers destined to go by rail from the state of Kansas more than fifteen hundred miles to California. Frederick Henry Harvey would bring comfort and satisfaction not only by supplying delicious food prepared under sanitary conditions, but by having it served by highly-refined and impeccably-groomed waitresses he dubbed 'The Harvey Girls'. Harvey would bring to the Southwest a new kind of food service and a new kind of woman.

Before the innovations of Fred Harvey, people travelling by train through the West suffered miserably. Typically, passengers would disembark at railroad station lunch counters or restaurants hardly better than shacks where they were given bad food served in the most slovenly manner. Menus offered rancid bacon and eggs brought in from the East that were preserved in lime, accompanied by soda biscuits the diners called 'sinkers'. Beverage choices were cold tea or stale and bitter black coffee, and the food was served in cracked and chipped crockery on tables covered with filthy cloths. Insects were everywhere. Customers were often asked to pay for their meals in advance, making possible a notorious scam in which restaurant owners would conspire with railway conductors to blow their train whistles to signal departure just as food was being served. The passengers, afraid of being left behind, would rush to the train, leaving their meals and their money behind. The same food, of course, would then be served to the next victims. As an alternative, passengers would sometimes bring along box lunches which in the summer could spoil, or at the very least attract masses of black flies, especially when a carload of people all ate at the same time.[1]

Harvey would change all this. After arriving in New York, he worked at the Smith and McNeill Café as a busboy, receiving two dollars a week. He soon left for New Orleans and later for St. Louis, where he and his partner started a restaurant in 1856. When his partner disappeared along with all of the money from the business, Harvey left St. Louis taking on a variety of jobs and eventually becoming the general western freight agent for the Chicago, Burlington and Quincy railroad. This position kept Harvey travelling and exposed him to the wretched food served along the tracks and to the unspeakable hotels located in small towns in the West. These experiences, along with serious bouts of yellow fever and malaria, caused him to search for ways in which decent food and accommodation could be provided for hungry and weary railroad travellers. When he could not convince his employer that the creation of appealing new restaurants could be profitable, he presented his ideas to Charles F. Morse, superintendent of the Atchison, Topeka and Santa Fe, the most rapidly-expanding railroad in America. Morse listened to Harvey and made a place for him within his organization.

The path of the railroad was the Sante Fe Trail, a well-worn route accommodating wagon loads of settlers heading west. In the 1860s, it became the base for the Atchison, Topeka and Sante Fe Railway which started in Topeka, Kansas, and by 1878 reached Albuquerque, New Mexico. By 1889, the company owned 7,000 miles of track which extended from Chicago to major cities in California. The Santa Fe brought prospectors to newly-discovered silver and gold mines, and settlers to newly-opened western territories. Heading east, the railroad delivered Texas cattle to Kansas City and Chicago. New towns were formed all along the newly-laid track.

The first Harvey House venture was at the depot in Topeka, Kansas. The room was scrubbed clean, English silver and Irish linen purchased, a large and moderately-priced menu was prepared, and the railroad delivered fresh food to an able chef. Travellers would find fresh fruit cups or salads waiting for them at places at the table, to be followed by ample helpings of roast beef served in dramatic fashion. The restaurant's manager would enter the dining room carrying above his head a huge tray of meat which he would swiftly carve into generous portions to be distributed by the circulating waitresses. Dessert pies were always on the menu, and the house rule was to cut them into four rather than six pieces. The price for the meal was fifty cents, which in the next decade went up to seventy-five cents.

The Topeka restaurant was so successful that the railroad grew concerned that passengers would detrain and refuse to travel farther west. They had no choice but to arrange for Harvey to operate additional facilities. His next undertaking was a hotel and restaurant in Florence, Kansas, for which he hired the former head chef of the Palmer House in Chicago at the astonishing salary of $5,000 a year. The chef bought local game and produce and served first-rate European cuisine that soon became famous throughout the area.[2]

By 1883, seven years after the Topeka opening, Harvey was operating seventeen Harvey Houses along the Santa Fe. Harvey was acutely attuned to the needs of his patrons for variety as well as quality: he made sure that menus rotated in such a way that travellers could be on trains and eat at a Harvey restaurant for four days without repeating meals. Harvey and his managers also arranged a system with the train crews which guaranteed that passengers would be fed properly within a limited amount of time. Before arriving at a restaurant, a conductor would find out how many meals were required, then telegraph the information ahead. By the time passengers entered the restaurant, the first course was already on dining room tables, and the rest of the meal was served in less than half an hour.

No aspect of the Harvey service has been commented upon as frequently as the way in which beverages were ordered and served. Immediately upon being seated, various beverage orders from as many as a hundred customers were taken by waitresses who never wrote anything down. Within seconds, the correct drink was poured from pitchers held by a line of servers marching in from the kitchen. This baffling stunt was made possible by a cup code that had developed during the 1880s:

> *Cup upright in the saucer:* coffee
> *Cup upside down in the saucer:* hot tea
> *Cup upside down, tilted against the saucer:* iced tea
> *Cup upside down, away from the saucer:* milk

The only time the system was likely to fail, of course, was when a customer unwittingly fiddled with the cup and saucer.

In co-operation with the railroad, Harvey, in 1882, went on to build and operate a resort hotel, the Montezuma, six miles west of Las Vegas, New Mexico. The Santa Fe had built a branch line that would deliver people to this massive wooden construction, over 300 feet long and four stories high. To feed his clientele, Harvey arranged for fresh produce from Mexico during the winter months, thus ensuring that canned foods were never served, and the railroad would deliver such luxurious and perishable foods as sea bass, shell fish, and live green turtles. Other resort hotels were to follow, all of them obedient to the high standards and a close attention to detail that were to characterize Fred Harvey's style of management for the rest of his life.[4]

In general, the Harvey restaurants all turned a profit despite their commitment to highly-priced ingredients and furnishings and generous portions. This was possible because no rent was paid to the railroad which also furnished free coal, water, ice, laundry service and transportation for Harvey

House employees. In return, the Santa Fe attracted many customers because of the popularity of the restaurants which were certainly a profound improvement over the abysmal food service that had previously characterized western travel.

In 1883, Fred Harvey introduced an employment policy that was to ensure not only his success in business but his place within the history of American culture. Tired of breaking up fights between rowdy male waiters, Harvey devised a plan to attract employees who would behave properly and in other ways meet the high standards of the Harvey operation. To this end, he placed the following ad in Eastern newspapers:

> Wanted – young women, 18 to 30 years of age, of good moral character, attractive and intelligent, as waitresses in Harvey Eating Houses and on the Santa Fe Railroad in the West. Wages $17.50 per month with room and board. Liberal tips customary. Experience not necessary. Write Fred Harvey, Union Depot, Kansas City, Missouri.[5]

The ads attracted immediate attention mainly from mid-western girls, the daughters of farmers and railroaders, who needed to earn a living. While waitressing was not a well-regarded profession, especially for young single women, being 'A Harvey Girl' promised something more. Guarantees of job training and decent living conditions within a benevolent community setting offered a secure life for girls already accustomed to working hard. Besides, there was something liberating about going west in the latter part of the nineteenth century, when American males had been hearing New York newspaperman Horace Greeley tell them, 'go West, young man'. Why not, young woman? Opportunities for travel and adventure awaited. Even the less adventurous-minded women who joined Fred Harvey's operation could argue that finding a husband in the West would be easier than in the East. The 1870 census listed 172,000 women to 385,000 men residing from the Mississippi River to the Pacific Ocean.[6]

Harvey's impeccable standards insisted upon a reliable workforce that could be shaped and made to heed to company regulations. Harvey Girls were required to sign a contract promising to stay for six or nine months and agreeing not to marry during this time. They had to accept mandatory living arrangements with roommates in supervised Harvey House dormitories which were often above the restaurants, and to obey a strict curfew. They also has to agree not to fraternize with male Harvey employees, violations being grounds for dismissal. Their personal appearance was also outlined in detail by Fred Harvey who decided upon a rather nun-like appearance for his Harvey Girls.

The Harvey Girls wore plain, starched black skirts, black high-collared shirts, and white aprons. Shoes and stockings were plain and black, and hairnets were required. Jewelry, make-up, nail polish and gum-chewing were forbidden. Introduced in 1883, the uniform scarcely changed over the next fifty years. Each employee was given several changes of uniform, since soiled clothing was not tolerated and had to be changed at once. The Railroad provided free laundering services, but the Girls were responsible for starching and ironing their work clothes.

Hard work was part of the Harvey family style. Staff were expected to work twelve-hour days for six and often seven days a week. When not serving customers, they were expected to polish silverware or to clean all of the tables and chairs in their work stations. Harvey Girls were never seen sitting.[7]

In return, the Harvey Girls received income, job security, and the companionship of other young women. Their oral histories are full of memories of going on enjoyable picnics and hikes with co-workers. Opportunities for free travel were also extended to them after their first year on the job when they had the option of requesting a transfer to another location. Some of the Harvey resort hotels were choice assignments which in addition to glamorous surroundings offered an affluent guest clientele who often tipped generously. For those looking to settle down, the chances to meet available men were abundant. The railroad, which was the life-blood of the Harvey House system, was full of single male workers looking for wives, and the entire Southwest was filled with ranchers and cowboys, many of whom married Harvey girls. Records indicate that sisters often came together to work for Harvey and in many cases several generations of a family had been Harvey Girls. In later years, company regulations eased a bit, allowing summers off for farm girls so that they could help their families with the harvest, and accommodating schedules in order for girls to take college courses.[8]

From the 1880s, when Fred Harvey began employing Harvey Girls, until the end of World War II when the Harvey House era was over, about 100,000 women were employed. Of these, more than 50,000 remained living in the West, on ranches, small towns, and sometimes in larger cities where some achieved prominent social positions.

Changes in the technology of passenger trains followed by the acceleration of air travel in the United States inevitably caused the disappearance of the Harvey Houses. At first, faster trains that could cover greater distances made obsolete many of the Harvey restaurants along the tracks. Then, the popularity of dining cars on trains gave passengers even less reason to disembark. Finally, the affordability of air travel to the masses of long-distance travellers ended the era of well-accommodated train travel in the United States. While long-distance passenger train travel still exists in parts of the United States, such trips are now considered somewhat quaint and the food service generally consists of plastic-wrapped sandwiches and bottled drinks.

The Harvey Houses experienced a brief resurgence during the Second World War when trains packed with servicemen criss-crossed the nation, but none of Fred Harvey's high standards could be maintained during this period. One traveller, a young bride from Ohio on her way to California to visit her soldier-husband, reports having eaten nothing but baloney sandwiches at one Fred Harvey Restaurant after another.[10] Mercifully, Fred Harvey, whose alleged dying words to his son and successor were, 'never cut the ham too thin' was long gone.

The story of Fred Harvey and the Harvey Girls touches on a number of major themes in American history: the development of the railroad system and how it contributed to westward expansion; the westward expansion movement itself, its history as well as the romance and mythology that has built up around it; the perceptions about women who settled in the West and finally, the reality of the lives of women who went there.

In 1946, *The Harvey Girls*, a popular Metro-Goldwyn-Mayer movie starring Judy Garland appeared with promotional material that announced:

> The Harvey Girls is a fast-moving epic set to repercussions of a fight typical of the west in the late 1800s – a battle between the civilizing influences of the Santa Fe Railroad and the Harvey House, as opposed to the lawless rule of outlaws, gamblers and crooked officials of the early west.

This endorsement left out the dance-hall girls featured in the film, with Angela Lansbury playing one of her memorable floozies as a foil to Judy Garland's innocent Harvey Girl from Ohio. The film, though entertaining, presents a panorama of familiar clichés about the American West, all hovering around the themes of good versus bad, law versus order, civility versus vulgarity.

Contemporary historians of American western history, especially those whose work focuses on women, are raising fascinating new questions about the meaning of the westward movement. Ever since Frederick Jackson Turner offered his famous 'frontier thesis' in 1893, most historians have accepted his belief that individuals who moved west were liberated from the constraints of civilized society, and that the free frontier acted as a democratizing force which kept the entire American society fluid and open. Many now wonder, examining the evidence, if the freedom Turner was talking about applied to women too? And if so, how much and what kind?

Most traditional accounts of US Western history depict heroic men conquering nature or hostile Indians, while women in poke-bonnets and gingham traipse behind them, silent and stoic. The Helpmate is just one of the stereotypes one finds about women in the west. The other two are the Wicked Women and the Civilizers. The Wicked Women are either fallen women, the dancehall girls and prostitutes of movie westerns, or would-be men, that is women, like outlaw Belle Starr, who behaved violently in ways usually identified with men. The stereotype of women as the Civilizers has served to suggest that women in the West created community and harmony just by their very presence, that with women in their midst, men naturally were inclined to build churches, schools and libraries. Such a portrayal overlooks the active participation of women as founders of organizations, fund raisers and lobbyists for good causes in the development of the American West.[12]

If we dismiss the myths of women in the West, what meaning will we find in the lives of the Harvey Girls? The most salient point about them is that they were ordinary women, and like most other ordinary people, they did most of the hard work of the world, in this instance, the serving of food. As with other women too, we can come to a truer understanding of who and what the Harvey Girls were by understanding the details of their daily survival and human community. We can hear the truth of their lives in their voices.

> I was respected and protected and the management at the house was wonderful...A bunch of us girls would get together and take a picnic out into the sand hills. That was our recreation: hiking and more hiking. I loved it.[13]

And this from the daughter of a widowed Harvey House worker who would go there every day after school:

> We were treated like royalty. The baker kept the broken cookies in a paper bag for us and everyone was always giving us sweets and food. It was a big family, our family. The manager and his wife took care of us just like we were their own.[17]

As for Fred Harvey, the founder, whose presence was felt within his organization for years after his death, the meaning of his life is less elusive, for it can be measured by his public successes. Through a combination of luck and great skill, he approached the right railroad at just the right time and established the first chain of civilized restaurants in the Southwest. He also created a system in which working women could have a piece of the dream Frederick Jackson Turner had seen for men, enabling them to travel alone and seek new lives and adventure. A Harvey Girl recalls:

> It was easy to travel alone, even for a woman. People on the trains were friendly and asked me about my life as a Harvey Girl. Everybody knew about the Harvey Houses. Even the cowboys were nice...They weren't that wild.[15]

All of these voices speak of personal connection – of family, mutual respect and a sense of belonging. Some also express a spirited sense of independence and adventure. This would suggest that like so many women before and certainly after the era of the Harvey Houses, the Harvey Girls tried to combined a desire to create and attend to family and community with a need to express some sense of self through work. Like all women, they measured the success of their lives at any given time by the presence or absence of equilibrium.

REFERENCES

[1] Keith L. Bryant, Jr., *History of the Atchison, Topeka and Santa Fe Railway*. New York, Macmillan, 1974, pp.106-122.

[2] Ibid.

[3] George H. Foster and Peter C. Weiglin, *The Harvey House Cookbook: Memories of Dining along the Santa Fe Railroad*. Atlanta, Longstreet, 1992 p.36.

[4] Bryant.

[5] Juddi Morris, *The Harvey Girls: The Women Who Civilized the West*. New York, Walker, 1994, p.20.

[6] Lesley Poling-Kempes, *The Harvey Girls: Women Who Opened the West*. New York, Paragon House, 1989, p.49.

[7] As discussed in Poling-Kempes.

[8] Ibid.

[9] Ibid.

[10] As told to Barbara Haber by Virginia Bartlett, May 23, 1996.

[11] Poling-Kempes, p.103.

[12] Susan Armitage, 'Through Women's Eyes: A New View of the West', In *The Women's West*. Ed. Susan Armitage and Elizabeth and Elizabeth Jameson, Norman, University of Oklahoma, 1987, p.13.

[13] Poling-Kempes, p.79.

[14] Ibid. p.81.

[15] Ibid. p.83.

How Arabic Traditions Travelled to England

C. B. Hieatt

It has long been recognized that English medieval cookery, as a part of western European cookery in general, was crucially influenced by the Arabic culinary traditions of the Near East.[1] Most students of the subject have assumed that, as C. Anne Wilson has suggested, these traditions came to England via Frankish (and other) crusaders who brought back Arabic recipes from their travels. Perhaps some did, but that is not the whole story;[2] many recipes went through more than one change as they moved to the West, and most are unlikely to have come directly from the East. We also now know that there are striking regional culinary differences from one part of western Europe to another throughout the period.

Thus scholars have begun to see that England, too, had its own distinctive regional cuisine.[3] The distinctiveness of English culinary recipes, right from the beginning, was a quality obscured for many earlier readers by the obviously French vocabulary of these works. Most writers on the subject took it for granted that, as Thomas Austin put it over a hundred years ago, 'Much of the scientific Cookery was of course French'.[4] Well, perhaps 'much', but there are major exceptions.

Anglo-Norman French was the normal spoken language of the courtly and ecclesiastical establishments from which the earliest recipes evidently came, and that of the clerks who wrote them down, whatever language the actual cooks may have spoken. The language does not, then, prove a French origin; and one has but to look at English feast menus to find that French visitors to the English court would not have recognized about half the items on the menu. Among the dishes which appear on a number of such menus, they would have recognized venison with furmenty, bruet of Almayne, 'gely,' blancmanger, and 'yrchons' – the latter name being derived from French *heriçons*. But no Frenchman would have been familiar with such popular English festive fare as 'Payn puff', long fritters, sambocade, blandesorry, or 'creme boiled'.

In fact, surprisingly few medieval English recipes correspond at all closely with contemporary recipes from France. My colleague Brenda Hosington quickly discovered this when she undertook a French translation of the late Sharon Butler's and my cookbook *Pleyn Delit*, in which the majority of the recipes were taken from fourteenth- and fifteenth-century English sources.[5] Professor Hosington had intended to substitute recipes from the *Viandier* and the *Ménagier de Paris*,[6] chief sources of medieval French recipes, for a great many English recipes, but she found this quite impossible.

When she did succeed in finding a similar recipe, a straightforward translation of our 'adapted' recipe often did not match the specifications of the French recipe at all well, which made it necessary for her to add footnotes pointing out differences between the English and French base recipes. Sometimes such notes had to go to considerable length. For example, one of her notes explains that a key ingredient in English 'Blanc manger' recipes was rice, and that shellfish were sometimes an alternative to other types of fish in a 'fishday' version of this dish. Without this note, her French-speaking readers would have been puzzled to find an adapted recipe entitled 'Turban de riz aux fruits de mer' placed after a *Viandier* recipe containing neither rice nor *fruits de mer*.

One section of her translation notably lacking French replacement recipes is that on 'Desserts'; of the twenty-three recipes, only seven borrowed from French collections vaguely parallel the twenty-two originally taken from English sources; and almost all of these required explanatory footnotes. That so few 'sweet' dishes were available in the French collections must be in part attributable to the greater use of sugar and other sweet ingredients, especially in the fourteenth century, by English cooks in dishes which were neither confections nor intended as medicinal.

But there is another significant factor to note here. Many of these dessert recipes are based on fruits, including strawberries, cherries, apples, plums, and pears. Such fruits were served in France, of course, but they are rarely called for as ingredients in pottages, sauces, and tarts, as they are in English recipes throughout the Middle Ages. Similarly, flower petals – such as the rose petals and elderflowers found in recipes in this section – do not occur as ingredients in medieval French recipes, except in the form of rosewater or in an occasional decorative garnish, witnessed by one 'gelée' recipe in the *Ménagier* which calls for a decoration of white violets.

When we look at recipes for dishes not normally thought of as 'sweet', it becomes apparent that English recipes also made much wider use of vegetables than was the case in France; vegetable dishes rarely make an appearance in the *Viandier*, although the *Ménagier de Paris* remarks on how to cook them in the section on the kitchen garden and includes a few in the chapter on 'potages communs'. Some do appear in full-fledged recipes, such as a poultry dish containing fresh peas or beans found in both the *Viandier* and the *Ménagier*,[7] but only a very few. Almost all close parallels to our medieval English vegetable recipes are to be found in Italian, not French, collections, strange as it may seem.

A number of recipes from the most influential later fourteenth-century English recipe collection, *The Forme of Cury*,[8] occur only in Italian contemporary culinary collections. These include English recipes for ravioli and lasagna in versions which are amazingly close to recipes found in the fourteenth-century Venetian text called, in its most recent edition, the *Libro di cucina*,[9] in the *Due libri di cucina* attributed to the 'Anonimo Meridionale',[10] and in the Tuscan *Libro della cucina*.[11] But most of these recipes were far from new in the late fourteenth century, when all of the works cited so far were written down.

The earliest English recipe for ravioli – and indeed the earliest recipe for this dish recorded anywhere – is in B.L. Additional MS. 32085, the manuscript designated as MS A in the edition of two Anglo-Norman culinary collections I edited in collaboration with Robin Jones.[12] This manuscript, which seems to have been compiled in the last decade of the thirteenth century,[13] antedates (if narrowly) the earliest surviving continental culinary collections. But there is at least one continental collection of *ca.* 1300 which has a remarkable number of parallels to Anglo-Norman, and later English, recipes: this is a manuscript thought to come from the Norman court of Naples, the Latin *Liber de coquina*.[14]

The *Liber* is clearly the source of the later Italian *Libro della cucina*, although that is, like other later recipe collections, much expanded. It is too late to be the source of Anglo-Norman MS A and of the slightly later B.L. MS Royal 12.C.xii, the manuscript we designated as MS B; however, its parallels are so striking that it may represent a version of a lost source of those Anglo-Norman recipes. Like MS A, the *Liber* contains an early recipe for ravioli, as well as a number of the vegetable dishes for which Professor Hosington could find no French counterpart. One is a recipe which is almost exactly the same as the *Forme of Cury*'s for mushrooms and leeks cooked in broth;[15] others include several for cooking fennel, which turns up a number of times in English recipes. Only *fennel* seeds are mentioned in the *Viandier* and *Ménagier*.[16]

A vegetable recipe of particular interest in the *Liber* is one for spinach: it is to be boiled, then, after the excess water has been pressed out, lightly fried in oil, with onion and spices. This recipe is almost exactly that given in the *Forme of Cury* for 'Spynoches yfryed' except that the latter recipe omits onions. While Professor Hosington substituted a recipe from the *Ménagier de Paris* for the English 'fried spinach', she realized that the French recipe was really quite different. She had to write an entirely new 'adaptation' and add directions for the English version as a 'variation'.

Neither of us knew this at the time, but the Middle English recipe, and the very similar one in the *Liber*, correspond closely to one in the *Baghdad Cookery Book*, a collection of Arabic recipes dating from the twelfth century.[17] And therein lies one of the most interesting facts about early medieval English culinary recipes: a number of dishes of documentable Arabic origin, retaining somewhat corrupted versions, or translations, of their Arabic names, are widely found in English and Italian cookbooks, beginning with the *Liber*, but not in northern French ones.

An outstanding example is the *Liber's* recipe for 'Mamonia,'[18] the name of a dish which appears in at least nine out of ten medieval English cookbooks for at least three centuries, beginning with the recipe for 'Maumenee' in Anglo-Norman MS B. This is a dish with so many variations that a thirteenth-century English diner would never have recognized any of the fifteenth-century versions.[19] It is thus not surprising that the B version differs in several respects from that of the Liber, which would in turn have been unrecognizable to the twelfth-century Arabian dignitaries whose *ma'munia* was a sweet porridge, sometimes containing (among other things) yogurt.[20]

Another dish of obviously Arabic origin found in the *Liber* is called *romania*, a stew flavored with pomegranates (Arabic *rumman* means 'pomegranates'). This is also to be found in one of the *Due libri di cucina* and the *Libro della cucina*, which also contains a version of 'mamonia', as do a number of unpublished Italian manuscripts.[21] 'Romania' also appears in a Languedoc Latin manuscript, where it is entitled 'Raymonia,'[22] and in one later English manuscript, B.L. MS Arundel 334, with the translated title 'Garnade'.

All of the Arabic recipes mentioned so far are recorded only in collections written in the Mediterranean area – and in England.[23] In the same chapter of the *Liber* there is also a recipe called 'Festigia'. The name of this recipe is not explained by the editor, but it looks suspiciously close to the Arabic 'Fustaqiya', which must be the base of the Anglo-Norman/Middle English word 'festicade', meaning a preparation of pistachio nuts (or possibly a confection including them, as in one of the Arabic recipes). There are no pistachio nuts in the *Liber's* 'Festigia', but there are no other distinguishing ingredients, either, so it appears likely that the pistachios dropped out by mistake.

At least one popular dish of Middle Eastern origin found in English collections (and elsewhere) is not to be found in the *Liber*. This is the recipe for meatballs 'gilded' with egg yolk called 'Poume d'oranges' in MS A and 'Pome dorreng' in the menu for Henry IV's coronation feast.[24] Gilded meatballs (or meatballs with a green coating to resemble apples) were also known in France, but there they were almost invariably entitled 'pommeaux' – little apples rather than 'oranges.'[25] Later English recipes for this dish appear to have been influenced by French variants, becoming, for example, 'Pommedorry', 'golden apples',[26] rather than 'oranges', but the original source of the English recipe was closer to the Arabic version than any known French recipe is.[27]

That this recipe is the first to appear in one of the very earliest English medieval culinary collections is significant in itself: the playful nature of meatballs disguised as oranges is typical of what English cooks (and presumably diners) valued most, a clever transformation of ingredients into what could be called 'subtleties.' While similar creations can also be found in French and other continental recipe collections, they have a particularly important status among medieval English recipes, beginning with MS A, which also includes a recipe bordering on a joke, 'Cooking Without Fire' (to be accomplished with the use of lime) and one of the most startling subtleties to be found in any early collection: 'Teste de Turke', 'Turk's Head'.

This elaborate creation also appears in MS B in an independent version. A's meat-day version (there is also a fish-day variant) contains pork and chicken, ground with spices, saffron, eggs, bread, and almonds, cooked in a pig's stomach; when this case is removed, the meat is to be basted with an egg yolk mixture, and presumably further roasted until the glaze has set. This 'gilded' giant sausage might indeed resemble a head, but it is a pretty tame creation in comparison with what we find in MS B. B calls for a pastry case filled with rabbits, poultry, dates, honey, cheese, and spices, topped with sugar, and – the crowning touch:

> a generous layer of ground pistachio nuts; the color of the ground nuts red, yellow, and
> green. The head (of hair) should be black, arranged to resemble the hair of a woman,
> in a black bowl, with the face of a man set on top.

As Professor Jones and I remarked, the black bowl presumably represented the hair of the 'Saracen', and the tints of the pistachio, his complexion.

The *Liber* contains a dish something like 'Teste de Turk', one called there 'Caput monachi', 'monk's head'.[28] To judge by its name, the dish must have started off as something shaped like a head: it appears to end up resembling a pastry castle more than a head, and may have resembled the *Forme of Cury*'s pastry castle rather more than an Anglo-Norman 'Turk's Head'. The late Rudolf Grewe suggested to me some years ago that both these dishes may be traced back to a hispano-Arabic recipe entitled 'Ras maimun', 'monkey's head'.

Now that I have had a chance to look at the recipes for this dish in Charles Perry's translation,[29] I heartily agree. The Arabic 'monkey's heads' are mixtures including sweet ingredients enclosed in pastry and cooked in a mold which would produce something resembling a head. In two of these versions, the resulting 'head' is to be decorated in a way which reinforces this resemblance, just like the more elaborate of the Anglo-Norman 'Turk's heads', and, like it, garnished with pistachios.

'Monkey' could easily have turned into 'monk' since the words are very similar in Latin and other European languages (see the *O.E.D.*). That a 'monk' could become a 'Turk' may have depended on the resemblance between the swirling folds of a turban and those of a monk's cowl. There is a tubeless version of the swirled mold used in making the sweet yeast bread known as 'kugelhopf' called a 'Turk's head pan': apparently because the shape resembles a turban; but an alternative name for this dish is 'gugelhopf', thought to be derived from 'gugle' meaning a monk's cowl. Thus, 'Turk's head' and 'monk's head' appear to be alternative names for similarly shaped pans or dishes.[30]

When I delivered a paper on Anglo-Norman recipes to the members of the Culinary Historians of New York in November 1995, one of that audience informed me that there is a traditional Sicilian dish called 'Turk's Head': an elaborate dessert in the shape of a head. Since then, several readers of *PPC* have responded to an inquiry I published there and sent me recipes for Sicilian Turk's Head: several surprisingly different recipes, but all consisting, like the medieval recipes, of pasta or pastry filled or surrounded by sweet ingredients.[31] The Anglo-Norman dish of this name, the Latin 'Monk's head', and the hispano-Arabic 'Monkey's Head' are, at least, all sweetened; such a dish could well have developed into a 'dessert', as the medieval poultry dish 'blancmanger' did.

An interesting point here is that Sicily was also a Norman kingdom from the early 11th century. This modern survival of a dish of the same name (and to some extent, nature) as one found only in England in the Middle Ages may again suggest the likelihood of contact between Normans in England and in Italy. While there are other recipes in the Anglo-Norman collections which resemble those in French cookery collections, most of them also have parallels in the *Liber*;[32] and at least two of the others are paralleled only in another Latin manuscript which may be of Norman origin.

This is the *Tractatus de modo preparandi et condiendi omnia cibaria*, which is of about the same date as the *Liber*;[33] a number of French glosses in this manuscript point to a French origin, and Bruno Laurioux has suggested that the frequent references to apples and two to cider point to Normandy. Two of its recipes which have no parallels elsewhere *except* in Anglo-Norman compilations (and the Middle English recipes derived from them) are 'Mistembec', which is MS A's 'Mincebek' (IV.2), and 'Claretum' (I.17), A's 'Claree': as Laurioux points out, the latter recipes have exactly the same ingredients, including one which is not usually found in such recipes, squinant.[34]

It remains that some of the most distinctively 'English' medieval culinary recipes have their strongest affinities with recipes which come from the Arabic areas to the east – usually, apparently, through Italy. Whether or not the Norman kingdoms in Italy were the primary source of Arabic culinary recipes in England, the culinary ideas to be observed in Arabic (and Italian) sources had a far-reaching effect on English cooking. And English cooks continued to be exceptionally innovative and experimental throughout the period, and beyond: for good or ill.[35]

The English emphasis on the unexpected is memorably expressed in one of the presumably Anglo-Norman recipes found in B.L. MS Additional 46919,[36] the earliest Middle English culinary collection. Here we find a remarkable dish of cherries stuffed with minced chicken and egg yolks, which begins, 'Now hear a great feat of cleverness of mind, how you shall make a dish of cherries: much comes of great cleverness.' This sounds the keynote: English courtly cookery aimed at 'subtle' (i.e., clever, surprising) combinations.

And, sometimes, jokey. The Middle English *Liber Cure Cocorum* begins with a series of kitchen practical jokes, for example. More serious culinary inventions of the fourteenth century include a stew of partridges and magpies garnished with peonies and a meat broth seasoned with ground rosehips.[37] Fifteenth-century English cooks have left us their recipes for, among other things, 'Lenten eggs' made of a paste containing fish and almond milk molded in empty eggshells, with carefully inserted 'yolks' coloured with saffron.[38] Nor did this tradition end with the Middle Ages. In many ways, the emphasis on innovation and 'cleverness' in English cooking is continuous from the Anglo-Norman beginnings, at least into the seventeenth century, and perhaps beyond.

A dish called 'Battalia Pie', with hollow pastry turrets variously filled around a central pork pie, was a recipe current in the eighteenth century, when it was indignantly denounced by Hannah Glasse. This is none other than *The Forme of Cury*'s pastry castle, a true 'subtlety': in its original form, it was a pork pie with crenellated towers filled with variously coloured custards and fruit mixtures. Its pedigree may go right back to that 'Caput Monachi', which apparently strayed from its Arabic origins by turning a head-shaped pastry into one with castle-like crenellations. Eighteenth-century versions hadn't changed much: except that the cookbook writers had forgotten the most 'subtle' touch of all, which was serving the 'castle' flambé. This is what *The Forme of Cury* means when it directs us to serve our castle 'with ew ardaunt' (brandy).

BIBLIOGRAPHY

Anonimo Meridionale, *Due Libri di Cucina*, ed. Ingemar Boström. Stockholm: Almqvist & Wiksell, 1985.
Austin, Thomas, ed., *Two Fifteenth-Century Cookery-Books*. Oxford, EETS o.s. 91, 1888; repr. 1964.
The Baghdad Cookery Book, trans. A. J. Arberry. *Islamic Culture* xiii (1939), 21-47 and 189-214.
Hieatt, Constance B., and Sharon Butler, *Pleyn Delit: Medieval Cookery for Modern Cooks*. Toronto: University of Toronto Press, 1976; trans. Brenda Hosington [then Thaon], *Pain, Vin et Veneison*, Montreal: Aurore, 1977; 2nd ed., Hieatt and Hosington, Toronto 1996.
     eds., *Curye on Inglysch: English Culinary Recipes of the Fourteenth Century* (*Including the* Forme of Cury). Oxford: EETS s.s. 8, 1985.
Hieatt, Constance B., and Robin F. Jones, 'Two Anglo-Norman Culinary Collections Edited from British Library Manuscripts Additional 32085 and Royal 12.C.XII', *Speculum* 61 (1986), 859-882.
Laurioux, Bruno, 'Les sources culinaires,' in *Comprendre le xiii* siècle, ed. Pierre Guichard and Danièle Alexandre-Bidon. Lyon: Presses universitaires de Lyon, 1995, pp. 215-26.
Liber Cure Cocorum, ed. Richard Morris. London: Asher, 1862.
Libre de Sent Sovi, ed. Rudolf Grewe. Barcelona: Barcino, 1979.
Libro della Cucina, ed. Francesco Zambrini. Bologna: Gaetano Romagnoli, 1863; repr. 1968.
Libro di Cucina, ed. Ludovico Frati. Leghorn, 1899; repr. Bologna: Forni, 1970.
Le Ménagier de Paris, ed. Jerôme Pichon. Paris: 1846; repr. Geneva: Slatkine, n.d (1970) 2 vols.; ed. Georgine Brereton and Janet M. Ferrier. Oxford: Clarendon Press, 1981.
Mulon, Marianne, ed., 'Deux traités inédits d'art culinaire médiéval', in *Bulletin philologique et historique*, 1971 for 1968, 369-435.
Perry, Charles, trans., *An Anonymous Andalusian Cookbook of the Thirteenth Century*, in *A Collection of Medieval and Renaissance Cookbooks*, II. Society for Creative Anachronism, 6th ed., 1993; pp. A-1 - A-80.

Rodinson, Maxime, 'Ma'muniyya East and West', trans. Barbara Inskip, *PPC* 33 (1989), 15-25.
    'Recherches sur les documents arabes relatifs à la cuisine', *Revue des études islamiques* (1949), pp. 95-165.
    'Romania et autres mots arabes en italien,' *Romania* 71 (1950), 433-449.
Santich, Barbara, '"Nondescript Gallimaufries" or Sophisticated Spicings? A Revaluation of Medieval Cuisine,' *PPC* 51 (1995), 15-26.
Le Viandier de Taillevent, ed. Jerôme Pichon and Georges Vicaire. Paris, 1892; repr. Luzarches: Daniel Morcrette, n.d., but post-1967; ed. Terence Scully. Ottawa: University of Ottawa Press, 1988.
Wilson, C. Anne, 'The Saracen Connection: Arab Cuisine and the Mediaeval West,' *PPC* 7 (1981), 123-22 and 8 (1981), 18-28.

NOTES

[1] See, e.g., Wilson.

[2] See Santich, *PPC* 51 (1995).

[3] See, e.g., Laurioux; see this article for some observations on basic differences between French and English cooking of the period.

[4] Austin, p.viii. Even so learned an expert as Karen Hess makes this mistake when she writes, 'English cookery manuscripts of the period were little more than translations from the French' (*Martha Washington's Booke of Cookery*, p. 208); it is dangerous to disagree with Mrs. Hess, who is usually right, but here she has surely made a wrong assumption.

[5] I.e., *Pain, Vin et Veneison* ; see Hieatt and Butler.

[6] The widely available editions are: for the *Viandier*, ed. Pichon and Vicaire and ed. Scully. The former is useful in that it includes the early 'Petit Traité' or *Enseingnemenz*, and, in the reprint, a photocopy of the earliest ms. of the *Viandier*; the latter edition gives all versions of every recipe, including those in the early ms., but does not include the (presumably) even earlier collection. The *Ménagier* was ed. Pichon (1846) and Brereton and Ferrier (1981); again, the more recent volume omits some useful addenda, in this case an appendix found only in later versions of the *Ménagier*. The recipes, and related matters, are in the second volume of the earlier edition.

[7] I.e., the 'Cretonnee' (with peas or beans) found in these collections.

[8] *The Forme of Cury* (hereafter designated as *FC*) is Part 4 in Hieatt and Butler, eds., *Curye on Inglysch*: hereafter designated as *CI*).

[9] The ravioli filled with herbs and cheese on p. 35 is parallel to the early Anglo-Norman recipe from which *FC*'s recipe clearly derives.

[10] The ravioli recipe is on p. 45, where it is numbered 55 (not the number in the table of contents).

[11] For ravioli, see pp. 38-39, lasagna, p. 77.

[12] Hieatt and Jones; see this edition for further information about the manuscripts and recipes included.

[13] See Laurioux, p. 219.

[14] One of the two Latin collections ed. Marianne Mulon, hereafter designated as *Liber*.

[15] *Liber* I.42.

[16] Except for a little fennel in the *Ménagier*'s enormously complex recipe for 'Composte': a recipe which calls for dozens of ingredients of all kinds.

[17] Trans. A. J. Arberry.

[18] *Liber* II.47, p. 407.

[19] See *CI* pp. 9-10 for some of this history.

[20] See Rodinson, (1949), p. 139, and trans. Inskip, (1989).

[21] Including two I saw some years ago in the library of the University of Reading, England; I am embarassed to say I apparently failed to mention these to my colleagues when we were preparing the 'Répertoire des manuscrits médiévaux contenant des recettes culinaires' published in *Du manuscrit à la table*, ed. Carole Lambert (Montreal: Champion-Slatkine, 1992), pp. 315-388.

[22] This is the ms. entitled 'Modus' in Carole Lambert's still unpublished edition of three important collections. – A delicious adaptation of the *Libro della cucina*'s recipe appears in Barbara Santich's *The Original Mediterranean Cuisine* (Kent Town, South Australia: 1995), p. 70.

[23] On the predominence of Italy in trade with the East after the First Crusade, see Santich, esp. pp. 17-18.

[24] Austin, p. 58.

[25] Carole Lambert has informed me that there is one French reference to these meatballs as 'oranges' in an as yet unpublished royal menu, but none of the French recipes for this dish retain the Arabic name.

[26] In Bodleian MS Douce 257, 'Diversa Servisa', Part 2 of CI.

[27] A recipe entitled 'Naranjiya' appears in the *Baghdad Cookery Book*, p. 190.

[28] *Liber*. V.5, p. 417.

[29] Perry.

[30] I am indebted to Ann McColl Lindsay, proprietor of Ann McColl's Kitchen Shop Ltd. in London, Ontario, for this information, and for sending me photocopied pages of kitchenware catalogues showing (and explaining) examples of these pans.

[31] The one which seems closest in general conception to the medieval recipes is one from V. Agnett's *La nuova cucina delle specialita regionali* (Milan, 1970), which calls for tubes filled with a ricotta-based cream, variously coloured and/or flavoured with chocolate, pistachios, and cochineal; this is to be presented 'a guisa di *turbante*'. I owe this recipe to Ulf Löchner. It is also worthy of note that Maria Kaneva-Johnson sent me a recipe called 'Arab's Head' from Bosnia: a filled pastry to be baked in a mold. This is certainly a recipe which can be said to be well travelled!

[32] Including 'crispis' and 'crispellas', crêpes (*Liber* III.5); 'mortarolum', a pottage ground to a paste in a mortar (II.63); the ubiquitous jelled meat or fish (II.4 and IV.1), and what MS B calls 'Browet sek', a dish of chicken in a sauce of verjuice, parsley, and spices (II.2). — I do not mean that *no* Anglo-Norman recipes come from vernacular French sources; some certainly do, e.g. 'Hauceleamye', which must be derived from a French 'Brout houssié'.

[33] This is the other collection in Mulon's edition.

[34] See Laurioux, p. 220.

[35] Some later commentators have been particularly appalled by such sixteenth-century inventions as carrots and other vegetables stuffed with 'puddings'.

[36] Printed as Part 1 of CI, 'Diversa Cibaria'. This collection translates all of the recipes in MS B and about half of those in MS A, with an additional seventeen almost certainly translated from two or more other Anglo-Norman sources.

[37] Both are found in *Utilis Coquinario*, Part 3 of CI, along with primrose pottage, violet pottage, and bean-blossom pottage; the latter has a parallel in the *Liber*, I.31.

[38] For an example of this dish, see Austin, pp. 41-42.

'The Fishy and Vegetable Abominations Known as Japanese Food'

Richard Hosking

It was in the sixteenth century that Japan began to become known to the Western world, through the long sea voyages of Portuguese explorers and missionaries. They arrived in Japan, introducing the Japanese to firearms in 1543, and to the famous Spanish Jesuit, Francis Xavier, who came to support the Portuguese Jesuit missionaries in 1593. After an initial period of success, Christianity, with its Jesuit missionaries, was firmly rejected. The firearms, however, were always welcome.

João Rodrigues arrived in 1577 as a youth of sixteen and soon entered the Society of Jesus. An excellent linguist, he became famous as an interpreter both of Japanese language and Japanese customs. What he had to say about Japanese eating and drinking habits is very interesting not least to show how little has changed. He was expelled from Japan in 1610 and spent the rest of his life in China, where he wrote a book on the history and customs of Japan.

> As the end of this pagan people is to serve their bellies in feastings and drunkenness, chiefly with wine, all the banquets, revelries and recreations are aimed at persuading them by various means to drink too much wine until they end up drunk and many of them completely lose their senses. The Chinese and Japanese do not consider drunkenness in banquets and revelries as something wrong although they will not countenance violent intoxication…in order to honour and favour the host who is holding the banquet and to show appreciation of his hospitality towards them, even those who do not normally drink exert themselves to do so. There are many among them who humour their host in these gatherings by pretending to drink….In order to show more gratitude towards the host and to excuse themselves from drinking many times in the middle of the feast, or because of the strength of the wine, they say, 'I am completely tipsy and cannot manage any more (as if they were owning themselves to be beaten), nor am I capable of returning home.'[1]

Concerning these banquets:

> They were wont to hold these banquets more as a rite to show honour and regard towards the person of the guest than to enjoy eating tasty dishes; hence the more entertainment provided in these banquets, the more formalities were there in drinking wine. They provided various appetising *sakana* which gave a thirst, as well as other entertainments of instrumental music, plays and other things which were interspersed throughout the banquet.
>
> The food was cold and insipid as it was cut up in portions and brought in on tables, and the only thing that was hot was the *shiru*, or broth, which one was able to enjoy. These were the principal dishes of the banquets and the rest was merely additional…The more solemn the banquet among the Japanese, and also in China, the greater number of different broths and *shiru* provided for each guest. Each of these is made from different things; some are made from high quality fish, others from the meat of birds which they prize, such as the crane, which ranks in the first place, the swan in the second, and wild duck in the third. This is still true even today, for on no account will they use anything but wild game and never the domestic animals and birds which they rear. They will not eat the latter…for on no account whatsoever will they eat ass, horse, cow, much less

pig (except boars), duck, or hens, and they are naturally averse to lard. They eat only wild game at banquets and their ordinary meals, for they regard a householder who slaughters an animal reared in his house as cruel and unclean; on the other hand, they do not show this compassion towards human beings because they kill them with greater ease and enjoyment than they would an animal.

The fourth kind of banquet.... is the modern banquet which has been held since the time of Nobunaga [1582] up to the present day and is now general throughout the kingdom...As regards the actual food, they did away with the dishes placed there merely for ornament and to be looked at, and also the cold dishes; in their place they substituted well-seasoned hot food which is brought to the table at the proper time, and is substantial and of high quality...They drink often and intermittently while they are eating....So food at banquets nowadays and at ordinary meals gives pleasure and enjoyment, all apart from the wine, and it is not only for the sake of ceremony and courtesy and merely to look at, as in former times.[2]

The Jesuits were expelled from Japan in 1630, and from 1639 to 1854 a strict policy of national seclusion was adopted. By the early nineteenth century the ramparts of isolation were being breeched, and in 1838 Lord Elgin led a mission to the Shogun. A meal which the Shogun served them was described by Laurence Oliphant:

When we arrived the floor of our dining-room was strewn with delicacies. Each person was provided with a little repast of his own, the exact ditto to that in which all his friends were indulging – and when anybody made a gastronomic discovery of any value, he announced it to the company: so at the recommendation of one we all plunged into the red lacquer cups on the right, or, at the invitation of another, dashed recklessly at what seemed to be pickled slugs on the left. We found it difficult even then to describe to each other the exact dishes we meant. How much more hopeless to attempt it now? There was a good deal of seaweed about it, and we each had a capital broiled fish. With that, and an immense bowl of rice, it was impossible to starve; but my curiosity triumphed over my discretion, and I tasted of every pickle and condiment, and each animal and vegetable delicacy, of every variety of colour, consistency and flavour; an experience from which I would recommend any future visitor to Japan to abstain.[3]

Somewhat later, in 1866, Prince Satsuma entertained Sir Harry Parkes in Kagoshima. The banquet was recorded by Jephson and Elmhurst, two officers accompanying Sir Harry. There were forty courses:

1. Bitter Green Tea (whipped)
2. Sweetmeats.

Band arrives and tobacco is brought on to fill up time between the courses

3. Fish, Soup, and Raw fish, with hot Saki.
4. Soup of Mushroom, Green Vegetable, and Fish.

Exit band, to the great relief of guests

9. Cold Fried Lampreys
19. Raw Cuttle-fish
23. Small bones of Chicken, and *Unlaid Eggs*
26. Raw Bonito, Rice, Apple and Chili Leaves.
30. A Tray with Rice, thick Soup, and Pickles.[4]

The constituents of this latter course, called *ichi ju, issai* in Japanese, quite clearly indicate the conclusion of drinking. For whatever reason, that did not happen here and they went on eating and drinking for another ten courses, and even then, 'it was only at the entreaty of the Minister that we were allowed to rise when this much had been gone through'.

Eating slices off a living fish has long been a problem for non-Japanese. In the early 1880s Christopher Dresser had this to say:

> Resting on a large kutani dish is a mat formed of rounds of glass, held together by plaited threads, on which is a living fish with gills and mouth moving regularly: at its back rises a bank of white shreds resembling isinglass, but in reality a colourless seaweed, while the fish itself rests on green algae. In front is a pile of small slices of raw fish garnished with a radiating tuft of variegated bamboo leaves. A portion of the raw fish from the pile in front of the living victim is now placed on a saucer and passed to one guest, and so with rest till the pile is consumed. Then, to my disgust, the serving-maid, not having enough in the pile for all, raised the skin of the upper side of the fish, which I now saw was already loose, and simply picked up slice after slice from the living creature, which, although alive, had been already carved; nay, even the pile of flesh already served consisted of the lower half of the creature's body. There is a refinement of barbaric cruelty in all this which contrasts strangely with the geniality and loving nature of the Japanese, for with consummate skill the fish has been carved so that no vital part has been touched; the heart, the gills, the liver, and the stomach is left intact, while the damp algae on which the fish rests suffices to keep the lungs in action. The miserable object with lustrous eyes looks upon us while we consume its own body; and rarely is it given to any creature to put in a living presence at its own entombment.[5]

Since this practice is still very much alive, let us hear what the Japan Society for the Prevention of Cruelty to Animals has to say about it:

> Eating live fish is part of our unique Japanese culinary culture. Westerners eat dead fish, we eat them live. Its just a cultural thing. We are not being cruel, we want to have the best-tasting fish. If the fish were prepared simply for show, like for TV, we would be very much against that.[6]

So the end justifies the means.

Christopher Dresser, like so many others, including myself, also had great difficulty with *mochi* (lumps of glutinous rice paste):

> I try to eat the putty-like compound with green exterior, but in attempting to bite a piece from the mass I encounter a serious difficulty, for instead of being wholly successful in my attempt I find that in removing my saucer from my mouth I am drawing out an attenuated string of the ductile dainty, and that the portion in my mouth is still connected with the larger mass now resting on the floor. The more I try to separate this connecting cord the more my difficulty increases and I verily believe that one mass of such food could be drawn into a thread which would span the Pacific itself: at last, in my agony, I swallow the mass, but even then it seems an age before I can break the thread which binds me to the dish on the floor. Being satisfied with one mouthful of this dainty, I try the gelatinous rice cake which with an effort I in part consume.[7]

Devotees of the film *Tampopo* might remember the scene in which an old man chokes on a *mochi*, and in fact many old men do choke to death on these lethal but much loved confections, especially at New Year, when the custom is to eat them in quantity.

By the 1880s, we are moving into a period in which Western visitors believed that only the Japanese could eat Japanese food. Major Henry Knollys expresses this point of view clearly:

> I have explained that nothing short of actual starvation would induce a European to face the forbidding native food. The country is absolutely without any supplies of meat, bread, milk, or coffee, and Japanese tea is exceedingly insipid, and even distasteful to English people. I have, however, come provided with the main elements of my meals in

the shape of tinned provisions: the only local additions are eggs, rice, pears which look like jargonels but which on being tasted prove considerably inferior to inferior turnips, and sometimes an exceedingly tough chicken, chiefly made up of legs as long and as thick as miniature stilts.[8]

The indomitable Isabella Bird, who travelled in the interior of Japan in 1878 was of a like mind:

> The 'Food Question' is said to be the most important one for all travellers...The fact is, that except for a few hotels in popular resorts got up for foreigners, bread, butter, meat, milk, poultry, coffee, wine, and beer, are unattainable, that fresh fish is rare, and that unless one can live on rice, tea and eggs, with the addition now and then of some tasteless fresh vegetables, food must be taken, as the fishy and vegetable abominations known as 'Japanese food' can only be swallowed and digested by a few, and that after long practice.[9]

Isabella went to Japan to recruit her health and embarked on a journey that would have finished most of us off. Travelling in American mountain dress and Wellington boots, she took an emergency supply of Brand's meat lozenges with her, as well as a collapsible bed and strong mosquito nets. Here's how she solved the 'Food Question':

> The 'Food Question' has been solved by a modified rejection of all advice! I have only brought a small supply of Liebig's extract of meat, 4 lbs. of raisins, some chocolate, both for eating and drinking, and some brandy in case of need.[10]

Nevertheless, food was a constant problem:

> On entering, a smiling girl brought me some plum-flower tea with a delicate almond flavour, a sweetmeat made of beans and sugar, and a lacquer bowl of frozen snow. After making a difficult meal from a fowl of much experience, I spent the evening out of doors, as a Japanese watering-place is an interesting novelty.[11]

> There was nothing eatable but rice and eggs, and I ate them under the concentrated stare of eighteen pairs of dark eyes.[12]

> I found nothing that I could eat except black beans and boiled cucumbers.[13]

> Much of the food of the peasantry is raw or half-raw salt fish, and vegetables rendered indigestible by being coarsely pickled, all bolted with the most marvellous rapidity, as if the one object of life were to rush through a meal in the shortest possible time. The married women look as if they'd never known youth, and their skin is apt to be like tanned leather. At Kayashima I asked the house-master's wife, who looked about fifty, how old she was (a polite question in Japan), and she replied twenty-two – one of many similar surprises. Her boy was five years old, and was still unweaned.[14]

> Besides a rack for kitchen utensils, there is only a stand on which are six large brown dishes with food for sale – salt shell-fish, in a black liquid, dried trout impaled on sticks, sea slugs in soy, a paste made of pounded roots [konnyaku], and green cakes made of the slimy river confervae [green algae–Suizenji nori], pressed and dried – all ill-favoured and unsavoury viands. This afternoon a man without clothes was treading flour paste on a mat....

> July 1. – I was just falling asleep last night, in spite of mosquitoes and fleas, when I was roused by much talking and loud outcries of poultry; and Ito, carrying a screaming, refractory hen, and a man and a woman whom he had with difficulty bribed to part with it, appeared by my bed. I feebly said I would have it boiled for breakfast, but when Ito called me this morning he told me with a most rueful face that just as he was going to kill it, it had escaped to the woods! In order to understand my feelings,you must have

experienced what it is not to have tasted fish, flesh, or fowl, for ten days! The alternative was eggs and some of the paste which the man was treading yesterday on the mat cut into strips and boiled! It was coarse flour and buckwheat, so, you see, I have learned not to be particular![15]

A coolie servant washed some rice for my dinner, but before doing so took off his clothes, and the woman who cooked it let her *kimono* fall to her waist before she began to work, as is customary among respectable women. . . .

We walked through the town to find something eatable for to-morrow's river journey, but only succeeded in getting wafers made of white of egg and sugar, balls made of sugar and barley flour, and beans coated with sugar...I was much mobbed, and one child formed the solitary exception to the general rule of politeness by calling me a name equivalent to the Chinese *Fan Kwai*, 'foreign;' but he was severely chidden, and a policeman has just called with an apology. A slice of fresh salmon has been produced, and I think I never tasted anything so delicious.[16]

We left Ichinono early on a fine morning, with three pack-cows, one of which I rode... I thought that I might get some fresh milk, but the idea of anything but a calf milking a cow was so new to the people that there was a universal laugh, and Ito told me that they thought it 'most disgusting,' and that the Japanese think it 'most disgusting' in foreigners to put anything 'with such a strong smell and taste' into their tea...In the afternoon [we] reached the village of Tenoko... Here Ito dined on seven dishes of horrors, and they brought me *saké*, tea, rice, and black beans. The last are very good.[17]

Shinjo has a large trade in rice, silk, and hemp, and ought not to be as poor as it looks. The mosquitoes were in thousands, and I had to go to bed, so as to be out of their reach, before I had finished my wretched meal of sago and condensed milk. There was a hot rain all night, my wretched room was dirty and stifling, and rats gnawed my boots and ran away with my cucumbers.[18]

I invited him [Dr. Nosoki] to dinner, and two tables were produced covered with different dishes, of which he ate heartily, showing most singular dexterity with his chopsticks in removing the flesh of small, bony fish. It is proper to show appreciation of a repast by noisy gulpings, and much gurgling and drawing in of the breath. Etiquette rigidly prescribes these performances, which are most distressing to a European, and my guest nearly upset my gravity by them.[19]

Poor Isabella! In the end the ultimate disaster struck:

My small stock of foreign food is exhausted, and I have been living here on rice, cucumbers, and salt salmon – so salt that, after being boiled in two waters, it produces a most distressing thirst. Even this has failed to-day, as communication with the coast has been stopped for some time, and the village is suffering under the calamity of its stock of salt-fish being completely exhausted. There are no eggs, and rice and cucumbers are very like the 'light food' which the Israelites 'loathed.' I had an omelette one day, but it was much like musty leather. The Italian minister said to me in Tokiyo, 'No question in Japan is so solemn as that of food,' and many others echoed what I thought at the time a most unworthy sentiment. I recognized its truth to-day when I opened my last resort, a box of Brand's meat lozenges, and found them a mass of mouldiness.[20]

Japanese breakfast has always been and still is a stumbling-block to foreign visitors. George Cullen Pearson vividly describes his experience:

Doing as the Japs do! This was to partake for early breakfast of bitter tea and to eat what were stated to be salted plums (the invariable native relish), but which looked and tasted like balls of blotting paper that had been lying for some months in bad red-cabbage pickle. To regale myself with what was by courtesy supposed to be breakfast, to wit:

One saucer, with a very flabby fish, cooked some days before.

One bowl of warm salt water, with a fish's eye and tail – extreme tip – and three shreads of green ginger floating in it.

One plate containing a section of something brown, with little holes in it, like a magnified piece of colts's-foot rock, very soft, very cold, and very nasty.

One slice of raw egg-plant.

A dozen beans coated with a sweet sticky substance like damp toffee.

A little pyramid of singularly offensive vegetable matter like cold boiled turnip-tops or neglected sauerkraut.

Two slices of pickled turnip radish (daikon as it is termed), which stands in the place of Roquefort cheese [Munster?] with the Japs, and 'smells so'. Phew!

Cold boiled rice *ad libitum*.

And this is what a weak European stomach was supposed to be able to receive at five o'clock on a hot summer morning, and what my base beguiler told me I ought to be truly thankful for, himself receiving it all in perfect faith, and having consumed, asking loudly for more.

For my own part it was useless to struggle with such a bill of fare. I could not eat the viands put before me...each attempt of mine to swallow the smallest mouthful brought on such a spasm of the throat, and such decidedly expressed objections on the part of my rebellious interior, that I was compelled to fall back on two eggs, boiled as hard as Japanese alone can boil them, and a glass of cold water, which tasted as though it had been dipped out of a globe containing goldfish. I construed this into one of the emergencies which demanded whisky, and acted accordingly.[21]

Sara Duncan and Orthodocia were more adventurous, but had their limits:

A delicate pink saucer was then presented to us, containing round slices of lilac-coloured vegetable matter with holes in it – the root of the lotus. It had a rubbery consistency in the hand, and a soapy suggestion in the mouth. 'Lovely culinary conception!' said Orthodocia, 'take it away!' And we decided that we did not care for boiled poetry.

We paused at the lotus. It had seemed a lengthy and elaborate repast, and yet we were conscious of a sense of incompleteness, a vagrant and uncared for gastronomic feeling.[22]

This sense of incompleteness after Japanese meals is something I have previously commented on with reference to myself.[23]

The Victorians were not alone in their negative attitude to Japanese food. Much more recently, the popular American comedian Dave Barry has expressed similar feelings:

As bold culinary adventurers, we experimented with all kinds of Japanese food for about fifteen minutes, then spent the rest of our trip looking for Kentucky fried chicken.[24]

He had the old problem of eating live fish:

I certainly would never say anything judgmental about another culture, but in certain food-related areas, the Japanese are clinically insane. The new culinary rage when we were in Japan was to eat fish that were still alive. I cannot imagine doing such a thing unless I were really desperate to get into a fraternity, but according to news reports, people were paying top yen in fine Tokyo restaurants for live, gasping fish. The waiter brings you your fish still gasping, then quickly slices it open at your table; then you are supposed to eat it while the fish is staring at you with its nearer eyeball and a facial expression that says, 'Go ahead and enjoy yourself! Don't mind me! I'll be dead fairly soon!'

And that's not the weirdest culinary activity that the Japanese engage in. There is also *fugu*. This is a kind of blowfish that the Japanese eat raw. So far you are not surprised. ...Well, what you are apparently not aware of....is that *fugu* contains a lethal poison. The liver of the male and ovaries of the female contain one of the most toxic substances in nature, for which there is no antidote, which means that if your *fugu* is not prepared exactly right, with all of the dangerous organs removed, you have encountered the Blowfish of Doom and soon are going to meet the Big Maitre d' in the Sky.

Clearly this is a fish that Mother Nature is telling us we should leave the hell under water, but to the Japanese it is a great delicacy. Every year they eat tons of it. They'll pay the equivalent of hundreds of dollars to eat it. And every year people die because their *fugu* was prepared wrong.[25]

After all these negative experiences of Japanese food, how refreshing it is to read M.F.K. Fisher's opinions and reactions. Her Introduction to Shizuo Tsuji's *Japanese Cooking: A Simple Art* is a superb study of Japanese food and cooking in relation to Western food and cooking. In October 1978 she went with her sister Norah 'for two peculiar and dreamlike weeks' to Osaka to the Tsuji Professional Culinary Institute. This is a large and very famous school with 2,500 students. What was her motivation in going?

I wanted to see for myself what was happening in a chancy modern field of East-West eating.

Aside from our watching some forty-five private demonstrations at the two Tsuji buildings in Osaka,...and coping with about thirty gastronomical onslaughts, no matter how gently subtle, in restaurants and inns and street-shops, we tasted seed pods and ginkgo nuts, and native fruits like 'twentieth century' pears, as juicy as a ripe melon and as crisp as a frosty apple...seaweeds, dried or fresh, poached or swished through broths...plum jam, sour as Hell's wrath, in a tiny bowl with two quarter-inch cubes of fried liver from a sea bass...the ovaries of a sea slug, buried in froth skimmed from boiling crushed soybean...slender cucumbers, faintly sour from their vat of fermenting rice bran...ices made from fruit pulps, beaten without sugar and pressed back into their hollow skins...

I was *curious*, and I still am. Shizuo Tsuji wanted, through his writings, to prove to readers of the Western world that traditional Japanese cookery can and should be a useful part of our own way of eating. At times I am not completely sure that he is right. The preparation and serving of fine as well as routine Japanese food is more obviously mixed, than is ours, with other things than hunger.

At its best, it is inextricably meshed with aesthetics, with religion, with tradition and history. It is evocative of seasonal changes, or of one's childhood, or of a storm at sea: one thin slice of molded fish purée shaped like a maple leaf and delicately colored orange and scarlet, to celebrate Autumn; and a chestnut made of fishpaste, to remind an honored guest that he was born on a far-north island; an artfully stuffed lobster riding on an angry sea of curled waves of white radish cut paper-thin, with occasional small shells of carved shrimp meat tossing helplessly in the troughs....

All this delicate pageantry is based on things that we Westerners are either unaware of or that we accept for vaguely sentimental reasons.... As children raised in lands of plenty, we do not learn to count on a curl of carrot and one fried ginkgo nut to divert us from the fact that the rest of the food on the plate consists of an austere mound of rice and two pinches of herb paste. We have never been taught to make little look like much, make much out of little, in a mystical combination of ascetic and aesthetic as well as animal satisfaction.[26]

Frances Fisher explains why she thinks she could be satisfied with Japanese food for the rest of her life:

> Students of the influence of gastronomy on [this] national taste, and therefore on politics and such seemingly distant subjects, from Brillat-Savarin in France of the early nineteenth century to Umesao[27] in present-day Japan, believe that what and how a man eats in his first few years will shape his natural appetite for the rest of his life. It will not matter if he begins as a potter's son and ends as an affluent banker. If he ate pure fresh food when he was a child, he will seek it out when he is old and weary, it is said…
>
> This theory, which I mostly agree with, has taken a double blow for me because of Shizuo's invitation to come to Osaka. Not only does my palate refresh itself daily with foods almost as simple as the first ones I knew, but I feel that it has stayed young because of my natural curiosity about the the best dishes that other countries have offered me. And now, after two weeks in Japan, I must admit with real astonishment that if I could eat as I did there under my friend's subtle guidance, I would gladly turn my back on Western food and live on Japanese *ryori* for the rest of my life.
>
> Such a pattern would be difficult for me to follow. There, few people without princely revenues and highly evolved palates are served the dishes Norah and I ate. I could never afford to buy them, even as an occasional luxury. For the same reason, neither could I go to the rare restaurants in Japan, where such intrinsically pure food is still prepared, even if for political or professional or social reasons my reservation might be accepted.
>
> Wealth is so much part of protocol in Japan that one must know this Personage in Tokyo, that Eminence in Osaka, in order to make reservation at a certain restaurant in Kobe for precisely 8:10 p.m. six months hence. This is out of my sphere of survival, except for the one such adventure in my life. I know, though, that the food I ate during those amazing days in 1978 has changed my whole palate, or, perhaps the gastronomers would say, it has simply strengthened the taste I acquired as a child...?
>
> This is not to say that I could not and would not live well in Japan, just as I manage to do here in the States. I would eat seasonal fruits and vegetables in either place, and honest fresh-caught fish when available, and would surely find a source there for noodle dough now and then…[28]

There was one important factor that Fisher seems to have been unaware of, a factor that has been very significant to me as a long-time resident of Japan, and which is one aspect of Umesao's view described above. That is the question of cultural identity.

So long as you are living safely enbosomed in your own culture at home, you can eat foreign food as much and as often as you like, knowing that your own food is always there should you happen to want it. When you live in a foreign country, there are three ways of life open to you. If you try to go native, among other things eating the local food all the time, you will put a very severe strain on your mental stability and probabably come to suffer from a serious loss of personal idendity. On the other hand, if you try to reject the local way of life completely, you will form your own little expatriate ghetto, make few local friends and not enjoy a reasonably full life. Some kind of middle way, or compromise seems the most practical and satisfactory approach. In this way of life, you start the day with your own familiar breakfast, then during the day mix with the locals and enjoy what you can of their way of life, and then in the evening, retreat to your accustomed ways and, so to speak, recharge your batteries. From time to time, more often as time goes by, you will feel a need for the foods of your childhood ('comfort foods'), and your home culture, a need which you would be wise to indulge. I think that if M.F.K.Fisher had been in Japan for two years rather than two weeks, she would have realised that she could not have lived there happily on Japanese *ryori* for the rest of her life.

For myself, as a resident of Japan for twenty-three years, I understand how those Victorians felt. I, too, have always had difficulty with Japanese breakfast and I, too, am revolted at watching a live fish wriggle and jump while one is eating its flesh. And I have to agree with Sara Duncan when she says that she was conscious of a sense of incompleteness, even after a lengthy and elaborate repast. I often have the same feeling. But I reject those Victorian attitudes of cultural superiority and narrow-mindedness, and try to enjoy what I can of the infinitely varied food culture that surrounds me. But not by any means all the time!

REFERENCES

[1] Cooper, Michael (tr. & ed.), *This Island of Japan. João Rodrigues' Account of 16th-century Japan.* Kodansha, Tokyo, 1973, p.211.

[2] ibid. pp.237-40.

[3] Cortazzi, Hugh, *Victorians in Japan. In and around the Treaty Ports.* Athlone Press, London, 1987, p.254. Excerpt from Oliphant, Laurence, *Narrative of the Earl of Elgin's Mission to China and Japan in the years 1857, '58, '59.* 2 vols, II, London, 1859.

[4] ibid. pp.254-5. Excerpt from Jephson, R.M. and Elmhirst, E.P., *Our Life in Japan.* London 1869.

[5] ibid. p.258. Excerpt from Dresser, Christopher, *Japan, its Architecture, Art, and Art Manufactures.* London 1882.

[6] *The Daily Yomiuri*, 29 April 1991.

[7] Cortazzi, 1987, pp.257-8. Excerpt from Dresser, *op. cit.*

[8] ibid. p.259. Excerpt from Knollys, Sir Henry, *Sketches of Life in Japan.* London, 1887.

[9] Bird, Isabella L., *Unbeaten Tracks in Japan*, Charles E. Tuttle, Rutland, Vermont, 1973, p.19.

[10] ibid. p.33.

[11] ibid. pp.63-4.

[12] ibid. p.89.

[13] ibid. p.93.

[14] ibid. p.95.

[15] ibid. pp.104-5.

[16] ibid. pp.107-8.

[17] ibid. pp.128-9.

[18] ibid. pp.139-40.

[19] ibid. p.142.

[20] ibid. pp.195-6.

[21] Cortazzi, 1987, pp.260-1. Excerpt from Pearson, George Cullen, *Flights inside and outside Paradise by a penitent Peri.* New York, 1886.

[22] Cortazzi, pp.261-2. Excerpt from Duncan, Sara, *A Social Departure: How Orthodocia and I went round the world by ourselves.* London, 1890.

[23] Hosking, Richard, 'Manyoken, Japan's First French Restaurant', *Cooks and Other People, Proceedings of the Oxford Symposium 1995*, Totnes, 1996.

[24] Barry, Dave, *Dave Barry Does Japan*, Fawcett Columbine, New York, 1993, p.69.

[25] ibid. pp.72-3.

[26] Fisher, M.F.K., Introduction in Tsuji, Shizuo, *Japanese Cooking: A Simple Art*, Kodansha, Tokyo, 1980, pp.7-8.

[27] Dr Tadao Umesao, anthropologist, formerly Director of the National Museum of Ethnology, Osaka. Dr Umesao lost his sight. His experience and opinions on eating food blind are described in Ishige Naomichi's Foreword to Hosking, Richard, *A Dictionary of Japanese Food*, Charles E. Tuttle, Rutland, Vermont, and Prospect Books, Totnes, 1996.

[28] Fisher, M.F.K., in Tsuji, Shizuo, 1980, pp.11-12.

Raw Liver and More:
Feasting with the Buriats of Southern Siberia

Sharon Hudgins

A wealthy Buriat and his wife.

The Trans-Siberian Express to Buriatia

I first became aware of the people known as Buriats when I was travelling across Russia on the Trans-Siberian Railroad in the winter of 1994. My husband and I had boarded the train in Vladivostok on a bitterly cold night in January, for a journey that took us through Siberian winter landscapes reminiscent of scenes from *Dr. Zhivago*. Through great forests of pine, birch, and larch, their branches burdened with snow. Past low mountain ranges along the borders of China and Mongolia. By old log houses, their windows decorated with carved and painted 'wooden lace.' Past lonely cemeteries, the graves marked with the eight-pointed crosses of the Russian Orthodox Church. Through Chita, place of exile and imprisonment for many of the Decembrists, Russia's most famous nineteenth-century revolutionaries. By steam locomotive graveyards, black and forlorn, next to modern snow-clearing equipment, shiny and proud. Past female road crews in worn-out work clothes and heavy eye-makeup. Near former gulags and present prisons. By herds of Mongolian horses, racing alongside the train. Over seemingly endless windswept plains, with blizzards blowing wildly and the snow piling deeper and deeper the farther we went into Siberia.

Late afternoon on the third day of travel, the train arrived at Ulan-Ude, the largest city along the route since we left the Russian Far East. As the train neared the station, we noticed several old wooden signs with peeling paint that still bore traces of words written in a cursive alphabet that was not Cyrillic.[1] On the station platform was a large group of people all dressed for the frigid weather, from the padded cotton jackets of the railroad crews to the fur-trimmed coats and hats of several stylish women. At least half the faces in the crowd were Oriental.

I was soon to learn that many of them were local Buriats, for Ulan-Ude is the capital of the Buriat Autonomous Republic, a section of Siberia about one and a half times the size of Great Britain, situated just north of Mongolia and east of Lake Baikal. Occupying part of the area known as Transbaikalia in tsarist and early Soviet times, the Buriat-Mongol Autonomous Soviet Socialist Republic was established in 1923.[2] Two other Buriat 'autonomous districts,' within larger administrative regions, were created during the Soviet period: the Ust'-Ordynskii Buriat Autonomous District (within the Irkutsk Region), west of Lake Baikal and north of the city of Irkutsk; and the Aginskii Buriat Autonomous District (within the Chita Region), east of both Lake Baikal and the Buriat Autonomous Republic. Under the new Russian federal structure established in 1992, these (non-Russian) ethnically based political entities still exist – as Buriatia, Ust'-Orda, and Aga.[3]

The largest minority ethnic group in Siberia, Buriats are divided culturally and geographically into two major sub-groups: the Western Buriats (or Baikal Buriats) who live west of Lake Baikal and on Olkhon Island in Lake Baikal, and the more numerous Eastern Buriats (or Transbaikal Buriats) who live on the other side of the lake. Buriats are closely related to Mongolians, whom they resemble in appearance and with whom they share many customs. Rev. Henry Landsdell's description of Buriats in his book, *Through Siberia*, published in 1881, echoes that of many travellers to this region, past and present:

> We first met these people a few miles on the western side of Irkutsk, and their physiognomy at once told us they belonged to a different race from any we had seen. They have large skulls, square faces, low and flat foreheads; the cheek bones are high and wide apart, the nose flat, eyes elongated, the skin swarthy and yellowish, and the hair jet black.[4]

Some Buriats claim that their people are descendants of Genghis Khan, the legendary thirteenth-century Mongol warrior whose empire extended from northern China across most of Central Asia, and whose grandson, Batu Khan, led the Golden Horde that terrified and subjugated much of Russia and Eastern Europe. In fact, the Buriats were a separate Mongolic group, distantly related to Genghis Khan's own clan, who lived in the woodlands and high steppes north of the Mongols and had a way of life very similar to them.[5] The Mongols fought the Buriats on several occasions, never conquering them but driving them farther north where, in the thirteenth and fourteenth centuries, the Buriats began to inhabit the land near the southern end of Lake Baikal.[6] Buriat folklore, on the other hand, identifies the Buriats as coming originally from around the shores of Lake Baikal.[7] And no doubt the Buriats mingled with the Mongol clans united under Genghis Khan and his descendants, as they swept through the Transbaikal region, producing a number of mixed Mongol-Buriat children, the ancestors of today's modern Buriats, many of whom proudly claim kinship with their warrior forbears.

Nomadic herders of cattle, horses, sheep, and goats, the Buriats were well established in the areas around Lake Baikal when the first Russian cossacks arrived there in the seventeenth century. These Buriats were expert archers and horsemen. According to W. Bruce Lincoln, in *The Conquest of a Continent: Siberia and the Russians*:

> While some of Siberia's natives offered little opposition to the Russians, the Buriats never missed an opportunity to strike against their new enemies. Buriat uprisings flared up around Lake Baikal several times during the seventeenth century, and Buriat arrows took the lives of tsarist tribute collectors even in times of peace. Only in the middle of the eighteenth century did the Buriats and the Russians come to terms and begin to intermingle, with Russian men marrying Buriat women but rarely the reverse. In the nineteenth century, Siberia's Buriats formed the backbone of the Transbaikal cossack regiments, intermarried frequently with the Russians, learned to farm, and became much more Russified than such neighbors as the Tungus [another ethnic minority group in Siberia]...[8]

It was the faces of these Buriats and part-Buriats that I saw among the numerous Oriental peoples – including Mongolians and Chinese – at the railroad station in Ulan-Ude that wintry day. The train stopped for only fifteen minutes before continuing its route around the southern tip of frozen Lake Baikal and on to Irkutsk, the capital of Eastern Siberia. My husband and I had been teaching at Far Eastern State University in Vladivostok during the previous semester, and now we were headed for our next assignment at Irkutsk State University. At the time, I thought my brief glimpse of Ulan-Ude and its exotic-looking inhabitants would be all I'd ever see of this particular part of Siberia.

Ulan-Ude, capital of the Eastern Buriats

Ten days after arriving in Irkutsk we were on the train again, travelling eastward back to Ulan-Ude to speak at a World Bank conference there. And it was in Ulan-Ude that I had my first contact with Buriat people, an encounter which ultimately piqued my interest in learning more about Buriat history, customs, and cuisine.

The capital of the Buriat Autonomous Republic, Ulan-Ude grew from a fort established in 1648 near the confluence of the Selenga and Uda rivers, into one of the major cities in southern Siberia by the mid-twentieth century. Today its population numbers 400,000, of which approximately 21 per cent are Buriats.[9] Originally named Verkhneudinsk (Upper Udinsk, in Russian, because of its location on the Uda River), its name was changed to Ulan-Ude (Red Ude, in Mongolian) during the early Soviet era. An industrial city known for its large locomotive plant and railway repair workshops, Ulan-Ude was off-limits to most foreigners until the early 1990s, primarily because of its strategic location on the Trans-Siberian Railroad and because of several military sites nearby. The city still has a number of its old wooden buildings; it also boasts an opera house, a ballet company, and several good museums, including an open-air ethnographic museum considered to be among the best in Russia. About twenty miles from Ulan-Ude is the Ivolginskii Datsan (monastery), the center of Buddhism in Russia.

We arrived in the city after an overnight train ride from Irkutsk. The weather was typical for the last day of January in southern Siberia: 42 degrees below zero (Celsius), with hazy sunlight and very little wind. Although we stayed in the city's newest and best hotel, we (as official guests of the regional government) ate all of our meals at a state-run *stolovaia* (canteen) two blocks away on the main square. This cafeteria-style dining facility was inside the government headquarters building of the Buriat Autonomous Republic (which still displayed its old bronze plaque identifying it as a 'Soviet Socialist Republic'). In front of the building – and dominating the central square – was a monumental bronze head of Lenin, the largest in the world.

Food at the canteen was what I had come to expect at such establishments: meaty, starchy, filling, and functional (although the quality was somewhat higher than average, probably because the government wanted to make a good impression on the conference participants who ate there). Breakfast, however, was worth noting: squares of fluffy baked eggs, slightly sweetened; yeasty white buns, fresh and hot from the oven; slices of densely textured Russian brown bread; large squares of white *tvorog* (similar to farmer's cheese or pot cheese) garnished with rich, thick *smetana* (sour cream) and sprinkled with sugar; leftover meats (hot and cold) from the previous day's meals; and chunky glasses of black tea liberally laced with milk.

That first morning in Ulan-Ude, several of our Russian colleagues from Irkutsk expressed great pleasure at being served this 'Buriat tea.' A Buriat student overheard their comments and later informed me that the canteen's tea, although admittedly tasty, was not authentic 'Buriat tea.' According to him, Russians call any tea diluted with milk 'Buriat tea' – whereas the Buriats themselves have specific methods of making tea that include other ingredients besides milk.

The Mongols are credited with introducing Russians to tea in 1638 when the Mongol Khan sent a gift of tea to the Russian court, where the foreign substance was received less than enthusiastically.[10]

According to Lincoln:

> Although often thought of (aside from vodka) as the Russian national beverage, tea did not become an important part of upper-class Russian life until the 1770s and 1780s. Before that, it was consumed more in Siberia than in Russia and was bought by the merchants of Kiakhta mainly in the form of hard-packed bricks, which the Siberians infused with mutton fat, salt, and rye meal.[11]

John Bell of Antermony was a British physician who travelled across Siberia between 1719 and 1721 on his way to and from China. His account of the journey, entitled *Travels from St Petersburg in Russia to Diverse Parts of Asia*, was published in 1763. Near Verkhneudinsk (Ulan-Ude) he met a group of Buriats and wrote detailed notes about their manners and customs. His description of the Buriat method of making tea remains one of the most authentic recipes in English for the preparation of this traditional Buriat drink:

> Our horses having swum the river, we went into one of the Buratsky tents [yurts] till they were dried. The hospitable landlady immediately set her kettle on the fire, to make us some tea; the extraordinary cookery of which I cannot omit describing. After placing a large iron kettle over the fire, she took care to wipe it very clean with a horse's tail, that hung in a corner of the tent for that purpose; then water was poured into it, and, soon after, some coarse bohea tea [black tea] which is got from China, and a little salt. When near boiling, she took a large brass-ladle and tossed the tea, till the liquor turned very brown. It was now taken off the fire, and, after subsiding a little, was poured clear into another vessel... The mistress now prepared a paste of meal and fresh butter, which was poured into the tea kettle and fried. Upon this paste tea was again poured; to which was added some good thick cream, taken out of a clean sheep's skin. The ladle was again employed, for the space of six minutes, when the tea, being removed from the fire, was allowed to stand a while in order to cool. The landlady now took some wooden cups, which held about half a pint each, and served her tea to all the company. The principal advantage of this tea is that it both satisfies hunger and quenches thirst. I thought it not disagreeable; but should have liked it much better had it been prepared in a manner a little more cleanly.[12]

The Russian explorer Colonel Nicholas Przhevalski, who travelled in Mongolia in the 1870s and 1880s, was even less favorably impressed than Bell about the way the Mongols made tea:

> The mode of preparation is disgusting...the vessel in which the tea is boiled is never cleansed, and is occasionally scrubbed with *argols*, ie dried horse or cow dung. Salt water is generally used but, if unobtainable, salt is added. The tea is then pared off with a knife or pounded in a mortar and a handful of it thrown into the boiling water to which a few cups of milk are added. To soften the brick tea which is sometimes as hard as a rock, it is placed for a few moments among hot *argols* which impart a flavour and aroma to the beverage. This is the first process, and in this form answers the same purpose as chocolate or coffee with us. For a more substantial meal the Mongol mixes dry roasted millet in his cup and as a final relish adds a lump of butter or raw sheep tail fat. The reader may now imagine what a revolting compound of nastiness is produced, and yet they consume any quantity of it![13]

Przhevalski added that the Mongols drank twenty to thirty cups of this tea each day.[14]

According to G. Tsyndynzhapov and E. Badueva, the authors of *Buriatskaia kukhnia (Buriat Cuisine)*, milk is the most important ingredient in making Buriat tea, and Buriats never drink their tea without it. They also point out that the Buriats have a saying, 'Tea with milk – for a friend!' since the serving of tea is an important part of Buriat hospitality 'where the door is always open to friends, strangers, and everyone who comes with open hearts to our homes.'[15]

In Ulan-Ude at the conference where I first heard the term 'Buriat tea,' my husband and I spoke in front of an audience peopled with more Oriental-looking faces than European ones. And at the buffet-style meal that capped the first day of the symposium, we found ourselves in the company of many of these same people, several of whom were taller and broader shouldered than other Orientals we had seen before.[16] As the conference participants stood around the heavily laden tables waiting for a signal to begin the feast,[17] one of them – a tall, bulky Buriat man in a gray-green suit one size too small – picked up a bottle of Russian champagne. Had I been making a film about Genghis Khan, I would not have hesitated to cast him in the leading role. In one swift move, he tore the metal foil off the top of the bottle and untwisted the wire, letting the plastic cork pop out with such force that it struck and shattered a light fixture over the table. Laughing loudly, he began swilling champagne, while the other people – apparently unperturbed about the debris that had fallen into the food – took this as a cue to start filling their plates. Later in the evening I spotted Genghis Khan plundering the leftovers, stuffing sandwiches, fruits, and cold meats into his pockets, no doubt for an after-dinner snack.[18]

Ust'-Orda, capital of the Western Buriats

Three months later we had an opportunity to attend another World Bank conference, this one in Ust'-Orda, the capital of the Buriat district west of Lake Baikal.[19] Smaller than the Buriat Republic, this 'autonomous district' within the Irkutsk regional administrative area is located about forty miles north of the city of Irkutsk. Although the district contains 79 'nationalities' (ethnic groups), 36 per cent of the population is Buriat.[20]

When we first visited this home of the Western Buriats, the winter snows had already melted but spring had not yet arrived. Strong winds blew across arid landscapes reminiscent of west Texas or the high plains of Wyoming and Montana. Mineral salt deposits streaked the surface of the steppes like sweat marks on silk. In small villages rows of unpainted wooden houses lined the narrow dirt streets. Everywhere we looked, the dominant color was brown.

Ust'-Orda, the largest town in the district, has a population of 13,000, most of whom live in traditional one-story, Russian-style wooden houses.[21] Many of them are farmers and stockmen; indeed, the Buriats are Siberia's cowboys (in fur hats instead of Stetsons). Cattle and horses wander down the unpaved streets, and clouds of dust fill the air. Except for a couple of paved roads, a few Soviet-era multi-story buildings, and a central square with a statue of Lenin, Ust'-Orda today looks much like it did when another American, Jeremiah Curtin, visited there almost a century ago.[22] It reminded me of sepia-toned photographs of small towns in the American West in the late 1800s.

While I was in Ust'-Orda I visited the local ethnographic museum, which has an interesting collection of Buriat folk art, tools, clothing, and jewelry, in addition to a display of traditional Buriat kitchen utensils, many of them wooden ones designed specifically for making the milk products that are central to Buriat cuisine. My guides and translators were Terry Alekseevevich Batagaev, an uncle of the chief government official of the district, and Elizaveta (Liza) Alekseevna Alekseeva, a local teacher of English – both of whom are of Buriat descent. Terry (who insisted on being called by his Anglicized first name) explained the function of a strange-looking tool in the museum: a large, two-pronged fork, wrought of iron, which was used for digging up the roots of *sarani*, wild lilies that grow in abundance in parts of Siberia during the summer. Terry recalled eating these roots during World War II when food was scarce – and he added that many people would have starved without this source of nourishment.[23]

Upon learning of my interest in Buriat cuisine, Liza arranged for me to interview her mother, Sof'ia Petrovna Garankina, a 72-year-old Buriat who was a retired geography teacher and a knowledgeable source of information about Buriat foods. When Sof'ia Petrovna arrived at our meeting the next day, she was wearing a black dress, white crocheted shawl, white mink hat, and a long necklace made of red coral, a favored material used in crafting traditional Buriat jewelry (and formerly also used by the Buriats as a medium of exchange).

Sof'ia Petrovna was indeed a wealth of information about Buriat cuisine. She began by emphasizing the importance of climate in influencing Buriat customs and Buriat foods – a point also made by the authors of the cookbook, *Buriatskaia kukhnia*.[24] And she explained that milk and meat are the two most important categories of food for the Buriats.

Marco Polo said the same about Mongol cuisine in the description of his travels across Asia 700 years ago: 'They live on meat and milk and game and on Pharaoh's rats, which are abundant everywhere in the steppes. They have no objection to eating the flesh of horses and dogs and drinking mare's milk. In fact they eat flesh of any sort.'[25] Marco Polo also noted that when the Mongol army set out on a long expedition:

> they carry no baggage with them. They each carry two leather flasks to hold the milk they drink and a small pot for cooking meat... In case of need, they will ride a good ten days' journey without provisions and without making a fire, living only on the blood of their horses; for every rider pierces a vein of his horse and drinks the blood. They also have their dried milk, which is solid like paste; and this is how they dry it. First they bring the milk to the boil. At the appropriate moment they skim off the cream that floats on the surface and put it in another vessel to be made into butter, because so long as it remained the milk could not be dried. Then they stand the milk in the sun and leave it to dry. When they are going on an expedition, they take about ten pounds of this milk; and every morning they take out about half a pound of it and put it in a small leather flask, shaped like a gourd, with as much water as they please. Then, while they ride, the milk in the flask dissolves into a fluid, which they drink. And this is their breakfast.[26]

According to both Sof'ia Petrovna and the authors of *Buriatskaia kukhnia*, dishes made from milk occupy first place in the 'national cuisine' of the Buriats. Buriats greet guests with milk and other milk-based dishes (a custom called *sagaalkha* in the Buriat language) in the same way that Russians greet guests with bread and salt. The Buriat writer Afrikana Bal'burova also noted that Buriats have a very old custom of putting milk products, including sour cream and sweet cream, on the table as a way of greeting guests.[27]

Sof'ia Petrovna described to me a number of Buriat milk-based drinks and dishes with (to me) strange-sounding names:[28]

- *Uurag*: a kind of flat cake made from coarsely ground flour, a little salt, and beestings (cow's colostrum), the protein-rich milk taken from a cow three to four days after the birth of its calf in the spring; the cake is baked in a heavy cast-iron pan, cut into wedges, served with melted butter, and accompanied by milky tea.
- *Urmen*: clotted cream made from whole milk (the fatter, the better) heated slowly in a wide, shallow pan (preferably cast iron), then placed in a cool place for 12 hours; the resulting 11/2- to 2-centimeter-thick 'skin' of white clotted cream that forms on the top is *urmen,* which is then removed and eaten as is; or salted and aged (during which time it yellows slightly); or preserved by drying (in summer) or freezing (in winter). Ten liters of milk will produce one kilogram of *urmen*.[29]
- *Tarag*: a thick, soured-milk drink similar to kefir and cultured buttermilk, made by adding a souring agent[30] to the milk remaining after the cream has been skimmed off; the *tarag* can be enriched before serving by the addition of sour cream or whole milk. Guests arriving at Buriat homes are often greeted with bowls of *tarag*, a refreshing drink.
- *Tarasun*: 'The Buriats' wine,' a clear, rather potent, alcoholic beverage distilled from milk and with the strength of sherry or other fortified wines.[31]

•*Aarsan*: a drink made from the thick mass that is left after distilling *tarasun* from milk; the mass is mixed with water and flour, boiled, and then enriched with more milk, fresh cream, or sour cream. It may be consumed hot or cold. Buriats say that this refreshing and nourishing milk drink is indispensable during hay-making time, and as a pick-me-up whenever the weather is hot (July and August).[32]

But I was most surprised by Sof'ia Petrovna's description of Buriat *salamat*[33] – a kind of porridge made by boiling sour cream in a cast-iron pot, then slowly adding flour (usually rye),[34] cooking over low heat until the butter separates from the milk solids, and continuing to cook until the mass is creamy, smooth, and thick. The rich porridge, often garnished with melted butter, is a Buriat favorite. *Salamat* is served on important occasions or as a special treat – for guests, for children, for convalescents, and particularly for nursing mothers. According to Sof'ia Petrovna, it is an old Buriat custom that when the *salamat* is ready – but before anyone eats a spoon of it – a small amount is tossed into the fire as an offering to the gods.

I immediately recognized this Buriat *salamat* as being the same as *rømmegrøt*, the sour cream porridge that is considered to be a 'national dish' of Norway, served for special occasions (weddings, baptisms, funerals), on holidays (especially in the summer), and to nursing mothers. But subsequent inquiries to food experts in Norway turned up no recorded connection between Norwegian *rømmegrøt* and Buriat *salamat*.[35] Likewise, none of my Buriat sources (nor my Russian ones) had ever heard of *rømmegrøt*. It would be interesting to determine whether these two 'national dishes' – widely separated geographically, but the same in ingredients, techniques, and taste – have any historical connection at all, or whether, as is more likely, they developed independently in these two countries where dairy products are such an important part of the cuisines.[36]

Among the traditional Buriat meat dishes that Sof'ia Petrovna described to me, one of the most appealing was *buuza* (*pozy* in Russian), steamed meat-filled dumplings very similar to ones that are popular all across Asia from Turkey to Japan.[37] Buriat *buuza* are made from an unleavened dough of flour, water, eggs, and salt, wrapped around a filling of ground meat (mutton, pork, beef, or horsemeat – which can be used singly or in combination) mixed with onion, garlic, black pepper or hot red pepper, and sometimes milk. The *buuza* are formed by hand into spheres, with the edges of the dough drawn together at the top and a small opening left at the top of each dumpling. They are steamed in a multi-layer pot called a *poznitsa,* which functions like a set of Chinese stacking bamboo steamers, but which is made of metal and has a tube through the center of each layer to circulate steam from the bottom of the pan to the top. To eat a *buuza,* you first drink the meat juices from the hole in the top, then bite into the *buuza* itself. Sof'ia Petrovna pointed out that among the Eastern Buriats *buuza* are prepared by the men, but among the Western Buriats women assist the men in making these dumplings.

From my own point of view, the least appetizing Buriat dish that Sof'ia Petrovna described to me is similar in appearance to chocolate-vanilla pinwheel cookies in the West, but is made from raw horse liver (for the dark part) and raw horse fat (for the light part). In Buriat villages several families join together in purchasing a horse, which they feed specially to fatten it for slaughter. The horse is killed in December – and, among its meat products shared by the collective owners, is a delicacy made from the fat and liver. The raw liver is sliced very thin and topped with a thin piece of the best yellow-white fat (*arbin*). The double layer is then rolled up (like pinwheel cookie dough) and put outside (in a place protected from hungry animals) to freeze solid in the Siberian winter. To eat this liver-fat assemblage, the Buriats cut the roulade crosswise into thin slices (hence my visual analogy to pinwheel cookies) and eat it raw, garnished with raw onion, garlic, and salt. Sof'ia Petrovna said that one horse liver, prepared and preserved in this manner, was sufficient for the several families who had bought into the horse. According to her, these raw liver roulades, which stay frozen throughout the winter, are eaten mainly in the spring, for reasons of health, by people who are anemic or who have bad eyesight. I got the distinct impression, however, that raw horse liver layered with fat was considered to be a tasty delicacy by many Buriats, regardless of their state of health.[38]

At the end of our interview, I gave Sof'ia Petrovna and her daughter each a small gift which I hoped would be appropriate for these descendants of the famed and feared Mongol horsemen: a tooled-copper picture of a galloping mare and foal, their manes streaming in the wind. The pictures had been crafted in my own native land of Texas which, in some places, is not unlike the lands inhabited by these Buriat-Mongols of Siberia.

The official conference in Ust'-Orda concluded with a banquet for fifty people in the dining hall of the district government – a room whose walls were decorated with stylized horses and Buriat motifs made of wood and brushed metal. The meal, which began at half past noon, consisted of a jumble of courses, with heavy emphasis on meat dishes, accompanied by tumblers of champagne and innumerable toasts with glasses of vodka. Before each Buriat knocked back a glass of vodka, he dipped the third finger of his right hand into the liquor and flicked a small amount of liquid into the air, or shook a drop or two on to the table. One man always tapped his finger on the right lapel of his suit coat.[39] These were gestures that we had seen before, not only among Buriats but also among some of the ethnic Russians in Irkutsk and Ulan-Ude. The act was meant as an offering to 'Burkhan,' the god or spirit of Lake Baikal and of the lands adjacent to it.[40] No vodka was drunk without this ritual first being performed.

The meal started with a plate of sliced fresh tomatoes and Russian *kolbasa* sausage, followed by a soup made of beef and beef broth, potatoes, onions, pickled red peppers, and paprika. Next was a large meatball accompanied by mashed potatoes, followed by a plate of stir-fried beef, onions, and pickled red peppers garnished with pickled cabbage. Dessert arrived in the form of a flaky pastry made with lard, shaped like a French *palmier*, accompanied by a glass of milky tea. Before we could even finish dessert, the waitresses put plates of sliced fresh cucumbers on the table, then platters of sausage, followed by stir-fried meat and onion strips, then another round of meatballs and potatoes – all accompanied by more bottles of vodka and champagne. Toast after toast, we gulped down the vodka in the name of international friendship, personal goodwill, everyone's health, and future prosperity – always after making the expected offering to Burkhan. We left the banquet at 3:30 that afternoon, stuffed to the gills and barely able to stand on our feet. The Buriats were still going strong, singing songs in their native language and ordering more rounds of vodka. We later learned that the banquet had continued for another twelve hours, until 3:30 the next morning!

The day of four feasts

Knowing my interest in Buriat foods – and in gratitude for some assistance I had given in providing educational materials for her school – Elizaveta Alekseevna (Liza) invited my husband and me to return to Ust'-Orda in late June of that year, to sample traditional Buriat cuisine. We were told only that someone would pick us up early in the morning in Irkutsk and drive us to Ust'-Orda – and that a 'full day' was planned for us.

Liza and a Buriat driver arrived in Irkutsk at 8:30 a.m. During the one-and-a-half-hour drive to Ust'-Orda, Liza told me the story of her family: how they lost their house and lands during the forced collectivization of the 1930s, how some of the men disappeared into the gulag, how her grandmother managed to hide some of her jewelry when the Communists confiscated all their household goods and personal property. Her family, which had lived in a rural area north of Irkutsk, had been forced, like so many others, to move from their own village into a designated town, in this case Ust'-Orda.[41] Without looking directly at me, Liza told the story quietly, dispassionately, as if such topics were matter-of-fact, daily fare. But she glanced at me occasionally as if to ascertain whether I really understood this hidden history revealed, these events that people had dared not mention for decades, and which, even today, some people still suppress or deny. As I listened to her stories, I felt like we were travelling through time across a landscape that had been ravaged by rulers from the Communist collectivizers all the way back to the Mongol khans.

Since my last trip to Ust'-Orda in April, the land itself had changed from the sere browns so reminiscent of west Texas into the lush greens of grasslands and rye fields that made me think of Germany. Here, as elsewhere in southern Siberia, summer had suddenly burst on to the scene, without the slow transition of a gradually blooming spring. Yet even that day in June the overcast sky and occasional drizzle tempered the enthusiasms of the season and hinted of winter storms to come.

The route to Ust'-Orda took us near the village where the log house of Liza's family had once been located, before they were driven off their land and the house sold to someone more acceptable to Stalin's regime. (The purchaser had dismantled the house and transported it elsewhere, to be reassembled.) We also passed a couple of old Russian Orthodox churches now being restored, a small Buddhist temple set back from the road, and – simplest yet most impressive of all – a pagan shrine, an *oboo*, consisting of two very tall poles with a horse's tail attached to the top of each one. The poles and connecting crosspiece were covered with strips of colored cloth that had been tied to them, and small offerings had been placed at the shrine: pieces of sausage and bread, cigarettes, a jar half full of some kind of homemade sauce, even coins and paper money. Empty vodka bottles littered the ground all around.

In less than forty miles, we had encountered symbols of the three very different belief systems (four, counting Communism) that had vied for the Buriats' allegiance over the centuries. Originally believers in a number of god-spirits who inhabited the earth, the water, and the sky, many southern and eastern Buriats converted to Buddhism in the mid-seventeenth century, whereas western and northern Buriats tended to remain pagan or converted, often only superficially, to Russian Orthodoxy.[42] When I asked Buriats in both Ust'-Orda and Ulan-Ude how many of their people were Buddhists, the answer was often a sideways glance and, in a quiet voice, the reply, 'Some... But of course we have our own religion, shamanism.'[43]

When I asked Liza why the shrine on the way to Ust'-Orda was situated in that particular (nondescript and rather desolate) spot, she answered that a shaman had chosen the location. To her, that seemed to be explanation enough. I had seen similar but smaller and less impressive shrines on the shores of Lake Baikal, in the Siberian forest, and on the steppes near Ulan-Ude. But this *oboo* in western Buriatia struck a primordial chord in me. Each time that I passed it on the way to and from Ust'-Orda, I felt the presence of something primitive, as if I were recalling memories formed centuries before I was born.

We arrived in Ust'-Orda at ten o'clock that morning and went directly to the official government dining hall for breakfast. Although there were only three of us – Liza, my husband, and me – the table was set for a formal dinner for twelve, with the best dishes, flatware, and linens available. As we dined on fresh tomatoes and cucumbers, buns known as *shan'gi* (made from Liza's own recipe),[44] sliced sausages, raw *omul* (fish from Lake Baikal),[45] milky tea, and the inevitable vodka, Liza outlined the day's culinary schedule. She felt obliged to advise us that in the afternoon something special was planned: we could choose to be present for the event or we could, of course, be excused from watching it, whichever we wished. When my husband quietly asked me what she was talking about, I whispered to him, 'The Buriats are going to kill a sheep for us, in the traditional manner. The sheep is going to die whether we watch or not – so we might as well be present.' My husband put down his forkful of raw fish and reached for a swallow of vodka, while I informed Liza that we would be honored to attend all the events planned for us that day.

The first stop after breakfast was at the headquarters of the District Education Committee, where it finally became clear to us that our trip to Ust'-Orda was at least partially sponsored by that organization. We met the chairman of the committee who, after making a formal speech to the two of us, surprised me with a set of jade-and-silver-filigree jewelry made in a traditional Buriat style, and presented my husband with a cow's horn drinking cup decorated with Buriat metalwork. After such largesse we could not politely refuse the offer of something to eat and drink: rich chocolate candies accompanied by cups of black coffee and glasses of cognac. At eleven o'clock in the morning, however, this combination of caffeine, sugar, and alcohol did not sit well on the raw fish and vodka that we had consumed for breakfast shortly before.

At the Education Committee headquarters we were joined by Terry Batagaev, the English-speaking Buriat who had been one of our escorts during our first visit to Ust'-Orda. Together with Terry, Liza, and two drivers, we travelled in two cars to a former Pioneer camp (similar to our Scout camps) several miles from Ust'-Orda, where we were scheduled for a midday meal of typical Buriat foods. About halfway to our destination, at a spot where we could see nothing but forest on either side of the road, both cars stopped. 'This is "Three Pines",' Terry said, 'a sacred place for Buriats. Buriat people always stop here when they pass this way.'

I looked around at the forest, but no three particular pines stood out from the hundreds of trees surrounding us. 'Why is it called "Three Pines", and why is it sacred?' I asked. (I was always asking 'Why?' in Russia – a question that most people were reluctant to answer.) 'Because the shaman said so,' replied Terry, as if that explained everything.[46]

Out came the vodka bottles. We clambered up a steep muddy embankment, through dense wet undergrowth, until we reached a place on the edge of the forest. 'This is it…I think,' Terry said. Nothing distinguished this spot from any other that I could see. Terry poured the vodka, and we all performed the ritual of dipping our finger into the glass and sprinkling some of the alcohol into the air as an offering to Burkhan. Then we stood around in rather uncomfortable silence until Terry suddenly said, 'Okay, time to go.'

A few miles down the highway, we turned off on to a road so deep in mud that we had to get out and stand aside while the drivers made several attempts to move the cars on to firmer ground. Finally leaving one car behind, we all got into the second car and bumped down the rutted, muddy track for about half a mile until we bogged down once more. Just then, as if out of a Fellini movie, a well-dressed Buriat woman in a tailored suit and high heels came walking toward us, with the news that the road was not passable beyond this point and that the truck bringing all the food supplies for our Buriat meal had not been able to get through to the Pioneer camp.

Terry was disappointed at this turn of events but, undaunted, we all got out of the car and walked the rest of the way to the camp. Despite the remoteness of the location and the lack of special food supplies, the camp's cook had prepared a copious and delicious meal: fresh fish, stewed chicken, and fried potatoes; a salad of finely chopped red radishes, green onion tops, and wild garlic; plenty of Russian brown bread, plus a special fried bread made from a Kirghiz recipe; and commercial chocolates for dessert. Pitchers of Kool-Aid-colored *sok* (watery, artificially flavored 'fruit' juice) were ignored in favor of bottles of Russian champagne. As we sat under two large handpainted banners – PRIIATNOGO APPETITA! (*Bon Appetit!* in Russian) and WELCOME (in English) – our hosts presented us with more gifts: a Russian wrist watch for me and a decorative ceramic samovar for my husband, plus a bottle of champagne and a bottle of vodka (which we promptly opened and passed around the table, as was obviously expected of us).

Barely able to stay awake after so much booze, we toured the Pioneer camp, then boarded a large Russian four-wheel-drive vehicle which succeeded in getting us back to the two cars waiting at the highway. On the way back to Ust'-Orda, we had to stop again at the sacred spot of the three pines to make an offering to Burkhan (and consume another round of vodka). Fortunately Terry didn't insist that we climb the embankment this time; apparently a roadside offering was sufficient for Burkhan, especially at this stage of our own fatigue and tipsiness.

It was four o'clock in the afternoon when we came to the home of the Tabikhanovs, a Buriat family in Ust'-Orda. Husband, wife, five children, and a grandmother lived in a typical Russian-style, single-story wooden house very similar to farmhouses that I remembered from my childhood in Texas in the 1950s. As we started through the door, someone warned us not to step on the threshold: to do so would bring bad luck.[47] However, the Buriats were pleased that it was raining when we arrived, for they consider it a good omen when guests bring wet weather with them.

The house was spotlessly clean, with blue-washed walls, Russian furniture, and a graceful, Oriental-looking peaked archway leading into the kitchen.[48] Although the house had electricity, there was no running water, and the toilet was located outdoors in a privy next to the barn.[49] To my surprise the Tabikhanovs had three cookstoves: a gas stove, hooked up to a large orange gas cannister, in the entry hall; a modern Russian electric stove in the kitchen; and a traditional Russian stove, used both for cooking and for heating the house, built into the kitchen itself.

After we had removed our shoes in the entry hall and changed into slippers, Olia Tabikhanova, the grandmother, greeted us in the traditional Buriat manner by presenting each of us with a bowl of *tarag*, a cool, refreshing, and (thankfully) non-alcoholic soured-milk drink. Under other circumstances I would have been better able to appreciate its taste and restorative properties. But soured milk was not the best substance to add to a stomach already brimming with vodka, cognac, and champagne.

As soon as we had finished drinking the *tarag*, we all went outdoors to watch the slaughter of the sheep. Rodion Tabikhanov led a ewe from his barn into the enclosed yard behind the house. He flipped the ewe on her back, swiftly made an incision in her breast, and reached inside with one hand to stop her heart. This is the Buriats' traditional method of slaughter, the way that they (and the Mongols) have killed their cattle, sheep, and even horses over the centuries.[50]

We watched as Rodion and his three sons butchered the sheep, first cutting off the forelegs and hind legs at the lowest joint, then gradually removing the sheepskin in one piece. The method of slaughter ensures that little blood is lost, and the carcass is butchered in such a way as to preserve as much blood as possible, to be collected and used in making one of the specialties of the feast. As the men proceeded to cut up the sheep, the women of the family worked on processing the innards. When the sheep's liver was removed, fresh and steaming, from the carcass, the raw liver was cut into chunks and distributed among all of us as a special treat. I have to admit that I busied myself with taking photographs at that point, but my husband could not avoid the inevitable. He saved face for both of us by picking up a piece of raw liver, sprinkling it with salt, and managing to swallow it, all the while smiling and saying how good it tasted.[51]

The sheep's heart, lungs, and trachea were removed in one piece and hung from a nail on the outside of the barn. The stomach and intestines were taken out and washed in cold water, while the muscle meat and the bones were thrown into an iron cauldron of boiling water, set over a wood fire. Soon the sheep's head – unskinned, with wool and eyeballs still intact – was placed next to the fire, to singe the wool a bit, before being thrown into the pot with the rest of the animal. Occasionally the grandmother also tossed a tiny piece of raw meat or innards into the fire itself, as did two other Buriat men who showed up to help with the butchering. When I asked Terry why they were doing that, he said they were making a gift to the gods and that, in earlier times, people knew the prayers they were supposed to say when making such offerings. I could see the grandmother mumbling something each time she tossed a piece into the fire, and I suspected that she, of all the Buriats present, was the only one who really knew the appropriate thing to say.[52]

During all of this activity outdoors, we and the Buriats drank mugs of *tarasun*, the potent clear liquor distilled from sour milk (and with a distinct aroma of soured milk). The ritual associated with drinking *tarasun* was one that I had not observed before. When someone was first given a mug of *tarasun*, he dipped the third finger of his right hand into the liquor and tossed some of it into the air or into the fire. Then he took one swallow from the mug and passed it someone else, who repeated the process. After that the mug was returned to the first person, who could then drink the rest of its contents.[53] All the Buriats were quaffing large quantities of this strong stuff as if it were water, and they were amused that my husband and I were unable to match them mug for mug. The family matriarch was the hardiest drinker of all. While processing innards and eating raw liver, she downed huge amounts of *tarasun*, which did not seem to affect her in the least.[54]

When the meat was cooked, we all went indoors and crowded around a large dining table in the living room. By that time there were twelve adults in our party; the five children ate in the kitchen or carried plates of food back to the bedrooms. There were no napkins at the place settings, but the hostess ceremoniously draped a large towel across our laps, for my husband and me to share. Bottles of vodka, Russian champagne, and Bulgarian white wine stood at each end of the table.

After our Buriat host offered the first toast, welcoming us to his house, we began the meal with appetizers of sliced sausage, fresh *omul* (raw), sliced fresh tomatoes and cucumbers, and thick, chewy white bread. These were followed by a soup course of hot mutton broth drunk from bowls. Before the broth was served, I noticed grandmother going outside to toss a small cup of it into the fire. Vodka and wine glasses kept being refilled, as we toasted our hosts and they drank to our friendship. Then we, as the honored guests, were served the most important part of the feast. The entire sheep's head, wool and eyeballs still attached, was placed in front of my husband. Terry explained that it was traditional for the guest to sing a special song about the sheep's head;[55] however, since my husband was not a Buriat and did not know any sheep's head songs, we moved on to the next ritual. He was given a hunting knife and instructed to cut off the sheep's left ear, to cut a cross on the top of the head, and to cut out a piece of the right cheek. Our host took the ear and cheek and went outside to throw them as an offering into the fire.

Then it was my turn. Placed in front of me was the sheep's stomach, which had been filled with a mixture of fresh cow's milk, fresh sheep's blood, garlic, and spring onions, tied up with the sheep's intestines, and boiled in the pot with the rest of the meat. I told myself that – despite all the food and alcohol I had already consumed that day – I was going to eat this thing without throwing up. I couldn't insult a group of people who had been so kind and generous to me. All the Buriats around the table waited expectantly for me to take the first bite. But I didn't know where to begin. Finally our hostess leaned over and sliced the top off the stomach. The contents had not been fully cooked and blood oozed out onto my plate. She took a large spoon, scooped out some of the semi-coagulated mass, and handed the spoonful to me. Trying to focus my mind on something else – anything else – far away, I swallowed the junket-like lump and forced a smile.[56]

The other guests still waited for me to make the next move. And suddenly it occurred to me: pass the dish around. That's exactly what they wanted. The Buriats happily and hungrily scooped out and devoured big portions of the blood pudding, while my husband and I concentrated on the huge platter of boiled mutton in the middle of the table. More vodka. More toasts. Declarations of friendship. Buriat songs. More vodka. More wine. More champagne.

Our hosts presented me with a large purple paisley shawl and my husband with a brown plaid shirt (like we had seen on Buriat cowboys near Ust'-Orda). We offered our own gifts in return, including a box of Belgian chocolates which the grandmother promptly opened and passed around the table before taking a piece for herself. The Buriats gave me a bottle of wine and my husband a bottle of vodka, both of which were shortly opened and consumed by all. I was hoping the food and alcohol would soon run out, but there was still plenty of boiled mutton on the table and a whole cauldron of mutton broth outside. When we protested that we couldn't eat another mouthful of their fine feast, the Buriats merely laughed, claiming that in the old days one sheep would not have been enough for twelve people: at least three sheep would have been needed to feed such a gathering. Just at that moment, grandmother came out of the kitchen and placed in front of us large bowls of sour-cream *salamat* bathed in melted butter – which we were not allowed to eat until she had put an offering of *salamat* into the fire.[57]

We had been at this feast for only five hours when Terry announced that it was time to leave for the *next* meal – at the home of Liza and her mother, Sof'ia Petrovna, the woman who had provided me so much information about traditional Buriat cuisine. Sick from so much food and alcohol, we just wanted to crawl away and hide somewhere, but we knew we couldn't disappoint them. So at nine o'clock that evening, we thanked the Tabikhanovs and bade them farewell, climbed into the car and bounced down the rutted, muddy streets to Sof'ia Petrovna's house, all the while trying mightily to keep down the meal we had just eaten.

The last feast of that long day remains only a blur in my memory. I recall a beautifully set table in a cheerful and immaculate kitchen. I remember cups of tea being poured, fresh vegetables from the garden outside, rich rounds of creamy *urmen*, tales of Buriat ancestors, a family photo album, a bottle of sweet berry liqueur that turned out to be an excellent *digestif*. I could have spent days in that house in Ust'-Orda, listening to Sof'ia Petrovna's stories of Buriat history, Buriat customs, and Buriat foods. But finally it was time to go.

Liza, our companion for that entire unforgettable day, insisted on seeing us safely home – for her, a round-trip journey of three hours, very late at night. On the way back to Irkutsk we were all too tired for much conversation. But I did learn that in August she would be taking a group of eighteen school children from Ust'-Orda to London to study English for two weeks. Liza's only other trip abroad had been to next-door Mongolia, and none of the children had ever been outside of Russia at all. While in England, they were planning to stay in the homes of several British families. As we drove across the steppes on that Siberian summer night, I wondered what kind of feasts the children of Ust'-Orda would encounter when they travelled to a strange and different land halfway around the globe. I trusted that the British would give them as warm a welcome as the Buriats had shown to us.

Postscript

Six months later, back in the United States, I read Jeremiah Curtin's account of his two-month visit to Ust'-Orda and the lands of the Western Buriats at the turn of the century. Only after having lived in Siberia could I truly appreciate the conclusion to his narrative:

> We left Usturdi September 13. I was glad to go from the Buriat country, where, though
> I had gained considerable knowledge, we had endured many hardships.

Curtin arrived in Irkutsk after a two-day journey, having travelled the same route that took us only ninety minutes by car almost a century later:

> That evening I dined with the governor of Irkutsk, and went with him to the opera. In
> this quick change from life among the Buriats to the refinements of civilized life in the
> capital of Siberia, I experienced the striking results of some centuries of social evolution
> – an evolution which through its effects upon humanity enables the man of cities to
> step back in a moment and with no mental effort from the wild, free life of fancy to the
> prescribed surroundings of material facts.[58]

ACKNOWLEDGEMENTS

I would like to say a special word of thanks to the following people for their assistance in providing information for this paper: *In Siberia:* Sof'ia Petrovna Garankina, Elizaveta Alekseevna Alekseeva, Terry Alekseevich Batagaev, the Tabikhanov family. *In Norway:* Astri Riddervold, Aase Strømstad, Brita Edland, Torunn Linneberg. *In the United States:* Darra Goldstein, Birgitta Ingemanson, Charles Perry, Helen Hundley, Glenn Randall Mack, Monika Kajstura. Special thanks must also go to Tom Hudgins, good sport and intrepid traveller, who agreed to go to Russia with me in the first place, who accompanied me to the outback of Siberia and the Russian Far East in search of culinary information, and whose skills as a food shopper and creative cook greatly enhanced our life in Russia.

BIBLIOGRAPHY

Bobrick, Benson. *East of the Sun: The Epic Conquest and Tragic History of Siberia.* New York: Poseidon Press, 1992.

von Bremzen, Anya, and John Welchman. *Please to the Table: The Russian Cookbook.* New York: Workman Publishing Company, Inc., 1990.

Brown, Archie, et al., eds. *The Cambridge Encyclopedia of Russia and the Soviet Union.* Cambridge: Cambridge University Press, 1982.

Buriatiia: unikal'nye ob'ekty prirody. Russian map with historical, cultural, and geographical information about Buriatia. No publisher or date of publication indicated. Purchased by the author of this paper in Ulan-Ude, Buriatia, June 1994.

Burat's [sic] *Origin.* Unpublished manuscript, author unknown. Given to the author of this paper in Irkutsk, Russia, May 1994.

Chang, K. C., ed. *Food in Chinese Culture.* New Haven: Yale University Press, 1977.

Curtin, Jeremiah. *A Journey in Southern Siberia: The Mongols, Their Religion and Their Myths.* Boston: Little, Brown, and Company, 1909.

Custine, Astolphe, Marquis de. *Empire of the Czar: A Journey Through Eternal Russia* (1839). New York: Doubleday, 1989.

Dmitriev-Mamonov, A. I., and A. F. Zdsidrski, eds. *Guide to the Great Siberian Railway.* English translation by L. Kukol-Yasnopolsky, revised by John Marshall. St. Petersburg: Ministry of Ways of Communication, 1900.

Dorje, Rinjing. *Food in Tibetan Life.* London: Prospect Books, 1985.

Goldstein, Darra. 'The Eastern Influence on Russian Cuisine.' *Current Research in Culinary History: Sources, Topics, and Methods,* pp. 20-26. Boston: Culinary Historians of Boston, 1986.

Halici, Nevin. *Nevin Halici's Turkish Cookbook.* London: Dorling Kindersley, 1989.

der Haroutunian, Arto. *A Turkish Cookbook.* London: Edbury Press, 1987.

Hudgins, Sharon. 'Rømmegrøt: Buttery Porridge is Cream of Norway's Culinary Crop.' *The Stars and Stripes,* May 24, 1984, pp. 8-9.

Hudgins, Sharon. 'Spicy Siberia: Hot Foods in a Cold Climate.' *Chile Pepper Magazine,* Vol. IX, No. 6, November/December 1995, pp. 16-23, 34-36.

Kennan, George. *Tent Life in Siberia.* New York: Putnam, 1871.

Kennan, George. *Siberia and the Exile System, Vol. II.* New York: The Century Co., 1891.

Kotkin, Stephen, and David Wolff, eds. *Rediscovering Russia in Asia: Siberia and the Russian Far East.* Armonk, New York: M. E. Sharpe, 1995.

Lincoln, W. Bruce. *The Conquest of a Continent: Siberia and the Russians.* New York: Random House, 1994.

Matthiessen, Peter. *Baikal: Sacred Sea of Siberia.* San Francisco: Sierra Club Books, 1992.

McGee, Harold. *On Food and Cooking: The Science and Lore of the Kitchen.* New York: Charles Scribner's Sons, 1984.

Newby, Eric. *The Big Red Train Ride.* New York: St. Martin's Press, 1978.

Perry, Charles. 'The Horseback Kitchen of Central Asia.' Paper presented at Oxford Symposium on Food, 1996.

Pokhlëbkin, V. V. *O kulinarii ot a do Ia: slovar-spravochnik [About Cooking from A to Z: A Dictionary - Reference Book].* Minsk: Polyma, 1988.

Severin, Tim. *In Search of Genghis Khan*. New York: Atheneum, 1992.

Sokolov, Raymond. 'The Cream of the Crop.' *Natural History*, December 1987, pp. 80-83.

Starostina, L. A., and M. N. Vechtomova. *Bliuda iz tvoroga* [Dishes Made from Fresh Cheese]. Moscow: Ekonomika, 1986.

Stephan, John J. *The Russian Far East: A History*. Stanford, California: Stanford University Press, 1994.

Stobart, Tom. *The Cook's Encyclopedia: Ingredients and Processes*. New York: Harper and Row, Publishers, 1981.

Strauss, Robert. *Trans-Siberian Rail Guide* (2nd ed.). Chalfont St Peter: Bradt Publications, 1991.

Sutherland, Christine. *The Princess of Siberia: Maria Volkonsky and the Decembrist Exiles*. New York: Farrar Straus Giroux, 1984.

Tannahill, Reay. *Food in History* (new and rev. ed.). New York: Crown Publishers, Inc., 1988.

Thomas, Bryn. *Trans-Siberian Handbook* (3rd ed.). Hindhead, Surrey, UK: Trailblazer Publications, 1994.

Toomre, Joyce. *Classic Russian Cooking: Elena Molokhovets' A Gift to Young Housewives*. Translated, introduced, and annotated by Joyce Toomre. Bloomington, Indiana: Indiana University Press, 1992.

Toussaint-Samat, Maguelonne. *A History of Food*. Oxford, UK: Blackwell Publishers, 1992.

The Travels of Marco Polo. Translated and with an introduction by Ronald Latham. London: Penguin Books, 1958.

Troyat, Henri. *Daily Life in Russia Under the Last Tsar*. Stanford, California: Stanford University Press, 1979.

Tsyndynzhapov, G., and E. Badueva. *Buriatskaia kukhnia [Buriat Cuisine]*. Ulan-Ude: Buriatskoe Knizhnoe Izdatel'stvo, 1991.

Ust'-Ordynskii buryatskii avtonomnyi okrug [Ust'-Ordynskii Buriat Autonomous District]. Pamphlet issued by the district government of Ust'-Ordynskii. No publication date. Acquired by the author of this paper in Ust'-Orda, Ust'-Ordynskii, Russia, April 1994.

Volokh, Anne. *The Art of Russian Cuisine*. New York: Macmillan Publishing Company, 1983.

Wheeler, Marcus, and Boris Unbegaun. *The Oxford Russian Dictionary*. Oxford, UK: Oxford University Press, 1984.

Wixman, Ronald. *The Peoples of the USSR: An Ethnographic Handbook*. Armonk, New York: M. E. Sharpe, Inc., 1984.

Wood, Alan, and R. A. French, eds. *The Development of Siberia: People and Resources*. New York: St. Martin's Press, 1989.

NOTES

[1] The signs were written in the Buriat language, which is one of the Mongolic languages and is closely related to Mongol (Khalka) itself. (Wixman, p. 33) The Soviets decreed in 1936 that Cyrillic would replace the other alphabets of non-Russian peoples living in Soviet territory. (Bobrick, p. 455) See also James Forsyth, 'The Indigenous Peoples of Siberia in the Twentieth Century'. (Wood and French, pp. 82, 91) Despite inter-ethnic marriage and the Russification (or Russianization) of minority groups in Russia, 90.2 per cent of Buriats in 1979 claimed that Buriat was their native language, while 72 per cent claimed to be bilingual in Buriat and Russian. (Wood and French, p. 91)

[2] 'Mongol' was dropped from the name in 1958. (Newby, p. 196) Today the Buriat Republic has a population of more than one million, comprising 60 ethnic groups of which the Buriats are the largest non-Russian group.

[3] Bobrick, p. 444; *Cambridge Encyclopedia*, p. 69. Marjorie Mandelstam Balzer, in her article on 'A State Within a State: The Sakha Republic (Yakutia),' points out that 'Of the more than thirty non-Russian ethnically based political entities recognized as viable for parliamentary representation within Russia, seventeen are within Siberia and the Far East... Most of these are only regions or districts within the hierarchically organized matrioshkalike structure of Russia, but four – the Sakha [formerly Yakutia], Tyva, Buriat, and Komi republics (formerly misnamed 'autonomies') – have higher status.' (Kotkin and Wolff, pp. 140-141) According to my own sources in the Ust'-Ordynskii district, 90 per cent of the district's operating budget in 1994 came from Moscow, an indication of how closely tied this 'autonomous' district still is to the central power structure of the new Russian Federation.

[4] Quoted in Newby, p. 193.

[5] Lincoln, p. 51.

[6] Lincoln, p. 51; Bobrick, p. 36.

[7] Newby, pp. 193-194; Curtin, pp. 97-99.

[8] Lincoln, p. 52. According to Kotkin and Wolff (p. 133), 'In the eighteenth and especially nineteenth centuries, immigration from European Russia increased substantially. Greatly outnumbered, subjected to tribute payments and Russification, frequently maltreated and occasionally slaughtered, many indigenous communities nonetheless managed to grow in size. Others have largely or completely died out. Today, perhaps thirty-five native-peoples groups remain' – out of the estimated 120 different language communities encountered by the Russians when they first arrived in Northern Asia in the late sixteenth century. Caroline Humphrey, in 'Population Trends, Ethnicity, and Religion Among the Buryats,' points out that in more recent times 'There is a significant imbalance in the sexes of Buryats marrying other nationalities: men do so to a much greater extent than women.... The explanation for this is not entirely clear. Certainly the colonial pattern of men taking 'native wives' is absent.' (Wood and French, p. 162)

[9] Thomas, p. 181. In 1994 several ethnic Russian residents of Ulan-Ude told me that the city numbered half a million people, of whom 50 per cent were Buriats. This claim about the size of the Buriat population could be a function of the Russians' own perceptions (and/or prejudices) regarding the largest ethnic minority group in the city – or it could be a result of the great disparities between reality and published statistics in Russia, a problem from tsarist times through the Soviet period and still today. Under the Soviets, city population statistics were considered 'classified' information, even though western guide-books routinely published population statistics derived from western sources considered reasonably reliable.

[10] Toomre, p. 17. Other Eastern foods that were introduced by various Asian groups and eventually incorporated into Russian cuisine include pasta; salt- and vinegar-preserved vegetables; fermented milk products; lemons, raisins, apricots, figs, and watermelons; capsicum peppers; and spices such as cinnamon, saffron, cardamom, ginger, and black pepper. (Toomre, pp. 15-20; Goldstein, pp. 20-25) On the other hand, some of the Decembrists exiled from European Russia to Siberia in 1826 introduced barley, aspara–gus, artichokes, tomatoes, cucumbers, melons, cauliflowers, and red cabbage to the Transbaikal area. (Bobrick, p. 294; Sutherland, pp. 211, 215)

[11] Lincoln, p. 145. Kiakhta (which the Marquis de Custine referred to as situated 'in the back part of Asia') is a Russian town on the border of present-day Mongolia, about 100 miles south of Ulan-Ude. When Kiakhta was established as a trading post in 1728, Russia bordered on China at that location. Both brick tea and loose tea entered Russia from China at this point, to be shipped overland and by river to the markets of major trading centers such as Nizhny Novgorod. (Lincoln, p. 144-146; Goldstein, pp. 22-23; Custine, pp. 517-518) According to Troyat, by 1900 imported Chinese tea was also known as 'Russian tea' in the markets of Moscow. From the Chinese frontier to the tea sellers of European Russia, 'it was carried in little boxes that were sewn up in skins, with the hair turned inwards to prevent the perfume from escaping. Compressed tea in tablets (*plitochnyi chai*) was also sold, and even a coarse tea in heavy bricks (*kirpichnyi chai*) which had to be broken with an axe before use.' (Troyat, p. 218)

[12] Quoted in Strauss, p. 133, and Tannahill, p. 269. This method also prevents the milk or cream from curdling when added to the hot tea. (Stobart, p. 298)

[13] Quoted in Severin, pp. 51-52.

[14] Severin, p. 52.

[15] Tsyndynzhapov and Badueva, pp. 7, 33. The authors give three recipes for tea: (1) *nogoon sai / zelenyi chai* (green tea, in Buriat/Russian), made from green brick tea and milk, to which can be added a bit of salt and melted butter, served hot; (2) *zutaraan sai* (zutaran tea, in Buriat; no translation available in Russian), made from black loose tea or green brick tea boiled in water and added to a paste of wheat flour fried in mutton or beef fat, lightly salted, and served hot or cold, with the fat cracklings either left in the tea or strained out; and (3) *ulaazhargyn sai / Ivan-chai s molokom* (rose-bay / willow herb / fire weed tea [with milk] in Buriat/Russian), made from the leaves picked in late autumn (when they roll up into a tubular shape) and dried slowly in a Russian stove. The dried leaves are added to boiling water and brought to a boil again; milk or sweet cream is added, and the mixture is brought to the boil once more, then simmered for 10-15 minutes. The herb tea can be served either hot or cold. The authors note that this kind of tea has been drunk since time immemorial by Siberian nomads who inhabited the *taiga* (dense forest land) and

who consumed the tea for their health. (Tsyndynzhapov and Badueva, pp. 35-37) Note that their recipe for *zutaraan sai* contains no milk. I have another recipe for tea of this same name, given to me by a Russian interested in Buriat foods, which is made from green tea, butter, flour, milk, and salt.

[16] We had lived in Japan and Korea, and had travelled in several countries of Southeast Asia, but this was the nearest we had ever been to Mongolia or Central Asia.

[17] The foods on the tables were not Buriat; they were standard Russian cold *zakuski* (hors d'oeuvres): salmon caviar; thinly sliced turkey and *kolbasa* sausage; preserved cabbage-carrot salad (*kislaia kapusta*); potato-beet salad (known as *vinegret*); meat-potato-carrot-pea salad, dressed with mayonnaise (*salat Olivier*); thickly sliced brown bread; unsalted butter; a light-brownish mustard as hot as standard Coleman's; and bowls of fresh whole fruit. In addition to Russian champagne, there were glasses of the same kind of milky tea that we had drunk for breakfast.

[18] Just before we left Ulan-Ude, we were given gifts by a high government official of the Buriat Republic: a large book about Lake Baikal, a traditional Buriat smoking pipe for my husband, and two bottles of Buriat-produced liquor (which our Russian colleagues said was very rare and not available in stores). Dark brown '*Buriatiia Bal'zam*' and '*Amrita Bal'zam*' both came in boxes printed with the information that these liquors – made from (unspecified) Siberian herbs and Siberian water, and 'based on Tibetan medicine' – were tonics beneficial to the whole human organism; it was recommended that they be taken with hot tea, coffee, or other drinks. I expected them to taste like Fernet Branca, but they were actually much better than that.

[19] There is a continuing confusion of names: The city limits sign at the edge of the town says 'Ust'-Orda,' but some maps (both Russian and American) identify the town as 'Ust' Ordynskii,' which is also the name of the autonomous district in which the town is located. Not far out of the town is a large statue of a Buriat on a horse, and in large letters the words 'Ust'-Ordynskii.' Jeremiah Curtin, an American who visited there in 1900, called the town 'Usturdi.' A local government official told me in 1994 that the name of the town was 'Ust'-Orda.' And in *Rediscovering Russia in Asia*, a 1995 publication, the entire district is referred to as 'Ust-Orda.' (Kotkin and Wolff, p. 141)

[20] Information from pamphlet entitled *Ust'-Ordynskii buriatskii avtonomnyi okrug* (*Ust'-Ordynskii Buriat Autonomous District*), published by the district government.

[21] Lincoln notes that 'As the Buriats began to farm instead of raising cattle in the nineteenth century, they also began to exchange their felt yurts for Russian-style wooden houses, especially in the land of Irkutsk province to the west of Lake Baikal.' (Lincoln, p. 283)

[22] Jeremiah Curtin, an accomplished linguist with a degree from Harvard, was Secretary of Legation of the United States in Russia from 1864 to 1870. In 1900 he travelled to Siberia, to the land of the Western Buriats, to study the Buriat language and Buriat customs. His interesting account, *A Journey in Southern Siberia: The Mongols, Their Religion and Their Myths*, published in 1909, details life in 'Usturdi' (Ust'-Orda) and the surrounding area during the two months that Curtin spent there between mid-July and mid-September. He also recounts a number of Buriat legends and myths. Many of Curtin's descriptions of Buriat life at the turn of the century are remarkably similar to what I observed during my short visits to Ust'-Orda in the spring and summer of 1994.

[23] Writing his own observations of life in northern Siberia in the 1860s, George Kennan described the food of the 'Kamtchadals,' native people living on the Kamchatka Peninsula: 'Bread is now made of rye, which the Kamtchadals raise and grind for themselves; but previous to the settlement of the country by the Russians, the only native substitute for bread was a sort of baked paste, consisting chiefly of the grated tubers of the purple Kamtchatkan lily…' (Kennan [2], p. 66) Bobrick also points out that 'The root of the sarana lily…took the place of flour and porridge, and was so much in demand that the wives of Cossacks as well as Kamchadal women used to dig up fieldmice nests (which were made of the root) and dry them in the sun.' (Bobrick, p. 124) A friend of mine in the Russian Far East, a woman who was born in Irkutsk and later lived in Yakutsk and on Sakhalin Island, remembers digging up these roots when she was a child. She described '*saranka*' as a flower, orange and round, which looks like a wild lily. The root is bulbous and white, shaped like a cluster of garlic pods. According to her, the root, which has a sweet taste, is cooked with milk – and is eaten only during late spring and early summer, when the flavor is best. Tsyndynzhapov and Badueva give two recipes using *sarana*, in addition to four recipes using *cheremukha*, a kind of meal (flour) made from another wild plant, the pits of bird-cherry fruits (chokecherries), which I have eaten in

Siberia. (Tsyndynzhapov and Badueva, pp. 27-30)

[24] Tsyndynzhapov and Badueva, p. 5.

[25] *The Travels of Marco Polo*, p. 28.

[26] *The Travels of Marco Polo*, pp. 100-101. A footnote to this passage (p. 100) adds that other manuscripts contain the information that in the absence of any other container, they use an animal's stomach as a pot in which to boil the meat and then eat it 'pot and all.'

[27] Tsyndynzhapov and Badueva, p. 7. Their cookbook gives recipes for 20 Buriat milk dishes – from porridge to cheeses to drinks (including *kumys*, which the Buriats call *segee*) – which they say can be made in a variety of ways by different cooks in different areas. They also point out that their recipes include only those milk dishes that are most important and best known, and that there are certainly other milk dishes also prepared by the Buriats. (Tsyndynzhapov and Badueva, pp. 7-25)

[28] Sof'ia Petrovna said the milk could be from cows, sheep, goats, or horses. (The Mongols use milk from horses, sheep, goats, cows, camels, and yaks – and sometimes mix different kinds of milks together for these dishes.) Unpasteurized, non-homogenized milk is necessary for most of these recipes, because pasteurization prevents the preservative lactic acid from developing, and hence the milk cannot sour naturally; it will only spoil. (Stobart, pp. 298, 455)

[29] This is the *kaimak/kaymak* of Eastern Europe, the Balkans, and Turkey (*qaymaq*); the *eishta/ushta* of many Arab countries; the *khoya* of India; the *shosha* or *churul* of Tibet; the *su* of China (during the T'ang dynasty); and the clotted cream of Devonshire. (Sokolov, p. 83; Tannahill, p. 126; Dorje, p. 76) In his paper on 'The Horseback Kitchen of Central Asia,' Charles Perry notes that the Khalka Mongol terms for clotted cream are *tsötsgii, zööhii,* and *öröm.* (Oxford Symposium on Food, 1996) Given that this is such a common – and delicious – milk product in so many countries (including parts of European Russia), I was surprised to find that the ethnic Russians I questioned in Siberia and the Russian Far East did not know the term *kaimak* and were not familiar with the product. I have cookbooks published in European Russia which mention *kaimak*, but none of the ones I have that were published in Asian Russia mention it. Only the Buriats I met were aware of it, although they knew it only by their own term, *urmen*. Furthermore, there is some confusion between the Buriats' translation of *urmen* into Russian as *molochnye penki* (milk skins), since European Russians distinguish between *kaimak* (thick clotted cream) and *penka* (the thinner skin of boiled milk), which are made and used in different ways.

[30] Sour cream can be used or *zakvaska*, a fermented mixture of rye bread and milk, similar to Polish *zakwas na zur.*

[31] The home distillation of liquor is supposedly outlawed in Russia, but it still occurs throughout the country. I myself have drunk the products of illegal Russian stills. (Unfortunately, several people die each year in Russia from consuming poorly processed or contaminated home-brews.) Jeremiah Curtin's description of how the Buriats made *tarasun* almost a century ago holds true today:
The most important work in a Buriat house and of a Buriat woman is to keep the milk barrels full, and to distill the milk into tarasun, a liquor looking like alcohol or pure water. When the milk is sour enough for the watery part to separate from the curd it is ready to distil. As much milk as is desired is taken out of the barrel and put in a large iron pot, then the pot is sealed up with a heavy paste made of mud and cow manure, and is placed over a slow fire burning on the ground in the center of the Buriat house. From the pot a pipe runs into a tub which stands four feet or so away. From the end of this pipe drips out the tarasun. If strong tarasun is desired the first is redistilled. The strongest is made by distilling the liquor three times. (Curtin, p. 92) Buriat *tarasun* is the same as the Mongolian *shimiin arkhi* described by Severin, pp. 123-124.

[32] Curtin describes 'arsá' as the 'substance left in the pot after the liquor is distilled. It hardens and is mixed with rye flour and cooked for laborers. Arsá becomes so solid that an axe is used in getting it out of the barrel.' (Curtin, p. 92)

[33] Sof'ia Petrovna called it *salamat*; Tsyndynzhapov and Badueva (p. 16) identify it as *shanahan zookhei* in Buriat and *salamat* in Russian. The *Oxford Russian Dictionary* gives the word as *salamata* '(obs. or dial.) (cul.)* salamata (*kind of porridge*).' The Russian Academy of Science Dictionary describes *salamata* as a gelatinous or watery (liquified) substance resembling kasha, made with flour and with oil or tallow. Another Russian dictionary identifies *salamata* similarly, as a gelatinized substance or watery kasha, often made from flour with suet or lard, or made with flour combined with oil. Several other dictionaries

published in Russia do not list the word at all. In addition to the spellings *salamat* and *salamata*, the word is sometimes spelled *solomat* or *solomata*. Presumably the root word is *salo*, meaning 'fat, lard, or suet.' It is evident, however, that the compilers of the Russian dictionaries had not actually tasted *salamat(a)* – as it is known to the Buriats and to some of the Russians living in areas inhabited by Buriats (and to the Norwegians, who have the same dish), for whom the primary ingredient is sour cream – because the descriptions are not accurate. It would be interesting to determine whether *salamat(a)* made in other parts of Russia, or by other ethnic groups, more closely resembled the Russian dictionary descriptions.

[34] Before the Russians arrived in Siberia and introduced the growing of cereal crops, Buriats used the dried roots of edible plants such as *sarani* (lilies) for making *salamat*. (Tsyndynzhapov and Badueva, p. 16) See also Note no. 23.

[35] Letters to the author from Astri Riddervold, Aase Strømstad, Brita Edland, and Torunn Linneberg in Norway, May-July 1994. My Norwegian sources said that *rømmegrøt* originated in Norway and dates at least back to medieval times; that it is not a dish found in other Scandinavian countries; and that it did not come to Norway from lands east of there, nor was it the result of eastern influences on Norwegian cuisine.

[36] I have eaten *rømmegrøt* on several occasions in Norway and *salamat* twice in Buriat Siberia; I have compared several recipes for both of these dishes; and I have made *rømmegrøt* at home. Therefore, I can attest to the fact that these two dishes are the same.

[37] These Buriat steamed dumplings are more closely related to the *manti* of Turkey than to some of the Central Asian dumplings made with a raised dough that are also called *manti*, or to the Chinese steamed breads known as *mantou*. Buriat *buuza* (Russian *pozy*) are made from the same dough that is used for making noodles. Larger in size than Siberian *pel'meni*, they are still smaller than many of the Central Asian and Chinese steamed dumplings and steamed buns to which they have sometimes been compared. (This confusion apparently arises because of the different uses of the term *manti/mantou/manju* by people in different parts of Asia, from Turkey to Japan). The Buriats also have a larger version of filled, steamed dumplings, made from the same dough and filling as *buuza*, with the dough twisted together to seal the dumpling at the top. These are known as *khushuur* in Buriat (*miasnye grushi* – 'meat pears' – in Russian), because in size and shape they resemble pears (*grushi*).

[38] When I described this liver dish to one of my ethnic-Russian students in Irkutsk, she knew exactly what I was talking about – much to the surprise of not only me but also the other Russian students within earshot. She said she had eaten this Buriat specialty several times and that it was very tasty. When questioned further, she explained that her father had a Buriat friend who provided her family with this delicacy, since it could be obtained only from Buriats living in villages, who still made it from the liver of horses fattened for slaughter in winter. I should add that the reaction of the more 'modern' Russian students in Irkutsk was a combination of surprise and revulsion.

[39] Severin describes a similar ritual in modern-day Mongolia: 'Before toasting the future of Mongolia in *arkhi*, he dipped the tip of the third finger of his right hand into the drink three times. Once he flicked a small drop of the alcohol away in the air, once toward the hearth, and once to the ground. It was a ritual gesture we had seen many times, the customary offering to the spirits of sky, fire, and earth. But he explained two extra details: the third finger was employed because it was the cleanest and least-used finger on the hand; and folklore said it was a test for poison in the cup. The poison would burn the fingertip.' (Severin, p. 164) Curtin also describes the ritual among Western Buriats in several places in his book. The Ainu – a paleoasiatic people who inhabit northern Honshu, Hokkaido, the Kuril Islands, and Sakhalin Island – have a similar ritual, in which they hold a 'drinking spatula' (a carved stick, about twelve inches long and pointed at one end) in front of their nose when drinking liquor. The pointed end of the stick is dipped into the cup of liquor and moved up and down in front of the face, in a ritual offering to the gods or spirits.

[40] Although the Russians and most of the Buriats we met in the area of Lake Baikal referred to 'Burkhan' as if that were the name of one particular spirit or god, in Curtin's book there are many Buriat myths and folk tales that include references to 'the thousand Burkhans' and also to specific Burkhans with individual names – which strongly implies that 'Burkhan' is the Buriats' general name for deities. Charles Perry informs me that 'The word *Burkhan* literally means "Lord Buddha" (Khan Buddha, that is). It was widely adopted by non-Buddhists, just like the word shaman, which comes from the Buddhist term, *shramana*.' (Letter to the author, August 1996)

[41] She was referring to the 'dekulakization' period in Siberia, under Stalin from 1932 to 1934, during which an estimated 10,000 Buriats perished. (Matthiesson, p. 38) Bobrick points out that 'At least fifty thousand once-productive Buriats and Mongols fled south to Inner Mongolia and China' and that 'Like peasants elsewhere, many Buriat, Mongol, and Yakut herdsmen slaughtered their own livestock rather than see them incorporated into collective herds....' (Bobrick, pp. 421-422)

[42] *Cambridge Encyclopedia*, p. 69. Wixman states that 'The religious adherence of the Buryats is a complex one. The eastern Buryats were primarily Buddhists. The religion of the western Buryats combined Buddhist and shamanist beliefs. Even a 'nativist' Buryat religion (called Burkhanism) developed. Eastern Orthodoxy was also adopted by some Buryats as their religion.' (Wixman, p. 33) Curtin observed in 1900 that 'The Buriats living west of that water [Lake Baikal], and those inhabiting the sacred island of Olkhon [in Lake Baikal], are the only Mongols who have preserved their own race religion with its primitive usages, archaic beliefs, and philosophy, hence they are a people of great interest to science.' (Curtin, p.1)

[43] A shaman is a person – male or female – who is believed to have the power to cure the sick and to communicate with spirits.

[44] *Shan'gi* are round, yeast-raised buns, with a circle of thick sour cream in a depression on the top – similar to Russian *vatrushki* and Czech *kolacky*. They can also have other toppings, such as *tvorog* (fresh cheese), or *tvorog* mixed with sour cream.

[45] *Omul* (*Salmo* or *Coregonus omul*) is a white-fleshed fish belonging to the salmon family and is found only in Lake Baikal. *Omul* are eaten raw or cooked; they are also salted or smoked for preservation. Another fish unique to Lake Baikal is *golomianka*, half of whose body weight is oil. *Golomianka* oil, rich in vitamin A, has been used by the Buriats for centuries for medicinal purposes and as fuel for lamps. (Newby, p. 186; Lincoln, p. 247)

[46] Curtin describes several kinds of Buriat 'sacred trees' and 'sacred groves,' and a number of customs related to them, in the area around Ust'-Orda. 'It has happened at times during past centuries that a Shaman seeing a beautiful tree or a fine clump of trees has thought that a Burkhan or the spirit of a dead Shaman if passing by there would surely like to stop and have a smoke; hence he has declared that tree or clump of trees to be sacred, and no man would be so foolhardy as to meddle with trees which they know have been given to the Burkhans or spirits.' (Curtin, p. 117).

[47] Marco Polo describes the same superstition at the court of Kubilai Khan 700 years ago. (*The Travels of Marco Polo*, p. 137) Russians are also superstitious about stepping on thresholds.

[48] At this house and the next one we visited, Terry kept saying to me, 'See how clean the house is. See how clean the people are. See, we aren't a dirty people.' I had no idea why he was making such a point of this, until later I read Newby's account of visiting a sheep station in Buriatia in the 1970s: 'The house was, of course, breathtakingly clean and it was difficult to believe that the Buryats, who are now among the most cultivated and well educated of all the Siberian peoples, were before the Revolution among the dirtiest – so dirty that the [Trans-Siberian] railway builders hesitated to employ them in case they spread typhus among the other workers....' (Newby, p. 211)

[49] Lack of such utilities as running water and indoor plumbing are typical of most of the old wooden houses in Siberia (and many places elsewhere in Russia), although electricity is common. Even in the larger cities where I lived (Irkutsk and Vladivostok), the old wooden houses were without basic utilities except electricity. However, we lived in recently built Russian high-rise apartment buildings which, although hooked up to city utilities, were often without electricity and running water (especially in Vladivostok) – which made life on the eighth floor of such buildings rather difficult at times.

[50] Descriptions of this form of slaughter have been written by visitors to the Mongol lands from Marco Polo to the present. See especially Curtin, pp. 46 and 99, and Severin, pp. 52-53. We were told that Buriats use a special knife, and only that one knife, to make the initial incision and to butcher the animal. An axe is used only once, and with only one blow, to split the pelvic bone.

[51] The Buriats said they ate raw sheep liver only in summer and raw horse liver only in winter, but when I asked why, no one could give me an explanation. Later in the meal, they said that Buriats slaughter sheep for food in the summer, but only cattle and horses in the winter.

[52] When I pressed Terry for more information about these customs, he confessed that he did not know much about such things. A middle-age former Communist, he was obviously one of the Buriats who, during the Soviet era, consciously rejected many aspects of their own traditional culture in favor of the more modern, career-enhancing values of the dominant culture.

[53] It was unclear whether these offerings were to a particular Burkhan, or to any number of burkhans, or –
as I later learned – to the Buriats' household gods known as *ongons*. (Curtin, p. 41) Marco Polo (pp. 99
and 109) described similar ritual offerings in the thirteenth century, as did Jeremiah Curtin at the turn of
this century: '...libations are made; that is a few drops of milk are cast into the air to the Burkhans, and
when tarasun is passed around some of it is also cast into the air.' (Curtin, p. 45) 'Small bits of the cooked
meat were thrown on to the blazing fire of the altars [during a horse sacrifice]...; soup from the kettles was
also thrown from small cups on to the fire of the altars.' (Curtin, p. 47) Curtin also points out that 'The
reality, the essence, of the milk and the tarasun goes to the Burkhans, immensely increased and incom-
parably better in quality. Thus a single drop may become a whole barrelful when it reaches the home of the
deities...' (pp. 44-45) ; and that the Buriats believe that 'Each drop of broth when it reached the gods'
mansions sufficed a hundred persons, each bit of flesh was increased in like manner, and so with tarasun, a
few drops of which would cheer thousands' (p. 49). As Curtin commented, 'Most interesting of all is that
strange philosophy, at least strange for us, by which gods are pleased and profited by a small material
outlay on the part of mankind' (p. 49).

[54] When I asked Terry where the *tarasun* had actually come from, he just grinned and said that *tarasun* was
something that could not be purchased in stores. Beyond that, he was unwilling or unable to identify the
owner of the illegal still that had produced the alcohol. See Note no. 31.

[55] One of my students in Irkutsk showed me a booklet published in Ulan-Ude, used in teaching English in
the schools. I copied the following English-language passage, in its entirety, from it: 'Do you know Buriat
tradition "torler" "sheep's head"? Sheep's head is a symbolic dish presented to the most honoured guest. It
is served with the nose turned to the guest. Taking it, the guest sings a song about the "torler". It's a
symbolic virtual [ritual?] meaning the highest respect to the honourable guest.'

[56] Curtin describes a similar meal in western Buriatia in 1900: '...a lamb had been slaughtered and cooked
for our nourishment. The great dish of honor at our table was the boiled head of that lamb, with the wool
on. There was also a species of soup made of blood and kidneys, which seemed much like diluted blood
pudding. It was relished by the Buriats, but strive as I might I could only make a very scant trial of its
qualities. There was an abundance of other food, however, hence I could let these Mongol dainties pass.'
(Curtin, p. 57)

[57] Newby (pp. 213-216) describes a similar culinary orgy with the Buriats that he visited near Ulan-Ude in
the mid-1970s. In late 1994 I saw commercials on Russian television for an investment company, which
used a romanticized Mongolian feast as a setting; the depiction of how the sheep was served was close to
accurate.

[58] Curtin, pp. 91-92.

Onions with no Bottoms and Chickens with no Tops: Shopping for Food in the Emerging Market Economy of Siberia and the Russian Far East

Tom Hudgins

A world in transition

The Soviet empire started to fall apart in 1989 when the Warsaw Pact countries of Central and Eastern Europe began to move away from the Soviet world and reform their governments and economies. The USSR itself disappeared at the end of 1991, and new nations have emerged from the old empire of the Soviet Union and the older empire of the Tsars. Russia, itself the largest part of the former Soviet Union, began the process of remaking itself into a different country with a new form of government and a different type of economy. Under the Communist system the economy was centrally planned; the state owned and directed the means of production. Government officials established targets for production and required the various producing entities in the system to strive to achieve the goals of the plan. Resources were allocated to factories and farms, which in turn were told how to use those resources to achieve the desired output. The system was top-down, inefficient, and often failed to meet its goals. It provided maximum employment, but not material well-being. From the perspective of the economies of the West, the Soviet system was riddled with inefficiencies and perverse incentives. From the viewpoint of the average Soviet citizen, it was a world of certainties in terms of price, a world of shortages in terms of availability, and a world of limits in terms of choices. The lack of material well-being was one of several factors that brought sweeping changes to the former Soviet empire[1]

This paper is an examination of some of the patterns of change that occurred in Russia in the early post-Soviet era. In general, it will consider the emergence of market-based economic activities in food markets during the period from August 1993 through December 1994. The focus will be on two regions of Russia: Siberia and the Russian Far East. These areas are less known to people in the West than is European Russia and cities such as Moscow and St. Petersburg. Life in Siberia, in a sense, reflects the situation of many average Russians who are located in isolated regions far from the centers of national power, and who are therefore more dependent on local production than on the activities of distant Moscow. The Russian Far East is in a very different situation, since it is located on the Pacific Rim and is less dependent on Moscow than many other regions. Its future will probably be governed more by the development of international trade.

The author of this paper taught economics for an American university that had undergraduate degree programs in two Russia cities: Vladivostok, in the Russian Far East, and Irkutsk, in Siberia.[2] Most of the personal anecdotes are related to those cities, or to smaller towns and villages which I visited near those major centers during the 16 months I was there. The emphasis of the paper will be on personal observations of what was happening in stores and markets during that time, including the products available, their prices, and changes in methods of marketing.[3] Less attention will be paid to official statistics of production and exchange. The reason for that is twofold: (1) many of the economic transactions occurring in Russia go through informal markets and hence official data does not reflect all of this activity; and (2) official data itself is often questionable – reflecting the older tradition of providing the politically correct numbers to the officials who required them, and/

or presenting the desired image of success to the external world.[4] In the first instance, the informality of the markets reflects, in part, the fact that market-based transactions used to be very limited under the Soviet system, and the new emerging markets are changing faster than government can monitor and measure them. In the second case, official statistics in Russia's emerging market economy are unreliable because many people want to avoid taxation and therefore tend to under-report their business activities. Furthermore, some of the economic transactions are controlled by, or deeply influenced by, organized crime. Therefore, official information available is generally not accurate and tends to understate market activity, in much the same way that Soviet figures used to overstate productive success.

In thinking about the emerging market economy in Russia, it is important to make a distinction between a market and a market system. People who live in countries where a market system forms the major basis for production and distribution, such as Western Europe and North America, are so familiar with the market system as to accept it as the natural order of things. Historically that is not the case. The market economic system is relatively new historically and has not always been the way that societies organized production and distribution. Markets themselves – in the sense of a place where buyers and sellers come together, or where exchange takes place – do have a very long history. The market system, however, dates from the eighteenth century and represents a major change in the way societies provided for their material well-being. As noted by Robert Heilbroner:

> If markets, buying-and-selling, even highly organized trading bodies, were well-nigh ubiquitous features of ancient society, they must not be confused with the equally ubiquitous presence of a *market society*. Trade existed as an important adjunct to society from the earliest times, but the fundamental impetus to production, or the basic allocation of resources among different uses, or the distribution of goods among different social classes was largely divorced from the marketing process. That is, *the markets of antiquity were not the means by which those societies solved their basic economic problems.* They were external to the great processes of production and distribution rather than integral to them; they were 'above' the critical economic machinery rather than within it.[5]

While Heilbroner is distinguishing between the markets of antiquity and a market economy system, this distinction could apply to the Russian experience as well. As noted above, the Soviet economy was a planned or command economy. Decisions about production and distribution were made centrally, and to the extent that market activity was permitted, it was external to the basic economic system.

In the planned economy of the Soviet era, food production was the job of the state farms and collective farms. Distribution and sale of most foodstuffs were also controlled by the state. This system was a particularly unsuccessful part of the Soviet planned economy.[6] As one Russian commentator wrote:

> The crisis of our agriculture was obvious to everyone. Capital investments are not the reason for this situation. More than enough of them have been channeled into the countryside in the last one and one-half decades. But they have in fact produced nothing. The crisis of our countryside is atonement for five and one-half decades of violence against common sense, against everything that encourages a person to perform normal, conscientious work. And today there are probably few who doubt that the basic reason for our agriculture's present grievous state, for its torpidity, is the unlimited power that the administrative stratum acquired during those decades over everything by which the countryside lives.[7]

Despite the Soviet system's reliance on collectivized agriculture, private economic activity was permitted on a limited scale. People were allowed to grow food on small plots of land. Some of these were adjacent to individual houses in villages; others were areas of land available outside of cities where urban Russians could build their country dachas (which can range from a very simple cabin to an entire house). Many Russians used the food grown on these plots of land to supplement the food available from official sources (or increase the variety of things available to them), and to supplement their income by taking excess products to small markets in towns and cities. It has often been noted that after the collectivization of agriculture in the Soviet Union (completed in the 1930s during the Stalin era, at a high human cost), small private plots still accounted for some 25 per cent of the total agricultural output, even though they represented only 3 to 4 per cent of the farmland.[8] Such small producers and small markets helped to alleviate the shortages which were a chronic condition of Soviet collective agriculture (due in large part to inefficiencies and waste).[9]

In contemporary Russia, the legacy of Soviet agriculture remains. Reforms and privatization have been slow in coming to agriculture.[10] People wanting to become private farmers, and former collective farms wanting to operate as a business, find many bureaucratic impediments in their path. Until land is privatized, until more collective farms and former state farms are converted to private businesses, and until excessive layers of bureaucracy are eliminated, agriculture will still lag behind many other sectors in the Russian economy.[11] Problems with infrastructure, especially transportation, also complicate the situation. Because of the continuing problems with agricultural production and distribution, Russia remains dependent on imports of food. In addition, production of food by individuals and families on their small garden plots remains a major way that many Russians are able to feed themselves – even if they live in a city and work in an office.[12] Also, for many Russians, 'dacha products' are the best in terms of quality. Russians are happier with what they have grown and preserved than with the products of the factories whether privatized or not.[13]

The emphasis on meats, fish, bread, and grains has long been characteristic of the basic Russian diet. One can read about and imagine the splendid tables of the Tsars, or the less splendid tables of the Communist Party élite, but for average Russians the diet was much more basic. This was in part due to the economic conditions during various periods of Russian history, and in part due to the political situation of the times. But another significant factor was climate. The realms of the Tsars and of the Soviet Union contained a variety of different climates and microclimates, but as one went farther north in the empire the growing season shortened. Also, much of the territory of present day Russia has less climatic variety than the larger territory of the former Soviet union. Areas such as Siberia, for example, have relatively thin soils as well as a short growing season.[14] Therefore, agricultural production was and is limited by climate and soil conditions. Large greenhouse operations help to some extent, but they are still caught in the inefficient domain of former state industries in transition.

The limits imposed by nature, and the bad decisions and excessive bureaucracy of the Communist era, are impediments enough to variety and freshness of foodstuffs, but these are joined by the problem of poor transportation systems to get the harvest from producer to consumer. Even today, much of Russia lacks adequate roads, railways, trucks, and rolling stock to move food products around the country. (When we travelled on the Trans-Siberian Railroad, it was always interesting to watch the people in the smaller towns where the train stopped, who came to the station and stood in line to buy whatever the dining car staff had to sell, whether it was sausages, oranges, vodka, or chocolates.) Variety and freshness were, and still are, luxuries. The types of foods that were produced had to fit the climate and had to be (for the most part) things that could be stored (such as grain) or preserved (cabbage made into sauerkraut) to last through the long winters. Traditional techniques such as canning, salting and smoking were common, as well as simply letting meat or fish freeze in the winter.[15] Spoilage is not a problem in Siberia in January!

Shop till you drop

In the planned economy of the Soviet era, distribution and sale of foodstuffs were through the channels of state transportation systems, state stores, factory canteens, and factory stores. In the post-Soviet era of the emerging market economy, there are now four basic places to purchase food items: (1) formerly state-run stores, most of which are now privatized; (2) 'farmers' markets,' many of which are open-air or partially covered; (3) kiosks and various street sellers (both independent and informal chains); and (4) other sources connected with one's place of work, such as company stores and canteens.[16] Most of the former state-run food stores were architecturally dull and often not very clean (by Western standards), with drab interiors and little or no sense of product display. Two exceptions in Vladivostok were *'Dary Taigi'* ('Gifts of the Forest') and a large *gastronom* (food store) on the main street of the city. The interior of *'Dary Taigi,'* a store which used to specialize in game, was decorated with huge hand-painted ceramic tile murals of the wild animals of the Russian Far East: deer, bears, tigers, ducks, pheasants. The *gastronom*, which was built before the Revolution, was decorated with mirrored walls, huge chandeliers, ornate brass fixtures, and Art Nouveau motifs. But these stores were by far the exception, not the rule.

The process of shopping for food in Russia is not always an easy one. For anyone who has lived in Russia, the slogan 'shop till you drop' has an entirely different meaning than in the West. Shoppers in Russia encounter many things that are different from the experience of shopping in a western supermarket. All of the familiar practices of modern food marketing in the West – including well-organized distribution, eye-catching displays, full shelves, grocery carts and plastic or paper bags provided by the store – are lacking in Russia. In some ways, the formerly state-owned food stores hark back to an earlier period in the West, when specialty shops were the rule rather than the exception. In most of Russia, if you want bread, you go to a shop that sells only bread, and if you want meat or sausage, you go to a shop that sells those products. Larger stores in Russia have separate sections or departments that sell separate products, but the customer still has to go to each counter to get the specific type of merchandise he or she wants. For instance, you might find cheese at one counter, meat at another, and flours and cereals at yet another (assuming that these products are available). (When I lived in Russia I was often reminded of the Soviet-era joke about the man in the fish shop who kept insisting that he wants meat. The clerk finally tells him to go across the street – that's the store where they have no meat![17]) If a product you want is available – cheese, for example – you must get the clerk behind the counter to cut and weigh the portion you want, then either tell you the cost of it or give you a slip of paper with the amount due on it. You then go to the cashier in another part of the store and pay for the item. The cashier will give you a receipt which you take back to the original clerk, where you finally pick up the item.[18] Each of these steps usually involves standing in line. In Russia, self-service shopping is only now being introduced.

In the case of farmers' markets, street vendors, and kiosks, the process of shopping is not as hindered by procedure, since the customer deals directly with the seller. Lines exist, but they move forward as each person gets what he or she wants, pays, and moves on. However, you may have to go through an entire market to find what you want (or to get the best quality/price combination), or even go to many different stores, kiosks, and markets to find what you need.

The amount of time people spend shopping in Russia is very high. In the 1970s, the Soviet press reported that citizens spent 30 billion man-hours each year just buying merchandise.[19] The process of shopping for food and other items was so time-consuming that many people were absent from work for a couple of hours each day, just to get their shopping done (hence adding to the low productivity of Russian workers).[20] When we were in Russia, we found ourselves constantly looking at whatever was for sale when we passed a street stand or kiosk. And, like Russians, whenever we saw a line of people we would check to see what was being offered for sale. I once commented that I knew I had been in Russia too long when an attractive woman walked by me and, instead of looking at her, I looked down at her shopping bag and wondered where she got those beautiful green vegetables!

Shopping at the open-air markets of Russia is particularly interesting. One of the first impressions one has upon visiting a Russian market is, in fact, the number of sellers with only a small number of items to sell. These are the babushkas (elderly women, grandmothers) who have come in from the country with a few surplus items to sell – such as onion tops. You can buy the dry onion bottoms from truck farmers, but not from the babushkas. The babushkas sell only the beautiful green tops of onions, the bottoms of which they have kept for themselves. And in Russia you buy onion tops to take home for your soup or for a salad – because otherwise you might have nothing green in either of them. In the market you also see people who have brought homemade products to sell. Many of these products are home-canned – such as tomatoes, cucumbers, garlic cloves, and mushrooms.[21] Other home-processed products include smoked salmon, horseradish sauce, sauerkraut, spicy carrot salad, fruit and berry preserves, sour cream, and *adzhiga*.[22] None of these 'dacha products' are tested by health inspectors, and so the buyer is at the mercy (and must rely on the competence) of the producer. Generally, these products are delicious – and of higher quality than factory-processed foodstuffs.

The two places where I lived and worked in Russia were very different in terms of both what was available for purchase, and where you could shop for it. Vladivostok, the home of the Russian Pacific fleet, is also an important trading port. Nearby is another important trading port, Nakhodka, which was open to foreigners during the Soviet era when Vladivostok was a closed military city. Vladivostok, the capital of Primorye territory on the Pacific coast, has a population of about 700,000. The Primorye territory is bordered by China and North Korea and lies only 400 miles from Japan. Within the region there is a large amount of food production. Most important in terms of volume are the fishing fleet and the fish canning industry, but this region is also the Russian Far East's leading producer of rice, milk, eggs, and vegetables. Another regional center, Ussurisk (about 60 miles north of Vladivostok), is a major food producing center and a town with a very interesting regional market. One source of the region's importance as a center of food production is the fact that the southern part of Primorye has a 200-day growing season, which is longer than other temperate parts of the Russian Far East (for example, the Amur region has 170 days) and much longer than the colder regions to the north (the Magadan region has only a 100-day growing season). Primorye is also very important in terms of total foreign trade (and is in fact the leading international trading region in the Russian Far East).[23] Given both the local food production and the amount of international trade, the markets, stores, and kiosks of Vladivostok are – by Russian standards – well-stocked. In terms of the entire Russian Far East, Vladivostok and Khabarovsk are the best places to shop for food items. Vladivostok is where I began to learn how to shop the Russian way.

Shopping for food in Vladivostok

In August of 1993, my wife and I arrived in Vladivostok to begin a semester of teaching in a joint Russian-American management degree program at Far Eastern State University. We were also able to observe many of the changes that occurred as the Russian economy shifted from the controlled world of state planning to the more bustling world of a market economy. At that time, Vladivostok still had many traditional Russian stores, complete with few products, low prices, slow service, and long lines. However, that first autumn in Vladivostok we were still surprised at the things it was possible to purchase in the more traditional Russian stores and especially in the farmers' markets. The stores had many kinds of grains (rice, wheat, buckwheat groats) and (usually) ample supplies of basic items like flour and sugar, when we first arrived.

Our Russian colleagues advised us early about a basic principle of shopping in Russia: if you see something you need or want, buy it immediately (don't wait)! The corollary was to buy more than you needed – for a friend, or for barter, or to hedge against future shortages. Russians had learned these rules under the Soviet shopping regime, but they still proved to be good advice since in the emerging market economy items such as flour or sugar or salt might disappear from the stores for a time and only be available at the farmers' markets at much higher prices. Good dairy products, such as milk, kefir, cheese, and sour cream were also available in Vladivostok. Meat was a more haphazard proposition (especially in the older stores), often consisting of fatty sausages, or poorer cuts of meat, or chicken that had eaten too little and walked too far. However, in Vladivostok fish was another matter. Stores that specialized in fish had a variety of products from the sea – some fresh, some frozen, some smoked, some canned. On a given day, one might walk in and find excellent salmon, freshly prepared salmon caviar, and smoked herring. If you wanted fish to cook, you could select among several varieties (often frozen whole). We knew when we saw the bounty of the seafood shops that the region lived up to its statistical reputation as a producer of fish.

Another pleasant surprise were the bread shops. Different shops in the city tended to make different kinds of bread, but all of them were good. We even came to prefer certain bakeries for their chewy white bread and yeasty buns, others for their basic Russian brown bread, and still others for their darker, grainier breads. Russia has historically been a country which sustained itself with bread, and to the average Russian no meal is complete without bread. Traditionally, Russians offer bread and salt to greet their visitors. Despite years of Communist rule (and reliance on wheat imports), good bread remains a part of the Russian culture.

The fruit and vegetable stores were another matter. The emphasis on fresh, high-quality produce so common in America or Europe was simply not to be found in the stores of Vladivostok. The selection was limited, with an emphasis on root vegetables such as potatoes, carrots, onions, and beets. All of these root vegetables came coated with plenty of dirt. As for green vegetables, there were the ubiquitous cabbages and often little else. Sometimes we could find cucumbers and perhaps tomatoes, but quality and size were always variable. Fruits were limited as well, perhaps only apples and pears. In general, the best sources for fruits and vegetables were the various farmers' markets scattered around the city. We were fortunate that our university department provided a van and driver to take the American professors food shopping one day each week. On these shopping days, we were able to visit many of the markets around the city and usually came home with our shopping bags full. Average Russians were more limited in their shopping possibilities (as we knew from shopping on our own), given the time and effort required to shop via public transportation, which was dirty, crowded, and seldom dependable.

The various farmers' markets around the city of Vladivostok had much more variety than what was available in the interior of the country.[24] These markets offered fresh produce, foreign products, and many homemade products that reflected the older Russian traditions of preserving foods. It was always interesting to see what people had made and brought to the market to sell. Among my fondest food memories of Russia is the day I bought a small smoked salmon from a person who had several very good looking fish to sell. I noticed that this salmon was not commercially smoked because there was a hole in the tail where a crude stick had been inserted to hold the fish over the smoke – and indeed, when I got home I found that the fish had a wonderfully different smoked flavor. I asked a Russian friend to taste it, and she said the salmon had been smoked over birch wood. Another pleasant surprise came later in the autumn when fresh tomatoes and cucumbers began to disappear from the market. A man and his wife were selling home-canned products displayed on their beat-up Lada automobile. On the hood of the car were two 3-liter jars of tomatoes and cucumbers mixed together. They looked so good that we purchased one jar, only to discover later that the canned vegetables had a smoky flavor from being processed over a wood fire. We regretted not buying more! Later in the autumn – on the edge of the Russian winter, when coats and fur hats were now a necessity – one man in the market had some jars of horseradish for sale. The seller clearly wanted me to know how good his product was, but given my lack of Russian, he was finding it difficult to communicate – until he mimed tasting a spoon of the horseradish, then quickly lifted his hat above his head and exhaled sharply – all the while saying that his horseradish was very good! (He was right.)

Aside from the homemade products (and the oddities such as bottomless onions) that were sold by babushkas and younger housewives, local farmers would also bring their produce to market and sell it directly from their trucks. There would be a line of people at the truckload of potatoes, another line at the truckload of cabbage, another at the truckload of eggs, and so on. You stood in line, told the seller how many kilos you wanted, then the purchase was weighed out and dumped into your shopping bag.[25] All except for eggs. In the case of eggs, which were sold in units of ten, you would ask for twenty or thirty eggs and be given an open egg carton with the number you asked for. You were expected to take the eggs, transfer them to whatever bag or container you had, and return the cartons to the pile beside the truck. One member of our faculty was lucky enough to find a special plastic egg-carrying case that held up to thirty eggs. The rest of us lacked such a 'high-tech' solution, and were left with the more sporting task of stacking eggs in a plastic bag, then placing the bag very carefully on top of our shopping bag, and then even more carefully carrying the shopping bag through the crowded market to get the eggs safely to the van. When I went shopping by public transportation, I faced the challenge of taking such a sack of eggs back home on the crowded buses. (Signs in the bus would say that the bus holds a certain number of passengers, but the number was routinely exceeded by people who jammed into the bus until the doors could barely close). Once, I even made it home with all the eggs intact.[26]

Another feature of the farmers' markets were the vendors from China, Korea, and Central Asia who had brought products from their parts of the world – including fresh or dried fruits and nuts. Of course these markets were very seasonal. We had arrived in Vladivostok in late August, when a variety of fruits and vegetables were still in the market. As autumn came, and then winter, the variety dwindled, the quality worsened, and the prices rose. Even the people who brought fruit from Central Asia, via ordinary passenger plane flights, ran out of things to sell. (The practice of bringing fruits and vegetables in via airplane diminished significantly when Aeroflot raised its ticket prices sharply to reflect the real costs of flying). Before winter closed in, we had been able to purchase apples, pears, berries, cucumbers, tomatoes, peppers, eggplant, and squash.[27] In early October, for instance, the markets were still full of eggplants, vine-ripened tomatoes, and a variety of peppers. A short time later, the only tomatoes left would be green, and the peppers and eggplants were gone for that season. Thereafter, the fresh vegetable choices were reduced to the root vegetables such as potatoes, turnips, beets, and the occasional cabbage. Otherwise, we looked in the produce shops for what was available from state greenhouses (usually a limited number of products of not very good quality), or whatever canned products, either Russian or imported, that we could find.

The farmers' markets were also the best source for fresh beef and pork, and such items as chicken parts. I remember our first day in the Russian Far East, seeing the sights of the city of Khabarovsk before our plane left that evening for Vladivostok. We were driving through the rain in a taxi when an open slat-sided truck came by, piled high with half carcasses of beef covered with mud from the road. I knew then that the meat markets of Russia would be more 'basic' that the ones we have in the West. In some American stores customers can get a glimpse of the butchers at work – either behind the counter or through a glass window behind the meat case. These are designed to show the customer the cleanliness of the operation, without offending shoppers sensitive to the realities of butchering. In Russia, whether you were buying meat from a meat counter in an enclosed market, or from the back of someone's station wagon, you always knew directly where the meat came from. Often the severed head of the animal was displayed to indicate the freshness of the product. I once watched a group of Chinese construction workers haggle with a Russian, at the back of his truck, over the price of the beef head itself; unable to communicate in a common language, they were miming the writing of numbers on the palms of their hands.

Not only is more of the animal on display, it is also not cut and packaged before you buy it. The butcher in an organized market may cut some steaks or roasts and place them unwashed and unwrapped, directly on the counter for people to choose. The butcher might also cut somewhat to your request from a quarter or half of beef hanging behind the counter. In more casual situations, the seller may be more of a farmer than a butcher – and in those cases it is more accurate to describe the meat as sold by the whack instead of by the cut. A quarter of beef pulled from the back of a station wagon – and cut up with an axe on a wooden stump brought along for the occasion – may indeed be fresh, but the cut is less precise and the process certainly is messier. Buyers also had to bring their own plastic bags, because meat in Russia is neither packaged before sale nor wrapped for you at the time of purchase.[28]

The beef and pork in these farmers' markets was good – the beef leaner than its American equivalent and not as tender, the pork fatter and darker. Pork itself commanded a premium price over beef in Russia; pork was valued for its tenderness and for the fat which could be used in other cooking or enjoyed on its own.[29] The Russian chickens sold in the markets tended to have a high bone-to-flesh ratio; therefore, we usually bought frozen chicken parts instead. The parts available were always the leg quarters – imported from the United States and sold individually by weight (or sometimes in American-packaged 5-pound bags). Chickens with no tops were the rule in Russia! Such leg quarters were known in market argot as 'gorbushki' – a word derived from the names of the two chiefs of state who signed the agreement permitting such trade between the USSR and the USA, Mikhail Gorbachev and George Bush.[30]

Occasionally we encountered fish in the farmers' markets as well. Often it was frozen fish, such as salmon.[31] On one memorable occasion we were shopping with a Russian friend who suddenly exclaimed, 'Tom, you want that salmon!' I asked why that one in particular, and she explained that it was a female and still full of roe. We took the fish home, thawed it, and took out the roe, which we processed according to her directions. The result was quite a nice amount of red caviar – so much I even ate caviar for breakfast for the next three days.[32]

If we could not find what we wanted in stores or at the farmers' markets, then we might find it at the private kiosks. The pervasive sight of kiosks selling everything under-the-sun has becomes a feature of the Russian landscape since the end of the Soviet era. In any Russian city you will find rows of kiosks, often purveying strange mixes of products. Some may carry mostly liquor, others cigarettes and magazines, still others will have some items of clothing, a few candy bars, a bit of food, some cosmetics, a few cans of beer or soft drinks, and so on. If you are shopping the kiosks, you must walk from one to the other to see what they have on that particular day. In downtown Vladivostok there is an entire three-block area of nothing but kiosks. They begin at the main bus terminal for intercity busses and go down the hill in two different directions toward the ocean. One group is the fresh flower market, but the other has an incredible jumble of small items. On a given day one kiosk might have Russian caviar and French champagne. A few days later it might have only canned mackerel and vodka.

The kiosks can be an important source of certain food items. For a time one kiosk in Vladivostok stocked canned peas of Russian origin, next to a wide selection of panty hose. Other food shops and kiosks had no canned peas, but this one did. Another kiosk had two types of Czech beer for several weeks; another was the only place that had American granulated sugar, a rarity in Russia. There seemed little rhyme or reason to the stocking: it depended on whatever the seller had acquired – either from abroad, or locally, through whatever legitimate or illegitimate channels. People who owned or supplied kiosks might acquire large quantities of a particular item from former state stores, then hold on to them until that item was in short supply and sell it with a high mark-up.

Such things as detergent and toilet paper were often found in kiosks when they had disappeared from the usual stores. Or, food products from a semi-defunct state industry's canteen would wend their way through the arms of the mafia to the many kiosks around the city. Again, the rule (as in the Soviet era) was if you see it today, buy it now, because it might be gone tomorrow – not to be restocked as one would expect in a more functional economy.

Street sellers were another dimension of shopping in Russia. They could range from the lone person near a bus stop selling toilet paper from a huge box that he had acquired from an unknown source, to stands set up by restaurants or canteens in front of their place of business to sell anything from prepared food to flour or sugar. Sometimes small food stores or bakeries would also have a table or stall in front of the shop, selling the same goods that were available inside (including such things as *testo*, fresh yeast dough, which we bought for making pizzas at home).[33] Again, we never knew what we might find. A standard Russian rule is to carry some cash and a shopping bag with you at all times, to take advantage of such opportunities. I remember one day when I was going to meet my wife and a friend of hers near the train station in Vladivostok, so we could all have lunch together at a passably decent restaurant up the hill from there. En route, I saw an unusual sight in front of a company canteen: a woman dressed in her canteen uniform was selling corn meal, apparently an overstock. I hurried to meet my wife and we all went back to stand in the line and figure out how many kilos we thought we were capable of carrying back to our apartments. I never saw corn meal in Russia again.[34]

Another small pleasure was finding people in the farmers' markets or on the street selling prepared food. Sometimes these would be individuals who had brought items from home to the market, and at other times a stand would be set up in front of a cafe or restaurant. My two personal favorites among the prepared foods were 'Russian pizza' and *piroshki*.[35] Russian pizza was available both inside and in front of a casual cafe on the main street of Vladivostok. These small pizzas were yeasty rounds of bread topped with pork and onions, or farmer's cheese, or mushrooms, or fiddle-head ferns. They were delightful snacks that were enjoyable with the very milky coffee sold along with them. *Piroshki*, my other favorite street food, are small savory pies made of fried (or sometimes baked) dough surrounding a filling of meat, rice, sauerkraut, vegetables or some combination of these ingredients. Sellers of *piroshki* could often be found at large streetcar and bus interchanges, as well as at the various markets around town. The first *pirozhok* I tried was not the best – way too fatty and the oil in which it had been cooked was rather old. When my wife walked up to me and asked, 'What in the world are you eating?' I replied, 'A doughnut of the last tsar' – a term that we continued to use whenever we encountered bad *piroshki* after that. But I found better examples as I went along, even to the point of seeking out individual vendors in certain markets.

It was always possible to buy ice cream on the street in Vladivostok. In summer it was sold from cool-cases and later, as the icy winter set in, straight from cardboard boxes. (In the Russian winter there was no problem of melting.) The ice cream cones came from the factory already filled but not wrapped in anything – the vendor would hand you one with tongs or let you pick up one yourself. Ice cream is the ultimate (and best) Russian fast food. Usually the flavor was vanilla, which was preferable, since the other flavors were either weak or artificial in character.

If you wanted something to drink with your snack, you could always find a kiosk or stand selling soft drinks, or kvass, or sometimes beer. At various times during our stay in Vladivostok, I found American, German, Australian, Czech, Japanese, and Chinese beer available. However, Russian beer – a type of top-fermented ale more in the style of English beers than American pilsner-style beers – leaves much to be desired. Russian beer was often watery in character or had off-flavors due to inconsistent quality control. Russians who liked domestic beer would try to find a reliable street stand as a source for draught beer. At the beer stand you could either drink from the stand's mugs – which were somewhat washed between customers – or bring your own container to carry the beer away. I once saw a smiling Oriental worker walking away from a beer stand with a plastic bag full of beer. I regretted that I did not have time to follow him and see how he drank it!

Ussurisk: a regional market center

Another special memory of shopping in Russia was the result of a combination shopping trip and excursion to the regional market town of Ussurisk, so that we could see more of the Primorye countryside and visit a farmers' market in a smaller regional center. We went in autumn after the leaves had changed. The market, which was located in an area that included both a large barn-like building as well as outdoor stands and tables, was large and teeming with people who had come into town from all around the countryside. There were no well dressed city people in this market, only country people in practical and often-repaired clothing, who came to buy or sell on market day. The vendors were both Russians and Orientals; Ussurisk is not far from the border with China, and some signs in the main stores of the city were even written in Chinese. The market offered the produce of the fall harvest, in all its color. Russian vendors sold home-canned cucumbers, tomatoes, or sauerkraut, in addition to a wide variety of mushrooms. Asian vendors had fresh vegetables, oriental salads, spicy carrots with squid bits, and kim chee. Hard cheese and sausage were also available. Inside the wooden building with its long plank tables were people selling fresh meat in one area, honey in another area, and dairy products in another. The dairy counters were covered with fresh cheese (*tvorog*) as well as the best sour cream (*smetana*) that I have eaten. Country sour cream was superior to anything we could get in the stores. At the Ussurisk market, the vendors prided themselves on the fact that a large, heavy spoon would stand upright in their bowls of extra-thick *smetana*.

The market was also full of people selling sweaters and track suits, fur coats and fur hats, car parts, tools, and hardware. Except for the modern items, I felt like I had gone back in time to the markets of the Tsarist era. (Historical descriptions of them sound much like the market in Ussurisk.)[36] When we visited some of the other stores in the Ussurisk, we could see why many people came to the open-air market or traveled to Vladivostok for basic items like pots and pans and tools, because so little was available elsewhere. However, one food store near the market was well-stocked – it even had sugar (which was becoming hard to find in Vladivostok at that particular time). A Russian friend accompanying us was also pleased to find salmon heads for sale, so that she could make aspic for her family. This was also the first store we had seen that had a large section of very reasonably priced products reserved solely for war veterans. On our way back to Vladivostok we stopped at the factory store of the Ussurisk distillery, where we purchased spiced rum and a very good type of vodka made exclusively from wheat grains. This was our introduction to the many varieties of vodka that are made in Russia – some much more drinkable than others.[37]

As the end of our first semester in Russia drew near, all of the American faculty (and our Russian friends) marveled at how much we had adapted to the unusual world of Russian shopping. Our colleagues who were headed back to the United States began to talk about the restaurants where they would eat and how good a supermarket would look to them. The two of us, however, were staying in Russia – taking the Trans-Siberian Railroad to Irkutsk to teach during the spring semester at Irkutsk State University. In mid-January, we left Vladivostok by train, departing after midnight and waking to find ourselves rolling through a winter landscape. The train itself was comfortable: we had a two-person cabin and plenty of hot water from the samovar at the end of the car. It was a 72-hour ride to Irkutsk, and we had come prepared with our own food – packages of instant oriental noodles, cans of sprats from the Baltic, a smoked salmon, and a salami. We did not expect to shop along the way, but I could not resist hopping off at the longer stops to walk among the vendors along the platform who were selling their homemade foods to the passengers on the train. Each stop seemed to offer different items. One had several *piroshki* vendors, another had *pel'meni* vendors, and in the very cold interior, one stop had only vendors selling cooked potatoes in paper cones (with bits of browned onions on top). At a stop near Lake Baikal we bought some of the famous *omul* (fish) which come only from Baikal.[38] Finally we arrived in Irkutsk, the capital of Eastern Siberia, our home for the next semester. It was minus 30 degrees Celsius and would be more than two months before we saw a thaw.[39]

Food shopping in Irkutsk

Irkutsk, with a population of 650,000, is located on the Angara river, approximately 40 miles from Lake Baikal, the world's oldest, deepest, and largest lake.[40] Founded as a military outpost in 1652, Irkutsk was historically important as a trading center for tea and silk from China, as well as fur and gold from Siberia.[41] A major stop on the Trans-Siberian Railroad, Irkutsk is the largest Siberian city between the Pacific Ocean to the east and Novosibirsk to the west.

Shopping for food in Irkutsk was different from Vladivostok because not only were we in Siberia, with its shorter growing season, but also it was the middle of winter. Irkutsk was far in time and space from the autumn markets of the relatively temperate Russian Far East. The limited growing season made Irkutsk more dependent than Vladivostok on food from elsewhere – whether it came by road or train or air. For people who like fresh fruits and vegetables, the choices were indeed limited (and sometimes nonexistent!). At one point in the winter, the only 'green vegetables' we could find were onions that had sprouted.

In Irkutsk during the winter, we were more dependent on the former state stores for food (especially for root vegetables and cabbage). The city also had a good central market which offered many products brought in by plane from Central Asia (a practice that may be less common now, since cheap Aeroflot fares are a thing of the past). Compared to Vladivostok, there were more products from European countries, especially Eastern and Central European countries that had been in the former Soviet sphere of influence. We were pleased to find such items as Bulgarian and Hungarian pickled peppers readily available, as well as wines from Hungary. Other Western products – Dutch cheeses, Italian pasta, Turkish olive oil, German beer, Swiss chocolates – would appear in the stores, be available for a while, and then disappear from the shelves.[42] Given the rail connections to Irkutsk, there were also many Chinese goods which made their way north, including food items such as noodles and tins of beef and pork. Again, we were seeing a pattern that became characteristic of Russia during this period – the increasing importation of a variety of food items, most of which had not been available to average Russian consumers during the Soviet era.

In Irkutsk we lived in a concrete high-rise development on the edge of the city, in a typical Soviet-style apartment building with all the charm of a parking garage. In the traditional central planning manner, the apartments were built and occupied long before the planned shops on the ground floors were completed.[43] Construction of the shops had also been put on hold by the recent changes in the government and the economy. Therefore, we usually had to go by bus to another area of apartments that did have a few places to shop. Most of the shops were former state-run stores with limited stocks, but it was possible to buy eggs, cheese, butter (and sometimes chocolate-flavored butter), pasta, and canned vegetables. One treasure was 3-liter jars of Russian canned green tomatoes. We used them for salads, to garnish meat, or to stir-fry with onions. As time passed, however, an increasing number of items became available as traders brought in more imports and as individuals and groups began to open more small stores and kiosks in the high-rise suburbs.

For more extensive food shopping we travelled once a week to the center of the city, where more goods were available, both at the central market and at other stores and kiosks. In the Irkutsk central market there were many vendors, including Central Asians, Russians, and Buryats. Most of the fruits and nuts that were available came from Central Asia, and prices were controlled by the Central Asian vendors to avoid price competition. Vendors also came from the Caucasus bringing fresh fruits, walnuts, and cilantro. Another group of Asian vendors (probably Chinese) sold kim chee and other similar products. Russian vendors offered sauerkraut, potatoes, beets, carrots, onions, and cabbages – when available. Roasted sunflower seeds and Siberian pine nuts were often for sale. Russians were also the purveyors of dairy products, especially fresh cheese, hard cheeses, butter, and sour cream. At the edge of the market we could purchase an excellent, chewy, white, yeast-raised flatbread, about one inch thick, called 'lavash' – a misnomer to people more familiar with the very thin flatbread of the Caucasus.[44]

The meat section of the market was roughly divided according to product. A few sellers (both Russian and Oriental) offered both beef and pork; others had only one kind of meat, whether fish or fowl or pork. All the posted prices were the same, but the Oriental pork sellers might whisper a lower price to get your business. The meat was cheap by our standards and was very good, particularly such cuts as T-bone 'roasts' (these were T-bone steaks, but 2 to 3 inches thick).[45] The only disappointment was the chicken. When we first arrived in Irkutsk, there was little imported fowl available, and Russian chickens, scrawny and stringy, were often the only choice. I referred to them as 'Russian roadrunners.' Only one shop in the city offered reasonably plump chickens – but the lines to purchase them were always long. So we were very happy when American *gorbushki* finally began to arrive in Irkutsk in the late spring.

The presence of topless chickens that we were so pleased to see in Irkutsk was, as mentioned earlier, the result of an agreement signed in the late 1980s between the American President George Bush and the Soviet Premier Mikhail Gorbachev. By the time we went to Russia, a significant number of chicken leg quarters were being shipped to Russia from chicken producers in the United States. At the retail level, a Russian seller might set up his operation on the street in front of a shop or at a farmers' market. He would have commercial cardboard boxes of frozen chicken leg quarters stacked up next to a small table with a scale on it. The seller would open the box and separate the pieces by hand or with whatever tool was available (perhaps a screwdriver), or simply drop them on the sidewalk to break them apart. They would then be weighed and dropped into the customer's plastic shopping bag. Other vendors might have prepackaged leg quarters in 5-pound plastic bags. For us, as well as other shoppers in Russia, *gorbushki* represented an excellent food product at a reasonable price.

One memorable surprise in Irkutsk was the sudden appearance of lettuce in the market on a cold day in early March. We had not seen lettuce since the previous summer in the United States. The sight of a box of Romaine lettuce in Siberia seemed a harbinger of spring. We purchased the best-looking head we could find but, unfortunately, the tips of the leaves froze and turned brown before we could get the lettuce back home. Winter was still very much with us. An American colleague of ours in Irkutsk had a similar experience when he bought fresh eggs at a local store, then decided to walk several miles in the snow back to his apartment. The eggs were frozen solid by the time he got home!

Actually the Russian winter provides an important means of food preservation. Meat, fish, and prepared items such as *pel'meni* can be sold frozen on the streets, without the need for additional refrigeration. (Icy blocks of fish are chopped apart with an axe or other tools before being weighed for the customer.) Milk was sold at the central market in the form of large 'Popsicles.' The milk had been placed in a bucket or shallow pan and allowed to freeze with a stick in the middle of it – which became the handle you used for carrying it home. Ice cream also required no special storage – although you had to hold your cone with a gloved hand in the winter. But winter is hard on fresh lettuce.

The first day that temperatures rose above freezing in Irkutsk was during the last week of March. Freezing nights continued until mid-May and frosts were still possible until mid-June. By the end of May, however, the days were becoming warm and pleasant, and winter was retreating before the sun. The food markets began to change as well, as more traders from southerly climes made their way to the Irkutsk area and, finally, as plants began to grow and be harvested from forests and fields. Two items that became increasingly available were fiddle-head ferns (*paparotnik*) and wild garlic (*cheremsha*).[46] Fiddle-head ferns were available at the central market, but we could also go to the nearby forests and pick them ourselves. We usually cooked them in the Korean manner, with onions, pork, and hot red pepper (a recipe we had acquired in Vladivostok, where this dish is quite popular).

Wild garlic was new to us. Bottomless onions were a distant memory, and wild garlic was a welcome new green after the long winter. We chopped its green leaves and small tips for salads, and we appreciated its subtle garlic flavor. We first encountered wild garlic in the central market, and later learned how to forage for it ourselves. In late spring, one of our older students invited us to go with his family on a picnic to an area where wild garlic was known to grow. While our student's wife and mother cooked shaslik over a fire, he showed us how to hunt for *cheremsha*. It was an interesting picnic, not only for the good food and wild garlic, but also for the location itself, the site of a former gulag camp near Irkutsk.[47] Only the occasional foundation remained as a reminder of where we were. Across the field ran a rail line to nowhere, now covered with spring flowers. We brought back some barbed wire as well as wild garlic from the site. I'll always wonder whose remains fertilized those plants.

Summer came with its bright warmth, and the fields and forests around Irkutsk bloomed with wild flowers. People were more cheerful, and fur hats and coats were finally put away for the season. Everyone rushed to their dachas to begin preparing the soil and planting their gardens.[48] They knew that time was short and another winter would come soon. And they would still need their dacha products, despite the increased availability of imported foods. At the beginning of July, we boarded the Trans-Siberian Railroad, heading east to Khabarovsk on the first leg of a two-month trip to America and England. This time it was a different Siberia that we crossed. The great open spaces were green and flowering, covered with wild iris and tiger lilies instead of snow. Vendors at stops along the route offered a wide variety of foods (often brought to the station in rickety old prams), including potato salad, cabbage salad, bunches of radishes and *cheremsha*, baked goods, and *piroshki*. Only a few days later we would again be in a world where supermarkets were full, where food products were fresh and well-displayed, and where meals could be planned in advance instead of being wholly dependent on the vagaries of the marketplace in Russia.

Returning to the food markets of Vladivostok

After a summer respite in the United States and England, we returned to Russia for the fall semester in Vladivostok. We had enjoyed the 'lazy' world of the West, where we could plan our meals before going shopping, drive our car to the store, pick the items ourselves from the shelf, and pay as we left. However, we were interested in seeing what changes had occurred in Vladivostok since we had left there the previous winter.

As 'old Russia hands' we were surprised at what we saw. Vladivostok was changing rapidly. Former state stores were being spruced up and stocked with a wider array of goods, many imported. Other food stores had been closed, and were now in the process of being transformed into much more fashionable shops or boutiques. Part of the transformations were predictable – such as food shops which added a coat of paint and increased the number of products they stocked. Some stores had closed for renovations, but continued to sell their products on tables in front of the shop, or in one case, from a bread truck parked on the sidewalk in front of a bakery that was under renovation. Other changes were less predictable. One former bread store eventually became a fashionable clothing shop with a bread boutique in one corner – the result of rules governing the transformation from state-run to privately owned stores, which required former food shops to continue selling food for a certain period of time after they had converted to the sale of non-food products.

The pace of change was noticeable in the number of construction projects, the number of shops being renovated, and the increased number of kiosks and vendors in the markets. In the fall of 1993 when we went to a farmers' market in Vladivostok, we might find a truck with only a load of onions for sale, or perhaps with a load of both potatoes and carrots. By the autumn of 1994, the markets had one or more trucks which were essentially mobile shops, with a wide array of goods displayed on shelves at the back and the 'shopkeeper' selling from the truck, sometimes from behind a Plexiglas front. The stores also had more products in them. Formerly state-run food stores that had once stocked grains, milk products, or meats (when available) had suddenly acquired shelves full of food products from China, Korea, Vietnam, Hungary, Australia, and America. For example, it was now possible to buy imported canned goods such as peppers from Hungary, pineapple from Vietnam, and vegetables from the USA, in addition to baking potatoes and frozen turkey legs from America. Fruit and vegetable vendors began to pay attention to display, and to shake a bit of the dirt and mud off the root vegetables before putting them out for sale. However, meat, fish, and chicken continued to be sold in the traditional Russia way – by the whack and bring your own sack.[49]

By the autumn of 1994, there were also more companies from abroad committing themselves to Russia and its emerging markets. Two examples were noticeable from the perspective of food shopping in Vladivostok. First was an American supermarket company, Globus, which had opened up shop on the outskirts of the city. While it had a small retail operation as part of the store, it mainly served as a wholesaler to other shops and kiosks of the city. Globus also had a van that travelled to the various farmers' markets in Vladivostok and offered a selection of American products for sale. The company's focus was on food products and household items (such as detergent), and it was doing a booming business. New products brought in by Globus would soon begin to appear in various shops, markets, and kiosks around the city. Globus' prices were usually reasonable at the parent store, and were competitively marked-up when sold by other vendors.[50] A second example of a foreign effort to market in Russia was from Australia. Australian products including canned vegetables and fruits, soft drinks, milk products, baby foods, soups, candies, and wines were being sold on the ground floor of one of the old state department stores on the main street of Vladivostok. The contrast between the older, drab, Russian store and this bright western corner was noticeable – and business was brisk.

The increased choices of products – from the Pacific Rim and from Europe – pushed many Russian products from the shelf. It was still possible to buy such things as Russian canned tomatoes or peas, but in many cases Russian customers preferred foreign products, even paying more for them, under the assumption that they were superior to their Russian counterparts. This was, of course, often the case. Many manufactured products such as tools and hardware imported from Korea and China were certainly better than the Russian versions. But this was not always the case in regard to food. Russians with whom we worked eventually began to discover that some of the imported food products were expensive for what they were. Some Russians also began to realize that they were paying a lot for the value added in food processing. For example, Uncle Ben's rapidly increased sales of its products when they were first introduced, mainly because of the company's sophisticated marketing strategy and extensive advertising campaign. Some of our Russian friends and colleagues, however, began noticing that the price of an imported seasoned rice product was much more expensive than the cost of locally grown rice which they seasoned themselves. The convenience of a new product and its novelty as a western import will often lead to a first-time purchase, but companies that hope to succeed in the long term in Russia will have to develop customers continue to prefer its products and buy them on a regular basis.

Another interesting example of western products crowding out their Russian counterparts is in the area of candy, especially chocolates. Vladivostok had a candy factory which produced chocolates and other candies that were as good as standard commercial candies made in the West. The outlet kiosk near the factory gates always had a long line of customers, even in the winter. Yet the stores and kiosks around the city began to stock more expensive western candies in place of the excellent local product. In particular, the Mars candy company has made a serious entry into the Russian market, with extensive distribution and heavy advertising. Even in Irkutsk the previous winter, we had seen vendors on the streets selling Mars bars – which had to be warmed up a bit before it was safe to bite into them. Likewise, imported western ice cream products were beginning to supplant locally made ones. Visitors to Russia in the past often commented on the excellent taste of Russian ice cream, which has long been one of the best products of the Russian food industry. By the time we left Vladivostok, however, imported ice cream products – in colorful cartons, on sticks, or wrapped in fancy foil – where the 'in' thing for Russians to eat, on the street or in their homes (if they could afford such expensive food items). We ourselves were unfamiliar with the imported brands of ice cream being marketed in Russia, and the ones we ate were inferior to most Russian-made ice cream, in terms of both taste and price.

In a country where the cuisine has often been limited by the lack of foodstuffs (due to the climate and to political and economic reasons), an increase in the availability of foreign products has been a welcome change both for foreigners living in Russia and for the Russians themselves. In the emerging market economy of Russia, one important question is to what extent Russian producers will be able to provide products of acceptable quality that meet the expectations of Russian consumers who are becoming increasingly acquainted with international products and their quality. In many cases, joint ventures between Russian companies and foreign companies are offering an opportunity for Russian firms to acquire the technology and know-how to upgrade their facilities and their products. And those of us who taught in the new management programs at universities in Siberia and the Russian Far East hoped that we were making a contribution to the continuing development of a functional market economy in Russia.

Outside of major cities such as Vladivostok and Irkutsk the pace of change is still slow. When we returned to the regional market town of Ussurisk in late 1994, we found far fewer signs of change than in Vladivostok. Although more imported products were now available, the same farmers and babushkas were in Ussurisk to market their home-grown products as they had been doing for years. The slower pace of change was especially noticeable to my wife and me when we accepted a Russian friend's invitation to stay at her house in a village 12 hours north of Vladivostok by train. The village was very small, and little was available in the town's only shop. Most of the shelves were bare, and no imported foods were to be seen. People either had to drive or take a bus to a larger place to find more goods. Or they could continue to do what Russian villagers have always done – grow and store their own food. We spent the weekend helping our friend put potatoes and turnips into the root cellar, tie up and hang onions to dry, shred cabbage for sauerkraut, and sort the seeds for next year's planting.[51] The market economy is coming to Russia, but it will be more noticeable in the larger cities, and the ones on major trade routes, long before it reaches the villages of the heartland.

Postscript on 'Gorbushki'

From the perspective of the chicken producers in the United States, the sale of broiler parts to Russia has become an important business. As noted in the industry magazine, *Broiler Industry*, the value of broiler meat sales to Russia reached $299 million dollars in 1994. That represented 24 per cent of the value of U.S. broiler exports at that time.[52] Most of the sales were of chicken leg quarters. Why leg quarters? In general, in the United States, chicken and chicken products tend to be dominated by white meat parts of the chicken. Chicken breast has become a popular food item, particularly among health-concious Americans. Some fast food products, such as chicken McNuggets are also based on white meat. Another chicken product that has become popular in the United states is chicken wings – especially 'Buffalo hot wings', chicken wings cooked in a spicy sauce and then dipped in blue cheese dressing. The American market obviously prefers chicken tops to chicken bottoms.

Since chickens come with both bottoms and tops, producers need to find markets for the less popular leg quarters or sell them at very reduced prices. The latter solution may not be as desirable as exporting them to places where they are more appreciated. For example, I presently live in a small town in north-east Texas which is the home of the fifth largest broiler producer in the United States, Pilgrim's Pride. The largest producer, Tyson's, is in the adjacent state of Arkansas. In this part of the country chicken breasts (bone-in) sell for $ .99 to $1.99 per pound (boneless and skinless breasts sell for appreciably more, $2.99 and up). Leg quarters sell for only $ .59 cents per pound or less. The local Wal-Mart has been selling 10 pound bags of leg quarters for $3.50 for several months. Given the cost of raising broilers, especially in a period with rising corn prices, profits in the broiler industry become chicken feed, in the slang sense, as the price of chicken feed continues to rise.

American chicken producers have sought export markets for products such as leg quarters, and Russia has become the largest single market for them. By 1995, the total broiler meat exports to Russia had reached $550.4 million, an increase of 83 per cent over the 1994 figure. This dollar value represented 674,447 metric tons of broiler meat, or 36.3 per cent of U.S. broiler exports.[53] These figures represent a boon to American broiler exporters, but they may be a short-run phenomenon. The United States has had a distinct cost advantage in the past due to low feed prices and efficient operations. In 1995, as noted in a *Broiler Industry* survey, costs of producing eviscerated whole birds in the United States were one-third of the cost of producing such birds in Russia. As noted in the article, there are difficulties in comparing the figures in question which may alter the size of the gap, but the general pattern of significant cost advantages to American producers is correct.[54] In 1996, however, rising feed prices in America threatened to narrow the gap. Corn prices recently hit a twelve-year high in the United States. In 1994, corn was $1.99 per bushel, but in January 1996 it reached $3.09 per bushel.[55]

The rising cost for American producers is only one factor that can alter the importance of imported chicken in the Russian market. The Russian government has been encouraging Russian chicken production, or at least discouraging importation of chicken, most notably through raising tariffs. Prior to 1994, there was only a relatively small tariff on imported broiler meat. In July 1994, however, Russia increased the tariff to 20 per cent and then increased it again in July 1995 to 25 per cent. Further attempts to discourage imports have taken the form of blustering – including recent Russian threats to ban poultry imports from the United States.[56] The ban, which was to have taken effect in March 1996, was cancelled due to both European and U.S. pressure. The ostensible reason for such a ban was concern over the cleanliness of American chicken production facilities. However, having seen the retail practices of the local Russian street sellers with their concrete-impact separation technique, I would conclude that this is a case of protectionism, not of public heath. Still, it is a matter of concern both for the Russian consumer who may have to pay more for scrawny domestic chickens, and for exporters who could lose a valuable market. One writer who is interested in this industry has encouraged American producers to form joint-ventures with Russian firms instead of counting on exports alone.[57] As Russian markets continue to evolve, Russian production of popular items such as chicken will certainly increase – but the pace of such changes is hard to predict.

BIBLIOGRAPHY

Abo, Paul, 'Dancing With the Russian Bear', *Broiler Industry*, August 1995, pp.24-28.

Bobrick, Benson, *East of the Sun: The Epic Conquest and Tragic History of Siberia*. New York: Poseidon Press, 1992.

von Bremzen, Anya, and John Welchman, *Please to the Table: The Russian Cookbook*. New York: Workman Publishing, 1990.

Chamberlain, Lesley, *The Food and Cooking of Russia*. New York: Penguin Books, 1983.

Custine, Astolphe, Marquis de. *Empire of the Czar* (1839). New York: Doubleday, 1989.

Evans, Terry, 'Broiler Production Costs Around the World', *Broiler Industry*, December 1995, pp.38-44.

Evans, Terry, 'Changes Ahead in the Broiler Trade?', *Broiler Industry*, December 1996, pp.28-36.

Goldstein, Darra, *The Georgian Feast*. New York: Harper Collins, 1993.

Heilbroner, Robert L, *The Making of Economic Society*. Englewood Cliffs, New Jersey: Prentince-Hall, 1962.

Herlemann, Horst, *Quality of Life in the Soviet Union*. Boulder, Colorado: Westview Press, 1987.

Hosking, Geoffrey, *The First Socialist Society*. Cambridge, Massachusetts: Harvard University Press, 1992.

Hudgins, Sharon, 'Spicy Siberia: Hot Foods in a Cold Climate', *Chile Pepper Magazine*, November/ December 1995, Vol. IX, No.6, pp.16-23, 34-36.

Jones, Anthony, and William Moskoff (eds.), *The Great Market Debate in Soviet Economics*. Armonk, New York: M.E. Sharpe, 1991.

Kennan, George, *Siberia and The Exile System*, 2 vols. New York: The Century Co., 1891.

Kennan, George, *Tent Life in Siberia* (1871). Salt Lake City, Utah: Gibbs M. Smith Inc., 1986.

Kort, Michael, *The Soviet Colossus: The Rise and Fall of the USSR* (3rd edition). Armonk, New York: M.E. Sharpe, 1993.

Kotkin, Stephen, and David Wolff (eds.), *Rediscovering Russia in Asia: Siberia and the Russian Far East*. Armonk, New York: M.E. Sharpe, 1995.

Lee, Steven H., 'Ruffled Feathers: Chicken Producers Cut Production to Survive Price Squeeze', *The Dallas Morning News*, March 9, 1996, pp.1F and 11F.

Lincoln, W. Bruce, *The Conquest of a Continent*. New York: Random House, 1994.

Massie, Suzanne, *Land of the Firebird: The Beauty of Old Russia*. New York: Simon & Schuster, 1980.

Miller, Elisa and Alexander Karp, *Pocket Handbook of the Russian Far East: A Reference Guide*. Seattle, Washington: Russian Far East Update, May 1994.

Newby, Eric, *The Big Red Train Ride*. New York: St. Martin's Press, 1978.

'Russia's Crisis of Capitalism', *The Economist*, October 15, 1994, pp.33-34.

'Selling the Sod', *The Economist*, June 29, 1996, pp.78-79.

Shifrin, Avraham, *The First Guidebook to Prisons and Concentration Camps of the Soviet Union*. New York: Bantam Books, 1980.

Smith, Hedrick, *The Russians*. New York: Ballantine Books, 1976.

Smith, Hedrick, *The New Russians*, New York: Random House, 1990.

Thornton, Lisa, 'U.S. Exports Hit 1.7 Billion', *Broiler Industry*, April 1996, pp.22-27.

Toomre, Joyce, *Classic Russian Cooking: Elena Molokhovets' A Gift to Young Housewives*. Bloomington Indiana: Indiana University Press, 1992.

Volokh, Anne, *The Art of Russian Cuisine*. New York: Macmillan Publishing, 1983.

NOTES

[1] See Smith (1990), pp.566-568 and Hosking, p. 488.

[2] Both of us were employed by the International Programs division of University of Maryland University College. UMUC had established an undergraduate degree program with two Russian universities, which granted both a Russian and an American degree to successful candidates. The two Russian universities are Far Eastern State University in Vladivostok and Irkutsk State University in Irkutsk. Established in 1991, this program was the first of its kind in Russia.

[3] The prices quoted throughout the paper are in dollar terms, based on the exchange rate at the time. The

difficulty in discussing prices more thoroughly is that this period was one of *giperinflatzia* (or hyper-inflation) in Russia. To convey a sense of this type of inflation: in September of 1993 shortly after we arrived in Vladivostok, the exchange rate was $1.00 = 990 rubles. By January of 1994 the rate was $1.00 = 1,594 rubles. By September of 1994 when we returned to Vladivostok, it was $1.00 = 2,222 rubles, and by the time we left in January 1995 it was approximately 4,000 rubles to the dollar after spiking even higher at one point. At present (late June 1996) one dollar is worth 5,091 rubles. Hyperinflation may have stopped for the present, but inflation remains a problem for the Russian economy. The hyperinflation has been largely blamed on Russia's Central Bank which does deserve much of the blame. However, a second factor should be kept in mind – prices in the former Soviet system rarely reflected the real costs of producing products. Much of the early debate on reforming the economy, beginning in the Gorbachev era, was on the question of how to reform prices so they reflected real costs. As reform gave way to complete change, prices had to change. Even now, there are still problems with the accuracy of some prices, since failing state industries are still supported by various subsidies. Interested readers should refer to Jones and Moskoff, pp. 160-180, and Smith (1990), p. 241.

[4] Problems with the accuracy of Soviet information have been noted before. The reform economists of the transition period have largely been from Akademgorodok near Novosibirsk, which has a long history of trying to measure what is actually going on in the economy. See Smith, pp. 9-10.

[5] Heilbroner, pp. 19-20.

[6] For one historical example of the problem, see Lincoln, p. 374.

[7] See Shmelev in Jones and Moskoff, p. 11.

[8] Kort, p. 25.

[9] Smith (1976), pp. 266-267.

[10] Smith (1990), pp 206-232.

[11] For an interesting perspective on the problem of shifting away from collective farming, see Buckley in Kotkin and Wolf, p. 224ff. The case is made that the collective farm served more social roles than that of a production facility alone. The Nizhny Novgorod region has been using 'cashless auctions' to allocate ownership of collective farms since 1993. The approach has led to increased agricultural production. See *The Economist*, June 29, 1996, pp. 78-79.

[12] One Russian professor and his wife grew the following items at their dacha near Vladivostok: tomatoes, cucumbers, carrots, potatoes, onions, garlic, gooseberries, blackberries, and strawberries. They also had cherry, apple, apricot, and plum trees.

[13] An interesting perspective on food preservation and storage in Russia historically can be found in Toomre, pp. 40-44. Many of the practices cited are still used in Russia. Modern technology and production techniques have not always supplanted traditional methods.

[14] A large amount of the Russian land area is permafrost. One estimate is that 50 per cent of Soviet territory, mostly in Siberia, is permafrost. Smith 1976, p. 440.

[15] Descriptions of the winter market in St. Petersburg, drawn from travelers' accounts during different time periods, are quoted in Toomre, pp. 51-54.

[16] During the semester we were at Far Eastern State Univeristy, people who worked in the office brought in both apples and flour for sale. It was also possible to acquire staples from the university canteen, if it had a surplus at all.

[17] Recounted by Kort, p. 283.

[18] Smith (1974), pp. 74-90.

[19] Cited in Kort, p. 283.

[20] See Smith (1976), pp. 76-90.

[21] Many Russians harvest plants from woods and fields. Mushrooms are among the most popular wild foods for people to gather. In the markets of Vladivostok in autumn, there were several vendors with a wide variety of mushrooms for sale.

[22] *Adzhiga*, a type of Russian 'salsa' usually containing peppers, tomatoes, and garlic, is used to flavor stews and soups. For more information (and a recipe) see Hudgins, p. 21.

[23] Miller and Karp pp. 20-21.

[24] The markets we frequented the most during our time in Vladivostok were the First River Market, Second River Market, Belayeva Market and Lugovaya Market. By the autumn of 1994 there was also a market area at

the main port. In addition, many smaller markets existed around the city, often near major transportation interchanges.

[25] To give the reader an idea of the prevailing prices in such a market, in October of 1993 we paid the following per kilogram: potatoes 30¢, carrots 50¢, cabbage 30¢, bread 30¢, and tomatoes $2.00.

[26] The price of eggs in Vladivostok changed quite rapidly that autumn (1993). When we arrived, eggs were readily available and very inexpensive – approximately 25¢ for ten. By October, eggs were harder to find and more expensive. The price rose from 25¢ to 60¢ per ten within two weeks. They became scarcer and more expensive thereafter. By December 1993 they were $2.00 for ten. (In ruble price, they went from 250 to 3,000!) Russians offered various explanations for the price rise, none of which could be proven. One explanation was that producers had slaughtered laying hens because they could not afford to feed them through the winter. Another story was that producers (or the mafia, in other versions) were controlling the price. In contrast, the price in Irkutsk in January 1994 was 70¢ for ten eggs.

[27] Prices in the farmers' markets were, of course, very much subject to the laws of supply and demand. In September 1993 tomatoes sold for 800 to 1,600 rubles per kilo, depending on their quality. By October, the price was 2,000 and rising. In the winter in Irkutsk, they might cost 10,000 rubles when they were available.

[28] The messiness is less of a problem in winter, when the meat is frozen. In the winter we also saw vendors with piles of frozen tongues, liver, hearts, and offal for sale.

[29] For example, in late November 1994, good cuts of beef sold for 15,000 rubles per kilo and pork for 22,000. In dollar terms this was approximately $4.55 vs. $6.67 per kilo. The dollar figures are approximate because of the gyrations of the ruble's foreign exchange rate at that time – the ruble fell 29 per cent against the dollar from September 1st to October 10th, then dropped 22 per cent in a single day on October 11th, and rebounded 25 per cent after Central Bank intervention (see *The Economist*, October 15, 1994). Students in our program, as well as other Russians with whom we talked, always referred to dollars (and other hard currencies) as 'currency' – a term they did not apply to rubles.

[30] *Gorbushki* sold for 2,500 rubles for a kilo (about $2.50) when we first arrived in Vladivostok. The price rose during the autumn, as the value of the ruble declined. As is the case with any imported product, the ruble price reflects the exchange rate, and the ruble went from 990 to the dollar in September of 1993 to 4,000 to the dollar by January of 1995. By the time we left Vladivostok in January 1995, *gorbushki* were selling for 12,000 rubles (approximately $2.67) per kilo.

[31] The harvesting of salmon has long been important in the Russian Far East. See Kennan (1989), p. 65.

[32] Salmon sold for 3,500 rubles per kilo in November 1994, approximately $1.06 per kilo, with no extra charge for the caviar! In general, fish was much cheaper than meat in Vladivostok, and far more affordable for the average Russian consumer.

[33] We usually made Italian-style pizza from the *testo* we bought, but we also made *rasstegai*, a type of Russian savory pie containing fish. Russian cuisine has a wide variety of savory pies. For a good introduction to Russian savory pies, see Volokh, Chapter 4.

[34] Historically, cornmeal came to Russia via Moldova and became an ingredient in Russian cooking. See Chamberlain, p.15.

[35] For an explanation of the various terms for Russian pies, as well as good recipes for several kinds, see von Bremzen and Welchman, pp. 430-454.

[36] For a sense of the food markets of Russia before the Soviet era, see Toomre, p. 51ff. For an interesting description of the historically famous market at Nizhny Novgorod, including food items, see Custine, Chap. 23.

[37] Aside from standard vodka based on potatoes or on a variety of possible grains, there are vodkas with special characteristics depending on the grain which is used (such as wheat vodka), or because of flavoring agents added (such as lemon or pepper vodka). Since we like spicy foods, we especially enjoyed good versions of *pertsovka*, the hot-pepper-flavored vodka. The best unflavored vodka we tasted was one made from the pure water of Lake Baikal.

[38] *Omul*, a white fish of the salmon family, can be eaten raw or cooked, smoked or salted. See Newby, p. 186.

[39] Russians we knew never bothered with the 'minus' when stating a temperature in the winter. They would only say 'twenty' meaning minus twenty. See Smith (1976) on his similar experiences, p. 436.

[40] Bobrick, pp. 29-32.

[41] See Bobrick, Chapter 4, p. 67ff., on the role of the fur trade in the settlement of Siberia.

[42] The pattern of items appearing in stores and then disappearing – sometimes to return later and sometimes never to be seen again – was also characteristic of the Soviet period. It is a type of rolling shortage. See Smith (1976), pp. 77-78.

[43] Herlemann, p. 37.

[44] See Goldstein, pp. 46-47.

[45] T-bones cost 3,500 rubles in January 1994, about $1.06. The price rose to 6,000 rubles later, but that represented only $1.50 per kilo at the prevailing exchange rate. The price hike was due in part to changes in formerly controlled prices.

[46] Wild garlic is known as ramsons in Great Britain. According to Russians in Irkutsk, it is supposed to be high in vitamin C and purportedly a favorite snack of bears emerging from hibernation.

[47] There were, of course, many gulag sites in Siberia. One sourcebook is Shifrin. For an interesting account of the tsarist exile system, see Kennan (1891).

[48] One friend in Irkutsk said that in addition to potatoes, she grew the following items at her dacha: cabbage, carrots, cucumbers, garlic, onions, pumpkins, and herbs such as parsley. She also grew peppers, tomatoes and winter squash in a greenhouse, and had several fruit trees.

[49] My wife went to the fisherman's dock one day in early December and brought home a whole, large Kamchatka crab which cost 25,000 rubles, about $6.00 at the time.

[50] Prices ranged from 1,700 to 2,500 rubles ($ .77 to $1.14) for cans of pineapple, carrots, yams, potatoes, green beans, pork & beans, and olives. Other product prices included: 3,300 rubles ($1.50) for a can of Dinty Moore Beef stew; 5,200 rubles ($2.36) for a liter of tomato sauce; and 6,600 rubles ($3.00) for Newman's Own Spaghetti Sauce.

[51] Our friends grew the following items in their village garden: pumpkins, beets, green cabbages, red cabbages, summer squash, winter squash, watermelons, white radishes, potatoes, carrots, onions, peppers, tomatoes, cucumbers, and various herbs.

[52] Both figures are from *Broiler Industry*. See Aho, p. 24ff.

[53] The figures are based on USDA Foreign Agricultural Service data and are quoted in *Broiler Industry*. See Thorton, p. 22ff.

[54] See Evans, pp. 38ff.

[55] Lee, p.1F.

[56] Lee, p.1F.

[57] It should be noted that in the world of Russia before the revolution, poultry of all sorts, both domestic and imported (except pigeons, due to their religious symbolism in the Russian Orthodox church), was available in the major cities. See Massie, p. 266.

Arabian Travellers' Observations on Bedouin Food

Philip Iddison

Badwiyyin – dwellers in the desert

These characteristics of the land, reacting on the inhabitants, render them in great part of unsettled predatory habit, intensely individualistic, jealous of the secrets of water and pasture which barely make life possible, and proud of an exclusive liberty, which has never been long infringed.

D G Hogarth (1904)[1]

Arabia attracted a sparse number of adventurous travellers from the developing European countries from the sixteenth century to the middle of the present century. Their published accounts identify various attractions ranging through exploration, scientific studies, political or religious intrigue to early ethnographic studies. The latter often concentrated on the bedouin, a case of the traveller observing his fellow traveller. The accounts record a consistent view of the Arabian character and society, epitomized by the harsh realities of bedouin life and the more urbane life of towns and villages. There are passing references to the food of the local people and that introduced by the travellers but this is usually a subsidiary element of the account, subordinated to the travellers' tales of extreme hardship, the mercurial character of the bedouin and a fascination with their social customs. The latter were characterized by the two extremes of the rules of hospitality and the rules of raiding. Tales of the coffee hearth are common and this key element of bedouin life is remarkably consistent through the centuries of travel.

Practically every part of the Arabian peninsula, an area of some 3.2 million square kilometres, was occupied to some degree, from the well-established trade and holy cities such as Jeddah, Mecca and Medina to the nomadic herdsmen of the vast sand deserts such as the Rub al Khali. However the bedouin seemed to dominate the Western perception of Arabia. This landmass included a variety of human habitations. Oasis villages and towns were scattered over the sand and stony deserts of the inland plateau. In the mountains on the southern and western fringes, altitude tempered heat, rain was more plentiful and a much more varied agriculture was possible. The Omani mountains sheltered groves of walnut and fruit trees and Yemeni valleys yielded sorghum and coffee. The long coastline had numerous trading ports and fishing villages where a rich haul of seafood was made.[2]

Despite failing to conquer Arabia the Romans divided it into two provinces, *arabia felix* and *arabia deserta*. *Arabia felix* occupied the whole of the peninsula and effectively controlled the spice trade from the Indies in the period before reliable seaborn commerce became established. It was also the only source of frankincense. *Arabia deserta* was the northern, Syrian desert.[3]

From the start of the Islamic era in September 622, Arabia was practically inaccessible to non-Muslims. The few Westerners who did penetrate Arabia either posed as Muslims or travelled with trepidation as the population were frequently hostile to *kaffirs* (unbelievers).

The earliest account by a European traveller to the Arabian interior was by Ludovico di Varthema, a Bolognese adventurer who accompanied the *haj* caravan from Damascus in 1503 and who reached Yemen where he noted fair orchards, an abundance of vines, fat-tailed sheep and the spice trade.

The discovery of coffee in Yemen was to attract interest from all the main trading nations from the end of the sixteenth century, but trading houses and their European settlers remained in the coastal towns such as Jeddah, Aden and Mokha.

The first party with any aspirations to a scientific assessment of the interior was not mounted until 1762. Carsten Niebuhr was the only member of the party of six to return and his account was published in 1772. The party travelled in Yemen, only reaching as far inland as Sana but amongst many observations gave a detailed description of coffee cultivation which was then supplying the coffee houses of Europe.

The first crossing of Arabia was made by accident rather than by design and yielded little apart from confirmation of the stark terrain. Thereafter a number of travellers made significant journeys into the interior deserts and started to flesh out the lives of the bedouin. Charles Doughty (travelling 1876-8) provides a substantial amount of anecdotal information on the food culture of the bedouin. He travelled extensively in the Hejaz and Nejd, spending periods in oasis towns such as Hail and Kheybar as well as travelling with the bedouin. His observations establish a strong connection between the requirement of the bedouin to travel to find pasture for their flocks which were their economic wealth and sustenance and their frequent visits to the oasis towns which often extended into short periods of residence.

By the early twentieth century the only unexplored area of significance was the great sand desert called the Rub al Khali in the south-western portion of the peninsula and it was to yield little additional information on the food of the region when it was finally crossed in 1931 by Bertram Thomas.

With the advent of oil wealth, bedouin life changed dramatically from an austere existence in exacting terrain to nationality in new wealthy nations and a transition into the modern world in a single generation.

The Bedouin

Several travellers' reports of the bedouin culinary regime are influenced by the rules of hospitality. If the host were expansive or wanted to impress, the quality and quantity of food offered would be lavish and hence create an unrealistic impression of routine consumption, not dissimilar to the situation in other cultures. However there would often be no backup supplies and playing host could seriously deprive the dependants of the host of their meagre rations or seriously deplete the host's flock. The dish of boiled mutton or camel calf served on rice or a 'mess of wheat',[4] *mansaf*, would normally only be a festival or major family event dish for the bedouin.[5] Doughty, Thomas and Thesiger who travelled extensively with small parties of bedouin record a far more basic and monotonous diet. Commonly it was so ordinary that it did not warrant a mention in their journals.

Light breakfasts and occasional impromptu meals of game or for hospitality during the day are recounted but the main meal was usually taken at the end of the day, after the evening milking.

Bedouin culinary requirements ranged from the need to sustain a small group travelling independently, probably with grazing flocks, to the provision for large tribal groups who might be settled in one area for several weeks. Access to fresh provisions might be close at hand in a nearby oasis or could be several days march away.

Thus bread, *'abud*, which was a staple, would be the simple mixing of flour with precious water from the waterskin (*girbeh*) to prepare dough to be cooked in the embers of the fire for wandering herdsmen. In a tribal encampment large quantities of *shirak* or *rukak* (thin unleavened bread) would be prepared and cooked on a *saj* (convex metal sheet), over a fire.

Small game was simply thrown on the fire to cook in its fur and was eaten in its entirety. On the other hand a butchered beast for a feast in a large camp would be cooked in a *jidda* or *qidr* (large stewpot) to be served with wheat or rice[6] and liberally drenched with rendered animal fat or molten butter (*samn*). Wheat is mentioned more in the nineteenth-century accounts and seems to have been replaced by rice as the latter became more readily available through trade.

Cooking utensils were simple and robust. The *jidda*, made of tinned copper,[7] came in a variety of sizes, large specimens were required to cook for feasts. It was accompanied by a shallow dish, *sahen*, for serving food. Wooden bowls and serving dishes were also used. Coffee making required its own utensils described below.

Much cooking was thus an improvised affair, three stones to make a tripod support and a search for dried plant roots in the desert sand or some dried camel dung, *jella*, for fuel.

With food resources at a premium there was little prospect of regular meals, one meal a day would be adequate and no meal was a common occurrence, perhaps a few dry dates and some camel milk sufficing. A bedouin herdsman could survive during the spring grazing, *rabia*, with the very barest of possessions. Doughty recounts meeting two young men several days from camp with their milch camels whose sole provisions were a cloak and stick each and one bowl between them so they could milk their camels for food and drink.

Hospitality

Bedouin hospitality made a great impact on Western travellers. The rules varied but the common version required that if anyone appeared at your camp who was not a sworn enemy, you were duty bound to provide at least a minimum of board and lodging for three and one third days. After that time your guest was required to leave and but was still under your guardianship for a further three days, the time it was believed to take for all the host's food to pass through the guest's body. Frequently a beast would be slaughtered for the first meal, as much to demonstrate the host's wealth and social standing and to uphold tribal honour which was on show on such occasions. Whilst this meal was being prepared, coffee or some other light refreshment such as dates and buttermilk would be served and the guest would be politely questioned to extract useful information. These gatherings were strictly male affairs, if women were in the encampment they would be segregated and would prepare the meal, although slaughter and butchery were men's work.

Meals were served on the ground to the guests first. Food was generally eaten speedily. Once you had taken your fill you would vacate your place at the food to allow someone of lower standing to have his turn. After rinsing your hands you would retire to wait for everyone to finish, after which more coffee would be served. After all the men had eaten, any remaining food would be taken to the women and young children. A host would often abstain from eating, taking a supervisory role to ensure that the hospitality was worthy.

Staples

Bedouin food was dominated by a number of staple items. Apart from water these had to have certain characteristics. They had to be self mobile or at least economical to carry. They had to be readily preserved in the harsh climate which ranged from freezing[8] on the central uplands in winter to 55° Centigrade shade-temperatures in the summer.

Apart from stock and their milk products the staple items were dates, wheat and rice, flour and *samn* (clarified butter).

Dates, *tamr*, were of prime importance to survival in the desert. They were ideal food, readily obtainable as they grew in all the oases, non-perishable, easy to consume, economical to transport, provided excellent nutrition as a balance to the other main dietary constituents and were relatively cheap. Thirty pounds of good dates cost 1 real (then equivalent to 4 shillings) in the 1870s whereas a goat cost 2 reals. Dates were also fodder for camels on a regular basis.

For a few months of the year during the date harvest, the fresh dates from the oases provided a welcome alternative to the usual fare of dried dates.

> The best stems, upon which hanged with the ripe, the half-ripe purple berries, which thus at the mellowing, and full of sappy sweetness, they call *belah*; the Arabs account them very wholesome and refreshing.[9]

Ba-theeth, a preserve of parched flour, dried dates and *samn*, heated together and kneaded into a solid mass was prepared for use on journeys. It had excellent keeping qualities and did not require any further cooking.

Wheat was grown in Arabia in the marginal land where enough winter rain would fall or collect to grow the crop. There are references to *burghul* but it is not clear whether this is the true par-boiled grain or broken wheat boiled as a starch staple for meals. Wheat was cooked in a variety of ways including *harees*, a dish with the consistency of porridge but little of the appeal!

Rice has already been mentioned and there is an interesting aside by Doughty that one of his hosts begged enough water from his guest to cook the rice for the usual mutton meal.

Wheat was ground to flour for bread, hand querns were a possession of larger Bedouin groups. Barley meal is also mentioned as a bread ingredient and millet was grown in some oases although considered fit only for invalids. One dessert plant, *samhh*, yielded grain which could be used for bread, porridge or a version of *ba-theeth*.

Samn was a major commercial product of the bedouin herds which was sold in the villages and towns. Doughty travelled with a caravan from Aneyza to Medina taking the annual production of 30 tonnes[10] of *samn* in goatskin bags, each camel carrying about 170 kilos. The *samn* was prepared by churning either fresh goat or sheep's milk or yoghourt[11] in a skin which was inflated by blowing into it at regular intervals. The fresh butter (*zibdeh*) was heated with flour and occasionally coriander and cummin. Once the samn had been poured off into the storage skin (goatskin for commerce, *dubh* skin for personal use), the curds and flour were eaten and not wasted. A family with a modest herd could produce 250 kilos of *samn* during the winter season, worth £18 at Medina in the 1870s.

Yoghourt, *leban*, was also prepared and was drained and salted to make a sun-dried food for storage, *mereesy* or *jamid*. Initially like a cheese, which is mentioned by several travellers, the drained yoghourt eventually becomes rock hard and well deserves its description by Doughty as 'milk shards'. It was reconstituted by pounding in a mortar and mixing with water or sieving into hot water. As a traveller's food it could be gnawed in its natural state.

Drinks

Water was a precious commodity. Throughout the interior it was only dependably found at some waterholes and at various springs associated with oases. There are no rivers in Arabia. On the rare occasions when a wadi was in spate due to heavy rain, the flow could be disastrous in its power and was likely to run for a day or two at most. With luck it would leave a few pools of water and would raise water levels in adjacent wells for a few months. There were only limited technical means of recovering ground water, the *haddaj* and *suany* or draw-well driven by a camel or ox was the practical limit of mechanization. Some permanent waterholes were 60 feet deep and required considerable effort to draw water with bucket and rope. If a large camel herd or caravan had to be watered the bedouin would work in relays for several hours, often with considerable fear of attack if there were *ghrazzu* (raiding parties) known to be in the vicinity.

The quality of the water was often poor. At frequently used waterholes several travellers noted the contamination of the water with urea percolating into the water source from the camel urine concentrated around the waterhole. Doughty comments on many sub-standard supplies, 'brackish water ...thick well water full of old wafted camel droppings...tasting like alum...mawkish water causing illness in my companions...salty bitter water...water full of wriggling white vermin drunk through the lap of the kerchief...muddy puddle water...'. Yet he claimed that he had never been ill from consumption of any of these doubtful sources.

Coffee, *kahwa*, was the prime social drink.[12] The ring of coffee pestle on the mortar as the freshly roasted beans were crushed was the signal for men to gather at the coffee tent for the exchange of news and recounting of stories. Guests were received by the host who would frequently prepare the coffee himself.

> We sat down to drink coffee with the sheikh, Misshel, who would make it himself. This
> ruler of seven tribes roasted, pounded, boiled and served the cheerful mixture with his
> own hand. Misshel poured me out but one cup, and to his tribesmen two or three.
> Because this shrew's deed was in disgrace of my being a Nasrany, I exclaimed, 'here is a
> great sheikh and a little kahwa!' Thus challenged, Misshel poured me out unwillingly,
> muttering some word of his fanatical humour.[13]

Coffee was always freshly roasted in a *mahmas* (roasting spoon) stirred with a *maqlab*. The
roast beans would be cooled in a *mabradah*, a wooden tray. They were brayed in a *mihbash* or *nijir*
made of wood, iron or brass. In some bedouin families the coffee was brewed in a dedicated pot
made of clay, *medlah*. It would be transferred to the classic beaked Arabian coffee pot of tinned
copper or brass, *dalla* and served in small ceramic cups, *finjeyn*. It was often flavoured with
cardamom.

Milk, *haleeb*, from camel, goat and sheep was consumed, although preference was for camel's
milk. Of the three the camel's milk was drunk whole and the other two usually after the butter had
been made. Doughty reports a hierarchy of bedouin views on the relative merits of the three milk
sources:

> Camel milk is the best of all sustenance, and the very best is that of the *bukkra*, the
> young camel with her first calf, as lightly purgative.
> Ewe's milk is very sweet and fattest of all, it is unwholesome to drink whole, it kills
> people with colic ... ewe buttermilk should be let sour some while in the *semily*
> (butterskin) with other milk, until all are tempered together, and then it is fit to drink.
> Goat milk is sweet, it fattens more than strengthens the body.

These observations are borne out by modern analysis of the milk. An appended table compares
the main characteristics with cow's milk from tropical breeds. Cattle were kept in the oases but are
recorded as being of poor quality.

The dromedary cow has a gestation period of 370 to 375 days and only breeds every second
year commencing at four years of age and continuing until 20 or so years of age. Calving is very
seasonal coinciding with the winter rains and the presence of good feed stocks. The lactation period
varies according to the camel's nutrition but is usually 18 months with yields of 1,000 to 3,000 litres
per year and individual milkings up to 5 litres being common. The milk is rich in vitamin C which is
of particular benefit to the bedouin who have little access to fresh fruit and vegetables. The milk
diet was however not satisfying in some respects; bedouin complained to Doughty of the 'creeping
hunger' and begged him for 'Damascus *kaak* (biscuit), it is six weeks since I have chewed anything'.

Tea drinking was introduced at a relatively late stage but has become well established. Doughty
may be held responsible in part for its introduction as he carried supplies for his own consumption
and several times offered it to bedouin who had not tasted it before. They were generally unimpressed
with the tea flavour, considering it insubstantial compared to coffee, but did enjoy the sugar.[14]

Flocks

Bedouin existence depended on their herds and flocks. The camel was the supreme possession
providing transport for man and his chattels, a mount for raids which would potentially add to his
wealth, milk for food and drink, meat, hair and hides and dung for fuel. Camels were wealth and
would rarely be slaughtered for meat. Any camel meat usually came from the slaughter of surplus
bull calves or injured or sick beasts. Camels enabled man's penetration of the extensive desert
areas as they are capable of sustained travel in search of pasture with only intermittent water supplies.
After the winter rains, rich spring pastures provided enough moisture in the feed to enable camels

to survive without access to water. Contrary to popular conceptions, camels do need regular feed to maintain satisfactory condition but this could be provided by meagre desert plants, some dates or even dried sardines traded up from the coast.

Where daily access to water could be assured, herds of goats and sheep were kept, primarily for milk and meat and also skins, hair and wool to make woven goods. There are references to fresh milk used for human consumption but apart from that dedicated to the rearing of young, *samn* production seems to have been the prime use. These herds were effectively tied to the permanent waterholes and oasis villages. Modern bedouin have overcome this handicap by using their four-wheel-drive vehicles to transport the water to the flocks. This is adding pressure to the limited amount of grazing.

The desert is remarkably fertile. Many plants are adapted to its demands, *halophyte* species are salt tolerant and *xerophytes* are drought resistant. Most of the seeds show remarkable long-term fertility.[15] A single thunderstorm can bring a flush of green plants which are established in a few days and will last for several months. A few days rain will trigger plant growth and revive desiccated shrubs that will be green for a year or two. The bedouin sought these rare storms in the deep deserts and would remember precisely where rain had fallen in recent months and hence there might be the chance of some pasture for their camels.

The bedouin were not recorded as consuming desert plants on any regular basis. However they were aware of what was edible and would consume them on finding. Many plants were known to have medicinal or veterinary value and are mentioned. There are several plants which have water storage capabilities in the roots and these were known to the bedouin for emergency use. The dessert truffle, *faga*, was harvested and eaten.

Apart from the date palm which rarely produces useful fruit in the true wild state, some trees of the stoney and mountainous dessert produced edible fruit; *sidr* and *haybed*[16] are relatives of the jujube and produce significant quantities of edible fruit, *nabak* and *dom*. Another palm tree[17] has edible fruit, *mish*, that will keep for up to a year and are ground up to make a nutritious meal, eaten raw or cooked.

Game

Game formed an important element of bedouin food though it was not available on any regular basis and would at times be an item of last resort, such as the eating of carrion and the prohibited foods (*harram* rather than *halal*). The decimation of the game supply by hunting with high power rifles or automatic weapons from four-wheel-drive vehicles is a phenomenon of the last few decades and is slowly being reversed by a more enlightened view of the natural fauna.

Game was caught in a number of ways. Hunting *salukis* and several hawk species have been used for centuries and are a part of bedouin culture just about surviving to the present day. There are records of large traps in use since Chalcolithic times. They were constructed in the stoney deserts from converging drystone walls with a ditch behind. Gazelle were driven into the trap by beaters and in leaping over the wall some would be killed by the hunters or break limbs and be caught for slaughter. This illustrates a serious problem concerning game consumption for the strict Muslim, as all meat had to be slaughtered in a prescribed way and the carcase bled.[18] The accounts show some laxity in this requirement, though given human nature it was usually ascribed to a neighbouring tribe with whom relations were not cordial or who were not considered to be true bedouin.

Matchlocks and rifles had become relatively common by the second half of the nineteenth century and were used for hunting. However their prime purpose was quite clearly for personal security or offensive action against fellow bedouin. Small game[19] such as jerboa and lizards could be dug out of burrows with a camel stick and some men were fleet enough of foot to run down the larger reptiles such as *dubb*, the spiny-tailed lizard which can grow to 60 cm long and whose tail is particularly good eating. Like most reptiles its flesh is likened to rabbit or chicken in taste and consistency. Sling shots and stones propelled from simple pop guns were also effective weapons in skilled hands.

Certain game had pre-eminent value to the bedouin, associated with the sporting element of the chase and kill. *Houbara* bustard was one such sought-after game bird taken exclusively with hawks. The Arabian gazelle, *rim* and oryx were also esteemed.[20] Conversely some game was not so welcome, *gatta*, sandgrouse were considered to be poor eating being dry-fleshed birds. There are several references to the relish with which the bedouin would consume the cud from the stomach of ruminants such as gazelle.

Jarad (locusts) can probably best be considered as game. There are many references to the consumption of locusts; it seems to have been an item of horrible fascination for many of the European travellers.

> The children bring in gathered locusts, broached upon a twig, and the nomads toast
> them on the coals; then plucking the scorched members, they break away the head,
> and the insect body which remains is good meat.[21]

In the nineteenth century locust plagues were still a serious scourge for the Arabians. Doughty recounts passing a large locust swarm heading for the Teyma oasis from which he had departed with his Bedu companions a few days before. His companions accepted the destruction of the burgeoning date harvest with fatalism. Several had date gardens at the oasis and realised that they would have few or no dates that year and that they would have to rely on other resources such as their stock.

Whilst locusts were a curse for the farmer, they at least supplied some instant food. They were generally roasted or parched over the fire. If not consumed immediately the dried flesh could be ground up into meal and stored in a skin to be added to stews at a later date.

Oasis life

If grazing was adequate near an oasis the bedouin would pitch camp and take a break from the nomadic life.

Many bedouin had land holdings in the oases where they would grow date palms to provide for their travels. At the date harvest in early autumn they would return to supervise their holdings which were frequently left in the hands of a slave farmer who would take half the crop for his sustenance. Beneath the date palms fodder could be grown for the flocks and vegetables and fruits cultivated. Fruits included pomegranate, citron, lime or lemon, grapes, plum, melons and watermelons. Vegetables included cucumbers, carrots, pumpkin, onions, garlic, okra, sorrel, thyme and other fresh green herbs.

The oasis village would have a *suq* or market. Apart from the basic foods such as *samn*, rice, wheat, flour and dates, some fresh vegetables and fruits would be on sale and there might be a butcher or someone who was offering cooked food.

Oasis rulers were expected to provide hospitality just as the sheikhs did in the desert. By the end of the nineteenth century these oasis rulers had started to develop political muscle through exacting taxes to pay for soldiers to enforce their new-found power. With the arrival of the internal combustion engine, the camel was soon displaced. The bedouin economy which was built upon the value of these beasts declined dramatically and many gave up their nomadic ways for good.

The bedouin recorded by Doughty and his fellow travellers in the nineteenth century no longer exist. Much of their culture has been handed down to their descendants and certainly elements of their food culture can still be identified in the Arabia currently on the threshold of the twenty-first century.

APPENDIX *Composition of ruminants' milk*

Constituent	Unit	DROMEDARY *Camelus dromedarius*	COW *Bos indicus*	SHEEP *Ovis aries*	GOAT *Capra bircus*
Fat	%	2.9-5.5	4-4.8	7	4.9-5
Protein	%	2.0-4.5	2.8-3.5	6	4-4.3
Lactose	%	3.4-5.4	4.5-4.6	4	4-4.1
Solids, non-fat	%	8.7-10.1	8.1	-	9.3
Total solids	%	12.9-14.4	13-13.5	18	14-14.2

Note: values for sheep are temperate breeds due to lack of statistics on tropical sheep

BIBLIOGRAPHY

Al-Fahim, Mohamed, *From Rags to Riches - A Story of Abu Dhabi*, The London Centre for Arab Studies, London, 1995

Al Taie, Lamees Abdullah, *Al Azaf - The Omani Cookbook*, Oman Bookshop, Sultanate of Oman, 1995

Brock - Al Ansari, Celia, *The Complete United Arab Emirates Cookbook*, Emirates Airlines, Dubai, 1994

Carles, A. B., *Sheep Production in the Tropics*, OUP, Oxford, 1983

Doughty, Charles M., *Wanderings in Arabia*, Duckworth, London, 1926

Dyke, Gertrude, *The Oasis - Al Ain Memoirs of Doctor Latifa*, Motivate, Dubai, 1995

Hogarth, David George, *The Penetration of Arabia*, Khayat, Beirut, 1966, preface dated 1904.

Keohane, Alan, *Bedouin - Nomads of the Desert*, Stacey International, London, 1994

Stark, Freya, *A Winter in Arabia*, Readers Union, London, 1941

Taylor, Andrew, *Travelling the Sands*, Motivate Publishing, Dubai, 1995

Thesiger, Wilfrid, *Arabian Sands*, Penguin, UK, 1964

Thomas, Bertram, *Arabia Felix*, Readers Union, London, 1938

Webster C. C., and Wilson P. N., *Agriculture in the Tropics*, Longman, UK, 1966

Weir, Shelagh, *The Bedouin*, British Museum Publications, London, 1990

NOTES

[1] Hogarth was summarising the explorations to date in Arabia and it is surprising what little of the peninsula had been comprehensively explored at the start of this century. His summary of the bedouin character is however concise and to the point.

[2] Some bedouin near the coastline split their activities between their flocks and fishing or pearl diving in the Arabian Gulf (Al-Fahim).

[3] Hogarth corrects the medieval error which assigned *arabia felix* to the south-western provinces of the peninsula, but the error has become accepted in modern usage probably emphasized by our modern perception that these areas are more blessed in resources than the remainder.

[4] The 'mess of wheat' or *harees* as described several times by Doughty was to be expected in Arabia where wheat was grown on the oasis fringes whereas rice, *temmn*, was generally imported by camel caravan from Iraq. The meat was boiled first and then the wheat cooked in the stock.

[5] Weir reports the slaughter of one camel and 86 sheep at one such feast in 1973 for the visit of a member of the Saudi royal family to a group of Jordanian bedouin. One dish contained 24 sheep on a mound of rice.

[6] The area bordering the southern Iraq marshes between the Tigris and Euphrates rivers was a major rice growing area up to the 1950s when Thesiger noted the importance of this crop to the Arabian economy.

[7] Copper has been replaced by aluminium. There is much evidence of prehistoric copper mining and refining on the peninsula.

[8] Snow was even recorded at high elevations every thirty or forty years.

[9] Doughty.

[10] Valued at £2,000 by Doughty.

[11] Dyke and Weir respectively, *samn* is called *dibn* in the UAE.

[12] 'Where there is not coffee, there is not merry company,' Bedouin saying quoted by Doughty.

[13] Doughty.

[14] And still do to this day, *shai* is invariably taken with a hefty sugar content.

[15] I have used dune sand in garden pot plants in the UAE and with regular watering have propagated seven different species from latent seed in the sand. One was *Portulaca oleracea*, purslane.

[16] *Ziziphus spina-christi* and *Z leucodermis* respectively.

[17] This palm, *Nannorrhops ritchieana*, also yields excellent strong rot-proof fibres for craft work.

[18] Unusual large game recorded included wolf, fox and hyena. Wolf flesh was considered to be medicinal, very good for aches in the shins.

[19] Small game included Cape hare, Ethiopian hedgehog, porcupine, and various rodents as well as many birds, some shot quite indiscriminately at hides. Snakes were not eaten but lizards were *in extremis*.

[20] Sadly they are still hunted, I saw a gazelle carcase from the small remaining population dangling from the back of a four-wheel-drive last winter.

[21] Doughty.

Eating the World: Foods of the United Nations

Eve Jochnowitz

Travel and travellers are never without some kind of controversy, or at least ambivalence. All of us who live with a love of food seek in travel the unfamiliar flavors we crave, but none of us wants to be seen as a tourist. Claude Levi-Strauss was speaking of this problem in *Tristes Tropiques* when he wrote 'Travel and travellers are two things I loathe – and yet, here I am, all set to tell the story of my expeditions' (Levi-Strauss, 17). Many social critics draw a line between respectable travel and despicable tourism, determined by the traveller's willingness to encounter strange foods. Paul Fussell attacks as a 'tourist of the grossest kind' a traveller who wrote a letter to the editor of the *New York Times* travel section asking for advice on how to avoid Chinese food while in Hong Kong (Fussell, 31).

One tourist site whose unusual relationship to its visitors makes it an interesting case study is the headquarters of the United Nations in New York City. The United Nations frames itself for visitors as a meta-nation, a country with a flag, national colors, a post office which prints valid stamps and issues postmarks, a national holiday and even an anthem with words by W.H. Auden. The United Nations, in its tours, tourist literature and iconography, presents itself as a sovereign country whose borders lie next to no one's, but rather above them.

In this paper I will not be discussing the United Nations' work as an official international body, but rather the UN headquarters in New York City as a destination site for travellers and the virtual travel promoted in various cookbooks of the United Nations.

If the United Nations is an independent country, who are the natives? Both tourists and tour guides inhabit the international territory of the UN's public areas. The women who work as guides are all young and gorgeous, and dressed to the nines in identical costumes. (For more on the touristic use of uniformed lovelies, see Barbara Haber's excellent piece in this volume.) If these are the citizens of the UN, then the UN is a bit like an all-female planet from the Star Trek series. The guide-tourist interaction is an inversion of the usual relationship between tourist and host, where the tourist is a stranger and the host a native. Three quarters of the visitors to the United Nations headquarters are Americans, and almost all the guides are from overseas, making the tourists natives and the guides strangers (Tatomirovic). The tour guides embody the supposed impartiality and objectivity of the United Nations, its multi-ethnicity and also its blandness and tidiness. Non-compliant tourists may attempt to get the guides to break character and express their own opinions.

The guides, the pamphlets, the video tour, the restaurants, the gift shops, the new on-line tour on the World Wide Web and all parts of the UN that are extended to tourists strive above all to avoid controversy, an admittedly daunting task. Visitors to the UN are pacified with the assurance that seeing is believing and believing is acting. Stickers on sale in the bookstore bear such goofy new-age slogans as 'Another family for peace' and 'Visualize world peace'. Just visualize peace and you've done your bit. 'Do you want to join the UN?' shouts a large display on the tour route, 'you already have!' You are taken care of at the UN, whether you like it or not.

Cuisines of the United Nations

There are many ways to eat the world. The cuisines of mysterious distant lands are represented in their cookbooks, in the work of their famous chefs at their best restaurants, at the kiosks and coffee shops on the streets and in the homes of the locals, where home cooking, always an important element of national identity, is performed. The United Nations purports to provide the traveller with all possible touristic dining experiences, and he need never leave New York.

It is in the delegates' dining-room that the United Nations gets its best opportunity to present its own specific culture through its cuisine, and the culture presented is consistent with the rest of the UN experience. Although the dining-room is supposed to represent all member countries, the cuisines that dominate are French, Italian, Chinese and Indian, in other words, New York mainstream cooking. The delegates' dining-room emphasizes prestige and elegance. The food is plentiful and very pretty, but not especially impressive. The clearest sign that one is in contact with an alien culture is that smoking is permitted in all areas at all times.

Norman Manjaka, the flamboyant maitre d', unconsciously continues the standard United Nations story when he says: 'I feed all these important people and they go away happy, but what really keeps me interested is that when you come to the United Nations, it is as though you are coming to another country, a country made up of every other country in the world. Nothing could be more interesting than that' (De Silva).

The pale blue and white ubiquitous in all other parts of the United Nations headquarters are nowhere to be seen in the restaurant area, where reds and golds gleam. The delegates' dining area has none of the oppressive tackiness that pervades the UN's other public areas. With views north and east, the dining-room is filled with light on sunny days. Diners can order from an a la carte menu, but almost everyone chooses to select food from the international buffet, which runs half the length of the dining-room. With respect for the myriad diet restrictions of dozens of religions, there are always plenty of vegetables. In the early part of lunch service, the crowd is almost all female, but as the afternoon progresses, more men arrive. One afternoon a retired couple from Arizona was enjoying lunch at the next table after their tour. They had a wonderful morning and wanted to end it with lunch for 'A complete UN experience'. A woman who works in the secretariat told me: 'The delegates and staff like to have a place where they can impress their friends. And enemies.'

The lunch buffet is served every day, and special promotional events, the most recent of which was co-sponsored by Air France, are staged occasionally, but what Norman Manjaka really lives for are the special events in the evenings, the receptions and national holidays (there is one for each country) when he can wear his tail coat and white gloves, and stand with a microphone at the entrance of the hall, where the flag of the honored country hangs beside the UN flag, and announce the distinguished guests as the crowd gazes on. Norman is proud to hold 'the second most powerful office at the United Nations,' and perform the protocols of an august institution.

Visitors who don't want to spend the time or money in the delegates' dining-room can grab lunch at the coffee shop, which is located in the basement, adjacent to the bookstore and gift shops. It is truly astonishing that such an awful and uncomfortable place can exist in New York, but of course, it is not in New York. The seating area is wide, windowless and shallow and the decorations – a showcase full of kitchen equipment bearing the United Nations logo – make the space even more depressing. No pretence is made to international cuisine here, unless you count the fact that eggplant parmigiani is always served with a side order of french fries.

For travellers who want to eat the world without leaving even their homes, there are the international cookbooks published by the United Nations. The Association for the United Nations did not choose to consult chefs, or cooks, or restaurateurs or even nutritionists or home economists from member nations to gather international recipes. Instead, they consulted individual women, most of them wives of delegates or United Nations staff, to come up with recipes they felt were representative of their home countries, making the United Nations cookbook a sort of international church supper cookbook. Each United Nations cookbook is very much a document of its time and the image the United Nations was seeking to put forward.

The United Nations was actually in the cookbook business a year before the UN charter was ratified. In 1944 the Committee of United Nations published a book of wartime recipes. The book contains five brief introductions about the importance of food and peace written by Roosevelt,

Churchill, De Gaulle, Chiang Kai Shek, and Stalin. Stalin's introduction urges workers on collective farms to produce more. Wartime recipes from Her Excellency, the Marchioness of Linlithgow, Vicereine of India, and Baroness G.H.H. van Boelz Laer of The Netherlands serve to show that all kinds of women deal with the troubles of wartime cooking. The sober dedicatory note underlines the seriousness of this cookbook as a wartime effort.

> We dedicate this book to those women throughout the United Nations – particularly in the invaded countries – who strive with ingenuity and fortitude in the face of severe food shortages, to sustain their families. (AWVS, 1944, n.p.)

The first United Nations cookbook, published by the American Home Economics Association in 1951, is titled *The world's favorite recipes* and has an introduction by Eleanor Roosevelt. It is a modest four-inch-high pamphlet with red stripes and a tiny United Nations logo in one corner. Eleanor Roosevelt's introduction brings up the issues of shared food and world-wide brotherhood, but emphasizes the observance of United Nations day as being the primary mission of the cookbook. In the introduction she writes:

> I hope many housewives throughout the nation will own one of these cookbooks before the next United Nations Day and will try to have at least one meal with recipes from different countries of the world. (AHEA, 1951).

Mrs Roosevelt is using locutions associated with the World War II era, which is hardly over, when she exhorts every American wife to do her bit for the greater good, even is she is just cooking a special dinner. Particularly evocative are the words 'at least one meal'. How could any housewife do less?

By 1956, the cookbook has been revised and expanded to nearly twice its original size. *Favorite recipes of the United Nations* is a spiral bound standard paperback with '170 authentic dishes from all countries of the United Nations'. The cover shows a place setting made up of a fork, spoon and knife, with the northern projection of the globe from the United Nations logo as the plate, and thus introduces the theme of eating the world. The long introduction, which is unfortunately anonymous, emphatically makes the point that the cookbook is an instrument for the furtherance of world peace:

> If we are increasingly aware of these fundamental elements common in the life of all of us, everywhere, basic similarities and needs can unite human beings around the world more than differences divide them. Food, clothing, shelter and mental and spiritual development are surely basic needs, and all humanity, in different ways, seeks to fulfil them. Knowledge of one another's way of life, and pleasure derived from that knowledge, unencumbered by political difficulties, or by the pressure of ominous problems, will help to contribute to that awareness, which precedes mutual friendship and respect.
> …Thus, there will be a steady and accumulating deposit of that awareness of one another's ways, at once basic and pleasant, which the world surely needs. (AHEA, 1956).

This introduction takes as given that the modest little housewifely recipes contained within are an accurate indicator of the ways of life of the peoples of the world, and that they wield immense power. The inclusion of 'mental and spiritual development' along with food, clothing and shelter shows the enormous shift in consciousness between the World War II era and the prosperous fifties. On the other hand, the disturbing reference to 'ominous problems' indicates that although the first hump of the cold war has passed, the terror of nuclear destruction is still a very solid presence in the lives of the book's intended audience.

The 1959 edition of the cookbook is an expanded version of the 1956 edition, but the introduction by Olga P. Brucher recalls Eleanor Roosevelt's concerns, or at least, one of them:

> Designed for year-round use, we hope [sic] that the book will be widely used, particularly on United Nations Day, October 24, when a growing tradition of a United Nations Day family meal in the home will again[!] be observed across the country. Eating internationally in the home on that occasion was initiated in 1958 by President and Mrs Eisenhower at the White House with a menu prepared by Mrs Eisenhower herself. (AHEA,1959)

United Nations Day is back, as well as an emphasis on housewifery – even Mrs Eisenhower is not above preparing an international meal for her family to honor the United Nations.

In 1964 the editorship of the cookbook passed from the AHEA to Barbara Kraus. With a new title, *The cookbook of the United Nations*, a completely new set of recipes, and a new, more attractive, cover that features a drawing of a copper pot full of colorful vegetables surrounded by tiny line drawings of familiar national symbols: a windmill, the Sphinx, the Arch of Triumph, a kangaroo, the Empire State Building, the Roman Colosseum. The cookbook has a new respectability. Still the same are the modest spiral binding and the peculiar insistence on the 'growing trend' of the observance of United Nations Day.

> The cookbook of the United Nations provides both information and inspiration for those planning international menus for United Nations Day, October 24, a growing trend here and abroad (Kraus, 1964).

In the slightly more sophisticated recipes of this volume, we can hear the first rumblings of the gourmet movement of the sixties. Cooking itself has a new respectability, and this respectability is reflected in an explosion of the cooking media, if not of actual cooking. In 1962 Marlene Dietrich writes:

> Judging by the vast amount of cookbooks printed and sold in the United States one would think the American woman a fanatical cook. She isn't (Dietrich, 46).

The 1970 edition of the United Nations cookbook is the largest, incorporating most of the recipes from 1964 and reviving most of those from previous editions. It is also the first published not by the United States Association for the United Nations, but by Simon and Schuster, in a hardcover, with flags of member nations in the shapes of dishes on the white cover. In the introduction to this edition, Barbara Kraus writes:

> Since ancient times, sharing a meal has been a traditional and happy way of sharing friendship. The United Nations is founded on the principles of sharing and of coming together for the purposes of improving human understanding (Kraus, 1970).

The United States is at war again in 1970, and peace and human understanding re-emerge as the goals of the United Nations and its cookbook. There is also a British edition of this final United Nations cookbook which omits the introduction. Of all the United Nations cookbooks, the 1970 edition appeals most overtly to tourism, including in the section for each country a short upbeat paragraph about that country's peoples and attractions.

* * * * * *

To get a clear view of the evolution of the cookbook, follow the two test cases of Israel and Iraq through all five editions. Even these two very controversial countries are handled without any reference to any kind of unpleasantness.

IRAQ

1951: Dolmas (Meat and vegetable rolls)
1956: Dolmas
1959: Same as 1956
1964: Kubba shalgum (Turnip soup with meat balls)
1970: Kubba shalgum; Dolmas; Bulgar with eggplant

'Iraq is based at the site of ancient Mesopotamia, the area of the oldest known civilization, which flourished from 3000 BC. From this rich historical past, there remain excavations, mosques, tombs, ruins, the famous hanging gardens and more, to make this historic land a great tourist and archaeological mecca. Most Iraqis are Arab, mainly employed with oil, with which Iraq is richly endowed. Iraq was admitted to the United Nations on December 21 1945.'

ISRAEL

1951: Fish soup (court bouillon)
1956: Kishium (squash with tomatoes); Cheese steaks (fritters); Nezid adashim (lentil casserole)
1959: Same as 1956
1964: Chocolate date nut pie; Boureka (Meat squares); Orange peel confection
1970: Boureka; Levivot Gevina (cheese 'Steaks'); Nezio [misprint] adashim; Chocolate date nut pie

'Israel today is a country of contrasts, the new side by side with historical evidence of past centuries. Verdant farms and orchards thrive where there was once swamps and deserts. New types of villages have been settled, especially the famous kibbutzim, where the community owns the land and equipment. Modern factories have risen and beautiful museums, the Israel philharmonic, National opera and Habima theatre provide cultural background. Vegetable and dairy foods are most popular with the Israelis. Israel became a member of the United Nations on May 11, 1949.'

The promotional paragraphs in the 1970 edition, which must certainly have been selected by the countries themselves, are very interesting choices indeed. The paragraph from Iraq, reduced to a one-line slogan, would read 'Come to Iraq and see the past!' The paragraph from Israel, similarly reduced, would run 'Come to Israel and see the future.' While both appeals are equally compelling, there is a tremendous consciousness gap between where Israelis and Iraqis locate their national pride and how they choose to produce their countries as tourist attractions. While the promotional paragraph on Israel emphasizes modernity and the future, the inclusion of *nezid adashim* (lentil pottage) in the delegation of Israeli recipes to the United Nations cookbooks beginning in 1956 is an interesting reference to Israel's past. *Nezid adashim* is the name of the pottage Jacob prepared for Esau (Genesis 25:29). Slipping *nezid adashim* into the United Nations Cookbook is a very political (albeit subtle) assertion that the modern state of Israel is a continuation of the ancient presence of the Hebrews in the Middle East. The recipe for *nezid adashim*, however, is a modern one. The patriarch Jacob would have had to redden his pottage with something other than tomatoes (see recipes).

In 1977, the United Nations Women's Guild picks up where the UN proper left off and publishes its own compilation of recipes by the wives of UN personnel. After all the evolution the UN cookbook has undergone, the UNWG starts completely from scratch with some truly awful recipes and a very shoddy hand-typed production. The United States is represented by 'Meat and Corn Casserole' which calls for '2 cups cubed cooked pork, beef, or chicken.' There are no recipes from Iraq, and Israel is represented by *hamentaschen* and gefilte fish. There is a bit of a hodge podge of countries in this seat-of-your-pants production, and along with member nations, there are entries from 'Middle East,' 'Mediterranean' and 'South Sea Islands'. Antigua is represented by 'Toad in the Hole,' and France by 'Brandy Alexander Pie,' made with Graham crackers and gelatin. Mrs Kurt Waldheim contributed the recipe for Sacher Torte, the recipe which introduces the volume. In 1992, the Women's Guild issued a professionally printed version of this cookbook, with a scenic view of the United Nations headquarters on the cover and the first recipe, for *khoshari* (lentils and rice), is from Mrs Boutros Boutros Ghali. Even in 1992, the United Nations Women's Guild puts the wives of its officers to use in the vestigial function of first ladyship.

A peculiar private contribution to the United Nations cookery book series came about in 1981, when the Governor of Tennesee invited all the ambassadors to the United Nations and their families to visit the future World's Fair site in Knoxville, Tennessee. This visit was the occasion for *Phila Hach's United Nations Cookbook*. While the United Nations permitted the cookbook author, writer and television personality Phila Hach to use the UN name and logo for her book, it is not an official United Nations publication.

Finally, there are the UNICEF cookbooks for children, and it is in these books that the UN finally succeeds, for better or worse, in presenting, through food, its chosen image as a sacred site. These gorgeously produced and colored books are unsigned and undated. Each recipe is illustrated by a picture of a little boy and a little girl with big round heads and tiny ears and noses wearing the traditional attire of their nations and appropriately colored (more or less) preparing the recipe. It is United Nations iconography cut completely loose. The second volume of the UNICEF cookbook is the same but even more so. The kids' heads are bigger and rounder, their ears and noses are tinier. Neither cookbook has a recipe from Israel or Iraq, but both have sections about the rights of children, the importance of good nutrition, and most of all, the vital role played in securing these by the United Nations. In much of its promotional literature, the United Nations uses children, and particularly third-world children as a soft sell. The UN's Web page explains that 80 per cent of the UN's work is devoted to saving children from starvation and disease. Their parents must also need the same kind of help, but this is not emphasized in UN literature. In the production of these charity cookbooks, as on the site of the United Nations itself, the UN performs the benevolence of its protection, both of real children and the child-countries of the third world.

RECIPES

Victory Whipped Cream

The wartime ban on heavy cream doesn't necessarily mean that whipped cream for dessert is out for the duration. The formula calls for one cup chilled cream, one level teaspoonful of vegetable gum, two tablespoons of sugar, and a few drops of vanilla. Mix the sugar and gum until free from lumps; then slowly add the mixture to the chilled cream while stirring, and whip immediately. The cream should whip satisfactorily in two or three minutes.

From AWVS, 1944

Cauliflower with Curry Sauce

Boil one or two compact cauliflowers carefully so that they are tender and unbroken. Drain thoroughly on hot cloth. Place them upright in a gratin dish containing some warm butter and pour a rich curry sauce over them sufficiently thick to mask them, and over the sauce scatter the sieved yolks of two hard boiled eggs. Cut three or four good size tomatoes into moderately thick slices and cook in butter until tender. Arrange these neatly around the cauliflower and scatter some finely chopped parsley over them and beyond the tomatoes put a line of croutons fried to a golden brown. Serve very hot.

> Recipe from Her Excellency, the Marchioness of Linlithgow, Vicereine of India, President of the women's voluntary service in India, for the AWVS, Washington Unit, United Nations cookbook. From AWVS, 1944.

Paludeh Seeb (Apple Delight Dessert), Iran

4 medium apples • 2 tablespoons lemon juice • 4 to 6 tablespoons powdered sugar
2 teaspoons rosewater • 4 ice cubes

Pare and grate apples. Sprinkle each apple immediately with lemon juice after grating to prevent apples from darkening (slight darkening is not objectionable). Add sugar and rose water. Stir lightly. Add ice cubes, which serve to chill and dilute the mixture. The finished product is delicate and rewarding. Serve in dessert dishes. Yield: 4 servings. From a private collection.

From AHEA, 1951.

Umintas (Baked Corn), Bolivia

5 ears fresh corn, or 2 cups corn kernels • 2 eggs • 1 tablespoon fat
1/8 teaspoon chili powder • 1/8 teaspoon anise seed (optional) • 1 teaspoon flour
1/4 pound swiss or goat's milk cheese

Scrape kernels from uncooked corn. Beat eggs and combine with corn. Heat fat, add chilli powder, anise seed and flour and cook for one minute. Combine with corn and egg mixture. Pour half of mixture into well oiled 1-quart casserole. Cover with thin slices of cheese. Cover with remaining corn mixture. Bake in moderate oven (350°F) for 1 hour. Yield: 4 servings.

From AHEA, 1956.

Perlau Rice (Chicken and Rice), Liberia

1 chicken (3 1/2 to 4 lbs) • 1 tablespoon salt • 2 to 3 teaspoons black pepper
1/4 cup flour • 1/4 cup drippings or vegetable fat or lard • 1/2 pound ham, cubed
3 quarts water • 1 onion sliced • 1/3 cup tomato paste
1/2 cup chopped cabbage • 2 1/2 cups (1 1/4 pounds) brown rice

Have butcher cut chicken into serving pieces. Wash, drain. Season with salt and pepper and let stand for about 15 minutes. Then sprinkle lightly with flour. Heat fat in heavy skillet over medium heat. With fork, carefully place chicken in hot fat. Fry until lightly browned on both sides. Remove chicken and place in large kettle. Fry ham in remaining fat. Add to chicken. Add water, onion, tomato paste and cabbage. Cover and simmer for 20 minutes or until chicken is tender. Remove chicken from stock. Add rice. Cover and cook about 45 minutes, stirring occasionally. If necessary, add boiling water during cooking. Return chicken to rice and heat thoroughly. Yield: 8 servings.

From AHEA, 1956.

Kubba Shalgum (Turnip soup with meat balls), Iraq

5 turnips, peeled and sliced • 1 large onion, chopped • 1 1/2 oz butter
3 1/4 pints water • 1 1/2 level teaspoons salt • 4 level tablespoons tomato concentrate
2 lb lean beef, minced • 4 1/2 oz rice flour • water • 1 1/2 lb shoulder of lamb, minced
1 large onion very finely chopped • 2 heaped tablespoons minced parsley
3 oz raisins • 3 oz blanched almonds, sliced • 2 level tablespoons rice flour
5 tablespoons lemon juice • 6 spinach leaves or sprigs of parsley

Cook turnips and onion in 1 oz hot butter in a large heavy pan until onion is golden. Add the water, salt and tomato concentrate. Bring to the boil and boil for 15 minutes. Reduce heat and simmer for 30 minutes.

Combine the beef, rice flour and sufficient water to mould mixture with your hands, set aside.

Mix the lamb, onion and parsley; cook in the remaining butter until meat is brown and thoroughly cooked. Add raisins and almonds.

Divide the mixture of beef and rice flour into four equal portions. Divide each of these into six equal portions. Flatten each portion into a 3-inch round or patty. Place 1 teaspoon of lamb mixture in the center of the patty. Shape into a round ball, keeping the lamb within the beef rice mixture.

Add 2 level tablespoons rice flour, lemon juice and spinach leaves to the soup. Bring soup to simmering point. Drop meat balls into the soup and simmer, uncovered, for 25 minutes. Serve soup piping hot with meat balls. Serves 8.

From Kraus, 1969

Nezid Adashim, Israel

1/2 lb lentils • 1 1/2 pints cold water • 1 medium onion, very finely chopped
1 level tablespoon very finely chopped parsley • 1/2 clove garlic, crushed
1 stalk celery, very finely chopped • 1/2 oz butter • 2 level tablespoons flour
2 level teaspoons salt • 1/8 level teaspoon pepper • 2 tablespoons tomato purée
6-8 small smoked sausages

Wash lentils and soak overnight in cold water. Drain and reserve liquid. Heat 3/4 pint of this liquid to boiling point and add lentils, onion, garlic and celery. Cook until tender (about 15 minutes). Drain and reserve liquid. Pour lentil mixture into a greased casserole. Make reserved liquid up to half pint with water in which lentils were soaked. Melt butter in saucepan, add flour, salt and pepper, and stir in the 1/2 pint liquid. Cook until thickened. Pour over lentils, then cover with tomato purée. Arrange sausages in attractive design on top of the mixture and bake for 30 minutes in a very moderate oven (350°F Mark 3), serves 6.

> This recipe is from the 1969 British edition of *The Cookbook of the United Nations* by Barbara Kraus. It is essentially the same as the recipe in the 1956 edition, but the style is a bit more awkward. '1 tablespoon minced parsley' in the 1956 book becoming '1 level tablespoon very finely chopped parsley'.

Peanut sauce for baked bananas, Barbados

2 tablespoons grated onion • 2 tablespoons olive oil • 1 ounce dark brown sugar
juice of one lime • 2 tablespoons peanut butter • 1/2 pint coconut milk • salt

Lightly fry onion in oil. Add sugar, lime juice and peanut butter. Blend thoroughly. Slowly add the coconut milk; stirring all the time. Cook slowly, until thick.

From Hack, 1981.

ACKNOWLEDGEMENTS

Inestimable thanks to Dalia Carmel for her thoughtful help and for access to her extraordinary library. All the rare United Nations cookery books cited here are from the Carmel collection. Thanks also to my colleagues on the Culture of the United Nations project, Maureen Aungthwin, J. Anton Elmquist, Gertrude Mead Embree, Miwa Nagura, Lorena Rodas and Craig Rosa, and to our intrepid advisor, Professor Barbara Kirshenblatt-Gimblett.

BIBLIOGRAPHY

American Home Economics Association, 1951, *The world's favorite recipes: over 100 tested dishes from the United Nations.* With introductions by Eleanor Roosevelt and William W. Waymack. New York, Harper and Bros.

American Home Economics Association, 1956, *Favorite recipes of the United Nations: 170 authentic dishes from all countries of the United Nations.* Unsigned introduction, Washington D.C., United States Committee for the United Nations.

American Home Economics Association, 1959, *Favorite recipes of the United Nations; 185 authentic dishes from all countries of the United Nations.* Introduction by Olga P. Brucher, Washington D.C., United States Committee for the United Nations.

American Women's Voluntary Services, 1944, *United Nations recipes for war rationed cooking.* District of Columbia, Nutrition Committee of the District of Columbia Unit of American Women's Voluntary Services, Inc.

De Silva, Cara, 1992, 'The international power lunch', *New York Newsday*, March 11.

Dietrich, Marlene, 1962, *Marlene Dietrich's ABC*, New York, Doubleday.

Fussel, Paul, 1988, 'Travel, tourism and "international understanding"' in *Thank God for the atom bomb*, New York, Summit Books.

Hach, Phila, 1981, *Phila Hach's United Nations cookbook*, Clarkesville, Phila Hach.

Kirshenblatt-Gimblett, Barbara, 1995, 'Theorizing heritage', *Ethnomusicology* 39:3 Fall.

Kraus, Barbara, 1964. *The Cookbook of the United Nations: 250 authentic recipes from 112 countries*, Introduction by Barbara Kraus, New York, United Nations Association of the United States.

Kraus, Barbara, 1969. *The cookbook of the United Nations*, British edition revised by Marion Howells. New introduction by Barbara Kraus, London, The Cookery Book Club.

Kraus, Barbara, 1970. *The cookbook of the United Nations: 350 recipes from 126 member nations of the United Nations*, New York, Simon and Schuster.

Levi-Strauss, Claude, 1968, *Tristes Tropiques*, New York, Atheneum.

Raufflet, Jean-Christophe and Valerie Pettinari, illustrators, n.d. [*ca.* 1992], *The little cooks; recipes from around the world for boys and girls*, (Brown cover) UNICEF.

Tatomirovic, Aleksandra, 1985, 'The United Nations as sacred place and tourist attraction: experiences of a tour guide', New York University Department of Performance Studies, unpublished paper.

Tharlet, Eve, editor and illustrator, n.d. [*ca.* 1988] *The little cooks: recipes from around the world for boys and girls*, (blue cover) UNICEF.

United Nations Publications E.95.I.31. n.d. [*ca.* 1996], http://www.un.org. A public relations website for the UN. Sections on 'The history of the UN' and 'Setting the record straight'.

United Nations Women's Guild, 1977, *United Nations Women's Guild cookbook*, New York, UNWG.

United Nations Women's Guild, 1992, *United Nations Women's Guild cookbook*, New York, UNWG.

The Gardeners of Europe

Maria Kaneva-Johnson

In the sixteenth century the Turkish Empire included Bulgaria as well as most of Hungary in its realm. The Bulgarians, known as the Gardeners of Europe, have always been famous for being able to make almost anything bloom. Having learned to cultivate paprika from the seeds given them by the Turks, many Bulgarian gardeners emigrated to Hungary during the sixteenth century.... There is ample evidence that the Bulgarians brought paprika to Hungary and started its cultivation.

George Lang (1971)

Vegetable production in cottage gardens, and commercial market gardening in the vicinity of larger towns, have been a long-established practice in the Balkans.

The earliest specialized market gardening areas grew up in the sixteenth century in Bulgaria, which at that time was part of the Ottoman Empire. This was to satisfy the demand of the Turkish government for fresh vegetables for their troops located in the conquered territories. In the seventeenth century, however, this demand was scrapped and the Bulgarian growers were free to look for markets further afield.

The phenomenon of massive market gardening abroad, known as *gourbetchijstvo* in Bulgarian (from the Turkish *gurbet*, foreign travel), is considered to have been initiated by the men from Lyaskovets, then a large village (now a town) located in central Bulgaria in the region of Veliko Turnovo.

Lyaskovets in those days was a soldiers' village – that is to say, it was obliged to send men to Istanbul to work in the Sultan's bakeries, which provided the army with bread and *peksimet* (rusks, resembling the old-fashioned British ship's biscuits). In return, the villagers enjoyed privileges granted by a Sultan's decree declaring that no Turk had the right to settle, stay overnight, or be born or buried in the village of Lyaskovets or its surroundings. The villagers were also under the protection of Roustem Pasha, Great Vizir and Commander-in-Chief of the army in Roumalia (the land south of the Balkan mountain range in central Bulgaria) during the sixteenth century. (4)

From the end of the seventeenth century, when their obligations were withdrawn, the villagers turned to what they could do best – growing vegetables, using seeds of new species given to them by the Turkish authorities, and in the process creating new sorts and improved varieties. (4)

Towards the close of the eighteenth century, professional gardeners from the village of Lyaskovets hired or bought vacant land in the countryside around larger European towns and cities, and started growing vegetables for the market. They were usually organized in 'companies' (singl. *kompania* in Bulgarian), functioning on a co-operative basis. (2)

Another village from which Bulgarian gardeners in their thousands went abroad was the village of Polikraishte. This is how a descendant of a market gardener describes the way his grandfather joined a company in Budapest.

It happened in the thick of winter, just before Christmas, more than seventy years ago. My grandfather on his way to Gorna Oryahovitsa passed through the village of Polikraishte. He stopped in the tavern of Martin the Lame to have a glass of wine and to read the newspapers. He had just sat down when the door was opened and several men, laughing and shouting, burst in. These men were obviously very rich! They were brilliantly decked out in long fur coats with astrakhan collars and astrakhan caps, and wore straight black trousers in the European fashion and scarlet knee-boots. After greeting the customers, they ordered a kilo of wine to be served at each table, and also some music – which happened to be a one-man affair performed by the tavern clarinettist. The newcomers then explained that they were *gazdi*,[1] heads of several market-garden companies, and owned extensive lands under crops and irrigation in the environs of Budapest, and that they have come to enlist new members for their companies. The companies, they explained, were flourishing and there was a great need for more hands. The next spring, my grandfather, together with over twelve hundred men from Polikraishte, joined the companies in Budapest. When he came home, in the late autumn, there were festivities that lasted a whole week!(9)

During the last century, the exodus of market gardeners to other parts of the Balkans and to Europe was considerable. Most of the nineteenth-century gardeners were from a submontane village called Tserova Koriya, in the district of Turnovo (Veliko Turnovo, the medieval Bulgarian capital).

The first to go to Serbia was someone called Georgi Moyanov. In 1845 he bought some land near Kragujevac and started a market garden helped by his family. Ten years later, Tsonyu Karadzhata and Neno Kandilarya followed his example and started their own gardens in the same town. Another fellow-villager, Panayot Madzharov, went to work in Wallachia in Romania. In 1855, in Ukraine, were established the companies of Peter Milev, Peter Penev and a few others, while in Kislovodsk, in the Caucasus, Radi Kovachev and Georgi Chatalov founded two more companies. In 1882 the first market garden near Vienna was set up by Mihail Savakov.

On the whole, during the nineteenth century, more than fifteen hundred *gourbetchii* (men working abroad) were known to have gone each spring to work in Austria, Czechoslovakia, France, Hungary, Moldova, Poland, Russia, Serbia, Ukraine and Wallachia in Romania. Large, privately owned or co-operative market gardens were established on the outskirts of Berlin, Bordeaux, Istanbul, Kiev, Kishinev, Mainz, Moscow, Petersburg, Tashkent and Vienna. In summertime, mostly the women, the children and the elderly remained at home. The male element was represented chiefly by the priest, the sexton, the teacher, the mayor and the tax-collector. In 1906, in the Turnovo region alone, the number of *gourbetchii* had increased to over twenty-five thousand, organized into one thousand six hundred and four companies.(2) The more determined ventured as far west as the United States – to Louisiana, New Mexico, North Dakota, Oklahoma, Texas, the State of Washington (1911-1912), and to the Canadian provinces of Manitoba and Saskatchewan (1904). Some even went to Australia and Brazil, though their success in all these faraway places was short-lived, lasting only a few years.

Tsani Ginchev (1835-1894), Bulgarian novelist, ethnographer and folklorist,(4) was the first to write about the lives of the Bulgarians gardening abroad. He himself had been a gardener in Serbia and Wallachia. According to him, there were twelve market gardens in the vicinity of Belgrade in 1853, about ninety throughout Serbia, and in Wallachia there were gardens in almost every large town and city.(9)

On their return home in late autumn, nearly all gardeners bought with their earnings new big houses, more land, or got married, or organized huge weddings for their sons and daughters. They also made large donations to the local schools and monasteries, built fountains, monuments and churches and helped the poor and needy.

The story of one *gazda*, Mihail Piperov (the Pepper) is so redolent of the period that it is worth recording. At the beginning of this century, Piperov and his brother founded a company in Russia, but soon after that Mihail on his own moved to Serbia. There he became owner and head of eight companies in which were employed about a hundred men from his village. In a newspaper of that time, *Gradinar* (Gardener), he writes:

My vegetable gardens are about 100 decares [10 hectares or about 25 acres]. In the past, I used to irrigate them by an electromotor, which cost me about 300 leva a day. In 1931 I introduced the newest invention of our times, the so-called *samokat-dolap*[2]. This mechanism only needs water, lots of it! Then it will raise one thousand litres of water per minute to a height of 5.5 metres.(9).

Piperov had vegetable gardens in Sarajevo as well. He was also the founder of the Gardeners' Association in Sarajevo and had won numerous prizes for his vegetables at the horticultural exhibition in the town.

The work of the Bulgarian gardeners abroad has contributed to the appearance of new vegetable species and varieties on the European table. In Budapest, in 1987, a book was published entitled *Bolgárkertészet máguar földön*, or 'Bulgarian horticulture on Hungarian soil'. The author, Czibulya Ferenc, is an horticulturalist and son of an horticulturalist. His father had been a partner for a short time with a Bulgarian gardener from Plovdiv, and later had developed and improved the Bulgarian irrigation system. The author also writes about the variety of vegetables grown in the Bulgarian market gardens in Hungary. Here is a list, which I have compiled, for some Hungarian fruits and vegetables, which still bear names acquired from or through the Bulgarian language:[3]

bab, bean, from the Bulgarian *bob*, bean[4]

cékla, beetroot, from the Bulgarian *tsveklo*, beetroot

cseresznye, cherry, from Bulgarian *cheresha*, cherry

dinnye, melon, from Bulgarian *dinya*, watermelon

karfiol, cauliflower, from the Bulgarian *karfiol*, cauliflower, itself from the German *Karfiol*, cauliflower, ultimately from the Italian *cavolfiore*, meaning, literally, cabbage and flower

kelkáposzta, literally, *kel* cabbage, meaning savoy cabbage, from the Bulgarian *kel*, savoy cabbage *málna*, raspberry, from the Bulgarian *malina*, raspberry

paprika, the capsicum pepper, from the Bulgarian *piperka*, the capsicum pepper

padlizsán, aubergine, from Bulgarian *patladzhan*, itself from the Turkish *patlican*

paszuly, bean, from *fasoul*, another Bulgarian word for beans, derived from the Turkish *fasulye*, bean

répa, turnip, from the Bulgarian *ryapa*, the winter black radish

szilva, plum, from the Bulgarian *sliva*, plum

There is also a popular Hungarian salad, *Bulgar Saláta*, similar to the Bulgarian 'Mixed Summer Salad', consisting mainly of vegetables introduced by the Bulgarian gardeners, such as peppers and tomatoes.

Irrigation system, showing the water-wheel turned by a horse, and the irrigation channels. From Ferenc.

The most important vegetable crops grown by the 'Gardeners of Europe' were varieties of locally developed peppers, aubergines and watermelons, tomatoes (from seed brought from Istanbul in the eighteenth century), beans, onions, cucumbers and cabbages.

The first gardener's train started travelling from the town of Gorna Oryahovitsa direct to Budapest in February 1936. The financial report of the railways for that year recorded the number of passengers on the first journey: from the village of Draganovo – 186 people; from Polikraishte – 84, from Tserova Koriya and the village of Pchelishte – 59.

A living history of the Bulgarian market gardening abroad is the ninety-year-old Nikola Karaivanov. For more than forty years he had been gardening in Czechoslovakia. He recalls:

'At fifteen I was a shepherd in my native village of Pchelishte. My uncle was a gardener in Czechia. He used to come home every winter and he kept saying to me: "You won't do well grazing the sheep, my boy. Listen to me, come and join me in Czechia!" After much thought, I took his advice. For four years I helped my uncle in his garden in Czechia. Then I left him and started a company of my own. What did I grow there? Why, peppers, tomatoes, pumpkins, cabbage, cauliflower, carrots, kohlrabi, the lot. And, of course, parsley [*magdanoz*, the flat-leaved type], because, as you know, no decent garden could be without it.'

Bulgarian market gardening abroad, which lasted more than two centuries, accounts for the spread of many Turkish imports from their first foothold in the Balkans to most of Europe. Their impact on the European horticulture of the near past was considerable. The way the Bulgarian growers lived, their gardening implements, the clothes they wore, the kitchens in which they cooked their food, are all displayed in the Museum of Gardening in Lyaskovets, the village which was the first to send its gardeners abroad to sow the seeds of their achievements.

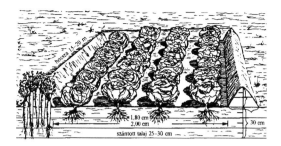

A Bulgarian cabbage-patch framed by carrots growing in ridges. From Ferenc.

BIBLIOGRAPHY

1. Boev, Nikolaj et al, *Alboum za Rasteniya i Zhivotni* (Album for Plants and Animals), Zemizdat, Sofia, 1980.
2. *Bulgarska Etnografia* (Bulgarian Ethnography), 'Vliyaniya na gourbetchijskoto gradinarstvo…' (The influence of market gardening abroad on the way of life and culture of the population of the Turnovo region), No.3-4, Bulgarian Academy of Sciences Publishing House, Sofia, 1978.
3. Daskalov, Academician Hristo, et al, *Zelenchoukoproizvodstvo*, (Vegetable Growing), Zemizdat, Sofia, 1965.
4. Ginchev, Tsani, *Gancho Koserkata* (the name of the main character), Bulgarski Pisatel, Sofia, 1961.
5. Kaneva-Johnson, Maria, *The Melting Pot – Balkan Food and Cookery*, Prospect Books, Devon, 1995.
6. Lang, George, *The Cuisine of Hungary*, Penguin Books, Great Britain, 1985; first published in the USA by Atheneum, 1971.
7. Petrov, Slavcho, *Rasteniya, Koito ni Hranyat i Oblichat*, (Plants, which feed and clothe us), Narodna Mladezh, Sofia, 1964.
8. Petrov, Dr. L., et al, *Bulgarska Natsionalna Kuhnya* (Bulgarian National Cuisine), Zemizdat, Sofia, 1978.
9. *Rodolyubie* (Patriotism), Committee for Bulgarians Abroad, Sofia, Grigor Nikolov, No.10: 'Polikraishte, Selo po Sveta' (Polikraishte, a village of the world), 1985; No.3: 'Kogato Balkandzhiite pravyat Zemedelie' (When the mountain-dwellers practise agriculture), 1988; No.8: 'Lyaskovskite gradinari' (The Lyaskovo gardeners), Sofia, 1987.
10. Vizvári, Mariska, *Treasure Trove of Hungarian Cookery*, fourth revised edition, translated from the Hungarian, Corvina Kiadó, Hungary, 1982.

NOTES

[1] *Gazda*, from the Hungarian *gazda*, master, leader of a group; also adopted in the Serbian *gazda* and the Romanian *gazda*

[2] *samokat-dolap*, a contraption with a water-wheel. From the Turkish *dolap*, water-wheel, and the Bulgarian *samokat*, self-moving.

[3] There are also other words stemming from the Bulgarian, which I have not included here, such as *bivaly*, from the Bulgarian *bivol*, water-buffalo, and *jérce*, from *yarka*, pullet. Terms for gardening tools, such as *lapat*, from *lopata*, spade, and *vasvilla*, from *vila*, pitchfork.

[4] Beans were the first American crop to come to Bulgaria. They appear for the first time in a document dated 1513(8). Beans were given the name *bob*, which in all Slavonic languages originally referred to the indigenous broadbean.

Food for the Lewis and Clark Expedition: Exploring North West America, 1804–6

Mary Wallace Kelsey

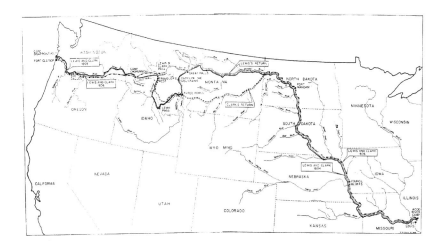

Thomas Jefferson, who became the third president of The United States of America in 1801, ordered this expedition. He had wanted someone to explore the west and to find a commercial (practical) land route to the Pacific Ocean. He had tried to find someone to do this five times before he was successful in finding Meriwether Lewis who agreed to lead the expedition.[1]

Jefferson was curious about Native Americans (Indians), animals, plants and the Great Salt Lake or salt deserts he had heard about. He knew that the land must eventually be of 'economic importance' to the United States. At that time, the British and French Canadians had most of the fur trade, entering the U.S. through western Canada. Trading with the Indians could be profitable, Jefferson thought, if a route could be found. He also wanted to know how much room there was for population expansion. In addition, there was concern about France reclaiming the Louisiana territory from Spain. If they did, the French could cut off trade with the west and the British were trading at the north, so the U.S. would be left out.[1]

Before the trip was planned, Jefferson had Meriwether Lewis in his employ, teaching him a great deal about plants and animals. It was expected that Lewis would return with detailed records of the terrain, its vegetation and its inhabitants, both human and animal. Lewis did this, and because so much detail was given about each plant and animal, and drawings were often made, scientists have been able to determine what the species were, if Lewis hadn't known.

Lewis chose William Clark to accompany him and to be his co-leader. Clark had a lower military rank than Lewis, but they agreed that each would be called Captain, and the men thought of them as equals.

It is mind-boggling in today's world to imagine planning the provision list and catering menus for more than two dozen men about to undertake a journey where there would be little opportunity for them to purchase anything and where there may be little food for which to forage for up to two years. How much more appreciative I've become of our many processed packaged 'instant' foods needing little or no preparation before consumption. These packaged foods are, of course, what would be taken on modern expeditions.

Lewis and Clark knew they would need to 'live off the land' and that there would need to be hunting of many animals to feed the men. Therefore, a large supply of ammunition was taken with gunpowder sealed in water-proofed kegs. The kegs were made from lead so that they could be melted to make bullets as the gunpowder was used. There was also an air gun included in the equipment in case there was no powder left.[1]

There are several accounts of provisions the explorers purchased before the journey. Lewis spent some time in Philadelphia buying needed items. One of these was 193 pounds of 'portable soup', a dried soup mix which proved to be unpopular with the men. This mix was supposedly made from concentrated meat broth.[1,2] Cutright reports that 20 barrels of flour, 14 barrels of parched corn meal (maize, also known as Indian meal), 42 barrels of pork, and lesser quantities of sugar, coffee, salt, preserved dried apples, and biscuit were purchased.[2] I am guessing that the pork was salted for preservation, but have not found documentation of this.

The biscuit was probably the same type that the wagon train travelers took with them as they traveled the Oregon Trail about half a century later. It has been described as being made only of flour and water, and so dry and hard that it must be dunked in liquid to soften it in order to make it chewable. Biscuit seems to be the same product as hardtack.[2]

In another notation, Cutright mentions that Lewis and Clark bought 5 barrels of pork, 5 barrels of flour, 25 and 1/2 bushels of lye-treated corn (hominy), and several gallons of Woodsford's whisky, paying $1 per gallon. He goes on to say that large quantities of corn were parched to be converted into meal.[2] It might be that the parched meal would keep longer than more moist meal; also, parched meal would not need to be cooked as long, which would be helpful on the trip. One can imagine how long it must have taken to prepare meals when there were none of the convenience foods that we might take on a camping or hiking trip in this era. Thinking about building a fire and having to cook everything (except the biscuit) from the beginning for each meal while traveling in open boats not equipped with galleys is overwhelming.

Further description of the provisions for the trip include melting of 200 pounds of beef tallow with 50 pounds of lard from hogs which, after being cooled, was stored in small whiskey kegs. 'All comestibles – pork, lard, beans, dried apples, coffee, sugar – were packaged and then stored away in designated places in one or another of the boats. Space was at a premium.' It has been suggested that the stores were divided among many boats so that if one met with an accident, not all provisions would be lost.[2] The journey was to be made, as far as possible, by boat, following the Missouri River and whatever other rivers led to the ocean. Lewis and Clark were charged with making maps of the land and waterways as they went.[2]

The last opportunity for the team to buy food before they left populated areas was at a small town in Missouri where they purchased milk and eggs. Then Lewis and Clark issued this order to the men:

> The day after tomorrow lyed corn and grece will be issued to the party, the next day Poark and flour, and the day following indian meal and poark, and in conformity to that routine provisions will continue to be issued to the party until further orders....no poark is to be issued when we have fresh meat on hand. [2]

The party had spent the winter of 1803 at a camp site in Illinois, just across the river from St. Louis in what is now the state of Missouri. The journey began on May 14th but not until 4 p.m., so the group traveled only four miles before camping for the night. Lewis was not with them for the send-off; he stayed in St. Louis and joined the boats down-river.

On May 31st, it was recorded that hunters – who left the boats and walked on land until they had game to bring to the boats – caught several very large rats in the woods.[1] There is no comment about them having been eaten, but the reader may accept that it was possible.

On June 4th, wild cresses and tongue grass were gathered along the shore. On a notation in a diary for June 7th, hunters, 'who had hitherto given us only deer', killed three bears and reported signs of buffalo nearby.[1] When there was extra meat, it was preserved by 'jerking' – thin slices of raw meat were hung to dry near fires, or in the sun. When jerky is kept dry, it lasts a long time. [2] Jerky from various animals is still prepared and sold in the U.S. as a snack food or a provision for camping and hiking trips.

It has been suggested that the men could have eaten four or five deer daily. The two French hired men who were part of the entourage complained about the small amount of food they were given. They were used to eating five or six times a day, they said, instead of just three meals daily as was usual during the trip.[2]

A headwind caused the party to stay in place on Stump Island in the Missouri River on June 11th. They dried some of the meat from animals the hunters had killed so as to have some for later use. At that location, the Osage plum 'of superior size and quality' was noted. The diary did not say the plums were eaten, but one can assume that any edible plants were consumed.[1]

During the next few days, hunters brought deer, bear, elk and a racoon to the boats. Then there is mention of a fat horse, which was probably lost by some Indian war party, having been eaten. Fowls, gooseberries, and raspberries were all found in this region.[1]

The entry in the diary for June 25 says that the prairies have many fruits, including wild apples, raspberries, plums, and mulberries (the latter were nearer the river than the other fruits). A few days later, grapes (called summer grapes by Cutright[2]) and more raspberries were found, along with pecan trees, 'large quantities of deer and turkies on the banks'.[1] Service berries and strawberries were eaten, and there is mention of 'choak cherries', which Cutright says were sand cherries.[2]

July 4, the day which Americans observe as independence day, the men were allowed to celebrate by receiving an extra gill of whiskey in the evening.[1,4]

Near the Platte River, in what is now the state of Nebraska, the report that game was scarce is followed by a statement that the hunters have seen deer, turkeys and grouse. Ripe grapes were picked, and a catfish was caught.[1] One catfish would not go far to feed the number of men on the expedition.

A Missouri Indian, found by the hunters as he was dressing an elk, gave the hunters some of the meat. The next day, several large catfish were caught, so the stores improved. A description in a diary said that one of the fish was nearly white, and that all of them were very fat.[1]

By the end of July, geese and beaver were shot along with deer and turkey. Within a few days. the explorers sent the Ottoe and Missouri Indians some roasted meat, pork, flour and corn meal in exchange for watermelons.[1]

In Townsend's version of the trip, a story about a colt wandering into camp is related. The colt was slaughtered and served for breakfast. Leftover colt was taken along for another meal later. After bartering with Indians for some salmon, the men invited one of the Indians to eat with them. He suddenly spit out the food, exclaimed 'horse!' (in his language), and left.[5] Perhaps horses were so valuable to the Indians as means of transportation that they were not used as food by that tribe; nevertheless, the Native recognized the flavor as being horsemeat.

As to what was drunk in addition to whisky and coffee, Cartright tells us that Missouri River water was consumed in spite of mud, and that there were reports of mild dysentery among the travelers.[2]

Between the Mississippi River and the Kansas River, 70 deer were killed by the hunters, along with 12 or more black bear (*Ursus americanus*), 3 wild turkeys (*Meleagris gallopavo*), 1 rabbit

(*Lepus sp.*), 1 woodchuck (*Marmota monax*), and 1 goose (probably *Branta canadensis*). Cutright says these figures are reliable because the journalists were interested in what they ate and kept records in their journals. If the meat were lean and tough, it was called 'pore'; if fat, tender and juicy it was noted to be in 'good condition'.[2]

Sometime in July or August of the first year of the trip, beaver were added to the diet. The next spring, near the Yellowstone River, good, fat beavers were found and beaver was listed as the favourite meat of the men. Lewis liked 'particularly the tale and the liver'. He wrote that boiled beaver tail tasted like the tongues and swim-bladders of codfish. The hunters learned to trap beavers overnight so there would be some to take on the next day's journey.[2,4]

The hunters killed the first buffalo of the trip on August 23, near what is now Vermillion, South Dakota. Roasted bison steaks were served to the men. Another day, a prairie dog was shot and cooked for the captains' dinners. A small animal would not have gone far in feeding the entire group, especially with the calorie expenditure each one must have had while performing the arduous tasks necessary on such a journey.

When the group spent four days with the Teton (Oglala) Sioux Indians, Clark wrote about the food the women prepared, such as 'ground potatoe' which Cutright tells us is a legume, *Psoralea esculenta*, also known as prairie apple, prairie turnip, white apple or pomme blanch. Cutright explains that this root was an important source of food for the Plains Indians, even though Lewis found it 'tasteless and insipid'. Lewis did suggest that United States epicures would use the roots in gravies and ragouts in place of truffles morella.[2]

The travelers received quantities of buffalo meat from the Tetons, as well as pemmican made from jerked beef and buffalo tallow which the women seasoned with fruits like wild cherry. When pemmican was sealed into skin bags, it would stay in good condition for four to five years. It needed no cooking.[2]

The Teton Indians kept dogs to pull loads of goods when they moved, but they also ate the dogs. Several of the diary-writers described these dogs as being domesticated wolves.[2]

The Arikara Indians grew corn, beans, squashes and sunflowers. The first three have been known as 'the three sisters' because of their importance to the Native Americans. All were grown in the same plots, with the sunflowers usually rimming the edges of the fields. In order to prepare and cultivate the plots of land, the Indian women used hoes fashioned from shoulder blade bones of elk or buffalo and fastened to wooden handles. Another farm tool was a rake made of reeds curved at the ends.[2]

Corn (*Zea mays*) was the staple crop for most of the Native Americans who did farming. Several varieties were grown and stored, along with other produce, in cellars dug in the fields or beneath the earthen lodges.[2]

According to Clark, the Arikira gave the explorers 'a large Been' robbed from the mice on the prairie. Cutright identifies this as the hog peanut or ground bean (*Falcata comosa*), a member of the pea family. This plant produces two types of fruits, one below ground, like lima beans in pods, and those above ground, the size of lentils. A species of meadow mouse (*Microtus pennsylvanicus insperatus*) digs up the mature underground beans and stores them in amounts of about a pint. The Indian women would rob the mouse bean stores but not without leaving some other food to replace the beans.[2]

The first winter encampment for the explorers was at the mouth of the Knife River where some Indian groups also lived. Providing food for the group was difficult. One full-grown buffalo, or its equivalent, was needed daily. The equivalent to the amount of meat from a buffalo was one elk plus one bear, or four deer. While the fort, called Fort Mandan, was being built for the winter, all the men were needed to work on it, so hunting was abandoned. This meant that the stores of pork brought from Missouri must be used; it was used sparingly, the diarists recorded.[2]

When the fort was ready, the hunters were sent out; they returned in a few days with 32 deer, 12 elk, and one buffalo, all of which lasted the party three weeks. The next five-day hunt brought 36 buffalo, and one deer. A successive hunt gave only nine buffalo, then just one wolf, which was eaten because there was nothing else.[2]

Mention is made in the diaries of the fact that the Mandan Indians liked putrid meat. It was usual for them to let their buffalo meat rot some before it was eaten.[2] It seems certain that the men on the expedition ate meat that nowadays would be considered rotten.

There is a report of the hunting party being accosted in mid-February by hostile Sioux Indians, who robbed the hunters of their knives and two of their three horses. On the other hand, the Mandan and Hidatsa Indians were eager to trade and brought pemmican, jerky, dried pumpkins, squash, corn and beans. Because of the variety of foods eaten by the men, no dietary diseases such as scurvy were reported.[2]

The foods the Indians brought were traded for beads, ribbons, mirrors and fish hooks. When the explorers' stores of such trifles for trading were depleted, a blacksmith in the group who repaired tools and guns began to do this for the Indians. Then iron battle-axes were requested, so the blacksmith made those. By spring, there was a store of Indian-grown corn to go with the men on the continuation of their journey. [2]

Just after leaving Fort Mandan, no game was seen. The diaries report that 'Indians had driven the game away'. After a few days on the river, lots of deer, antelope, elk and buffalo were seen. Accounting was made of buffalo drowning in the early spring as they tried to cross the frozen river. The ice was beginning to melt, and the heavy animals broke through it and were swept downstream. A traveler through this region in 1811 wrote about seeing 30-40 buffalo carcasses in the river daily.[2]

As they got nearer the Marias River, it was noted that fuel for cooking was more difficult to find.[2] It might be thought that the meat would be cooked for shorter times, or that more jerky would have been processed, but I could not find mention of this.

Much game, including bear, was found between the Yellowstone River and the Marias. One supper meal described as having gone down 'uncommonly well' consisted of buffalo humps, tongues and marrowbones; trout; and parched meal with salt and pepper.[2]

Modern-day visitors to the various Lewis and Clark interpretive centers are often surprised to hear that the men of the expedition were near starvation during parts of the journey. Why, the visitors wonder, when the trip took the explorers to some of the parts of the land which were lush with flora and fauna did this happen? The harsh winters spent when food was hard to come by are understood; what about the other times?

During part of the journey the travelers were spending all their time negotiating the rugged landscape; portaging at Great Falls, in what is now Montana, for example, and crossing part of the Rocky Mountains when the boats had to be left behind took the energy and efforts of all. There was no time for hunting or foraging. When the group got to the deep canyons of the Snake River, it was too difficult to leave the river to do much searching for food.

Some distance down the Columbia River, Lewis and Clark encountered the Skilloot Indians, of the Chinookan Tribe just after the party left the river they called the Quick Sand River, now known as the Sandy River. From these Indians they learned about 'Wap-pa-to which the Chinese cultivate in great quantities called the Sa-git-ti-folia or common arrow head'. The description in the journals was that the plant had an agreeable taste and was a good substitute for bread. The men bought four bushels of wappato. Cutright comments that these starchy tubers are used by the coastal Indians as well.[2]

From November 9-15 at the mouth of the Columbia, the party was stuck on a small edge of shoreline because of winds and rain. They drank rainwater and ate pounded salmon. One factor in deciding the party to establish their winter camp on the coast instead of upriver was that they would be near a source of salt; another was that elk were available, larger than deer, and as Lewis wrote, 'better meat and Skins better for the clothes of the party'. Clothing was an urgent item at this stage because the men had been so often wet that the fabric was rotting and falling off them.

While still scouting an appropriate winter campsite, Lewis and five others left Clark and the rest of the men for eight days on a point of land where they had only dried fish, a few squirrels and some 'fat and delicious' hawks to eat.

The spot chosen for quarters in which the second winter would be spent, Fort Clatsop, was established four miles east of the ocean on the Lewis and Clark River (called Netul by the natives then). This is located in what is now the west coast state of Oregon. The men had been out of salt for several weeks by the time the fort was built, so a trail was blazed to the ocean for the salt-makers to follow and hunters were sent to find elk. It was almost Christmas. The Christmas dinner that year consisted of 'pore Elk, so much Spoiled that we eate it thro' necessity, Some Spoiled pounded fish and a few roots'. One of the group wrote in his diary that 'we have no ardent Spirits, but all are in good health which we esteem more than all the ardent spirits in the world'.[2]

On December 28, 5 men left the fort and hiked the trail to the seashore to make salt. They chose a spot about 15 miles southwest of the fort. Seawater was evaporated in 5 large kettles. By January 5, the salt-makers were able to send a gallon of salt to the fort. Lewis described it as 'excellent, fine, strong & white'. The kettles boiled day and night, so that three or four quarts of salt were made daily. After about 20 gallons were made, 12 were put into kegs for the return trip to the United States. The cairn where the salt was made has been reconstructed and can be seen now in the town of Seaside, Oregon.[2]

Nell has made a study of the references to salt in the diaries. He calculates that the expedition started with between 700 and 800 pounds of salt, which was relatively expensive at one dollar per pound, when the average monthly wage at that time was twenty dollars, and was a considerable amount; yet the men were out of salt before they reached the west coast. There are several mentions of salt being used to add some flavor to foods which were otherwise not very palatable.[3]

Historians seem to believe that much of the meat killed by the hunters on the expedition was preserved by salting. Nell tells us that salting takes a lot of effort, a great deal of salt, and plenty of time. Except for the winter months spent at Fort Mandan and Fort Clatsop, the men were constantly on the move, so Nell questions that much 'salting down' of meat would have been done. However, he does suggest that it is possible that the men used salty water, from some of the brackish rivers or springs that were found, to 'pickle down' buffalo and venison.[3]

Rainfall helped prevent food-getting at the fort; also, the hunters had to travel through bogs, often 'immersing themselves to midriff'. Elk moved further away from the fort as winter progressed, so when game was shot it had to be carried many miles to camp. There was a need to hurry with this transport, because the winter of 1805-1806 was a mild one so the meat spoiled quickly. Between December 1 and March 20, 131 elk were killed and consumed. This elk described in the Lewis and Clark journals was, years later, named as a new species, *Cervus roosevelti* to honor Theodore Roosevelt, but now is a subspecies, *Cervus canadensis roosevelti*.[2]

Sometimes the men described their favourite parts of the elk. Lewis praised a meal of a marrowbone and boiled brisket. He said of the meal, 'this .....is living in high style'. The diet of elk was tiresome, so the men were delighted when, in January, the Clatsop Indians sold them some whale meat, Lewis wrote that this was 'verry palitable and tender', saying that it tasted like beaver or dog. Then Clark took some men to the place where the whale was located to get about 300 pounds of whale meat and a few gallons of whale oil from the Natives.[2]

The next month, the Indians brought to the fort white Columbia River sturgeon, *Acipenser transmontanus*, to sell, and a small fish that had just begun to run. Clark described the little fish as being so fat that they could be roasted on a wooden spit without any other preparation and needing no sauce. He declared them the most delicious fish he had ever eaten, including his previous favourite, white fish from the lakes. The fatty fish he described were eulachon, or candle fish, *Thaleichthys pacificus*. When dried, the fish can serve as a candle if a wick is drawn through it.[2]

While at Fort Clatsop that winter, Lewis described in his journal several roots which were foods for the Chinook Indians. *Shannetahque* (edible thistle), *Cirsium edule*, was as wide as a thumb, and about 9-15 inches long. It was white and about as crisp as a carrot. When cooked, the root turned black and tasted sweeter than any of the other roots.[2]

Horsetail rush, *Equisetum telmateia*, was also as wide as a thumb, but only about an inch long. Its pulp was noted as brittle and white; mention was made that it could be easily chewed. Preparation was usually done by roasting. Lewis thought the flavor of horsetail was insipid.[2]

The root of Western bracken fern, *Pteridium aquilinum pubescens*, ranged in size from that of a goose quill to as large as a finger. It was divided into two equal parts by what Cutright calls a ligament. On each side of the divider was a white substance. Lewis wrote that when this was roasted in the coals of a fire, it tasted like wheat dough except for 'a pungency which becomes more visible after you have chewed it for some time'.[2]

Cattail, also know as Cooper's flag, *Typha latifolia*, was made up of a number of strong white flexible fibers. Among the fibers was a starch-like or mealy substance which dissolves in one's mouth. Lewis said the fibers 'are then rejected', a polite way of saying expectorated. (2)

Wappato, mentioned previously, was considered the most valuable of the roots. It didn't grow around Fort Clatsop but was gathered from 15 miles away. *Wappato* bulbs, about the size of hen's eggs, were roasted and eaten like potatoes. The harvesting of *wappato* was unusual. The plants grow in swampy places, so the native women took canoes into the swamps, left the canoes and got into the water, often up to their necks. The women dug the bulbs with their toes. When the bulbs floated to the surface, they were scooped into the canoes.[2] Other native groups, including the Klamath of southern Oregon and northern California, have harvested *wappato* this way for a long time.

The fruit of salal plants, which Lewis named shallon (*Gaultheris shallon*), was a deep purple berry about the size of our black cherries. The Clatsop Indians baked salal berries into large loaves, says Clark's account. He describes having been served a kind of soup 'made of bread of the Shelewell berries mixed with roots', by an Indian woman.[2]

Another berry, bearberry (*Arctostaphylos uva-ursi*), also known as *saccocommis*, was bright red and about the size of a small cherry. Lewis called them 'tasteless and insipid', but commented that the ripe fruit remained on the bushes all winter waiting to be picked. Sometimes the Natives dried bearberries.[2]

Lewis also described wild crab apple (*Pyrus fuscu*) whose fruit differed from eastern wild crab apple in that the western fruit 'consists of little oval burries which grow in clusters at the extremities of the twigs like black haws'. He said the fruit was brown, and after a frost tasted agreeably acid. This is now known as Oregon crab apple.[2]

The explorers discovered cranberries (*Vaccinium oxycoccus intermedium*) in marshy areas and said it was the same fruit as found in the United States. This northwest territory was not a part of the United States in 1806.[2]

Evergreen huckleberries (*Vaccinium ovatum*) were eaten as picked by the Natives, or dried, or pounded and baked into loaves of about 10-15 pounds. Lewis said 'this bread keeps very well during one season and retains the moist jeucies of the fruit much better than by any other method of preservation'. He wrote that the Indians broke up the loaves and stirred the fruit into cold water to make a thick mass.[2]

There was a root mentioned in Lewis's journal which Cutright, in 1969, said had not been definitely identified. Lewis wrote that it was a liquorice like that cultivated in gardens in the United States. The Indians roasted it and pounded it to separate it from the strong 'liggament' making up the center of the root. He said the roasted root tasted something like 'sweet pittaaitoe'. Elliott Coues said the plant is *Glycyrrhiza lapidota*, wild licorice, but David Douglass identified it as *Lupinus littoralis*, seashore lupine. It is sometimes called Chinook licorice.[2]

Animals Lewis identified as being eaten by the Natives included seal, sea otter and porpoise. Ducks, geese and swans were consumed in season.[2]

Salmon were the most important animal food to the Chinookans. There are five different species, all belonging to the genus *Onchorhyncus*. Most important was the king or Chinook (*O. tshawytcha*) which Lewis called 'common salmon'. It has been of greater commercial value than any other fish; as the largest, it averages 20 pounds, and sometimes one weighs about 100 pounds. King salmon may travel as far as 1,000 miles up the Columbia River during its spring run to spawn.[2]

The next most important salmon is sockeye (blueback), *O. nerka*, usually about five pounds in weight. This fish was called 'red charr' by Lewis and Clark. The men found them excellent eating. Silver or coho salmon, *O. kisutch*, averages from five to eight pounds and is the next most important of the salmon to the natives. The journalists called it 'white salmon trout'.[2]

The other two species of salmon were not mentioned by Lewis or Clark. All of the salmon had been identified a few years before this expedition. So these men were not the first to technically name the fish.[2]

Chinookans usually cooked the fish by dropping hot stones into water-tight baskets. Some fish were sun-dried. Eulachon were hung in the smoke of the lodges. Lewis wrote that it was not necessary to clean the fish first, and that they would cure in 24 hours. Sturgeon were steamed on hot stones with small boughs laid on top, then all was covered with mats; water was poured on top. It took one hour for the process and was better than boiling or roasting, said Lewis.[2]

And so the winter on the Pacific coast passed; in the spring, the explorers headed back to the United States, checking maps, distances, and notes on flora and fauna for accuracy. They reached St. Louis about two years and five months after embarking on their remarkable journey.[2]

BIBLIOGRAPHY

1. Biddle, Nicholas, ed.: *The Journal of the Expedition under the command of Captains Lewis and Clark to the sources of the Missouri, thence across The Rocky Mountains and down the river Columbia to the Pacific Ocean, performed during the Years 1804-5-6 by order of the Government of The United States*. Volume 1. New York: The Heritage Press, 1962.
2. Cartright, Paul Russell: *A History of the Lewis and Clark Journals*. Norman, Oklahoma. University of Oklahoma Press, 1976.
3. Nell, Donald F.: *Where is the salt? We Proceeded On*. The Official Publication of the Lewis and Clark Trail Heritage Foundation. Volume 17, number 2, p.14, 1991.
4. Thwaites, Reuben Gold: *Original Journals of the Lewis and Clark Expedition. 1804-1806*. Volume 1. New York: Dodd, Mead and Company, 1904.
5. Townsend, John Kirk: *Narrative of a Journey across the Rocky Mountains to the Columbia River*. Lincoln, London: University of Nebraska Press, 1978.

Paximadia (Barley Biscuits):
Food for Sailors, Travellers and Poor Islanders

Aglaia Kremezi

'The staple food of the common people is a biscuit made of barley from which only the very outer husk has been discarded. They bake it two or three times a year. It is so black that when I showed a piece to one of our monks in Naxos, he sincerely told me that in France it would be bread to give to the dogs, but he doubted that even the dogs would eat it. Nevertheless, here the small children eat it from early morning on with great appetite, and they seem to be thriving. But it would cause haemorrhaging and death to those unaccustomed to it,' writes François Richard,[1] who visited the island of Santorini in the seventeenth century. 'With this biscuit, which many soak in water before lunch, they eat their vegetables, their usual meal, because they only rarely taste meat, with the exception of the rich, who buy it once a year in order to secure that they will not go without it.'

Thevenot,[2] who visited Santorini a few years later, describes somewhat finer biscuits: 'Their bread, which they call *schises*,[3] is a kind of biscuit made with half wheat and half barley flour, black like tar, and so rough that one cannot swallow it; they only fire the oven twice a year... maybe they do it because they don't have wood to burn and have to import it from Nio...'[4]

Paximadi (plural *paximadia*) was and still is the Greek word for this barley biscuit (rusk or hard-tack), although in recent years the word came to mean all kinds of twice-baked bread. Many believe that the word *paximadi* comes from Paxamus, a cook and author who probably lived in Rome in the first century AD.[5] As Andrew Dalby[6] points out, from this Greek word came the Arabic *bashmat* or *baqsimat*, the Turkish *beksemad*, the Serbo Croatian *peksimet*, the Romanian *pesmet*, and the Venetian *pasimata*.

Barley, cultivated in the Mediterranean from the beginnings of civilization, was for many centuries the basic food of the regional populations. It was roasted so that some of its husk could be rubbed off, then ground and mixed with water, spices, and maybe honey, to be made into a gruel, or it was kneaded with water, shaped into cakes and then baked. The barley cakes were called *maza*, and according to the laws of Solon,[7] *maza* was the everyday food of Athenians in classical times, while the more refined breads, made of wheat or a combination of barley and wheat, could only be baked on festive days. 'When we come to our regular daily food we require that our barley cake (*maza*) be white, yet take pains that the broth which goes with it be black, and stain the fine colour of the cake with the dye,' writes Alexis.[8] *Maza* was probably a kind of heavy unleavened flat bread, unlike *paximadi*, which is first baked as a leavened bread. The way *maza* was eaten though, dipped in a more or less rich broth, as this paragraph reveals, was very similar to the way *paximadi* is consumed to this day.

Since barley contains less gluten than wheat, the bread made with it is heavy, darker in colour, and dries faster. So it is not surprising that it was baked again in order to be preserved. 'The flavour is good, with an unmistakably earthy tang – anyone who has ever eaten a good barley or Scotch broth will recognise the taste and the aroma,' writes Elizabeth David.[9] She advises modern bakers to add a small amount of barley to their usual wheat flour when making bread, a widespread tradition in most Mediterranean countries.

C.S. Sonnini,[10] who visited Greece and Turkey in the last years of the eighteenth century, writes that in Kimolos (then called Argentière) and in the other islands of the Aegean, people only baked barley bread. He is one of the very few who agree with David on its taste: 'Having lived there for a long time, I did not find this bread disagreeable, but thought it tasty and appetising.' Sonnini also claims that all over the Orient barley bread was the usual food, and the Jews used it a lot in their diet.

Either baked in the form of a loaf, or shaped like a large doughnut, the bread destined to be made into *paximadia* is sliced – vertically in the case of the loaf and horizontally in the case of the doughnut – and left to dry for many hours in a low oven. *Dipyros artos* (twice-baked bread) was the ancient word and both the Italian *biscotti* as well as the French and English biscuit, derive their names from the description of the technique in Latin (*bis-coto*).

During Byzantine times, *paximadia* 'was probably the food that the future Emperor Justin II, uncle of Justinian, carried in his knapsack, the food that kept him alive on his long walk from Illyria to Constantinople; it was certainly food for soldiers and for frugal priests as well,' writes Dalby.[11]

In the mid-eighteenth century, Nicolas-Ernest Kleeman[12] writes that after the fall of the Byzantine Empire the Turks served biscuits to the army during their sea and land expeditions.

European travellers of the seventeenth and eighteenth century also carried with them biscuits during their long journeys over sea and land, but their biscuits were probably made with white wheat flour, much more refined than the rough *paximadia* of the poor inhabitants of the Orient.[13] During his wanderings on camelback, through the vast Ottoman Empire – or the Levant as the eastern Mediterranean region was often called – Carlier de Pinon[14] thought that the Arab camel drivers were extremely grateful when offered a taste of the European biscuits. He describes with contempt the Arab flat breads prepared fresh each time the caravan stopped and baked using camel's dung as fuel. My impression is that Europeans misjudged the big gestures with which Arabs politely thanked them. I have no doubt that the locals definitely preferred their fresh breads to the dried European biscuits, especially as they often rolled their warm pitas over stuffings of fresh cheese and dates, as documented by Sauveboeuf.[15]

From the islands to the city

An old man from Mykonos told me that not so long ago, merchant ships preferred their island as a stop-over because sailors loved to stock up on *paximadia* from the local bakeries made with a combination of barley and wheat flour. Similar biscuits are still baked in most islands of the Aegean and the ones from Crete are the most popular throughout Greece. One can get Cretan *paximadia* in specialty shops around the central market of Athens, as well as in grocery stores and, recently, even at some supermarkets. Although the people belonging to the generation that traditionally fed on this kind of dried bread has either died or switched to more refined foods, there is a new generation of consumers who have tasted *paximadia* during their summer vacations in the islands and loved them. Once back in the city they started to look for them in their local bakeries, so now in most Athenian neighbourhoods one can find darker or lighter *paximadia*, baked using mixtures containing more or less barley flour in addition to the wheat flour, that makes lighter and crunchier biscuits which need no soaking.

Paximadia were not just eaten as an accompaniment to cheese, olives or dried fish and meats, but were used as the main ingredient of cooked dishes. Villamont[16] describes a soup made with 'black biscuits', water and salt, which was prepared by a Genoan, during his voyage from Cyprus to Jerusalem. Similar soups, with the addition of vegetables, herbs, pulses or even a little meat or fish, can be found in the peasant cooking of Greece, Italy, Spain and other Mediterranean countries. In the island of Santorini people make a kind of sweetmeat, pounding together in a mortar the very black local *paximadia*, with sultanas and shaping the thick dough into walnut size balls which they often roll on toasted sesame seeds. Briefly dipped in water drizzled with olive oil and sprinkled with coarse sea salt and oregano, *paximadi* becomes a delicious snack which is called *riganada* in the Peloponnese. In the island of Kea, I recently tasted soaked *paximadia* with *kopanisti* – the local sharp fermented soft cheese – and chopped tomatoes, an excellent combination. Food writer Colman Andrews[17] mentions a very similar dish served in Triora, the back country above San Remo. There the medium brown biscuits are usually soaked in a combination of water and vinegar.

In the Calabrian bakeries and grocery stores on Arthur Avenue, in New York's Bronx, one finds barley biscuits very similar to the ones from Crete. Their taste complements fantastically the spicy *cacciocavallo* cheese of southern Italy, which is covered with crushed dried *peperoncini* (hot chillies). In a similar way one couldn't find a more perfect combination than *paximadi* and the hard sharp *anthotyro* of Crete.

When, in the fifties, Ansel Keys[18] and his colleagues studied the eating habits, the state of health, and life expectancy of various peoples in seven countries, they decided that the inhabitants of Crete were faring best of all. *Paximadia*, in those days, were the staple food of the Cretans. But when their traditional eating habits became the model for the now famed Mediterranean diet, the barley biscuits were translated into 'wholewheat bread' for the unaccustomed and refined northern Europeans and Americans. Barley flour has now completely disappeared from the shelves of the supermarkets and one can only find it if one goes to a healthfood shop or to a wholesale distributor of animal fodder.

My version of
barley and wheat Cretan *paximadia*[19]
from a Cretan recipe

For 16 large (12 cm) biscuits.

2 tablespoons honey • 11/3 cup (325 ml) warm water or more if needed
2 tablespoons dried yeast • 1 tablespoon coarse sea salt • 1 tablespoon green aniseeds
2 - 21/2 cups (330g) unbleached all purpose flour • 2 cups (260g) whole barley flour
1/2 cup (125 ml) olive oil • 1/2 cup (125 ml) sweet red wine such as Mavrodaphne or port
1/2 cup (125 ml) dry red wine • olive oil to brush the dough and baking sheets

In a 4 cup bowl, dilute the honey in 1/3 warmwater. Add the yeast, stir and let prove for 10 minutes.

In a mortar beat the salt together with the aniseeds to get a coarse powder. In a large bowl stir together the wheat and barley flours and the aniseed-salt powder. Make a well in the center and pour in the olive oil, the sweet and dry wine, the yeast mixture and 1/2 cup warm water. Draw the flour towards the center, mixing it with the liquids to form a rather sticky dough. Knead patiently, adding a little more warm water or flour to obtain a smooth dough.

(Alternatively, work this dough in a food processor, equipped with dough hooks. Add all ingredients to the processor's bowl, and process for 11/2–2 minutes, at high speed. Scrape the bowl with the spatula, let rest for 5–10 minutes, and process another 1–2 minutes.)

Turn the dough on to a lightly floured board and continue kneading, folding, pushing, turning and folding, for another 2–3 minutes. You must end up with a soft, very slightly sticky dough. Form a ball, oil it all over with a few drops of olive oil, place in a 3-quart bowl, cover with plastic film and let rise in a draft-free place for about 11/2 hours, until it has doubled in size.

Cut the dough in half and divide each piece into quarters. Form each piece into a one-inch-thick cord, then shape each cord into a small circle with overlapping ends (like a large doughnut). Place them on lightly oiled baking sheets, spaced 11/2 inches apart. Cover with plastic film and let rise for about 11/2–2 hours.

Preheat the oven to 400° F/204°C. When you place the bread circles in the oven, reduce the temperature to 375° F/190°C. Bake for 30 to 40 minutes, until the breads are light golden on top and sound hollow when tapped. Let them cool for 5–10 minutes. Turn the oven down to its lowest setting (175°F/80°C). Using a very good bread knife slice the circles in half horizontally. Place the halves on the oven rack and leave for about 1 1/2–2 hours, until they are completely dry. Let cool and keep in tins in a dry place.

Cretan Barley Paximadia will keep for up to 6 months.

ACKNOWLEDGMENTS

I would like to express my deep gratitude to Aliki Asvesta, of the Gennadios Library in Athens, for her invaluable help.

NOTES

[1] Richard, F., *Relation de ce qui s'est Passé de plus Remarquable à Saint-Erini, Isle de Archipel*, Paris: S.Cramoisy 1657, pp.38-39.

[2] Thevenot, de, *Relation d'un Voyage fait au Levant*. Paris: T. Iolly, 1857, p.203.

[3] Εκιζες from the verb 'schizo' (to tear off) is a word still used in Santorini by some old people, to describe the thick squarish barley biscuits, distinguishing them from the round doughnut shaped ones that are called 'paximadia'.

[4] Ios or Nios, another island of the Aegean.

[5] Athenaeus, *Deipnosophistae*, trans. C.B.Gulick, Cambridge, Mass., Loeb 1987, volume IV, p. 205, '...my own authority, Paxamus, mentions...'.

[6] Dalby, A., *Siren Feasts, A History of Food and Gastronomy in Greece*, London: Routledge 1996, p.197.

[7] 7-6th centuries BC.

[8] Alexis comic. (4th-3rd centuries B.C), *The Woman who drank Belladona*, as cited by Athenaeus.

[9] David, E., *English Bread and Yeast Cookery*, London: Penguin 1977, p. 62.

[10] Sonnini, *Voyage en Grèce et en Turquie*, Paris: F.Buisson 1801, 2nd volume, p. 30.

[11] Dalby, A., 1996, p.196.

[12] Kleeman, N.E., *Voyage de Vienne à Belgrade et à Kilianova*, Neuchatel: Société Typographique 1780, p.193.

[13] The Eastern Mediterranean was often referred to as The Orient at this time.

[14] de Pinon, C., *Voyage en Orient*, annotated by E.Blochet, Paris: Ernest Leroux 1920, p.202.

[15] Ferrière-Sauveboeuf, Comte de, *Mémoires Historiques, Politiques et Géographiques des Voyages fait en Turquie, en Perse et en Arabie (1782-1789)*, Paris: Buisson 1790, 2nd volume p.97.

[16] de Villamont, L.S., *Les Voyages de la Terre Saincte et autres Lieux Remarquables*, Paris: Guillaume Loyson 1627.

[17] Andrews, C., *Flavors of the Riviera*, New York: Bantam Books, 1996.

[18] Keys, A., et al., 'The Diet and 15-Year Death Rate in Seven Countries Study', *American Journal of Epidemiology*, 124, no.6 (1986).

[19] Kremezi, A., *Mediterranean Pantry*, New York: Artisan, 1994, pp. 58-59.

Space, Time and Food
(Barbecued Elephant, *Saucisses mi-Cheval-mi-Porc*,
Whale's Milk)

Nicholas Kurti

The reader may rest assured that this is not a paper on relativistic gastronomy. The title simply indicates that, as in other human activities, so in eating and drinking, historical variations are just as important as geographical ones. However, apart from two examples of travel in time, this article will deal with travel in space – not to be confounded with space travel.

The first example is Paris, more particularly the Quartier Latin which I have known for 70 years. I was an undergraduate from 1926 to 1928 at the Sorbonne, the name by which the Faculté des Lettres and the Faculté des Sciences and the buildings they occupied were known. The Quartier Latin was full of hotels – as it is today, but they were largely used by students. They were relatively inexpensive but they usually had the basic modern comforts, running hot and cold water in the room and central heating; but to have a bath was a major, and costly, operation. During my second year in Paris I lived in the Hotel du Panthéon in the Place du Panthéon. It is still there but much more luxurious than it was in my days. I had a room in the mansarde and, stepping out onto the roof, I could see Sacré Coeur in Montmartre. There were just as many restaurants as today but the main clientèle was students. Most of them offered Prix Fixe meals but not one of the most popular ones, the Bouillon Chartier in the rue Racine, one of a chain of some 50 restaurants in Paris, all with the same à la carte menu, the same Art Nouveau décor. Today there are only two left. Most of the restaurants served French food and the only 'foreign' restaurants in significant numbers were the Indo-Chinese, probably because most of the foreign students came from Indo-China. You could also get a satisfying meal of *Saucisses-pommes frites* from a corner stall. The fried potatoes were excellent, the quality of the sausages was variable. In those two years I never discovered whether the sausages described as *mi-porc, mi-cheval* contained equal weights of pork and horse flesh or were prepared from an equal number of pig and horse carcases. As a student of modest means I did not frequent any restaurants serving memorable or exotic dishes. My only gastronomic delight was the breakfast in the corner coffee bar: steaming, frothy café-crème accompanied by a fresh croissant. I continued this habit on subsequent visits to Paris and eschewed hotel breakfasts until the late 1960s, by which time the quality of the coffee-bar breakfasts had diminished – or so it seemed. I wonder whether others have noticed a similar deterioration in café-bar service over the last four or five decades.

My second 'time-travel' example is the change of North American drinking habits. I first visited the USA in 1943 and the custom then was to offer before the meal excellent, but very strong, chilled cocktails, and iced water and hot coffee to go with the food. My first experience of American cocktails was when I was having lunch with friends who lived in a university residence. We had pre-prandial drinks in their apartment and I was offered a refreshing, very cold fruit drink which tasted innocuous so I accepted a second glass and then a freshly mixed third glass. My host looked rather surprised when I said 'yes' to what was left in the cocktail shaker. When I tried to get up to go to lunch I understood my host's wonderment. He had given me a very strong Daiquiri. I could hardly get out of my chair. I thanked fate that the corridors were narrow and I could walk in an approximately straight line but I had the crowning humiliation of listening to my own speech, stumbling over slurred words in the most exaggerated stage-drunk fashion.

California seemed to be in those days the only exception to the rule of wineless meals, at least as far as private houses were concerned. I still recall a dinner with friends in 1953 in Berkeley when we drank a superb 1945 Cabernet Sauvignon from Louis M. Martini.

A real breakthrough occurred three years later, when at the banquet of the American Physical Society's West Coast meeting, white and red wine from Mondavi was served *à discretion*. This historic event was mentioned in the official report of the meeting published in the *Bulletin of the American Physical Society*.[1]

The serving of wines at scientific conference dinners took some time to get established. Thus at a conference in Toronto in 1960 (by then Toronto was no longer dry) we were offered a small glass of sherry each as a pre-prandial drink but no wine with the meal. After the dinner I ran into a French colleague who was seething with rage. He explained that the waiter asked him whether he wanted coffee, or tea or iced tea or Coca-Cola with his meal and, when he refused, he was offered a glass of milk to go with his steak: the crowning insult to a Frenchman!

While the wine-with-meals situation has greatly improved in the USA, the pre-prandials are becoming weaker and weaker: thin white wine or Perrier are fashionable. It seems that where prohibition failed, the continued efforts of the medical profession and of wine buffs ('don't spoil your taste buds') have succeeded and it may well be goodbye to the intoxicating pre-prandials.

I shall now turn to food and travel in space. This has two aspects: the names of the dishes on the one hand and their actual composition and taste on the other. As to the first of these, culinary terminology or the language of cookery books and of menus is a rich source of merriment and annoyance. There seems to be no attempt to harmonize terms, to eradicate misnomers or to discourage new names for variants of existing dishes.

One of the most widespread misnomers is 'goulash' which is used to describe a meat stew flavoured with onions and paprika (powdered capsicum). 'Goulash' comes from the Hungarian word *Gulyás* which denotes a soup flavoured with onions and paprika and containing meat, potatoes, vegetables – a meal in itself. To call a *pörkölt* or a *paprikás*, both of which are meat stews, 'goulash' is a bit like calling a fish stew *bouillabaisse*.

Another example of misusing a well-defined culinary name was the first course of an Oxford college menu announced as 'Quenelle' on the menu card. I asked myself would it be *quenelle de brochet* or *gnocchi al formaggio*, or perhaps *Topfenknödel* (curd-cheese dumplings) but what turned up on the plate was a salmon mousse, shaped like a quenelle but without having its spongy firmness.

The mania for frenchifying or translating the names of typically native dishes can have odd consequences. Thus the menu for a Christmas dinner in an Oxford college was given entirely in French. Calling Christmas Pudding 'Poudingue de Noël', though silly, is harmless, but calling Roast Turkey, Bread Sauce 'Dindon Rôti, Sauce Pain' may well give the uninitiated the idea that there may be a printing error and that the English Christmas Turkey is a *Dindon en casserole*.

French having been for a long time the language of cooking and gastronomy it is natural that there are many well-established culinary terms and to translate them into English is unnecessary, just as musical terminology remains Italian and allegro, vivace, con amore, con brio are rarely translated. But, surprisingly, Mrs Beeton who is usually circumspect in her use of expressions, trips sometimes. Thus in the 'Analytical Index' of the first edition of *Book of Household Management* we find under 'Sauces' the entry 'Dutch, for fish' followed by 'Dutch green, or Hollandaise verte'.

Menu French can become annoying when the term is non-existent or rarely used or misused. Thus, what is one to make of *Filets de viande à la Charentaise*? The first three words are ill-defined, the last is unknown to me and to some knowledgeable friends I have consulted. The dish was actually mixed grill on a skewer. I have also come across *Carottes en robe des champs*. *Pommes de terre en robe des champs* is used for potatoes served in their jackets, i.e. unpeeled. Persistent enquiries about the use of this term for carrots revealed that the carrots, instead of being scraped, were only scrubbed.

The growth of international travel makes the restaurateur's life difficult if he wants to produce bills of fare understandable by guests from many countries. We all have our cherished examples of absurd or amusing translations. My favourite one is from a German restaurant which prided itself on its excellent *Schweinebraten auf bürgerliche Art*. There was no difficulty with the French version, *Roti de Porc à la Bourgeoise*. For the English version they wisely discarded 'Roast Pork in the Middle-class Fashion' and opted for the concise yet poetic version 'Pig in the Family Way'.

I now come to a discussion of examples of food one can find nowadays in different parts of the world. Although I have travelled a fair amount, I will rely for really unusual food experiences on the accounts of others. However, I will mention one brief journey I made more than 30 years ago, mainly because it can no longer be undertaken; it was taking the Mistral, one of the French crack trains of a previous era, from Paris to Lyons. By the time it reaches Dijon one is comfortably seated in the *Wagon Restaurant*, preferably on the right hand side, and is enjoying the excellent table d'hôte luncheon. But during the twenty-odd minutes the train takes to reach Beaune one's enjoyment of the lunch is enhanced by visual stimuli. The railway line skirts the Côte d'Or and, although the Mistral is fast, one can decipher the names of the stations as the train whizzes through: Gevrey-Chambertin, Vougeot (I believe that the French army still presents arms when it passes the Clos Vougeot), Nuits-St.-Georges, Aloxe-Corton. Alas, the TGV follows a different route and the local trains using the old line have no restaurant cars, so this particular tourist attraction can no longer be enjoyed.

Since my experience of the unusual, the unfamiliar – and often unpalatable – is rather limited, I shall quote from the papers of more enterprising travellers.

Let us begin with the southernmost part of the globe: Antarctica. Dr. R.M. Laws who worked for 18 years in the British Antarctic Survey (BAS), for 14 years as its Director, wrote an interesting essay on Antarctic fare and here are some excerpts from it:

> When I first went to the Antarctic in 1947 with the Falkland Islands Dependencies Survey (FIDS), now British Antarctic Survey (BAS), it was to spend 25 months on small Signy Island in the South Orkneys. There were only three of us in the first year and four in the second; we took it in turns to be cook for a week at a time. Facilities in general were primitive since, with an open plan floor area of 12 ft x 24 ft, the kitchen area was naturally very small, though with a solid-fuel Esse cooker. Water was obtained for most of the year by melting snow. The food provided was greatly lacking in variety: tinned stew, tinned meat and vegetables, tinned pilchards, dried, diced vegetables, dried or tinned fruit, rice, flour, spices, pickles and bottled sauces. The only alcohol was an excess of full strength Navy rum, but we made cider from dried apple rings and baker's yeast.

> Because we lacked refrigeration, fresh material soon went off, although we acquired mutton carcasses, some fresh vegetables and fruit when ships visited us, no more than twice a year, we were, however, able to introduce variety by eating off the land, or rather ice!

> Delicacies included young crabeater seals, especially filet or liver, leopard seal brains, seal chitterlings (the small intestine of one species can be several hundred feet long), fish and shag. The eggs of several sea birds were appreciated though the whites of penguin eggs are an off-putting translucent bluish grey and are better in cakes and omelettes than fried or boiled. Particularly to be avoided were giant petrels (flesh or eggs), and elephant seals which, although the subject of my PhD thesis, are repulsive, however cooked.

Dr. Laws then gives detailed recipes:

The following recipes are typical of those employed to make the most of local products. They are taken from *Recipes of an Antarctic Cook* by Gerlad T. Cutland (Polar Record 9, No. 63, pp.562-9). There follow detailed recipes of the following delicacies: Tournedos of Seal Portugaise, Braised Seal Heart, Savoury Seal Brains on Toast, Escalopes of Penguin.

The diet now provided at the BAS Antarctic stations is very similar to what is eaten at home in Britain. Variety is somewhat less because all food has to be brought in infrequently by ship...

Professional full-time cooks produce a wide range of dishes representing a variety of national cuisines, from French to Indian. The kinds of food provided have changed. Walk-in deep freezes (even installed at Halley Station which is 60 ft down within the shelf ice) mean that a wide variety of frozen foods can be kept year round. To some extent the diet reflects changing tastes in the U.K., and increasing interest in foreign food such as pasta and rice in place of potatoes, and a wider range of herbs and spices. The personnel on our stations probably feed better than their contemporaries in Cambridge colleges.

The early explorers managed mainly on salted or dried meat and biscuits. Captain Scott's sledging rations in 1912 consisted only of pemmican, biscuits, butter, sugar, cocoa and tea. Pemmican was originally developed from a North American Indian recipe based on dried caribou meat, fat, and wild berries, pounded together to make a bar. As used later by Polar travellers it was made from dried beef and beef fat and added vitamins. We were still using it in the 1950s. For present-day sledge travel rations are light, compact, easy and quick to prepare (to save fuel). The food is well-packed in standard BAS sledging ration boxes to last for twenty man-days. There are three kinds of freeze-dried meat, several varieties of dried soup, dried vegetables, rice, tea, coffee, drinking chocolate, orange drink, biscuits, chocolate, butter, sugar, dried milk and multivitamin tablets supplemented by a few extra 'goodies' to personal taste. Water is from melted snow and paraffin primus stoves are still the most dependable and compact system. These special sledging rations are expensive and it costs almost twice as much to feed a person at a field camp as it does at a research station.[2]

We now move north, but still in the southern hemisphere, to Papua-New Guinea. It was here that N.W. (Bill) Pirie, nutritionist, for many years Head of the Biochemistry Department of the Rothamstead Experimental Station, practised *Popularizing Unconventional Foods*, the title of his essay from which the following quotations are taken.

My personal experience is confined to the popularization of protein extracted from leaves (LP). This is not proposed as a substitute for leafy vegetables, prepared in the normal manner, but as a supplement to them. It is now generally agreed that many people in industrialized countries eat too little fibre for the proper functioning of their guts. Nevertheless, there are limits. Structural fibre in leaves restricts consumption to an amount which would supply only 2g to 4g of protein daily. That is not insignificant, it is as much as fish supply in the UK. LP contains little fibre, about 60% protein, and a useful amount of carotene; 19g to 20g is the usual amount eaten. In many parts of the world, the carotene (pro-vitamin A) is as important as the protein: vitamin A deficiency blinds 0.5 million people (mainly infants) annually. The technique of extraction is simple enough to be a village, or even family, process... The real problems arising with novel foods involve a study of local dietary habits to see where and how an unconventional food can be fitted in neatly, and with which conventional components it will be complementary. For example: LP, like several legume seed proteins, is somewhat deficient in sulphur amino acids, whereas maize and wheat grains are relatively rich in them. Experiments on rats confirm that LP and wheat are complementary.

Tasting panels can judge no more than the extent to which the qualities of a well-known food have been mimicked by one containing novel components. F.U. Shah and his colleagues in Pakistan were very successful in introducing LP in a manner which satisfied the tasting panel. My colleagues M. Byers, S.H. Green, J.E. Morrison and I approached the problem by making things which looked interesting and could be eaten in one or two bites, and were portable so that they could be demonstrated away from the laboratory. LP is very dark green, it can be decolourised but the carotene would then be lost. A dark colour causes less comment when pieces are small. My technique of presentation is simple and effective. Instead of politely offering what we had made to visitors first, I, while still explaining the merits of LP, started eating. After a few seconds one of the visitors invariably said, 'Could I have some too?'; all the rest then joined in. If personal initiative is not encouraged in that manner, there is more initial hesitation and suspicious nibbling of minute pieces instead of straightforward eating.

In Papua New Guinea I met some resistance to LP from charming, able and conventionally minded Australian nurses, but none from local children. At a school where English was taught, I handed out samples. When they were eaten I said, 'Who would like another one?' Every hand went up. In a village, I wandered round munching. Children followed expectantly and ate all I had with me. No problems arose with feeding trials in India. The subjects in these trials were in institutions: valid measurements of growth etc. can be made in no other way. The charity 'Find Your Feet' (FYF) has organised and/or supported LP production, and use by people coming voluntarily for it, in Bolivia, Ghana, India, Mexico and Sri Lanka; projects elsewhere are being planned. As before, there were no problems when familiar foods, fortified with LP, were intelligently presented.[3]

While in New Guina let us turn from leaf protein to real meat and see what P.G.H. Gell, an Emeritus Professor of Experimental Pathology, has to say about it in his essay *The Banquet of Atreus*. As the title indicates (Thyestes was served his sons in a pie by his brother Atreus), it deals with cannibalism and the quotation with its reference to Kuru, related to Kreutzfeld-Jacob desease, is of topical interest in view of the debate about mad cow disease. (Note, having had cheeses called *La vache qui rit* and *La vache sérieuse* shall we now be offered by an enterprising cheese manufacturer *La vache folle?*)

I make no claim to be a professional anthropologist, merely a philosophic observer, but perhaps with that proviso I may be allowed a little off-the-cuff analysis going somewhat beyond my specific sources. Firstly, it seems to me that the sources make it unlikely that cannibalism was ever practised purely for nutritional purposes. Apart from availability there is absolutely no nutritional advantage to humans of human meat over pig meat and the tribes who practise ritual cannibalism are precisely those who do not have any great difficulty in getting adequate amounts of animal meat. There is also the considerable disadvantage that eating of fresh uncooked human flesh carries an appreciable chance of transmitting infections. I will consider the special case of Kuru in a moment, but, although the normal stomach is pretty efficient at killing off most infective agents, some viral infections (poliomyelitis, AIDS, hepatitis, infectious diarrhoea) and many bacterial and parasitic ones can certainly be transmitted from foodstuffs taken by mouth; moreover any agents derived from man will be often well, or indeed uniquely, able to infect man. Many of these agents will be largely eliminated by efficient cooking through, but primitive cooking is evidently seldom efficient, and quite often the ritual of anthropophagy demands uncooked meat anyway. It surprises me that cannibalism has not been eliminated in social evolution for these reasons, but men, whether primitive or not, always suffer from an over-supply of imagination and generally prefer a fanciful explanation which fits in with their ideological obsessions to a rational one. Cats know better.

The case of Kuru is an interesting, though not a particularly unique one, except that it has been used to confound sceptics who did not believe in the existence of cannibalism at all. The practice of eating the brains of dead neighbours was established in the relevant New Guinea tribes (Gimi, Fore) as a rite of the third type, confined, like many others, to females and pre-adolescents; this practice was thought to strengthen females but actually to be weakening to adult males. Though there is no documentation, it is likely that the ritual persisted harmlessly perhaps for centuries until the advent of a quite new, highly stable and intensely virulent slow virus, present in quantities in the brain of sufferers, possibly brought from Europe and possibly derived from, or at least related to, the virus of Kreutzfeld-Jacob disease, a European virus infection, causing, after a long incubation period, senile dementia with rather similar symptoms to Kuru. The sex and time incidence of the disease, confined to women or to men who could as boys have shared their mothers' meal, makes the association with female cannibalism almost certain, though historical evidence is rather sparse and, presumably as a result of indoctrination, both moralistic and hygienic, about the ritual, the disease is now disappearing.[4]

We now cross the equator and meet again Dr. Laws whom we last saw in Antarctica, this time in sweltering Uganda and sun-dried Texas. I give in full his brief essay on *A Barbecue on a Large Scale*.

This is a true story which draws on my experiences in North America and East Africa. I was in Texas, staying with my old friend Professor Sayed el Sayed (an oceanographer well away from the ocean) at College Station. One evening we went out for a steak dinner at a plain and basic restaurant - board floor, checked gingham tablecloths and excellent barbecued T-bone steaks.

During the meal the proprietor suggested that we might like to see his kitchen facilities around at the back. There was a splendid stainless steel marinading cabinet and other equipment, but his pride was clearly the barbecue pit – a new term to me – of which he was inordinately proud. It was, he said, 'The biggest barbecue pit in Texas'.

Although it was splendid, I couldn't resist the temptation to compare it with my facilities in Uganda when I was engaged on my research on elephants. I told him that we had had a much larger set-up altogether. First, I said, we dug a pit in the ground fifteen yards by five and several feet deep. Next we brought in a large number of trees for fuel and made a fire. We then shot ten elephants and barbecued them in the pit – which took a long time of course. The meat was distributed to a large number of local people and was received with delight; we did this most nights. He was at a loss for words, but looked at me rather strangely and I returned to my meal. My host Sayed followed in a little while and said, 'You've really upset him. He says, "I don't know whether that Limey is pulling my leg or not."' Sayed assured him I wasn't – but every time he goes back to that steak bar the proprietor raises it again – 'That godamned Limey was pulling my leg wasn't he?'

The irony is that it was all true. In the course of my work we culled large numbers of elephants for management and research purposes. The elephant population was destroying the habitat it depended on, so there were thousands upon thousands of dead Terminalia trees for fuel. To help pay for the operation we sold the carcasses to a local butcher who cut them up and smoked great quantities of meat in these large pits for sale to the local population. I'm sure that Texan is still uncertain though![5]

Lest it be thought that unusual food can be found only in out-of-the-way places the last example will show that uniquely unusual food has been consumed on at least one occasion in Oxford. The noted entomologist Dr. Miriam Rothschild (Mrs Lane) wrote in a charming essay on milk:

> Great was the excitement when it was announced that the Lanes were about to become the first family in the UK to drink whale's milk for breakfast.
>
> Derek Frazer and Professor Huggett had been to the Faroe Isles to conduct some scientific investigations on the female animals brought ashore by the local inhabitants. Derek Frazer had secured the milk and preserved it in a thermos flask which was despatched to Elsfield, near Oxford from St. Mary's Hospital. We all knew that whale's milk was as solid as blue cheese and had to be eaten, not drunk. It was 49% fat and was squeezed into the baby's mouth from the mother's teat, like toothpaste out of a plastic tube. This is a practical solution of the difficulties involved in suckling under water. It avoids a loss of milk flowing into the sea, or conversely the baby whale imbibing gulps of salt water rather than its mother's milk. Furthermore, all mammals, such as seals, which live in cold waters, have a very high concentration of fat in their milk, which is consequently solid rather than fluid.
>
> The moment I handled the hospital thermos I knew something was wrong. There was a sloshing around in the body of the flask suggesting water rather than thick cream or cheese. I gingerly unscrewed the top and looked in. The children craned their necks and held out their plates. Inside the thermos was a transparent yellow fluid, the colour of sweet Rhine wine. There had been a mix-up of bottles at St. Mary's and we were about to serve whale's urine instead of milk! Eventually the right container was located and despatched to us. Whale's milk, as anticipated, was as solid as Stilton cheese. It could no longer be described as fresh, and perhaps it was not a fair trial for taste and flavour. Small chunks were eaten very thoughtfully and voted revolting, and compared with rancid soap.
>
> In the afternoon there was a party at All Souls College and I passed around the jar, offering a prize to anyone who could identify the contents correctly. There was not a single guess which came within even reasonable distance of the correct answer. So much for the great brains of Oxford. Next day the Royal Entomological Society did better. The jar was again handed round. It stopped in the grasp of the President, the late Norman Riley. 'This' he announced confidently, 'is cheese. But not one I have ever tasted'. He won the prize, a bottle of Claret, Lafite 1947.[6]

A cheerful finish to a rather cheerless bill of fare.

REFERENCES

[1] *Bull. Amer.Phys.Soc.*, 1957, Vol.2,157.
[2] Laws, R.M., 'A Perspective on Antarctic Cookery' in *But the Crackling is Superb*, 1988, ed. N. and G.M. Kurti (hereinafter abbreciated as BCS), 157.
[3] Pirie, N.W. 'Popularising Unconventional Foods' in *BCS*, 170.
[4] Gell, P.G.H. 'The Banquet of Atreus' in *BCS*, 151.
[5] Laws, R.M., 'A Barbecue on a Large Scale' in *BCS*, 179.
[6] Rothschild, M.L. 'Whale's Milk for Breakfast' in *BCS*, 162.

The Pavlova Cake: the Evolution of a National Dish

Helen M. Leach

It is a well-known fact, and source of heated nationalistic debate, that both Australia and New Zealand lay claim to the invention of the pavlova cake. For over half a century, the dish bearing this name has taken the form of a large, soft-centred meringue, usually topped with cream and fresh fruit. The West Australian chef, Herbert Sachse, claimed to have invented it in 1935, a statement which has been thoroughly researched by Michael Symons in his history of Australian eating.[1] New Zealand does not acknowledge a single creator, but was certainly using the name pavlova and making large soft-centred meringues before 1935. The New Zealand evidence is not straightforward, however, and in the interests of historical accuracy (if not trans-Tasman relations), Symons' conclusion as set out below, deserves some reconsideration:

> We can concede that New Zealanders discovered the secret delights of the large meringue with the 'marshmallow centre', the heart of the pavlova. But it seems reasonable to assume that someone in Perth attached the name of the ballerina. As Bert Sachse implied, he distilled, or codified, a widespread New Zealand idea, to which was added a catchy name, and all of this was legitimate, common and like the crystallising of genius.[2]

Proponents of the New Zealand case have cited the *OED* (2nd edition), which gives two 1920s examples of dishes called pavlovas. Examination of these sources shows that neither is a large meringue topped with cream and fruit. The earliest to bear the title, from *Davis Dainty Dishes* (1927), is a rather elaborate moulded gelatine dish, consisting of four layers of different coloured fruit-juice and milk jellies with inset orange slices.[3] This can be dismissed as an independent application of the name pavlova. Since Davis was a company with subsidiaries in Australia, South Africa and Canada, as well as New Zealand, we cannot even be sure that this particular recipe was developed in New Zealand. The artist who illustrated this dish, M.V. Leith, may not have worked in New Zealand, for he or she does not appear in contemporary directories.

Turning to the second *OED* reference to pavlovas, the 1929 book which included it within a section of contributed recipes, attributes it to a Dunedin woman.[4] But the recipe is for small meringues, containing chopped walnuts and flavoured with coffee essence. This was not a true precursor to the modern pavlova, and does not represent a stage in its evolution. From 1929 to 1940 or later, small coffee-flavoured walnut meringues were given this name.[5] For at least a decade they coexisted with the evolving large meringue cake, which came to share the name pavlova and eventually took it over exclusively.

Of course meringues are a European, not an Australasian invention. The *New Larousse Gastronomique* attributes them to a Swiss pastry-cook, Gasparini, who invented the small meringue in 1720 in the town of Mehrinyghen,[6] but since the word meringue predates 1720 (*OED*), the origins of both word and food item clearly need further investigation. The larger meringue cake may have been a nineteenth-century development. According to J. Thudichum (1895):

> The pure *meringues* of *albumin* and *sugar* only are known in France as *baisers*, or as *Spanish foam*, and a large confection of the kind is called *Spanish tourte*; this latter is a construction in layers of sheets of meringue paste baked, iced, and stratified with whipped cream.[7]

Not surprisingly, European variants reappeared in the Antipodes. Most colonial meringue recipes were for the small types, but the larger layered version appears in the 1920s. For example, a c.1926 New Zealand cookbook by E. Futter lists 'Meringue with Fruit Filling'. In this recipe a large meringue was baked crisp, split and then filled.[8] The obvious difficulties of this operation were avoided in subsequent recipes by baking two meringues in tins, like sponges, and then sandwiching them with a cream and fruit filling. Such was the 'Meringue Cake' recipe contributed by a Mrs McRae to a Wellington cook book *Terrace Tested Recipes* in 1927. With three egg whites, eight ounces of sugar, and a dessertspoonful of cornflour, it was baked in two well-greased sandwich tins. The two halves were sandwiched together with cream and cherries or strawberries, or served as two cakes (presumably topped with the cream and fruit).[9] In this same tradition, Miss I. Finlay's *Cookery*, published in Dunedin c. 1934 provides a recipe for a 'Meringue Sponge Sandwich'.[10] With 12 ounces of sugar for three egg whites, it lacks the vinegar and/or cornflour of the later pavlova, and was cooked at a higher temperature, presumably to become crisp right through (see Appendix for Miss Finlay's successive meringue cake recipes).

Significantly, the next edition of Miss Finlay's book adds the words 'Or Pavlova' to the original recipe title.[11] The exact date of this edition is not known, but as one of the advertisers had changed their address by 1936, a 1935 publication date is a strong possibility.[12] For this third edition, the recipe was modified by a reduction in the quantity of sugar from 12 ounces to 7-8 ounces for three egg whites, and by the addition of a teaspoon of vinegar. As with the previous version, the mixture was divided between two sponge sandwich tins, and when cooked the cakes were fastened together with whipped cream and fruit such as raspberries or loganberries. Readers were given the option of piling more cream and fruit on top. In her instructions Miss Finlay referred to a 'special Pavlova cake tin', but this did not reappear in a subsequent enlarged edition of her book. No information is available about this special tin, nor the name of its manufacturer. But her later recommendation of an 8 inch diameter tin with sloping sides, may give some clue to its shape.[13]

This next stage in the evolution of Miss Finlay's pavlova sees the further reduction in the amount of sugar, to 3-4 ounces for three egg whites, and the addition of both cornflour and vinegar, which together would have resulted in a softer centre. Now the cake was cooked as a single layer and was served in the 'modern' style with whipped cream and fruit piled on top.[14] The chief difference from a modern pavlova lies in the instruction to cook the meringue cake in a tin. It was not until the 1940s that the tin began to be dispensed with.[15]

Because we cannot date Miss Finlay's first 'Pavlova' earlier than 1935, it cannot be used to dispute Michael Symons' claim that the naming was the critical Australian contribution. However, there is firm evidence for the New Zealand application of the name to a large soft-centred meringue cake in 1934. It appears in Daisy Basham's *The N.Z. 'Daisy Chain' Cookery Book*.[16] Aunt Daisy, as she was known, compiled listeners' and readers' recipes, so not surprisingly this book contains two different recipes for pavlovas and one for meringue cake. 'Pavlovas No.2' was the familiar coffee and walnut-flavoured small meringue, but 'Pavlovas No.1' was a large cake made from four egg whites, one breakfastcup (eight ounces) of sugar and one teaspoonful of vinegar. It was cooked in a high-sided tin in a cooling oven. Frustratingly, this particular recipe (on which New Zealand national pride seems to depend) provides no instructions on serving. For those, we may turn to the virtually identical recipe for 'Meringue Cake'.[17] This was cooked in a loose-bottomed tin and when turned out was intended to drop in the centre with the resulting hollow to be filled with whipped cream and fruit.

It is now clear that New Zealand has won this particular contest, using the name pavlova by 1927, developing the large soft-centred meringue by at least 1934, and putting the name and dish together at about the same time, which was definitively before 1935. It is equally obvious that we have not been dealing with a single act of creation (on which the Australian claim depended), but with culinary evolution, which is a process, not an event.

The evolution of the modern pavlova from the 1920s meringue cake required several transformations:

- a shift towards top decoration with cream and fruit, eventually replacing the layered filling;

- a change in egg white and sugar proportions and the introduction of cornflour and vinegar, to promote the soft centre;

- the abandonment of the tin in favour of cooking on greaseproof or baking paper alone.

These changes occurred between 1927 and 1950. Simultaneously the name pavlova shifted in its referents from a moulded gelatine dish, to small coffee and walnut meringues, to the large soft-centred meringue cake. We have already seen that the last two usages of the word coexisted for several years before one was dropped. Such semantic shifts are typical of cultural evolution.

A simplistic conclusion to this research would be to accuse the late Mr Sachse of plagiarism. Since we now know that New Zealand cooks applied the name pavlova to the soft-centred meringue cake before 1935, and since Michael Symons established the fact from Sachse's wife that he read women's magazines which contained New Zealand recipe contributions,[18] the case for his creative 'crystallising of genius' can be strongly challenged. In such a conclusion, all the ingredients are present to stir up national outrage yet again, with the added spice of gender exploitation, and of rivalry between professionals and amateurs. The imaginary headline 'AUSSIE CHEF STEALS KIWI WOMEN'S CREATION' expresses the divisive and polarising potential of my findings.

My preferred, more diplomatic conclusion is that we are dealing with a case of convergent cultural evolution. The meringue cake was widely known in Australasia in the decade 1925-1935, and the name Pavlova was so highly topical following the ballerina's two visits and her early death in 1931, that it had been applied to at least two other dishes before the meringue cake. Given these circumstances, it is a mistake to believe that the Pavlova cake was 'created' only once. As with various mechanical inventions, national rivalry has promoted and perpetuated such an error.

Historians of technology dealt with the myth of the heroic inventor many decades ago.[19] It is now widely accepted that new artefacts are based on objects already in existence, and that instead of a discontinuous development of technology, there has been a continuous stream of cumulative innovations. Food historians may need to rethink the role of the creative master chef just as historians of technology have repositioned the inventor. Innovation in cuisine has always been constrained by the powerful principle of neophobia, the fear of unfamiliar foodstuffs.[20] In consequence innovative cooks recombine culturally acceptable ingredients within a culturally approved repertoire of techniques. A true novelty, such as premasticated badger tail, would fail to gain acceptance in Western cuisine, on the grounds that neither method of preparation nor foodstuff were permissible. The influence of cultural restraints on culinary creativity may explain the high degree of reworking and repetition (even to the extent of plagiarism), in the long history of cook books.[21] The story of the pavlova should be read as an example of this evolutionary process.

Since this paper was presented at the Oxford Symposium, an even earlier pavlova recipe has come to light. It was found in the *Rangiora Mothers' Union Cookery Book of Tried and Tested Recipes*, bearing the printing date of 1933. The recipe, contributed by Mrs W.H. Stevens, was entitled 'Pavlova Cake' and consisted of an unfilled meringue cake, topped with whipped cream, pineapple and chopped walnuts. It called for the addition of corn flour but not vinegar and was cooked for one hour in a single sponge sandwich tin. It represents the earliest example of the modern pavlova cake both in name and concept.

ACKNOWLEDGEMENTS

Thanks are due to the staff of the Hocken Library, the University of Otago Library, and the Otago Settlers' Museum for their assistance in locating early recipe books. I wish to express particular gratitude to Mrs Elizabeth Hinds, Miss Noeline Thomson, and Mr Robin Charteris for their sustained interest in this debate.

APPENDIX

The following recipes show the development of the dish in the various editions of Miss Finlay's recipe book.

1. Finlay, Miss L., *c.* 1934 *The Osborne Cook Book* [front cover]. *Cookery* [title page]. 2nd edition [Dunedin City Gas Dept.], p.125.

No.452 Meringue Sponge Sandwich
I
Whites of 2 eggs • 8 oz sugar • pinch of salt
6 in. diameter sponge tins
II
Whites of 3 eggs • 12 oz sugar • pinch of salt
Suitable tins, 8 in. diameter sponge tins

Method: Whisk egg whites with salt until mixture is stiff. Carefully fold in sugar. Grease the tins, and place in the bottom a round of grease-proof paper; fill with the meringue mixture. Heat the oven to butter sponge or biscuit heat; cook for about 5 minutes at that heat, then reduce temperature considerably. Bake from one and threequarter to two hours.

When cooked, turn out carefully. Brush outside of paper with hot water; leave a few minutes; then remove paper. Fasten cakes together with a filling of whipped cream. Some tart fruit, such as raspberries or loganberries, may be added to cream. Cream may also be piled on top, finishing off with fruit used in centre.

2. Finlay, Miss I., *c.* 1935, *Cookery*, 3rd edition [Dunedin City Gas Dept.], p.125.

No.452 Meringue Sponge Sandwich or Pavlova Cake

Whites of 3 eggs • 7 or 8 oz sugar • 1 teaspoon vanilla essence
1 teaspoon vinegar • pinch of salt
suitable tins, 8 in. diam. sandwich tins or special Pavlova cake tin.

Method: add salt to egg whites. Whisk them stiffly; add sugar gradually and continue beating for a few minutes. Carefully mix in vinegar and essence. Place in greased tins and cook in a slow oven for one to one and a half hours.

When cooked turn out carefully. Fasten cakes together with a filling of whipped cream. Some tart fruit, such as raspberries or loganberries, may be added to the cream. Cream may also be piled on top, finishing off with fruit used in centre.

3. Finlay, Miss I., [between 1936 and 1940] *Cookery*. [Dunedin City Gas Dept.], p.125.

Meringue Sponge Sandwich or Pavlova Cake

Whites of 3 eggs • 3 or 4 ozs sugar • pinch of salt
1/2 oz cornflour (optional) • 1/2 teaspoon vanilla essence (optional)
1/2 teaspoon vinegar (optional)

Method: Whip egg whites stiffly with pinch of salt added. Beat in one-third of the sugar and continue beating for a few seconds. Add another third of the sugar and whisk again. Repeat using remainder of sugar. Mixture should be stiff.

Suitable tin, 8 in. diameter (sloping sides best).

Cut large round piece of greaseproof paper and press it into buttered tin. Cook in slow oven for about an hour. Remove paper and serve with whipped cream and fruit piled on top.

NOTES

[1] M. Symons, *One Continuous Picnic: a history of eating in Australia*, Duck Press, Adelaide, 1982, pp.147-152.

[2] Symons, *op.cit*, p.151.

[3] Anon, *Davis Dainty Dishes*, 6th ed., Davis Gelatine (N.Z.) Ltd., Christchurch, 1927, p.11.

[4] Rose H. Rutherford, 28 Royal Terrace, Dunedin. Her recipe appeared in *Practical Home Cookery Chats and Recipes written and selected by 'Katrine'...* [Mrs Katrine J. McKay], Simpson and Williams Ltd, Christchurch, 1929, p.155.

[5] E.g. D/ Basham, *The N.Z. 'Daisy Chain' Cookery Book by Aunt Daisy*, Harvison and Marshall Ltd., Wellington, 1934, p.49; Flora M. Crawford and Mary J. Lousley (comp.), *The Southland Patriotic Cookery Book*, Whitcombe and Tombs Ltd., 1940, p.155.

[6] P. Montagné, *New Larousse Gastronomique*, p.587.

[7] J.L.W. Thudichum, *The Spirit of Cookery*, Baillière, Tindall and Cox, London, 1895, p.411.

[8] E. Futter, *Home Cookery for New Zealand*, Whitcombe and Tombs Ltd., c.1926, p.141.

[9] Symons, *op.cit.*, p.150.

[10] I. Finlay, *The Osborne Cook Book/Cookery*, 2nd ed. Dunedin City Gas Dept., c.1934, Recipe No.452.

[11] I. Finlay, *Cookery*, 3rd ed., Dunedin City Gas Dept, c.1935, Recipe No.452.

[12] Paterson and Barr whose address was listed as 142 Princes St., Dunedin in Miss Finlay's 3rd edition, relocated their premises to 142 High St., in time for the new address to appear in *Stone's Otago Southland Directory* for 1936.

[13] I. Finlay, *Cookery*, 4th or later ed., Dunedin City Gas Dept., [between 1936 and 1940], Recipe No.467.

[14] Curiously Miss Finlay forgot to remove the original title of the recipe 'Meringue Sponge Sandwich', despite the fact that it was no longer a two layer cake.

[15] The *Southland Patriotic Cookery Book*, *op.cit.*, provided a Meringue Cake recipe [p.128] with the following instructions; 'Grease square of grease-proof paper. Run cold water over paper and shake well before placing mixture on same.' Apart from its name, this recipe and the manner of serving are identical to that of a pavlova. In 1940, these Southland women were restricting the name pavlova to the small coffee and walnut meringues.

[16] D. Basham, *op.cit.*, pp.48-9. This book would have been undated, but for a publishers' note that from January 1935 they would be occupying new premises.

[17] D. Basham, *op.cit.*, pp.26-7.

18 M. Symons, *op.cit.*, pp.150-1.

19 G. Basalla, *The Evolution of Technology*, Cambridge University Press, 1988, pp.21-4.

[20] P. Rozin, 'Acquisition of Stable Food Preferences', *Nutrition Reviews* 48(2), 1990, pp.106-113.

[21] For a brief review of this theme see A. Davidson, 'Acknowledging Sources: A Message from Adelaide: And Two Further Notes' in T. Jaine (ed.) *Oxford Symposium on Food and Cookery 1984 and 1985. Cookery: Science, Lore & Books. Proceedings*, Prospect Books, London, 1986, pp.2-7.

Beyond Old Cookbooks: Four Travelers' Accounts

Margaret Leibenstein

While sitting in the Denver airport waiting for a plane to Boston I saw three men deplaning through the adjacent gate. They were dressed in the universally recognized garb of motorcycle gangs; black boots, black leather pants, a black T-shirt emblazoned with a picture of a motorcycle and the words 'Hogs Make Great Lovers,' and metal-studded black leather vests. They could not have been more conspicuous had they been riding their Harley-Davidsons through the lounge.

Imagine my surprise when, as they passed me, I overheard one say, 'The rabbit was tolerable, but Portabellos would have given the sauce a more robust flavor.' Unlikely as this sounds, it really happened. These three men, however unconventional, were behaving in the grand tradition of the traveler. They were commenting on food.

Social Scientists have long used the reports of travelers in their research[1] but food historians have tended to rely on old cookbooks. I would suggest that travelers' reports of foods encountered in the countries in which they found themselves, such as the ones that follow, can be equally interesting and useful sources of information for culinary historians. To indicate the wide ranging material to be found in such authors I've chosen four disparate men, living in disparate times and places as examples.

Our four reporters will take us to Egypt in the thirteenth century, to India in the fourteenth, to a tropical island in the seventeenth, and on a polar expedition in the nineteenth century. They will tell us of such improbable foods as bear, seagulls and bread made from the poisonous root of the cassava. They will relate ways in which wealth and circumstances determined what people ate. And, if cannibalism piques the researcher's interest, one of our travelers supplies first-hand information on the manner in which people were prepared during a prolonged famine.

When using such sources the question of reliability inevitably arises. John le Carré in his novel *A Murder of Quality*,[2] has one of his characters say 'Until you know the pedigree of the information you cannot evaluate a report.' It is always, therefore, necessary to learn something about the reporter in order to determine how useful an account is. This requires a bit more digging than is necessary with old cookbooks. The rewards, however, can be the more satisfying since these accounts constitute a body of knowledge acquired through first-hand personal experience (the historian's dream, a primary source). Since the topic is the description of foods, it can be assumed that the traveler had no other intent than to inform.

* * * * * *

Our first traveler, Abd al-Latif al-Baghdadi (1162-1231) was a physician, anatomist and religious scholar whose writings covered almost all fields of the knowledge of his times.[3]

At the age of twenty-eight he began the travels that carried him from Baghdad to Greece, Turkey, Egypt and Syria where he served Saladin. Then in 1197 he left Syria and went to Egypt as a teacher and physician. It was during his sojourn in Egypt that he proved that the human lower jaw was made up of more than one bone – a revolutionary anatomical discovery that went counter to Galen's long accepted single bone theory. Abd al-Latif's discovery was the more remarkable for its having been made by so devout a Moslem through the observation and dissection of cadavers.

In the years 1200 to 1202 Egypt experienced a terrible famine. Cannibalism was rampant and murder for meat became the norm. Our traveler was appalled by it, yet his descriptions of the practice are unique for their detail, perceptiveness, and reportorial objectivity (pp.223-43). Students of the bizarre might find his recital of the various ways human flesh was prepared of some interest. We, however, will concentrate on his descriptions of more conventional comestibles.

He died in 1231. He'd left Egypt planning to settle in Damascus. Before doing so he wished to make a pilgrimage to Mecca via Baghdad. It was in Baghdad that he fell ill and died.

In his book he describes in detail the means of cooking foods he considered peculiar to Egypt. He tells of a preparation of germinated wheat with added flour, cooked in water, removed from the fire and sold at the 'price of bread'. It was probably a form of gruel such as was eaten by ordinary people in many countries at that time and that was not usually cooked in private homes. It may have required long cooking and, since elsewhere he tells us that the cost of fuel was high, we can assume it was cheaper to buy prepared than to cook at home.

Oil was pressed from the seeds of radishes, turnips and lettuce and used for cooking. These same oils (colored by the seeds) were used in the making of soap. Not surprising that a nougat resembling the colored bars was called *sapouniyyèh* after the word for soap.

He relates that Egyptian 'sour' or ordinary stews were similar to those in other countries, but 'their sweet stews [were] of a singular kind...they cook a chicken with all sorts of sweet substances.' His recipe describes boiled fowl put in julep (rose-water), placed on a bed of crushed hazelnuts or pistachio nuts, poppy seeds, purslane seeds, or rose hips, cooked until 'coagulated', spices are then added and the stew is taken off the fire. These stews were called *fistakiyyèh* (pistachio), *bondokiyyèh* (hazelnut), *khaschkhaschiyyèh* (poppy seed), *wardiyyèh* (rose hip) or *sitt alnoubèh* (purslane) called 'Nubian woman' because it is black.

He found so many varieties of sweetmeats it would have required a special book to describe them all. But he singles out *khabis*[4] of pumpkin or carrot which were given to convalescents and those on diets. Sweets were also made from roses (*wardiyyèh)* and ginger (*zindjebiliyyèh*), and pastilles were made of aloes wood, lemon, and musk.[5]

The Egyptians, he writes, used pistachio 'in the place of almond' and to illustrate his point he gives us a recipe for making a 'very delicious' pistachio *hérisèh* which is so explicit one could duplicate it today (p.193).

The ordinary folk lived on simple fare and drank *mezer*, a 'wine' fermented from wheat and another made from 'green water melon.' And though specific spices do not often appear in his receipts we learn that many spices were available to the Egyptian cook including *sumach*, the sour aromatic plant which both colors and flavors so much of today's Middle Eastern food.

While he writes primarily about dishes prepared and eaten by the general public, he also describes a dish that only the wealthy could afford. *Raghif alsiniyyèh*, a dish fit for kings, and best prepared for hunting trips because 'it is easy to transport, difficult to break, pleasing to the sight, satisfying to the taste, and keeps hot a very long time.'

> One of the most singular foods made in Egypt is that called *raghîf*[6] *alsiniyyèh*. This is how it is made: they take 30 *rotls* [Baghdad weight][7] of wheat flour. They knead with it 5-1/2 *rotls* of sesame oil in the same way as they make the bread called *khoschcnana*. They divide the whole into two parts, spreading one of the two in the round shape of a *raghîf* in a copper plate made for this purpose of about 4 spans[8] in diameter, and which has strong handles. After that they arrange on the dough three roasted lambs stuffed with chopped meats fried in sesame oil, crushed pistachios, various hot and aromatic spices like pepper, ginger, cloves, lentisk [mastic], coriander, caraway, cardamom, nuts and others. They sprinkle rose water in which they have infused musk, over all. After that they put on the lambs and in the spaces left, a score of fowls, as many pullets, and fifty small birds, some roasted and stuffed with eggs, other stuffed with meat, others fried in the juice of sour grapes or lemon or some other similar liquor. They put above them pastry, and little boxes filled, some with the meat, some with sugar or sweetmeats.

If one would add one lamb more, cut into morsels, it would not be out of place, and one can also add fried cheese.

When the whole is arranged in the form of a dome they again sprinkle rose water in which musk has been infused, or wood of aloes. They cover it again with the other part of the dough, to which they begin to give the shape of a broad cake. They are careful to join the two cakes of dough, as one makes pastry, so that no vapor escapes. After that they put the whole near the top of the oven until the pastry is solid and begins a degree of cooking. Then they lower the dish in the oven little by little holding it by the handles, and leave it until the crust is well cooked and takes on a rose red color. When it is at this point it is taken out and wiped with a sponge, and again sprinkled with rose and musk water, and then brought out to be eaten (pp.195-97).

We can only guess at quantities or the number of people required to produce and consume it.

Students of medieval cookery will note the similarities between this construction and those appearing on banquet tables of the aristocracy in Europe. There, perhaps, the variety and quantity of spices would have been somewhat curtailed because of cost and availability, but in Egypt these spices were commonly home grown.

* * * * * *

Our next correspondent, Ibn Battuta (1304-1378)[9], considered the greatest Moslem traveler of all times, was born in Tangier. He began his wanderings at the age of twenty-one and continued for the next twenty-eight years. He made three pilgrimages to Mecca, acquired six wives, traveled through Asia Minor visiting Russian Mongolia, crossed the Russian steppes to Bokhara then to Kabul and over the Hindu Kush to India. In 1333, at the invitation of Sultan Mohammed Tughlak he went to Delhi where he remained for eight years before his debts caused him to move on.

This chronicle is a highly personal report on what befell him in the course of his travels including his experiences with, and prejudices about, food. For example, on his way to Delhi he writes of a meal to which he was invited, provided for a nobleman with whom he is traveling: First thin round cakes are served, 'like those called *jardaqa*' (assumed to be *chapati*) (Vol.III, p.607). Then a sheep is cut into 4 or 6 pieces – one piece per person. Then 'round dough cakes made with ghee' stuffed with a mixture of starch, almonds, honey and sesame oil, and topped with a brick-shaped sweet cake made of flour, sugar and ghee called *kishtï*, are served. Then, in large porcelain bowls, 'meat cooked with ghee, onions, and green ginger' followed by five pieces of 'something …they called *samusak*' (from the Persian *sanbusa* [footnote 47, p.608]) – a triangle of very thin fried bread filled with 'hashed meat cooked with almonds, walnuts, pistachios, onions and spices' are served. Something like an elaborate Tunisian *briks* perhaps. Next, he tells us, rice cooked in ghee topped with chickens is followed by mouth-of-the-judge (probably a small sweet cake) which the Indians called *hāshimi* , and another sweetmeat. Before eating they are served glasses of *shurba*, (sherbet) sugar syrup diluted with water. When finished 'they are given jugs of barley water (footnote 51), betal and areca nut (footnote 52).

Those with an interest in Indian cuisine will find Ibn Battuta's description of the cereals and fruits of India useful. He reports that Indians gather green, unripe mangoes (*anbahs*) when they fall from the tree, and salt and pickle them 'as limes and lemons are pickled in [his] country'. This is eaten with meat – 'taking after each mouthful a little of these pickled [fruits].' Is this, perhaps, the first description of mango chutney?

* * * * * *

Our next traveler is a mystery. He is the author of *A True and Exact History of the Island of Barbados*[10] who signs himself Richard Ligon, Gent. (1596- ?). His book appeared in London for the first time in 1657 dedicated to Dr. Brian Duppa, Lord Bishop of Salisbury, who paid for the publication. It must have had a degree of success because it was reprinted in 1673. '…by that time, it had been already translated into French in 1669 and, in 1674, it was issued in the Billaine collection of voyages and travels.'[11] Not much more is known of him except what appears in his book.

Claiming that, 'Need makes the old Wife trot,' he left for the West Indies because '… having lost (by a Barbarous Riot) all….. by which means I was stript and rifled of all I had, left destitute of a subsistance, and brought to such an Exigent, as I must famish or fly….' at the age of 'more than sixty years old' (p.17). He sailed from England on June 16, 1647 on the good ship Achilles (p.1).

Ligon was a shrewd and accurate observer who claimed to be unlettered yet his education is always evident when writing about food and women. For example, Ligon's passion for detail and good food comes through clearly when he describes a meal taken on the Cape Verde island of Sao Thiago, then called St. Jago.

Padre Vagado, Chief Governor of the island, invited a group from the ship to dine at his home and Ligon was disgusted to find the Governor's home so primitive. He likened the appearance of the house to 'the meanest Inns upon London-way'. '….Cobwebs serv'd for hangings, and frying pans and grid-irons for pictures,' and when a 'Cloath was laid of Calico, with four or five Napkins of the same to serve a dozen men.' he was surprised. Though the house disappointed him, the food did not. The first course was made up, he tells us, of six dishes 'with every one a different fruit…' 'Millions [could he have meant melons?], Plantines… Bonanos… Guavers… Prickled Pears… the Custard Apple; but to fill up the table and make the feast yet more sumptuous, the Padre sent his Mollotoes, into his own Chamber for a dish which he reserv'd for the Close of all the rest; Three Pines in a dish, which were the first I had seen and as far beyond the best fruit that grows in England as the best Abricot is beyond the worst Slow or Crab.' He never lost his appreciation of pineapples as the best of all fruits.

The first course was followed by a glass or two of Red Sack, 'a kind of wine growing in the Maderas.' Then a course of 'flesh, fish, and sallets,' which he 'took great heed of, being all Novelties to me, but the best and most savoury herbs that ever I tasted.' The salads were dressed with 'salt, Oyle, and the best Vinegar.' The meats were served separately, 'not mixt, but in several dishes, all strange, and all excellent. …a wild Calf of a year old, which was the Colour of stags flesh, and tasted very like it… strong meat and very well Condited: boyl'd tender, and the sauce of savoury herbs, with Spanish Vinegar.' They were also served roasted turkeys and hens, a 'gigget' of young goat, and many different kinds of fish 'some fryed in oyl, and eaten hot, some souc't, some marinated: of all these we tasted, and were much delighted' (pp.11-12).

Ligon's obvious knowledge of art and his skill as a social commentator are put to good use when the meal was over and the Padre's mistress entered. She was, 'a Negro of the greatest beauty and majesty together; that ever I saw in one women'. He was smitten, gave her some presents, but refrained from going further. As he says, 'other addresses were not to be made…for they are there as jealous of their Mistresses as the Italians of their wives' (pp.12-13).

Later a meeting with a group of 'pretty Negro virgins' inspires him to fill two pages with descriptions of 'creatures of such shapes, as would have puzzel'd Albert Durer, the great Master of Proportion, but to have imitated; and Tition, or Andrea de Sarta, for softness of muscles and curiosity of Colouring…' Could a man with such sensual appreciations be indifferent to food? Impossible. As we see, he devotes eleven pages to food, its taste, its preparation, its origins, its distribution, even its use as a means of furthering social stratification.

In sections such as 'Meat and drink for the supportation of life', 'Bread and drink', 'Several sorts of meat', 'The manner of killing a Turtle', 'Victuals broght from forraign parts', 'A Feast of an inland Plantation', and 'The like of a Plantation near the Sea', he tells all. He reports that flour was produced from the root of the 'Cassavie' (cassava) tree, and describes how the root is grated, the poison extracted, and the pulp left to dry producing flour. He describes in detail how the dough is prepared, and what the utensil on which the bread is made looks like. Finally, how it is best eaten. He even suggests how to improve it (pp.29-39 inclusive).

His detailed description of how slaves and indentured servants were employed, what they were fed, and how they were treated has made him today one of the major sources for economic and social historians of the West Indies.

Winding down his history, he says: 'And now I have as neer as I can, delivered the sum of all I know of the Island of Barbadoes, both for Pleasures and Profits, Commodities and Incommodities, Sicknesses and Healthfulness. So that it may be expected what I can say to perswade or disswade any that have a desire to go and live there.' He returned to England in 1650 and by July 12th 1653 he had completed his manuscript while in the Upper Bench Prison into which he had been 'cast...by the subtle practices of some, whom I have formerly called Friends.'

I truly hope that the sale of his book delivered him from that prison, 'which the burning fire of a Feavor, nor the raging waves of the Sea, [were] so formidable' (p.122). He deserved better.

* * * * * *

In 1850, at the behest of the wife of Sir John Franklin who was lost en route to the Arctic Ocean five years before, the U.S. navy was sent to search for him. The expedition was mounted and financed by Henry Grinnell, a New York merchant. Elisha Kent Kane (1820-1857) was ordered to serve as the medical officer for the expedition.

His adventure began, Kane wrote, 'on the 12th of May, while bathing in the tepid waters of the Gulf of Mexico, I received one of those courteous little epistles from Washington which the electric telegraph has made so familiar to naval officers.' [12]

Kane, who was born to a distinguished Philadelphia family, became a respected surgeon and naval medical officer. He was also a gourmand, skilled writer and artist whose curiosity prompted him to record in drawings and words his every experience. For the culinary historian the result is a cache of information about foods consumed under extreme conditions.

On August 14 he reports: 'We are living luxuriously. Yesterday our French cook, Henry, gave us a salmi of Auks (black and white birds abundant in the Arctic) worthy of the *Trois Frères* ; and today I enjoyed an Arctic imitation of a trussed partridge...' He tells us, 'bear is strong...and withal most capricious meat...One day he is quite beefy and bearable; another hircine, hippuric, and damnable.' His description was not designed to increase appetite. He was determined to eat everything, 'albeit I esteem a discriminating palate...' He claimed to have 'convert[ed] several outcast eatables to good palatable food.' Seal, he says, 'is not fishy, but *sealy*; ...with patience and a good deal of *sauce piquante*, is very excellent...' The mollemoke (a word used interchangeably for any large oceanic bird) he declares the 'hardest to manage'. The breast he allows is the only part worth eating and only when rubbed with soda, washed, parboiled and pickled. Seagulls, on the other hand, were worthy of 'honorable mention'. The filet of the large ivory ones he likened to a 'morceau between a spring chicken and ....canvas back.' But the 'perfection of good eating' were 'all birds feeding on crustaceal life.' He describes them as 'very red in meat, juicy, fat, delicate, and flavorsome...'

On August 27th the first traces of Franklin's party were found on Beechy Island – artefacts and the graves of three crew members. It was determined that Franklin's ship had not broken up there so the search continued into the dark Arctic winter. 'The first thing that really struck me was the freezing up of our water-casks...and our inability to lay the tin cup down for a five minutes' pause without having its contents made solid. ...On the 4th of October we had a mean temperature below zero.' By early December, 'all our eatables became laughably consolidated.' They learned how to 'manage the peculiarities of their changed condition. ... 'Dried apples became one solid breccial mass of impacted angularities...Dried peaches the same.' To get the fruit out of the barrels in which they were stored they had to 'cut up both fruit and barrel ...with a heavy axe,' then thaw the lumps and remove the wood. 'Sauerkraut resembled mica.... Sugar formed a very funny compound.' Only a saw would work to extract it. Butter and lard changed less but required a 'chisel and mallet' to remove. Flour changed very little and molasses at -28°F could be 'half scooped, half cut by a stiff iron ladle.' At -30°F, 'pork and beef are rare specimens of Florentine mosaic,' that require, 'crow-bar and handspike,' because an axe would hardly chip them.

'Ices for the dessert come of course unbidden.' Despite the alcoholic content, he produced Roman Punch ice, at -20°F. 'Some sugared cranberries, with a little butter and scalding water, and you have an impromptu strawberry ice.' These were served on the shaft of a hickory broom used as 'a stirrer first and a fork afterward.' The danger inherent in this frozen cuisine was that one's spoon might 'fasten to your mouth.' Yet despite the obvious discomfort, these reports are laced with humor.

'Thus much for our Arctic grub. I need not say that our preserved meats would make very fair cannon-balls, canister shot!!' And with this statement he goes on to tell of grimmer things. After bouts of scurvy and other hardships the Grinnell Expedition finally left Baffin's Bay on the 6th September, 1851 and arrived in New York some 24 days later.

It was not until 1859 that Franklin's fate was finally revealed. Sir John's ships had been trapped by ice in September of 1846 and he died the following year. Ironically, Kane himself died in 1857 never knowing.

These travelers' accounts are only a few of the many such reports available to us. Since it's possible that the answers to questions food historians have may lie hidden in such accounts, it behoves us to dig more deeply into this cache. To paraphrase H.L. Mencken, 'there is in [travelers'] writing the constant joy of sudden discovery, of happy accident.' [13]

ACKNOWLEDGEMENTS

I should like to acknowledge the inestimable help I received from Professors David Galenson, University of Chicago, and Stanley Engerman, University of Rochester, and my Web correspondents: Jack Campin, Neil Fazakerley, David Friedman, Alec Shuldiner, and Cassandra Vivian. Finally, I must thank Harvard University for its incomparable and accessible libraries. I thank you all.

REFERENCES

[1] See K.C. Chang, *Food in Chinese Culture,* New Haven and London, Yale University Press, 1977, and Sidney Mintz, *Sweetness and Power: The Place of Sugar in Modern History*, New York: Viking Press, 1985

[2] Victor Gollancz Ltd., 1962

[3] *The Eastern Key*, Cairo, 1204. Translated by Kamal Hafuth Zand and John A. and Ivy E. Videan, London 1965, pg. 5

[4] This is described by the translator as 'dates and butter'.

[5] It's not clear whether these last three confections were meant to be eaten or burned as incense.

[6] A broad thin cake.

[7] 1 rotl weighs between 1 and 5 pounds depending on local conventions.

[8] 1 span is the distance between the thumb and small finger when the hand is opened.

[9] *The Travels of Ibn Battuta*, H.A.R. Gibb, Vol.III, Cambridge: Hakluyt Soc., 1962.

[10] London: Humphrey Mosley, 1657.

[11] Elsa V. Goveia, *Historiography of the British West Indies: to the end of the nineteenth century*, Washington D.C.: Howard University Press, 1980.

[12] Elisha Kent Kane, M.D., U.S.N., *U.S. Grinnell Expedition in Search of Sir John Franklin, A Personal Narrative*, New York: Harper and Brothers, Publishers, 1854.

[13] Henry L. Mencken, *A Book of Prefaces,* 1917, chapter 1.

European Food in the Eighteenth Century as Viewed by a Venezuelan Traveller

José Rafael Lovera

When describing eighteenth-century Caracas, historians agree that it was like a village as well as being the birthplace of several influential politicians and admired Independence army officers. In fact, it is appealing to learn that in such a small provincial city, where neither big palaces nor public monuments were commonly found, there were schools and great teachers who helped to train several generations of heroes whose enterprises went beyond the borders of Venezuela, even beyond the American continent.

My main goal at this time is introducing one such character, widely respected for his contribution to the Independence movement as both a military strategist and a soldier. This patriot is also regarded as one of the first Spanish-American gourmets, as well as a distinguished explorer of the gastronomical world (the world of tastes and flavours), that is to say an accomplished 'gastronaut'.

Our character was born in Caracas on March 28th, in 1750, at Hoyo in the district of San Pablo. Son of a merchant, immigrant from the Canary Islands, and a middle-class native of Caracas, the child who would become the precursor of Venezuelan independence enjoyed from the very beginning of his life very close contact with the basic tastes of bread: at home there was a small bakery where wheat bread was sold daily to the neighbours.

The family business allowed our character to enjoy contact with this basic taste from childhood. At the same time it was an obstacle to the social rise of his family, because the Caracas upper class regarded bakers as inferior people. That his father acquired a beautiful house in the neighbourhood of the Cathedral, the most prestigious and expensive residential area in Caracas, where he moved with his family, made no difference; with just a few exceptions the neighbours paid no attention to the newcomers. On the contrary, what they did was to show their traditional disdain for working-class people.

In the new house at Padre Sierra the child grew into an adolescent and, far away from the bakery, lived close to an area that was very picturesque in terms of food experiences: nearby was the Plaza Mayor that, on specific days, was also the biggest market in the town. There food, both produced in the country and imported from both the Caribbean Islands and Spain, made up a very diversified offering. It is possible to imagine that the child profited from that privilege, not only with his eyes, but also by tasting.

Opposite the new house was located a convent of Concepcionistas. The nuns not only used to pray and practise celibacy, but, following the old Spanish tradition of mixing the profane and the sacred, they also used to cook. They were famous for highly elaborate desserts, sold on a regular basis to help pay their living expenses. Spanish desserts as well as Venezuelan ones were among their specialities.

The Xerez de Aristigueta y Lovera de Otañez house was not far away. This family house, where the beauty of the young ladies and a well-supplied and well-served table were famous, would become legendary after several French courtiers, members of General Rochambeau's army, such as the Prince de Broglie, General Dumas, and the Comte de Ségur, paid visits to the Xerez family. The French stopped at Caracas en route to France after fighting in the War of Independence of the Anglo-American Colonies.

Our Caraqueño used to converse with the famous nine Caracas Muses, a nickname given to the young and attractive inhabitants of the Xerez House. When, in Russia many years later, he ran into the Comte de Ségur, they would recall the famous ladies, and our character recorded his memories in his diary.

However he did not spend much time at the new house. In fact, he left the Capitanía General (Venezuela) in 1771, and would not return until three decades later. Due to the prejudice against his background, our character could not join the army. As a consequence of this social failure, the young man was sent abroad looking for improvement as well as the opportunity to feel free after the hardships he had had to face during his early life in colonial Caracas.

His father sent him to Spain where the position of captain in the Spanish army was purchased, as was customary at that time. In this way he started a military career. Soon he was sent on duty to Cuba and the Anglo-American colonies. In the United States he did not get along with the Spaniards and returned to Europe, via London. From this time on he concentrated on fighting against Bourbon power.

However it is not his European public life that we are interested in. On the contrary, let us study his private life, looking for the gastronomical details included in his personal diary, which is a very rich source of information for the history of food in Europe. It is the testimony of a South American: a foreigner who registered his impressions and experiences of the old continent, or if you prefer, a foreign palate that tried European food. The diary was kept from 1771 until 1800.

Between August of 1785 and December 1805, he travelled round Italy, Greece, Turkey, Russia, Holland, Sweden, Denmark, Germany, Switzerland, Austria, France, and England and I will give a glimpse of some anecdotes of this extensive travel showing the historical importance of our character's personal diary.

On November 12th 1785, he arrived in Venice. Amazed by the superb view of the Grand Canal, he wasted no time before tasting the famous Venetian ice creams. He acknowledged that his favourite was sweetened sour cherry, 'with the whole fruit, delicious'. Next day he headed for the best coffee house, in the Piazza San Marco, which noblemen used to visit. (Later on he discovered that the best sorbets were prepared in Pisa, 'better than in any other place'.) After a very hard trip, he stayed overnight at a very bad inn where, 'I slept well after having a good bottle of Montepulciano'. After crossing the River Po he arrived at Parma, whose first glimpse he had from a carriage crossing a bridge.

> The city looks pretty. The streets are wide, made of stone, and there are plenty of handsome buildings. The Parma river waters the city walls, which are in decay. The countryside looks splendid and well cultivated; grass, above all, is excellent. This is the reason for the superior quality of Parma cheese. Experience has shown that if cow's milk other than that from Parma is used, the quality comes down.

Later, in Rome, he was received at Anna Manzoli's house on the Strada Papale. There he was treated as a member of the family; every morning breakfast was brought to his room: a delicious cup of hot chocolate, fresh baked bread, and butter. After Angelus time, it was common to find him at the café 'Al arco de Carbognano', trying its renowned sorbets with delight. Some time later, in Naples, recalling classical references, he went to Monte Falerno, where he tasted a glass of the famous wine produced there since ancient times. However, after trying it, he acknowledged his disappointment. 'It is not as described by Horace.' After traversing the Apennines en route to the Adriatic sea, he praised with grateful memory a *capretto* served to him by the village priest of San Casimiro.

He continued his travels, and Greece was the next country he visited. There he tried with delight Corinth raisins and the legendary Helicon honey, whose quality according to him depended on the thyme and myrtle found on the land.

At Constantinople he was lodged as a special guest in the Swedish Embassy, where he enjoyed the diplomats' worldly pleasures, though this did not prevent him from going occasionally to the taverns of the ill-famed Galata neighbourhood. For the first time he tried Turkish coffee and noted the way it was made and drunk. He also had the opportunity of eating Turkish traditional food: among other dishes, he tasted several done with lamb and *pilaw*, which he liked a lot.

Later on he crossed the border of the Russian Empire where, with valuable skill and unusual celerity, he entered the highest social levels, sharing the luxurious tables of ministers, ambassadors, counsellors and princes. Once he was one of Potemkin's guests and even enjoyed being a favourite of Tsarina Catherine II, who according to the diary, used to talk to him 'with affection'. At table she used to serve 'Russian dishes for me to try'. It was a time full of parties and dinners when wine was drunk freely, particularly a Hungarian variety, whose price was six ducats a bottle. During this time the diary includes several entries about caviar, beers, *kinchlesti* and hydromel, ice creams, and coffee.

But he did not share the table only with the élite. Our character also had opportunities to taste soldiers' meals. 'I tried their food and I found sour black bread (they say that it is not a bad food, though). I also tried cold cabbage with just some vinegar as a seasoner.' Obviously what he is referring to are rye bread and sauerkraut products he had not tasted before, which he found 'miserable'.

In Poland he was invited several times to Prince Stanislas' palace, whose kitchen he had the privilege to enter: 'I was very pleased to visit this magnificent office where the most exquisite meals are prepared. The prince's table is the best table I have ever tried. The kitchen is clean, orderly, well arranged and spacious; it deserves attention. ... We entered the very decent room of the pastrycook, who presented us with excellent chocolate biscuits, Chios oranges, etc. It is amazing to put it this way, but the kitchen exceeds proportionally the whole palace.'

After leaving Poland, he visited Sweden, Denmark, and Germany. In the latter, at Bremen, he was invited to a banquet at the Consistorial House. 'Nothing else in my journeys has reminded me so much of Roman bacchanalia.' In Holland, he enjoyed more gastronomical pleasures, going for instance once to the small city of Gouda, well-known for its cheeses and pipes. He found the city 'clean and gracious'.

In Switzerland, near to Constanz, he arrived starving at an inn and decided to eat one of the fat farm chickens he had seen in the henhouse. The amphytrion rejected such an idea by telling him that his order was not possible because that day it was a religious holiday, and eating meat was forbidden. The traveller, who was very hungry, got very angry, and confessed he was a Protestant or an agnostic in order to be served a farm chicken! After several demands the innkeeper decided to ask the village priest who, open-minded, advised serving the dish that he wanted so much.

Later on, in Appenzell canton, he was invited by a peasant to a frugal dinner, which our character found unique. 'I can tell you that this meal has been so far the most delicious one I have ever eaten. I could not avoid comparing it with the table of the great Catherine.' Adding that he would have liked her to be a guest at such a plain table, being confident that the Tsarina would have liked it. 'She would know how to enjoy the superlative value of such a simple meal.'

He came back to Italy for a short period of time, and then headed for France. He got to Marseilles, where, thanks to letters of introduction, he met the famous abbé Raynal. They became friends and he visited him regularly, acknowledging that he enjoyed not only the wicked ironies of the religious man, but also 'the best chocolate I have ever tasted'. The comment on chocolate is a very serious statement, particularly coming from somebody who was a native of the land where the famous Caracas chocolate was produced.

He left Marseilles, went to Aix, and continued his travel by stopping at Salon to visit the tomb of the physician and astrologer Michael of Nostradamus, who was distinguished at the French court thanks to his art of making predictions as well as preparing marmalades. Later on the Caraqueño went to Bordeaux where he visited the Pauillac vineyards whose Château Latour and Château Lafite wines are the glory of the region and the honour of France. In the southern city, he befriended a wine merchant who gave him a rare booklet, *Notice sur les vins de Bordeaux*, which has been preserved in his personal archives available at the National Academy of History in Caracas.

After a short visit to Paris when he headed for Versailles, he came back to Great Britain. He was in London till March of 1792, when he returned to France to participate in the exciting events of the Terror. After his arrival he joined the Revolutionary Army, occupying several important positions. But at the same time, he was thought to be a counter-revolutionary. Because of this he was sent to La Force prison. After a famous defence, that helped to establish his fame as an orator, he was released.

It was the first years of the 1790s and Paris prisons were full. As food supply was very irregular, prisoners ate badly at Saint Pélagie and La Force prisons: green peas had grubs, vegetables were frequently not available, and when available they were rotten; meat was in no better condition.

Life in France's capital city presented violent contrasts. Citizens who enjoyed freedom did not eat in an egalitarian way. A minority, particularly the ones holding public office, feasted lavishly, not paying much attention to the fraternity principle they claimed to defend. Meanwhile, most people suffered from shortage of food, which included, for instance, meat rationing through ration books that indicated the maximum amount people could get.

Restaurants began at this time. In Paris Beauvilliers, Véry, Café Riche, Café Hardy, Le Savard, were among the first ones to open. Our character kept a menu from Le Savard, which is today a bibliographical treasure. Regarding the food served at the new places, Cambacérès, chairman of the Committee of Public Safety, said: 'I have as a principle that men working at the Assembly and the Committee should enjoy good restaurants, because otherwise they would die soon due to the hardness of their jobs.'

Once out of prison, our character, following the wave of the times, became an epicurean, which contrasted with the restrictions suffered by most of the citizens.

The Duquesa de Abrantes, retelling the Parisian events of 1795, recalled that Napoleon had said at Madame Permon's, a common friend, the following: 'I ate yesterday at the house of a very special man. I think he is a spy paid by the Spaniards and the English at the same time. He lives on a third floor and is settled with every kind of luxury. He complains of hardship in the middle of this condition and after serving meals prepared by Méot on silver vessels. I had dinner along with very important people... this man has sacred fire in his soul.' Who was the shining character, the sophisticated gourmet? Where was his house located? Well, Napoleon was referring to the sparkling Venezuelan whose destiny, as I said before, took him to the troubled France of the Revolution. When he met M. Bonaparte he was living in rue Saint-Florentin, close to the famous guillotine installed in the square later known as La Concorde. He was living in a flat that also impressed the Danish poet Emmanuel Baggesen, who met him at that time. The poet wrote that he found his friend, 'dedicated exclusively to the Muses and the Graces living in a superb apartment located behind the Tuileries Palace. After his peregrination through the world like a real Don Quixote of republicanism, he has not been able to save his head without all kinds of troubles. He consoles himself with art and science. He possesses the most exquisite library, reduced though, and a flat settled with such good taste as I have never seen: one would think of being at Pericles' house in Athens.'

This exquisite library showed not only his interests towards traditional Muses, but also for 'Gastrea', the tenth Muse, so praised by all gourmets. After a review of the inventory of the library we found that he possessed *The Deipnosophists*, by Athenaeus, rich source and almost the only one to approach classical Greek gastronomy. He also had a copy of *Observations Historical, Critical and Medical on the wines of the Ancients, and Analogy between them and Modern Wines* (1775), a work by the English wine expert, Sir Edward Barry; he also owned a copy of the very rare wine treatise *De Naturalis vinorum historia*, by Baccius (Rome, 1797), one of the most important books ever published on the wines of France, Spain, and the rest of Europe; Rabelais' *Works* (Amsterdam, 1725), where he would have followed with hilarity the pantagruelic meals of the characters; *The Satyricon*, by Petronius (Bruman edition of 1743) with the unforgettable Trimalchio's banquet; the curious *Eloge de l'Ivresse* (The Hague, 1714); and the three volumes of *Palais Royal* (1790) by his contemporary Restif de la Bretonne, among the many titles that prove his epicureanism.

This Venezuelan, whose taste for gastronomy and literature surprised both the great Corsican and the Danish poet, used to be served by one of the most famed and first restaurateurs of eighteenth-century Paris: the already mentioned Méot, owner of the favourite restaurant during the time of the Revolution. Méot had opened his business in 1791 at the old Argenson Palace, located on the rue Valois. This restaurant was closed 60 years later, in 1847. In the main dining room the sinister members of the Revolutionary Court celebrated Marie Antoinette's execution on October 16th 1793. Méot had worked in the house of the Duke of Orleans, the well-known 'Philippe Egalité', who betrayed his class by becoming an ardent revolutionary and was killed at the guillotine as a reward.

This cook had the idea of decorating his restaurant lavishly in a period when restaurants lacked comfort, were rustic and for instance did not have tablecloths. One of Méot's clients, Mercier, praised him in the book *Tableau de Paris*. He wrote: 'The beautiful dining room, golden, full of sculptures, theatrical; pyramids of fresh fruit; delicious fumes that stimulated the appetite even of people without one.' Another fellow-diner at the restaurant, Héron de Villefosse, described in one of his works the charming architectural style of the place: the ceiling frescoes showing Jupiter with his daughter, his cupbearer and Juno, as well as the numerous mirrors on the walls, which were a novelty at that time. Praising Méot's skills, Mercier added: 'When one eats in Paris even if we do so at the best places, the meal is not worth a single dish at Méot's: warm, fast and well done.'

This restaurateur followed the fashion of the time by offering in the menu original dishes of the aristocracy of the Ancien Régime with changed names that today sound like a childish act of the moment. For instance, the turbot fillets *à la maître d'hôtel* became known as *à l'homme de confiance*, and the *Noix de Veau à la Reine* was named *à la directrice*.

Méot's menus were varied and numerous, even in the worst moments of the Terror; Robespierre, Danton, Saint-Just and other fanatical leaders had no scruples about appearing at his restaurant. It is said that Grimod de la Reynière's famous *Mystificateurs* dinner took place there; among celebrities who attended was the Marquis de Sade. The mystification consisted in pretending that Restif de la Bretonne had been elected a member of the Académie Française. It is likely that our Caraqueño had been a fellow-diner at that memorable banquet. What we do know for certain is that our character attended the same year, in August, another famous meal offered by Barras, a member of the Directory. The menu had six entrées, two roasts, and six side dishes. Barras' comments written at the bottom of the menu read: 'too much fish; remove mackerels. The rest is right. Do not forget to put cushions on the chairs of citizens Tallien, Talma, Beauharnais, Hinguerlot, and Miranda. At five o'clock ask to bring over Veloni's ice creams; I do not want any but those.'

After his stay in the rue Saint-Florentin, the gentleman from Caracas got in trouble and the Directory issued a deportation order. After his departure, he settled in London for two years and eight months. He then returned to France in November of 1800, where he was sent to prison by an order of Fouché, who was in charge personally of tormenting him with a very tedious questioning. In March of 1801, he was expelled definitively from France.

England welcomed him and lent support in forming a fleet which was meant to liberate Venezuela from Spanish power. He landed at Coro, northern Venezuela, in 1806. He spent several days at the house of Señor Antonio Navarrete and Señor Francisco La Bastida, acknowledging to the latter one evening, when they were talking of Venezuelan food – the palate tired of so many courtly tables, of so many foreign tastes, and not without nostalgia – that the 'regular lunch at my father's was *hallaca*

SAVARD, RESTAURATEUR.

PRIX DES METS POUR UNE PERSONNE

Potages.

A la purée de navets	12
Au Riz au naturel	12
A la Crecy	12
A la Faubonne	12
Aux laitues	12
A la Julienne	12
Aux choux	12
Aux herbes	12
Aux légumes	12
Au Vermichel	12
A la semoulle	12
Au macaroni	15
Consommé	12

Hors d'œuvres.

Œuf frais	1 f.
Beurre de Vanvres	
Cornichons	10
Anchois aux fines herbes	15
Boudin noir	
Boudin blanc	10
Saucisse	5
Rognons au vin de Champagne	1
Raves & radis	4
Petit pain	
Artichaux à la poivrade	

Relevé de Potage.

Bœuf au naturel	10 f.
Bœuf garni de petit pâté	15
Bœuf garni de légumes	12
Bœuf à la sauce	12
Bœuf d'Hambourg	15
Bœuf à la royale	18

Entrées de Pâtisseries.

2 Petits pâtés au naturel	1 6 f.
2 idem au jus	10
2 idem à la béchamelle	1
2 idem à la baraquine	1
Tourte de saumon	10
Tourte d'anguille	1 10
Vol-au-vent à la financière	1 10
idem de cervelle à l'Allemande	1 10
Pâté à l'Anglaise	
Pâté de légumes	1

Entrée de Volailles.

Chapon au consommé, le quart	2 L.
Poularde au ris, le quart	1
Poularde à l'oille, le quart	10
Poularde au nouille, le quart	1
Poularde à la tartare, le quart	1
Moitié de poulet à l'estouffade	1
à la gelée	1
Moitié de poulet à la ravigote	5
Salade de volaille	1
Salade de volaille à la gelée	1
Aileron de dindon aux légumes	1
Fritaux de volaille garni	10
Côtelette de poulet	1
Cuisse de poulet grillé	18
Filet de poulet au suprême	1
Filet de poularde à la maréchale	1
Blanc de poularde aux concombres ou laitues	10
Fricassée de Poulet garnie	1
Filet de caneton à l'Orange	1
Filet de pigeon grillé	4
Pigeon à la crapaudine	10
Marinade de Poulet	
Macédoine de volaille	1
Caille au consommé ou légumes	1
Pigeons aux pois	4
Chipolata de volaille	1
Marinade de poulet à crud	1

Entrées de Gibier.

Lapereau en caisse aux fines herbes	1 f.
Lapereau en papillote	
Filet de lapereau au beurre	1
Lapereau aux pois	1
Perdreau au laurier ou Verjus	1
Filet de perdreau glacé	1
Caille aux laitues ou au consommé	1

Entrées de Bœuf.

Filet de bœuf piqué	1 f.
Bifteck aux pommes de terre	18
Entre-côtes aux cornichons	15
Queue de bœuf au hochepôt	1
Palais de bœuf à l'Allemande	1
Langue de bœuf à l'écarlate aux épinards	1
Langue de bœuf en papillotes	18
Langue aux Épinards	1
Emincé de filet de bœuf aux laitues	1

Entrées de Veau.

Côtelette de veau panée	1 12 f.
Côtelette de veau glacée à l'Espag.	1
Cervelle de veau au velouté	1
Cervelle au beurre noir	1
Cervelle en matelotte	4
Cervelle frite	1
Cervelle en Mayonnoise, à la gelée	10
Tendron de veau aux petits pois	1
Tendron de veau à la Flamande	1
Tendron de veau à l'Anglaise	1
Tendron de veau au ginguinoise	1
Tête de veau en tortue	1
Tête de veau au naturel	1
Ris de veau piqué aux laitues	10
Foie de veau grillé, à la ravigote	1
Filet de veau glacé à la chicorée	15
Filet de veau à l'Anglaise	1
Noix de veau à la bourgeoise	1
Blanquette de veau de Pontoise	1
Grenadin glacé à la purée d'oseille	1
Côtelette de veau aux fines herbes	18
Côtelette de veau en papillote	1
Côtelette de veau au naturel	15

Entrées de Mouton.

2 Côtelettes au naturel	1 f.
2 Côtelettes à l'Anglaise	16
2 Côtelettes à la purée	1
2 Côtelettes sautées glacées	16
Tendron aux racines	1
Carbonnade aux laitues	1

Entrées d'Agneau.

Côtelettes à l'Italienne	1 4 f.
Côtelettes glacées à la chicorée	1
Tendron aux petits pois	1
Emincé à la ravigote	1
Pieds à la poulette	1
Tendron pané	

Poisson.

Saumon frais	1 10
Raie au beurre	
Esturgeon	10
Solle	10
Truite à la Genevoise	1
Perche	10
Anguilles à la broche	10
Macédoine de carpe & d'anguille	1
Brochet à l'Anglaise	
Carpe frite	1 10

Rôts.

Veau rôti	1
Quart de Poularde au creston	1
Moitié de poulet normand	1
Moitié de poulet gras	1
Lapereau	1
Caille	1
Canneton de Rouen	1
Perdreau	
Dindon	
Pigeon rôti	
Salade	

Entremets.

Petits Pois	1 5 f.
Asperges	
Artichaux	1
Concombre	
Aricots verds ou blancs	1
Choux-fleurs	1
Petites fèves	1
Croûte aux Champignons	
Macédoine	1
Céleri au jus ou en salade	
Chicorée au blanc	
Œufs pochés à l'oseille ou à la chicorée	1
Œufs brouillés au pointes d'asperg.	20
Omelette aux fines herbes	12
Omelette soufflée	1
idem aux confitures	4
idem à la Célestine	1
idem aux rognons	4
idem au jambon	1
Pommes au riz	4
Charlotte de pomme	1
Beignets idem	4
Beignets d'abricots	1
Pommes de terre à la maître-d'hot.	15
Soufflées de riz	1
Macaroni	1
Soufflé au café	1
Crème	

Desserts.

Orange & sucre	1 f.
Poire crue	
Pomme crue	
Compote de cerises	15
idem diaboutes	
idem pêches	
idem Portugaise	8
idem poires	15
idem Pommes	15
Fruits à l'eau-de-vie de toutes esp.	1
Confitures idem	15
Fromages de toutes espèces	1
Biscuit	4

VINS.

Vin de Bourgogne ordinaire	1 L. f.	
Chablis	10	
idem première qualité	1	
Mulseaux	1	
Beaune	1	
Pommard	5	
Volnay	10	
Nuits	4	
Clos de Vougeot	4	
Chambertin	4	
Morachay	5	
Champagne Sillery	6	
Champagne Ay	4	
Champagne mousseux	6	
Bordeaux la Fitte	4	
Médoc	10	
Bordeaux blanc Prignac	3 10	
Sauterne	4	
Côte-rotie	4	
L'Hermitage	3	

VINS DE LIQUEUR.

Vin de Malaga, la bouteille	4 L.	
Palme, idem	5	
Rota, idem	5	
Alicante, idem	4 10	
Frontignan, idem	5	
Malvoisie, idem	9	
Chipres, idem	9	
Muscat sec, idem	9	
Tokal	16	
idem Constance	30	
Du Cap	15	

LIQUEURS, le petit verre.

Liqueurs des Isles de toutes espèces	1 L.
Marasquin & Rosolio Bologne	1
Liqueur ordin. de toutes espèces	1
Anday & kervalar	1
Anisette de Bordeaux	1
Cognac	
Café	

Copy of menu and account from Savard, preserved in the Miranda archive. Because of its condition, the marginal annotations have had to be sacrificed in the cause of a cleaner reproduction.

[a kind of *tamal*], *olleta* [cock soup], *mondongo* [viscera soup], and *hallaquita* [wrapped corn bread]. I have not tried these dishes since I left the country, thirty years ago.'

After the failure of his liberationist attempts he returned to England. In 1810 Simón Bolívar, Luis López Mendez, and Andrés Bello went to London to look for him; they came back to Venezuela in December of the same year. The result of this new independent enterprise was tragic: our character was captured and sent to Spain, to Cadiz prison, where on July the 14th 1816 – when incidentally the 27th anniversary of the taking of the Bastille was celebrated – he died forgotten by all. His name was Francisco de Miranda.

BIBLIOGRAPHY

Miranda, Francisco de, *Archivo del General*. Caracas, Editorial Sur America, 1929-50, 24 vols. (The complete archive is kept at the Academy of History in Caracas)

Rodriguez de Alonso, Josefina, *Le siècle des lumières conté par Francisco de Miranda*. Paris, Editions France. Empire, 1974

The Availability of Exotic Vegetables and Herbs as a Reflection of Ethnic Populations in Great Britain

Michael Michaud & Mark Redman

Great Britain is a multicultural society. Though the majority of Britons are white, a significant proportion are members of a minority group. According to a survey taken in the spring of 1995 by the Central Statistical Office, ethnic minorities represented just under 6 per cent of the population. This included 869,000 Blacks (Caribbean, African and other Blacks of non-mixed origin), 844,000 Indians and 725,000 Pakistanis/Bangladeshis.

This diversity of cultures is reflected in the wide range of exotic foods available in the shops, especially in those catering to the ethnic populations. These foods, often unknown to mainstream whites, include fresh tropical fruits, vegetables and herbs; dry goods including pulses and flours; and canned and bottled products, both sweet and savoury.

While shops catering to ethnic tastes have a tremendous and, to the uninitiated, often overwhelming selection of strange foods, they are not the only source of exotic food eaten in the ethnic communities. Many members of the various communities are also allotment holders and are, therefore, able to grow a significant quantity of food for their own use. Many of the foods they grow parallel those found in the allotments tended by the whites, though a number of them reflect their ethnic backgrounds.

A preliminary study was conducted in 1996 to characterize the exotic vegetables and herbs found in the shops and allotments in ethnic communities. The study took place in Sandwell Metropolitan Borough, located in the West Midlands and adjoining Wolverhampton, Dudley, Walsall and Birmingham. Of the total population of 289,000, 7.9 per cent are Indian, 2.7 per cent are Afro-Caribbean and 4.1 per cent are Bangladeshi, Pakistani and East African. According to information supplied by the council, 'Sandwell has one of the largest and most culturally diverse ethnic minority populations outside of London'. Because of this diversity and size of the ethnic community, it was considered to be an ideal locale for such a study.

The study focused on two communities: the Asians and the West Indians. The Asian community, however, was a cultural mix based to some extent on the geographical origin of its members, who have roots either in India, Pakistan or Bangladesh. In the context of any other study, however, it was felt that the vegetable and herb eating habits of the Asian community as a whole were more or less the same and, therefore, no distinctions were made between Indians, Pakistanis and Bangladeshis.

Results of shop visits

Some of the exotic vegetables and herbs found in Sandwell shops are given in the checklist. The list is incomplete since some food items have still not been identified, nor were all the shops in Sandwell visited as part of this preliminary study. There is also the possibility of seasonality, meaning that vegetables and herbs peculiar to a season may have been missed because of long time lapses between visits. Nevertheless, some interesting foods were found, and were often a combination of imports from the tropics and produce of local origin. Descriptions and discussions of many of the vegetables and herbs listed in the table can be found in the Grigson and Knox book *Exotic Fruits and Vegetables*, and it is highly recommended as a reference. Some comments, however, are made here about a selection of the vegetables found in the Sandwell shops.

Fat hen (*Chenopodium album*). Fat hen is a common weed in waste places and cultivated land in both Europe and North America. Richard Mabey states in his book *Food for Free* that it was apparently an important food plant in Anglo-Saxon times, but went out of favour with the introduction of spinach. In India too it is a common weed of waste land as well as cultivated fields. Some forms, however, are grown as a vegetable, with their tender shoots eaten raw or cooked. They are also dried and stored for future use. In Sandwell young stalks of fat hen were found for sale in one of the Asian shops. Because they are so common, the plants could have come from a nearby allotment or someone's garden when the weeding was done.

Tinda (*Praecitrullus fistulosus*). This vegetable, found in Asian shops, is related to the water melon. It has a light green skin; firm, white flesh; and a shape and size similar to a turnip.

Bottle gourd (*Lagenaria siceraria*). Under the guise of bowls, ladles, musical instruments and shells carved for decorative purposes, bottle gourds are probably more familiar as tourist items from Africa and South America. The thick-shelled varieties are, in fact, used extensively by the inhabitants of the tropics, though they tend to be bitter and, thus, non-edible. Non-bitter edible forms, without hard shells, have been selected, especially in India, and a wide range, varying in both shape and size, were found in the Sandwell shops. They included small, oval-shaped types that fit comfortably in the hand up to large club-shaped ones at least 30 cm long.

Mango (*Mangifera indica*), papaya (*Carica papaya*) and jackfruit (*Artocarpus heterophyllus*). A number of fruits that doubled as vegetables were found in the Asian shops. They included both green mangoes and papayas, the unripe flesh of which are used in cooking. Huge, ripe jackfruits were also found in the shops catering to the Asian community. While the sweet flesh is used as a fruit, the dry, ripe seeds, which can be bought separately, can be boiled or roasted for use in savoury dishes.

Breadfruit (*Artocarpus communis*). In the same botanical genus as the jackfruit, this vegetable was found in Sandwell in a shop selling mainly West Indian goods. Though it is grown in India, breadfruit were not found in the Asian shops during the study. This may, however, be an indication of the inadequacy of the shop visits rather than a reflection of the eating habits of the Asian residents of Sandwell.

Calalloo (*Amaranthus sp.*) and thyme (*Thymus sp.*). Both were for sale as bunches in a shop apparently owned by West Indians. Calalloo, closely related to the ornamental 'Love Lies Bleeding', consists of a succulent tender stem along which are attached heart-shaped leaves. The leaves have margins of golden green, with an overlay of red emanating from the centre part. There was nothing exceptional about the thyme, which appeared to be the common English type. Both the calalloo and thyme seemed to be locally grown.

Results of allotment visits

Allotment sites managed by members of the Asian and West Indian communities were visited and the holders interviewed to determine the type of vegetables and herbs they were growing, the origin of the propagating material, and the growing methods that were employed. In those instances where the original planting material, either seed or vegetative parts, originated outside Great Britain, it was collected so that it could be grown on for further study.

Generally speaking, climatic constraints dictated to some extent that the 'potato, cabbage and onion' planting routine normally associated with white allotment holders was followed. It was found, however, that some vegetables and herbs specific to the cultural background of the ethnic allotment holders could also be grown.

Asian allotments

Herbs: Coriander (*Coriandrum sativum*) and fenugreek (*Trigonella foenum graecum*) were grown in relatively large areas by the Asians, who often made sequential sowings in order to guarantee a continuous supply. So extensive were the plantings that the herbs could be smelled from the roads that passed through the allotments. During the course of the study, bunches of fenugreek and coriander were usually found for sale in the local shops. Considering the extent of their production in the allotments, it seems likely that the holders were selling some of their produce.

Kale (*Brassica sp.*). There is some uncertainty as to the exact identity of this vegetable, which is reminiscent of the 'Hungry Gap' kale found in Great Britain. One allotment holder had seed of three different types which he brought back from India. He claimed that two of them grew better when they were sown direct rather than transplanted. He also managed them differently, cutting one at a young stage of growth and allowing it to regrow before recutting, while allowing another to grow to a larger size before cutting. As with the fenugreek and coriander, these kales were found in the local shops, suggesting the allotments as being a possible source.

Radish (*Raphanus sativus*). The popularity of the long white mouli radish in the Asian community was reflected in the area devoted to its cultivation in the allotments. Radishes, however, were not grown just for their roots by the Asian allotment holders. They were purposely allowed to flower so that pods, which are eaten, are produced. While ordinary radishes are used for this purpose, there are varieties in Indian that have been specifically bred for their pods. They can reach lengths of 75 cm, and one of the holders was hoping that his wife, who was in India at the time of the interview, would be bringing seed back with her.

Chickpeas (*Cicer arietinum*). This vegetable was sold fresh in their pods in the local shops. Though probably imported for sale in the shops, they are also grown through the summer in the allotments. The seed used for planting is the same that is sold as a dried pulse for cooking.

West Indian allotments

Calalloo (*Amaranthus sp.*). Large areas of the West Indian allotments were devoted to the cultivation of calalloo. Though a number of types were being grown, one was significantly more prevalent than the others. Its leaves had golden green margins and red centres, and was for sale in one of the West Indian shops. One holder grew three distinct types: two originally from Jamaica and one given to him by an African friend. Sowing techniques varied between the types, with the African type sown each year with seed collected from the prior year's plants. In contrast, seed of the Jamaican types were allowed to fall to the ground at the end of the growing season, thus reseeding themselves annually. The various calalloos cultivated by the allotment holders were often easily distinguished from each other by differences in leaf colouration and plant morphology. In addition, some had black seeds, while others had pink ones. It is difficult at this point to determine the exact number of species being grown, though this is an important consideration in terms of cross pollination found in *Amaranthus* and the practice of saving seed from year to year.

Thyme (*Thymus sp.*). Because it is normally associated with temperate regions, it was a surprise to discover the extent to which West Indian allotment holders cultivated thyme. Not only was the proportion of holders growing it considerable, but the large area in each case was significant. Though cultivated for home use, some was probably being sold locally.

Scallion (sic) (*Allium sp.*). The consensus among the allotment holders places Jamaica as the origin of this plant. With its small bulbs and round hollow leaves, it is similar in appearance to the Welsh onion. Also, like the Welsh onion, it is propagated from bulbs put back in the soil after harvesting.

French beans (*Phaseolus vulgaris*). Though grown for their tender green pods, French beans seem to be mainly grown as a pulse crop. The varieties were mostly of the dwarf bush types, though some climbing types were grown. The original seeds came from a number of sources, including local food shops selling it as a pulse and, in one case, an African friend. One allotment holder even made reference to a 'Polish' bean he had, suggesting East European origins. After procuring the original seed, subsequent supplies were saved from the annual harvest.

Small-scale farmers in the tropics tend to intercrop corn and beans in order to increase yields and reduce the risk of crop failure. The West Indians in Sandwell were no exception, and many of them planted bush beans in between rows of sweet corn. As one holder explained, more could then be harvested from the same piece of land.

Pumpkin (*Cucurbita sp.*). Though called pumpkins by the West Indians, these vegetables are, in fact, winter squashes with hard skins and thick, orange or yellow flesh. They come in various shapes, sizes and skin colours, and seem to be ubiquitously grown by the allotment holders.

Squash seed is frequently bought in small packs from local shops. Despite the ready availability of these packets, it seems more popular to save seed from the best tasting fruit from one year to the next. Though seemingly a reasonable strategy for producing tasty vegetables, such a practice can have surprising results. This is due in large part to cross pollination by insects. As long as squashes of only one variety are grown together and isolated by a sufficient distance from those of other varieties, then seed collected from the fruit will breed true and produce replicas of the parents. Given the variation in the population of squashes in West Indian allotments and the close proximity of the individual plots, it is more than likely that insects are moving pollen from one variety to another, producing a random mix of types in the offspring. Saving seed under these circumstances can be something of a lottery, since the type of fruit that will be produced cannot be predicted. An allotment holder had heard of a case where seed collected from a green-skinned fruit produced offspring with brown skin. Though this anecdote cannot be verified, it does illustrate the problem of saving squash seed.

Comments

As this preliminary study has shown, at least some of the eating habits of the Asians and West Indians have immigrated with them to Great Britain. Not only are vegetables and herbs familiar to them available in the shops catering to their communities, but many of the foods are being grown in their allotments. Judging by their availability, these foods play an important role in maintaining cultural identity and will continue to do so, at least for the first generation of immigrants.

The study of exotic vegetables and herbs will continue to be carried out, expanding beyond the confines of Sandwell into other areas of Great Britain. It will begin to focus only on allotments, and will encompass those managed by other ethnic minorities. Looking 'over the fence' into some Italian allotments has already revealed some interesting salad crops as well as bottle gourds (*Lagenaria siceraria*) cultivated not for their fruit (which would be difficult in the cold of Great Britain) but for their tender stems and leaves. As the study progresses, other exotic foods will undoubtedly be discovered.

Checklist of exotic vegetables and herbs sold in Sandwell shops catering to Asian and West Indian clients

English Name	Scientific Name	Part sold
Betel	*Piper betel*	Fruit
Bitter gourd	*Momordica charantis*	Fruit
Bitter gourd(spiny)	*Momordica cochinensis*	Fruit
Bottle gourd	*Lagenaria siceraria*	Fruit
Breadfruit	*Artocarpus communis (or altilis)*	Fruit
Calalloo	*Amaranthus sp.*	Leaves/stems
Cassava	*Manihot esculenta*	Root
Chayote	*Sechium edule*	Fruit
Chickpea	*Cicer arietinum*	Pod
Chile pepper	*Capsicum annuum* and *C. chinense*	Fruit
Cowpea(blackeye pea)	*Vigna unguiculata*	Pod
Fat hen	*Chenopodium album*	Leaves/stems
Fenugreek	*Tigonella foenum graecum*	Leaves/stems
Guar (cluster bean)	*Cyamposis tetragonoloba*	Pod
Hyacinth bean (bonavist bean, valor bean)	*Lablab purpureus*	Pod
Ivy gourd	*Coccinia grandis*	Fruit
Jackfruit	*Artocarpus heterophyllus*	Fruit/seed
Kale	*Brassica sp.*	Leaves/stems
Mango	*Mangifera indica*	Fruit
Mouli(white radish)	*Raphanus sativus*	Root
Okra	*Abelmoschus esculentus*	Fruit
Papaya	*Carica papaya*	Fruit
Pigeon pea	*Cajanus cajan*	Pod
Plantain	*Musax paradisaica*	Fruit

Snake gourd	*Trichosanthes cucumerina*	Fruit
Sweet potato	*Ipomoea batatas*	Root
Taro(dasheen)	*Colocasia esculenta*	Leaves/runners/corms
Tinda	*Praecitrullus fistulosus*	Fruit
Yams	*Dioscorea sp.*	Root
Yard-long bean (Asparagus bean)	*Vigna unguiculata sesquipedalis*	Pod

BIBLIOGRAPHY

Achaya, K.T. 1994, *Indian Food – A Historical Companion*, Oxford University Press, Delhi.

Ashworth, D. 1991, *Seed to Seed*, Seed Savers Exchange, Decorah, Iowa.

Central Statistical Office, 1996, *Social Trends*, HMSO, London.

Chadha, Y.R. (ed.-in-chief) 1985, *The Wealth of India*, Vol.1: A. Council for Scientific and Industrial Research, Delhi.

Food and Agriculture Organisation, 1988, *Food and Nutrition Paper 42 – Traditional Food Plants*, FAO, Rome.

Grigson, J. and Knox, C. 1986, *Exotic Fruits and Vegetables*, Jonathan Cape, London.

Jacquat, C. 1990, *Plants from the Markets of Thailand*, Duang Kamol, Bangkok.

Joshi, S.K. (Chair), 1992, *The Wealth of India*, Vol. 3: CA-Ci. Council for Scientific and Industrial Research, Delhi.

Kay, D.I. (rev. by E.G.B. Gooding), 1987, *Crop and Product Digest No.2 – Root Crops,* Second Edition. Tropical Development and Research Institute, London.

Krishnamurthi, A. (ed.-in-chief), 1969. *The Wealth of India*. Vol. 8: Ph-Re. Council for Scientific and Industrial Research, Delhi.

Mabey, R. 1989, *Food for Free*, Collins, London.

The Horseback Kitchen of Central Asia

Charles Perry

The speakers of Turkish languages were originally nomads. Some groups, such as the Turkmens, Kazakhs and Kirgiz of Central Asia, still are to a considerable extent, and others, such as the Tatars, retain many nomad traditions though settled. The Turks originally had much in common with their fellow nomads the Mongols, though history has separated them, culturally and religiously as well as physically.

Turk or Mongol, the nomads primarily herd sheep, goats and horses, to a lesser degree cattle and camels. The Mongols also herd yaks. Everything else in their material life is subject to the necessity that it be carried on horseback. For this reason, the only traded foodstuffs that could find a market on the steppe until recently were grain, dried fruit, spices and tea. (Some nomads were able to practice casual agriculture themselves, but all nomads despise farming as a primary way of life.)

The entire *batterie de cuisine* must also be portable. The basic cooking utensil of the Turkish nomads is the *qazan* or *qazghan* (literally, 'the hollowed-out thing'), a hemispherical vessel, typically half a meter in diameter, made of cast iron or, in modern times, aluminum. The name is usually translated as 'pot,' but it looks to us more like a cauldron. In place of a bail for supporting it over a hearth fire, or the familiar handles of European pots, which are designed for picking up by the hands, it has four small horizontal extensions spaced around the rim by which it can be supported. These semicircular lugs may also be convenient when the pot has to be lashed to a pack animal for travel.

In the most primitive cooking situations, the *qazan* can be set over a grass or dung fire on rocks, or a shallow hole may be dug for a hearth and the *qazan* set on that. A more advanced solution is an iron ring on three legs similar to the *sajayaq* (see below) for supporting the *qazan*. Central Asian town dwellers set *qazans* into large holes built into their kitchen ranges, or (on picnics, and for cooking outdoors during the summer months) on cylindrical charcoal burners made of sheet metal.

Nomads steam certain foods in the *qazan*, such as the traditional meat dumpling *mantu* and various dim-sum-like pastries introduced by Muslim refugees from China during the nineteenth century. The wooden rack on which they put the foods to be steamed is called a *qasqan*, which seems to be a dialect form of *qaz(gh)an*.[1]

In Turkey, the *kazan* was the unifying symbol of the Janissary regiments, and they would indicate a quarrel with their superiors by the violent step of overturning the unit's *kazan*. Even today, the expression *kazan devirmek* – 'to overturn the *kazan*' – is a synonym for mutiny in Turkish. However, in Turkey the *kazan* has adopted the typical Middle Eastern flat-bottomed shape, because it is usually set on a range or in an oven, rather than over a campfire on the steppe.

The *qazan* seems to have been invented by the medieval nomadic Turks. It resembles the Chinese *wok* or the Indian *karhai* in general shape, but not in size or how it is made or used, and unlike those utensils, it lacks a handle. The Scyths and other Iranians who inhabited the western steppes before the Turkish invasions of the early Middle Ages had round-bottomed clay and bronze pots (though the latter were rare), but all had the big-bellied shape of a witch's cauldron, not the strict hemispherical profile of the *qazan*.

Some of the Turkish peoples' neighbors have adopted the *qazan* because of its usefulness, particularly in making pilaf – for special occasions like weddings, professional pilaf-masters may use *qazans* two meters in diameter. Another Turkish cooking utensil has been even more popular, having been adopted widely in Iran, Afghanistan and the Levant: the *saj*, a slightly domed griddle shaped like – and perhaps originating from – a shield. It can be set over a fire on stones, or on a tripod known as the *sajayaq*. In cities, a bakery may install a *saj* on a charcoal or gas fire.

The last of the principal cooking utensils is the *shish*, or skewer. Originally the word probably meant a sharp stick. The first written notice of it, in the eleventh-century *Dîwân Lughât al-Turk* by Mahmud of Kashgar, defines it not only as a skewer but as 'a tool for arranging noodles' (*minzâm tutmâj*). This has been interpreted as a stick for eating noodles with, like the Chinese chopsticks, though logically it might refer to something for drying noodles on. In any case, every other mention of the *shish* through history clearly refers to the skewer we know from shish kebab.

The Turks originally had no such utensil as a frying pan, and eventually adopted the pan (along with its name, *tava*) from the Persians. The *Codex Cumanicus*, a fourteenth-century glossary of Persian and Turkic words for the use of European merchants in the Black Sea area, does translate *patella* (pan) as *yaglaou*, which seems to be *yaghlaq*, 'place for grease.'

The medieval Turks also knew small earthenware pots called *eshich* and *butaq*, but these were of relatively little use to nomads.[2] Throughout history, the Turkish herding peoples have done nearly all their cooking with the *qazan* (for toasting or boiling grain, preparing dairy products and boiling or frying meat), the *saj* (for cooking flatbread, the daily staple of nomad dining) and the *shish*. The favorite utensil was the *qazan*; despite the difficulties posed by its shape, most nomadic groups even contrived ways to cook flatbread in it.[3]

Food was served in a carved wooden bowl or soup dish called *chanaq*. If there was a large piece of meat in the soup or stew, the diner might finish the liquid portion, remove the meat with the point of his knife, turn the *chanaq* upside down and use its flat bottom as a carving board for the meat. This word has spread to some foreign languages, e.g. Hungarian *csanak*.

Turkic tableware includes the knife (*bichaq*) and the carved wooden spoon (*qashïq*), the latter sometimes made with a sort of double bowl – looking almost like a figure 8 – for ladling kumyss. *Qabaq* means both gourd and a lidded vessel made from a dried gourd, but it, the word, is a diminutive of *qab*, small sack, so to the Turks the gourd was evidently a container before it was a vegetable. Several leather containers are used in making traditional dairy foods.

The ancient food preparation utensils included *oqlaghu* (later *oklava*), a thin rolling pin (from *oq*, 'arrow'); *süzgüch*, a colander especially used for straining curds; and *tägirmän*, a stone for grinding grain. Most Turkish languages use the Iranian word *hâwan* for mortar.[4]

All sources seem to agree that Mongol cookery is much less developed than that of the Turkish nomads. I have not been able to find any Mongol cookbooks to verify the claim (this absence may be eloquent in itself).[5] In any case, the Mongol *batterie de cuisine* includes most of the same utensils, though the pot *toghughan* (in modern Khalkha Mongol pronunciation, *togoo*), which has the *qazan* shape, is apparently often made from sheet metal, rather than cast, lacks the lugs and may have a flat bottom. *Tulgan*, the Mongol device for supporting a cauldron over the fire has four legs, rather than three. The Mongols do not have the *saj*.

Nomad cookery revolves around dairy products. The Turkic words for milk (*süt*), butter (*yagh*), buttermilk (*ayran*), cream (*qaymaq* – usually a sort of clotted cream made by simmering whole milk), yogurt (*yoghrut*), yogurt starter (*qor*), dried yogurt (*qurut*) and kumyss (*qïmïz*; fermented mare's milk) have come down from very early days. Words for yogurt thickened by straining (*süzmä*) and for a cheese-like product made by boiling soured milk to curdle it (*bishlaq*) are so widespread that they must also date from the early Middle Ages.

Buttermilk is a favorite beverage, and the word *ayran* is also widely used for a similar drink made by diluting yogurt with water. This diluted drink, similar to the Iranian *dugh*, the Armenian *tan* and the Indian *lassi*, also has its own specific name, *chalap*. (Kirgiz makes the distinction that *changït* is less diluted than *chalap*.) However, some dialects have lost the word *yoghrut* and now use *ayran* in the sense of yogurt, or a word (*qatïq*) which originally meant any condiment to go with bread or noodles – or both, with *ayran* referring to a more liquid and *qatïq* to a more solid form of yogurt. Camel's milk *ayran* is known as *shubat*.

The Turkic nomads of the Golden Horde – ancestors of the Kazakhs, Kirgiz, Tatars and a number of smaller groups – developed new ways of using dairy products during the Middle Ages, often depending on the different cooking qualities of milk from different species. Besides the dairy products already mentioned, the Kazakhs and Kirgiz make the following products (the Tatars make most of them also):

- *Koirtpak*: cow's milk or water is added to yogurt, *ayran* or kumyss in a leather bag (*torsuk*). Eventually, it is said, the sour taste is lost and the result is a beverage.
- *Irkit*: a mixture of raw (unboiled) milk and yogurt is aged in the small leather barrel called *saba*. It is churned to obtain butter, then the curd is removed and converted into *kurt* (as the Kazakhs call *qurut*) by boiling it down until solid and then drying it on a board. The whey, *irkit*, is served as a beverage.
- *Irimchik* or *irimshik*: a sort of dried cheese, made from milk curdled with rennet. The curd is boiled and then dried quite hard in leather sacks; it turns a tawny color and keeps well. Sometimes meat broth is added during the boiling stage to improve the flavor. *Irimshik* is eaten by itself, added to other dishes or made into a sort of porridge (*talkan*) by pounding in a mortar and adding milk or sour cream.
- *Ak irimshik* (white *irimshik*): this is made by boiling milk with yogurt or the sour buttermilk left after churning butter from yogurt.
- *Ejegei* or *ezhegei*: yogurt is added to boiling milk and cooked for 30-60 seconds so that it curdles. The curd is filtered out with a cloth strainer and mixed with sweet butter. Exceptionally (for culinary borrowings nearly always went from Turk to Mongol), this is a Mongolian word for curds, *ezegei* (the modern Khalkha Mongol pronunciation is *eezgii*).
- *Akalak*: whole cow's milk and sheep-milk yogurt are boiled together. When the mixture curdles, the whey is removed and the curd is mixed with sheep milk, boiled cow's milk or butter.
- A favorite dish of the southern Kazakhs, *turniyaz*, consists of milk cooked with butter, *kurt*, flour and toasted millet.

Meanwhile, *kurt/qurut* has diversified. *Qurut* made from whey, called *qara qurut* ('black *qurut*'), is cooked down to a very thick consistency; there are tales of automobile radiators being patched with it. (A medieval Arab source said of *qara qurut*, 'It is very acid and disagreeable and dry and lowers blood pressure.') The fattier upper layer of *qurut* after boiling is traditionally given to children and old people. At the boiling stage, *qurut* can be mixed with thickened yogurt and salt for a richer product. Dry *qurut* can be pounded in a mortar and added to soups, stews and porridge, or mixed with sweet butter to make a light meal for a hurried guest.

Likewise the nomads make fine distinctions among kumyss. Ordinary kumyss is made by putting mare's milk into a leather sack (*torsuk*) and churning it 10-12 times a day. In 24 to 48 hours, the fermenting whey separates and is ready to drink. But there are three-day, four-day and even five-day kumysses. *Tünemel kïmïz* ('returned kumyss') is ripened in a special *torsuk* with old kumyss for two days, and eaten with *kurt*, *irimishik* and butter. Slowly ripened kumyss, or kumyss made with the addition of fresh mare's milk during the fermentation, is called *saumal*. A sort of weak vodka, *arqi*, is distilled from kumyss.

The Mongols ferment their yogurt (*ayrag*) in a leather sack called *hühüür*. Their equivalent of kumyss is called *ösög* or *bozo*, the latter being the same as the Turkish word for beer, *boza* (to be sure, the Kazakhs often make *boza* with the addition of dairy products). The Mongols make milk vodka (*arbi* or *tarasun*), and they also make stronger versions by further distillation (*arz*, for instance, is distilled twice; *sharz* is a fourth distillation).

They make *qurut* (*huruud*) and the Turkish-style boiled cheese *byaslag*. Their usual cheese, *aaruul*, is made by thickening curds from sour milk (*aarts*).[6] Some sources describe it as a sort of *bishlaq* made from buttermilk, rather than whole milk. A Khalkha Mongol specialty is *horhoi aaruul* ('worm *aaruul*'), cheese rolled into spaghetti-like strands. They also make butter (*tos*) and clotted cream (*tsötsgii*, *zööhii*, *öröm*), which they store for months at a time in tightly sewn lamb gut. The average Mongol consumes about a pound of butter a day.

Most of the medieval Turkish grain dishes are still prepared by the Central Asian nomads. Apart from the porridgy beer called *boza*, they fall into the following categories:

- Preparations of whole grain: *talqan* (crushed grain, or a porridge made from it; sometimes flour or toasted flour); *qawïrmach/qawïrmaq* (fried or toasted grain), *yarma* (split barley).
- Soups and soup adjuncts: *botqa* (porridge or soup with small pasta), *töp* (thick porridge), *köchä* (crushed grain cooked with dairy products), *bulamïq* (thin porridge), *ovmach* (pea-shaped noodles), *salma* (broad noodles of varying shape; in Kazakhstan, where *salma* is usually rectangular, more often served with boiled or roasted meat, as we might serve rice, than in soup), *kesme* or *kespe* (literally, 'cut'; this is the modern name for sliced noodles, replacing the medieval word *tutmaj*).
- Breads and pastries: *bawïrsaq* (lumps or disks of rich fried dough; when fried in mutton fat, they keep indefinitely and are carried by travelers as provisions for the road), *quymaq* (thick pancake of leavened dough containing egg), *chälpäk* (pancake or thin bread fried in deep fat), *kömäch* (thin bread fried in ashes; the coin-sized Kirgiz version is served in hot milk with butter and thickened yogurt), *toqach* (usually a bun; used as the general word for bread in Kirgiz), *chöräk* (fine bread; among nomads, only known to the Turkmens and Kazakhs), *yupqa* (thinnest flatbread, often served or made in layers), *qatlama* (fried bread made from dough rolled out thin, greased or sprinkled with dried fruit or fried meat, rolled up tightly and then sliced crosswise, jellyroll-fashion), *qatïrma* (thin bread fried in a *qazan*), *böräk* (small savory pie; among nomads, only known to the Kazakhs and Turkmens; among latter, a sort of ravioli).

The present-day Kazakhs make *belish* (literally, pillow), a class of pies with various fillings, but this is doubtless a borrowing from the settled Tatars, who have a vast repertoire of pies of various shapes and compositions. It requires a tandoor or other oven, so it is not nomad food.

The Khalkha Mongols use the Turkic word *talh* (<*talqan*) as their name for any kind of bread. Among them *budaa* (<Turkic *botqa*) means porridge, but the Ordos Mongols of Inner Mongolia use *buda* as their word for noodles. The Khalkha Mongols also make *zaram* (<*yarma*), *hoimogh* (<*quymaq*) and boorsogh (<*bawïrsaq*). In recent centuries, they have adopted a number of Chinese pastries such as *baozi* and *bianshi*.

Meat plays a smaller role in day-to-day nomad diet than many people suppose. Every animal that is slaughtered reduces the herd, the measure of a nomad's wealth. Most slaughtering was done in winter to thin the herds (the Turkic word for winter-slaughtered meat is *sogïm*). At the winter camp, the ancient ways of preserving meat are the usual sort of sausage (*sujuq*), blood sausage (*qan*, although this is ostensibly forbidden to Muslims) and a sausage stuffed with fat horse belly-meat (*qazï*).

The Golden Horde Turks developed a new sausage of ground meat and offal mixed with rice, *hasip*. The Kazakhs make a product called *sur et* by salting horsemeat for several days and then smoking it over elm, juniper, spruce or meadowsweet. They also preserve meat by pickling it in brine, covering with oil, *kurt* and garlic and wrapping in cheesecloth, or by slicing thin and drying over a fire.

The Turkish nations have a strong taste for chopped meat; their word for it (*qïyma*) has entered languages from Greek to Hindustani. Other nations tend to make chopped meat into meatballs or meatloves or forcemeat. The Turks use it as forcemeat, but their characteristic method is to fry it loose, each tiny bit of meat remaining separate. *Qïyma* has also been the name of a sausage, particularly one frozen for winter use.

At one time the nomadic Turks must have had a dish of fried meat called *qawïrma*, to judge from the presence of the word in India (*korma*), Iran (*ghormeh*) and the Levant (*qawirma*). In the latter two places, the name refers to mutton preserved in fat, a sort of mutton *confit*. The modern nomads (and their settled Tatar cousins to the north) call a fry-up of meat, usually including various organ meats and offal, *qawïrdaq* (in Kazakh, *kuïrdak*), and this word has entered Russian as *kavardak*, 'confusion, disorder, mess.'

In ancient times, spit-roasted meat was called *söklünch* (from a root meaning 'to snatch or tear off'). Today it is simply known as kebab. There was no ancient word for a stew or dish of boiled meat, but virtually all Turkish-speaking peoples have adopted the Persian word *shorba* for meat soup. In Kazakh, the word means broth, and soup proper − consisting of *sorpa* with meat and added salt, spices and onions − is *tuzduk* (among the Nogai Tatars, however, *tuzluk* is a sauce or condiment of garlic and salt). A Kazakh *sorpa* with yogurt, buttermilk or kumyss added is *akirim*. The Kazakhs and Tatars make a special soup of fat meat with dough, the Kazakh *koldama* adding little balls of dough, while the Tatar *kullama* uses a cavatelli-like dumpling (*salma*).

The Kazakhs also cook meat in some rather rough-and-ready ways. *Zhau büirek* is mutton stuffed into its own tripe and thrown on the coals. *Sïrbaz* is lamb wrapped in its own plucked skin and boiled. The last recalls the Mongol technique of disemboweling a whole lamb carcass, filling it with water (or in winter, ice) and setting it on a hot hearthstone while still in its skin. The meat is said to fry on the outside and bake on the inside.

Technically it does not really fry. Although the Mongols are great connoisseurs of fat, and derive the largest proportion of their caloric intake from animal fat of any people in the world, frying is not part of their culinary tradition. They boil meat, roast it on the fire or set a pan of meat on the coals and cover that with another pan and hot coals. In the dish *horhog*, they preserve the Stone Age technique of placing meat and water in a skin or rumen sac and adding heated stones to cook it.

The Mongols make sausage, especially blood sausage (*shavai*) and a sausage of blood and tripe that is frozen for winter use (*biaram*). Their primary way of preserving the winter slaughter is by slicing the meat into ribbons and drying them in the wind. This product, *borts*, may be eaten as is or boiled in kumyss, making a dish called *bolhörük*. Much use is made of offal, and, like the Turks, the Mongols enjoy boiled or roasted gut by itself, without any stuffing.

The reader may have noticed a virtually studied absence of vegetables in this diet. At least in the Middle Ages, the nomadic Turks, although they knew of carrots and turnips, scarcely used any non-grain plant foods but herbs and wild onions and garlic. Even today, the Mongols, believers with a vengeance in plain and simple food, rarely add anything to meat but wild onion (*mangir*).

More substantial plant foods can be found in the steppe if you look − berries, wild apricots, the bland fruit of the Russian olive (*Eleagnus angustifolia*), edible roots and greens − and *The Secret History of the Mongols* relates that the young Genghis Khan grew up on such gathered foods after his fatherless family was dispossessed of its flocks and sent into the wilderness to starve. But the point of the story is that this was the measure of his later triumph. The steppe is no home for vegetarians.

BIBLIOGRAPHY

Arkheologia SSSR, *Stepnaia Polosa; Aziiatiskie Chasti SSSR v Skifo-Sarmatskoe Vremia*, Nauk, Moscow, 1992.

Azarovym, V., et al., *Kazakhskaia Kukhnia*, Kainar, Alma Ata, 1981.

Baskakov, N.A., *Nogaisko-Russkii Slovar'*, Innostrannykh i Natsionalnykh Slovarei, Moscow 1963.

Clauson, Gerard, *An Etymological Dictionary of Pre-Fourteenth Century Turkish*, Oxford, 1972.

von Gabain, Anne-Marie, *Das Leben im Uigurischen Königreich von Koco*, Otto Harrassowitz, Wiesbaden, 1973.

Hangin, G., *A Modern Mongol-English Dictionary*, University of Indiana, 1986.

Iudakhin, K.K., *Kirgizsko-Russkii Slovar*, Sovietskaia Entsiklopediia, Moscow, 1965.

Lessing, Ferdinand, *Mongolian-English Dictionary*, University of California, Berkeley, 1960.

Levin, M.G. and Potapov, L.P., eds, *The Peoples of Siberia*, University of Chicago, 1964.

Pokhlëbkin, V.V., *Natsional'nye Kukhni Nashikh Narodov*, Pishchevaia Promyshlennost', Moscow, 1978.

Shamsutdinov, R.G., *Tatarskaia Kulinaria*, Tatarskoe Knizhnoe, Kazan, 1981.

NOTES

[1] This may be pointed to by the definition of *qazghan* given in Sanglakh, a fifteenth-century Persian dictionary of Central Asian Turkish (though in no other source): 'a circular object made of wood and reeds; when they take a pot off the hearth, they place it on it.'

[2] The *güveç*, which has spread from Turkey to most of the Balkan countries, is somewhat mysterious. Mahmud mentioned something called *küväch* in his eleventh-century dictionary, but his definition is incoherent. In any case, the *güveç* of Turkey and the Balkans has little of the nomad about it, being a squat clay casserole with a lid.

[3] The Kazakhs, for instance, carefully fit flattened dough to the inside of the *qazan* and overturn it on the coals. Contriving this so that the dough doesn't fall out requires some skill; the Kirghiz simply leave the *qazan* right side up and cover it with a lid on which they set hot coals. The Uzbeks use a relatively crude method, cooking the flattened dough in the *qazan* until done on one side, removing it and breaking it in several places so that it can be fitted to cook on the other side.

[4] The Codex Cumanicus calls it *toguch*, but this appears to be the merely the word *tängüch*, a name applied to any implement half a cubit high.

[5] Since this was written, Sharon Hudgins has kindly drawn my attention to a 94-page Buriat Mongol cookbook, *Buriatskaia Kukhnia*, by G. Tsydynzhapov and E. Badueva (Buriatskoe Knizhnoe Izdatel'stvo, Ulan-Ude, 1991). Of the roughly 100 recipes, 20 are for dairy foods, 8 for preparations of wild fruits and nearly all the remainder meat dishes.

[6] The classical Mongolian forms of these two words, *agaruul* and *agarcan*, suggest borrowings from the Turkish *aq*, white.

Kalakukko: Food for the Home and Travel

Jaakko Rahola

This ancient eastern Finnish fish or vegetable pie used to be served warm, directly from the oven, on Saturday evenings, when the family had finished their weekly sauna bath and gathered in the living room for supper. It was also baked for family feasts and for serving to guests.

The Finnish name *kalakukko* means, literally translated, 'fish cock'. *Kala* is the Finnish word for fish. There is no reliable explanation for the origin of the latter part of the word, *kukko*. Probably, it comes from the Germanic word for cake, *Kuchen*. This word may have originated from the language of the Hanseatic tradesmen, who loaded their homeward-bound ships with furs from the hunters, and pies for their ships' supplies for the voyage. This is, however, only a guess; no proof exists for any explanation.

The *kalakukko* also made good food for travelling. The loaf was usually dimensioned so that it made a day's food for a forest worker, and it could be kept a long time. There is a special travel version with a 'built-in' carrying handle made of wicker. This model is called *ripakukko*, *ripa* meaning handle. This model was originally developed for the long journey to church on Sundays. Upon arrival on the Church Hill, the pies and food sacks were hung on the branches of a large rowan tree growing outside the church. After the service, the food was eaten before commencing the journey home.

The crust of the pie, usually about ten millimetres thick, was originally made of rye, with water, pork fat, and salt, and the dough was unleavened. The flour was rather coarsely hand milled in a quern. It was important to stick to a proven quality of flour to avoid sweetening in the oven, and to keep the inside of the crust top from falling down on the filling, which would have caused drying-out of the crust and hollowness in the pie. With modern, industrially produced flours, rye alone does not give good enough results, so wheat or barley is used for the crust in addition to rye. Even oat flakes may be used to absorb moisture, thereby preventing leakage through the crust in the oven.

The most common filling is made of small fresh fish, normally vendace. If perch is used, then the name of the pie becomes *ahvenkukko*, perch cake. Earlier, if fresh fish was not available, dried or even salted fish could be used. During very bad times, pies could be baked with a filling of salt herring heads — but they were removed when eating; only the taste remained.

For a succulent and delicious pie, fat has to be added. For this, fresh or salted, fat bacon is used, the amount being nearly half of the weight of the fish. In households where bacon or other fat pork was not available, butter was used.

There are numerous other versions of the pie, with different fillings and also with different types of crust dough. One common version was the potato pie, with potato slices, bacon fat and possibly mutton. It was usually made on baking days, after the bread was baked. The last piece of dough was used for the pie, just as the bakers in Naples made a pizza from the last scraps of the day's dough. Potato as a filling is not a very old custom, as potatoes were not grown in Finland until the late eighteenth century. Meats, mostly cheap stewing cuts, were often used instead of fish. Udders and lungs were also common as fillings — even squirrel meat has been used.

Of the vegetable fillings, turnip and cabbage have been the most common. Pearl barley porridge has also been used, often mixed with bacon and onion, much like the *kasha* in Russia (*kasha* means porridge). But the pies were not strictly vegetarian — bacon or bacon fat was still used. The most bizarre filling was snow with coarse salt. Naturally, the snow melted immediately, leaving a hollow, but succulent pie crust with delicious crystals of salt inside.

How to eat the *kalakukko*

For the purists from the district of Savo, the only way to open a *kalakukko* pie is to cut a round hole on the top of the loaf, just like cracking open a boiled egg. Then, thin slices are cut from the crust edge around the hole. They may be coated with cold butter and are eaten like bread. Filling is taken with the knife from the middle and eaten with the crust. The remaining bottom used to be served for Sunday breakfast with rice gruel. Also, if the *kalakukko* was served as a lunch dish, it was followed by rice or other gruel. Today, potatoes are usually served with *kalakukko*.

In the south of Savo, the pie was cut vertically into thick slices for serving. This method is recommended today, when the *kalakukko* is served mainly as a curiosity to tourists. Pies are often sold in halves. Then, the fish in the filling has been arranged in parallel, so that the cutting surface looks appetising, and it is easy to cut into neat slices.

Food in the Sephardi Diaspora: from Spain to Istanbul

Claudia Roden

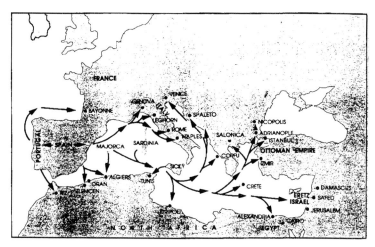

The Routes of Departure in 1492/1497

The history of the Jews is one of migration and exile, of the disintegration and dispersion of communities and the establishment of new ones. They moved to escape persecution or economic hardship and for trade. Culinary memories from old homelands are part of their culture, beginning with the Bible which recalls, in Exodus, the yearnings of the Jews for the foods they left behind in Egypt. Dishes are always that part of the immigrant cultures which survive the longest, long after clothing, music and language have been abandoned. They are kept up because they represent a link with the past, a symbol of continuity, a celebration of roots. There is nothing like a kitchen smell and an elusive taste to evoke vanished worlds and generations past.

The adoption of dishes by Jewish communities in two or more homelands produced an interweaving of traditions and a hybridisation which created some distinctive cuisines. The Jewish dietary laws of Kashruth which prohibit ingredients such as pork and seafood and combining meat and dairy foods; and during Passover, the use of leavening agents, flour and wheat; have influenced the cooking, as have the laws of the Sabbath which prohibit any work, including lighting fires and cooking. Also, dishes adopted to celebrate the Sabbath and religious festivals have usually been transformed into something particular and unique.

Jewish history spans more than three millennia and has touched most parts of the globe. We cannot say that everything that Jews have eaten is Jewish, but there are a number of distinctive cuisines which came out of important centres of Jewish life, where the legacies can be traced.

The style which has been known as 'Jewish' in the Western world is the cooking of the Ashkenazi Jews, who came from Poland, Eastern Europe and Russia, whose emigration to America and Western Europe in the late nineteenth and early twentieth centuries was the greatest mass movement of Jews ever to take place. Although the immigrants came from a vast territory their foods, like their language, Yiddish, and their culture, was similar, because they shared the same roots and the countries they came from had similar foods.

In contrast, the cooking of the Jews whose roots are around the Mediterranean, in the Middle East and Asia, now broadly classed as Sephardi, is regional and immensely varied. It varies not only from one country to another but sometimes even from one city to another. In the strictest sense, the term Sephardi designates only the Jews whose ancestors lived in the Iberian Peninsula (Sepharad means Spain in Hebrew). I will be focussing in this paper on the Jews who went from Spain and Portugal to Turkey.

Each group – Ashkenazi and Sephardi – developed its own separate culture in separate geographic areas. Broadly, the dividing line was the mountains that divide the north and south of Europe all the way from the Caucasus via the Alps to the Pyrenees. That the significant migrations in Jewish history have been between east and west, and not between north and south, encouraged the division between Sephardi and Ashkenazi. There were few cases where the two worlds overlapped geographically and when they did it was a matter of one culinary culture taking over the other – there was no fusion of styles and, with a few exceptions, no Ashkenazi-Sephardi hybrids and no unifying element.

While the Ashkenazi world was in the Christian world, all the lands where the Sephardim lived before the seventeenth century, with the exception of Italy and Christian Spain, were under Islamic rule. Even the Jews of Spain came for the most part with the Arabs, mainly from North Africa, and when they were expelled in 1492 they returned for the most part to Islamic countries.

While Ashkenazi cooking was the cooking of a people closed in on itself in ghettos and restricted areas, who suffered constant persecution and restrictions, Sephardi cooking developed in communities which had an intimate contact and symbiotic relationship with the world they lived in. This, in a way, explains the regional character of the cooking. The Sephardim had a sunny, hedonistic nature. They were less concerned with the inner spiritual life than the Ashkenazim, more sensitive to beauty and pleasure. The warm and sunny world they lived in had something to do with it, as had the way of life. Hospitality had an all-important place. To honour a guest was the ultimate joy. The Sephardim entertained warmly, graciously and constantly and festivities went on for ever. Good eating was an important part of traditional Jewish life.

The Sephardi Diaspora began in the sixth century BC when the Babylonian King Nebuchadnezzar overthrew the Kingdom of Judah, destroyed Jerusalem and its temple, and carried most of its inhabitants back to Babylon (near present Baghdad). When they were allowed to return to their Holy Land fifty years later by the new Persian ruler many decided to stay. They formed what was to become the leading and most influential community of the Jewish Diaspora until the eleventh century.

Babylonian Jewry – under the Sassanian Persian Empire and later in Baghdad which was the seat of the Abbassid Caliphate and the capital of the Islamic Empire – was the centre of learning of the Jewish Diaspora. It was here that the foundations of Sephardi culture were laid, and here too, among the Jewish elite of courtiers and merchants, physicians, mathematicians and philosophers, poets and musicians, that many of the grander dishes entered the Sephardi repertoire. There was even a Jewish nobility with its own court which took its styles and culinary practices from the local aristocracy.

Many elements of the grand medieval, Persian-influenced, Abbassid tradition are recurring themes in Sephardi cooking today – more so than in the cooking of their host countries. For example, Jews have a great fondness for sweet-and-sour flavours which they obtain by mixing sour pomegranate syrup, tamarind, sour grapes, lemon or vinegar with sugar or honey; and for meat cooked with fruits such as apricots, quinces, peaches and dates, apples and pears. They use ground almonds in their pastries and also to thicken soups and sauces. Of course the Jews may have picked up those styles in different parts of the Arab world. But when you think that Babylonian Jews were the leaders of world Jewry for more than ten centuries, that they travelled backwards and forwards, spreading their religious traditions and also setting the tone in matters of taste for their co-religionists it seems likely that they passed them on through their own channels of communication.

When the Arabs invaded Spain in 711 the indigenous Jews, who had been persecuted by the Visigoth Kings, fought on the Arab side and helped them to set up a new order. Jewish communities flourished in Moslem Spain which attracted a mass immigration of Jews from around the Mediterranean. Large communities came into existence in southern Spain which was given the name Al-Andalus. Jews participated in the flowering of the extraordinarily rich new civilisation which became known as the 'Golden Age of Spain'.

As Spanish cities filled with palaces and mosques, public baths and caravanserais, orchards and running water; and as harems were established in the royal courts, so the pattern of social life, etiquette of manners, and style of living and eating was set in the mould of Baghdad, Damascus and Morocco. The Jewish community in particular became a cultural colony of the Baghdad community to whom they turned for advice on all matters.

By the eleventh century, when Judeo-Spanish culture was in full flower and Baghdad was in decline, the Jewish community of Moslem Spain took over the mantle of the Babylonian community, assumed the leadership of the Jewish world and became the most influential community in Europe. Jewish life in Spain at that time was at its most glorious, noble, and gracious.

The chemistry of the three cultures and three religions that was Moslem Spain produced a convivial civilisation which loved music, song and dance and story-telling; where everything that exalted life and made it beautiful, like good food, was cultivated. That experience had a great impact in shaping the Sephardi character.

When the Jews of Andalusia fled to the Christian states in the North when the Almoravids and the Almohads (Islamic Berber sects who conquered Andalusia in the twelfth century) tried to force them to convert to Islam, many of the foods they introduced to the North, like marzipan and aubergines, which the Arabs had brought, were associated with them. What became known as the 'Jewish manner' of cooking – such as frying meat with onions and garlic or combining it with fruits and garnishing dishes with raisins and pine nuts – was a mix of Baghdadi, Syrian, and North African styles. Cooking with olive oil was also associated with the Jews. The French historian, Fernand Braudel, in his book *The Mediterranean* credits the Jews for introducing it as the main cooking medium, instead of pork fat.

For the first two hundred years in Christian Spain the Jews enjoyed royal protection and rose to high positions of state. In 1391 Christian mobs, furious at their privileged position, destroyed the Jewish quarters of the main cities. There were massacres and persecutions and forced conversions. Jews were made to eat pork publicly to prove their allegiance to the new faith. Marrano, which means pork in Spanish, came to signify these converted 'New Christians' or Conversos, who were suspected of keeping their old faith in secret. The Inquisition was established in 1480 by King Ferdinand and Queen Isabella to root out and destroy those who continued to practise Judaism in secret. Thousands were brought to the tribunals and witnesses were called who had noticed strange behaviour which could be a sign of reverting to the old faith. Many women went in front of the Inquisitors because they were discovered cooking their Saturday dish *adafina,* a lamb stew with onions and chickpeas, on the Friday. (It is said to be the basis of the Spanish, *cocido,* a meat stew and the only dish to be found, in different versions, in every region of Spain, and also of *olla podrida* which has meat, chicken, chickpea and a large sausage). Another clandestine dish mentioned in the records of the inquisitional courts was an aubergine, cheese and egg bake. Barbara Haber mentioned it in a paper she gave at a conference in Spain (see bibliography, below).

On March 30th, 1492 Ferdinand and Isabella signed the decree expelling all Jews who had not converted. The Inquisition continued until the end of the eighteenth century and was also instituted in all colonies of Spain, including Southern Italy, Sicily, Sardinia, Provence and the New World of South America. Many of the banished found refuge in Portugal only to be forced to convert there five years later without being given the chance to leave. Some of the exiles found refuge in Italian cities and large numbers fled to North Africa, but above all, the Jews from Spain headed for the lands of the Ottoman Empire where the Sultan Beyazit II welcomed them and even sent ships to collect them. (On the 500th anniversary of the expulsion, the wife of the owner of the Pera Palace in Istanbul, called Suna Suzer, baked a huge cake which was a model of the first ship which sailed.)

The Sultan needed the exiles to populate and help administer the war-depleted empire of Byzantium that the Ottoman armies had destroyed. The Jews settled in Anatolia (Turkey), the Balkans (Greece, Bulgaria, Rumania, Yugoslavia), Cyprus and Crete. They were moved and relocated by Imperial decree from one part of the Empire to another, and were joined by Jews banished from Southern Italy and Provence. Many went on to centres of the Islamic world such as Aleppo, Damascus, Alexandria and Jerusalem, which were dominated by Ottoman dynasties. The Ottoman Empire became the centre of the Sephardi world.

The emigration of thousands of Marranos from Spain and Portugal continued until the end of the sixteenth century. These later waves of immigrants had been wealthier and more educated than those who left in 1492. They were the ones who had stayed behind and converted because they had more to lose. Many had become part of the higher strata of society and had intermarried into the aristocracy. Many settled in Atlantic ports like Amsterdam, Rotterdam, Antwerp and Hamburg where they established trading and finance houses. In 1593 Ferdinand II, Grand Duke of Tuscany, invited New Christians to settle in great numbers in Pisa and Livorno and allowed them to reconvert to Judaism. At the same time, France opened its doors to New Christians who settled in Bayonne, Toulouse and Bordeaux, Marseilles Avignon, Carpentras and Cavaillon which became important Marrano centres. (Almond confectionery and pastries are one of their legacies in the South of France where they were famously in the almond trade.) They ended up scattered everywhere, including the Americas, the Caribbean islands, Surinam, India and England, where they remained secretly as Portuguese Christians until Cromwell allowed Jews in officially in 1656.

Many Marranos followed their Sephardi brethren to North Africa and the Ottoman lands and reconverted to the Mosaic faith. Even though they may have been of Spanish origin they had had one or two generations in Portugal and they were seen as Portuguese. Their cooking was Portuguese and one of its characteristics is that it made use of all of the products of the New World which had been brought back by the Conquistadores. Based in ports around the Mediterranean, and as the main maritime merchants dealing with Spain and Portugal, they were largely responsible for introducing the new products to the region. It is through them that chocolate cakes and vanilla flavouring, tomato sauces and pumpkin and bean dishes spread in a big way through the Sephardi world. Many Marrano families also had interests in the sugar trade, and the grain and spice trades.

Very little remains of Marrano food in Northern Europe. A few things have passed into the Ashkenazi style (in Britain: fish fried in batter, fish in egg and lemon sauce, sponge cake and macaroons), but old Portuguese-type dishes are much in evidence in Mediterranean centres like Livorno and Tunis.

In the Balkans and Anatolia, where they settled in great numbers, the Sephardim very quickly became the leading social and economic force within the local, mostly Greek-speaking, Byzantine and Romaniot communities. By their numbers, not to speak of their cultural superiority, the Iberians overwhelmed the indigenous communities, and came to constitute the bourgeoisie and merchant class and in some cases a kind of Jewish titled aristocracy. Some of the communities they joined took on an Iberian character including the Spanish language and dress.

Some cities became bastions of Jewish life. Salonica (now Thesaloniki), Smyrna (now Izmir) and the island of Rhodes, where Jews became the majority of the population, were like diminutive

Jewish republics. Salonika had the largest Jewish community and became the most important Sephardi city that ever was. Spanish was the language of the land. Istanbul had the second largest community. Being at the administrative core of the Ottoman empire it acquired considerable authority over the communities in the provinces of the empire. It dispensed spiritual inspiration and material support and set the mould for all aspects of community life. Istanbul and Salonika delicacies became fashionable in the far-flung communities of the Eastern Mediterranean.

The sultans allowed the Jews internal autonomy. Within their quarters they lived according to their own administration and managed their communal affairs in a style adopted from Spain. The communities were divided into groups according to regional origin called *cales*. In many big towns there were dozens of these *cales*, each with its own synagogue, rabbi, school and charitable organisations. In Salonica in the early seventeenth century there were forty four of these *cales* including an Apulian, Sicilian, Neapolitan, Calabrese, Catalan, Aragonese, Majorcan, North African, Greek, Provençal, Lisbon and one Ashkenazi. This explains why some Sephardi dishes are neither Spanish nor Turkish but Italian or something else.

As an effort at unification, the Iberian synagogue ritual, the prayers and music, were adopted, with a few exceptions, by Jewish communities all over the Mediterranean, the Balkans and Middle East. This is why these communities were later labelled 'Sephardi'.

When the Empire and the Islamic world declined, the Jewish communities declined even faster, both economically and educationally, and their culinary repertoire was much impoverished as a result. A kind of renaissance came through the intervention of the Jews of France. In 1860 the Alliance Israelite Universelle was established in Paris for the emancipation and 'moral progress' of the Ottoman Jews who were seen, according to Alliance reports, as living in grinding poverty, ignorance and insecurity. Secular Alliance schools that taught children French and also trades opened in the far corners of the Ottoman world, and French became the common language of the Sephardim. In gastronomic terms it meant exposure to French ways and a certain refinement.

It is sometimes difficult to disentangle what are Iberian from what are Turkish, Greek, Balkan or Arab dishes, because Spanish cooking was influenced by Arab styles and Ottoman gastronomy was itself based mainly on the Arab, Persian and Byzantine cooking. And you cannot always tell by the names, because Judeo-Spanish speakers gave everything a Judeo-Spanish name. But many dishes have obvious Iberian roots, like the fish pies called *empanadas,* the garlicky mayonnaise-type sauce called *ajada,* orange and almond cakes and little egg and almond pastries such as *marunchinos* and *almendrada,* the quince paste called *bimbriyo* (membrillo in Spain), and the sponge cake called *pan d'Espanya.*

The Jews adopted the kebabs, pilafs, milk puddings, and all the famous dishes which developed in the Sultans' court in Istanbul and which spread through the main cities of the empire. But most of their cooking is different enough for the Turkish food writer and gastronome Tugrul Savkay to ask why, after five hundred years, it has remained unknown to the general population.

One of the peculiarities of the cooking of the Jews of Turkey is a sauce made from sharp plums, called *avramila,* which came with a wave of Jewish immigrants from Georgia, who settled in Turkey. It is used in many dishes, especially with eggs and with fish. Among the many distinctive features of Sephardi cooking are their dairy dishes. Because the dietary laws forbade the eating of meat and dairy products at the same meal, it was usual to have a meat meal at lunch and a dairy one in the evening. These dishes – *almodrotes* (gratins), *fritadas* (omelettes) and stuffed vegetables – are combinations of vegetables such as spinach, courgettes, aubergines, leeks, pumpkins, peppers and tomatoes with cheese and egg. Some of their pies, like *borekas* and *borekitas* (half-moon turnovers), *tapadas* (large pies), and *bulemas* (coiled filo pastries), are different to the ones made by Turks, with different doughs, different shapes and different fillings. There are *borekas* stuffed with mashed aubergine and cheese or with *handrajo* – an aubergine, onion and tomato filling; *empanadas* filled with fish and walnuts, and *bulemas* and *tapadas* with cheese, spinach, aubergines, or pumpkin.

Another type of food that is unique to the Jews of Turkey is a range of meat balls called *albondigas* which are mixtures of meat and vegetables. One of the most popular is *rulos de berencena* – a meat ball rolled up in a slice of aubergine, cooked in tomato sauce. Some of their pasta dishes are different too, like *skulacha* - vermicelli fried then cooked in water or stock.

The Sephardim specialise in almond pastries, and marzipan made in the Spanish way. *Tishpishti* is a walnut Passover cake soaked in sugar syrup. *Uevos haminados,* hard-boiled eggs cooked for many hours with onion skins, acquiring creamy yolks and brownish whites, epitomise Sephardi food. Until about twenty years ago the Jews of Istanbul cooked everything - even hot meat dishes, in olive oil. Now that is considered heavy and old-fashioned and they have switched to sunflower oil.

The menu of the Symposium dinner at Saint Antony's College in 1996 was of Jewish dishes from Istanbul. Several of the recipes were from the book *Sefarad Yemekleri,* a collection put together by a group of women to raise money for an old peoples' home. I met the elderly ladies in Istanbul when they were preparing it. They had made little pies for me to taste. They talked to me in French and to each other in *Judesmo* (Judeo Spanish), which I could just about understand because my grandmother was from Istanbul. Their preface begins: 'Our ancestors who moved from Spain to this land five centuries ago, brought their traditions, their customs and their eating habits. Some of these eating habits are still being used.' They added, 'Our housewives are spending less time in their kitchens – our Sephardi way of cooking is slowly vanishing'. I am glad to say that it does live on in the new countries where the Jews of Turkey emigrated since the nineteenth century.

TARAMA
Fish roe cream

APYO
Celeriac and carrots in a sweet and sour lemon sauce

BOREKAS DE HANDRAJO
Little pies with aubergine, onion and tomato stuffing

* * * * *

HAMIM DE KASTANYA
Lamb with chestnuts

ALMODROTE DE BERENJENA
Aubergine gratin

ARROZ Y PINYONES
Rice with onions and pine nuts

SALATA VEDRE
Green salad

* * * * *

GATO DE NARANJA
Moist almond and orange cake with orange syrup

DATILES REYNADAS
Dates stuffed with a nut paste

HALVA DE BIMBRIO
Quince paste (Spanish *membrillo*)

Menu for the Symposium dinner
at St Antony's College, Saturday 7 September 1996.

BIBLIOGRAPHY

Much of the above material reflects research which I have been doing for a forthcoming book to be published by Alfred. A. Knopf in the USA in November under the title 'The Book of Jewish Food' and in the UK by Viking/Penguin in February 1997 perhaps under a different title.

Ashtor, Eliyahu. *The Jews of Moslem Spain.* JPS, 1973.

Baer, Yotzhak: *A History of the Jews in Christian Spain.* Philadelphia Jewish Publication, 1992.

Bolens, Lucie. *La cuisine andalouse, un art de vivre XIe - XIIIe siècle.* Albin Michel, Paris, 1990.

Cooper, John. *Eat and be Satisfied. A Social History of Jewish Food.* Jason Aronson, London, 1993.

Elazar, Daniel. *The Other Jews.* Basic Books, New York, 1989.

Haber, Barbara. *The Sephardi World, A Culinary Dispersal.* Talk given at an Oldways International Food Symposium in Spain,1992.

Israel, Steve. *The Story of the Jews in Spain. The Sephardi Diaspora.* Part of the Educational Kit of *Exile 1492 - The Expulsion of the Jews from Spain.* Ben Zvi Institute, Jerusalem, 1991.

Lewis, Bernard. *The Jews of Islam.* Routledge and Kegan Paul, 1984.

Nehama, Joseph. *Histoire des Israelites de Salonique.* Communauté Israelite de Thessalonique, 1935, 1978.

Perry, Charles. Annotated translation of *Kitab al Tabikh fil Maghrib wal Andalus.* In a Collection of Medieval and Renaissance Cookbooks. David Friedman and Betty Cook. Volume II, fifth edition 1992, Chicago.

Schwartz, Oded. *In Search of Plenty. A History of Jewish Food.* Kyle Cathie, London, 1992.

Stillman, Norman. *The Jews of Arab Lands: A History and Source Book.* Philadelphia, 1979.

Cookery books

Badi, Meri. *250 recettes de cuisine juive espagnole.* Jacques Grancher, Paris, 1984.

Benbassa Esther. *Cuisine judeo-espagnole.* Editions du Scribe, Paris, 1984.

Sefarad Yemekleri. Collected by Viki Koronyo and Sima Ovadia and printed by the Society of Assistance to Old People, Istanbul, 1985.

Stavroulakis, Nicholas. *Cookbook of the Jews of Greece.* Cadmus Press, N.Y., 1986.

'Messing about in boats', the York Chamberlains' Accounts, 1444-5

Ann Rycraft

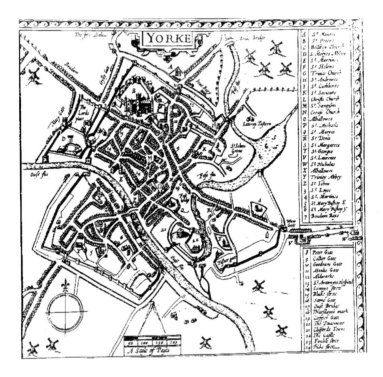

John Speed's map of York, 1610.

Throughout the middle ages, the city of York (Fig.1) depended on the river Ouse to maintain its position as an inland port; at the end of the fourteenth century, the city jurors described the river as 'a highway', used by merchants coming from the sea, up the Humber and the Ouse, to trade in York and thence elsewhere in the region. There were quays along both banks of the river, and a usually thriving merchant community. From time to time, however, the city's prosperity seemed insecure: then the city government, looking for a simple, domestic and quickly remedied cause, tended to blame difficulties of river passage. One of the causes of this was silting but another, in theory much more easily remedied, was the presence of traps for fish – 'fishgarths'.[1] These were wicker and wood constructions with nets, extending well into or right across the river.[2] During the mid-fifteenth century, the city council undertook what was to be a long-running legal dispute with St. Mary's Abbey, York, one of the chief offenders in the placing and maintaining of fishgarths. The case eventually reached the Privy Council, though its exact process, and the final result are not known. The conduct of such litigation was expensive and the city council, determined to have a favourable result, added to its costs by ostentatious entertaining of Lord Beaumont and others, who stayed at the Augustinian Friary in York for consultations about the case, and by generous gifts of food and wine to others concerned.[3] The council had to raise extra revenue in order to pursue the case and did so by taxing the city parishes. The officials responsible for finance were the three chamberlains, whose rolls of account, in Latin, survive (though many are damaged, and there are gaps in the series) from 1396-7. Two of these rolls, for 1444-5 and 1445-6, are concerned, not with general city finance, but with receipts and expenses concerning the case against St. Mary's, including accounts for four voyages, made by the mayor and others, down the river Ouse to inspect the fishgarths.[4]

These journeys were made, at unknown dates between 3 February 1444 and 3 February 1445, in a boat called 'le Barge', which either belonged to the city, or on which they had first call. There are various references to boats with this name (one was sent from York to Southampton for a muster in 1378 and arrived in such dilapidated condition that the mayor and bailliffs were commanded by royal writ to effect immediate repairs) but no evidence that they are the same; the name is probably generic – a flat-bottomed boat for river navigation – the type indeed, in which merchants' goods were transported between York and Selby (which was usually the limit of navigation for the larger sea-going ships). This 'Barge' needed new rivets, rudder and cover during the inspections (and an oar was broken, but apparently the rowers were responsible for their own), On the first voyage, there were two (certainly), and on the second, two (probably), small boats, which may have been no larger than rowing boats or skiffs.[5] The inspections were undertaken by an unknown number of persons – 'the mayor and other commissioners and legal experts'. Presumably the three chamberlains were among the commissioners, and the 'common clerk' (the salaried official responsible for keeping the City records), or a similar scribe, accompanied them. On the first and second inspections, the largest sums expended are to five and six persons, respectively, 'for their advice and work'; these were the 'legal experts'.[6] Fourteen (on the first and third inspections) and twelve (on the second) sailors worked 'le Barge' and the smaller boats; there were two or more cooks present, at least on the first and second journeys, and also, on the second 'servants'.[7] On the second outing the party was accompanied by Thomas Cuke, chaplain. The maximum number present, therefore, was probably about thirty persons.

The account for the first journey, to Blacktoft (near the confluence of the Ouse and the Trent, 43 miles down river from York, see fig. 2), starts with the purchase of food in York; the prices paid are given, but the quantities, as usual in medieval accounts, are not.[8] Bread (3s 4d), two dozen ale (3s 3d), wine (17d), meat (8s), three dozen pigeons (16d), wheat flour 'for baking of flour and for pigeons' (91/2d), spices (3s 2d) and some salt. If the flour bought for cooking was wheaten, then presumably the bread was fine white; city bakers, according to the 1301 ordinances, baked wastel, simnel and cocket bread, as well as the extra-fine pandemain (called 'mayne brede' in York). Ale was sold in York in the sealed gallon, pottle and quart; the quantity here is uncertain, as is the strength, strong or small: it is more expensive than the ale bought for Lord Beaumont and others staying at the Augustinian Friary, which cost just under 1s a dozen. The far greater cost of the ale than the wine is interesting, in view of repeated opinion that ale was the common, low-status, drink; this might reflect the composition of the group. The wine could possibly be an indication of the date of the journey; it might be the slightly better wine imported in spring or early summer, rather than the previous year's vintage, imported young the previous autumn and kept through the winter. Of course the quantity is not known: for a feast celebrated by the York Merchants Adventurers, probably in 1448, the wine cost 8d the gallon (though the Merchants were responsible for importing wine into the city; and on this occasion they were buying 211/4 gallons, so perhaps some quantity discount applied). The only definite prices for meat which can be compared to those here, are from a proclamation concerning the prices of birds and other victuals, made in Thursday Market at an unspecified date about the middle of the fifteenth century, according to which small pigs were to be sold for 4d each and pigeons for 5d the dozen. Six pigs (no size given) were bought for the Merchants' feast for 3s and forty-four pigeons for 2s 1d. The wheat flour, presumably intended for

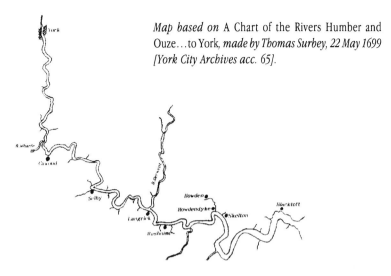

Map based on A Chart of the Rivers Humber and
Ouze…to York, *made by Thomas Surbey, 22 May 1699*
[York City Archives acc. 65].

pigeon pie, is an unknown quantity; the Merchants bought wheat at 4s the quarter and paid 4d for
grinding. The sum paid for spices is, of course, comparatively large. There are at least two sources
for the price of spices in mid-fifteenth century York; the Merchants' feast and the inventory of the
goods of Thomas Gryssop, chapman, made on 20 October 1446, after his death. He dealt in a large
variety of goods, including spices; one of his debts was for 30s 6d to a spicer in London.[9] Neither
can tell us on what the sum in the Chamberlains' accounts was actually spent, but both witness to
the variety of spices available in the city.

   The food bought in York might have been eaten before the voyage began; that a meal was
prepared on this day is indicated by payment to two cooks for five days work.[10] None of the accounts
mention any landing before Selby, and one hopes that the work in hand – 'examining the problems
caused by the fishgarths' – would take precedence over a water-borne picnic. However, calculating
when the party set out from York is almost impossible, since the time of year is unknown. Presumably
the journeys did not take place early in the year, when the days would be short, the weather possibly
bad and the river running high; the same reasons would exclude the late autumn. The boats would
need to have left York on the ebb tide, with enough time (probably about five hours, depending on
whether they were rowed or sailed, which is not stated) to reach Selby before dark; a journey which
would also have involved arriving at Barlby, just above Selby, on a tide suitable to negotiate the
notoriously difficult bend in the river below there. Drinking vessels were also bought in York,
presumably to be taken on the boats; each man would have a knife but need a drinking bowl or
goblet. The food itself may have been carried and only supplemented at the other stops; the prices
paid for victuals at the various stops could support this.

   The first night was spent at Selby, where horses were needed, either to land the party or to
convey them and any baggage the (very short) distance into the town. An alternative interpretation
of this part of the document is that most of the party were actually landed at Barlby (given the
difficulties of the river between there and Selby), crossed on the ferry there, with the horses being
used for the mile or so into Selby. At this time Selby was a busy port, with probably a little under a
thousand inhabitants. The account roll does not record where the mayor, commissioners, legal
persons and others stayed. There was an expenditure of 8s 7d (no individual prices are given) on
bread, ale, wine, meat and 'other foodstuffs', and payment to the cooks for preparing a meal. On
the following day, a light meal of bread, ale and meat, at a total cost of 4s 4d, was taken at Langrick
(probably an older, or local name for Long Drax); the account implies that the food was bought at
Langrick, though it is difficult to see how a hamlet could provide it with, presumably, no notice.

Bread, surely, would be a problem.[11] Perhaps the food came from the nearby Augustinian Priory at Drax (who had themselves, at an earlier date, caused problems with their own fishgarths). Another possible explanation could be that the mayor, Richard Bukden, a wealthy merchant and later a member of parliament for the city, or one of the chamberlains, Thomas Curtays, also a merchant and later a city sheriff, had actual property or trading connections along the river, either of which might be used for supplies. Thomas Curtays himself traded from Hull, and had some interests along the river, since he left legacies to the church at Riccall and to a woman in Barton on Humber.

The second night the party was at the hamlet of Blacktoft. This was at the point of the river beyond which the city claimed no jurisdiction; it was the focus of the journey and had to be reached. Here, 11s 10d was spent on bread, ale, wine, meat and other foodstuffs. In addition to wondering, as at Langrick, how food was actually acquired in such a place, there are now two other questions – where did the party spend the night, and how did the cooks prepare the meal? It is difficult to see how there would have been anywhere at Blacktoft, small, remote, surrounded by wetland, for even a smaller party to have stayed. No payment is recorded for accommodation, other than 'expenses' included in the sum of 11s 10d spent on food and drink. The payment to the cooks implies that they prepared a meal here; and the party had not eaten since the small meal at Langrick. So, presumably, the meat was cooked (though lack of wood here – and there is no mention of fuel being carried – would have made this difficult), and the party ate, and remained, in the open air: there are enough depictions of such meals being eaten at, for instance, both real and fictitious hunts, and also of food being cooked out of doors, to make this a real possibility.[12] Such eating might also, of course, have implications for the time of year when the expedition took place.

During the third day, the party returned to Selby, where they stayed for that night, sat in session on the following day, and stayed for the fourth night. 2s 8d was spent on fuel, candles and beds for these two nights, and the largest sum expended in this account, 34s 31/2d was spent in Selby on bread (16s 4d), ale, wine, beef and pork (8s), mutton and sucking pig (4s 6d), chickens, pigeons, five capons, fish (4s 3d), mustard, honey, eggs (141/2d) and cooking fat. There would have been no difficulty in obtaining this food and drink in a market town. The variety of it suggests a richness of meals, in contrast to the previous plain eating; composite dishes perhaps, rather than simple roast or boiled meat. The lack of either spices or salt in this list may indicate that those bought in York on the first day were still being used. The lack of game may indicate the time of year, or simply that this is not feasting; game features more prominently in the Merchant Adventurers' 1448 feast and also in the extravagant food provided by the city for those staying in the Augustinian Friary. The accounts for the latter also list the freshwater fish – pike, small salmon, trout, bream, perch, eels and lampreys – in contrast to the undifferentiated 'fish' which were bought in Selby for the mayor and party.

The second inspection of the fishgarths were undertaken by a slightly smaller party: the mayor and commissioners, twelve sailors and two 'mayor's cooks', who had not been paid in the previous account.[10] There were also mounted servants, probably three, who assisted with the work; possibly the banks were drier on this second excursion and the bankside ends of the traps could be investigated. The inspection also lasted a slightly shorter time, four days instead of five. Again they travelled in 'le Barge' and smaller boats, though this time they also hired a 'barge' as well. 14s 71/2d was spent in York on bread (2s), ale (3s), beef and mutton (5s 6d), 2 dozen pigeons (10d), a gallon, a pottle and three pints of red wine (181/2d), wheat flour for cooking pigeons (13d), salt and an ounce of saffron (8d); very similar to the purchases for the first journey.

The first night was again spent at Selby. This time, despite the smaller number present, more was spent on food than on the previous outward visit; 12s on bread, ale, meat and other foodstuff. The light meal on the next day was bought at Rusholme, a smaller hamlet than Langrick, and a little further from York. Here 3s 3d was spent on bread, ale, meat and other foodstuff, and again, one wonders how this food was obtained. They reached Blacktoft for the third night, apparently buying bread, ale, meat and other foodstuff there (11s 7d), this time for 'supper and breakfast'. They returned to Selby for the third night, and spent 13s 5d on the same food as at Rusholme and Blacktoft, in contrast to the return stay during the first inspection. However, fuel, candles and beds for the two nights at Selby cost 3s 7d, an increase on the 2s 8d spent on these on the previous visit.

For the third inspection legal advisors were again included, though the account does not record how many of them there were. The journey was shorter still, this time only three days, and the accounts are very short. There is no mention of sailors, cooks or servants. Again, food is bought in York; bread (2s 8d), ale, wine (4s 10d) and beef (2s). At Selby, on the first night, 13s 1d was spent on bread (20d), ale (2s 3d), meat and other foodstuff (9s 2d). The light meal on the second day was bought at Howden, which, being a small town, was a more likely place in which to be able to buy the bread (12d), ale (2s), fish, wine (2s 5d) and 'other foodstuff' than Langrick or Rusholme. The party stayed at Skelton, a village only two miles or so from Howden, on the second night, where they bought, for 3s 10 1/2d, the customary bread, ale and meat. There was presumably a lot of work to be done in this area, to account for the comparatively long time spent near Howden (unless the proximity of the town was itself the reason). On the third day the party returned to York, stopping only at Langrick to buy bread, ale and three geese.

The fourth inspection was the shortest, lasting only two and a half days and the accounts are the least informative. The mayor and commissioners made the inspection; fourteen sailors travelled, but there are no details of the boats, although 'le Barge' was presumably used, since a cover was bought for it. They were, as customary, at Selby on the first night, where they spent only 6s 4d on bread, ale and fish (not priced separately). The second night they were at Howden, buying bread, ale, meat and other foodstuff for 3s 5d. They returned to York on the third day, presumably in very favourable conditions, since this was the longest day's journey of all their inspections, and included the difficult passage north of Selby. They stopped only at Cawood, about a third of the way between Selby and York, to buy bread, ale, fish and 'other things' for the total – and large – sum of 10s 111/ 2d. It is possible that the length of this day is reflected in a payment which occurs only in this account, of 14s 31/2d to the sailors 'in addition to their meals'.

This description of the food purchased and the meals eaten during working journeys undertaken by the mayor of York and others in 1444-5 shows what can, or more accurately, what cannot be done with one record from one place. We know, from descriptions in both literary and historical sources and from collections of recipes both in manuscripts and in early printed books, quite a lot about the food, eating habits and cookery of the English royalty and gentry. At the other end of the social scale, we know something of the diet of labourers and of prisoners. The middle, especially the urban middle is, at the moment, all too often missing. Trying to find out more can be very frustrating: but information about provisioning, cooking and eating is now being extracted, recognised and made known; soon, perhaps, it will be possible to discuss daily meals as analytically as royal feasts. Meanwhile, we still do not know how exactly the mayor, chamberlains and company ate on the farthest extent of their river journeys; perhaps, as in the medieval poem:

> Yete I do you mo to witte
> The gees y-rosted on the spitte
> Fleeth to that abbey, God it wot,
> And gredeth, Gees, al hot, al hot,
> Hi bringeth garlek gret plentee
> The best y-dight that man may see.
> The laverokes that beeth couth
> Lighteth adown to mannes mouth
> Y-dight in stew ful swithe wel
> Powdred with gilofre and canel.[13]

The Chamberlains' Rolls are quoted with the permission of the York City Archivist. The Merchant Adventurers' Feast Account is quoted with the permission of the Governor of the Company of Merchant Adventurers of the City of York.

NOTES

[1] Known in other parts of the country as 'weirs'. The system often used was that a landowner could 'farm' (franchise) the rights to a local man; payment in an agreed amount of fish, with the 'fisher' retaining any excess. The fish caught on the Ouse were salmon and salmon fry, also trout, tench, roach and pike.

[2] As well as being an obstruction (particularly in summer), the fishgarths were a danger: for instance, on 25 June 1376, a ship, all merchandise and two Austin friars lost; on 22 September 1377, a ship, cargo and three men lost; on 26 July 1390, two ships fully laden with woollen cloth totally lost.

[3] For the accommodation of Lord Beaumont and others, for a month or less, the City provided a pipe of red wine costing £4.5s, meat including swans, heronsewes, pheasants, quails, and lapwings, and an extensive spice account – almonds, saffron, mace, sanders, sugar, cinnamon, raisins, honey, dates, and anise comfits. In London, the custodian of the Privy Seal was given a pike and a tench 'for his goodwill'; the Chief Justice of the King's Bench was given a swan, two herons and other, now illegible, items; and Lord Beaumont himself was given a tun and eight gallons of red wine, at a cost (including carriage and a sum for 'the selection of it') of £6.10.4d.

[4] York City Archives YC/F;C2:1, C2:3, C2:4; printed in Surtees Society vol.192, R.B. Dobson (ed) *York City Chamberlains' Rolls 1396-1500* (1980). These are final account rolls for audit; the less formal, and fuller, account books do not survive for this period.

[5] These small boats, and the horses which were used later, were possibly to allow the margins of the river to be closely examined.

[6] The City 'retained', for £1 per year, eight or so legal experts, to be called on when needed.

[7] In York (as in other cities) the medieval cooks are a difficult group to distinguish; their craft overlaps that of so many other victuallers – saucemakers, innholders, bakers, poulterers, fishmongers. In 1445, the whole Cooks Guild apparently numbered only sixteen men (one of whom, John Chaumbre, cooked or supervised the cooking for Lord Beaumont's party at the Augustinian Friary). They tried to maintain a monopoly of cooking for all feasts and for public eating but seem never to have been able to prevent 'wives of other craftsmen' from selling their products.

[8] The food, considering for whom it was being purchased, was probably bought at Thursday Market (by St. Sampson's church, M on Fig.1), where the Council was trying to concentrate retailing, rather than having food sold at Pavement Market (by All Saints Church, at 0), from 'windows' or hawked in the streets. (The two other city markets were for freshwater fish, on Foss Bridge, and for sea fish, on Ouse Bridge).

[9] For their feast c. 1448 [York Merchant Adventurers' Archives, Feast expenses 1] the Merchants paid, per pound, 10d for pepper, 20d for ginger and cinnamon, 2s 8d for mace and cloves, 16d for white sugar, 16d for annise comfits, 4d for dates, 6d for raisins, 12s for saffron, 4d for gum tragacanth and 5d for an unspecified quantity of saunders. These prices might perhaps be low, since it was the Merchants Company who imported the spices. In Gryssop's inventory, the values of the spices, per pound, are, 2s 6d for raisins, 2s 4d for cloves, 2s 8d for mace, 12 1/2d for galingale, 7d for pepper, 12d for saunders, 12d for ginger and cinnamon powder, 12d for sugar, 14d for cinnamon, 10d for cinnamon powder, 12s for saffron and 2s for cinnamon and saunders powder. These are values, not prices; they might be low, to keep down the value of the estate. Thomas Gryssop's – very uninformative – will was made on 4 October 1446 and proved on 7 October 1446; one of his executor's was John Shaw, cook [York Minster Library, Wills I, fol.260']. The inventory of his goods is printed, with some errors, in Surtees Society vol.45, *Testamenta Eboracensia III* (1845).

[10] The two cooks on the first journey were each paid 4d per day; no payment is made to cooks on any other journey except in the account for the second, when two 'mayor's cooks' were paid approximately 2d per day for 'helping with the preparation of food' on the first two journeys. The payments seem low: the three

cooks who worked at the Merchants' feast were paid 3s 2d between them, plus 5d in 'fees'; the spit-turners 8d; a woman 91/2d for scouring the pewter vessels and 'swilling'. Presumably these payments were for serving a larger number of people. In other part of this account, a London cook is paid 1s per day.

[11] Though there is a miniature in a mid-fifteenth century French manuscript of Dioscorides *De herbis* of a woman cooking unleavened bread in a large flat pan over an outdoor fire [Modena, Bibl. Estense ms.lat.993].

[12] For instance, in the mid-fourteenth century *Romance of Alexander* [Oxford, Bodleian Library, ms.Bodl.264] there are detailed foot-of-page depictions of both roasting on spits and boiling in a pot in the open air.

[13] 'I would also have you know that spit-roasted geese fly to that abbey – as God's my witness – crying "Hot geese, hot geese!" They bring plenty of garlic, the best prepared you'll see. Tasty larks, excellently cooked in a stew spiced with cloves and cinnamon come straight down into your mouth.' [London, British Library, ms.Harley 913]

Travel and Food in Afghanistan

Helen J. Saberi

Travel and food. The subject might have been specially devised for people who know Afghanistan. The interface there between the two things is complex and fascinating, partly because travel covers so many different experiences, most of them totally unfamiliar to people in the western world.

What I have tried to do in this paper is to describe travel first – the foods associated with it only make sense in this context – and then to discuss the foods which the various sorts of traveller might eat.

But first I must say that, although the subject is perfect for me, the timing is completely wrong. At present travel to or in Afghanistan is definitely out. There is no security for the people of Afghanistan, let alone the foreign traveller. Travelling from one city to another is virtually impossible. It is even difficult to travel from one part of Kabul to another. Mines litter the countryside and food is scarce. It is for this sad reason that the approach of this paper must be mainly historical.

Certainly there is no lack of history. Over the centuries travellers, merchants, pilgrims, conquerors and their armies have criss-crossed the mountains and the deserts of this rugged but strategic country, often facing tremendous hardships. A glance at the atlas is enough to explain why there have been so many travellers through Afghanistan. The country is situated literally at the crossroads of Asia – and I mean crossroads in the plural. It was crossroads of the ancient Silk Road which played a vital role in the exchange of food, plants, skills and knowledge. It was and is the cultural crossroads of four major cultural areas: Persia and the Middle East; Central Asia; the Indian sub-continent; and China and the Far East. Finally, its fate has been to be a crossroads of power: you name them, they've been there – Alexander the Great – Genghis Khan – the Moghul Babar – the Persian Nader Shah – the British in the nineteenth century and the Russians in the twentieth.

What Afghanistan has not yet become is a crossroads for tourism. There was a brief flowering with the hippie trail and some pioneer modern tourists in the 1960s and 70s – people who visited the beautiful sites of Afghanistan, often en route to exotic places such as India, Nepal, Tibet and overland to as far away as Australia.[1] But with the Russian invasion in 1980 opportunities for travel became severely restricted and unfortunately the situation has recently deteriorated even further, the whole country being now in the grip of a disastrous and destructive civil war.

One very important group of people who have been travellers – permanent travellers – in Afghanistan are the nomads, to whom I will return later. Finally, of course, there are the ordinary Afghan travellers visiting relatives, going on pilgrimages, etc.

Many problems have faced the traveller in Afghanistan. The terrain is rugged and often dangerous, the mountains are steep with high snowy passes, deep ravines and dizzy precipices, and the air is thin with little oxygen. The deserts are vast and are searingly hot and dry in the day; freezing cold at night. The climate elsewhere can also be extreme, unbearably hot in summer and freezing cold in winter. In spring the rivers flood causing bridges and roads to be swept away.

The method of travel can also be a problem. In the past, horses, donkeys and camels were used for transportation, journeys often taking weeks or months. More recently some main roads were built and travel can be by bus or car although even these journeys can be bumpy and uncomfortable off the beaten track. The buses or lorries in Afghanistan are amazing; they are often highly decorative and can be so overcrowded with travellers that people have to sit on the top or hang off the sides. On the steep hills or mountain areas the people have to get off and place wedges behind the wheels to stop them rolling back down the steep mountain passes. Dick Parsons, who travelled around Afghanistan in his quest to obtain beautiful rugs and carpets, gives a graphic description of travelling by lorry in his book about the carpets of Afghanistan:

> These much used lorries operate from a designated staging point, usually a tea house near the entrance of a town or village. Here the passenger is enticed or bullied by a *dallal* (broker) or the *kleenah*. As the name suggests, the *kleenah* keeps the vehicle clean, but is also the driver's apprentice. He stands just below the tailboard, clinging onto the lorry's superstructure, ever ready to jump down and place a wooden chock under a rear wheel should an incline prove too steep for the overladen lorry.
>
> Passengers are seated on benches facing each other; the overflow squat on the floor filling every space available. As the lorry lurches over culverts, rocks and dried river beds, the passengers sway and pitch in rhythm, protecting their faces with the ends of their turbans or as best they can from the blast of fine dust that envelops them each time two lorries pass each other, and may Providence keep you from a following wind! Another hazard of such a trip is the unforeseeable risk of the seasick traveller. Many a disaster has occurred in the packed interior of a lorry, with the poor victim unable to extricate himself in time. He is sometimes punished by being made to spend the rest of the trip standing on a foot-step at the outside of the truck, hanging on for dear life. The more fastidious drivers, before starting up, will demand of the prospective passengers: 'Are there any *istefragis* among you?' literally, 'any thrower-ups'. If a shamefaced man comes forward, he is made to sit at the very end of the lorry facing the open void.[2]

Many travellers take their livestock with them and one can imagine the squawking and cacophony as the bus clatters and bumps along on its journey. In many parts where there is no real road, perhaps just a track, sturdier vehicles are required, such as a landrover, or one has to resort to two feet or at best a sturdy donkey.

Despite all these hardships travelling in Afghanistan can be a great pleasure and an unforgettable experience. The scenery, though stark in many places, has a special beauty: the snow-capped mountains contrasting with the brilliant blue skies, the colour of lapis lazuli; the bright sunshine and the lush green valleys; the friendliness and hospitality of the people have all beckoned the traveller. The journeys are exciting and different. Travelling in Afghanistan has always been an adventure.

Travellers, who are called *musafer*, are usually given special treatment in Afghanistan. For example Muslim travellers are exempt from fasting during the month of Ramazan. (They are not, however, exempt from praying and it was a common sight for travellers to see a bus stopped and a row of people facing the setting sun and praying by the roadside.) As noted above, journeys were not without hazards or dangers, even for the Afghan traveller going on a pilgrimage or visiting relatives in a far off town. There was no telephone or reliable postal service and loved ones would perhaps be gone for a long time and perhaps might never return! So, when a traveller was setting off from his home the custom or tradition was that a member of his family would pour water behind him. This, it was believed, and still is, would ensure his safe home-coming.[3]

One tradition I remember very well, and one which my mother-in-law insisted on whenever my husband and I returned from travelling, was the burning of grains of wild rue (*esfand*). She would burn them with hot charcoal and the sweet-smelling smoke would be carried from room to room to freshen and sweeten the air and, superstitition has it, ward off any evil spirits which we might have inadvertently brought back with us.[4]

Caravanserai

In the past most travellers would travel for safety in a 'caravan' and each night would break their journey to rest at a *caravanserai*. (Caravan comes from the Persian word *karwan* which means a convoy of travellers. Our word 'caravan' [a wheeled conveyance for travellers] derives from this. *Serai* is again a Persian word and means 'a place enclosed by walls', thus a caravanserai is a place for the reception of caravans…) It is a pity that most *caravanserai* have crumbled to ruins (even before the Russian invasion and present disastrous civil war). Strategically placed along the trade routes or between the main towns and cities and at a distance of one day's journey to ensure the caravans arrived by sunset, they used to provide warmth, food and shelter for the weary travellers, their animals and their merchandise on their long and arduous journeys and giving a safe haven from possible attack by wolves (mainly in the winter) or the occasional marauding bandits. And they were romantic and picturesque.

Nancy Dupree in *An Historical Guide to Afghanistan* (1977) describes a stay at a *caravanserai* which was still operating in the 1970s in the north of Afghanistan:

> Should you wish to experience life in a caravanserai, you may stop for the night at the village of Atin Jalao…From the guest rooms on the second floor, you watch the busy activity of settling in the horses for the night in the stables directly below you. When all is ready the big gateway is closed and bolted and small groups of men gather around trays of pilau and tea to swap stories about the day on the trail. Outside, there is a vast stillness. When the nomads are on the move, this silence intensifies all the little noises made by thousands of resting sheep and the sudden shrill cries of their shepherds bounce from hill to hill. They keep each other alert this way, and hopefully persuade the wolves to stay beyond their flocks.[5]

Caravanserai were usually built of mud walls surrounding a courtyard where the animals could be tethered and around which were rooms for lodging and storage purposes. The resthouse attendant, called a *seraiwan*, provided water for the animals and fodder for a small fee. Extra money was earned by selling the droppings of the animals left in his care. Droppings, which were dried and formed into cakes, were also sometimes used as fuel for cooking and the smoke served the added purpose of driving away insects and mosquitos, although the preferred fuel was charcoal or wood.[6]

It is at this point ('At last!' someone will say) that I get down to the main subject of food. Caravaneers had a restricted diet while travelling. Two meals a day – morning and evening, so that they do not interrupt the slow progress of the camels. In the morning they would probably eat *nan* (bread) with *chai* (tea), often purchased fresh from the *chaikhana* (tea house), which would be attached to or part of the *caravanserai*. In the evening they would have a more substantial meal either prepared with their own 'travel food' and provisions or purchased from the *chaikhana*. Pilaus or *aush* might be prepared. *Aush* which is a noodle-type soup, would be made with dried noodles and *quroot* (a strained, salted and dried yoghurt which is formed into hard round balls resembling greyish/white pebbles) which is reconstituted with water when required for cooking. Another simple dish which might be prepared is *qurooti*. *Quroot* is reconstituted and added to boiling *roghan-e-dumbah* (rendered fat from the tail of the fat-tailed sheep) and hunks of *nan* added to the mixture. If available, garlic and mint would be thrown in for extra flavour.

Perhaps they would finish their meal with some dried fruit, such as green or red raisins called *kishmish sabz* and *kishmish surkh* respectively and nuts such as almonds (*badam*), walnuts (*charmaghz*), pistachios (*pistah*) and pine nuts (*jalghoza*). Dried fruits and nuts are a very convenient travel food because they are easy to carry and provide quick sustenance and energy. They are often tied in the end of turban cloths of travellers.

Mulberries, which are highly nutritious, also abound in Afghanistan and in summer the fresh fruit is spread out to dry, usually on the flat roofs of the mud-brick houses. Sometimes the dried fruit is mixed with ground walnuts into a combination called *chakida*. *Talkhan* is another dried mulberry preparation and Nancy Dupree describes *talkhan* as dried berries ground 'and made into hard bars called *talkhan* which is such a nutritious concentrate that a villager can go on a week's journey with no other food except a few bars of *talkhan* tucked into his cummerband. All he needs is water.'[7]

In thinking about foods such as *talkhan* one must remember that there are no hard and fast dividing lines twixt travel and ordinary household foods in Afghanistan. Food is often scarce and Afghans have devised many ways of preserving their food, not just for travelling. Aitchison in *Notes on Products of Western Afghanistan and North-Eastern Persia* (1890) also remarks:

> The dried fruit, *tut-i-maghz*, is met with in every household, for eating as a relish with their ordinary bread diet, or it is made into flour, *talkhan*, to be mixed with corn-flour and baked into bread, ...[8]

Another dried fruit which is a popular travel food and which is also described by Aitchison is the *sinjed*, which, he says, has been nicknamed the 'caravan date' because of its popularity and usefulness on long journeys:

> The fruit of the indigenous Elaeagnus and of the Jujube cannot be distinguished from the cultivated forms except by size; these are chiefly carried and eaten on journeys, hence one of the names for the fruit of the Elaeagnus, 'Caravan-dates.'[9]

In another passage Aitchison gives a most unflattering description (with which I entirely agree) of this fruit: 'Much cultivated in orchards for its fruit, which to a European palate does not seem worth eating, to me resembling in the mouth a mixture of dry cotton wool with ashes.'[10] The jujube (*Zizyphus vulgaris*) known as *anab* in Afghanistan is another useful fruit for journeys. Aitchison tells us that

> it is cultivated in all orchards... for its fruit, which is largely eaten by the natives, especially on journeys, in the same way as the fruit of the Elaeagnus, and this may account for the spread of the tree throughout the whole of Asia, wherever caravan journeys were made....[11]

Yet another food described by Aitchison, which is in common use by travellers as a convenience food, is called '*kulcha*'. *Kulcha* has the general meaning of biscuit in Afghanistan but this is a special kind of '*kulcha*' made from yellow split peas. The split peas which are called *dal nakhud* in Persian, are roasted and mixed with sugar and butter.[12]

I have linked the foods I have just been describing to the *caravanserai*, but I should say that any travellers could use the same foods and I should repeat that anyway the *caravanserai* no longer

Sherwa-e-chainaki *(teapot soup)*.

exist. The long trade caravans no longer traverse Afghanistan. Fortunately, as the *caravanserai* crumbled into ruins, another traditional Afghan institution for travellers, the *chaikhana*, has survived and travellers would break their long, arduous journeys by stopping at them.[13]

Chaikhana

Chaikhana (literally, 'tea houses') provide all the basic requirements needed by the travellers, although the type and standard of *chaikhana* can vary considerably. Some are very basic and serve only tea, either green or black, from a constantly boiling samovar (tea urn). The larger *chaikhana* can be quite luxurious – with tables and chairs, and the mud floor covered with the beautiful red traditional carpets and rugs of Afghanistan. They provide not only meals but accommodation which is usually quite basic consisting of a 'guest' room which is shared by all those planning to stay the night. The *chaikhana* itself often accommodates any overflow of travellers who may have been cut off by bad weather, such as snow storms or flash floods etc. Most travellers will have brought their own *liaf* (like a duvet) or bedding which is unrolled but the owner of the *chaikhana* will provide a *toshak* (a thin cotton-filled mattress), and maybe even a *bolesht* (pillow).

Before ordering his refreshments the traveller may be brought a *haftawa-wa-lagan*, a bowl and pitcher containing water, to wash his hands. Apart from the ubiquitous tea, most of the larger *chaikhana* can provide a basic breakfast of *nan* and tea with perhaps some fried eggs. The tea may be *sheer chai* (tea with milk) which is quite popular for breakfast. For lunch various dishes may be available depending on the local specialities of the region. A *sherwa* (soup) or *aush* (a noodle soup with yoghurt) will probably be on the menu served perhaps with a kebab such as the fiery hot and spicy *chappli* kebab (a minced meat kebab which is mixed with *gandana* [Chinese chives] and hot spices and made into a shape like a sandal – *chappli* means sandal – before being fried in oil).

The most traditional food served at a chaikhana is *sherwa-e-chainaki*, which means teapot soup. This soup is made, as the name implies, literally in a teapot! The soup ingredients, lamb, onions, a little salt, perhaps some split peas and perhaps a little coriander for added flavour are all put into the teapot with water and the whole teapot is then placed among the hot embers from either a charcoal brazier used for grilling kebabs or from the fire of the boiling samovar. This soup is usually made early in the morning and then left to simmer slowly among the burning embers. When the traveller orders his soup, he is served with the teapot, containing the soup, a bowl and one large *nan*. He then breaks up some of the bread into pieces and adds them to the bowl. The soup is poured over the bread. The bread soaks up the juices of the soup which are then scooped

*A chaikhana
(tea house)*

up by hand or with a spoon. The chunks of lamb meat are usually eaten last with the remaining bread.

The main service of the *chaikhana* is, however, as its name indicates, to serve tea and this will always be served at the end of the meal. Each customer will have his own individual teapot plus a small bowl for dregs. When the tea is served the traveller will first rinse out his small glass tumbler (or little Chinese-type tea bowl) with the hot tea. Sugar will then be added (usually quite a lot, although this is charged extra) and then the fresh hot tea added.[14]

Nomads

The nomads who have criss-crossed the mountains and deserts of Afghanistan for as long as anyone can remember do not stay at *caravanserai* or *chaikhana*. They migrate with their livestock and other worldly belongings from winter to summer camp or vice versa, setting up camp each evening until they reach their destination, often living in extreme and harsh conditions. They are sometimes called *kuchis*; the word comes from the Persian word meaning belongings, *kuch* meaning belonging; it can also mean leaving – leaving one dwelling place for another.

Nomadic life in Afghanistan is extremely complicated, too much so for a detailed description here. But I will sketch out their lifestyle and discuss their food. According to Louis Dupree (1973) about two million Afghans remain nomadic or semi-nomadic.[15] Generally speaking the nomads fall into three main groups: Pushtun, Baluch and Kirghiz.

Pushtuns generally speaking live in the south and south-eastern part of Afghanistan and since time immemorial have been moving their flocks from the summer pastures on the high plateaux of the Hindu Kush to winter quarters on the river banks often as far as the Indus in Pakistan. Continual search for water and food for their animals is of utmost importance. They live in tents called *khaima-e-sia* (black tents) which are quite distinctive and which many people have likened to black bats. Sabrina and Roland Michaud in their book *Afghanistan* describe a Pushtun nomads' camp:

> A Pathan camp set up during migration is a memorable sight. At dawn, wisps of blue smoke rise from the conglomeration of black tents resembling bats – the Persians call them leather butterflies – that hug the dun-colored hills. Around the camp slender, supple women with a wild beauty and warm laughter walk barefoot, their features masked by mysterious tatoos, heavy silver ornaments around their necks, their red dresses billowing out in the wind.
>
> When the camp is struck, the tribe starts marching slowly and inexorably through a breathtaking landscape under starry summer skies, the cavalcade accompanied by the baaing of sheep and the bleating of goats mingled with the curious roar of camels and the barking of dogs.[16]

The Baluch nomads, who generally live in the very dry southern part of Afghanistan spend only part of each year in their villages on the river banks cultivating meagre plots which hug the irrigation ditches.[17] In spring they abandon their villages and set up camp at the base of mountains. The Baluch also live in tents similar to those used by the Pathan nomads.

The nomads who live north of the Hindu Kush, for example the Kirghiz and Turkomen, live in circular felt tents of the Turko-Mongolian peoples, usually called yurts (pronounced *uii* by the Kirghiz). The Kirghiz live in the high mountains of the Pamirs and their style of life is quite different from their nomadic cousins, the Pathans and the Baluch.

The size of a nomad group varies considerably but most own their own camels, donkeys, horses, dogs, sheep and goats. The camels and donkeys are the beasts of burden and are used to carry the tents and storage boxes called *sanduq* with all the household things – cooking pans, pots, *tawa*, bedding etc. Sometimes they carry small lambs, kids or chickens which sway in panniers tied onto the camels' backs. Children also often ride on the camels when they are tired, but most of the time the nomads walk alongside with their huge, ferocious guard dogs called *sag-e-ramah* (literally meaning dog of the flocks).

The type of food the nomads eat depends a lot on their environment and the time of the year. It is safe to say, though, that the diet of a nomad, wherever they may be, is usually quite limited and that life is very hard, especially for the women. (The women put up the tents when they set up camp, they bake the bread, milk the goats and sheep, make the dairy products, do the cooking and in the evenings spin and weave.) The staple foods for most nomads are bread and dairy products. The sheep and goats furnish the milk for making butter (*maska*), cheese (*panir*), yoghurt (*mast*), strained yoghurt (*chaka*), (*quroot*) etc. (*Quroot* is often the only milk-based food of the Kirghiz in winter.) They often barter dairy products in exchange for grain and luxury products such as tea, sugar and salt. Sabrina Michaud, in *Caravans to Tartary*, says that,

> Tea is worth so much that each camel driver carries it about his person in a beautifully embroidered little bag, which is cautiously produced to put tea in the kettle. Sugar is so precious that tea is drunk with salt not sugar, and salt is so scarce that it is only used in tea...[18]

Aitchison describes how the nomads make their butter:

> The ordinary method of making butter amongst the nomads is by putting freshly warmed milk into a leathern skin, adding to it some sour butter milk, a little water, and then hanging the skin on a tripod over a light fire just hot enough to prevent the warmed milk from losing its temperature; the milk is now churned by swinging the skin backwards and forwards by pulling on a piece of string. The butter is here usually called *maska*, the fresh butter milk *dogh*. The butter to enable it to keep and allow of exportation is clarified; it is then called *roghan-i-zard*, or the Hindustani term *ghi* may be employed by the traders.[19]

Cheese (*panir*) is usually made by using rennet to curdle the milk. Different cheeses are produced. The most basic one is called *panir-e-khom* or *panir-e-tazah* (*khom* means raw, *tazah* means fresh). To make this cheese most of the cream is skimmed off the milk before curdling takes place. The curds are drained in a cloth and the cheese left to harden for a day or two. It is this cheese which is brought to the cities by the nomads in the spring and sold in the bazaars on green leaves, accompanied by red raisins (*kishmish surkh*). This popular and traditional spring treat is known as *kishmish panir*.

Another type of cheese made by the nomads is *panir-e-shour* (*shour* meaning salty). This keeps for much longer as salt is added before all the whey has drained off, and is stored in a pottery container. *Panir-e-aushawi* or *panir-e-roghani* (*roghani* means oily or fatty) is a richer, creamier cheese. It is is formed into round 'cakes' of about 2 inches in diameter and about 1/2 inch thick. It is not salted and my husband tells me that it is dried to a consistency rather like cheddar.

The bread the nomads bake is also often very basic and unleavened. The Pashtun nomads make a kind of chapati bread called *nan-e-tawa* or *tawagi*. A dough is made from flour and water which is then slapped on to the portable *tawa* (a curved cast iron plate) which is heated underneath. The most primitive bread can be made by slapping bread dough on to large stones which have been previously heated. Kirghiz nomads also make a special bread for their journeys which keeps for months. Sabrina Michaud in recounting her travels, wrote in *Caravans to Tartary*: 'The secret is to work fat into the dough so as to make a kind of shortbread, not unlike ship's biscuit.'[20]

The sheep and goats also provide the meat which is only eaten as a luxury by the nomads, the animals being kept mainly for their valuable milk which is made into various dairy products mentioned above. When an animal is killed the meat is often dried for use when travelling or for when food may be scarce.

Dried meat, called *gosht-e-qagh*, is not only made as a kind of convenient travel food for nomads and travellers but it is also made all over Afghanistan, usually during the summer months when meat is plentiful, for use in the winter when food is scarce. The fresh meat is sprinkled first with salt, then with powdered asafoetida.[21] It is then left to dry in the hot summer sun. This process helps prevent the meat from deteriorating or 'going off'. When required for cooking the dried meat is first soaked in water and then rinsed to remove the salt and asafoetida. Another type of dried meat is also prepared called *landi*. This is usually prepared at the end of the autumn. A fat sheep is slaughtered and the wool sheared off, leaving the skin with a thick layer of fat underneath. The carcase is then hung to dry. A special pilau is prepared from this meat called *landi pilau*. The sheep and goats also provide the wool, and goat hair is used for making the felt for the yurts. These items are also traded for other foods such as grains, vegetables, fruits and nuts.

Nomads use their environment, even if it is a very temporary one, to their full advantage. They collect plants and roots from the surrounding countryside. One such plant is the liquorice plant called *mahk* which grows abundantly in Afghanistan.[22] There is a kind of symbiotic relationship between the nomads and the landowners/farmers. The farmers benefit from the dung left behind by their animals.

I don't want to close this essay with an image of nomads scrabbling about in the parched soil for liquorice roots or handing pats of dung to farmers. So, if I may, I will end with a personal reminiscence.

I travelled quite a bit in Afghanistan. Not 'rough' (by donkey, horse or camel) but we did eat at the local *chaikhana* whenever possible, buying melons or grapes along the roadside when we could. And our journeys have left me with some wonderful memories – as when we travelled as a large group, a sort of caravan, if you like, to the Panjshir valley. We were given freshly caught fish, called *sheer mahi*, from the Panjshir river, which was fried, and then eaten while we were lazing in the shade under the apricot trees. Breakfast was *nan* straight from the tandoor with fresh *qymaq* and followed by the inevitable but deliciously sweet green tea...bliss. This is the picture I would like to leave with you.

Buying melons by the roadside.

REFERENCES

[1] Places to visit included the Buddhas at Bamian, the Lakes at Band-i-meer, the Mosque at Mazar-e-Sharif, the Mosque and minarets at herat, Balkh, the Hindu Kush mountains ..... the list is endless.

[2] R D Parsons, *Oriental Rugs*, Volume 3, 'The Carpets of Afghanistan', Woodbridge, Suffolk, 1983, p 23.

[3] The significance of this is that water is a scarce and valuable commodity in Afghanistan. Furthermore, when the traveller had gone on his way, friends, relatives and neighbours would call on or greet the family of the traveller and wish them '*Joy-esh sabz bosha*', which means 'may his place be green'. In other words, let him return to a prosperous and healthy home.

[4] Dr J E T Aitchison in *Notes on the Products of Western Afghanistan and North-Eastern Persia*, Edinburgh, 1890, p 149, describes the wild rue of Afghanistan as follows: 'The wild rue, *barmal, isphathan, ispand, isfand, spand, spandan, spanj, spangaoli, spinguli*. This shrub was common over the whole country traversed up to an altitude of 4000 feet. The natives employ it in medicine, as it is supposed to be efficacious in many diseases. On the occurrence of an epidemic, as cholera, they collect it in heaps and burn it through the villages; they consider it drives away evil spirits...' I also noticed recently that a similar tradition is carried out in Ethiopia.

[5] Nancy Hatch Dupree, *An Historical Guide to Afghanistan*, Kabul, 1973, p 422.

[6] Roland and Sabrina Michaud, *Caravans to Tartary*, London, 1978.

[7] Nancy Hatch Dupree, p 116.

[8] Aitchison, p 135.

[9] Aitchison, p 83.

[10] Aitchison, p 63.

[11] Aitchison, p 224. On all these fruits see Philip Iddison, 'Azarole, Oleaster and Jujube' in *PPC 48*.

[12] Aitchison, p 41.

[13] In the 1950s, 60s and 70s a number of modern hotels were built, especially in the main cities. The type of food served was similar to that of the *chaikhana*.

[14] For more detail, see my paper 'Public Eating in Afghanistan', in *Public Eating – Oxford Symposium Documents 1991*, pp 258-9.

[15] Louis Dupree, *Afghanistan*, Princeton, New Jersey, 1973, p 164. It is very difficult to know just what the population of Afghanistan is, or was, especially with regard to the nomadic population. A demographic survey was carried out by the State University of New York (SUNY) in the 1970s but as far as I know it was never completed; and since the Russian invasion of 1980 the situation has been further complicated by the movement of internal and external refugees.

[16] Roland and Sabrina Michaud, *Afghanistan*, London, 1980, p 17.

[17] Irrigation ditches are called *jui* in Afghanistan. These are channels of water re-directed from streams or rivers to water crops etc. Other water channels called *kareze* or *qanat*, are underground water tunnels connecting 'wells' or shafts intercepting the water table. (This ancient underground system brings the valuable water to the surface for use in irrigation.)

[18] Michaud, 1978.

[19] Aitchison, p 29.

[20] Michaud, 1978.

[21] See my paper 'Rosewater, The Flavouring of Venus, Goddess of Love, and Asafoetida, Devil's Dung', in *Spicing up the Palate – Oxford Symposium Documents, 1992*, p 232.

[22] Aitchison, p.89.

Tin Plates and Silver Christening Mugs:
Travels with Madame Gary

Alice Wooledge Salmon

Her experience and writing are filled with adventure and nuance. For instance:

> More Gypsies squatted along the kerb selling huge bunches of flowers, and rugs – the celebrated Bessarabian Aubusson which are just as bright and bunched with flowers as the Gypsies' baskets. I have longed for such rugs all my life – but there, confronted at last by them, we were also confronted by problems of inflation, exchange, devaluation.... Was it an astronomic price, or given away? No one was able to face such intricacies. The menu was problem enough. So I retired beaten to the restaurant kitchen, where...over all, as over all Bucharest, challenging and conquering the blasts from the ovens, hung that heady, drenching perfume, combination of expensive French scents and cheap local essences, hair oil, and the make-up which was the most striking aspect of the crowds swarming about their nocturnal business. Just as, in the Midi, an overpowering blast of garlic...strikes the newcomer as being the very essence of the land, so, in Bucharest, it was this heady perfume, exhaled by not only the more seductive female passers-by, but by trim, richly-medalled officers, coachmen, and policemen too; all of them swam in musk and patchouli and *violette de parme*. The cook, who mopped his brow with a cotton handkerchief reeking of attar of roses, gave me several recipes.[1]

And:

> *Ashe* is Persia's basic soup, a thick mixture of every imaginable vegetable, and often accompanied by *köfte* – meat balls – heavily spiced and marble sized. I came to know *ashe* well, when staying in the province of Mazanderan in a house beside the curiously sullen, greyish waters of the Caspian. There winter comes down early. An incessant fine damp mist swirled mysteriously through the lush groves of orange and mulberry trees, and then *ashe* came into its own. We consumed it beside a fire of scented apple boughs, and as the autumnal gales tore round the wood-tiled roof, blowing straight in from the Russian steppes northwards across the Caspian, our appetites were keen. In that house, the cook, a gifted boy from the region, finding us enthusiastic, offered us a different kind of *ashe* each of the six days we lingered there.[2]

And also:

> A curtain which divided the room was now drawn back and the Professor's sister was revealed in the manner of a conjurer's assistant, beside a table piled with surprises. The immemorial samovar dominated an array of cakes, *piroshki*, pies and fancy breads, while there were seven kinds of jam – 'home made' from special Siberian berries, *brousnika*, *smorodina*, *rassetki* and such.
>
> 'All must be tasted,' said the Professor, as I began this agreeable experiment, to the evident satisfaction of his sister.... While she filled and refilled our glasses of tea and the samovar puffed and hummed, the Professor and I continued talking with our mouths full; he, waving his glass of tea dangerously to emphasize a point or using a spoon as a

'book-marker'. When at last I was torn away by the exhausted interpreter I realized I had been the recipient of an entire academic address, delivered to, and for, myself alone. Coming down to earth after this heady triumph, I found the Professor's sister pressing a pot of the *brousnika* jam into my hand, while he presented me with one of his own books on Siberia.[3]

This is a woman who has lived for nearly ninety years, her earliest memory the thud of her head against the nursery floor where she beat it in frustration 'because I couldn't get my way', her latest achievement the restoration of a burnt-out home in the South of France and the formidable rewriting of a flame-lost autobiography. The latter is bound to be opulent, and tough; suffused with curiosity; brimming with hungers both literal and scholarly; well-laced with humour and sharp-eyed, fine-nosed affection for life's incongruities – in the spirit, to be certain, of these passages quoted from three earlier volumes.

The author is also a fair-skinned beauty, heavily scented with jasmine; a fatal English *femme* with a warm and commanding manner, her voice polished and not of the current era, her elegant mode what my mother would have called, without undue censure, 'bohemian'. Of ten published books, the most instantly linked with her name is the first, *The Wilder Shores of Love*, a luxuriant account of four European women who 'found…glowing horizons of emotion and daring' in nineteenth-century North Africa and the Near East. A multi-translated best-seller, it has stayed in print for forty-two years and added a phrase to the English language.

What remains, for me, her most *sympathique* work – *Journey into the Mind's Eye* – spins the tale of her fascination with Russia and Russians, conceived at the age of four, while the author's *tour de force* – 'the book I was meant to do in my life' – is a scintillating chronicle of the nineteenth-century Murid Wars, the decades of Muslim resistance to Russian domination of the Caucasus, led and personified by one extraordinary figure, the Imam Shamyl, 'lion of Daghestan'. The name of this volume – arguably a masterpiece – is *The Sabres of Paradise*, and the author of all is Lesley Blanch.

Blanch devotees (who abound throughout the world) are uncommonly partial to her characteristic rendition of life, travel, and history with vibrant, engaging atmosphere – a distinctive synergy of subject (well-researched or intensely-lived), imaginative *élan*, and the penetration of an empathetic mind. The subjects are unusual and almost always exotic: the French Orientalist Pierre Loti; Queen Marie of Romania; Russia's Dekabristi rebels; a neglected harem in Tunisia; the feel of Bulgaria, post World War II. Sentences cascade, names drop, the prose is frequently florid; the involvement is contagious and at all times genuine.

Born in Chiswick, London, to 'unconventional' and cultivated parents who, like herself, rarely 'suffer[ed] fools', Lesley Blanch was educated by wide and promiscuous reading, the influence of her parents' friends and her father's taste for museums, a stint among the pupils at St. Paul's, trips to France and Italy, attendance at The Slade School of Fine Art, where Rex Whistler and Oliver Messel were two of her contemporaries. 'I was,' she says, 'always very aware of other horizons.'

Obliged to earn a living at a period when women of her background generally did not do so, she illustrated and drew, became a journalist, and joined British *Vogue* where, before and during the second World War, she worked as Features Editor, covering 'everything *except* fashion', acquiring and shedding at least one husband *en route*. In 1932, she visited the USSR on the first of many journeys to as much as possible of '"All the Russias" that were the landscape of my heart.'

In 1945, she married the naturalized Free Frenchman, Romain Gary (né Kacew, 'somewhere in Russia; he changed his birthplace according to his mood'), one of numerous fabled and temperamental versions of the tinselled *bel homme* – as fond as she of the grand gesture – for whom Lesley Blanch has had an explosive and lifelong penchant, both incarnate and historical. With Gary, a diplomat and writer (two eventual Prix Goncourt), she lived in Paris, Liguria, and 'en poste' in Sofia, Berne, New York, and Los Angeles, while starting to journey in earnest.

'I've rather hopped on some trains in my time,' she reflects. And steamers across the Bosphorus, lorries through Afghanistan, any form of available transport to wherever she was able around Mexico and the American Southwest, Egypt, the Balkans, Persia, North Africa, the Caucasus, Turkey, the Uzbek cities of Central Asia, the Yemen, India, and beyond.

She tended to 'travel heavy', and largely alone, with 'creature comforts', an ikon, a silver miscellany of christening mugs from which to drink 'in remote areas', and a great deal of knowledge absorbed from extensive and disciplined reading of history, literature, nineteenth-century travel writing, old guidebooks, and memoirs. From the 1930s to the 1980s, she liked to move about unplanned, savoured the unexpected circumstance, the juxtaposition of kebabs, tin plates, and licked fingers 'along the road' with digging out portable splendour and dining the next evening, much admired and listened-to, at a particularly good embassy.

Others have travelled with high romance and shades of grandeur, or roughed it comprehensively; no one has done so with quite the Blanch amalgam of unapologetic nineteenth-century style and modern self-reliance, or reached so effectively certain places of twentieth-century ferment before they became, as now, tragically inaccessible or banally open to all.

Though long divorced from Romain Gary, who died in 1980, she is frequently known as Madame Gary; 'in France,' she observes with a sparkle of malice, 'it improves my place at table'. But what's *on* the table or the picnic rug, what's served beneath the tent or sold round the corner from the spice-redolent alley has always been paramount for its own sake – 'All my life I have liked to eat well' – and, as often as not, for the 'centuries of history, travel, exploration, and adventure behind each dish'. Not to mention – as in Bucharest, Persia, and at tea in Siberia – an overwhelming presence of the *genius loci*.

Blessed with resistant digestion rarely disrupted – and then put right by a brief but exclusive regime of 'raw green apples, peeled ... grated' and escorted by 'very weak tea' – Lesley Blanch has steadily tucked in with gusto, 'relished both fat and lean', and vividly conveyed the experience – by inference, circumstance, and often, so little direct description as to suggest magic – as native to the human and topographical drama at which this writer excels.

She has published two what I'll call cook-ish travel books – *Round the World in 80 Dishes* (1955), and *From Wilder Shores* (1989) – whose largely summary recipes are the least generally interesting, least reliable aspect of what Lesley Blanch herself calls, in the latter instance, 'a sketch book ... for those who fiddle around, have had a little basic experience, enjoy experimenting and ...cooking as much as eating and travelling.' Dishes like *moussaka*, *brandade* of salt cod, Swiss fondue, Hungarian 'goulash', mushroom *risotto*, aubergine 'caviar', various kinds of *dolmas*, or yoghurt and cucumber soup, which 1950s readers would have found exotic – 'Take 1 cup rose-water (from the chemist)...Vine leaves can be bought in jars at certain progressive delicatessen shops... If you cannot get aubergine...' – have, forty years later, been thoroughly analysed by thousands of English-language cookbooks and sweepingly entered, in some version or other, the stock-in-trade of such as Birds Eye Foods.

But few purveyors of recipes have quite achieved her sense of occasion. To introduce *sarma*, the Balkan stuffed cabbage, Lesley Blanch has written:

> I was taught to make this by Raiina, my much-loved...Bulgarian maid, who could, when she chose, cook like an angel.... When she... had been particularly trying, she always knew how to wheedle herself back into my good graces....she would arrange that one of the few remaining 'medicine bears' was hanging around outside, so that of course, enchanted, I had him fetched in. These bears, rather large brown ones, are trained to shuffle up and down the spine of anyone who dares let them, thus giving a sort of tonic massage, highly beneficial, according to local opinion. Raiina herself favoured such a furry treatment, and when she felt low, or to brace herself to cook a big dinner, she

often had the bear in. These docile creatures shuffle and pad uneasily, a few paces forward, a few paces back, treading delicately along each side of the spinal cord. It seems to work wonders. Raiina always sprang up revivified. The only time I tried it I was too stiffened with terror to relax in the required manner, said Boris, the bear's owner. A glass of *slivovitz* (a plum brandy) was then ritualistically offered and drunk by all, the bear included.[4]

The recipe section of *From Wilder Shores* contains brief jottings for five Egyptian dishes – red pottage, *foul medammess*, macaroni Kom-Ombo, *kounifa*, *muhallabieh* – but, unlike cooks of the 1950s, I've been rather spoiled (and more conclusively tempted) by the well-detailed pages of now-classic Middle Eastern cookbooks which first appeared in the 1970s and 1980s. Nothing, however, could equal the Blanch description of how she learned about Egypt's food:

> My knowledge and appreciation of the Egyptian cuisine has come from many unexpected quarters – from the hospitality of government officials, a religious leader, exiled Caucasians settled in Cairo, musicians, architects, and journalists. Among the most cherished sources [was a wonderful, massive] matriarchal figure…with the huge painted eyes of an idol. She had long been treated as such, for she had been the most celebrated of belly-dancers from Cairo to Alexandria. In her old age she was still considered the finest teacher of that undulating art which in its purest form stems from the temple rituals of ancient Egypt. She was also an excellent cook, delighting to pass on as many kitchen tips as I demanded. But first, something about her profession.

Lesley Blanch recounts her own interest in 'the tradition behind this vanishing art', its decline into 'night-club stuff which the old lady deplored loudly', her conversations with the reminiscing dancer

> over a luncheon table loaded with steaming casseroles, pickled fish, and a cherished tin of Everton's toffee. After lunch, the six-piece set of gilded armchairs, a gigantic buffet adorned with paper flowers and the massive table were pushed around to make room for the classes about to begin.

The succession of young Egyptian disciples had 'grave' faces

> as they concentrated, postured, writhed, writhed again, advanced and retreated with small, slipping steps, a pantomime of seduction which the old teacher mimed with them, corrected sharply, or praised. Some of her pupils were already star performers, returning for a refresher course.

A variety of family and hangers-on watched the lessons through 'a bead-hung *portière*', a Nubian woman made lemonade and wound up 'an antique gramophone', and

> Everyone seemed aware of the sacred elements which the old teacher upheld. These were no ordinary dancing classes. 'The belly movements – the hips – all that can be learned easily enough,' said my hostess, sucking a piece of toffee noisily. 'It is by the hands, the language of the hands and arms that *real* style is seen.'[5]

As the dancers' activities summoned historic images to her guest's inner eye, the teacher interrupted: '"If you come back tomorrow I will make you *sitt alnoubéh*", said my hostess, who had noticed that my appetite for traditional Egyptian food was as keen as my appreciation of her art.'

I can taste this cooking as realistically as from any exhaustive set of recipes. As a connoisseur, moreover, of mystery, of civilisations where much is withheld from view, Lesley Blanch knows the power of what is *not* revealed – 'those dominant yet subtle wafts of unnameable and probably unobtainable spices which rise from the plate, or drift about one's memory…'.

Her prose is always selective, her subjective writings adept at elusive chronology, forming a pattern which suggests mosaic, the weave of a Karabagh carpet, 'the intricate brick-work of…ancient mosques'. My favourite among her books, *Journey into the Mind's Eye* (subtitle: 'fragments of an autobiography'), while telling (selectively) more about her life than any other volume, retains this patterned quality. It expresses deep yearning for Russia, loved since the age of four – though not visited till Lesley Blanch was twenty-five – and for the man, named only as The Traveller, who kindled that love, inspired and returned an intense passion, and disappeared from her life on the eve of her twenty-first birthday. She looked for him in her memory, in her mind's eye and their shared knowledge of Russian history and culture, through frequenting some of the urban multitudes of his exiled fellow citizens.

She had first visited Paris in The Traveller's company – 'it was not his fault, but rather his force, that I could only see the city as a frame for his compatriots' – and in that metropolis, during the 1930s, she seemed to find his trace. Her representation of a Paris provisioner says a great deal about more than just groceries:

> In Russian Paris there were a considerable number of small food shops where every imaginable Russian speciality could be obtained, something the exiles of London had been unable to achieve.... Passy was the quarter where the best Russian foodstuffs were to be found, for it was here the more prosperous émigrés congregated, and here I came on regular pilgrimages.
>
> No lover waited below the window of his adored with more longing, with a more ardent wish to unite, than I, loitering outside the Russian grocers. Flattened against the glass, I would gaze spellbound at the delicacies within; *bublitchki*, great slabs of sturgeon, the noble *koulibiak*, feathery dill, pyramids of Easter *pashka* and the curious wooden moulds in which this rich dish is made. Entering, I would spin out my more modest purchases, in order to breathe the unmistakable, spicy-sour flavour of Russia, a compound of cabbage, salted fish, and poppy seeds.
>
> I would dawdle over the evocative merchandise listening to the deep, dark voices of the Russian customers. The simplest household orders were music to my ears, though applied to the émigrés, the words *simple* or *household* did not ring quite true. They were seldom simple or, if they were, then they were unlikely to possess a household of their own, being generally part of someone else's.
>
> But within this, whatever its style, they lived in their own nomadic fashion, taking with them wherever they went that sense of impermanence, of the tent, even though garnished by the extravagances that are so characteristic of them as a race....
>
> So, looking and listening, I spun out my purchases, deliberating between a jar of dill pickles, some *kasha*, or a loaf of that close-textured white bread...from the Boulangerie Moscovite, sprinkled with poppy seeds, and to me, a thousand times more evocative of Russia than the celebrated black loaf. I generally came away with a packet of Caravan tea which, although it tasted like hay, was irresistible on account of its wrapping paper. Across a yellow desert a camel caravan plodded towards a Chinese trading post backed by a blue pagoda. Coolies scuttled about, ant-like, unloading the tea boxes, while a scarlet sun sank behind a yellow horizon. *Kiakhta Tea Company* said the label, in Russian, and I ached to have known the little frontier town at that depicted, quintessential moment, before lorries, telephones and the twentieth century were imposed on even the confines of the Gobi Desert.[6]

REFERENCES

[1] *Round the World in 80 Dishes*, 75-76.
[2] *From Wilder Shores*, 68.
[3] *Journey into the Mind's Eye*, 367-68.
[4] *Round the World in 80 Dishes*, 81-82.
[5] *From Wilder Shores*, 95-97.
[6] *Journey into the Mind's Eye*, 225-26.

Books by Lesley Blanch

The Wilder Shores of Love, 1954, London, John Murray.
Round the World in 80 Dishes, 1955, New York, Gramercy Publishing.
The Game of Hearts, 1957, London, Gryphon Books.
The Sabres of Paradise, 1960, London, John Murray.
Under a Lilac-bleeding Star, 1963, London, John Murray. Soon to be republished in a new edition by
    Quartet Books.
The Nine Tiger Man, 1965, London, Collins.
Journey into the Mind's Eye, 1968, London, Collins.
Pavilions of the Heart, 1974, London, Weidenfeld & Nicolson.
Pierre Loti: Portrait of an Escapist, 1983, London, Collins.
From Wilder Shores, 1989, London, John Murray.

Bread and Travel: Travelling Sourdough

Dan M. Schickentanz with Silvija Davidson

Ethnic bread & travel

Bread is a perfect travelling companion, both as a nutritionally valuable food staple, and in terms of its form and consistency. Its history represents an epic travelogue, spanning many diverse cultures and societies; indeed, wars have been fought over bread.

I would, however, like to narrow the topic a little and look at how sourdough breads travel. Sourdough fermentation increases the longevity of the baked loaf, thus permitting a certain amount of long-distance travel. What interests me particularly, however, is the infinite range of intricate subtle nuances of aroma, texture and flavour which ensure that sourdough breads remain uniquely regional.

In my time as a baker I have been inundated with requests from ethnic customers to bake them the loaf of their homeland. Rising to the challenge, I invariably found that the breads I created from old traditional recipes appeared to come close to what was desired, but never met with full approval. I began to wonder why.

Quizzing my ethnic customers further, I discovered that they themselves tended to be avid home-bakers and had indeed attempted to replicate the loaves that lived on in their memories – more vividly than any other foodstuff. They admitted to failure.

I brought the problem up with many other food professionals and gleaned many inside views. Silvija Davidson, author of one of the few English books about bread that I know, has undertaken considerable research into different types of bread. Silvija comes from a Baltic background and bread has always been a main staple of both her and her parents' diet. She confirmed that her parents, and their expatriate countrymen, had been unable to bake or to commission 'their bread' in this country.

I myself am a double expatriate, having moved from Germany to the USA, and from there to the UK. Thus I have my own share of similar experiences, which in themselves triggered my interest in the subject.

When you leave your native country everything changes drastically. Your environment, of course, and gradually your habitual behaviour; but the last element to change, in so far as at all avoidable, is your diet. You will adapt partially to the culinary customs of your adopted country, but you will always seek out, or reproduce for yourself, your traditional foodstuffs. It is part of your home, your security.

I don't wish to dwell on this in any detail, but feel that a little personal history is called for. In the USA my family and I found ourselves longing for our familiar bread. We sought it far and wide, and constantly attempted to bake something similar. The results were, by most standards, good, but authenticity eluded us. It was then I recalled my parents moving away from my birthplace (in Germany) when I was three years old. The distance was a mere 100 miles, but far enough removed for them to demand that friends and family should mail us the bread produced by the baker in our old home town. As a young boy I failed to see the attraction of eating three-day-old bread; now, however, I began to understand and grew curious as to what part was played by mere sentiment, and to what degree the bakers in the new area were simply inept. Sentiment is a factor not open to scientific investigation; and I felt sure that there was as fair a spread of good as of bad bakers everywhere. Perhaps the history and regionality of my parents' sought-after loaf rendered it inimitable. And perhaps it had this in common with all sourdough raised breads.

What follows is a quick look at the history of breadmaking, followed by a technological brief on the nature of sourdough, concluding with some observations on regional differences in the make-up of sourdough breads world-wide.

History of breadmaking

The history of breadmaking is that of a 'kitchen accident' to use von Stokar's apt phrase; in other words, we cannot trace or describe the exact beginning.The first 'bread' consumed was undoubtedly based on broth or gruel. Cooked over an open fire or on hot stones, this produced a flat, rough kind of loaf, coarse and far from moist, which probably required soaking to render it edible. It would have been a useful travellers' staple, as it might keep almost indefinitely.

One day, we surmise, a little gruel was left over, unbaked. It was forgotten and rediscovered some days later, by now a rather bubbly, airy mass which had undergone fermentation. Once baked – waste not, want not – it was found to be both lighter in texture and considerably more palatable. We cannot attribute this to a particular period in history; what we do know is that by around 4,000 BC leavened bread was regularly produced in Egypt, some 4,000 years after the first seed plants – wild wheats and barley – began to be cultivated in the fertile crescent of Mesopotamia. After writing this paper I became aware of the book by Ed Wood, *World Sourdoughs from Antiquity*, unfortunately only available in the USA at the moment.

Ed Wood was invited to participate in an excavation experiment in a new-found baking site for a National Geographic project. What followed makes a fascinating story, charting how he reproduced sourdough as known to the ancient Egyptians, using their bakery and recreating their equipment as depicted in a bas-relief that amounts to an instruction book in ancient baking.

The ferment was started in Egypt near the succulent date and fig trees which helped to create a powerful sourdough starter. Besides barley Ed and his team used spelt (*Triticum speltae*), still readily available today, emmer wheat (*Triticum dicoccum*) and kamut (*Triticum polonicum*). The dough was then baked in cylindrical cones. After a few errors and misjudgments the result was deemed to be a full success.

Biblical mentions of bread include the well-known passages of the Book of Exodus, describing how the Jewish peoples had no time to ferment their bread during their exodus from Egypt, but had instead to bake unleavened bread, and the resonant pronouncement of Deuteronomy: 'Man shall not live by bread alone.' When I remembered the Exodus passage from my German bible lessons, there it said ' Du sollst kein *gesäuertes* Brot essen' meaning 'soured'. The term 'leavening' was on a par with souring. A Jewish friend then enlightened me that they have two words: 'souring' and 'leavening' and the original passage should certainly denote 'leavening'.

But the making of the Jewish Passover bread or 'Mazzo bread' is meticulously regulated. From the beginning to the end – 18 minutes – the dough has to be handled all the time to avoid even the tiniest chance of accidental fermentation through resting and souring. Only cold water is to be used, again to avoid spontaneous fermentation which would result from the inevitable souring of warm dough.

More revealing, however, is a mural from the tomb of Rameses III, giving witness to the ingenuity of Egyptian bakers (at least 50 varieties of variously shaped breads, some flavoured with seeds, some scented with honey, others enriched with eggs and milk, were baked in the first closed-chamber clay ovens), and indications of the process of sourdough fermentation. Excavations in the Nile delta have brought to light a wheaten sourdough dating back to 1400 BC. In 450 BC, Herodotus reported that 'all men are afraid of food spoiling, but the Egyptians produce bread dough which has to be spoiled'.

We know, however, that already by 800 BC the Greeks had adopted sourdough fermentation, and indeed improved on Egyptian methods. Where the Egyptians had made use of spontaneous fermentation, using a piece of leftover dough for the fermentation of the new batch, the Greeks invented what might be termed the first commercial sours: the prime sour and the dry sour. 'Prime sour' was produced in large batches after each vintage. It consisted of ground millet mixed with freshly fermented wine and under favourable conditions remained usable for a whole year. 'Dry sour' was produced from wheat gruel mixed with three-day old wine, then dried out in the sun. A piece would be broken off when required soaked in water, mixed with spelt flour and subsequently used for baking.

It seems that the resultant sourdough breads were a delicacy for the privileged and indeed consumed only on Sundays and holidays, as decreed by Solon (*c.* 600 BC). Xenophon reported upon return from his battle at Kunaxa, in *Anabasis* VIII 3.21 that he ate 'something delectable by way of soured bread and meat' as dinner guest of a Thracian king.

At around this time in Egypt commercial sourdough production became regarded as a profession. In Rome by contrast, Cato was unaware of the harnessing of the technique. For him a soured dough represented a contamination to be avoided. In *On Agriculture* he instructs that you must wash your hands and mortar before commencing breadmaking.

In his *Natural History*, however, Pliny described sourdough production in fine detail (though the grain he commends is barley, considered more healthful than wheat).

Archaeological excavations north of the Alps have revealed that sourdough bread was known around 800 BC. In 1981 in the vicinity of Twann in Switzerland a bread was uncovered which had burned in a village fire some 5500 years previously. This would put it in the timeframe of the first Mediterranean breads; some sources suggest it is as much as 1000 years older than this, placing it alongside the earliest ratified breads recovered from Sumer and Egypt.

European breadmaking

Excavations at Mondsee in Austria revealed perfect leavened flatbreads made around 1800 BC. It is, however, uncertain when the Germanic region first became a user of sourdough fermentation. Certainly it was widely used by around 500 AD, as revealed by written evidence. The Goths, Franks, Alemanns, Bavarians and Anglo-Saxons were all familiar with the method at around 800 AD.

European breadmaking in the Middle Ages fell to the monasteries, who were mainly responsible for improvements in quality and variety. Such breads were generally made of soured rye-grits, fresh barley grits and occasionally the addition of oats, although wheat breads were also produced using sourdough fermentation, and they began to form a daily staple.

Only at the beginning of the nineteenth century were natural fermentation and the use of ale barm largely discarded in favour of other forms of yeast. Brewers' and distillers' yeasts – the foam or froth produced during fermentation, which was collected and dried for later use – were the first to be employed, particularly in the production of white wheaten loaves. It undoubtedly gave more consistent results, yet the quality of the risen loaf was still unpredictable. In England it became customary to add a piece of old dough to the fresh batch, in addition to a dose of brewers' yeast, and leave this to ferment for a day. This often gave rise to complaints about its disagreeable level of sourness; several generations later, however, the gold diggers of San Francisco turned the very same method into a mark of distinction.

1856 saw the introduction of baking powder, and a year later Louis Pasteur discovered that yeast was a unicellular organism propagated by cell division, leading to the development of baker's yeast.

In the USA Sylvester Graham fought a feverish campaign against these modern leavened breads, and indeed against all yeasted breads, claiming yeast to be a poisonous and impure substance. In his 1858 pamphlet, *Good Bread, How to make it light without yeast or powders*, he insisted that 'bread today is rotted by fermentation, poisoned with acids and alkalis to the point that the staff of life has well nigh become the staff of death'. His suggested alternative unfortunately produced an almost unpalatably dense loaf.

The Chorleywood bread process

The Chorleywood bread process introduced in the 1960s was hailed as the progress of the century. At last we had consistently light-textured bread, produced fast enough to feed a mass market. Heavy mixers shredded the dough in seconds, replacing slow fermentation. A loaf could be produced from scratch in two hours, a loaf of high volume, soft texture, uniform consistency, and low cost. Unfortunately, the method (which accounts for the vast majority of breads produced today) relies on additives to 'age' flour rapidly via chemicals and mechanical agitation, and to provide increased dough and fermentation tolerance; in addition, high quantities of yeast and of water are added to gluten-rich flours to enable the dough to withstand such 'heavy-handed' treatment.

This technological success is not, however, the bread of which I am writing. Lacking in any discernible flavour, it is readily copied world-wide. The bread that concerns me is a craft bread, traditionally made, full of nuances of flavour that reflect regional difference. This is the bread you may recall eating when your grandmother baked it, or perhaps a baker who had resisted the pressures levied by banks, convenience shopping and greed. What accounts for its infinite range of flavours, the regional differences such a loaf reflects? I believe, and recent research indicates, that sourdough fermentation plays an important part in the process.

Definition and role of sourdough

With typical efficiency, the Germans have defined sourdough as 'a wheat product with the addition of micro-organisms and fluids in an active state in which their proliferation is not interrupted and fermentation occurs continuously'.

We can divide sourdough into two categories: natural sour and pure sour. Natural or spontaneous sour is the modern version of the Egyptian method.

Leave wheat or indeed any grain in a moist state for long enough and it will develop some form of sourdough culture. As you might imagine this is not a very reliable method in terms of the technological accomplishments of today, but none the less yields interesting results.

Pure sour is an industrial product consisting of a range of cultures in varying degrees of concentration available in either dry or liquid form.

Both types of sour are subject to regional variation, simply because in any sourdough culture a multitude of micro-organisms are participating in differing proportions and levels of activity in the construction of a perfect loaf. There are over one hundred such micro-organisms, roughly divided into lactobacilli (stick like, static bacteria, anaerobic to microaerophilic, acidity-tolerant and capable of intensive carbohydrate fermentation) and saccharomyces (yeasts). All make a particular contribution towards flavour, leavening, crumb-structure, crust and keeping qualities.

The principal functions of sourdough could be divided as follows (in order of perceived importance):
- to enable the leavening and production of rye breads,
- development of flavour and of aromatic substances,
- protection against undesirable wild fermentation,
- synergistic support to the action of yeast,
- antagonistic action against mould fungi and rope (a disease of wheat which causes doughy patches inside breads, particularly highly moist styles, and can be visibly pulled into threads or 'ropes').

While in wheat doughs it provides the arguably desirable final four functions, sourdough is an essential in the production of rye breads. Rye bread is barely bakeable without souring, and its digestibility is impaired. Even mixed-grain breads containing only 20 per cent rye need a certain degree of sourdough fermentation.

In contrast to wheat, rye flour has:
- less starch,
- less gluten,
- more soluble sugars,
- more water-binding fibre,
- more enzymes.

To describe the implications for rye bread baking in more detail: starch builds the binding agent in breads. In wheat breads it gelatinizes at about 650°C and helps form the loaf's structure along with gluten, the stretchy, rubber-like substance formed by adding water to an amino acid contained in flour, and agitating the mixture. Rye flour is lacking in both important elements. The filling and water-binding substances specific to rye are pentosane and a specific starch, both of which lead to a more complete gelatinization and water retention, and hence keeping qualities, than is the case with wheat flour. The darker the flour, the more pentosane it contains, ranging from 3.5 per cent in light rye floors to over 7 per cent in dark ones.

Rye flour is also generally milled at a higher extraction rate than wheat, meaning that more fibre is left in the flour, allowing greater water retention in the baking process.

One problem area with rye flours is their aleuron enzyme content. These include the starch-reducing amylase and the protein-reducing protease. Rye is prone to what we might term overgrowing: if the weather is wet and warm at harvest time, and the grain cannot be dried quickly enough, it may start sprouting to a degree where green sprouts are visible to the naked eye. This common process increases the above-mentioned enzymes, which in turn destroy the starch and amino acids in a series of complex chemical and physical processes.

Sourdough, and indeed salt, provide a solution to the problem. The starch-reducing alpha-amylase and protein-reducing protease are sensitive to acidity, which reduces their destructive activities. Laboratory testing can reveal the degree of sprouting present, and indicate the amount of acidity needed to counteract its effects. Salt in solution splits into ions, creating an electric current which also slows the activities of the enzymes present. But the amount of salt needed to counteract the enzymatic action in rye flour would adversely affect both the flavour and the rising properties of the dough. Only a judicious combination of salt and sourdough can guarantee the successful containment of destructive enzymatic forces.

Souring, incidentally, also increases levels of gelatinization, and additionally speeds transformation of pentosanes into pentose, which in turn gelatinizes to a higher degree, binding yet more water and assisting keeping qualities.

But would some other form of acid do?

The chemistry of sourdoughs

The chemistry of sourdoughs is so complex that only an introduction can be given here.

A soured dough can be roughly divided into
- lactic acids,
- acetic acids,
- alcohol,
- amino acids.

What is creating these substances? We need to return to the earlier division of micro-organisms into lactobacilli and polysaccharomyces, or yeasts.

The lactobacilli form the starter cultures for the sour. The main cultures are:
- *delbrueckii*
- *plantarum brevis*
- *brevis ssp. Linderi/Sanfrancisco*
- *leichmannii*
- *casei*
- *fermenti*
- *pastorianus*
- *buchneri*

to name but a few important ones.

These are the main building blocks that account for much of the regional differentiation of breads. When bread doughs and cultures are transported to another environment, they tend to adapt to local conditions as do those other living substances, unpasteurized cheese and wine. One such example was given to me by a cheese expert who recalled that when he bought young cheeses of diverse origins and left them to mature in his cellar, their regional characteristics altered over time and took on elements of the microclimate of his cellar. Cheeses also depend on the action of lactobacilli – the connection between sourdough breads and cheeses is, in this respect, remarkably close. Research so far conducted has shown that in every town examined world-wide, the presence and proportions of lactobacilli are different. But before listing certain examples, it is necessary to explain two different types of fermentation methods involved in the production of various breads.

Homofermentation & heterofermentation

Essentially, the difference between them is that during homofermentation lactic acid is formed from the glucose present in the flour, while during heterofermentation both lactic and acetic acids are produced:

Homofermentation

$C_6H_{12}O_6$ (sugar) 2 x $[C_3H_6O_3]$ (lactic acid)

Heterofermentation

$C_6H_{12}O_6$ (sugar) 3 x $[C_2H_4O_2]$ (acetic acid)

Delbrueckii, leichmannii, plantarum, casei are for example homofermentative and *brevis, fermenti, pastorianus, buchneri* are heterofermentative.

The craftsman can manipulate the required result of these fermentation processes through what I call the '3T' Method: time, temperature, texture (i.e., the consistency of the dough).

While tradition and time-proven methods handed down through generations ensure the desired qualities in breads produced by craft bakers, I doubt that many of these bakers could give a precise chemical explanation of the complex reactions inherent in their particular sourdough. They will however have some understanding (if not that of the chemist) of roles played by the '3Ts'.

Temperature plays the main role in developing a sour to the required result. In spontaneous fermentation (fermentation from scratch) undesirable acids may develop, such as butyric acid (giving a rancid smell to the bread), alongside bacilli which might affect the well-being of the consumer. Temperatures over 30°C are favourable for developing homogenous fermentation with lactic acids.Temperatures up to 45°C are tolerated. Different temperatures within this range favour the development of different lactobacilli. Under 30°C heterofermentation is sponsored, and more yeasts develop. In terms of texture, a loose dough fosters heterofermentation and a tight dough homofermentation. By combining a number of variables, a bread can be tailored to the baker's liking.

My aim in providing these technical details is largely to stress the point of the complexity of sourdoughs. I could go into further detail but feel that a practical demonstration would be of more interest. I should, however, perhaps mention one or two other flavour-affecting elements. First of all, a broad range – 25 per cent to 75 per cent dough proportion – of lactic and acetic acids is deemed desirable. Secondly, in addition to brewers' and bakers' yeasts, a good number of natural yeasts have a role to play. Not all of them are involved in producing the carbon dioxide that leavens the dough; a number have a subordinate, or negligible role, but one that none the less affects flavour.

In addition to acids and carbon dioxide, alcohol, esters and amino acids are produced by the fermentation process and each in its turn contributes to the final flavour of the bread.

Techniques of sourdough bread production

If we were to mix together a little flour and water and let the mixture sit for a few days at room temperature, we would end up with a sour-tasting mixture. Mixed in the right quantities with more flour and water this would produce a bread dough suitable for baking. The method and result would not be accurately controlled, and suffer a great deal of variation in repetition, quite possibly leading to absolute failure.

In Germany we have developed a vast array of techniques all based on the same principle – proliferation of the sourdough cultures. Whether you start from scratch, 'spontaneously', or use commercial cultures, or other methods such as sponge and dough, the principle remains the same. From a small amount of base starter you can develop the full dough in a matter of hours, or of days. To give you an idea of the quantities involved, 350g of old dough can give you 100 kg of finished dough within a day or so.

The base starter is mixed with a certain amount of flour and water and is then fermented under controlled temperature and time conditions, proliferating the lactobacilli and yeasts. A new base starter is taken away for use the following day, and the rest is used in baking.This description is rather crude in that many different techniques are employed in bakeries working with natural sourdoughs, ranging from a five-step method, through a three-step method to a one-step method, a short-time sour or a salt-delayed sour. A three-step method, for example, would involve fermenting the base sour with a flour/water mix for 8–15 hours; this in turn would then be mixed with more flour and water in different proportions and fermented for a further 3–8 hours; this would then be used for the final dough which would be bulk fermented and then baked.

Timing depends on the workflow in each bakery. A baker might prefer to do the first step overnight or during the day, or use a shorter method at higher temperatures. It all depends. But this indicates what variations are possible when dealing with sourdoughs.

Analysis of sourdough cultures in different areas of the world

German bakeries show a majority of *L. delbrueckii, leichmannii, plantarum, casei, brevis, fermenti pastorianus* and *buchneri*. But samples taken from 30 different sourdoughs isolated 200 groups of bacteria, which were further divided into four sub-groups.

Research in Dutch bakeries has revealed mainly *L. Sanfrancisco* and *Saccharomyces exiguus*.

Black bread sourdoughs in Russia showed a strong presence of *L. leichmannii*. Scientists found three basic types of sourdough in use in Russia and found traces even of the *Streptococcus lactis Lohne*, but were unable to confirm a regularity in geographical distribution. No differences were found between Russian rye and wheat sours; both used *L. plantarum* and *brevis* for their production. Both homofermentative and heterofermentative methods were in use.

In Czechosolvakia, *L. plantarum* was found in both hetero- and homofermentation processes and it was suggested that the consistency and microbiological breakdown of the microflora of the sourdough in different bakeries were differently proportioned, accounting for the regional variety of breads.

Polish, Finnish. Swedish and Italian doughs showed variations despite using the same types of flour and/or methods of production.

The famous San Francisco sourdough, well known for over a century, showed a characteristic culture of bacilli only reproducible when maltose is present in the culture (also 70–80 per cent lactic and 20–30 per cent acetic acid).

Ed Woods's expedition, which I mentioned earlier, revealed an interesting fact, supporting my theory of travelling sourdoughs. Ed Wood had bought grains in the USA from specialized growers after extensive research. He felt that in order to reproduce something approaching original ancient Egyptian breads, the flours had to be 'neutral'. He faced the task of sterilizing the flour without impairing the baking properties. Irradiation was the answer. But supporting my conclusion was his realization that this 'New World' flour had inert properties which would probably not recreate the Egyptian 'original sour' he proliferated in situ.

In conclusion

When I am quizzed about the origin of my breads I always reply that my breads are English with ethnic influences. I feel I cannot bake 'German', 'Italian', or 'Russian' bread in England because I use different flours, the water is English, the air and climate are English, as are the microflora of the environment. Commercial starter-cultures can isolate and induce a specific culture in dough, but as I have elaborated, the variety of some 200 substances and their infinite combinations makes it impossible to replicate breads outside their specific place of origin.

The Portuguese Influence on Bengali Cuisine

Colleen Taylor Sen

Aquas do Gange, e a terra de Bengala
Fertil de sort que outra não lhe iguala

Here by the mouths, where hallowed Ganges ends
Bengal's beauteous Eden wide extends

Camões, *Os Lusiadas*, Canto VII, Stanza xx[1]

Introduction

The Portuguese conquests of the fifteenth and sixteenth centuries are a remarkable chapter in the history of empire. Throughout the sixteenth century the Portuguese retained a dominant position in the maritime trade of the Indian Ocean and an important share of the trade east of the Strait of Malacca. At the heart of this mercantile empire was India, with its wealth of cloth, luxury goods, and spices. The Portuguese even used the expression *Estado da India* (State of India) to describe their conquests between the Cape of Good Hope and the Persian Gulf on one side of Asia, and Japan and Timor on the other. At its height, *Estado da India* comprised a chain of more than 40 forts and factories (*bandars*) extending from Brazil to Japan. Portuguese was the lingua franca of this far-flung empire.

The products traded included gold from Guinea, South-East Africa, and Sumatra; sugar from Madeira, São Tomé, and Brazil; pepper from Malabar and Indonesia; mace and nutmegs from Banda; cloves from the Spice Islands; cinnamon from Ceylon; gold, silks, and porcelain from China; silver from Japan; horses from Persia and Arabia; and cotton textiles from Gujarat, the Malabar Coast, and Bengal. The merchandise was bartered in the interport trade of Asia or taken round the Cape of Good Hope to Lisbon and Antwerp, a major distribution center for Asian spices and other goods.

This vast empire was launched in 1415 when a fleet of 59 galleons and 50,000 men attacked the Arab stronghold of Ceuta on the African side of the Straits of Gibraltar. By 1515, the great conqueror Albuquerque had seized the three most important centers of the spice trade: Malacca, Ormuz, and Goa, wresting control of this trade away from the Arabs. However, the glory days of the empire lasted little more than a century. The task of maintaining such an extensive empire was too great for a small nation of around 1 million population. Sufficient sailors could not be found to man their fleets, so that convicts and outlaws were recruited. The Portuguese system of administering the spice trade was also inefficient, if not obstructive.[2]

In 1580, the crowns of Spain and Portugal were united under Philip II of Spain, who treated Portugal as a conquered country. The real blow came when Portuguese ports were closed against the rebellious Dutch. Forced to get an empire of their own, the Dutch wrested much of the trade in Southeast Asia, Ceylon, and India from the Portuguese. The French, English, and other European powers followed. By the middle of the seventeenth century the Portuguese role as the dominant mercantile power in Asia was virtually over (although they left Goa only in 1961 and will leave Macau in 1998).

The Portuguese in India

On the Indian subcontinent, the Portuguese established trading posts in three areas: along the Malabar coast at Calicut, Cochin, Goa, and other towns; on the island of Ceylon (Sri Lanka); and in Bengal in the northeast. Goa was the capital of the Portuguese empire in the east and a central clearing house for merchants from Arabia, Siam, Java, Malacca, Persia, China, Japan, even America. So great was Portuguese influence that at one point it looked as if King Sebastian (1557-78) might occupy the throne of the Great Moghuls.

According to legend, when Vasco da Gama reached Calicut in 1498, a Moor from Tunis asked him in Castilian, 'May the devil take you. What brought you here?' His answer was, 'We have come to seek Christians and spices.' The conversion of local people was always a major Portuguese objective and was accompanied by widespread intermarriage with local inhabitants at all levels of society. Today, the major Portuguese legacies in India, especially on the West Coast, are the Catholic religion and churches, the Portuguese language, and the prevalence of such surnames as (Da) Souza, Castro, Cruz, Dias, Fernandes, Gonsalves, Fonseca, Pereira, Rodriques, (Da) Silva, Correa, etc. Because of internal migration, these names are also found in Calcutta and other Indian cities.

Gastronomically, the Portuguese legacy was widespread, profound, and enduring. Their main heritage was, of course, the fruits and vegetables brought from the Western Hemisphere, Africa, the Philippines, and China and Southeast Asia which were rapidly and thoroughly integrated into local cuisines. Another was the creation of Goan cuisine, which combined Portuguese techniques and dishes with Indian spices.

The Portuguese in Bengal

The Portuguese first visited Bengal in 1517, just 33 years after Bartholomew Diaz landed at Calicut on the East coast. Bengal was an independent kingdom under the Muslim Lodi dynasty, which was replaced by the Moghuls in 1576. Bengal was then an extremely wealthy land known far and wide as 'the Paradise of India.' Rich in rice, cotton, and other agricultural products, it had long been the center of a luxury trade in spices and cloth. The famous muslins of Dacca, much sought after by Roman women, were exported in large quantities to Provence, Italy, and Languedoc in the seventeenth century. The chief port was Chittagong and the capital was Gaur. Kalikatta, which was to become Calcutta, was an insignificant village on the left bank of the Hooghly River.

In 1580 Akbar granted the Portuguese a charter to settle in a village on the banks of the Hooghly River 25 miles upstream from the site of present-day Calcutta. Called Hooghly or Porto Pequeno, it became the common emporium for vessels from other parts of India, China, Malacca, and The Philippines. Merchants took advantage of the cheapness of goods in Bengal and sold them at an enormous price in their numerous ports in the east. At first the Portuguese traders would remain there in the rainy season buying and selling goods and return to Goa when the rains were over, but eventually they formed permanent settlements.

In the 1670s, there were said to be at least 20,000 Portuguese and their descendants in Bengal, although only about 300 were pure Portuguese. About half lived in Hooghly, the rest in Satgaon (Porto Grande), Chittagong, Banja, Dacca and other ports. They lived in great luxury, dressed in the style of the local nawabs, and 'made merry with dancing slave girls, seamstresses, cooks and confectioners'.[3] Slavery was widespread, so that households often had dozens of domestics. One of their specialties was the preparation of sweetmeats from mangoes, oranges, lemons, ginger, and pickles. Portuguese bakers were also known for their bread, cakes, and other forms of pastries, filled and flavored for various occasions.

The Bengali settlements were under the authority of the government in Ceylon, not the viceroy in Goa because of difficulties with communications. However, in reality, neither this government nor the home government in Lisbon had much to do with them, especially after the merger with Spain. Authority was weak, and adventurers tried to set up independent kingdoms, often in alliance with local rulers. Their men, convicts and outlaws, became plunderers and pirates in alliance with the Arakanese and Moghs, a semi-tribal Buddhist people who lived around Chittagong. Known as Feringhi (from the Arab word 'Frank', once applied to the Crusaders), these brigands exercised a reign of terror over the rivers and swamps of eastern Bengal.

These Moghs were to play an interesting role in culinary history. For centuries they had worked as deckhands and cooks on Arab ships trading with Southeast Asia. The Portuguese continued this tradition by employing the Moghs as cooks and they quickly learned the culinary arts of their masters, becoming skilled confectioners and bakers. The British likewise had high regard for Mogh and Goan cooks, and today both are encountered running Indian restaurants around the world.[4]

Meanwhile, the first Dutch ships arrived in Bengal in 1615 and were given permission by the Moghuls to trade there. A struggle ensued and over the next century, Portuguese trading posts in the Moluccas, Ceylon, and India gradually passed into Dutch hands. In 1651 the English built their first trading post in Bengal and in 1690 Job Charnock founded Calcutta. The Moghuls eventually subdued the pirates and conquered Chittagong and Hooghly. By the eighteenth century the Portuguese presence had almost disappeared.

In contrast to Western India, in Bengal there are only a few physical vestiges of the Portuguese presence: a few churches and some ruins. Some geographical place names remain: the Dom Manik Islands, Point Palmyras on the Orissa Coast, the town of Bandel, and Feringhi Bazaar in Dacca. But the Portuguese influence lives on in other ways. Many people living around Chittagong in East Bengal have fair skins and blue eyes and are popularly considered to be descendants of the Portuguese. A fair number of Bengalis have Portuguese surnames. They fall into several categories: Luso-Indians (descendants of the offspring of mixed unions between Portuguese and local women), descendants of Christian converts, descendants of Goans who migrated to Bengal for economic reasons in the early nineteenth century, and others who for various reasons adopted Portuguese surnames, including Anglo-Indians.[5] There has also been a merging of the Anglo-Indian and Luso-Indian communities in Calcutta and other metropolises.

The Portuguese language remained a lingua franca in Bengal as late as the eighteenth century. Clive, who could never give an order in any native language, was said to speak fluent Portuguese. The first three books printed in the Bengali language were printed in Latin characters in Lisbon in 1743, and it was a Portuguese who composed the first Bengali prose work and the first Bengali grammar and dictionary. In Modern Bengali, articles of common use, items used in Christian services, and plants often go by their Portuguese names; e.g., *ag-bent* (holy water), *alpin* (pin), *altar* (altar), *ananas* (pineapple), *balti* (bucket), *bispa* (bishop), *botel* (bottle), *spanj* (sponge), *girja* (church), *tamak* (tobacco), *piyara* (pear), *ata* (custard apple), *veranda*, etc. Other Portuguese words have passed into the English language, including caste, peon, padre, papaya, plantain, cobra, mosquito, pomfret, and palmyra.[6]

The evolution of Bengali cuisine
Pre-European Bengali food

Before the arrival of Europeans in the early sixteenth century, the staple of Bengali cuisine was locally grown rice, as it is today. A Portuguese traveler wrote 'The rice here is far better than the European one, especially the scented variety, for besides being very fine and of a most agreeable flavour, it has after being cooked a nice smell which one would think a blending of several scents.'[7] Other dietary staples were wheat, fruits, vegetables, and milk, milk products such as yogurt, and clarified butter (ghee). The basic diet of poor people was rice with a little salt and green vegetables.

However, according to one source, Bengali texts make no mention of lentils or methods of preparing them until well into the fifteenth century and even today, most of the dals consumed in Bengal are grown outside the state.[8]

One reason may be that fish and even some kinds of meat were readily available and widely eaten in Bengal, even by Brahmins, who were strict vegetarians in other parts of India. However, like Orthodox Hindus in other parts of India, they avoided onions, garlic and mushrooms. There were also restrictions on what kind of fish was to be eaten and when. According to one text, a Brahmin could eat fish that are white and have scales but not those that have ugly shapes or heads like snakes or lived in holes. Venison and other kinds of wild game were allowed and, in ayurvedic medicine, recommended for certain medical conditions. Snails, crabs, fowls, both domestic and wild, cranes, ducks, camels, boars, and, of course, beef were prohibited to Brahmins.[9]

In the ninth and tenth centuries, there were over 40 varieties of rice, 60 kinds of fruits and more than 120 varieties of vegetables in Bengal. Vegetables included cucumber, carrot, various kinds of gourds, garlic, fenugreek, radish, lotus root, mushroom, eggplant, and green leafy vegetables. Among the fruits eaten were peaches, water melon, banana, mango, amalaka, lime (nimbu), grapes, oranges (imported from China or Indochina around the beginning of the Christian era), pear (also introduced by the Chinese), jujube, almond, walnuts, coconut, pomegranates, and many fruits with no Western equivalent.

Until the twelfth century, spices used in Bengali cooking were limited to turmeric, ginger, mustard seed, long pepper, poppy seeds, asafoetida, and sour lemon. Long pepper was replaced first by black peppercorns brought from the west coast of India and later by the cheaper chili, which thrived in Bengali soil. Spice traders also brought cinnamon, cardamom, and cloves. Various methods of preparation were used, including frying in both shallow and deep fat. Cooking media included ghee by those who could afford it, mustard oil, still popular today in Bengal, and sesame oil.

The Bengali love of sweets goes back into the Middle Ages. Sugar has been grown in Bengal and India since ancient times, as indicated by its Sanskrit name, *sharkara*, which passed into other languages (except, ironically, in Bengali where it is known as 'Chini' from the word for China.) Texts dating back to the twelfth and thirteenth centuries describe a number of dishes based on milk, partly thickened milk, and milk solids.

The introduction of New-World ingredients and techniques

Appendix 1 lists the most important plants and foods introduced by the Portuguese into Bengal, with some comments about their history and their role in Bengali cuisine. Today it is impossible to imagine a Bengali meal without potatoes, tomatoes, and chilies, so thoroughly have they been integrated into the cuisine. 'Next to the Irish, Bengalis are probably the largest potato-eaters in the world,' says one writer.[10] Other common fruits and vegetables include okra, sweet potato, eggplant, guava, and papaya.

At the same time, the role of the 'imports' is somewhat less visible than on India's West coast. In Bengal, for example, peanuts and cashews are eaten mainly as snacks and do not generally form part of main dishes, as they do in Maharashtra (roasted potatoes with peanuts) or Kerala (shrimp with cashews.) In fact, the Marathi word for potato is the Portuguese 'batata.' Gujaratis prepare bread from corn-flour and Maharashtrians make a corn curry from the kernels. The only way Bengalis eat corn is on the cob, perhaps smeared with a little oil and chili, and purchased from a street vendor.

To show how these ingredients are incorporated into the cuisine, let us examine a typical Bengali meal. It starts with *shukto*, a bitter dish intended to stimulate the appetite. *Shukto* is a mixture of diced vegetables, such as white radish, potatoes, beans, and bitter gourd or *karela*, a vegetable also used in Chinese cuisine (though apparently indigenous to India). The vegetables are lightly sautéed in ginger, mustard seed, and cumin, and then cooked with milk and water. Potatoes are almost always a component of *shukto*.

Shukto is followed by rice and dal (spiced lentil soup), accompanied by one or more fried, boiled, and sautéed vegetable dishes. Cut and sautéed tomatoes are often added as a flavoring to dal. *Poshto* is a mixture of potatoes and other vegetables cooked in a paste made of white poppy seeds. *Chheshki* consists of julienned root vegetables, usually potatoes, and onions stir-fried in a little oil with chili, mustard seed, and cumin seed. In a non-vegetarian household, fish and meat would now be served, cooked in a light gravy and perhaps accompanied by one or two vegetable dishes in gravy, a rice pullao and bread. Typical seafood dishes are *lau chingri*, prawns cooked with vegetable marrow, said to be of Portuguese origin; *macchher jhol*, a pungent fish stew; and *malai* curry made with coconut milk. Plain boiled rice accompanies every course. If bread is served, it could be *luchhi*, unique to Bengal in that it is made of white flour, not wheat flour – perhaps another legacy of the Portuguese bakers.

The next-to-last course is a sweet and sour chutney made with tomatoes, apples, mangos, pineapples, or other fruits. This quintessentially Bengali dish may also reflect the influence of the Portuguese preserve and pickle makers. Chutney plays the role of sorbet in European cuisine: it is intended to clear the palate for the pièce de resistance: the sweet or dessert course.

Bengalis are famous for their love of sweets, which borders on an addiction. In Calcutta there is a sweet shop on almost every corner. In homes, sweets are served at the end of meals (not throughout a meal, as in Western India) and with afternoon tea. Tea is an important meal since dinner is traditionally eaten very late (10.00 p.m. or even later in some Calcutta households). Tea also includes salty and fried snacks, Western-style cake, delicate cucumber and tomato sandwiches, and, of course, tea, served English-style with milk and sugar (never with spices.) Sweets are also eaten as snacks throughout the day; in the old days, very rich landowners were said to have lived on a diet of sweets alone.

The two basic ingredients of Bengali sweets are sugar and milk. The milk is thickened either by boiling it down to make a thick liquid called *khoa*, or by curdling it with lemon juice or yogurt to produce curds, called *channa*. There is some debate as to whether the latter was a traditional technique or a Portuguese contribution. Portuguese cheesemakers in Bengal used to produce curds by breaking milk with acidic materials. One of their products was a salted smoked cheese called Bandel Cheese, which is still made and sold in Calcutta. According to Achaya,[11] this routine may have lifted an Aryan taboo on deliberate milk curdling and given the traditional Bengali sweetmaker a new raw material. While some historic texts seem to indicate that curds were used in Indian sweets in the Middle Ages, Achaya argues that these texts are ambivalent and that what was actually used was *khoa*.

It is a fact that the extensive use of *channa* by Calcutta sweetmakers began in the mid-nineteenth century when they greatly expanded their repertoire by inventing new varieties, often with fanciful names. The most famous include *rasgolla*, a light spongy white ball of *channa* served in sugar syrup; a dark-colored fried version called *ledikeni*, named after Lady Canning, the wife of the first Viceroy of India; *cham-cham*, small patties dipped in thickened milk and sprinkled with grated khoa; *ras malai*, khoa and sugar balls floating in cardamon-flavored cream; sausage-shaped *pantuas* fried to a golden brown and dropped in sugar syrup; and the most exquisite of all, *sandesh*. *Sandesh* (the word means 'message' in Bengali, perhaps because it was once sent as a gift) is basically *channa* mixed with sugar, fried in a little clarified butter, and pressed into pretty molds shaped like flowers, fruit, or shells. Like all good Bengali sweets, *sandesh* has a delicate, subtle flavor that must be carefully savored. Connoisseurs debate the virtues of their favorite variety and manufacturer with the passion and expertise of a French oenophile.

New dishes

Bengali cuisine is one of the most eclectic of Indian regional cuisines and has been the most open to foreign influences for a number of reasons. Throughout history, caste has always been much weaker in Bengal then in other regions of India. Until 1947, Calcutta was an extremely cosmopolitan city, with large communities of Jews, Armenians, Chinese, Anglo-Indians, Tibetans, and people from all parts of India. Moreover, the British had a presence there for 350 years and until 1911 Calcutta was the capital of the Indian empire and the second city of the British empire after London. From the mid-nineteenth century a westernized Bengali middle class emerged who studied in British universities, sent their sons and daughters to English-language schools, belonged to English-style clubs, adopted Western political ideas, and were not adverse to exploring other cuisines. Rich people in Calcutta used to have houses with three or four separate kitchens for preparing Muslim, Western, Hindu, and Hindu vegetarian dishes. In the first half of the twentieth century, Calcutta social life centered around the English clubs, the Great Eastern Hotel, and fashionable restaurants like Firpos and Fleuries, founded by Europeans and serving European cuisine.

In Bengali middle-class homes, breakfast tends to be Western-style: fruit or juice, toast, porridge, and perhaps a spicy omelette cooked with chilies, onions, and tomatoes. Lunch includes dishes such as cutlets and chops, recreated in forms totally unlike their English originals. Chops are a spiced round or oval potato cake filled with ground fish, meat or vegetables, dipped in egg and breadcrumbs, and fried. Cutlets are long, flat, oval patties made from ground fish, meat, or vegetables mixed with eggs, spices, and perhaps fresh herbs, coated with breadcrumbs and fried until golden brown. Common household desserts include such western dishes as soufflé, caramel custard, Jelly, rice pudding, and trifle.

Portuguese-Goan dishes also found their way into Bengali menus. *The Indian Cookery Book* written in the last century by an anonymous 'Thirty-five year Resident of Calcutta' contains a recipe for *vindaloo*, which it calls 'this well known Portuguese curry.' This hot and sour pork dish made with vinegar and red chilies is derived from the Portuguese *Carne de Vinho e Alhos*, or pork with wine and garlic, a Madeira specialty made with vinegar and dry white wine.

More recently, the *Calcutta Cookbook* (1995) includes recipes for *buffath* (a beef or duck and vegetable stew); *temperado* (prawns cooked in coconut milk); chicken *xacuti* (hot and sour chicken in coconut milk); *sorpotel* (a very spicy stew made from beef and pig offal); and *vindaloo*. Appendix 2 lists some Goan dishes and their ingredients. Generally, Goan cuisine is characterized by a strong rather than subtle flavoring that comes from a liberal and, to some tastes, rather indiscriminate use of spices, including cardamoms, cloves, cinnamon, nutmeg, ginger, garlic, chilies, cumin, perhaps poppy seeds, mustard seeds, fenugreek, and coconut. In Bengal, these dishes may be made with mustard oil.

In Calcutta, Goan cuisine has merged with the cuisine of the Anglo-Indians, who are a distinct and legally recognized minority community. Under the British, places in schools and certain professions were reserved for Anglo-Indians, but after Independence, many left for Canada, Australia, and Britain. Today, the once flourishing community in Calcutta is small. A cookbook published in Calcutta in the 1950s, *Anglo-Indian and Portuguese Dishes*, is an interesting compendium of several cuisines:

> British: e.g., tongue stew, roast goose, roast chicken, baked mutton breast, roast mutton, sardine toast, Irish stew, Yorkshire pudding, sausage rolls, fish pie, shrewsbury biscuits, ox-tail soup, Indian Worster (sic) sauce.

> North Indian/Moghlai: tandoori chicken, kabob, pilaus, burfee, firni.

> Bengali: steamed hilsa fish, moong dhal, cutlets, chops, rasgoolahs, chutney, Lady Canning.

Goan: vindaloo, kuziddo, buffado, richadoo, baradoo, prawn temperadoo, fish vindaloo, prawn curry with coconut milk.[12]

Portuguese: Bebin Ka Lacy, Bole Memosoo, Bole de Leithe, Bole Comadree, Bole de Amandrue Pudding, guava cheese.

By far the largest chapter is 'Cakes, Portuguese Sweets, Halwa, Custard Puddings, Marmalades, Toffees, Ice Creams, Bread, and Biscuits', which includes cakes and pastries with Portuguese names. The very first recipe is for a lavish Christmas Cake, made with almonds, raisins, dried and candied fruits, cream, cardamom, cinnamon, and nutmeg and impressive quantities of eggs and butter. Rum is usually an ingredient, though omitted in this recipe. The ingredients are handed over to the local baker several weeks before Christmas and the cakes given as gifts to family and friends. An obvious precedent is the Portuguese *Bolo-Rei* (King's Cake), a Christmas cake made with raisins, nuts, candied fruits, and port. Another intriguing recipe in this cookbook is for guava cheese, a kind of paste made from boiled and mashed guavas, lime juice, sugar and butter that is cooked, poured into a mold, and cooled.

Conclusion

The gastronomical legacy of the Portuguese was widespread, profound, and enduring. Their far-flung trading posts were the hubs of a global exchange of fruits and vegetables between the Western Hemisphere, Africa, Oceania, Asia, and India. The Portuguese brought potatoes, tomatoes, chilies, okra (ladies fingers), corn, papayas, pineapples, cashews, peanuts, guavas, and tobacco to India, and these products were thoroughly assimilated into the regional cuisines. In Bengal, the Portuguese may have introduced the technique of curdling milk that became the basis of the famous Bengali sweet industry. Goan dishes such as *vindaloo*, *buffath*, and Chicken *xacuti* also became part of Calcutta's cosmopolitan cuisine.

Appendix 1: Some plants introduced by the Portuguese into Bengal and their use in Bengali cuisine.

English name (& botanical)	Bengali name	Comments	Use in Bengali cuisine
Cashew (*Anacardium occidentale*)	Kaju, hijli badam	Native of S.E. Brazil, introduced on W. coast of India to check erosion. Today India is the world leader in production. 'Kaju' is Port. corruption of Brazilian 'acajau.' 'Hijli' is a coastal region in Bengal where it is grown.	Snack
Pineapple (*Ananas Sativa*)	Ananas	Introduced in Bengal in 1594 from Brazil. The Tupi Indian name is 'nana'.	Fresh in chutney
Peanut (*Arachis Hypogaea*)	Chinar badam	Introduced from America, perhaps via Africa. The Bengali name means 'Chinese nut' so could have arrived via Manila or China. However 'Chinese' is also used by Bengalis to denote anything foreign.	Snacks.
Papaya (*Carica Papaya*)	Papaya	Orig. in C. America. Came to India via Philippines (where the Spanish took it) and Malaysia.	Unripe as vegetable. Paste used as meat tenderizer.
Mangosteen (*Garcinia Mangostana*)	Mangus- tan	Brought from Malacca.	
Sweet Potato (*Impoaoea Batatas*)	Ranga alu, chine alu	Introduced from Africa or Brazil. Bengali name means 'red potato'.	Vegetable dishes, shrimp dishes.
Potato (*Solanum tuberosum*)	Alu; vilayati alu ('European potato')	Spanish took first potatos to Europe in 1570. On the west coast of India, called 'batata' (sweet potato). In 1780, a basket of potatos was presented to Sir Warren Hastings in Calcutta. Grown in the foothills of the Himalayas in 1830. By 1860, had become popular in Calcutta, but orthodox people avoided them until this century.	In curries with meat and seafood. Filling for samosas. Vegetable dishes, dried and with gravy; i.e., shukto, poshto.
Tomato (*Lycopersicon Lycoperiscum*)	Vilayati begoon ('Euro- pean eggplant')	Orig. in Mexico or Peru. Came via England in late C18.	Chutney. Flavoring for dals.
Chilies (*Capsicum frutescens*)	Lanka	The Bengali name indicates it may have come via Sri Lanka. Orig. in C. America, chili in all its forms spread rapidly in India as substitute for long and black pepper. By the mid C16 Europeans were calling it 'Calcutta pepper'.	Fresh, dried, and powdered. Used as flavoring and decoration.
Custard Apple (*Anona Squamosa*)	Ata	Native to S. America, came to India from West Indies via Cape of Good Hope or the Philippines. Well naturalized in Bengal.	
Tobacco (*Nicotiana Tabacum*)	Tamak	Introduced into South India by Portugal in the early C16.	

Appendix 1 continued.

English name (& botanical)	Bengali name	Comments	Use in Bengali cuisine
Guava (*Psidium guyava*)	Peyara	May have orig. in Peru. Known in Eastern India as early as 1550. Widely grown in Bengal.	Eaten as fruit. Also guava cheese, jelly.
Corn or Maize (*Zea Maya*)	Bhutta	Originated in Central America. Achaya notes temple carvings from C12 A.D. showing what he claims are corn cobs.	Roasted and eaten on the cob, usually purchased from street sellers.
Sapodilla (*Manilkara achras*)	Chiku	The bark of the tree yields chicle used by Aztecs for chewing; hence Bengali 'chiku'. Brought from Mozambique to Goa or Philippines to Malaysia, and thence to east coast.	
Litchi (*Niphelium litcvhi*)	Lichi	Native to southern China. Portuguese brought to Bengal in late C17.	Eaten as fruit. Goans make litchi wine
Okra, Lady's Fingers (*Abnelmoschus esculentus*)	Bhindi	Probably from Africa.	Popular vegetable. Fried, cooked in stews.

Sources: Campos, pp 253-258 ; Achaya, esp. pp 218-238; M. Toussaint-Samat, Yule and Burnell. pp 284-286 .

Appendix 2: Some Goan recipes found in Bengali cookbooks

Goan Dish	Ingredients	Spices
Buffath, Buffado	Beef, potatoes, carrots, radishes, green onions, vinegar	Ginger, garlic, turmeric, chilies, mustard seeds, cumin, coriander seeds
Buffath II	Duck, potatoes, onions, coconut milk, vinegar, lime juice	Cloves, green cardamoms, cinnamon, coriander, green chilies
Temperado	Prawns, gourd or pumpkin, coconut milk	Kashmiri chili powder, green chilies, cloves, cardamoms, cinnamon, sugar
Chicken Xacuti	Chicken, coconut milk, onion, tamarind pulp Marinade: lime juice, ginger, garlic, chilies, coriander leaves	Grated coconut, green chilies, nutmeg, garlic, coriander, cumin, pepper, aniseed, poppy seeds, mustard seeds, fenugreek, green cardamon, caraway seeds
Sorpotel	Pork, pork liver, pork kidneys, ox tongue, beef heart, vinegar, onions	Garlic, ginger, cumin seeds, cloves, green cardamoms, cinnamon, black pepper, dry red chilies
Pork Vindaloo	Pork Marinade: vinegar, ginger, garlic, and spices Mustard oil for frying	Red chilies, coriander, cumin, cloves, green cardamoms, cinnamon
Kuziddo (Mutton curry)	Mutton, white radish, onion, lime, water. Cooking medium, ghee	Ginger, garlic, green chilies
Richadoo (Baked crab)	Crab, onions, lime, butter. Crab is boiled, minced with other ingredients, put in shells and baked	Fresh herbs, pepper
Bolo du Portugal	Semolina, ground sugar, butter, eggs, almonds, rose water, brandy	
Bole Comadree	Grated coconuts, cardamoms, rice flour, cinnamon, lemon essence, eggs, butter, milk	
Bole de Amandrue Pudding	Eggs, sugar, chana (curd), sliced almonds, bread soaked in milk	
Bibingka (Coconut pudding)	Coconut milk, sugar syrup, rice flour	

Sources: Gupta, et al; Limond.

BIBLIOGRAPHY

Achaya, K.T. *Indian Food: A Historical Companion*. Delhi: Oxford University Press, 1994

Anderson, Jean. *The Food of Portugual*.New York: Hearst Books, 1994.

Andrews, Jean. 'Around the World with the Chili Pepper: Post Columbian Distribution of Domesticated Capsicums,' *The Journal of Gastronomy*, Vol. IV No. 3, Autumn 1988, pp 21-36

Banerji, Chitrita. *Life and Food in Bengal*. New Delhi: Rupa & Co., 1993

Boxer, Charles R. *The Portuguese Seaborne Empire, 1415-1825*. London: Hutchinson, 1969

Burton, David. *The Raj at Table*. London, Faber and Faber, 1993.

Campos, Joaquim Joseph A. *History of the Portuguese in Bengal*. Calcutta, London: Butterworth, 1919.

Das Gupta, Minakshie, Bunny Gupta, and Jaya Chaliha. *The Calcutta Cookbook*. New Delhi, Penguin, 1995

Disney, Anthony R. *Twilight of the Pepper Empire: Portuguese Trade in Southwest India in the Early 17th Century*. Cambridge: Harvard University Press, 1978.

Limond, (Late) Mrs. Dora. *Anglo-Indian and Portuguese Dishes*, Calcutta: L.O.H. de Silva, n.d.

Prakash, Om. *Food and Drinks in Ancient India*, New Delhi: Munshi Ram Manohar, La., 1961

Raychaudhuri, Tapankumar. *Bengal Under Akbar and Jahangir*. Calcutta: A. Mukherjee & Co. Ltd., 1953.

Roy, Pratap Kumar. 'The Food and Sweets of Calcutta,' in *Calcutta: The Living City*, Volume II. Ed. Sukanta Chaudhuri. Calcutta: Oxford University Press, 1990. pp 337-340.

Roy, Atul Chandra. *History of Bengal. Mughal Period*. Calcutta: Nababharat Publishers,

Sarkar, Sir Jadu-Nath. *The History of Bengal. Muslim Period 1200-1757*. Patna: Janaki Prakashan, 1977.

Sen, Colleen Taylor. 'Exotic Delights: The Cuisine of West Bengal,' *Yoga International*, May-June 1995, pp 50-56.

Toussaint-Samat, Maguelonne. *History of Food*. Trans. Anthea Bell. Cambridge, Ma.: Blackwell, 1992.

Yule, Henry, and A. C. Burnell. *Hobson-Jobson: A Glossary of Colloquial Anglo-Indian Words and Phrases*. 2nd edition. London and New York: Routledge & Kegan Paul, 1986.

NOTES

[1] Quoted in Campos. Published in 1572, this great Portuguese epic celebrates the Portuguese encounters with the East, starting with Vasco da Gama's voyage to India. Camões himself spent part of his life in India.

[2] See Disney. Factors contributing to the decline of the Portuguese spice trade included undercapitalization; a deteriorating global market for pepper; and lack of support and even outright hostility on the part of the governments in Lisbon and Goa. The Viceroy in Goa and his advisors had an 'aristocratic disdain for merchants', many of whom were converted Jews, and even turned some over to the Inquisition in India.

[3] Minakshie Das Gupta, et al, p. 148

[4] Several years ago the head chef at the Gymkhana Club in New Delhi was a Mogh, as was the owner of a Bangladeshi restaurant I met in New York City in the 1970s.

[5] Campos, pp. 177-188.

[6] Ibid., pp 204-220. See also Sarkar, pp 368-370.

[7] Atul Chandra Roy, p. 478

[8] Banerji, p. 9.

[9] Achaya, pp 128-133.

[10] Banerji, p. 122.

[11] Achaya, pp 132-33.

[12] Banerji, p. 122.

[13] Indians might have taken quite naturally and quickly to tobacco because of a long tradition of smoking. In ancient times Indians smoked a form of cigar called *dhumavartis*, which was said to have medicinal value. One version was made of cardamon, saffron, sandal wood, aloewood, resin and thinly cut bark of trees like the banyan and pipal, which burn quickly and have fragrance. The mixture was finely ground, made into a paste, and coated on a hollow reed 6 inches long. The reed was removed when dry and the 'cigar' was smeared with ghee and lit. Many virtues were ascribed to smoking: it was said to soothe the nerves, put the smoker in a cheerful mood, strengthen his teeth and hair, sweeten his breath, and cure many diseases. However, one medical writer found it necessary to state that smoking indulged in excessively could lead to ill health. Prakash, pp 254-257.

Hard Rations

Roy Shipperbottom

Froissart, describing the Scots invading England, marvelled at the rapid advances achieved by their self-sufficient horsemen who each carried his own food and cooking equipment; oatmeal and a broad plate of metal.

> When they have eaten too much sodden flesh, and their stomach appears weak and empty, they place this plate over the fire, mix with water their oatmeal, and when the plate is heated, they put a little of the paste upon it, and make a thin cake, like a cracknel or biscuit...

This frugal approach was echoed in World War II when small Long Range Desert Groups, operating behind enemy lines in North Africa, relied on parched oatmeal mixed with water to form a soup. Thirst was quenched by chewing an onion. Tea was important to them: made with water boiled on a biscuit tin filled with sand soaked in petrol. When ignited this served as a useful stove.

The British response to feeding numbers of men in difficult circumstances in the field was canned bully beef and biscuits. Biscuits baked to endure and be stored indefinitely and which, in World War I, were hard and almost useless. Jeremy MacClancy reports a gunner saying, 'you had to put them on a firm surface and smash them with a stone or something.' They were soaked in water for days to make them edible; in World War II they were said to have improved, but difficult-to-eat food continued to be issued and some soldiers carried a curiously hard chocolate block kept in a tin in the hip pocket and only to be consumed in an emergency. It could not be smashed and would only succumb to a persistent sucking and gnawing.

In World War II British troops envied American rations, and referred to them all, erroneously, as 'K rations'. A.B. Keys, an American physiologist, developed the 'K' ration for the US armed forces – it was a lightweight pack, nutritious and sought after for the small comforts the pack held, particularly cigarettes. Douglas Allanbrook, in his excellent memoir, *See Naples*, described K rations as:

> smallish oblong boxes wrapped in waterproof paper containing concentrated food: dried beef with carrot chips, thick crackers resembling compressed cardboard, rounds of processed cheese, lemonade or coffee powder and always, thanks to the American tobacco industry, little packs of cigarettes. Constipation was the order of the day with K rations.

'C' rations, which were canned and heavy, consisted of pork and beans and had the opposite effect on bowels and 'erred on the side of looseness'. As the group trekked through the Italian mountains they met goatherds and were able to exchange K rations for cups of foaming goats' milk.

A Piper Cub dropped a new ration, the D ration, which

> turned out to be concentrated chocolate bars, rocklike in consistency, and, as their wrappers informed us, jammed full of vitamins and life sustaining grains. They were difficult to eat, the best method being to whittle them with a knife and to eat the shavings or mix them with hot goats milk.

An inventive dish, named by Douglas Allanbrook, 'Welsh rarebit aux herbes de montagne' consisted of melted K-ration processed cheese with crumbled sawdust biscuits topped with wild thyme and rosemary.

Some ration boxes, abandoned by returning US forces in South East Asia, contained 2 small cans of stew, biscuits, a small, difficult to open, can of pork and some welcome comforts including toothpaste, Lucky Strike cigarettes, tightly packed toilet paper and a cube of chewing gum. Chewing gum enclosed in some rations was said to 'relieve facial tension'.

Despite the jokes, the food served in British Army barracks was adequate and sometimes excellent and the capacity of the army to serve regiments on the move was impressive. These skills were the result of good training and logistics and developed to deal with large numbers. However, there are times when advances are so rapid and movement so fluid that catering facilities are impossible. Then the Defence Ministry is able to use its special phrases to describe the adverse factors that soldiers have to endure. In a war – 'a high intensity conflict' – soldiers have 'environmental insults' (extremes of heat and cold) and problems with food, short or poor rations or no food at all, which are 'nutritional insults'. Insults may occur when men are isolated from the main body or are part of special forces engaged in clandestine operations. In the Falklands War a hidden SAS observation post overlooked Stanley, then occupied by Argentinian forces, and for over 20 days existed on cheese by day and soup by night. There is an SAS 7–14 day ration but the speed of setting up an operation, and sometimes a hazy knowledge of the time it might take, means that food is almost forgotten and, when packs have to be carried, and weight has to be considered, there is a natural tendency to prefer ammunition to food. Some rely on boiled sweets and Mars bars, as do some members of United States SEAL forces who have no official ration policy. They argue that the nature of the operations they undertake should not occupy more than 24–48 hours and their men should be able to cope with that.

The US forces' MRE (Meals Ready to Eat) rations in the Gulf War were considered by British troops to be inferior to their rations, but British Special Forces admired the small packs of M & M sweets and the tiny bottles of Tabasco sauce that enlivened the meal. Scrounged bottles enhanced the British foil packs of sausage and mash. It will be interesting to see how the privatization of some front-line support services will influence rations. In the United States, the Logistic Civilian Assisted Provisions scheme, let to Brown and Root, supplies provisions worldwide and there are proposals to use civilian contractors to supply the British Army.

Special forces are extremely interested in survival food and they are told that they can survive three weeks without food but only three days without water. Training in obtaining water and edible wild food is given and assistance from aboriginals adept at survival in hostile environments has proved invaluable, for example in the preparation, by Australian Special Forces, of 'snack maps' which include details of plants and animals which will assist survival.

MI9, the department involved in escape and evasion, approved a ration kit issued to aircrew. This pack was designed to be used by those who had escaped by parachute or been fortunate enough to survive an emergency landing. Originally based on what could be housed in a standard flat cigarette tin, it contained boiled sweets, malt tablets, a fishing line (that was seldom used as such but was useful), benzedrine, a compass and water purification tablets.

Round-the-world sailors and lone mariners, when writing of their voyages, usually include a helpful chapter about the considerable amounts of provisions carried. The weight of food, which is a problem to the soldier, never occurs to the sailor. Based on research and experience, and using the latest technology, with satellite navigation, and solar stills to ensure a water supply, it would appear that little could go wrong. But disaster is swift when a boat is holed by whales or smashed by floating debris or freak waves. Time to quit the boat is minimal and there is little chance of salvage, although anything that can be retrieved may be useful to assist life on a raft. The shipwrecked mariner who achieves a place in a lifeboat or raft has considerable problems; what had seemed safe is now lost, and the swiftness of disaster, loss of personal possessions and possible loss of shipmates, all have considerable impact. The main problem is that of water. S.T. Coleridge's *Ancient Mariner*, has the memorable line, 'Water, water, everywhere nor any drop to drink,' a paradox which sums up the problem.

Lifeboat and liferaft rations are now carefully considered and do not include thirst-provoking food. Fresh water is imperative and around 1.5 litres per person per day is advised. The Admiralty *Manual of Seamanship* advocates a survival pack that will last each person in a 20-man liferaft for five days. Presumably modern search and rescue techniques should discover any survivors within that time: a modern marine beacon hitting the sea immediately contacts a satellite giving a distress signal and position. A suggested lifeboat ration is:

	Desirable	Compromise	Minimum	Calorific Value
Water	1400cc	800cc	500cc	-
Boiled sweets	100g	100g	100g	400
Toffee 40% Fat	100g	100g	-	500
Biscuits 20% Fat	100g	-	-	500
Sweetened Condensed Milk	100g	100g	-	350
Net weight	1800g	1100g	600g	-
Total calories	1750	1250	400	-

Source: Harvey and McCance

This was adopted by the Royal Navy as adequate for wartime conditions when rescue could take five days; in peacetime, supplies for two days are thought to be adequate because search and rescue are more easily undertaken. The digestion of protein involves the use of body-water and is best avoided. It is advised that fish or birds should not be eaten unless there is plenty of water available.

The WHO advise the taking of seasickness remedies to minimize dehydration and there is general agreement that not drinking water for the first 24 hours is a prudent saving (except for those who are injured or have been sick), thereafter, 500ml (1 pint) a day until supplies run low when the ration is cut to 100ml. An intake of 600ml of water will keep an average person fit for five to seven days and although there will be a loss of 5 per cent of body weight, it is expected that a seaman will, when rescued, be fit to resume duty within a few hours.

However a period of 10–14 days on liferafts will case loss of 10 per cent of body weight and the survivor will be lethargic, depressed and irritable. After this time the survivors, without food and water, will sink into a state of being beyond coherent thought. Dr. Alain Bombard claimed, in 1952, that it was possible to survive on sea water until one could catch fish and express liquid from them. Bombard states that sea water is dangerous and causes death by nephritis (inflammation of the kidneys). He argued that he would consume the permissible intake of sodium chloride, or common salt, by swallowing sea water, about a pint and a half a day. He maintained that the other chemicals in sea water were equivalent to the minerals in French mineral waters such as Vichy and Contrexéville. He reckoned that he could last five days on sea water, after which the danger of nephritis became acute. His brave experiments at sea confirmed the importance of mental endurance and demonstrated that for sixty-five days he could live exclusively on what he could catch from the sea. Bombard, however, was a medical doctor who monitored his own body with iron self-discipline and never touched the sealed food reserves that he carried. It is unlikely that the experiment is capable of being repeated unless one finds extraordinary people to undertake the hazards involved.

The current belief held by some is that it is possible to consume small amounts of sea water provided you do not need to, but this is not the official view: 'Never drink sea water, do not even moisten the mouth with it as the desire to swallow is overwhelming', states the Admiralty Manual, continuing, 'during World War Two, the mortality rate in lifeboats where salt water was drunk ranged between 700% and 800% higher than in boats where only fresh water was used. Rain must be caught when possible and it is useful to spread clothing which can be wrung into a container.' There is a psychological benefit gained if the rations are given three times a day as distress has been observed at meal times if nothing is given and a set ration does restore confidence.

This advice has been gained by interviews with survivors and experiments with courageous volunteers. A study of the voyage of the launch of H.M.S. *Bounty* under the command of William Bligh (1754-1817) would have revealed much about the techniques of survival at sea.

Bligh has been ill-served by legend and Hollywood films; he was certainly hot tempered and tactless, but his seamanship, navigation skills and discipline in the launch saved his men. He wrote to his wife that the launch was hoisted out and 18 people put into her and he was forced to join them making 19 in total in a launch '23 feet from stem to stern and rowed by six oars … We were so deep and lumbered that it was believed we could never reach the shore and some of them made their joke of it.' They rowed about thirty miles to Tofoa, landed, looked for food and water, were attacked and lost a man, took to the boat and were pursued with canoes loaded with stones 'which they threw with much force and exactness'. Fortunately night fell and they escaped.

Bligh told the men that there was no hope of relief until they came to Timor, a distance of 1200 leagues (3,600 miles) and secured their agreement that they would live on 'one ounce of Bread a day and a Gill of water'. Bread meant ship's biscuit. Bligh,

> after recommending this promise for ever to their memory bore away for New Holland and Timor across a Sea but little known…without any single map of any kind and nothing but my own recollection and general knowledge of the situation of Places to direct us. Unfortunately we had lost part of our provisions, what we had was 20 lbs of Pork, 3 bottles (of wine), 5 Quarts Rum, 150 lbs Bread and 28 Galls of Water. I steered to the WNW with Strong Gales and heavy Rains…

Biscuit, they estimated, would last six weeks issued at 2 oz per man per day. However, simple division reveals that it would have lasted nine weeks – presumably Bligh was being prudent. The ration was initially guessed but Blight made a pair of scales from coconut shells and utilised pistol balls found in the boat as weights. At twenty-five to the pound one ball gave each man about a third of his daily bread ration, which was issued at 8 a.m., noon and sunset, with a quarter of a pint of water. The water problem was relieved because they were able to catch rainwater.

After twenty-two days Bligh estimated that he had enough bread left for another twenty-nine days and he estimated that Timor would be reached in another thirty days but also allowed that they might have to go on to Java and so he stopped the supper ration. It was a bold decision and Bligh said,

> I was apprehensive that this would be ill received, and that it would require my utmost resolution to enforce it; for small as the quantity was which I intended to take away, for our future good, yet it might appear to my people like robbing them of life, and some, who were less patient than their companions, I expected would very ill brook it.

He put it to the men and said he would increase the ration when he could and they agreed with his decision. They caught three sea birds and they were divided into eighteen pieces and shared by a man pointing at a portion saying, 'Who shall have this?' and another, with his back turned, called out a name. The blood was given to those most in need. Some dipped their bread in salt water to make it more palatable but Bligh preferred to use part of his water allowance mixed with bread and eat it slowly, 'so that I was as long at dinner as if it had been a more plentiful meal.' Bligh did increase the ration and doubled it when he realised that he would reach Timor and did not have to go on to Java; he also at this time gave wine to everyone.

Bligh wrote in his 'Narrative',

> In our late situation, it was not the least of my distress, to be constantly assailed with the melancholy demands of my people for an increase of allowance, which it grieved me to refuse. The necessity of observing the most rigid economy in the distribution of provisions was so evident that I resisted their solicitations and never departed from the agreement we made at setting out.

Landings on small islands searching for food yielded oysters, which were stewed, and some seabirds, but the great benefit was the relief from cramped conditions. With an improved feeling of well-being, stupid disputes arose about the preparation of the oyster stew and Bligh's intention to increase a stock of dried oysters was abandoned because the men were apathetic and weak. They were emaciated, limbs full of sores and their bodies 'nothing but skin and bones habited in rags'. But eventually Bligh reached Kupang where he was able to restore his crew to health. Bligh had assessed the food available, informed his crew of the rations policy, obtained their consent and promises, issued the food fairly, three times a day at the usual mealtimes – all procedures that are now considered correct survival techniques. Bligh proudly recorded,

> Thus happily ended through the assistance of Divine Providence without accident a voyage of the most extraordinary nature that ever happened in the world, let it be taken in its extreme duration and so much want of the necessities of life.

For forty-two days Bligh had, in an open and overloaded boat, sailed three thousand, seven hundred and one nautical miles.

ACKNOWLEDGEMENTS

I am grateful to the Librarian, United States Military Academy, West Point and Harlan Walker for their helpful information.

BIBLIOGRAPHY

Admiralty Manual of Seamanship, Vol.2, HMSO, 1967.

Danton, Graham, *Theory and Practice of Seamanship*, 8th Edition, Routledge & Kegan Paul, 1980.

Hervey, G.R. and R.H. McCance, *Proc. Nut.Soc.*, 1954, Vol.13, No.1.

World Health, January 1963, 'Advice to Castaways'.

Brunton, P., ed. and introduction, *'Awake, Bold Bligh', William Bligh's Letters*, State Library of New South Wales, Alan & Unwin, 1989.

Callahn, Steven, *Adrift*, Bantam Press, Transworld, 1986.

Allanbrook, Douglas, *See Naples, A Memoir*, Peter Davison, Boston, 1995.

Bombard, Dr. Alain, *The Bombard Story*, André Deutsch, 1954.

Danielsson, Bengt, *What happened on the Bounty*, George Allan & Unwin, 1962.

Growing Momentum towards a Global Cuisine

Art Siemering

One development that concerns culinarians worldwide is the growth of a global cuisine that blurs the long-nurtured local and regional distinctions among our foods and beverages. Some fear permanent losses as a result.

Even now, the pace at which foods and culinary ideas sweep across cultures and continents is intensifying and accelerating swiftly. Formerly remote ingredients and cooking styles are creating a whole new mosaic as they are transplanted and reinterpreted all over the world.

Where we stand

The seeds for a global cuisine sprouted first at top restaurants in national capitals and other business destinations worldwide. This process has escalated with the multitude of American fast-food and casual dining outlets turning up in so many of these cities.

Over time, virtually every chef employed by the great hotel chains gathers global experience in locales as diverse as Singapore, San Juan, Toronto and Dubai. And at each stop, the chefs carry away ideas and techniques for which they will find future use elsewhere. A key question is whether indicators like these foretell a dandelion effect that someday will carpet every corner of the world.

Though the day is already at hand when visitors to nearly any country must trek further off the beaten track for a true taste of native cooking, I am one who doubts that global cuisine will overwhelm the world's local and regional eating patterns within the near future.

What to expect

The world's future culinary map may soon resemble nothing so much as a complex circuit board. As the main circuit, global cuisine will feed on interconnections with thousands of subsidiary lines that carry its local and regional roots. A by-product of this is fresh appreciation from a much broader audience for the most worthy or unique points of difference. But ironically, this will also be the means by which an umbrella cuisine redoubles in strength as more of the once-obscure ingredients and cooking styles are drawn into the global mainstream. Look for the immediate rise of what I call 'Global Roadfood' drawn from many cultures to meet the needs of a fast-expanding class of international road warriors whose customers, suppliers and employees are spread in all corners.

One of the earliest and most crucial culinary battles of the twenty-first century will be fought over how this rising demand is to be met – and the most likely scenario will set many of us on edge. Within the next ten to twenty years, there is a strong likelihood that menus everywhere will be Americanized to an alarming degree. Even now, certain aspects of American culture are credited with worldwide dominance. And it seems certain that every movie, music video, CD or television series that crosses all those borders will stimulate greater demand for American culture in its other forms – specifically, for American food on a level more elevated than the McDonald's, Pizza Hut and KFC stores that circle the world even now.

But that's only one aspect of what I have in mind. Whether we like it or not, the USA's highly entrepreneurial, ethnically diverse culture will also serve as a springboard for the most widely accepted versions of Italian, Asian, Hispanic and other ethnic cuisines as they make their move internationally.

At least in commercial terms, the notion of strictly authentic ethnic food will be viewed increasingly as narrow-minded and out of date. Soon, much of the world will be dining on American-modified or 'improved' versions of ethnic foods as more of them follow the same trail blazed by the pizza. The underpinning for this process is that outsiders (read Americans) can make the most objective judgements about another country's cuisine by eliminating pride and emotion from the process of choosing those elements most likely to succeed in markets around the world. Our best hope may lie not in avoiding this likelihood, but in seeing that it is conducted with a measure of integrity. For one thing, we shouldn't overlook the possibility of strategic alliances in which American companies seek ethnically pure partners to lend cachet to their world-circling efforts. And then there's the tantalizing prospect of turnabout. We'll see more of what I call a 'Fast-Food Boomerang'. If McDonald's prospers with its American menu in Moscow, how long will it be before they're testing Russian fast foods – say, *shashlik* and *pierogi* – in the USA? And it won't be long before Japanese-owned restaurant and hotel chains aim new concepts straight at the American market.

In the USA, global cuisine is gaining ground even at the highest levels. A recent story by Michael Batterberry in our *Wine Spectator* magazine concluded that 'Today's star American chef needn't even be American.' In support, the author borrowed a remark by French-born, Los Angeles-based Michael Richard (chef-owner of the prestigious restaurant, Citrus): 'Yes, I'm a French regional chef,' Richard said, 'Only my region is Southern California.'

Agents of change

- In country after country, society's most ambitious and aspiring elements will lead the way. Global cuisine will manifest a generational appeal ranging far beyond the attraction of American hamburgers and french fries.

  Youthful enthusiasm will be far from unanimous, of course, but there seems little doubt that worldly influences will make their biggest inroads among the younger set. We know that many in the generation coming of age will stake their own futures on internationalization, treating world-ranging food knowledge and experience as a key element in furthering their own ambitions.

- The Infobahn will make global contacts a matter of routine. In any country, computer networks will permit curious eaters or cooks to link directly with the best authorities on unfamiliar cuisines, bypassing such traditional interpreters as the chefs, cookbook writers and journalists in their own nations.

  Many culinarians are destined to become 'Virtual Globetrotters' as world-ranging interviews, consultations and exchanges among journalists, chefs and other professionals become quite the norm, facilitated by simultaneous translations even as they speak, and by technological leaps by which one may establish an instantaneous, face-to-face presence anywhere in the world.

  To sharpen our Japanese cooking skills, for example, we might work *virtually* side by side with chefs at Tokyo's Imperial Hotel. Or in a research mode, we might be escorted on a counter-by-counter walking tour of the basement food halls in major Ginza-district department stores.

- The global economy will fertilize the spread of a global cuisine, pushing it forward as a defining expression of growing wealth and worldly sophistication. To see the truth in this supposition, one has only to review the various reports documenting China's potentially boundless appetite for meat. One of these noted that Chinese consumption of pork has grown by 11 million metric tons over the past five years, which is more than the *entire* US pork market.

Most experts agree this demand is fuelled by growing affluence and the notion that meat is what people eat when they can afford it. A recent report in *Forbes*, one of America's leading business magazines, concluded that what's true for China is mirrored throughout much of Asia. 'Large, populous countries such as Indonesia, Thailand and the Philippines are rapidly urbanizing. They're gaining purchasing power, losing farmland and adding more animal proteins and processed foods to their diets,' *Forbes* reported.

- As culinarians, one of our central concerns is the direction that global cuisine will take in terms of quality. Will it become a mish-mash with few redeeming features, as did America's own Cajun-style food once it gravitated from Louisiana to commercial kitchens that were blissfully or wilfully ignorant of its true tastes and traditions? Or will the global approach serve as a worldwide window on healthful and otherwise deserving ingredients such as tofu or tropical tubers?

Most likely, we'll see evidence to confirm both directions as this trend advances. And that's the best possible reason why culinary thinkers must stay actively involved. Someone has to insist that the impending wave of ethnic adaptations and cross-cultural hybrids be at least as satisfying as the originals that inspire them.

- Finally, there is the delicious possibility that undiscovered foods – by way of necessity or their own virtues – may gain worldwide acceptance in what, by historical precedents, will be a very brief period of time.

We're correct in fretting over the very real dangers of confining our favorite foodstuffs – from fruits and vegetables to grains and the various proteins – within a dangerously small range of strains. But the fact is there's an infinite range of potential foods out there – and within the next several years we'll be eating many more of them. More than 700 species of potatoes have been registered in Peru, for instance, and a recent story in *The Economist* magazine estimated that the earth nurtures 40,000 species of flora and fauna that have yet to be classified.

This leaves a whole lot of breathing room before we're reduced to eating what are currently referred to as 'microlivestock', or in plain English, bugs.

Rocambole, a Short Journey

Colin Spencer

A short journey or a long one into oblivion? Rocambole (*Allium scorodoprasum*) – from being cultivated in the medieval garden to growing wild quite near (in one case only fifty yards away) where five hundred years ago it was once cultivated.

It was still cultivated in the seventeenth-century walled gardens where John Evelyn speaks of it when he prefers it to garlic, remarking 'it is much better for ladies palates: a light touch on the dish with a clove thereof, much better supplied by the gentler Roccombo.' The botanist, Richard Bradley in 1718 laments that though rocambole, for its high relish in sauces has been greatly esteemed formerly, 'is nowadays hardly to be met with.' He adds that 'considering how small a quantity of it is sufficient to give us that relish which many onions can hardly give, it ought to be preferred.'

I first came across rocambole thirty years ago on the Greek island of Corfu, where I was drawn to stop and examine it because of its twisted stem and strangely beautiful seed head. It is these bulblets which cooks used to add when flavouring a sauce. When I chewed parts of the stem it was obviously a cousin of garlic. I then entirely forgot about it until last year walking around the hilltop town of Winchelsea, I found it growing profusely all over the steep banks. Again its seed head draws one's attention because it is so individual. One wonders that dried flower arrangers have not used it – perhaps they have.

In fifty years of roaming around the British countryside I have not stumbled over rocambole before. Why should it be growing here? The answer seems obvious. Winchelsea was built in the 1280s after the sea had destroyed old Winchelsea. The new town built on the grid system on a steep hill became a flourishing port, the houses had deep vaulted cellars beneath them (many of them still in existence) to store the imported French wines. They all would have had 'herbers' or small enclosed gardens, or directly above the port, terraced gardens that used part of the steep hill which the town was built on. There, herbs and vegetables, grown for immediate use, would have included several members of the allium family, including, I surmise, rocambole.

But during the fourteenth and fifteenth centuries, the French attacked the town seven times in all and by the 1600s the churches and hospitals were in ruins, while the river Brede had silted up and ships could no longer use the port. Winchelsea was almost deserted. The remains of the houses were pulled down, their stones used for new buildings, the walls around the small herbers were demolished and larger gardens made for grander houses. In all this destruction and reorganisation many of the old plants were lost.

It is interesting to see where the rocambole grows now. On the north and east sides of the steep hill there is thick forest, home of many badgers, where only shade-loving plants grow at ground level. On the west side where the hill is not so steep there is good pasture for sheep. On the south side where the trees merge into pasture, near one of the old medieval gates, rocambole grows on the grass verge where the sheep can't touch it. There also I have found lovage and angelica. But the biggest clump is on a very steep part of the east hill, the only part that is unwooded and also, because of its steepness, untouched by the cows which pasture below, between the terraced gardens and the old port. It is the obvious place for seeds from the original gardens to have blown down and rooted. It travelled fifty yards, if that.

It is thought that rocambole was unknown to the ancient world. In Loudon's *Encyclopaedia of Plants* (1855) he claims it was a native of Denmark, formerly cultivated in England, but now thoroughly neglected. John Ray in 1688 does not mention it, though it was grown by Quintinie, Louis XIV's gardener, but Townsend in *The Complete Seedsman* (1726) says 'it is mightily in request'. Interestingly enough, American gardeners mention it among the garden esculents up to 1832.[1]

Why after that, should it journey into oblivion on both sides of the Atlantic? I suppose because in the epoch of the rising bourgeoisie which in a growing mercantile society also aspired to ever greater social heights, pungent aromatic smells upon the breath were considered only to come from the vulgar working classes. Rocambole was banished together with garlic and leeks and now we have almost forgotten it ever existed.

Culinary uses

Rocambole appears above ground early in the year, in February, about the same time as sorrel. The green shoots can then be cut and used as chives. The flavour is that of garlic chives. The green shoot will slowly harden and become unusable, but by July you have the seed pods to pick and use in a sauce. If half the sauce is blended you will have an aromatic, faintly garlicky sauce, which is attractively speckled green and purple. The cloves in the root are indistinguishable from garlic in appearance and flavour.

REFERENCE

[1] Mrs Grieve's, *A Modern Herbal* (1931) usually so reliable, misses rocambole out entirely.

Dancing with the Mermaids:
Ship's Biscuit and Portable Soup

Layinka Swinburne

The ship that sailed to 'Noroway over the foam' in 1189 to bring back a little princess as future queen of Scotland was provided with all the comforts that the noble passengers could expect. She was victualled for 34 days and carried many luxuries: sturgeons, lampreys, rice, beans, peas, onions, leeks, cheese, nuts, almonds, figs, raisins, gingerbread, biscuit, many spices; and napkins. Wax torches, tallow candles, cressets and lanterns were fitted to lighten the gloom but the 10 year old Margaret did not survive to appreciate them.[1] According to the ballad of Sir Patrick Spens she drowned when the ship went down with all hands in the Orkneys. In fact she lies buried in Bergen and some say that she died of sea-sickness.

The diet of ordinary mariners was predictable and monotonous. A stew of whatever was available was cooked in a brass cauldron on deck. By the fourteenth century, according to Sir John Froissart, the French fleet was provisioned for three years with biscuit, wine and salt meat. This soon became the staple fare of other sea-farers. Biscuit was always known as bread at sea. The knack of drying bread for keeping was known to the Romans who provided *buccellata*, a type of dried bread or hard biscuit for the troops on the march.[2] Unleavened bread was traditionally used by nomadic people as it kept better than dough raised with yeast and it is difficult to maintain a stable 'sourdough' on the move. No doubt the Hebrews took their unleavened bread with them in their flight from Egypt as a symbol of a return to the nomadic life rather than through not having time to wait for the dough to rise.[3] The method of making a durable and almost indestructible biscuit, by prolonged baking and drying, was adopted by mariners early on. The coast-hugging, and island-hopping early sailors did not plan for long journeys and depended on topping up supplies of fresh bread and meat, fruit and vegetables whenever they touched land.

De Joinville related that when the crusaders in the mid-fourteenth-century seventh crusade overcame a coastal city they commandeered the local supplies of wheat and even took standing corn to supply their expedition.[4] He described as a novelty a report that the Sultan of Cairo sent people up the Nile 'who took with them a kind of bread called biscuit because it was twice baked... and lived on this until they came back again to the Sultan'. He also mentions that the crusaders' ship left three bags of biscuits on the shore of an island for a deserter, to sustain him after he had disappeared to become a hermit.

Queen Margaret of Provence, who accompanied King Louis on the same voyage, sent a party to an island to hunt for fruit for her children. They stayed so long on land to eat fruit themselves that they were nearly left behind when the ship sailed. After a long time at sea the mariners made for the nearest inn or sought out ladies of pleasure round the harbour whilst the officers made for gardens and monasteries. When one such party ventured on shore they recorded 'he gave us our handkerchiefs full of sallats and some sweet herbs, fruit now not being in'. Elsewhere they 'took dry fish to the monastery in Sicily, Messina. We went into a fine garden.' However, even in the Mediterranean, ships might still be at sea for several weeks at a time during which perishable foods would rapidly deteriorate. Bread in particular becomes mouldy and inedible in those conditions. Damp air and salt soon impregnated the stores in spite of the skill of the coopers in making water-tight barrels.

Later maritime powers developed large fleets and haphazard ravaging for supplies was replaced by more careful assembling of food as well as ships and men at major ports before embarking on a venture. Victuals were 'taken into the ship's hold for the pre-fixed time of service abroad.'[5] The provisioning of ships was carefully calculated and officially supervised to prevent graft and ensure adequate food for the crews of sailing ships, galleys and the troops they carried. Any shortfall in quantity or quality would endanger not only the lives of the men but the success of the enterprises whether military or commercial. In the sixteenth century the *veedores* of Phillip II were empowered with overseeing the supplies of the Naples galleys and even on the Turkish galleys the ordinary rations included a generous distribution of biscuit. In Venice in 1606 the total grain consumption of the city was 483,000 *stara* of which 47,500 *stara* were consumed in biscuit for the fleet and these quantities were a serious drain on the resources of the local population.[6] In Henry VIII's ships, the daily amounts of food needed to sustain a man had been agreed as one pound of biscuit, one pound of salt meat and one gallon of ale which in more southerly countries was replaced by wine. Sir Richard Grenville's ship, the *Daintie*, renamed from the *Repentance* which Queen Elizabeth did not approve of, was provisioned in Plymouth in 1597 and naturally took the local product, cider, on board.

For the provisioning of the Spanish Armada, special ovens were set up in Naples, where wheat was cheaper than in Spain at the time, and the demand far exceeded the amount that Andalucia could produce. The biscuit was baked six months ahead of need to ensure the supply. The Armada's needs over-ruled the needs of the local population in Sicily who were reduced to eating chestnut bread and near famine. By the time the fleet set off, the water was putrid and the food decayed and many of the seamen were sick. The English fleet in contrast made up its supplies only six weeks ahead of need with the result that by the time of the battle the crews could only be supplied with half rations as they had only two days supply in reserve.

After the defeat of the Armada the Spanish raids on ports in the south of England continued. To supply even one of the smallest expeditions ordered by Phillip II, the following provisions were taken on board:[7]

> 12,837 barrels of biscuit
> 696 skins of wine
> 1,498 barrels of salt pork
> 1,031 barrels of fish
> 6,082 barrels of cheese
> 2,858 barrels of vegetables
> 2,900 barrels of oil
> 850 barrels of vinegar
> 2,274 barrels of water
> 631 barrels of rice

A barrel or puncheon generally held 224 lb of biscuit so the fleet was supplied with several months rations for ten or twelve thousand men. Rivalry in exploration of the New World and beyond, entailed large numbers of men on prolonged voyages. Huge quantities of biscuit had to be prepared in advance of journeys across the Atlantic or to the Far East. Anson's expedition to the Pacific to capture the Spanish treasure ship set out in 1740 with seven ships and two thousand men, victualled for eighteen months and biscuit was always the largest and most essential component.

The method of making biscuit and the allowance per head remained virtually unchanged for the next three hundred years. In the *Encyclopaedia Britannica* in 1773 is the description 'Sea-bisket is a sort of bread much dried by passing the oven twice to make it keep for sea service. For long voyages they bake it four times and prepare it six months before embarkation. It will hold good for a whole year.'[8]

Biscuit is derived from the French meaning twice cooked, or Latin *panis biscoctum*, *bizcocho*, in Spanish and *Zwieback* in German. In France the hard biscuits were known as *biscuits de guerre*.

These hard biscuits were not to be confused with more delicate confections and dishes for the table of the same name. Even Eliza Smith's recipe for 'the hard biscuit' which will keep a year contained sugar and eggs like Sir Hugh Plat's bisket bread, for which the simple dough was bound with egg white. It was to be baked 'in a long roll as big as your thigh', left in the oven for an hour and cut when it was a day old 'overthwart' before drying out in the oven again. It was to be dusted in sugar and boxed 'and so you may keepe it all the yeare'. The sea biscuits could contain neither sugar, eggs, yeast, nor fat so that there were no ingredients which could putrefy. The baking was brief enough to avoid caramelisation, which would also encourage deterioration, and was followed by prolonged, slow drying to remove any residual moisture.

The basic naval ration in the mid-eighteenth century still consisted of the following, with some variation in quantity in different conditions when food supplies had to be eked out by reducing the allocation or increasing the group sharing it:

	Biscuit	Beer	Beef	Pork	Pease	Oatmeal	Butter	Cheese
Sunday	1 lb	1 gall	-	1 lb	1/2 pt	-	2 oz	-
Monday	1 lb	1 gall	-	-	-	1 pt	2 oz	4 oz
Tuesday	1 lb	1 gall	-	-	-	-	-	-
Wednesday	1 lb	1 gall	-	-	1/2 pt	1 pt	2 oz	4 oz
Thursday	1 lb	1 gall	-	1 lb	1/2 pt	-	-	-
Friday	1 lb	1 gall	-	-	1/2 pt	1 pt	2 oz	4 oz
Saturday	1 lb	1 gall	2 lb	-	-	-	-	-

(C.C. Lloyd 'Victualling the Fleet (18th and 19th centuries)' in *Starving Sailors*, ed. J. Watt, E.J. Freeman and W.F. Bynum, National Maritime Museum 1981.)

The meatless days were known as Banyan days and were only abolished in 1824. The oatmeal was unpopular and was used to make a porridge or 'Burgoo', a gruel with gobbets of 'salt horse' and molasses, served for breakfast . The name is probably derived from *burghul*, the cracked wheat of the Middle East. The cheese like the biscuit was of the hard variety for long keeping. Suffolk cheese, originally from ewes' milk, was issued to the fleet but developed an evil reputation as sometimes it was so hard as to be more suitable for making sailors' buttons than eating.[9] Even locally it was said ,

> Those that made me were uncivil
> They made me harder than the devil,
> Knives won't cut me, fire won't light me,
> Dogs bark at me but cannot bite me.[10]

Cheshire or Cheddar cheese was issued in later years. When in a home port bum-boat women would bring their boats alongside with fresh provisions of bread, cheese, greens and liquor for the sailors.[11] Calculations of the food value of old diets show that they officially amounted to about 4000 calories per day. This compared very favourably with the uncertainties of life and food for the average working adult of the labouring classes. Boteler claimed that 'in particular of victual, especially bread, it is more than can be eaten,' although there were abuses in the weight of meat supplied. Unfortunately prolongation of journeys meant that food often deteriorated. Roderick Random experienced 'putrid salt beef (Irish horse), salt pork of New England, neither fish nor flesh but favoured of both, biscuit of the same country – moving like clock-work, butter served out by the gill.' Also diets which were adequate nutritionally when topped up with fresh meat, fruit and vegetables, could not alone supply all the elements needed for health as they basically were devoid of vitamin C. Scurvy showed up after a few weeks away from shore, and as some of the mariners might well have been ill-nourished before they came aboard, sometimes sooner. It increased the susceptibility to infections and interfered with the healing of injuries and wounds. In spite of the keeping of livestock on board and putting in for fresh vegetables whenever possible, for the next three hundred years scurvy remained a scourge.[12]

The Victualling authorities made arrangements for reclaiming and reissuing unused biscuit after a voyage or campaign. French officials also reissued biscuit from stores of ships that were laid up. Jacques says to Touchstone in *As You Like It*, 'his brain which is Dry as the remainder biscuit after a voyage,' referring to a fool. In one case biscuit was said to have been issued after 40 years storage. The meanness of the Admiralty made certain that Captains kept inventories of all stores and every item had to be accounted for. Before even badly deteriorated biscuit could be disposed of as uneatable, three officers, preferably from another ship, were required to form a board of survey to certify the fact and instruct the boatswain to throw it overboard.[13] Butter was given to the boatswain for the rigging but cheese was to be thrown overboard as by infecting the air it might endanger the health of the ship's crew. To allow for such wastage there was a long standing unwritten agreement that the purser could issue bread at 14 ounces to the pound, endorsed in a successful petition of the Pursers in 1776 in which they asked for an allowance to cover their losses 'of bread by its breaking and turning to Dust: of butter, by that part next to the Firkin being not fit to be issued: of cheese, by its decaying with Mold and Rottenness, and being eaten with Mites, and other insects: of Peas, Oatmeal and Flower, by their being eaten by Cockroaches, Weavels and other Vermin.' This was one of the grievances which later lead to the famous mutiny on the Nore in 1797.

The food of the ship's company was prepared on the mess system by the cook and his assistant in the galley down by the hold. In Nelson's time either or both might be old salts, retired petty officers or Chelsea pensioners who had some disability such as a wooden leg. Pope comments that their only function was to watch water boil and neither literacy nor agility were prime needs. 'Jack Nastyface' or 'Slushy' were some of the cook's soubriquets. A man who wished to evade the press gang disguised himself by smearing his face with grease and soot in the hope of passing for a cook as the cook had the reputation of being the most useless person on board.[14] They were greasy and dirty from tending the fire and skimming the grease as it rose to the top of the pot of boiling salt meat. There was a belief that the greasy scum provoked scurvy. For that reason, as Captain Cook said, 'it was never suffered to be given to the people,' but forbidden as food and destined to be thrown overboard or used to grease the mast or waterproof boots and hats. Cooks illicitly sold the men some of the fat to smear on their biscuit or use in their own concoctions and puddings. On arrival in port a cook might be besieged by grease-dealers bidding for slush.[15] Perhaps this is the origin of the slush fund. It is true that fats soon became rancid in poor conditions of storage and recent work has shown that rancid fat increases the severity of the diarrhoea which often accompanies scurvy. It continued to be discarded until well into the nineteenth century. In the Crimean campaign Alexis Soyer stopped the practice which was also the habit of army cooks as by then the quality of meat was much improved and it was no longer necessary.

Cooking for the ship's crew was done in a huge copper cauldron (one has been recovered from the *Mary Rose*, Henry VIII's flagship), and they continued in use until the last century. Each mess or group of 6-8 men had their food boiled in a bag with a button or tally to identify it. The elected mess 'cook' had to collect the food for his group including the bread ration carefully doled out by the Steward. From the time of Queen Elizabeth, the biscuit was marked with the broad arrow, the royal mark (along with guns and other stores), and from the reign of Charles II, the number of the oven at which it had been baked. The biscuit was stored in barrels and canvas bags in the bread-room. This was almost as important as the gun-room. It should be lined with tin, mats, or deal planks, well caulked, according the ship-wright's instructions in the 1773 *Encyclopaedia Britannica*. Before use it was to be warmed through with charcoal for several days. Old biscuit crumbled to dust and the bread-room was a dirty dusty place in spite of the precautions. The steward's assistant was nick-named Jack the dust, Jack of the bread-room, or Dusty because of it. Weevils and rats were the enemy to be kept out but with such huge stocks kept for many months, contamination was inevitable. Fresh 'bread' was known as hard tack but in a moist atmosphere at sea it gradually became softer. Infestation by weevils in the dry state gradually made the biscuit lighter so that in the end it might be so riddled that a light tap on the table would completely reduce it to dust. There is a record of 41,400 lb of biscuit yielding 2,420 lb of dust after storage. In 1520 after three months and twenty days at sea Ferdinand Magellan recorded,

> having in this time consumed all their Bisket and other Victuals, they fell into such necessitie that they were inforced to eate the powder that remayned thereof, being now full of Wormes and stinking like Pisse, by reason of the salt water.[16]

Spreading the biscuits on a tarpaulin in the sun or re-baking for two hours would kill the weevils. A freshly caught fish placed on top would entice the maggots to crawl out to their destruction.[17]

The taste of weevils was said to be bitter whilst maggots or 'bargemen' tasted cold. Some men preferred to eat in the dark so as not to be too conscious of the 'fresh meat with bread' (weevily biscuit) or the bargemen with their big black heads. The mess allocation was kept in a bread barge, originally an open wooden trough but later not only closed but kept in a locker as the meagre rations were precious. The bread barge contained the allocation for the group and was put out on the table at mealtimes. A watch was kept for anyone stealing bread or taking more than a fair share or 'swapping net for net' when meat was being hooked out of the cauldron. Bread for the men on each watch was stored in a canvas bread-bag. It could not be locked but the experienced bo'sun tied a deceptive bread-bag knot, an underhand reef-knot, round the neck to help them detect theft. A tyro would retie the bag with a standard reef knot, which the expert would easily spot and go searching after the novice thief.[18]

The standard biscuit was 'very dry, bone-hard little slabs of cooked flour and water paste made to keep for ever (unless destroyed by sea-water or weevils) on voyages in old sailing ships. So hard were the biscuits that they had to be soaked before use, and many an ancient mariner has broken his teeth on them. Ship's biscuit have long been extinct and would cause a mutiny on a modern ship.'[19] One well-known and particularly hard brand made in Liverpool was named 'Pantiles'. Passengers in the nineteenth century might be provided with gavels with which to reduce them to manageable fragments.

If the ship's cooks had little latitude in menu planning, the ingenuity of sailors found ways of dressing the boring hard tack and preparing something a bit more interesting with the basic rations. Simply crumbled ship's biscuit could be stirred into the stew of salt horse (jargon for salt beef or pork) and earn the name 'lobscouse'. The land-lubber's version of this dish, a stew of meat, onion, and potato or barley to replace ship's biscuit, became popular in Liverpool and other parts of Lancashire.[20] Sea pie was meat and vegetables layered with crumbled biscuit. Dunderfunk (thunder and lightening), a Dutch contribution to the colourful international jargon of the sea, was a concoction of biscuit, soaked in water, mixed with fat and molasses and baked in a pan. 'Dancing with the mermaids', the title of this paper, was a Dutch term for getting to know the life of the seamen.[21] The Navy also copied the Dutch in using sauerkraut as a preventative for scurvy. Midshipman's crab was a mixture of pickles, salt beef, biscuit crumbs and cheese no doubt sprinkled with 'galley pepper' – soot and ashes in the food. Various duffs (northern pronunciation of dough) were made up of whatever was available to add to the oatmeal, flour, or crushed biscuit base.

A special treat at the Captain's table was Figgy-Dowdy:[22] Captain Aubrey in one of Patrick O'Brian's novels offers his guest 'A Navy dish that might amuse you. I find it settles a meal, but perhaps it is an acquired taste.' Each of the officers contributed a line of the recipe:

> We take ship's biscuit and put it in a stout canvas bag.
> Pound it with a marline spike for half an hour.

Add bits of pork fat, plums, figs, rum; currants.
Send it to the galley, and serve it up with bosun's grog.

Scotch coffee was another improvisation – a drink made of biscuit burnt brown and pounded to a powder and stirred into hot water. A little real coffee was added if available. After setting off on his adventures with Midshipman Easy in charge of the vessel, Mesty, the assistant cook, says 'Somebody else burn the biscuit and boil the kettle for the gentlemen tomorrow'.[23] Taken still further biscuit burnt to charcoal could be used to purify foul water.

Hard tack was difficult to eat even with a healthy mouth. Food for the invalids on board was the responsibility of the ship's surgeon. Essential stores of medicaments and dressings and other 'Objects for the sick' were allocated to him. In the *Mary Rose* his equipment included an iron cauldron possibly for this purpose. Many of his patients would suffer from sore gums and loose teeth, one of the most troublesome symptoms of scurvy. Dysentery, food poisoning and other forms of diarrhoea were common and debilitating at sea and diet was not neglected even in the difficult conditions below decks. John Woodall, Surgeon General to the Honourable East India Company, advised for such patients that the surgeon should 'make him some comfortable spoone meate, such as you can make at sea, namely, an oatmeale caudell would not be a misse of a little beer or wine, with the yolk of an egge and a little sugar made warm and given him to drink'.[24] A gruel made of crushed biscuit and water was known as loblolly. It was similar to a West Indian maize or hominy porridge. Gervase Markham in his essay on the virtues of oats wrote 'nay, if a man be at sea, he cannot eat a more wholesome and pleasant meate than these whole greets boyl'd till they burst and then mixt with butter, and so eaten with spoones, which although seamen call simply by the name of loblolly, yet there is not any meate how significant soever the name be, that is more toothsome or wholesome.'[25] Later it was mainly associated with the sick and the assistant who doled it out to the sick came to be known as the loblolly boy. Other concoctions which crop up later as skilly or skillygolee, were similar to the water gruels served in prisons and work houses, and the morning oatmeal gruel served to ordinary seamen was anything but toothsome.

Interest in the health of those at sea stimulated Sir Hugh Platt to offer a recipe for trosses for the sea, pills 'gilded here and there' composed of gum tragacanth, cinnamon, ginger, sugar and a little musk to combat sea-sickness.[26] 'Being kind to ye fishes,' as a servant said of a sick passenger on a crossing to Dieppe,[27] was a problem above and below decks. Ginger is recently back in favour as an effective remedy for nausea. Platt was consulted by Sir Francis Drake and Sir John Hawkyns and amongst his hints was a method of getting rid of the excess salt from salt meat by dragging it in a cage behind the ship, a method used right up to the nineteenth century.[28]

He published a broadsheet in 1607 addressing his remarks to noblemen about to set out on a voyage and proposing his own method of preserving – *Certain Philosophical Preparation of Foods and Beverages for Seamen in their Long Voyages*. No one knows whether his method was more than a method of bottling and keeping out the air with a layer of olive oil, but he advertised a broth 'preserved by philosophical fire free from all mouldinesse, sournesse, or corruption, to last sweete 2, 3, or 4 yeares together. A necessary secret for all sicke and weake persons at sea.'

His secret died with him as he withdrew the offer when no one took it up.[29] He felt that the method would work with 'any broth or colase that will stand clear and liquid and not jelly or grow thicker,' that is without letting it gel. However amongst his *Victual for Warr*, a few of which were published in the *Jewelhouse of Art and Nature,* there were many other ingenious ideas. In particular he described the exact opposite in a new invention.

C Qre of strong & restoratif broathes kneaded up, in a paste & the paste baked sustinently.
C drie jelly wherin there is no suger in pieces like mowthglew. Disolve them in water, to make a good broth, mix it with spice swetten it with liquerice in steade of suger make cheape gellie with meat suet & legge of beff, and som calfes feete amongst them. qre of

strengthening ye gellie with isinglass. qre how long ordinary gellie will last in boxes being first boiled to a great stifnes.[30]

'Mouthglew' was glue which was to be moistened with spit as opposed to liquid common glue which was painted on. Whether or not the suggestion was taken up at this time it occurs again as 'veal glew' described by Anne Blencowe in 1694. A leg of veal trimmed of all fat was boiled down to a strong broth and then heated more gently over boiling water until 'ye jelly grow of a Glewish substance.' It was then to be put into sweetmeat pots until quite cold and then wrapped in flannel and paper 'and it will keep many years'. [31]

Hannah Glasse called it 'pocket soup', and added a more appetizing version of 'portable soup for carrying abroad' starting with two 50 lb pieces of beef boiled with herbs for 8–9 hours in 9 gallons of water. The final product was to be cut into rounds and dried in the sun, then wrapped in flannel and stored with sheet of paper between each layer. She recommended it to ships' captains saying in the recipe for pea soup 'if you add a piece of the portable soup it will be very good'.[32] She included a chapter for ships' captains in her book not only because passengers took their own comforts with them but captains expected their friends to send hampers on board to stock the larder before a voyage. Preserves and pickles, especially dried and pickled mushrooms were popular. Hannah Glasse gave a recipe for ketchup 'to keep twenty years'. Dripping, well salted, was to be taken for frying fish with the recommendation that it should be stored upside down so that the rats could not get at it.

Later writers of recipe books and household manuals followed Hannah Glasse in suggesting food for travellers by sea with many recipes for portable and pocket soup. Most start with three large legs of veal, one of beef and the lean part of half a ham well seasoned with 'chyan' pepper.[33] Elizabeth Moxon recommended starting with a leg of veal and a large cock. The little cakes were to be stored in a paper bag where there is a fire, 'as damp will dissolve them'.[34] All comment that the material was easier to make in frosty weather. Isabella Byron's manuscript of 1756 includes several for pickles and one recipe for a sorrel preserve for those at sea.[35] John Varley copied several of Hannah Glasse's recipes including the soup but with even less attention to the reality of life at sea although entitled 'Necessary articles for sea-faring persons'. The chapter included such pompous remarks as 'As pickled mushrooms are very handy for captains to take with them to sea, we shall here give directions for that particular purpose,' and was given a lift with 'Admiral Sir Charles Knowles receipt to salt meat.' All these were aimed at adding a little spice to the dreary menu on board British vessels. Boteler complained that our common seamen were besotted in their beef and pork, and spoke wistfully of the 'lusty subsistence of the Italians'. He wrote that it was

> to be wished that we did more conform ourselves to the Spanish and Italian nations, who on board ship (and at land, too) live most upon rice, oatmeal, biscuits, figs, olive oil and the like; or at the least to our neighbours the French and Dutch , who content themselves with a far less portion of flesh and fish than we do, and instead thereof do make up their meals with peas, beans, wheat [flour], butter, cheese, and those white meats as they are called.[36]

When a French prize was taken by an English ship the fine wines and refreshments in the captain's store were one of the perks; whilst it was said that the French taking an English vessel set store on the salt beef which, for all the complaints, (sometimes being hard enough to carve into trinkets or snuff-boxes) was of higher quality than they were used to.

John Woodall's advice that 'if the patient is grown very feeble,' you should 'appoynt him a diet that may warm and comfort the stomache, namely broathes of chickings or the like,' was not easy to achieve at sea. Lloyd and Coulter consider that the introduction of portable soup was a most important innovation for the health and comfort of seamen.[37] James Lind, ship's surgeon, who conducted the famous experiments on the effectiveness of various foods in treating scurvy on board the *Salisbury* in 1746-7 wrote to the Commissioners of the Sick and Hurt Board of the Admiralty in 1754 recommending portable soup as one of the commodities which should be supplied for the sick. He proposed that it should be made from the shins and feet of cattle. It is not clear whether he regarded it as anti-scorbutic in itself, but it was taken up and produced by the Board soon after. In 1755 the staff of the headquarters included a clerk with responsibility for 'attending the souphouse', but decided that it should be made of offal with one third mutton added to make it more nutritious. In 1756 the contract was awarded to Mrs Dubois in Deptford and Mr Cookworthy in Plymouth and Portsmouth. In 1757 salt and vegetables were added to the recipe. An advertisement in 1761 in the *London Chronicle* offered it for sale as particularly recommended for gentlemen on journeys at sea. It was sold by ships' chandlers. Large quantities were made from then on and by 1793 the output of the main establishment, Ratcliffe's Soup House, was 897 tons per annum. By that time the Army were purchasing it from the Navy but corruption crept in and one of the main suppliers was disgraced for illicitly selling off the fat and bones.

The Board arranged further tests of its efficacy in treating scurvy by instructing Captain Wallis to take a supply with him on his circumnavigatory voyage in the *Dolphin* in 1766. He loaded 3000 lb on board for a complement of 150 men and 33 officers. It was to be boiled up with cranberries for men with scurvy. Captain James Cook emulated him on his voyage to Tahiti of 1768 in the *Endeavour* and also tested a number of other antiscorbutic remedies including wort, sauerkraut, and sallop. He reported that 'portable soup was another essential article of which we had likewise a liberal supply'. He gave an ounce to each man, boiled with oatmeal, pease or celery, three times a week[38] and considered that, 'it was the means of making the people eat a greater amount of greens'. He fed it to fit and ill alike. On the return of Commodore Byron who commanded the *Dolphin* in 1766, the Navy Board sent orders for 'some of the portable soup which has been on the voyage of his Majesty's ship the Dolphin, that their Lordships may taste the same.'[39] A sample from Captain Cook's stores found its way to the Royal United Services Museum and was analysed by Professor Drummond in 1938 and still found to be uncorrupted.[40]

At first it was allowed only as one of the objects for the sick on the requisition of the ship's surgeon and like other stores had to be carefully accounted for in the captain's records. It came to be regarded as essential and was referred to by Captain Bligh who had a set of Lind's works on board the *Bounty*. In his own notes on the prevention of scurvy he wrote ' but the scurvy is really a disgrace to a ship where it is at all common, provided they have it in their power to be supplied with dried malt, sour Krout and portable soup.' Along with saloop and later, arrowroot, it remained one of the esssentials both for sea and land expeditions for many years to come. Lind wrote that '2 lb of salep and 2 lb portable soup will afford a wholesome diet to one person for a month because they contain the greatest quantity of vegetable and animal nourishment that can be reduced into so small a bulk.' From then on all eighteenth-century explorers were amply supplied with salep as well as portable soup.

The naval version was not so luxurious as those described in the household manuals and unfortunately Lind was quite wrong on attributing to it any useful nutritional powers. In Nelson's time it was put up in 25 lb containers and issued as a sheet from which the requisite pieces were broken off. Father explains in the *Swiss Family Robinson*:

> My wife placed (on the fire) a pot filled with water, having first dropped therein several cakes of portable soup. Little Francis had in his simplicity taken these cakes to be pieces of glue but his mother explained to the child that these cakes were the essence of meat reduced to a jelly; that in long voyages ships were always provided with them, in order that soup might always be at hand , when fresh meat could not be prepared.[41]

Dr Kitchiner agreed that it 'is really a great acquisition to the Army and Navy, – to Travellers, Invalids &c.' He suggested that the soup could be made most cheaply by digesting shin-bones in a patent Digester – almost as cheaply as Salisbury glue (the best make of glue). For long keeping it was to be stored in bladders as *tablettes de bouilllon*. He was mainly interested in the soup as a useful aid in the kitchen for making soups and glazes. Moreover after preparation the meaty residue could be used up as potted beef which would be very acceptable to many poor families.[42] He pointed out an advertisement offering large quantities of portable soup at Leipzig imported during the late war with Russia. Russia was also a substantial exporter of glue!

Whilst soup had been under the control of the Sick and Hurt Board it was taken over by the Victualling Board when the arrangements were reorganised in 1820. Baking biscuit was still important in many ports until well into the nineteenth century. The Victualling Board, which took over the supplying of food for the fleet from the time of Charles II, established depots at Deptford, where Samuel Pepys was in charge, and at Portsmouth. Alas! during the Commonwealth even the fine old royal palace at Greenwich was stripped by Cromwell and used as a biscuit factory before being demolished. This was to supply both land and sea forces although the army was relatively better cared for than the navy. There is good evidence of the dietary allowances of Cromwellian soldiers and the importance of biscuit or 'biscake' and the efforts made to organise the commissariat. An officer wrote in 1650, 'Nothing is more certain than this, that in the late wars both Scotland and Ireland were conquered by timely provisions of Cheshire cheese and biscuit.'[43] On the march General Monck ordered Colonel Cooper to furnish 'the soldiers snapsacks with 7 days bread and cheese to be carried on horseback, and as much bisquett besides the cheese as the horse can carry.' This was defined as 200 weight of biscuit to be carried on each baggage horse.

Francis Markham wrote of his experience in the Dutch Army and described the allowance as 'likewise a pound of biscuit and a poor John between two men for one day, or two pounds of biscuit and a haberdine between four men for one day is a great proportion; half a pound of biscuit and four herrings is one man's allowance for one day, and so is a quart of peas boiled, or a pint of rice with the ordinary allowance of biscuit.'[44] These were identical with the allowances on board ships of the time.

The Victualling Board concentrated production at several other ports. At Plymouth in the eighteenth century two bakehouses containing 4 ovens were fired up as many as eight times a day to produce biscuit for 16,000 men. The bakery at Deptford was named Old Weevil, whilst Weevil Lane lead to Weevil, the Gosport establishment. The time-honoured method of baking it involved a five-man team for each oven which was a marvel of human precision: the turner, the mate, the driver, the breakman and the idleman working in a 'singular and often disgusting method' according to Sheridan Muspratt.[45] After mixing by hand in a trough the dough was put on a wooden platform called the break and kneaded by the breakman sitting on the end of a pivoted beam and shuffling about until it was mixed. The dough was cut up and chopped into balls with a huge knife and shaped by hand. It was then handed to a second workman who stamped it with the number of the oven and the king's mark and after docking (piercing with holes) each biscuit was thrown accurately onto the end of a peel held in the oven by another man standing before the open door. The baker could deftly arrange 70 biscuits a minute on the floor of the oven, carefully graded in size to allow for the longer baking time of those at the back. Mr Grant of the Royal Clarence victualling station improved on the method by introducing steam machinery and replaced the round cutters with an octagonal cutting plate, leaving no waste. With these innovations the streamlined production team turned out 1,378,409 pounds of biscuit in 116 days (77 working days) from 9 ovens as well as saving about £900 a year in wages. In time of war the big yards were supplemented by local contractors such as the small baker Mr Bartle of Hull, listed as 'bakers of bread and ships biscuit' in the gazetteer for 1822.

Further improvements occurred in 1852 when Mr Slater of Carlisle invented a biscuit oven on a new principle – an endless chain with trays of biscuits passing through a long tunnel. A fifteen minute bake in a controlled temperature was followed by 3 days in the drying room. This development lead to a huge new biscuit industry, a precursor of modern mechanized food production.[46]

Several of today's biscuit manufacturers such as Carrs of Carlisle, and Huntley and Palmers started their business as makers of ship's biscuit. The Jacob brothers of Waterford, owners of a bread and ships' biscuit bakery and a yeast brewery, came over to study the new methods in 1851 and later established the factory at Dublin. With the new mechanized methods they were able to make vast quantities. The new packet-steamers, emigration and empire-building created a demand for a range of refined biscuits; and so did the home markets. Captain's biscuit and Cabin biscuits were made of finer flour, with milk instead of water. A water biscuit for the table was the fore-runner of the present water biscuit. Mrs Beeton refers to the difference between the plain ship's biscuit and the captain's version made with finer flour but extols the variety of the new manufactured biscuits.[47]

By the time of the Army and Navy Stores catalogue of 1907, the range was even wider. They were still supplied in the traditional way even though Captain Cook had pointed out the superiority of tin liners for storage:

Ship Biscuit
> Captain's biscuit
> Cabin Biscuits Extra Fine
>> First: in barrels only
>> Second
>> Third
> Ship Biscuits
>> Extra Navy: in bags only
>> Navy

Over the same period there were commercial preparations for a boiled-down stock for ships and pharmacies derived from the French bouillon bar developed by the chemists Proust and Parmentier. It was supplied to the French Navy. It was superseded in the 1860s by the immensely popular von Liebig's meat extract. Faster ships, better storage and new methods of preservation lead to great improvement in naval diets which made the old stand-bys less necessary. Nevertheless Dorothy Hartley's description of her great aunt's methods of kitting poultry for long voyages in the nineteenth century was reminiscent of Hugh Platt's method – rapid salting, parboiling, and storing in a layer of fat to keep out the air. The chicken legs were used to make soup squares for the sea-sick on the voyage to the West Indies. Watercress which passengers used to grow in their cabins on these same transatlantic voyages became a weed choking the waterways when discarded at the other end.[48]

Improvement in sailor's diet based on new methods of food preservation made them less dependent on ship's biscuit. Tinned meat, first labelled '*boeuf Bouilli*', was prepared by a French process and gave origin to the term 'Bully beef.' Fresh bread could be safely baked on board although the English were a long time in following the example of the French who had found this feasible in 1776. Soft bread and flour were issued instead of biscuit and portable ovens were sometimes provided for use of distant expeditions on shore. More refined versions of commercially made biscuit were still supplied to the captain and passengers in a variety which paralleled the enormous expansion of the trade on shore and for export.

However as ship's biscuit was displaced from the standard naval diet it remained a compact source of energy useful for explorers needing concentrated rations. They were taken to Africa by Stanley, to the Arctic by the Franklin expedition (along with arrowroot), and by Shackleton, and Scott to the Antarctic in 1907.[49] A 'serviceable but unpalatable' meat biscuit was another imperishable food suited to travellers developed by Gail Borden for the adventurers in the Gold Rush. He came to London in 1851 to receive a medal from Queen Victoria for the product. More recently the Cambridge nutrition team devised a biscuit as the best way of supporting undernourished children and pregnant women in West Africa.

In the Great Exhibition of 1861 a number of other novel concentrated foods were displayed. There were biscuits with added gluten, consolidated milk, reminiscent of the solid cream made by Cornish housewives for fishermen. Lactone was an artificial milk for long voyages composed of egg yolk and gum acacia which 'keeps 1-2 years'. Mme Danielle St. Etienne of Totnes offered a hybrid vegeto-animal compound for long voyages made of wheat gluten, beef, veal, gelatine etc and 'the same with fruits. Used in the preparation of soups, pudding, pies and other dishes.'[50]

The common factor in many of these interesting, durable, and safe products is thorough dehydration and absence of fat. Banishing fat from foods to be kept for long periods was common to both the ship's biscuit, a simple dried-out baked flour, and portable soup which was to be skimmed until free of any trace of fat. Ship's biscuit, beef extract and even scotch coffee were all recommended by doctors for people with dyspepsia at different times and the virtues of the biscuits may have been the high amount of bran and B vitamins as well as the freedom from adulterating chemicals and fat. They were the forerunners of other diet biscuits such as the Bath Oliver and the Abernethy, named not after the Doctor but after the village where they were baked. Gervase Markham[51] advised that some 'Physitions appoint bisket bread for such as are troubled with a rheume'. Pereira[52] sanctioned the use of ship's biscuit by including it in his *Introduction to Materia Medica* as *Panis nauticus* for the same purpose. Dr Chase[53] was keen on scotch coffee for dyspepsia, basing it on a dry biscuit made from Graham flour.

Innovations for the sick often preceded improvements in the diet and welfare of sailors in general, and portable soup played a big part in changing attitudes as well as making the essential green vegetables more palatable. The conservatism of seamen was as much a hindrance as the ignorance of doctors and officialdom in bringing about improvements and Lloyd and Coulter have emphasised the immense influence of nutrition on the history of the Navy, suggesting that it is as important as the tales of battles at sea.

In these wasteful days of plastic bags, and refrigeration, sell-by dates are often applied to well-preserved and non-perishable goods whilst eggs and milk remain undated. It is salutary to remember the case of a 40 year shelf-life for ship's biscuit and the 160 year survival of a sample of portable soup now at the National Maritime Museum.

REFERENCES

[1] J. J. Keevil (1961), *Medicine and the Navy (1200-1900),* vol I p.20.

[2] Graham Webster, *The Roman Imperial Army,* 3rd edition p.262.

[3] Oded Schwartz (1992), *In Search of Plenty,* p.27.

[4] de Joinville (1256), *The Chronicle of the Crusades and the Life of St Louis,* Penguin Classics p.212.

[5] W G Perrin Editor (1929), *Boteler's Dialogues* (1635), p.59.

[6] Fernand Braudel (1973), *The Structures of Everyday Life,* p.139.

[7] Oliver Warner (1979), *Fighting Sail,* p.74.

[8] *Encyclopaedia Britannica,* (1768) second edition facsimile, p.382.

[9] Dudley Pope (1981), *Life in Nelson's Navy,* p.71.

[10] Dorothy Hartley (1930), *The Countryman's England,* p.52.

[11] Tobias Smollett (1747), *Roderick Random,* p.144.

[12] K J Carpenter (1981), *The History of Scurvy and Vitamin C,* p.46.

[13] Dudley Pope (1963), *The Black Ship,* p.128.

[14] Dudley Pope (1981), *Life in Nelson's Navy,* p.118.

[15] W H Dana (1835), *Two Years Before the Mast,* p.9.

[16] J C Drummond and A Wilbraham (1958), *The Englishman's Food,* revised edition p.134.

[17] C Lloyd and J L S Coulter (1961), *Medicine and the Navy,* volume III.

[18] C W Ashley (1947), *The Ashley Book of Knots,* p.221, 411.

[19] Tom Stobart (1980), *The Cook's Encyclopaedia,* p.47.

[20] Helen Pollard (1991), 'Lancashire's Heritage', in *Traditional Food East and West of the Pennines,* ed. C Anne Wilson, p.124.

[21] Lew Lind (1982), *Sea-jargon.*

[22] Patrick O'Brian (1972), *The Post Captain,* p.225.

[23] Captain Marryat (1836), *Mr Midshipman Easy,* p.87.

[24] John Woodall (1617), *The Surgion's Mate,* facsimile edition, edited John Kirkup (1978).

[25] Gervase Markham (1631), *The English Housewife,* Fourth edition, p.242.

[26] Sir Hugh Platt (1607), *Delightes for Ladies,* pp.35,76.

[27] Vita Sackville West (1922), *Knole and the Sackvilles,* New edition 1991, p.130.

[28] Sir Hugh Platt (1653), *The Jewel House of Art and Nature.*

[29] Sir Hugh Platt, Broadsheet quoted in Keevil (1961), vol 1 p. 108.

[30] Sir Hugh Platt (c 1588), *Victual for Warr,* British Library, Sloane MS 2244, ff 29-30. I am indebted to Malcolm Thick for this discovery amongst the Platt papers.

[31] *The Receipt Book of Anne Blencowe AD1694,* (1925) p.23.

[32] Hannah Glasse (1747), *The Art of Cookery,* facsimile edition (1983), pp.121, 65.

[33] Elizabeth Raffald (1769), *The Experienced English Housekeeper,* p.2.

[34] Elizabeth Moxon (1769), *English Housewifery Exemplified,* 10th edition p.30.

[35] Isabella Byron (1656), *My Receipt Book,* Castle Howard Archives J 13/1/4. By kind permission of the Howard Family.

[36] W.G.Perrin, *Boteler's Dialogues,* p.65.

[37] C Lloyd and J L S Coulter, *Medicine and the Navy,* volume III,1714-1815.

[38] K J Carpenter (1981), *The History of Scurvy and Vitamin C,* p.82.

[39] Note from National Maritime Museum on Portable Soup (1996).

[40] J C Drummond and A Wilbraham, ibid. p.315.

[41] Johann Wyss (1822), *Swiss Family Robinson,* p.20.

[42] William Kitchiner (1840), *The Cook's Oracle,* New Edition p. 219.

[43] C H Firth (1992), *Cromwell's Army,* 3rd edition p.223.

[44] C H Firth, ibid. p.211.

[45] Sheridan Muspratt (1870), *Chemistry Applied to Arts and Manufacture,* p.382.

[46] Jack Goody (1982), *Cooking, Cuisine and Class,* p.161.

[47] Isabella Beeton (1861), *Book of Household Management,* p.837.

[48] Dorothy Hartley (1954), *Food in England,* p.312.

[49] J Watt, E J Freeman and W F Bynum, editors (1981), *Starving Sailors,* p.168.

[50] Illustrated Catalogue of the Great Exhibition (1861), p.308.

[51] Gervase Markham (1616), *Farewell to Husbandry,* p.132.

[52] Jonathan Pereira (1853), *Introduction to Materia Medica,* part II p.992.

[53] Dr Chase (1893), *Trade Secrets, Receipts for Everything,* p.297.

Salt Cod, a Portuguese Obsession

Edite Vieira

A little introduction

Portuguese food is not bland and one of the strongest and most beloved tastes in Portugal is that of salt cod. Strange, in a country where a long, Atlantic coastline offers such a rich variety of fresh fish, also profusely used. Salt cod, however, is so special there, that it has earned the nickname of 'faithful friend'. Perhaps because it is always ready to be used, either waiting in the larder or (already soaked) in the freezer. A convenience food par excellence.

Although salt cod is sometimes called 'the national dish', the actual number of dishes that can be prepared with it is quite astonishing. There are hundreds of recipes (the Portuguese say one could have a different cod dish every day of the year) and while many do have a strong taste, some are very mild and delicate, such as those made with cream or béchamel sauce.

Attempts at cooking salt cod may turn out slightly disastrous sometimes – as some people may have found out. But the truth is that once knowing the simple basic procedures for its preparation, salt cod responds so well that it may become addictive, both to cook and to eat. Its texture and flavour are rich and satisfying – if you are hooked you cannot get enough of it. But it is advisable, if eating out, to be well informed about the places where to try it for the first time, to avoid risking disenchantment from the start. Non-Portuguese chefs may not be the best source for this introductory effort. And even Portuguese restaurants may offer you such a diligently prepared massive dish that the effect may be off-putting. In fact, it may be better to ask for a half-portion, which, knowing the amount usually served (of any dish) is perfectly acceptable. Order (safely) milder dishes, like *bacalhau com natas* (cod with cream) or *pasteis de bacalhau* (salt cod cakes). You cannot go wrong with these and I bet you will be hooked for life.

Although salt cod is used in incredible amounts in Portugal, it is not obtained in its territorial waters. Cod is a son of colder climes. However, the Portuguese pioneered cod fishing centuries ago in Newfoundland and used to unload it in large quantities, already gutted and salted, around the northern region of Aveiro, for some more salting and the essential drying out in the sun. Nowadays, however, this task has been all but totally abandoned and most of the cod is bought ready salted and at least partially dried, from Iceland and Norway – and even Spain – though (surprisingly) salt cod is also prepared this way in Britain (Hull and Grimsby) and equally exported to Portugal, albeit in smaller amounts than those supplied by other countries. Salt cod sold in Britain goes almost exclusively to ethnic communities, despite the fact that centuries ago, when the Vikings had a say in Britain and, after that, up to the time of the Reformation, salt cod used to be served at English tables. Since then it seems to have been forgotten and now it is true to say that in Britain salt cod is looked upon with suspicion by many, while others only show a reluctant interest in it. Lately, however, it has become apparent that the flavour of salt cod is slowly and cautiously creeping back into favour with British palates, due perhaps to the many tourists visiting Portugal (and of course other countries where this fish is also served). This is excellent news. Salt cod is nutritious, very good value for money and extremely versatile. It is also widely available now, so there is no excuse for not trying it.

The history

The difficulties about tracing the history of salt cod in Portugal are almost insurmountable. The National Library has precious little about the subject and any references or documents that do exist are scattered in various dusty and practically inaccessible vaults God knows where, or out-of-print books. Those that have come to light do not offer a systematic and proper overview of the facts and are almost exclusively confined to notes on taxes, amounts of fish caught and imported, and details of this sort. I hear that, fortunately, there is someone at the moment trying to do something about this. Recipe books of old (such as the now famous Princess Maria's book from the fifteenth century[1] and *A Arte de Cozinha* by Domingos Rodrigues, a royal cook, first published in 1693[2] and considered the first proper cookery book published in Portugal, offer no trace at all of salt cod recipes and very few of fish, as such, anyway. The point is that these books reflected the customs of the nobility, who considered fish (and especially salt cod) as food fit only for the poor (a view that has prevailed until not very long ago, when salt cod used to be very cheap). Meat of all kinds, including a large chapter on game, are the mainstay of these books, as well as the indispensable desserts – proving that the Portuguese love of sugary and eggy confections goes back a long way and has a very respectable tradition.

More 'modern' books, such as *O Cozinheiro Moderno* (1780)[3] by Lucas Rigaud (probably of French origin) and *Arte de Cozinha* (1876)[4] by João da Mata, do mention just a few salt cod recipes – precisely the fish-cake and the white sauce varieties, but little else, still considering salt cod as a very low-ranking food. It is just possible that curing methods in those times were not at their best, and so the taste of salt cod may not have been always very desirable. Nevertheless in those days fish of all kinds was part of everybody's diet, even the rich (however reluctantly) at least on Fridays. The Church would see to that. Salt cod, by its very nature, would be the best choice inland, in those fridge-less times. It would, also, be a good staple for men at sea: if we think of the many sailors, soldiers and missionaries taking part in the Portuguese expeditions of discovery and commerce throughout the world, during the sixteenth century and beyond.

Alan Davidson, in his fascinating *Guide to the Seafood of Spain and Portugal*[5] points out that salt cod originated in early medieval times, as far back as the tenth century and that in 1497 various countries, Portugal included, started serious cod-fishing off Newfoundland. In Portugal, the oldest official document referring to cod-fishing[6] dates back to 1353 and is nothing less than a treaty between Portugal and England, establishing the rights of Portuguese fishermen to operate off the English coast, for a period of 50 years. It is fair to imagine that this treaty did not come out of the blue but on the contrary merely confirmed what had already been going on for some time – how long we cannot ascertain.

One reason that might go some way to explain why salt cod took such roots in Portugal is the fact that salt itself was produced by the Portuguese in such quantities that its export constituted a major and very profitable industry, mainly around Setúbal and Aveiro, which became the centres for the drying of cod. Due to various climatic and geographical factors, this salt was of the highest quality and very much sought after, especially by Scandinavian countries, who found it ideal for preserving fish (kipper and cod).[7] There is evidence of intensive interchange in this respect between Norway and Denmark, and Portugal. In fact, there was great understanding between the Crowns of Portugal and Denmark since, at least, the twelfth century and, much later, a Danish pilot was dispatched to Portugal to take part in the so-called 'school of navigation' created by Prince Henrique, the initiator of the discoveries. This pilot (Wollert or Abelhart) had apparently the mission of participating in the Portuguese explorations of the North Atlantic.[8] The activities of the Portuguese were such, in that area, that it is known that in 1504 there was a colony of Portuguese fishermen from the Minho province and the Aveiro region, established in Newfoundland.[9] Their descendants are actually still there (still fishing), as reported on TV not long ago.

The 60-year Spanish domination of Portugal (1580-1640) was disastrous for the country in every respect, including the North Atlantic fishing. This was directly caused by the drafting by the Spanish of all Portuguese vessels capable of taking part in the Invincible Armada.[10] During those times the Portuguese continued to eat salt cod, of course, but were reduced to importing it all. It was only by the nineteenth century that they rebuilt their fishing fleet again. The industry developed enormously but due to the very high expenditure involved with maintenance and replacement of the vessels it has gradually declined, since 1965 or so.[11] At present the amount of cod caught by the Portuguese is negligible and the vast quantities they consume have to be imported. An attempt to calculate the consumption per capita is somewhat difficult because there are stark variations between regions. Interestingly, the areas of Lisbon and Oporto are at the top of the list – about 16 kilos of salt cod per capita per year, despite the much greater abundance of varied foods. The Minho and Aveiro regions come next with between 7 and 9 kilos per capita, then the Trás-os-Montes, Beira Litoral, Estremadura and Ribatejo provinces, with an average of over 5 kilos, and finally Beira Alta, Beira Baixa, Alentejo and Algarve, with a little over 2 kilos per capita[12] although it must be noted that these figures refer to the 1950s – the latest available in this respect. A very puzzling distribution, which may have something to do with price and the amount of meat – mainly pork – consumed in some areas (although the Trás-os-Montes province is poor and also has pork as a priority item).

Imports come from many sources and it seems that the Portuguese will buy willingly any amount available. I have recently had the chance of talking to the Manager of Cawoods in Hull and he told me that he could sell any amount to Portugal but provides about 200 tons per year. Another 40 tons are sold by the same firm (which has been turning out salt cod for more than 100 years) to the main Portuguese shop in London (Lisboa Delicatessen) which then distributes some of it to other Portuguese shops in the capital but sells most of it on its own premises. Other main suppliers to the Portuguese market are Iceland, Norway and… Spain! Some of it is imported already dried and ready to be sold, but the rest (about half) is finished in Portugal itself. All these supplies came to a total of almost 30,000 tons per year during the 1970s[13] though again present figures are hard to come by, because the industry is no longer co-ordinated by a central body, as it used to be.

The nutritional value of salt cod is very high, and according to research carried out by FAO, one kilo of salt cod is equivalent to 3.2 kilos of fresh fish (information given by the Norwegian Embassy). Apart from its protein content, comparable to that of meat, it is rich in fatty acids (the beneficial kind), minerals, trace elements and vitamins. So the Portuguese seem to be quite justified in their utter dedication to salt cod.

Where do we go from here?

It is not conceivable to imagine Portugal without salt cod, unless every Portuguese disappears from the face of the earth. But with their ability to spread their wings everywhere and create new communities in the most unlikely places, chances are that the use of salt cod will be on the increase, as more 'foreigners' around them learn to like or at least tolerate it. If there are countries where salt cod is appreciated, even nowadays, when Friday abstinence from meat is rarely observed, surely there must be something to it. I think that the best way of really savouring salt cod is to make the effort of preparing it at home. After the essential good soaking, salt cod gets tamed enough to be skinned and boned, cut or shredded, and cooked like any other fish. There are no mysteries. The only difference (and it is a big difference) is that salt cod is infinitely more versatile than anything else, and one can start creating new ways with it almost from the beginning. It is then that the Portuguese glorious trilogy of olive oil, garlic and coriander (or parsley, in many cases) comes into its own with endless variations to delight and subjugate the palate.

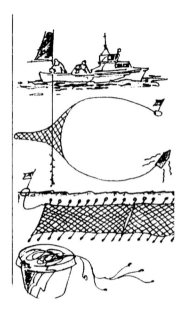

Cod fishing equipment.

REFERENCES

[1] A compilation published as the *Tratado da Cozinha Portuguesa do Século XV* by Instituto Nacional do Livro, Ministério da Educação e Cultura, Lisboa 1963, transcribing the medieval book into modern Portuguese.

[2] Reprinted in 1995 by Colares Editora, Sintra, Portugal.

[3] Published by Oficina de Simão Thaddeo Ferreira, Lisboa, and reprinted in 1798.

[4] Published by the author in Lisboa, 1876.

[5] Davidson, Alan, *The Tio Pepe Guide to the Seafood of Spain and Portugal*, Gonzalez Byass S.A., Jerez, Spain, 1992, 28.

[6] Moutinho, Mário, *História da Pesca do Bacalhau*, Imp. Universitária Editorial Estampa, Lisboa, 1985, 15.

[7] Ibid. 16.

[8] Ibid. 18.

[9] Ibid. 29.

[10] Ibid. 22.

[11] *Lello Illustrated Dictionary*, Lello & Irmãos, Porto, 1977, 290-1.

[12] Moutinho, 180-1.

[13] Ibid 157.

Travel and Contemporary Australian Food

Hugh Wennerbom

I wish you were here.
I wish…
I wish you were…
I…

graffiti, Darlinghurst wall, Sydney.

'Revolution' has passed into culinary parlance

The term 'revolution' has passed into Australian culinary parlance, as it has in many parts of the western world. I remember being a little surprised at how casually Claudia Roden used the term in her introduction to *Stephanie's Seasons*. 'The band of chefs who lead the revolution in Australian cooking and eating,' she wrote [Alexander, 1993a, vii]. It was the first time I had heard the changes in Australia's culinary landscape referred to as a revolution (though this says more about my ignorance than the state of culinary affairs). For me, this reference to a revolution was surprising and exciting because it gestured beyond this cook, this writer, this grower, this table to their multiplicity and interconnectedness.

It is a revolution that has changed the way we eat, what kinds of ingredients we use, and how we cook them. Yet these are not straightforwardly good or bad changes, but a mixture of both. A mixture of agribusiness, supermarkets, pre-prepared microwave meals, fast-food chains as well as restaurants, cafés, delis, specialty shops, boutique producers and providers. It seems that each end of the spectrum necessitates the other, insofar as, for example, agribusiness opens the space for small, localised, boutique markets. I would suggest that it is only because the anonymity and mechanical efficiency of industry has become the norm, that we value produce of integrity and helpful, personable service. The trend towards homogenization in food has opened the space for foodism, epicureanism, gastronomy and, possibly, the emergence of an Australian culinary identity.

Since the early eighties, food talk in this country seems to have gravitated around the prospect, whether yea or nay, of an Australian Cuisine. Indeed, the very first Symposium of Australian Gastronomy gathered in large part to investigate the possibilities and potential of what was cast by Gay Bilson as an 'upstart cuisine'. This is a cuisine that mixed and matched from here and there and that read Elizabeth David before Escoffier, resulting in an eclectic blend that continues to assert itself as somehow particular, or rather peculiar, to this place, this kitchen, this table.

It was almost as if that with the First Symposium, and Michael Symons' catalytic book on the history of Australian cuisine *One Continuous Picnic*, food in Australia became conscious of itself for the first time. And ever since, we've been piecing the jigsaw together, telling the story of our culinary arrival over and over again, talking ourselves into it [Marian Halligan, 1984].

Multiculinarism – selling an Australian cuisine

At its simplest, the story of Australian cuisine is a transparent one of multicultural success. After World War II, European migrants brought with them a rich food heritage which was gradually incorporated and assimilated into the mainstream. A second wave of migration in the early eighties, this time mainly Asian, saw our palate expanded once again. Add a few indigenous ingredients and *voilà*, Australian cuisine is born, an eclectic blend of (Fr)Anglo meets Med meets Asian meets Aboriginal. So that in a recent publication Crême Fraiche, Polenta, Wakame and Bunya nuts sit together as Australian ingredients, on the same menus, and sometimes on the same plate [Periplus Publications, 1995].

More than multiculturalism

The story of Australia's culinary gestation is not without its nuances, and the debate rages as loudly as ever over what constitutes a cuisine. There are concerns about the integrity of our meals, as some feel a little rushed by the urge to sell ourselves, our products and services to the world behind a coherent façade of freshness, hotness, and fastness (as the logo reads on the side of a popcorn vending machine in my local street). There are concerns for the substance behind the style. There are concerns about the speed of the transformations. The desire to be the latest with the swishest leaves some a little dizzy, as they become paralysed by the vast variety of ingredients available, and suffocated by a spiral of self-consciousness. Clearly, now is as good a time as any for a little reflection, a calming tonic with which we might take stock of our bearings.

Multiculturalism is a precondition of multiculinarism, and it would be churlish to ignore the enormous influence it has had on Australian food habits. Postwar migrants, both European and Asian, have created spaces and rhythms – the markets, the delis, the coffee shops, the restaurants – from which we continue to learn. Migration made available new ingredients. But it is the quality of this influence which is debatable. As such, multiculturalism is a necessary condition of an Australian cuisine, but as a commentator such as Michael Symons points out, it is not necessarily a sufficient one.

Symons notes that there isn't a straightforward correlation between immigration and changes in food habits. As evidence, he cites the nineteenth-century presence of Chinese migrants on the gold fields, and how their food was never taken up with any gusto until much later [Symons, 1982, 224]. Then, in our own century, there is the preoccupation with French international cuisine, despite a scarcity of French migrants [Symons, 1982, 223]. And so on.

Travel

A more likely explanation of the importance of ethnicity in the postwar transformation of food habits is travel. In the sixties cheap airfares became available, effecting a deregulation of the 'grand tour'. Symons refers to Frank Margan's *The Grape and I*, which chronicles how 'Australians had hitch-hiked around the vineyards of Bordeaux and the Bourgogne, had sat for lunch on the side of the road in some Italian village and eaten flour-dusted bread, salami and a bottle of unlabelled red,' and had been enamoured by 'the stinking cheeses in their little wooded boxes in the south of France and the hot scampi in little paper cones from the fantastic place on the corner in Venice' [Symons, 1982, 225].

Such a passage evokes well the pathos of Australians abroad: hardy yet naive, with more than a little romance, 'as if in a dream'. At any rate, and as Symons points out, by the seventies the number of Australians embarking on the grand tour had increased twenty-fold since the fifties (Symons, 1982, 225). So on top of the wealth of migrants arriving in Australia, Australians in the thousands were developing a taste for the European, and later Asian, flavours and styles. As a result of deregulated travel, there emerged a desire for the exotic and the ethnic. And when these travellers returned to Australia, this desire prompted them to seek out the spaces of the recent migrants, in order to buy ingredients and relive the aromas of other lands and cultures.

This is a view shared by Gay Bilson. She too makes the point that our current culinary situation 'is still dependent on the celebration of what we learn by travelling' [Bilson, unpublished MS, 2]. In these days when we travel 'with the ease of a flying trapeze', travel has given us the impetus to explore what our migrants have always been eating in Australia. Our newly defined palate did not develop because of what was here, but because of what we opened our minds and palate to by leaving this country so far away. We came back and then asked to taste what was here in other cultures and cuisines [Bilson, unpublished MS,2].

Travel produced desire: desire for the rhythms and pleasures of other places; a desire to recreate them at home, 'to place them onto our tongues, to swallow them'. So it was travel which caused middle Australians 'to use what were once exotic ingredients and to begin to expect them.[2]

Talking about the influences on her own style of food, Ms Bilson acknowledges the importance of travel. For her, travel 'enhances the way I feel about being a restaurateur – the sense of a room, the gestalt of a restaurant' [Bilson, 1995, 5]. But, for Ms Bilson, even more important than travelling is reading [Bilson, 1995, 5]. For reading is a migration of the mind, the imagining of other worlds through words. Reading evokes experiences, just as writing attempts to translate them.

Here lies the significance of Elizabeth David. Her books facilitated this desire for exotic aromas and experiences, and permitted them to be consolidated, naturalised, as it were. I was to argue that her influence, and that of Jane Grigson, Claudia Roden et al., whom she metonymically represents, was particularly profound in Australia, where a mediocre and flimsy tradition of Escoffier-derived French international cooking provided fertile ground for the emergence of a distinctively Australian style. Just as important as the information Mrs David provided was the imparting of an ethos towards food and life that has been developed with great passion in Australia.

Elizabeth David

A lecturer of mine has implicitly encouraged some of my everyday habits by ascribing a certain sacredness to their profanity. In our secular day and age, we no longer say a meditative morning prayer, yet we read the paper. Similarly, we no longer say grace before dinner, but thank the cook. In this vein, I acknowledge that this paper plays into a reverence for Elizabeth David. And I presume someone, somewhere is busily at work writing the tome of her life, Saint Elizabeth, warts and all.

It is no coincidence that Mrs David began to write her first book, *Mediterranean Food*, as a way of comforting herself when she returned to England in 1946. Sick ('my health in a precarious state, I was returned like a badly wrapped parcel'), cold ('as autumn turned to winter I shivered in my barely heated top-floor London flat'), and somewhat alone ('without a job, and with precious little to do except cook'), Mrs David 'took refuge from reality in writing down memories of the food I had cooked and eaten during my Mediterranean years' [David, 1991, 5]. Writing transported her from her relative misery to the lands in which she had lived and travelled. This imaginary world provided her with solace 'during those icy, hungry weeks' [David, 1991, 5]. It provided a space in which to dream.

Emerging from such personal roots, the driving impetus behind what would become *Mediterranean Food* was to be true to her own experiences, to write in a way that heeded the nuances of her influences and passions. Indeed, it was only through the process of writing that she came to realise the extent of her passion. Through the deprivation of that winter in London Mrs David came to realise that she had 'become addicted to the food and cookery of the Mediterranean and the Middle East' [David, 1991, 5]. So that when *Mediterranean Food* was published in 1950, it was presented merely as a selection of dishes that hoped to evoke a tableau 'of those blessed lands of sun and sea and olive trees' [David, 1991, x]. It aimed 'to give some idea of the lovely cookery of those regions to people who do not already know them, and to stir the memories of those who have eaten this food on its native shores' [David, 1991,x].

Mrs David's style of writing mirrors the food she describes: it is honest writing about 'honest cooking', with none of 'the sham Grande' of International hotel cooking. Instead of describing the dining rooms of International Palace Hotels, Mrs David is more interested in evoking the pathos of hillside olive orchards, the aromatic perfume of rosemary, the pungent local wines, the brilliance of market stalls in provincial villages, and the sound of air gruesomely whistling through sheep's lungs frying in oil [David, 1991, ix]. Her images are a precursor to Margan's images of Australians lunching roadside on flour-dusted bread, salami, and an unlabelled red.

Further, she sensitively lets slip her intellectual passion for food, quoting appropriate epigrams at the beginning of chapters, from Norman Douglas on the ideal cuisine, and the true cook, to Henry James on the poetry of butter and punctual eggs, to D.H. Lawrence on a great mass of colours and vegetable freshness. The words of these epigrams, in turn, open out on to other worlds, enriching her already substantial tableau. They represent ideals that lift her and carry her on her way. For she can be seen to live the life of Norman Douglas' true cook: she possesses 'a large dose of general worldly experience' and is a blend of artist and philosopher: sensitive and enthusiastic, yet passionately rigorous and informed. And she is the champion of his ideal cuisine insofar as her books offer a 'menu' of individual character drawn from the kitchen workshops of diverse lands and peoples; kitchen-workshops that are ever evolving in response to modern techniques and new ingredients [David, 1991, xiii].

Her passion would continue to grow ever more rigorous and informed, through *French Country Cooking* to *Italian Food* and *Summer Cooking* onto what is arguably her masterpiece, *French Provincial Cooking*. As her style developed, her scholarship became more pronounced, and her prose ever more authoritative, informed and sensible.

In *French Country Cooking* she reaffirmed her pathos towards living scenes as opposed to rarefied museums. She is interested in those everyday restaurants and recipes that see the production of pleasure through thrift, that blissful experience of value (a much devalued word these days, but which still retains a smidgen of valour). Her Europe is alive, as opposed to the endless travel routine of galleries and packaged holidays. Hers is a world full of characters, whether known or projected: of fishermen, sailors, ship-chandlers, port officials, lorry drivers as well as shopkeepers, lawyers, doctors, priests, gendarmes and 'even those stony-faced post-office officials'. She seeks them out like a bloodhound, for she knows that these locals 'are exceedingly addicted to the pleasures of the table; and, being thrifty as well, you may be sure they know where the cheapest and the best of everything is to be obtained' [David, 1979, 7]. What Mrs David offers us is her, and their, resourcefulness.

It is a resourcefulness that she celebrates, as it offers not only the prospect of good food, but the healthy ethos of a life lived with love, passion and pleasure. It defines itself not only against the drab mediocrity of English cookery, but also against 'the absurd lengths of the complicated' *haute cuisine* of professional cooking [David, 1989, xix; 1979, 9]. What distinguishes the dishes Mrs David enthuses about is their provincial logic ('honest, sincere and simple'), and the spirit which this inspires; a devoted and determined spirit; one that is never slap-dash, nor 'it is to be hoped, one of martyrdom' [David, 1979, 9].

In *Italian Food*, Mrs David's style becomes more authoritative, retaining the pathos of the earlier books but adding to it an explicit and remarkable scholarship. It is a rehearsal of her masterpiece to come. There are still the evocative passages, of lunching at a *trattoria* in the heart of Venice and being told by the waiter that 'the last batch of *risotto* is finished and that you must wait twenty-five minutes for the next lot. Do you want it or not? There will be enough only for six portions.' [David, 1989, 108]; or of 'the light of a Venetian dawn in early summer, so limpid and so still that it makes every separate vegetable and fruit and fish luminous with a life of its own' [David, 1989, 142], and so on in imitation of Garzoni-esque still-lifes. Mrs David's style mimics the Italian cuisine she describes, a cuisine of 'their memories, their instincts, and, literally, their hands' [David, 1989, xxi].

But she also speaks with rigour about a range of historical incidents, such as the widespread exaggeration of the importance of Catherine de Medici in the development of French food, and the reception in Italy of Marinetti's futurist 'bombshell' [David, 1989, xiii and 66]. Her recipes are littered with delightful and intriguing references, from Guiseppe Marotta on the importance of adapting 'your dish of spaghetti to circumstances and your state of mind' [David, 1989, 69], to Norman Douglas on a diabolical fish soup [David, 1989, 139], to Stendhal [236], Apollinaire [284], Montaigne [295] and others too numerous to mention. She also includes a number of chapters towards the end concerned solely with references: one on Italian wines, another on Italian cookery books, yet another on guidebooks to Italy, and a consummate one on 'Visitor's Books'. The latter comfortably surveys five hundred years of writing about Italy, and is nothing less than extraordinary in its scope. It is as if, when Mrs David puts her mind to something, her dedication and passion is seemingly boundless and all-encompassing.

Summer Cooking is a light and accessible book, that consolidates Mrs David's achievements. She uses it as an opportunity, in the face of the 'perversity' of 'the tin and the deep freeze', to argue for a seasonal approach to food [David, 1980, 9 and 7]. Again, it is a reaffirmation of resourcefulness and value: to seek out produce 'at its best, most plentiful and cheapest' [David, 1980, 7]. Frozen peas with everything not only marginalises the pleasure of eating 'those delicate, fresh, sugary green peas' but also homogenizes the rhythms of the year. A homogeneity of rhythm that distances us from a sense of place, from belonging, not just to this land, but to the air, the feel of the place, the seasons. Once again we can see that Mrs David's concern is not just cooking, but the capacity to live with 'sensitivity and enthusiasm'; the 'capacity to capture the essence of a fleeting moment' [David, 1980, 11]. The ethos of her food is concerned with bringing 'some savour of the garden, the fields, the sea, into the kitchen and the dining-room' [David, 1980, 9]. Significantly, no dish is delicious in and of itself, but delicious only in its appropriateness to time, place and circumstance. So that Mrs David is as equally enraptured by Viola and Arthur Johnson's Grottaferrata in a Frascati restaurant as she is by cheap coarse red wine diluted with ice close to a Mediterranean shore [David, 1989, 300 and 1980, 12]. Mrs David has an enviable sense of empathy towards a place, and seems to quickly and easily meld into a *mis-en-scène*.

French Provincial Cooking is rightly described by Paul Levy as 'a masterpiece'. It is a consummate piece of work. Consummate not only because it describes and evokes the best of French provincial cooking, but also the ethos of French provincial life. An ethos which we may heed to enrich our own lives. In *French Provincial Cooking* Mrs David gives much of herself. It is in her chapter on the provinces that she recalls the archetypical story – a story recited in the lives of others such as M.F.K. Fisher, Alice Waters, and Stephanie Alexander – of going to France as a student and learning to appreciate French food [David, 1970, 22]. Again she paints vivid tableaux of middle-class French life: of Madame Roberto twice a week returning from the marketing at Les Halles, 'two bursting black shopping bags in each hand, puffing, panting, mopping her brow, and looking as if she was about to have a stroke' [David, 1970, 22]; of the greedy daughter Denise who, on soufflé days, 'would suddenly find she was in fearful hurry to get back to work', meaning that she not only got to the soufflé before it had a chance to sink, 'but if there was enough for a second helping she had first go at that too' [David, 1970, 24]; and so on. Here, Mrs David's prose feels close to Ms Fisher's of *Long Ago in France*. In this way, *French Provincial Cooking*, and indeed all her books, fulfils the task of evoking the pathos of other places, the rhythms other times.

All of Mrs David's signature traits are in this *French Provincial Cooking*, only more refined and complete. There is the sage advice to avoid tourist traps, to eat seasonally with a mind to the quality of the produce ('A little fine oil, or true, clear stock, or double cream from Jersey herds, or a few fresh eggs laid by decently-fed, humanely-reared hens go a lot further than twice the amounts of third-rate makeshifts'), and to generally manage oneself with due care if one wishes to avoid disappointment [David, 1970, xv and xiv]. There are also the subtle and extensive references to literature and history, and the comprehensive chapters on kitchen equipment, cooking terms and processes, wine, herbs, spices, condiments and cookery books.

She restates that her concern is with 'sober, well-balanced, middle-class French cookery, carried out with care and skill, but without extravagance or pretension'; she is interested in food of 'taste, moderation and simplicity'; 'consistent' food of 'smell, texture and much character' which often looks beautiful too, and amounts to 'the rational, right and proper food for human beings to eat' [David, 1970, ix, xii and 19]. And in a note to later editions of the book [1983], she distinguishes the terrain of her interests not only from the mediocrity of English cooking ('skimping the work or the basic ingredients, throwing together a dish anyhow and hoping for the best') and the 'unnecessary complication and elaboration' of *haute cuisine*, but also from the affectations of *nouvelle cuisine* [David, 1970, 17]. Here, her sardonic wit is at its sharpest. Although she shares a concern for 'simplicity' with *nouvelle* (and, as she acknowledges, with Escoffier) her main point of objection is 'a certain coldness and ungenerosity of spirit, and indifference to the customer' [David, 1970, xvii]. In short, an absence of hospitality and restoration derived from a misunderstood mimicry of Japanese food, and an element of narcissism on the part of a number of chefs. To substantiate her position, she deploys her formidable scholarship, showing how the rhetoric of *nouvelle cuisine* is a repetition of a new wave that swept French cooking in the 1740s. Quoting Marin and Menon, she shows how 'nouvelle cuisine then, as now, meant lighter food, less of it, costing more' [David, 1970, 476]. What also offends Mrs David is the singular lack of resourcefulness and value in *nouvelle* kitchens. Her assessment of Paul Bocuse is that he is addicted to conspicuous waste, offering in *La Cuisine du Marché*, a dish of sea perch in a crust stuffed with lobster mousse: 'you do not have to eat the crust, it is there to keep the juices in the perch; nor do you have to trouble to eat the lobster stuffing in the centre. 'It is there to retain a certain moistness without which the perch has a tendency to dry out' [David, 1970, 479]. Mrs David's comment is, 'Wonderful'. She is as dry as a Spanish fino.

Elizabeth David and Australia

So what has all this chat about Elizabeth David got to do with Australian food? On one line, the line I have been following thus far, I want to argue alongside Michael Symons and Gay Bilson that it was travel, rather than multiculturalism, that was the primary reason for our culinary renaissance. Further, it was the books of Elizabeth David that consolidated the desire, generated through travel, for exotic – in this case European – food. Further still, Australia – like parts of America and Great Britain – was primed to be leavened by the ferment in Mrs David's books.

But if Australia shares this general condition with California and perhaps Britain, then what is it that distinguishes Australian food from Californian or modern British? Quite simply, I would say, not much. And the differences that are discernible are the effect of individual contributions rather than anything more coherent. Individual character is particularly pertinent in Australia where most of our leading first-wave food practitioners were not formally trained and therefore brought an inordinate multitutde of influences to bear on the style of their food. That is, our leading food practitioners were, and are, extraordinarily strong and diverse characters: from Gay Bilson to Stephanie Alexander, Damien Pignolet to Maggie Beer, Cheong Liew to Phillip Searle, even Leo Schofield and Barbara Santich, and so on. Notably, of this list only Damien has any formal training. Free from the formal reference points of an Escoffier-based schooling, most of these cooks adopted another central reference: Elizabeth David's *French Provincial Cooking*. As such, it is not an exaggeration that Elizabeth David's work is one of the foundations on which modern Australian food is built.[3]

The only cook whose story approaches the fairy-tale dimensions of, say, Alice Waters, is Stephanie Alexander. At its simplest, and like Elizabeth David, M.F.K. Fisher and others before her, Alice Waters went to France as a student, was enamoured by the ethos of the place, notably the food, returned to

California, cooked her way through *French Provincial Cooking*, interpreting it in the light of her own French experiences and with due respect to the actualities of California, and *voilà*, a distinctively Californian food style was born. Similarly with Stephanie. A librarian by trade, she went to France to work as an au pair and a language assistant. She was enamoured not only by the pathos of painters such as Toulouse-Lautrec and Van Gogh, but also by the extraordinary enjoyment of ordinary French meals:

> Meat was eaten only two or three times a week. Many meals were multi-coursed, often with simple soups, and always with delicious vegetable dishes and carefully dressed soft-leafed salads. Always a perfectly ripe cheese and, of course, always the bread brought fresh with each meal. [Alexander, 1993b, xiii].

These experiences profoundly influenced Stephanie, entailing, as they did, the simple rhythms of pleasure. Even the plainest French meal entailed a beginning, a middle and an end, later leading her to be one of the first restaurateurs in Australia to offer a fixed-price structure.

Stephanie's style is very personal, being the culmination of her experience ('the more one travels to eat, the more one reads, the more one listens…') as opposed to the logical result of a formal culinary schooling [Alexander, 1988, vii]. Drawing, in the first instance, on her mother's passion for food, in the second it was the figure of Elizabeth David that she took on as a mentor. Often referring to Mrs David as the greatest food-writer of our time ('her attention to the detail that so often determines the difference between the ordinary and the superb is unequalled in the English language'), Mrs David's very name was 'synonymous with unquestioned authority' [Alexander, 1993a, 4 and 109]. Mrs David's writing provided a fertile and comprehensive reference for Stephanie, and she 'returned to them constantly, always gaining some new insight and being stimulated to a new culinary adventure' [Alexander, 1993a, 109]. Mrs David encouraged Stephanie to understand 'cookery as a craft, to be practiced with care and love with a proper understanding of detail, an appreciation of what had gone before' [Alexander, 1993a, 109].

The magnitude of Mrs David's influence can be read, not only in Stephanie's solid French provincial style but also, in her appreciation of the pathos and *mis-en-scène* that food is capable of evoking [Alexander, 1993a, 4]. In Mrs David's writing, in her stories about food, the food itself tells stories, evokes rhythms and spaces, relations and faces. 'Her evocative, witty yet never fulsome prose brought to life the French and Italian countryside, remote Greek islands and cities all over the Mediterranean. Almost every recipe is interspersed with stories and anecdotes connecting the dishes to daily life' [Alexander, 1993a, 109]. Stephanie perceives that this intimate entwining of food and stories is 'very important in order to understand who we are and where we have come from. Through stories we can learn old skills, old traditions and, of course, old dishes. We can glimpse the continuity of human life and learn of places we shall probably never visit' [Alexander, 1988, vii]. In Stephanie's own writing, Mrs David's influence is notable, as Stephanie too lodges recipes in stories and contexts. Through her books, as well as her restaurant, Stephanie has been enormously influential in determing the mood and style of first-wave contemporary Australian food.

I include Leo Schofield as a leading food practitioner because, as a critic, he too was extremely influential in setting the tone of first-wave contemporary Australian food. He vividly remembers the excitement of coming across Elizabeth David's work in the late sixties, and was particularly taken by her refreshing aesthetic and deft use of citations. He recalls her citation of 'Wyvern's' instructions for making an omelette, with whom she shares a delicately observed wit:

> Books that counsel you to turn an omelette, to fold it, to let it brown on one side, to let it fry for about five minutes, etc., are not to be trusted. If you follow such advice you will only produce, at best, a neat-looking egg pudding' [David, 1991, 32].

Leo Schofield shares Mrs David's generous dose of worldly experience, and brought a straightforward, yet intellectual aesthetic to his restaurant criticism. Articulating the changes occurring in restaurants during the seventies and eighties, he was something of a latterday Curnonsky, and he had the power to launch careers. One career that he helped to launch was that of Gay Morris.

Like Stephanie, Gay worked as a librarian, and brings a highly personal sense of style of cooking and running restaurants. Together with Tony Bilson, whose name she took on, she made a name for herself at Tony's Bon Gout; a reputation which was consolidated in earnest at Berowra Waters Inn. Indeed, according to Michael Symons, not only did Tony and Gay Bilson have a major impact on the Sydney restaurant scene, but more than this they showed 'that cooking could at last be regarded as an honourable Australian profession' [Symons, 1982, 232]. This is because they recast the profession in artistic and performative metaphors; they brought to it an informed passion and a concern for, not just food, but the relations which food enables. Symons chronicles the political and intellectual vivacity of Tony's Bon Gout: of Labour advisers; of journalists and editors from the *Financial Review*, the now defunct *National Times* and occasionally from the *Herald* or the *Bulletin*; of Gay 'sitting in the Bon Gout kitchen, on an upturned rubbish tin, reading the *New York Review of Books*' [Symons, 1982, 236].

After the Bilsons split in 1982 Gay stayed at Berowra, ever 'the great idealogue on the river', and maintained it as arguably our first distinctively Australian, world-class restaurant [Brugman and Butt, 1992, 187]. Where Stephanie falls into a romantic mould, Gay can be cast in an idealistic one. She is passionately hungry for words, the worlds they open up, the relations that they imply. Elizabeth David's work does not figure as seminally for Gay as she does for Stephanie, which is not to say that it is not significant, and which no doubt has something to do with the fact that Gay started her cooking career in pastry – not one of Mrs David's strongest points. Though familiar with Mrs David's work since the early seventies, it was not until the early eighties that Gay really engaged with it. At this time, Gay's interest was driven not only by the responsibility created by Tony's absence, but also as a reaction against *nouvelle cuisine*. She recalls making pasta from *Italian Food* in 1982, and thinking at the time that it was one of the great cook books. That she does not necessarily think this now is not so much a poor reflection on Elizabeth David's work, as an indication of the depth of Gay's intrigue and the breadth of her influences.

Though she points out it was travel, rather than multiculturalism, that drove Australia's culinary renaissance, the primary influence on Gay was her passion for reading. Or, perhaps, simply her passion for passion: a passion for ideals, and a passion for life. She was attracted to cooking because of 'the conviviality of the table' and the pleasures of 'a tender, loving sense of hospitality', characteristics more than compatible with Mrs David's ethos [*Sydney Morning Herald*, 22/1/83]. But even more intensely than Elizabeth David, Gay is driven by these ideals of conviviality and hospitality in much the same way as an artist or a writer is driven by the ideal of representing, or recreating, the purity of experience. As such, her humility is astounding. She respects it as 'a great privilege to be able to practice passionately self-education towards an ideal, and to be supported by enough clients to make a viable business out of those interests' [*National Times*, 19/10/1980].

Between them, and in their different cities and styles, Stephanie and Gay have made defining contributions to contemporary Australian food. Not only in their writing, but also in the cooks they have ushered through their kitchens and the diners they have fed. These are contributions either styled on, or compatible with, Mrs David's ethos. What she offers us is rigour and resourcefulness, consistency and coherence.

NOTES

[1] It is worth noting that this book – called *The Food of Australia* – was heavily supported by the Hilton chain of hotels, featuring many of their chefs, and belongs to a series of cookbooks covering Thailand, Bali, Indonesia, China, Singapore, Malaysia, India and Japan. In other words, it is a sophisticated form of marketing: selling Australia as a tourist destination by selling Australian food and Hilton hotel chefs.

[2] Ms Bilson also points out that not only did travel produce desire, but another form of travel – namely transport – has made it possible to procure the fresh produce, seemingly from anywhere in the world, with which to attempt to satiate this desire for the exotic (Bilson, unpub.ms.,7).

[3] If I were to paint a more comprehensive picture, I would also point out the importance of *nouvelle*. But as this is presented merely as some thoughts towards a description of contemporary Australian food, I will limit myself to Elizabeth David.

BIBLIOGRAPHY

Alexander, Stephanie (1988) *Stephanie's Feasts and Stories*. Sydney: Allen and Unwin,

    (1993a) *Stephanie's Seasons*. Sydney: Allen and Unwin.

    (1993b) *Stephanie's Menus for Food Lovers*. Melbourne: Mandarin. First published in 1985.

Bilson, Gay (unpublished manuscript) 'Are we what we eat?/The Upstart Cuisine/We are still what we ate'.

    (1995) Interview, *Cafe Magazine*, No.5, June/July.

Brugman, M. and Butt, L. (1992) *Proceedings of the Australian Symposium*, No.6.

David, Elizabeth (1970) *French Provincial Cooking*. London: Penguin. First published in 1960.

    (1979) *French Country Cooking*. London: Penguin. First published in 1951.

    (1980) *Summer Food*. London: Penguin. First published in 1955.

    (1989) *Italian Food*. London: Penguin. First published in 1954.

    (1991) *Mediterranean Food*. London: Penguin. First published in 1950.

Halligan, Marion (1984) 'The Word made Flesh: can we talk ourselves into an Australian Cuisine?' in Santich et al, *Proceedings of the Australian Symposium*, No.1, 68-76.

Ripe, Cherry (1993) *Goodbye Culinary Cringe*. Sydney: Allen and Unwin.

Symons, Michael (1982) *One Continuous Picnic*. Adelaide: Duck Press.

Note: Informal conversations were had with Gay Bilson, Cheong Liew, Damien Pignolet and Leo Schofield during June 1996.

Symposiasts 1996

Dr. Michael Abdalla, ul. Szydlowska 53/10, 60-656 Poznan, POLAND
Carol Agnew, c/o Dorothy Duncan, 34 Parkview Avenue, Willowdale, Ontario M2N 3Y2, CANADA
Dr. Joan P. Alcock, 24 Queensthorpe Road, Sydenham, London SE26 4PH
Pepita Aris, 57 Hyde Vale, Greenwich, London SE10 8QQ
Josephine Bacon, 82 Stonebridge Road, London N15 5PA
Mrs. Anne Bamborough, 18 Winchester Road, Oxford OX2 6NA
Ann Barr, 36 Linton House, 11 Holland Park Avenue, London W11 3RL
Rosemary Barron, 12 Centenary Way, Cheddar, Somerset BS27 3DG
Gillian Bell, Old Manor House, Clive, Shropshire SY4 3JZ
Michelle Berriedale-Johnson, 5 Lawn Road, London NW3 2XS
Gay Bilson, Flat 15, 4 Ithaka Road, Elizabeth Bay, NSW 2011, AUSTRALIA
Dr. A. Blake, Firmenich SA, 1 route des Jeunes, CH 1211, Geneva 8, SWITZERLAND
Fritz Blank, Deux Cheminées, 1221 Locust Street, Philadelphia, PA 19107, USA
Carole Bloom & Jerry Olivas, 7067 Rockrose Terrace, Carlsbad, CA 92009-5015, USA
Prof. Phyllis P. Bober, 29 Simpson Road, Ardmore, PA 19003-2812, USA
Angela Bowman, Pear Tree House, Broadway WR12 7AL
Catherine Brown, 4 Belhaven Terrace, Glasgow G12 0TF
Deirdre Bryan-Brown, Rose Cottage, 14 Henley Road, Shillingford, Wallingford, Oxfordshire OX10 7EH
Stuart Burlinson, College of Higher Education, Francis Close Hall, Swindon Road, Cheltenham GL50 4AZ
Moira Buxton, Bulls Hall, Yaxley, nr. Eye, Suffolk IP23 8BZ
Aynsley Cameron, c/o Royal Prince Alfred Hospital, Camperdown, N.S.W., 2050, AUSTRALIA
Charles Campion, 5 Lea Close, Claines, Worcester WR3 7PR
Kathleen Cardlin, c/o Dorothy Max, 251 West 89th Street, NYC, NY 10024, USA
Ruth Carroll, Hill View, Fishers Lane, Charlbury, Oxon OX7 3RX
Mollie Chadsey, 19 Finlay House, Phyllis Court Drive, Henley on Thames RG9 2H
Lisa Chaney, 15B Upper Price Street, York YO2 1BJ
Robert Chenciner, 11 & 12 Lloyd Square, London WC1X 1NZ
Janet Clarke, 3 Woodside Cottages, Freshford, Bath BA3 6EJ
Dr. Helen Clifford, 38 Cheviot Close, Tonbridge, Kent TN9 1NH
Dr. Albert Coenders, Prof. Regoutstraat 77, 5348 AA - Oss, THE NETHERLANDS
Katarzyna Cwiertka, Van der Palmstraat 100, 3022 VZ Rotterdam, THE NETHERLANDS
Andrew Dalby, 5 Primrose Way, Linton, Cambridge CB1 6UD
Alan & Jane Davidson, 45 Lamont Road, London SW10 0HU
Caroline Davidson, 5 Queen Anne's Gardens, London W4 1TU
Silvija Davidson, 12 Lords Close, West Dulwich, London SE21 8EZ
Joy Davies, 501 Cinnamon Wharf, 24 Shad Thames, London SE1 2YJ
Andrea Dearden-Esty, Shamrock Quay, Southampton SO1 1QL
Mr. & Mrs. Hroar Dege, Segma, P.B. 2491 Solli, N-0203 Oslo, NORWAY
Carol Déry, Department of Classics, University of Wales, Lampeter, Dyfed SA48 7ED
June di Schino, Via Orazio 31, 00193 Roma, ITALY
John Doerper, 610 Donovan Avenue, Bellingham, WA 98225-7315, USA
Christopher Driver, 6 Church Road, London N6 4QT
Dorothy Duncan, Ontario Historical Society, 34 Parkview Avenue, Willowdale, Ontario M2N 3Y2, CANADA
Hugo Dunn-Meynell, The International Wine & Food Society, 9 Fitzmaurice Place, London W1X 6JD
Margaret Dyke, 63 Southfield Road, Oxford OX4 1NY
Professor Gladys Earl, 1022 Wilson Avenue, Menomonie, WI 54751, USA
Sarah Edington, 4 Bushwood Road, Kew, Richmond TW9 3BQ
J. Audrey Ellison, 135 Stevenage Road, Fulham, London SW6 6PB
Michael Erben, 21 Dorchester Court, Ferry Pool Road, Oxford OX2 7DT
Rachael Evans, Kiln Cottage, Culham, Abingdon, Oxon. OX14 4NE
Sarah Jane Evans, Crescent Wood Cottage, 6 Crescent Wood Road, London SE26 6RU
James Fallon, 128 Penn Green Road, Landenberg, PA 19350-9106, USA
Clare Ferguson, 5 Colville Terrace, London W11 2BE
Ove Fosså, Parkveien 11, N-4300 Sandnes, NORWAY
Jean Freemantle, Hill House, Waddesdon, Bucks HP18 0JF

Dr. Robert Frey, 194 Sutherland Avenue, London W9 1RX
Susan Friedland, Harper & Row Publishers Inc, 10 East 53rd Street, New York, NY 10022-5299, USA
Barbara Haber, Radcliffe College, 10 Garden Street, Cambridge, MA 02138, USA
Nevin Haliçi, P.K. 88 Naláaci, 42005 Konya, TURKEY
Vicky Hayward, Hortaleza 102, Atico Uno, 28004 Madrid, SPAIN
Jane A.D. Hedges, Fulscot Manor, Didcot, Oxfordshire OX11 9AA
Anissa Helou, 67 Littlebury Road, London SW4 6DW
Professor Constance Hieatt, 304 River Road, Deep River, CT 06217, USA
Prof. Richard F. Hosking, 9-4-703 Hakushima kukenko, Naka-ku, Hiroshima 730, JAPAN
Sharon W. & Tom C. Hudgins, 7 Sun Hala Drive, Pittsburg, Texas 75686-9318, USA
Phil & Patsy Iddison, 3 Upper Grotto Road, Twickenham, Middlesex TW1 4NG
Abed Jaber, 20 Reighton Road, London E5 8SG
Jane Jakeman, 33 Merewood Avenue, Sandhills, Oxford OX3 8EG
Bee Jasko, 3 Martin Terrace, Burley, Leeds LS4 2JY
Eve Jochnowitz, 21 East 10th Street #2a, New York, NY 10003-5924, USA
Mrs. Rosemary Joekes, The Hermitage, St. Catherine, Bath BA1 8HE
Kate Joll, 17 Battersea Square, London SW11 3RA
Maria Kaneva-Johnson, 6 The Limes, Stratton Audley, Bicester, Oxfordshire OX6 9DA
Jesse & Shirley Kaye, 4300 Tenth Avenue North, Suite 2, Lake Worth, FL 33461-2313, USA
Neil S. Kaye & Susan Donnelly-Kaye, 3 Hayloft Ct., Wilmington, DE 19808, USA
Professor D.T.Kelly, Royal Prince Alfred Hospital, Camperdown, N.S.W., 2050, AUSTRALIA
Mary Wallace Kelsey, Oregon State University, Milam Hall 108, Corvallis OR 97330-5103, USA
Shirley King, 162 E. 82nd Street #1D, New York, NY 10028-1829, USA
Aglaia Kremezi, 33 Robertou Galli, 11 742 Athens, GREECE
Giana & Nicholas Kurti, 38 Blandford Avenue, Oxford OX2 8DZ
Elizabeth Ladimeji, Flat 5, 10A Airlie Gardens, London W8 7AL
Professor Helen M. Leach, University of Otago, Anthropology Dept., P.O.Box 56, Dunedin, NEW ZEALAND
Shane Lehane, The Yellow House, Vicarstown, Co. Cork, IRELAND
Margaret Leibenstein, 47 Larchwood Drive, Cambridge, MA 02138-4638, USA
Jane Levi, 26 Hurst Street, Herne Hill, London SE24 8EG
Mrs. Audrey Levy, 60 Gloucester Road, Kingston-upon-Thames, Surrey KT1 3RB
Paul Levy, P.O.Box 35, Witney, Oxon OX8 8BF
Pat Llewellyn, 48c Kentish Town Road, London NW1 9PU
Professor José Rafael Lovera, P.O.Box 80394, Caracas 1080-A, VENEZUELA
Elisabeth Luard, Brynmeheryn, Ystrad Meurig, Dyfed SY25 6AH
Jenny Macarthur, 13 Wavell Road, Maidenhead, Berkshire, SL6 5AB
Jeremy MacClancy, School of Social Sciences, Oxford Brookes University, Gipsy Lane, Oxford OX3 0BP
Professor Gerald & Valerie Mars, 53 Nassington Road, London NW3 2TY
Laura Mason, 4 Saint John Street, York YO3 7QT
Stephen W. Massil, 138 Middle Lane, Crouch End, London N8 7JP
Dorothy Max, 251 West 89th Street, NYC, NY 10024, USA
Carolyn McCrum, 57 Oakthorpe Road, Oxford OX2 7BD
Christine McFadden, 71 Prior Park Road, Bath BA2 4NF
Tessa McKirdy, Cooks Books, 34 Marine Drive, Rottingdean, Sussex BN2 7HQ
Dr. Michael Michaud, Sea Spring Farm, West Bexington, Dorchester, Dorset DT2 9DD
Richard C. Mieli, 4 Longfellow Place #1703, Boston, MA 02114, USA
Janny de Moor, Ulco de Vriesweg 29, 8084 AR 't Harde, THE NETHERLANDS
Dr. H. & Mrs. F. Morrow Brown, Highfield House, Highfield Gardens, Derby DE3 1HT
Dawn & Douglas Nelson, Passe Renard, Avéron-Bergelle, 32290 Aignan, FRANCE
Jill Norman, 1 Rosslyn Hill, London NW3 5UL
Sri Owen, 96 High Street Mews, Wimbledon Village, London SW19 7RG
Helen Peacocke, Rose Cottage, 43 Acre End Street, Eynsham, Oxford OX8 1PF
Susan Parham, 1102 Victoria Tower, 199 Castlereagh Street, Sydney, NSW 2000, AUSTRALIA
Dorothea A. Pelham, 6 Portland Road, Oxford OX2 7EY
Charles Perry, 12912 El Dorado Avenue, Sylmar, CA 91342, USA
Karin Perry, The Lawns, 16 South Grove, Highgate, London N6 6BJ
Terry Peters, 3706 Kimble Road, Baltimore, Maryland 21218, USA
Edite Vieira Phillips, Garden Flat, 503a Liverpool Road, London N7 8NS

Maya Pieris, 17 Grays Lane, Hitchin, Herts SG5 2HG
Gae Pincus, PO Box 59, Glebe, NSW 2037, AUSTRALIA
Hawys Pritchard, 46 Church Crescent, London N10 3NE
Daniel Quirici, 8 Montpelier Square, London SW7
Jaakko Rahola, Pihlajamaentie 18 B, SF-02320 Espoo, FINLAND
Hannah Rapport, 4 Harbour Road, London SE5 9PD
Iris Raven, Catscradle, Newchurch West, Chepstow, Gwent NP6 6DA
Gillian Riley, 11 Kersley Road, London N16 0NP
Alicia Rios, Avenida General Perón 19 - 8°C, 28020 Madrid, SPAIN
Cherry Ripe, 1 Tivoli Street, Paddington 2021, NSW, AUSTRALIA
Joe Roberts, 31 Brock Street, Bath BA1 2LN
Claudia Roden, 8 Wild Hatch, London NW11 7LD
Owen Rossan, 66 Fellows Road, London NW3 3LJ
Ann Rycraft, 1 Mill Mount, The Mount, York YO2 2BH
Alison Ryley, 14 Howard Drive, Huntingdon, NY 11743-3033, USA
Helen Saberi, 75 Haldon Road, London SW18 1QF
Rena Salaman, 145 Tufnell Park Road, London N7 0PU
Alice Wooledge Salmon, 14 Avenue Mansions, Sisters Avenue, London SW11 5SL
Dan M. Schickentanz, Pakenham, Park Lane, Long Hanborough, Witney, Oxon OX8 8JU
David E. Schoonover, The University of Iowa Libraries, 100 Main Library, Iowa City, Iowa 52242-1420, USA
Philippa Scott, 30 Elgin Crescent, London W11 2JR
Liz & Gerd Seeber, 27 Meads Street, Eastbourne, East Sussex BN20 7RH
Dr. Colleen Taylor Sen, 2557 West Farwell Avenue, Chicago, IL 60645, USA
Maria José Sevilla, Foods from Spain, 66 Chiltern Street, London W1M 1PR
Regina Sexton, The Yellow House, Vicarstown, Co. Cork, IRELAND
Margaret Shaida, Teulades V, Apt. 201, Els Vilars/Escaldes, ANDORRA (Via Poste française)
Roy Shipperbottom, 9 Southgate, Heaton Chapel, Stockport SK4 4QL
Ralph & Kate Shirley, 39 Uttoxeter Road, The Studio, Foston, Derby DE6 5PX
Art Siemering, Trend/Wire, P.O.Box 6217, Leawood, KS 66206, USA
Helen J. Simpson, Burton Court, Eardisland, nr. Leominster, Herefordshire HR6 9DS
Raymond Sokolov, 34 1/2 Barrow Street, New York, NY 10014-3735, USA
Colin Spencer, Winchelsea Cottage, High Street, Winchelsea, East Sussex TN36 4EA
Gareth Spencer Jones, 501 Cinnamon Wharf, 24 Shad Thames, London SE1 2YJ
Rosemary Stark, 6 Chamberlain Street, London NW1 8XB
Jeffrey L. Steingarten, 29 West 17th Street, New York, NY 10011, USA
Margaret Sullivan, 1812 Thornbury Road, Baltimore, Maryland 21209, USA
Dr. Layinka M. Swinburne, 16 Foxhill Crescent, Leeds LS16 5PD
Anne Tait, Ridgeway Cottage, Glanvilles Wootton, Sherborne, Dorset DT9 5QF
Dr. Gábor Tasnádi, H-1113 Budapest, Villányi út 60, HUNGARY
Martha Brooks Taylor, 101 Westcott Street, Apt. 1906, Houston, TX 77007-703, USA
Malcolm Thick, 2 Brookside, Harwell, Oxon OX11 0HG
Elizabeth Thomas, 1372 Summit Road, Berkeley, CA 94708, USA
Jane Thomas, Dept. of Nutrition & Dietetics, King's College, Campden Hill Road, London W8 7AH
Kim van Gestel-Maclean, Oude Amersfoortseweg 12, 1213 AD Hilversum, NETHERLANDS
Harlan Walker, 294 Hagley Road, Birmingham B17 8DJ
Jennifer Walker, 10 Whitley Park Lane, Reading, Berks
Stuart Walton, 2a Walpole Terrace, Brighton BN2 2EB
Ann Watson, The Forge, High Street, Barford, Warwick CV35 8BU
William Woys Weaver, P. O. Box 131, Paoli, PA 19301, USA
Robin Weir, 104 Iffley Road, London W6 0PF
Hugh Wennerbom, 15/130 Campbell Pde., Bondi 2026, AUSTRALIA
Barbara K. Wheaton, 268 Elm Street, Concord, MA 01742-2247, USA
Margaret Willes, 17 Appleby Road, London E8 3ET
Mary Wondrausch, The Pottery, Brickfields, Compton, Guildford, Surrey GU3 1HZ
Dr. Theodore Zeldin, Tumbledown House, Cumnor, Oxford OX2 9QE